Nation and politics in the Soviet successor states

Edited by

Ian Bremmer
Department of Political Science,
Stanford University

and

Ray Taras
Hoover Institution,
Stanford University

CAMBRIDGE
UNIVERSITY PRESS

Published by the Press Syndicate of the University of Cambridge
The Pitt Building, Trumpington Street, Cambridge CB2 1RP
40 West 20th Street, New York, NY 10011-4211, USA
10 Stamford Road, Oakleigh, Melbourne 3166, Australia

First published 1993
Reprinted 1993

Printed in Canada

A catalogue record for this book is available from the British Library

Library of Congress cataloging in publication data is available

ISBN 0-521-43281-2 hardback
ISBN 0-521-43860-8 paperback

The final months of 1991 witnessed the disintegration of the vast Soviet empire of different nations which had, since the time of Lenin, perhaps never represented anything more than an illusion of true union. As Gorbachev struggled, then failed, to hold together the collapsing central authority of the Party and the Kremlin, fifteen diverse republics simultaneously embarked on the new task of building the institutions necessary for independent statehood. As they did so, national minorities rediscovered long-suppressed identities, and sought new rights.

This comprehensive collection of specially commissioned studies of the new states which have grown from the old Soviet Union provides the first systematic and rigorous analysis of these nation- and state-building processes. International specialists, each with unique individual knowledge and experience of these new state, capture their distinctiveness and character. Their studies, bringing together historical and ethnic background with penetrating political analysis, offer a fresh and invaluable record of the different roads to self-assertion and independence being pursued by these young nations.

IAN BREMMER is Hrair Hovnanian Fellow in the Department of Political Science at Stanford University. He is a specialist on nationalities questions in the post-Soviet context. His publications include *Soviet Nationalities Problems* (1990), with Norman Naimark.

RAY TARAS has been National Fellow at the Hoover Institution, Stanford University, and has taught at universities in Canada, England, and the US. His earlier books include *The Road to Disillusion: from Critical Marxism to Postcommunism in Eastern Europe* (1992), and *Ideology in a Socialist State* (1984).

Nations and politics in the Soviet successor states

Contents

Maps

Tables

Notes on contributors

Muriel Atkin is Associate Professor of History at George Washington University. She received a Ph.D. in history from Yale University. She is the author of the monographs *The Subtlest Battle: Islam in Soviet Tajikistan* and *Russia and Iran, 1780–1828* as well as numerous articles on Tajikistan and Russian/Soviet relations with Iran.

Ian Bremmer is Hrair Hovnanian Fellow and Doctoral Candidate in the Department of Political Science, Stanford University. A specialist on nationalities questions in the post-Soviet context, he has conducted research in the successor states and has published extensively on problems of Soviet transition and disintegration including, recently, *Soviet Nationalities Problems* (1990) with Norman Naimark.

Robert Conquest is Senior Research Fellow at the Hoover Institution, Stanford University. He has authored and edited numerous books on Soviet and international affairs, including *The Nation Killers*, *The Harvest of Sorrow*, *The Great Terror*, and *The Last Empire: Nationality and the Soviet Future*. Much of his work has recently been published in Moscow, Petrograd, and Kiev.

Nora Dudwick is a doctoral candidate in cultural anthropology at the University of Pennsylvania, where she is writing her dissertation on the national movement in Soviet Armenia. Since September 1987, she has visited and conducted research in Armenia on four occasions. She is the author of a number of articles on the subject.

John Dunlop is Senior Fellow at the Hoover Institution, Stanford University. He is author of *The Faces of Contemporary Russian Nationalism*, *The New Russian Nationalism*, and a number of other studies which treat the position of ethnic Russians in the Soviet Union.

Daria Fane is foreign service officer with the Department of State. She has just finished a two-year tour in Washington as a political analyst of Soviet nationalities and is currently serving at the U.S. Embassy in Moscow. She is presently working on a comprehensive volume on the nations within Russia.

Gail Fondahl is Assistant Professor in the Department of Geography at

Middlebury College. She is a specialist on the impact of industrial development on indigenous peoples of the Circumpolar North. Having recently conducted field research in Siberia, she has written several articles and is presently completing a volume entitled *Reindeer Herders and Railroad Building; The Cultural Ecology of Trans-Baykalia.*

Gregory Gleason is Associate Professor of Political Science at the University of New Mexico. He is the author of a number of articles on Soviet federal relations and on public policy in the Central Asian states as well as the book *Federalism and Nationalism: The Struggle for Republican Rights in the USSR.* He has held visiting research appointments at the Kennan Institute, the Hoover Institution, the Institute of Economics of the USSR Academy of Sciences, and the Turkmenistan Academy of Agricultural Sciences.

Shireen Hunter is Deputy Director of the Middle Eastern Program at the Center for Strategic and International Studies in Washington. Her most recent publications include *Iran and the World: Continuity in a Revolutionary Decade* (1990) and *Iran After Khomeini* (1992). She is currently working on a monograph on "Nation Building in the New Islamic States." Her articles have appeared in most major journals, including *Foreign Affairs, Foreign Policy, SAIS Review, Current History,* the *Washington Quarterly* and the *Middle East Journal.*

Eugene Huskey is author of *Russian Lawyers and the Soviet State*, numerous articles on Soviet law and government, and a study of elections in Kyrgyzstan. He has just edited a book on the rise and fall of the Soviet state apparatus, *Executive Power and Soviet Politics.* Huskey was educated at Vanderbilt, Essex, and the London School of Economics. He has taught at Colgate University, Bowdoin College, and Stetson University, where he is currently Associate Professor of Political Science.

Cynthia Kaplan is Associate Professor in the Department of Political Science at the University of California, Santa Barbara. She is the author of *The Party and Agricultural Crisis Management in the USSR* and is currently conducting surveys in Estonia and the Russian Federation on political participation.

Bohdan Krawchenko is Professor of Political Science and Director of the Institute of Ukrainian Studies at the University of Alberta. He has written extensively on Ukrainian politics and national identity, including *Ukraine After Shelest* and *Social Change and National Consciousness in Twentieth-Century Ukraine.* He presently serves on the council advising President Leonid Kravchuk.

Richard Krickus is Professor of Political Science at Mary Washington College. The co-founder of the National Center for Urban Ethnic Affairs, he was one of two American academics invited by Sajudis to witness the

1990 Lithuanian elections. He currently is conducting research on ethnic conflict in the former Soviet Union and has published several books including, most recently, *The Superpowers in Crisis.*

Stephen Jones is Assistant Professor of Russian Studies at Mount Holyoke College. He has written extensively on Georgian affairs in specialist journals and books. His own book, *The Georgian Democratic Republic: 1918–21,* will be published in 1993.

Nils Muiznieks is a doctoral candidate in the Department of Political Science at the University of California, Berkeley. The working title of his dissertation is "The Baltic Popular Movements and the Disintegration of the USSR." He has conducted numerous research trips to the Baltic States since 1984 and has worked as an intern at Radio Free Europe/Radio Liberty in Munich.

David Nissman received his doctorate from Columbia University in Turkic Studies. Author of *The Soviet Union and Iranian Azerbaijan* and numerous articles on ethnic identity and relations in the Middle East and Central Asia, he has conducted extensive research in Turkmenistan. He presently serves as a Fellow in the Seminar on Turkic Studies at Columbia.

Martha Brill Olcott is Professor of Political Science at Colgate University. She has been studying Soviet nationality problems since 1973; since then, she has traveled to the USSR more than a dozen times, and has spent nearly three years in residence in eleven of the fifteen successor states. She has authored numerous books and articles including *The Kazakhs, The Soviet Multinational State,* and, most recently, with Cambridge University Press, *Soviet Central Asia in Modern Times.*

Jane Ormrod is a doctoral candidate in the Department of History at the University of Chicago. She has presented work on Russian peasant popular culture and has conducted research and field work in Russia and the North Caucasus. She is currently investigating cultural self-representation and the development of ethnic and national identity among the peoples of the North Caucasus.

Ray Taras was educated in Canada, England, and Poland, and has served on the faculty of universities in Canada, England, and the United States. He has published a number of books on comparative politics including *The Road to Disillusion: From Critical Marxism to Postcommunism in Eastern Europe* (1992) and *Polish Communists and the Polish Road to Socialism: A History of Self-Destruction* (1993). Taras's previous book with Cambridge University Press was *Ideology in a Socialist State* (1984).

Michael Urban is Associate Professor of Politics in the University of California, Santa Cruz. His recent books include *More Power to the Soviets: The Democratic Revolution in the USSR, An Algebra of Soviet Power: Elite Circulation in the Belorussian Republic 1966–86,* and the edited volume, *Ideology and System Change in the USSR and East Europe*. Currently, his research focuses on the development of a party system in Russia, and the evolution of Russian political identity and political language.

Ronald Wixman is Professor in the Department of Geography at the University of Oregon. Since the age of seventeen, he has made over twenty-five trips to Eastern Europe, the USSR, and the Middle East, where he has studied ethnic, cultural, religious, and ethno-territorial problems. To date he has published two books and a number of articles on these issues; his handbook of Soviet nationalities (*The Peoples of the USSR: An Ethnographic Handbook*) has become the standard reference on the various nationalities and ethnic groups of the USSR.

Jan Zaprudnik is a graduate of Louvain University and received his doctorate at New York University. He has taught in the Department of History at Queens College and has served as correspondent and Editor at Radio Liberty. He has contributed articles on Belarus to numerous volumes, including *Handbook of Major Soviet Nationalities*, *The Journal of Byelorussian Studies*, and *ZAPISY of the Byelorussian Institute of Arts and Sciences*.

Victor Zaslavsky is Professor of Sociology at the Memorial University of Newfoundland. He has taught at the University of California, Berkeley; Stanford University; and the University of Venice. His publications include *The Neo-Stalinist State: Class, Ethnicity, and Consensus in Soviet Society*, *From Union to Commonwealth: Nationalism and Separatism in the Soviet Republics* (with Gail Lapidus and Philip Goldman), and *Soviet-Jewish Emigration and Soviet Nationality* (with R. Brym).

Foreword

ROBERT CONQUEST

Anyone who has even a moderate knowledge of Soviet nationality problems has long known that a "democratic Soviet Union" would be a contradiction in terms. For it was plain that nationality problems in the USSR had not been solved; that feelings repressed, rather than satisfied, over several generations would re-emerge if and when any civil liberty was restored; and that given freedom to do so citizens of the peripheral nationalities would vote against the system.

It was asserted by Soviet propaganda, and believed by some in the West, that the national problems which had beset the area under previous regimes had been accommodated by a program of autonomy within a greater sphere. This notion has now collapsed. Yet, right up to the end, it was not uncommon to read of members of this or that Western foreign policy establishment regretting the break-up of a unitary centralized Soviet Union.

They have two major plaints. The first is that the greater the number of sovereign states, the more difficult it is for diplomats to operate. The same objection may have been made to the break-up of the Austro-Hungarian and Turkish Empires, to the emergence of scores of African and Asian successor states to Britain and France, and perhaps – earlier – to the disintegration of the Spanish Empire into the many countries of South and Central America. Yes, of course new problems are presented, but coping with such matters is what diplomats and Secretaries of State are for. If they don't like it (an impatient citizen might say), they can retire and retrain as auctioneers or esteem-enhancement counsellors. In any case the breakup of the USSR (and Yugoslavia) would add no more than a score or so to the present large roster of independent states.

But this fairly frivolous objection is linked with a more substantial argument: that the status quo, the unified USSR, was stable, as against the anarchic repercussions of the freed forces of nationalism.

No. The Soviet Union did not provide stability; it froze instability. Its attempts to transcend and transform national feeling are now seen as a total failure; and its claims to have done so as a total fraud.

Nor is a status quo to be desired for its own sake. If you live under a dam with cracks in it you may feel safe, especially if the cracks have been plastered over. But when they are visible and spreading, and the whole structure is beginning to shake, it would be unwise to rely on the status quo, rather than seek other methods of containing or diverting the force of the waters.

Moreover, it is obviously untrue that the Soviet Union, in the seventy-odd years of its existence, contributed to world stability. On the contrary, it was always a major focus – and for the past forty years *the* major focus – of conscious efforts to destabilize all other states. Even within the past decade it was still instigating and financing a whole cycle of civil wars on foreign soil. And this was precisely because it denied the validity of all other principles, including the national principle, where these presented any sort of obstacle to Marxism-Leninism – that is, to the whole Soviet *raison d'être*.

Of course it is true that emergent nationalism, and not only in the USSR and Yugoslavia, may in some circumstances have highly damaging effects. Negative, destructive forces have emerged and are emerging. But it is a central error and distortion in much of Western argument on the subject to note the extremisms and xenophobias which are sporadically visible, and to write off *all* national feeling on that basis. For there are also positive and prudent phenomena. The elected leaderships not only in, for example, the Ukraine, but in Russia itself, are overwhelmingly against the virulent strains of race-hatred and of police imperialism. There are, in fact, various possible ways in which reasonably equitable relationships, reasonably satisfactory to all parties, might be established among the nations which formed Moscow's empire.

It is in the interests of the whole world that this evolution should be peaceful. But if the West is to help, or even advise, it is essential that our knowledge be as full as possible, and that we see the possibility, let alone the desirability of a restabilization of anything like the old order as a mirage.

Even before the present situation declared itself a number of useful studies of these problems were produced in the West. But with the predicted emergence of the realities of national sentiment, it has become more urgent than ever that a general understanding of the often complex and intractable detail should be given a much higher priority than has so far been the case. The academic and the political and the public mind in the USA, and in the West in general, needs to educate itself quickly if we are to understand, and react intelligently, to the processes now seething away over the huge area of what was the Soviet empire.

The contributions to this collection make a priceless addition to such knowledge and understanding.

Preface

The collapse of the Soviet Union in December 1991 ended an extraordinarily Orwellian chapter of history in a preposterously Schweikian fashion. To echo the sentiment of virtually every scholar studying the momentous changes taking place within the Soviet bloc between 1985 and 1991, the magnitude and swiftness of the transitions from Communism to post-totalitarianism, and from Soviet to post-Soviet government, were unanticipated and yet somehow inevitable. While a vanguard of scholars – Amalrik, Brzezinski, Conquest – had insisted collapse would come, the scenario of a reform-minded Communist Party General Secretary producing a series of unintended consequences that led inexorably to regime change still seemed implausible in March 1985 when Gorbachev succeeded Chernenko.

Understandably, therefore, at the outset of the six-year Gorbachev era specialists were preoccupied with the agenda of *reform* of the Soviet political and economic system. After all, such large-scale institutional changes as envisioned by Gorbachev were unprecedented in a Communist state. But over time *nationalities* within the USSR came to dominate the agenda of scholars and policy makers alike. Emergent nationalism was widespread, involved much of the public, brought to the fore new leaders, and often produced violent encounters with Soviet security forces. A failed coup in August 1991 briefly rekindled kremlinological-type analysis, but within a month the USSR officially recognized the secession and independence of the three Baltic states, and attention came to be focused on the future of the remaining twelve republics which had declared independence. Soviet federalism as advocated by Gorbachev was stillborn. And while the stability and strength of the Confederation of Independent States remained an open question in 1992, the study of the successor states – and the restless national minorities within them – became more important than ever.

The nationalities "explosion" has led those interested in its study to focus their attention primarily upon its origins. A common belief held by *perestroishchiki* of both East and West was that the crisis resulted almost exclusively from mistakes made in the Soviet past. Political scientist and one-time Gorbachev advisor Fyodor Burlatsky provided an example when he implored observers to "look at the intense national feelings and hatreds that are erupting around the country. All these problems were created by the authoritarian past.'[1] Similarly, self-proclaimed "half-dissident" Len Karpinsky noted: "we ourselves created this danger by trampeling these republics, disregarding their national interests, culture, and language. Our central authorities planted the roots of the emotional explosion of national sentiment we are now witnessing."[2]

Much of the extensive recent Western literature, if more sophisticated in analysis, none the less shares this underlying assumption. Thus a major study of the nationalities question by Bohdan Nahaylo and Victor Swoboda concentrated, in the words of the authors, "on the relationship between the Russians and the non-Russians." The central thesis of *Soviet Disunion* was that Russian domination exercised through the Soviet state was responsible for nationalist unrest. Not surprisingly, the purpose of the book was to describe "the way in which an empire masquerading as a new model society crushed resistance, imposed alien values and even an alien language on its subject peoples, and left many of them fearing about their very survival as distinct nations."[3] This "perspective from above" also informed the pioneering work of Hélène Carrère d'Encausse, *L'Empire Eclate*, written a decade earlier.[4]

According to this perspective, then, expressions of nationalism have represented little more than outgrowths of anti-communist sentiment, and communist rule was closely linked to Russian domination. Under these circumstances, the corresponding policy response was clear: if the nationalities problem had its origins in Soviet authoritarian rule, then doing away with authoritarianism through perestroika and introducing a new democratic socialism could right the situation.

An analytic approach focusing on Russia is not without its merits. It was the Russian-dominated Soviet state which ultimately bore responsibility for its own domestic instability. Reasons for this range from the inadvertent and belated negative consequences of promoting socio-economic mobility and, correspondingly, of migration, to outright polices of Russification or "sovietization." Yet such analysis ignores the fact that Soviet nationalities were more than merely a product of the Soviet era. This study therefore proceeds from a different set of assumptions. We consider the roots of the nationalities problems to be more complex, transcending the nature of direct Soviet rule. Indeed, as some observers have noted, in certain cases of relations between the nationalities, Soviet authoritarianism may well have provided stability, calming what had otherwise been a violent history. We are aware that, in the long run, to claim that Soviet rule had *any* single effect upon the Soviet nationalities is rife with difficulty, because the nature of nationalities issues in the Soviet Union escapes generalizability. To take a fundamental issue, the sharing of "union republic" status does not imply that the majority groups therein can be analyzed using the same conceptual framework as for national movements.

Numerous scholars have remarked upon the political difficulties which the Soviet nationality conflicts posed for Gorbachev and upon his consequent inability to deal with them. In *The Nationalities Factor in Soviet Politics and Society*, Lubomyr Hajda and Mark Beissinger note "Mikhail Gorbachev originally placed the nationalities issue at the very bottom of his agenda . . . [he] did not even raise the need for a reevaluation in nationalities policy until he was almost two years in office."[5] Generally speaking, Western scholars have operated upon the assumption that there exists one single nationalities "issue," that a nationalities "policy" can be formulated, and that the Soviet nationalities constitute one uniform problem, albeit a critical one, among (and, indeed, linked to) the many faced by the Soviet Union. While this approach may be justified by the fact that Gorbachev himself, especially during his first two years in office, did treat nationalities relations as a unified issue, the underlying assumption is nevertheless incorrect. By 1991, Gorbachev's statements consistently highlighted the differences among the Soviet nationalities, with particular emphasis placed upon the uniqueness of the Baltic situation. It may be argued that Gorbachev made this change due to political expediency, in the hopes of making more difficult the use of the Baltics as a precedent for national movements elsewhere. Beneath the rhetoric, however, many of the relevant Soviet policies enacted – such as economic decentralization, openness, and cultural policies (not to mention, more generally, the numerous drafts of the union treaty) – tended to deal with nationalities precisely in an undifferentiated manner.

Nationalities scholarship can fall into a related trap of assuming that the Soviet "national problem," treated in a way distinct from the approach to nations outside the USSR, existed homogeneously throughout the country. Studies of Transcaucasian nationalism, for example, insofar as they have drawn comparisons with other national movements, often have done so with other nationalities in the USSR, and not with those of neighboring states. The common denominator of shared institutions coupled with some examples of cooperation among unlikely partners (for example, the Baltic mediation attempt in the Armenian–Azerbaijani conflict) makes this approach especially attractive. Yet we believe that precisely the opposite approach holds more promise: Soviet nationalities are highly differentiated, and comparisons, to the extent that they may be made at all, are often more appropriate with nations lying *outside* the USSR. We would expect, for example, Turkmen nationalism in Turkmenistan to resemble Turkmen nationalism in Iran or Afghanistan (or, indeed, Iranian or Afghan nationalism) more closely than Latvian nationalism. Up until now, the traditional approach to the study of Soviet nationalities has not been informed by such a rationale.

This book proceeds from the view that while integration into the Soviet Union undoubtedly marked an extraordinary period of political development in the course of many national histories, the Soviet period may be perceived as anomalous. Henry Huttenbach, the editor of *Nationalities Papers*, has illustrated this point by making the following observation. Visiting Lithuania in 1988, he witnessed one of the early national front demonstrations during which schoolchildren joined hands and sang first the national anthem and then native folk songs. These folk songs had never been taught to the children in the state schools and had never been heard through the halls of the Komsomol, yet the children were singing them none the less. Huttenbach concludes, "Lithuanian wine was poured into Soviet bottles."[6] The Soviet Union was a political reality for much of the twentieth century, yet it did not put an end to the singing of folk songs, did not destroy national cultures entirely – despite Stalinism – and did not eliminate nationalist sentiment.

It is true, to be sure, that our generation has witnessed the unraveling of the Kremlin-ruled Soviet empire. The historic significance of this development remains unclear. Yet irrespective of the magnitude and the rapidity with which changes have taken place and, indeed, of their desirability, the central question concerns less why the Soviet Union fell apart than how it managed to remain together in the first place. While Victor Zaslavsky's remark that the Soviet Union is effectively "a union of Norway and Pakistan" may at first sound exaggerated, we are sympathetic to the sentiment behind it.[7] For it makes clear that *sovetsky narod* has not, does not, and will not exist. Sovietology as a field of inquiry was therefore well-equipped to study the Soviet nation, which in fact did not exist, and yet ill-equipped to handle the nations of the USSR, which did.

This is not to argue that studies of the Soviet successor states must start from a *tabula rasa*. In many ways, the echoes of Gorbachev's call for *novoe myshlenie* that permeate Western scholarship have created a crisis in post-Sovietological research. However, a complete break from previous models and methodologies, however seductive, would be imprudent. The Soviet historical legacy is of great importance (as, of course, is the Tsarist legacy). The impact of directed migration, of bureaucracy, ideology, and a central economy, as well as of imposed territorial divisions have had significant results across the country. While the lasting effects may be hard to gauge, we should expect some nationalities to have been less profoundly affected than others by the Soviet period. Western "new thinking" must build upon the influence of both the pre-Soviet and Soviet periods to help understand developments in the post-Soviet period. Both earlier periods have affected nationalities issues, and both are therefore central concerns of this book.

This volume deals, then, with what we might call "fraternal illusions": the facade and the reality of national relations in the Soviet Union. For seventy years, these relations were depicted by Soviet ideology as fraternal – there supposedly existed constitutional equality of republican nationalities and the protection of the rights of minority groups. Yet, for a long time, it has been apparent that the claim to national harmony was in fact illusory. With the countenancing of Gorbachev of criticism of the dominant political discourse, the fictional nature of this fraternity was revealed. *Nations and Politics in the Soviet Successor States* serves to demystify the multinational Soviet state.

Each chapter in this book treats a separate Soviet nationality and then focuses on the dynamic of its political mobilization. To this end, two questions have been posed by the authors: To what extent has nationalism played a role in mobilizing peoples of the USSR toward political action? And what have been the fundamental cleavages dividing Soviet society, and what role has nationalism played in creating them? Western scholars have recognized the pervasiveness of the nationality dimension. Paul Goble, for example, contends that "[n]ationality affects virtually everything in the Soviet system; it is not, as is sometimes thought, confined to issues such as language and culture. . . . But, while it affects everything, it determines relatively little, allowing both the authorities and the nationalities room to maneuver in achieving their goals."[8] And while Hajda and Beissinger also assert that "[t]here is a nationalities component to every facet of Soviet politics," this is certainly not true of *nationalism*.[9] The answers to the two questions posed above invariably differ greatly across the Soviet Union, and it is from this difference that the chapters diverge. From this perspective, other questions, such as the role of a diaspora, the increasingly explosive issue of refugees, the importance of religious differences, and regional economic relationships are considered. Questions touching upon more recent history, such as the role of anti-communism, are also addressed. None of these questions can be answered definitively without first having examined the specific features of a given region.

In order to describe the processes of political mobilization, we focus upon the distinctiveness of various national agendas. Much as Gorbachev's calls for a new Soviet federation based upon a new set of integrative principles failed to deal with the distinctiveness of Soviet nationalities, *any* abstract prioritizing of the conflictual issues dividing nationalities, or between nation and state, would be misguided. Only a systematic consideration of individual nations may yield such an agenda. Different relationships weigh more heavily in different regions; different cleavages have varying effects upon political mobilization. Each chapter highlights such variations.

Now that we have described the framework behind the individual chapters, let us present a brief description of the structure of the volume as a whole. The introductory chapter proceeds from an analysis of traditional Western approaches towards the nationality question in the USSR and then offers a framework for a theoretical treatment of nationalism, understood in terms of the variegated relationships between center, titular nationality, and non-titular nationality in the Soviet Union. The way in which nationalism emerges when a nation must maintain a relationship with a larger state is different from the results of its dealing with minority groups under its own jurisdiction. Particular attention is therefore paid to the theoretical aspects of nationalism; *applications* of nationalities theory are left to the other chapters.

The traditional "view from above" approach is presented in chapter 2, and it serves as a brief transition to the "perspective from below" taken in the remainder of the volume.[10] Such a macro-approach is valuable in reassessing the national myths which were propagated by the Soviet center and circulated throughout the country until the time of Gorbachev. That such spurious ideas still have some currency is remarkable. As late as 1989, a respected long-standing critic of the Soviet system, Roy Medvedev, appeared none the less, like Gorbachev himself, to show incomprehension and even insensitivity to the nationalities issue: "I do not agree with those who say there is no 'brotherhood of peoples' in the USSR. There was and there is cooperation among nations. There is a new historical and social community: the 'Soviet people.' All this is not a 'myth.'" Medvedev's only qualification about the harmony existing within the *sovetsky narod* was limited to invoking the complex cultural mosaic of the USSR: "The friendship among populations," he observed, "does not exclude the rise of disputes when more than a hundred different nations, each with its own traditions, live side by side."[11] In his contribution, Victor Zaslavsky describes how this short-sighted Kremlin perspective contributed to the system's inability to respond to nationalities issues.

The volume then proceeds to treat each of the republics separately. While certain nationalist movements have implicitly contained irredentist claims, few have expressed the desire for reunification of lands in existence in pre-Soviet times.[12] Breaking with an approach which would, for example, lump Central Asia into a single homogeneous analytical unit, our study disaggregates it. This approach provides greater explanatory power for understanding the complexities inherent in the Central Asian region. Much the same would apply to the Baltics and to the new Eastern Europe which, while at times sharing the same history, have distinct cultures and languages. In the case of Ukraine, even history differs and the incorporation of the western and eastern parts into different states before 1939 provides a focus of analysis. In the Caucasus, the differences are especially stark, with religion often being perceived as a decisive factor. The significance of each national group, of course, differs widely on several axes, including: historical role, population, natural resources, levels of economic development, and degree of national self-consciousness. The treatment of each national group in individual chapters should not in any way serve to blur these distinctions; on the contrary, we feel that only such a division does them justice.

A separate section of the book is devoted to what were the Soviet non-union republics – now the "nations without states." While an exhaustive examination of these entities would require another study, we have attempted to cover enough ground in this volume to draw conclusions about their national development. For this reason, we have opted in favor of a regional approach instead of individual case studies, with chapters devoted to the Middle Volga, North Caucasus, and Siberia – the areas with the highest concentration of nations enjoying limited autonomy.

A further clarification about this section, given its relative unorthodoxy, seems warranted. The territorial breakdown of the Soviet Union into fifteen union republics (and, upon its collapse, fifteen successor states), coupled with the lack of attention afforded to national groups not so represented, has led to their neglect in nationality discourse. None the less, as national groups they share many qualities. Their recent assertions of sovereignty have only heightened this similarity. This has led to the peculiar emergence of nations within nations, the phenomenon of *"matrioshka* nationalism." Those who supported Soviet federation might wish, for example, to apply this concept to Russia itself.

In contrast to this disaggregated framework for the study of Soviet nationalities, the concluding chapter adopts a cross-national comparative perspective. While seeking to identify the commonly-held patterns of nationalist assertion posited in the introductory chapter – thus enabling a better understanding of nationalism as a phenomenon – this final chapter also employs the findings of the empirical chapters to establish various irregularities among national movements. One methodology used to examine these trends is the qualitative comparative case-study approach.

The scholars contributing to this volume are regional specialists, each of them having worked extensively in their particular areas. They come from a variety of disciplines: political science, history, sociology, geography, and anthropology. Such diversity is welcome, given the wide scope of the topic being analyzed. It is the hope of the editors that this diversity will assist in the creation of a guidemap to the intricately woven national movements in the former Soviet Union. We hope that our readers, like ourselves, will come away from this volume with a knowledge of the diversity of the Soviet nationalities – impressed with how difficult they have been to maintain, however loosely, under a single roof, but also sensitive to how they will continue to function now that the roof has been blown off.

In this spirit, the toponymic approach informing the book is use of the most recent, national appelations for countries and places. Soviet-period toponyms are retained to designate a historical context.

The editors would like to acknowledge the constructive suggestions which have been made by a number of scholars concerned with nationalities questions. The following have read parts of the manuscript and offered valuable insights: Alexander Dallin, Partha Dasgupta, Julius Moravscik, and Kenneth Schultz at Stanford University; Henry Huttenbach at the City University of New York; Ron Suny at the University of Michigan; Rodolfo Stavenhagen at El Colegio de Mexico; and Valeri Tishkov at the USSR Institute of Ethnography.

Rich Barnett, Reid Schar, Rich Stifel, and Cory Welt tirelessly assisted the editing process by typing, re-typing, and last minute fact-finding. Administratively, Linda Reilly and Ora Hurd at the Department of Political Science at Stanford have been continually helpful.

Our maps were expertly designed by Amanda Tate. The funding was provided by Tulane University.

We would like to thank the Hoover Institution, and especially National Fellows coordinators Tom Henriksen and Wendy Minkin, for providing the generous resources that made this study possible. We are also extremely grateful to Louise Simone, President of the Armenian General Benevolent Union, and Anita Anserian for their continued unwavering generosity.

John Haslam, desk editor and our principal go-between at Cambridge University Press, assured the high professional quality of the volume. Lyn Chatterton, production manager, and Con Coroneos, copy-editor, also provided expert assistance in this regard.

And finally, our thanks to Michael Holdsworth at Cambridge University Press, whose professionalism and uncanny sense for what we should be doing next is greatly appreciated. After several conference meetings, countless written correspondence, numerous phone calls and faxes, you would think we would be tired of him . . .

Stanford University
1992

Notes

1 Stephen F. Cohen and Katrina vanden Heuvel, eds., *Voices of Glasnost* (New York: W.W. Norton, 1989), p. 195.
2 *Ibid.*, p. 303.
3 Bohdan Nahaylo and Victor Swoboda, *Soviet Disunion* (New York: Free Press, 1990), pp. xii–xiii.
4 Hélène Carrère d'Encausse, *Decline of an Empire* (New York: Newsweek Books, 1979).
5 Mark Beissinger and Lubomyr Hajda, "Nationalism and Reform", in Hajda and Beissinger, eds., *The Nationalities Factor in Soviet Politics and Society* (Boulder, CO: Westview, 1990), p. 306.
6 Henry Huttenbach, "Nationalism in the Baltics," presented at the Annual Meetings of the American Association for the Advancement of Slavic Studies. Washington DC, October 18, 1990.

7 Victor Zaslavsky, "Traditional Nationalities Policies," in Ian A. Bremmer and Norman M. Naimark, eds., *Soviet Nationalities Problems* (Stanford: Center for Russian and East European Studies, 1990), p. 9.

8 Paul A. Goble, "The Fate of the Nationalities," in Walter Laqueur, ed., *Soviet Union 2000: Reform or Revolution?* (New York: St. Martin's Press, 1990), p. 122.

9 Hajda and Beissinger, eds., *Nationalities Factor*, p. 305.

10 The term "perspective from below" in regards to the Soviet nationalities first appears in Rasma Karklins' study, *Ethnic Relations: The Perspective From Below* (Boston: Allen and Unwin, 1986).

11 Roy Medvedev and Giulietto Chiesa, *Time of Change* (New York: Random House, 1989), pp. 246–7.

12 In a study which applies to the post-Soviet period, recognition of this factor is essential. We therefore retain the republic – as opposed to the national majority – as the basic unit of analysis.

Part I
Introduction

1 Reassessing Soviet nationalities theory

IAN BREMMER

The Soviet Union was perhaps the most extensive single case of the conflict and coexistence of national groups in history. While precise estimates vary, there were more than a hundred nations in the Soviet Union, *most* of which laid claim to Soviet territory as their homeland.[1] All of these nations were incorporated into a single state, creating what was – considering the geographic, cultural, economic, and religious implications – a state of virtually unprecedented diversity.

Having suffered through the distress of economic crises, the siege and devastation of war, and the terror of Stalin, the Soviet Union was a state which had survived tremendous adversity. Yet, after seventy years of Soviet rule preceded by centuries of Tsarist rule, it was national conflict that became the fundamental threat to Soviet stability. National demands surfaced with a vengeance, bringing about the disintegration of the Soviet state system. That this came as a surprise to Soviet citizens and Sovietologists alike is a serious understatement, highlighting the need for thorough analysis of nationalities issues.

The politico-demographic situation in the Soviet Union makes the importance of nationalism particularly difficult to gauge. Soviet national groups typically lived together, with Armenians, Chuvash, Kazakhs, Kyrgyz, Yakuts, and others living in generally ethnically homogeneous regions. Even more significantly, administrative divisions and ethnic divisions within the Soviet Union were largely delineated along the same territorial lines. For this reason, regional movements in the Soviet Union tended to be national in *form*, regardless of content. Environmental groups in Uzbekistan, anti-nuclear groups in Kazakhstan, Belarus and Ukraine, and workers' movements in non-Union republics within the RSFSR have all been assailed by Gorbachev (and, indeed, Western scholars) as nationalist. In each of these cases, however, it is unclear whether these organizations deserve such a title.[2]

This chapter attempts to clarify the issues at stake regarding Soviet nationalities problems. The first section introduces our analysis by briefly outlining the Soviet national system. The chapter then turns to consider the origins of Soviet nationalities policies, tracing Marxism, Leninism, and Stalinism in relation to the national question. The third section presents a

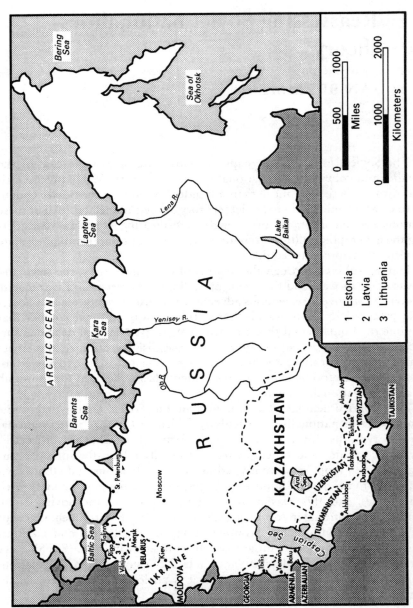

Map 1.1 The Soviet successor states

comprehensive framework for analysis of the underlying cleavages leading to conflict in the former Soviet Union. In the fourth section, recent developments are considered in this framework. The study concludes with an assessment of the possibilities for resolution of national conflict in the Soviet successor states. It is hoped that such an analysis will shed light upon not only post-Soviet cases but also the articulation of nationalism in general, particularly in today's increasingly interdependent world system where greater understanding of the national phenomenon may be essential for the avoidance of large-scale conflict.

Nationalism and the former Soviet Union

The Soviet political structure was federal, divided into four levels of regional, ethnically-based administrative-political units. Soviet nationalities policy was implemented similarly within each administrative level. Institutions were set up identically, with replications of not only party and state apparatuses but also cultural, scientific, and educational facilities. Economic policy also appeared egalitarian in structure, based upon the premise of giving to each according to his needs and taking from each according to his ability. Economic leveling could thereby occur, with state-controlled subsidies following policies of redistribution. It was, in essence, a massive state program of nation-based affirmative action. In all appearances nations possessed substantial, although by no means complete, control over their own governance.

All Soviet national groups were not treated equally, however. Only fifty-three of the over one hundred Soviet nations were officially identified with a particular territory and so afforded rights by virtue of their national status – the so-called "titular" nationalities.[3] The nature of these rights varied widely. Fifteen national groups were designated by the highest status of Soviet Socialist Republics (SSRs) or "union republics," which together encompassed the entire union. Directly accountable to and within the territories of the union republics, in order of descending status, were twenty Autonomous Soviet Socialist Republics (ASSRs), eight Autonomous Regions (*oblasti*), and ten Autonomous Areas (*okruga*). The rights of each of these formations were enumerated in the Soviet Constitution, including areas of dependence, guaranteed institutions, rights of autonomy and – in the case of the union republics – secession.[4] Significantly, obligations of obedience under Soviet rule were the same for all national groups while only the fifteen union republics were given the right to secede.[5]

Three factors underlie these administrative distinctions. First, each union republic bordered upon a foreign state. Were this to be otherwise, secession would leave a hole in the center of the union, an impractical arrangement for the republic and an intolerable one for the Soviet Union.

Second, larger, concentrated nations typically merited a higher administrative bracket. The vast majority of nations in the former Soviet Union are numerically small – typically numbering in the tens of thousands but occasionally as few as several hundred. Other nations, most notably the Tatars, had populations spread across the Soviet Union. Not deemed to constitute a credible threat to the stability of the union, they were not granted the right to secede. Third, nations which were part of a recognized diaspora instead of having their homeland within the Soviet Union fell into a lower administrative bracket. When this was the case, demands for statehood were either already actualized elsewhere or otherwise would be focused in the homeland.

With few exceptions, these factors applied evenly throughout the Soviet Union. The Buryats, Karelians, and Tuvanese – each bordering on foreign states and as large or almost as large as, for example, the Estonians and Moldavians – were the only nations which had been denied union republic status despite their apparent suitability. The Karelian case is interesting in that it was initially afforded union republic status upon its admission into the USSR in 1940 but was downgraded to ASSR in 1956, because of concerns about its size and the possibility of an outbreak of Finnish nationalism in the area. Thus, while there may have been elements of arbitrariness in categorization, for the most part administrative status was delineated according to a consistent plan.[6] Distinctions between ASSRs and Autonomous Regions and Areas were largely based upon the size of the national group, but here too administrative hierarchical divisions were clearer than national ones.

None of this is to neglect the fact that fully half or more of the Soviet Union's national groups had *no* political recognition as nations. If all nations in the Soviet Union were equal, some were clearly more equal than others.

Traditional approaches toward the Soviet nationalities question: Marxism, Leninism, Stalinism

Traditional explanations of nationalism have started from analyses of the state. Nationalism has been a principal ideological current since the time of Napoleon and the political imperative of successive Empires – Ottoman, Hapsburg, British, and Russian, to cite a few – has been to disarm national aspirations whether through the use of force, provision of economic development, or skilful use of intrigue within indigenous elites.

It is useful to recall, however, that nationalism has often been thought responsible for the suppression of individual rights and initiative. In his study, *The Myth of the Nation and the Vision of Revolution*, J.L. Talmon wrote of late nineteenth-century Europe in these terms:

Far from constituting the basic element and goal of society, from being his own autonomous lawgiver and free and equal partner to the social contract, as he was seen in the eighteenth century, man was made to appear more and more a function of collective forces, past traditions, the social setting, the organizational framework, the spirit of the nation, the Zeitgeist, their milieu, group mentality, finally the race ... Not man, therefore, but the nation, was the measure of all things, and the dominion of the dead was depicted as infinitely more potent than the deliberate decisions of the living.[7]

In some respects, therefore, the ideology of nationalism is reminiscent of the ideology of communism.[8] In states governed by nationalist or communist principles, the individual is important only as the embodiment of collective spiritual values. Man is no more the starting point of communism than he is the starting point of nationalism. But let us again invoke Talmon and consider a description that might aptly convey the relationship between nation and individual in the USSR. Talmon concluded about Europe on the eve of World War I: "Every nation was a world of its own, a unique blend. Since it fashioned countless men and determined their fate and well-being, the nation's interests, the imperatives of its particular situation, the conditions favouring its survival, cohesion, strength and influence contained its truth, morality and justice."[9]

Despite their apparent similarities, however, World War I revealed the inherent contradiction between socialist and nationalist ideologies. The leaders of the Second International believed that war could not break out between proletariats in different states because class loyalty was considered to transcend national loyalty. For them, socialism was viewed "as the purified product of the endeavors of European liberalism and democracy, and the crowning achievement of an ancient common European heritage."[10] The swift mobilization of war machines in Russia and Germany thus came as a bitter disappointment to most socialist leaders.[11]

Probably the most realistic of all Marxist currents concerning the national question was put forward by two Austrian socialist thinkers of the 1920s, Karl Renner and Otto Bauer. Contrary to Luxemburg and even Lenin, who generally recognized the progressive nature of national struggles, the Austro-Marxists were committed to the notion of an "evolutionary nationalism" that incorporated the history and traditions of a nation in the forging of a socialist order. Furthermore, as Talmon observed, they saw it as "the aim and destiny of socialism to enable the lower orders, for so long kept out of the national community, to join the national culture, to become co-heirs of the national heritage." As the Austro-Marxists contended, "Far from being anti-national, from working for the disintegration of the national community and for the effacement of its distinctness, socialism was aspiring to raise the nation to much loftier heights."[12]

Renner and Bauer ultimately underestimated the explosive nature of nationalism that could so quickly derail the socialist project. As Talmon noted, they had failed "to grasp the demoniacal, obsessive character of nationalist passion. They genuinely believed in the possibility of drawing and maintaining a line between the legitimate urge for collective self-expression and the passion for ascendancy, power, prestige and domination. A socialist nation could not by definition become imperialistic."[13] The Soviet Union had clearly become an imperialist state, as illustrated by its signing of the secret protocol to the Ribbentrop-Molotov Pact in August 1939, its aggression against Finland during the Winter War of 1939–40, Stalin's "sphere-of-influence" agreement with Churchill concluded in Moscow in October 1944, and finally his understanding of the 1944 Yalta treaty which left Soviet-liberated territories in Eastern Europe to Generalissimo Stalin's discretion. For other nations of the USSR – the peoples of former Turkestan, of Georgia, Armenia, and Azerbaijan – Soviet imperialism had been witnessed earlier, from 1921 when the Menshevik governments of the Transcaucasus were overrun, to 1927 when the last of the Basmachi revolts in Uzbekistan was crushed.

In Renner and Bauer's defense, it could be argued that Soviet power never gave legitimate expression to the national aspirations of the many peoples who were subordinated to it. In turn, suspicion of the central leadership about all but the most ritualistic manifestations of nationalism in the periphery exacerbated the subjective sense of colonialization felt by local peoples. As one observer put it, "The effort to cast all aspects of life in an ethnic mold brought ethnic considerations into areas that would otherwise have remained unaffected by them and gave sinister political implications to relatively harmless manifestations of ethnic assertiveness."[14] Even if we hold the view that the Soviet leadership neither launched a *Kulturkampf* against nationalities nor tried to forcibly russify them (culturally or linguistically) in the first decade after the October revolution, it may be enough that the life of these peoples could no longer take the traditional forms of national customs, habits, and cultural pathways. The ambiguous Soviet culture was presumed to dominate all other cultures save the Russian.

There was something peculiar about the formation of the Soviet state that went beyond the issue of Marxist experimentation. Following Alexander Gerschenkron, who studied the linkage between nation-building and industrialization,[15] Roman Szporluk underscored how the Russian industrial revolution had preceded the processes of modern nation-building, and consequently, "Marxism had taken hold before nationalism." The country's liberal nationalists were swept aside by the Bolsheviks and failed to have much of an influence in either elite circles or among the population. From the outset, Russia was slow in building a liberal civil society and a modern nation.[16] Put somewhat differently, Szporluk showed how "Relations between nations, and not just classes, played a vital role in determining the outcome of the Bolshevik Revolution." These included more illiberal Russian nationalists opposed to Communism who were convinced that the Bolsheviks "would best be able to preserve the territorial unity of Russia against the separatism of its non-Russian nationalities."[17] In a similar vein Deutscher identified the nationalist dilemma of the Bolsheviks in 1917: "The Leninists still believed that socialism demanded equality between nations; but they also felt that the reunion of most, if not all, of the Tsar's dominions under the Soviet flag served the interests of socialism."[18] These early calculations by certain Russian nationalist and Communist circles were to govern the formative years of the Soviet imperial state.[19]

So far we have discussed Marxist rather than Marxian approaches to the question of nationalities under socialism. In Szporluk's study of the early writings of Marx on the issue of German nationalism, he found a contemptuous attitude by Marx toward German backwardness as represented in its bourgeoisie, which lagged far behind its English and French counterparts in undertaking a world-historical mission. Yet by focusing on social relations, Marx was unprepared to attribute a historical role in social development to the nation. Szporluk concludes: "There can be no doubt that he considered nationality to be a minor factor, a 'dependent variable,' in the process of social development."[20] Nationalism was a historically determined phenomenon that emerged as a result of the rise of capitalism and was primarily a device of the imperialists, who could use it as a means to further their own parochial class interests by unifying the entire society.[21] But nations would eventually fade away in favor of a new community based upon class solidarity. The capitalist nation-state system would thus force itself into ruin.

Given this thesis, it is not surprising that many second-generation Marxists felt incapable of offering a doctrinal guide for the managing of national revolutions. There was nothing in Marx's model of successive social formations that pointed to nationalism as a historic force capable of accelerating or retarding progress to the next stage of development. Accordingly, the only solution to the national problem required the elimination of national differences.[22]

Before the Bolshevik Revolution, Lenin generally discounted the significance of nationalism and supported a policy of regional autonomy, whereby state political-administrative divisions would not be based upon ethnic lines.[23] After the revolution, however, many of the nations which had successfully gained their freedom from Tsarist Russia – such as the independent Soviet republics of Azerbaijan, Armenia, Belorussia and the Ukraine – were firmly opposed to domination from an imperial center. It thus became increasingly apparent to Lenin that the formation of a stable union would require substantial concessions to national rights.[24]

Lenin was thus caught uncomfortably between two poles, needing a modicum of national assimilation for state survival but unwilling to alleviate the national crisis through substantive action for fear of destabilizing the union. Consequently, even though complete assimilation of all national groups was the desired goal, it was deemed necessary to erect a façade of equality and sovereignty. Lenin compromised by allowing the creation of a Soviet federal structure based upon the dictum "national in form, socialist in content."[25] The primary policy enacted towards this end was *korenizatsia* (nativization), through which titular national cultures were promoted and members of titular nationalities were given preference for state-controlled benefits such as education, housing, and employment. Lenin's nationalities policy was necessarily transitional, since while nations would be allowed to remain distinct, they would eventually be assimilated. Where nations did not exist, they were created, with the intention of accelerating their inevitable demise. This process led to the paradoxical creation of modern national identities in Central Asia and the strengthening of national identities in the Caucasus.

The national right to secession became part and parcel of this new federal structure. Titular nationalities, embodied in union republics, were granted the right to unilaterally withdraw from the union. The granting of such a right was expected to be sufficient to placate the nationalist spirit. Closer analysis of the issue of secession, however, uncovers a central dilemma of Soviet nationalities policies – namely, the need to justify the constitutional contract between union republics and the Soviet state. Under this contract, each republic was responsible to the Soviet Union for carrying out the policies of the center and participating fully in socialist development. The Soviet center, in turn, was responsible for allowing republican secession were the republic so inclined.

This reasoning was based upon a circular logic. Given a right to secession, the republics would pledge to fully acknowledge and participate in a union under Soviet leadership; in return for such a pledge, nationalities would not choose to enact their right to secession. National instabilities would be constrained by the popular feeling of a freely entered contractual arrangement, thus providing a justification for empire that lies at the foundation of Soviet nationalities policy.

De jure nationalities policy was far divorced from Soviet reality, however. Neither Lenin nor any of his successors ever harbored any intentions of allowing the republics to exercise their right to secede. This understanding does not imply that a contractual arrangement never existed in social relations between center and periphery, but that its actual form was quite different from that prescribed by the Soviet Constitution.

What was the unofficial "nationalities contract"? At the most general level, it consisted of the central authorities providing a package of economic benefits to the republics, to be used largely at the discretion of the local elites, in exchange for the compliance of republic citizens with Soviet rule. This deal effectively "bought off" the loyalties of target leadership cadres, such as economic managers, trade union officials, administrative and party heads, and intellectuals. Those not fortunate enough to be so targeted were effectively excluded from the nationalities contract.

Reliance upon national passivity to maintain the stability of the union was therefore not left completely to the Constitution. The Soviet center hoped to undermine the fomenting of "nationalism in content" and eventually to assimilate titular nationalities into a Soviet model.[26] Throughout the Soviet period, Russian migration was extensive, indoctrination through schools and youth groups was maintained at a high level, religious organizations were coopted, and local economies were made dependent upon the Soviet center. Massive bureaucratic institutions were created, emanating from the center with symmetrical vertical lines of authority reaching down to the local level. Particularly in the non-Slavic areas, the Soviet center attempted to convince the varied nations that they had no culture prior to the Soviet period. This movement constituted the Stalinist "merging of nations" [*sliyanie*] and the Brezhnevite "creation of a new historical society – the Soviet people [*sovietsky narod*]."

Lenin's shift from a policy of regional autonomy to one of assimilation foreshadowed more ominous developments after his death. The accession to power of Stalin led to a deterioration of national rights in the Soviet Union. The national egalitarianism which had prevailed under Lenin became national regimentation and hierarchy. Russia was acknowledged to be the greatest nation while many others (most notably Chechens, Germans, Kalmyks, and Crimean Tatars) were deported by the hundreds of thousands to Central Asia and Siberia, punished *qua* nations for crimes against the Soviet Union.[27] Russification took place to a far greater extent under Stalin, and "somewhat national in form, Russian in content" became the rule.[28]

Lenin and Stalin improvised on the national question, therefore, rather than extrapolating from Marx (as they did in other areas such as economics and culture). Perhaps the Soviet state would not have been better served by an identifiably-Marxian approach to the subject; especially concerning this potent force, the Marxian paradigm and the theories of Marxist writers systematically wavered – often in a way transparent to even unideological and illiterate groups – thereby calling into question the visibility of Marxism as a guide to action generally. The inability to incorporate a *de jure* dynamic for national development in Soviet doctrine essentially stems from this inadequacy.

An alternative framework for national analysis

Traditional Sovietology has been Moscow-based, top-down, and monolithic. That there have been understandable ideological and practical reasons for this approach is beyond question; most notable among these are the Cold War context of Western scholarship and the relative inaccessability of Soviet sources. But as a result, the Soviet Union has been viewed as a unified bloc, and many internal Soviet cleavages have been either dismissed or ignored. To the extent that the Soviet periphery has been recognized as significant, nationalities have been perceived as reacting to and dependent upon center-initiated policies. The few scholars working on the Soviet periphery through this period were thus effectively marginalized.

It was only after the recent national explosions, which were widely perceived as threatening to the stability of the Soviet regime, that the study of Soviet nationalities became significant. Sovietologists immediately focused upon the factors contributing to destabilization.[29] Why had the Soviet Union suddenly fallen apart? What, if anything, could be done to keep the process from progressing further? Yet, as research agendas of Soviet study changed, perhaps the more analytically interesting questions concerned not so much the disintegration of the Soviet Union but how it remained together in the first place.

These questions, implicitly recognizing the inadequacy of state-centric analysis of Soviet nationalities issues, have not passed unnoticed. Indeed, much has been written recently about the importance of a "perspective from below" – a regional approach explaining nationalism in the Soviet periphery.[30] This approach necessarily discards many of the methodological assumptions latent in traditional Sovietology, putting the overworked paradigm of state-civil society relations on the backburner and making corporatism no longer satisfactory. In short, hidden nationalities in the Soviet Union would no longer be hidden; the Soviet periphery would no longer be peripheral.

But, if recent scholarship recognized that Soviet methodology must consider nations first and foremost, the question of how to formulate such an approach remained. The study of nationalities in the Soviet Union recognized the poverty of previous analysis without offering a comprehensive theoretical framework to replace it. As a consequence, recent scholarship has been characterized by the methods of area-studies rather than the canons of political science.[31] In the same vein as Stephen Cohen's revisionist replacement of the totalitarian school of Sovietology, a thorough alternative to the state-centric framework is desperately needed in the study of Soviet nationalities.[32] The emergence of fifteen successor states following the disintegration of the Soviet Union makes the need for such a framework all the more pressing.

In formulating such an alternative, we proceed from an analysis of the varied national relationships within the Soviet Union, breaking national conflict into its constituent actor-types: center, titular nationality, and non-titular nationality. Use of the term *center*, as opposed to state, here recognizes the Weberian notion of that institution which holds a monopoly over the right to use coercive force.[33] Authority rests in this institution. In most cases, center and state are interchangeable. Traditionally, this was true of the Soviet Union. Use of the term "center" allows for more accurate portrayal of the so-called "neocolonial" relationships between imperial powers and underdeveloped states, where authority lies outside the state in question. The ties between ruler and ruled may be discrete and indirect. The ruled may have gained a nominal sense of "statehood," but the national sentiment levied against perceived outside exploitation is no less substantive.

The *titular nationality* is of particular importance. This entity is the nation which, for any number of economic, demographic, cultural, or political reasons, has been vested with administrative power in a given region. In Russia it is the Russians, in Moldava the Moldavans, in Yakutia the Yakuts, and so on. The titular nationality has a special relationship with the state, being in a position of privilege *vis-à-vis* those nations not so empowered – the *non-titular nationalities* – and wary of any erosion of this position.

Although defined clearly under Soviet law, an analytical categorization of "titular" must show it to be a relative modifier. In other words, while "titular" relates to the special status of a nation in relation to the center, this status varies widely in a state with hierarchical titular rank. In such a realm, the relations between legally defined titular nationalities are not necessarily based upon a framework of equality. Nations may thus be considered titular in relation to other nations in certain contexts (i.e. titular Russians and non-titular Georgians in Russia; titular Uzbeks and non-titular Tajiks in Uzbekistan) while not in relation to others (non-titular Russians and titular Georgians in Georgia; titular Tajiks and non-titular Uzbeks in Tajikistan), depending upon their relative hierarchical status. Equality may be the foundation of a relationship between titular nationalities (on the union republican level – Estonians and Latvians, Armenians and Azeris), but it is important to remember that this need not be the case. Accordingly, it is useful to speak of *first-order* (union republic – Belorussians, Kyrgyz, Ukrainians) and *second-order* (ASSR – Abkhaz, Chechens, Yakuts) titular nationalities. This analysis thereby contextualizes the composition of a titular nationality.

Given these four actor-types, there are fifteen different possible interactions: center (A) – first-order titular nationality (B); A – second-order titular nationality (C); A – Non-Titular Nationality (D); $B - A$; $B - B$; $B - C$; $B - D$; $C - A$; $C - B$; $C - C$; $C - D$; $D - A$; $D - B$; $D - C$; and $D - D$.[34] Nationalism, defined as the political ideology aspiring towards the congruency of nation and center, particularly over the right to make decisions on issues perceived as important by the nation, will play a role in each.[35] Although the magnitude of this role will likely be determined or at least constrained by the relative strength of the center, its *form* may be expected

Table 1.1. *Patterns of inter-ethnic relations*

		A	B	C	D
		Center	First-order titular nationality	Second-order titular nationality	Non-titular nationality
A	Center		Integration	Integration	Assimilation
B	First-order titular nationality	Liberation	Competition	Domination	Domination
C	Second-order titular nationality	Collusion	Liberation	Competition	Domination
D	Non-titular nationality	Collusion	Liberation	Liberation	Competition

to change markedly depending upon the interaction. Nationalism is thus not only Janus faced, pointing upwards towards the state and downwards towards other nations, but also looks *across* to other nations.[36] These dyads may be shown graphically on a 4 × 4 matrix; the interactions and their contextual objectives are so represented in table 1.

This table, very loosely, represents the hypothesized objectives of each actor-type, given a certain interaction. This matrix more precisely depicts relationships usually implicitly differentiated in Soviet studies. Of course, room for maneuver exists within each interaction and objectives may be pursued in many different ways, from the most gradual policies to the most radical. Many factors may assist in determining the means involved, including the specific nature of actor grievances, the existence and consequent severity of a relationship of dependency, the internal and/or external support for the pursuit of given means, the perceived potential of success and the consequences of failure, and so on.

Each of these interactions may be briefly outlined. The center's interaction with all titular nationalities is one of *integration*, whereby the center attempts to establish a singular set of overarching norms and values (and thus a singular "nation") to maintain social cohesion. Nationalism is recognized as strong enough to remain troublesome even in the face of determined efforts to extinguish it, and continued nationalism among these groups undermines the ability of the state to apply unitary and direct rule.

Center-driven motivations to maintain a position of strength in relation to the periphery thus lead to integrative policies. The Soviet state's relationships with Azeris, Bashkirs, Evenks, Georgians, and Uzbeks all fall under this category. Integration is consistent with the traditional "perspective from above" – analyzing the Soviet state's justifications and actions towards its constituent nations in maintaining the integrity of the union – and is necessarily gradualistic in approach.

The center's relationship with non-titular nationalities follows the somewhat different pattern of *assimilation*. While the center's desire for relative strength remains, in these cases, the center feels for any number of reasons – historical, ideological, cultural, or demographic – that gradual integration is unnecessary. Instead, the center seeks to make the non-titular nationalities an immediate part of the state culture. Significantly, the essential difference between center policies towards titular and non-titular nationalities is therefore one of time-frame: the eventual expected outcome is the same. Denied rights of their own as nations, non-titular nationalities find it very difficult to maintain their national heritage. Linguistic rights are not protected; cultural practices, if not forgotten altogether, are weakened, and so on. This process was exemplified by relations between the Soviet state and, in Stalin's time, the Germans, Kalmyks, and Tatars. More generally, those between the Soviet state and the Jews, republican minorities such as Tabasaranis and Laks in Dagestan, Finns in Karelia, and the "peoples of the north" in Siberia revealed a similar assimilation phenomenon.

The interaction of first-order titular nationalities with the center was the traditional referent frame of the Soviet periphery – the "perspective from below" – and expressed itself as a manifestation of nationalism as *liberation*. This relationship takes into account titular nationalities' intentions to thwart Soviet rule and claim independence for themselves. Nations no longer wishing to yield to the dictat of central authority and desiring both a monopoly of control over the state apparatus and the ability to impose their norms and values upon surrounding populations first required liberation from external rule.

Nationalism as liberation may manifest itself through national demands for increased regional control of economic mechanisms, as in Central Asia, or through drives for independence, such as in the Baltics and Georgia. It may also affect the leading titular or "hegemonic" nation of an empire. The Russians are not only the titular nationality of the RSFSR; to some extent, they may also be considered titular nationality for the entire Soviet Union. Historically, to quote Paul Goble, "Russians were offered the choice of being free or being powerful"; perhaps not surprisingly they chose the latter.[37] Yet many have recently reconsidered, pressing for liberation from the burdens of empire and the corresponding desecration of Russian national values. In some strains of Russian nationalism, groups advocated the dismantling of the Soviet Union and the creation of a Russian nation-state. They perceived Central Asia and Transcaucasia to be a burdensome drain on valuable resources which, it is argued, could be better allocated to ethnic Russians.

Titular nationalities' intentions to improve their position *vis-à-vis* other titular nationalities of the same order are expressed in terms of *competition*. Desire to attain self-determination leads the titular nation to view as threatening other nations which it perceives as either encroaching on its own position or potentially able to make such an encroachment. Similar to the behavior of states in the international arena, the existence of mutually desired scarce resources create a perceived zero-sum relationship between titular nations, resulting in competition.[38] The focus of competition may be easily distributable (as in the case of natural resources such as precious metals, oil, food), or its resolution may be exceedingly difficult (such as when it takes place over land or political power).

Nationalism as competition can occur at all levels of national relations: between Uzbeks and Tajiks, Armenians and neighboring Turks, and even Russians and Western nations. The precise issues over which conflict is waged, as well as the methods of resolving conflict once competition occurs, are extremely wide-ranging. Competing claims over territory comprise the most longstanding and pernicious objects of competition (the conflict between Armenia and Azerbaijan over Nagorno-Karabagh provides the most obvious example); easily observable indicators such as economic indices and military force levels also have significant impact.

The relationship between titular nationalities and lower order titular and non-titular nationalities is one of *domination*. By virtue of their privileged status, titular nationalities reap considerable educational, employment, and social benefits. Non-titular nationalities represent a threat to this near-monopoly and therefore, far from the national integration pursued by the center, must be excluded from these benefits. Domination is the logical response. This relationship is expressed commonly in Russian relations with Bashkirs, Buryats, Chechens, Darginstis, Evenks, Jews, Tatars, Tuvanese, and many other nations within the RSFSR. Here the relativistic use of "titular" comes into play, with ASSR "titular" nationalities dominated as non-titular nationalities in relation to the hegemonic Russian nation. Similarly, Georgian relations with Abkhaz and Ossetians in Georgia, Azeri relations with Armenians in Azerbaijan (particularly in Nagorno-Karabagh), and Latvian, Lithuanian, and Estonian relations with Russians in the Baltics all display this essential characteristic of domination.

Yet, just as first-order titular nationalities express nationalism to keep lower order and non-titular nationalities from acquiring the fruits of power – be they economic, political, cultural, or otherwise – so too do lower order and non-titular nationalities express nationalism to attain those privileges from which they are excluded. Paralleling the actions of first-order titular nationalities toward the center, this is also nationalism as *liberation*, whereby lower order and non-titular nationalities attempt to avoid domination and attain authority and self-determination. These relationships typically appear as the backlash of titular/non-titular inter-actions and are reactive in nature. If developments in Chechen-Ingush against Russian rule is one particularly explosive example, nationalism as liberation among lower-order titulars such as Abkhaz, Kalmyk, Komi, North Ossetia, and Udmurt fit this model equally well.

Lower-order titular and non-titular nationalities interacting with the center are in perhaps the most interesting position, expressing nationalism as *collusion*. Ultimately non-titular as a consequence of center-initiated policy, they none the less find themselves immediately ruled by the titular nations above them. These ruling nations pose the most direct threat to lower-order titular and non-titular nationalities, and only the center possesses the power to restrain them. Lower-order titular and non-titular nationalities thus collude with the center, favoring such mechanisms as a strong unitary state apparatus to keep the titular nationalities directly above them in line.[39] Particularly in the case of Bashkir, Buryat, Chukchi, Chuvash, Karachai, and Tatar relations with the Soviet center, nationalism as collusion has been apparent.

Finally, there are interactions between non-titular nationalities which also express nationalism as *competition*. While mimicking titular-titular relationships through competition over such scarce resources as property rights, housing, and basic sustenance, non-titular nationalities typically lack the organizational skills and resources to engage in direct competition with one another. Yet, in the relatively small number of cases where they do, such competition may be fierce. Dagestan provides perhaps the best example, with a host of non-titulars engaged in competition with one another (Kumyks and Avars, Lezgins and Avars, Lezgins and Kumyks, and so on). One may add relations between Meshketians and Kyrghyz in Uzbekistan, and Russians and Crimean Tatars in Ukraine to this list.

Essential to this framework is the recognition that different impulses may be found among the same nations, and indeed, may contradict each other. For example, first-order titular nationalities may employ the rhetoric of liberation when dealing with the center, while at the same time rejecting such claims (and exerting domination) when they are made by lower-order titular or non-titular nationalities within their borders. These impulses are not mutually exclusive, but represent different simultaneously-operating motivations which may lead not only to the strengthening or weakening of nationalist sentiment but also to the articulation of those demands. For example, cooperation may occur among titular nationalities instead of competition, but only as a tactic which persists in the face of another relationship perceived to be of greater immediate importance (i.e., liberation from the Soviet center).[40] In addition to the fundamental threat of the center and its potential to be dominated by national or other interests, any nation which either has such influence or the potential to attain it may also become a threat.[41]

Few scholars have proceeded upon this recognition. Szporluk's division of Russian nationalists into "empire savers" and "nation builders" is a start in this direction.[42] Specifically, we may consider each impetus to be firmly grounded in the primacy of different nationalist interactions. "Empire savers" express their nationalism primarily in terms of titular nationality *vis-à-vis* non-titular nationalities, expressing nationalism as domination.[43] "Nation builders," alternatively, focus on the Russian relationship with the Soviet center and carry a strong liberative element.[44]

Continuing with Szporluk's categorization, not all non-Russian nationalists are empire destroyers. While such a tendency may have existed throughout the Soviet periphery, it may have been diluted or even overwhelmed by other impulses, equally nationalist, which played themselves out against other nations. Only a case by case consideration of national agendas, dynamic national forces, and pertinent social cleavages will enable a clear determination of which impulses predominate.

It should be noted that the general theoretic framework, intended for use in describing national relations within a Soviet Union in transition, should also apply more generally, and is envisioned to be particularly useful in reference to the Soviet successor states. As long as power structures among national groups remain hierarchical, this typology should serve to characterize the nature of national relations.

The Soviet nationalities explosion

How can this analysis assist us in understanding the disintegration of the Soviet Union? Contrary to Lenin's reasoning, the road to socialism has turned out to be a drastically insufficient incentive to maintain the integrity of the Union. Beginning in earnest in 1988, national explosions rocked the entire country and, by the end of 1991, the Soviet Union had disintegrated with all fifteen Soviet republics having achieved independence and more than twenty ASSRs, autonomous regions, and autonomous areas having declared sovereignty and formed national movements with widespread popular support. Many even had official nationalist parties standing for election and supporting programs of national self-determination (made possible by the 1989 abolition of Article 6 of the Constitution which granted a monopoly of state power to the Communist Party). The resistance of many national groups to Soviet power was thus considerable.

With the possible significant exception of coopted local elites (the so-called "state-dependent sector"), Soviet citizens never came to feel that a

Soviet nation existed. Even among Russians, the Soviet state was effectively perceived to be the natural extension of the Russian nation. And while the potential ramifications of a tougher nationalist policy are unclear (i.e. dissolution of sub-union administrative-political units or reorganization along non-ethnic lines), there should be no doubt that the same Soviet policy of "national in form", which coopted national elites, also allowed for the persistence of strong popular national feeling. Consequently, the Soviet Union could emasculate the Orthodox Church, but it could not stop people from believing its tenets; it could teach songs praising the victories of Marxism-Leninism in the schools, but it could not cease the singing of ethnic songs at home; it could publicly Sovietize its people, but it could not strip them of their ethnic identities.

Although some measure of integration was probably inevitable given the exigencies of Soviet rule, even this move typically was attributed to Russian more than Soviet initiative. *Sovietsky narod* essentially became a variant of *russky narod*, and the traditional Soviet policy of "national in form, socialist in content" was turned on its head, giving way in practice to socialist in form, national in content.[45] On the whole, Soviet policies of integration met with failure.

This analysis does not imply that nations had a tradition of challenging Soviet policy. Indeed, while many socialist principles were widely criticized under Khrushchev, little significant dissent arose over the Soviet nationalities question until after Gorbachev acceded to power.[46] Instead, outward adherence to Soviet policies was given, while much of the substance of day-to-day life remained the same. Soviet rule was circumvented, but not challenged, through subterfuge and corruption

Once Gorbachev came to power, however, many national groups directly challenged Soviet rule. Several factors worked in conjunction with this dissension. Those Sovietologists undertaking class analysis have been quick to point out the nefarious effects of perestroika upon the interests of the industrial proletariat.[47] Yet a parallel process set off by perestroika, though less perceptible, was also damaging to the interests of national elites in the Soviet Union. This process involved *khozraschet* and the related effective tightening of public monitoring of accounts; attacks on previously widespread corrupt practices; large-scale reductions in state-sector employment; and cutbacks in center-periphery capital transfers. The net effect was to economically alienate peoples in republics who could previously count on reasonable (and, in some cases, lavish) living standards.

Thus dissatisfied with the increasingly disadvantageous content of the nationalities contract, glasnost further spurred national elites, allowing widespread criticism with lessened fear of retribution. Those who had previously chosen to "exit" were given a "voice" under glasnost and motivated to air their grievances openly.[48] Together, the Soviet "carrot" of economic incentive diminished across the board, and its "stick" became less ominous as the state apparatus appeared increasingly fragmented and weak.

Soviet suppression of national preferences therefore appeared increasingly ineffectual at a time when imperialism had become inextricably linked with Soviet socialism in the minds of discontented national groups. If the totalitarian Communist order had perhaps succeeded in bringing about forced *sblizhenie* (coming together), perestroika could not help but produce the spontaneous *otdalenie* (distancing) of neighboring national groups.

Tracing the recent nationalities explosions in the Soviet Union (see Appendix A) clearly demonstrates the multiplicity of interactions posited in the previous section; the direct challenging of Soviet rule (the national movement as *liberation*) does not accurately describe national movements across the board. Some movements demanded independence, others opted for more limited increases in national autonomy; some attacked party representatives, Soviet army installations, and state institutions, while others targeted neighboring ethnic groups. These fundamentally different types of national conflict should be considered as such.

Perhaps not surprisingly, the most serious national uprisings were liberative, rising in particular from first-order titular national movements. There are four factors which help to explain this. First, only in the union republics did legitimate contractual grievances form the central plank of national demands. This dissent was strongest in the Baltics where, because of the Molotov-Ribbentrop Pact, no contractual basis for their incorporation into the union existed. In other union republics, the validity of the initial contract had been acknowledged and titular national movements demanded that the Soviet center recognize their right of secession. This was even true of Russia, which in 1990 joined its republican brethren in declaring itself sovereign.

Second, the state-dependent sector, which stood to lose the most from a sudden shift in Soviet policy, was most extensive in the union republics. To the extent that elite mobilization had been responsible for national uprising, movements among first-order titular nationalities were successful.

Third, the national rights of first-order titulars had been most staunchly supported by Soviet policy. This support especially applied to linguistic and cultural autonomy. These nations would thus expect easier consolidation in the transition period.

Finally, first-order titulars occupy the most ethnically homogeneous administrative divisions in the Soviet Union. According to 1989 Soviet census data, titular nationalities of union republics were national majorities in all but Kazakhstan, where they represented a plurality of the population.[49] This situation was typically not the case in the former autonomous republics, such as in Bashkiria, Buryatia, Karelia, Komi, Mari,

Mordvinia, Udmurtia, and Yakutia, where titular nationalities did not even comprise a plurality of the population.[50]

In the past, even first-order titular nationalities held virtually no power, with their administrative divisions being little more than hollow institutional caricatures of the state. Having increased their demands for the devolution of authority, these groups gained the opportunity to increase their voice in the workings of government. Yet, while national expression in this instance had been liberative, the related demands have emphatically *not* been total independence, as most national movements sought to dissolve the union in order to create a new one based upon more satisfactory, looser arrangements. With the exception of the independent Baltics, only Georgia consistently rejected all calls for a new-union treaty and pushed for complete secession. What these national movements typically demanded is greater independence than had been offered by the central Soviet leadership in the past.[51]

Under these circumstances, the trend of widespread Russian outmigration from the Soviet periphery, particularly the Caucasus and Central Asia, should come as no surprise. Yet, recent national assertions of sovereignty, while not totally free from irredentist claims, have nonetheless expressed no desire to revert to pre-Soviet territoriality. First-order titular nationalities generally have not attempted to expel non-ethnic nationals or reunite with their national brethren (with Nagorno-Karabakh, northern Kazakhstan, and the Crimea the major exceptions). Forced migration policies have thus created few territorial squabbles. Indeed, some independence movements explicitly recognized their representation of all those living within republican territory. In particular, Rukh, the Ukrainian independence movement, stated in a recent Congress that it "seeks power . . . in order to better the lot of all the people of Ukraine, as well as appeals to peasants, the military, youth, teachers, and Christians of all denominations."[52] More surprising is the response of ethnic Russians living in the Baltics, with public opinion polls finding that over 40 percent favored Baltic independence.[53] The overwhelming voter support for independence in Estonia and Latvia confirmed this trend.

While elite *dissimilation* may appear particularly strong in explaining anti-Soviet nationalist demonstrations among first-order (to a lesser extent, second order) titular nationalities, such an explanation is less compelling for other expressions of national sentiment which were either markedly less anti-Soviet, lacked reference to the Soviet state altogether, or embraced continued Soviet rule. It is not that the relationships of these movements with the Soviet state were fundamentally different, but rather that other relationships with neighboring national groups were considered to pose the immediate problem. This is first and foremost the case of the non-titular nationalities.

Many representatives of lower-order titular nationalities have chosen the "exit" option (many more have simply chosen to physically leave), but others have opted to directly confront disagreeable national rule. A large number of non-union republic-based national groups have voiced unequivocal demands for sovereignty (included among them the Chechen-Ingush, Chuvash, Karelian, Komi, Mari, Tatar, and Udmurt ASSRs and autonomous regions and areas including Adigei, Chukchi, Gorno-Altai, Karachai, Komi-Permyak, and Koryuk), although they only came after most union republic declarations. This list does not exclude the numerous "counter-movements" of ethnic Russians in the peripheral autonomous republics, Azeris in Armenia, Armenians in Azerbaijan, and so on. Yet almost without exception, these movements challenged republican (most typically Russian), as opposed to Soviet rule – concomitantly expressing nationalisms as collusion and liberation. These conflicts came from the peculiar existence of nations within nations, a phenomenon which may be referred to as "*matrioshka* nationalism." Reactionary movements resulted, with further consolidation of republican power making the republican government an immediate and dangerous threat. The same demonstrations asserting the rights of first-order titular nationalities often hurt lower order titular and non-titular nationalities as a direct consequence.

Our theoretical framework would lead us to expect extremely complex and fragmented nationalities movements in a Soviet Union under transition, with conflicting objectives sought not only by different national groups but also different tendencies appearing within the same national group. To the extent that preexisting power structures have remained intact since the disintegration of the Soviet system, we would expect such dynamics to persist in the successor states. The preliminary overview presented in the final section of this chapter seems to substantiate these hypotheses, but it is impossible to draw further conclusions without rigorous, case-by-case consideration. It is to this approach that we now turn.

Notes

1 There has been considerable debate on nation counting in the former Soviet Union, particularly concerning the difference between the ill-defined Soviet conceptions of "nation" and "ethnic group." See S.I. Bruk, "Ethnicheskie protsessy i voprosy optimizatsii natsional'no administrastivnogo deleniia v SSSR," *Natsional'nye problemy v sovremennykh usloviiakh* (Moscow: Institute of Marxism-Leninism, CPCC, 1988), pp. 128–143; and M.A. Abdullaev, "Osobennosti razvitiia dukhovnoi kul'tury malykh narodov SSSR v usloviiakh sovershenstvovaniia sotsializma," *Filosofiia razvivaiushchegosia sotializma* (Moscow: 1988), pp. 139–144.

2 There is, of course, another side to this problem. Cleavages which appear national in form by virtue of continued association with co-nationals may well *become* nationalist in content. Similarly, even though groups may be mobilized for diverse non-national purposes, to the extent that they are perceived as national movements, this perception may become self-fulfilling.

3 "Nation" and "nationality" are used indiscriminately throughout this chapter. The distinction in Soviet usage is an artificial one, based upon the Stalin-propagated notion of hierarchical relations among nations.

4 "Constitution (Fundamental Law) of the Union of Soviet Socialist Republics," in Donald D. Barry and Carol Barner-Barry, *Contemporary Soviet Politics* (Englewood Cliffs, NJ: Prentice Hall, 1982), pp. 372–375.

5 Not considered but none the less interesting is the resultant jurisdiction of those administrative divisions within the territories of union republics were the republics themselves to secede. Abkhazia and Ossetia – both located in Georgia – are presently grappling with precisely this difficulty.

6 There are also elements of fictitiousness – in particular, the attempted legitimizing of Soviet treatment of the Jews through the creation of a national Jewish territory, Birobidzhan, in Siberia.

7 J.L. Talmon, *The Myth of the Nation and the Vision of Revolution* (London: Secker and Warburg, 1981), pp. 544–545.

8 Peter Zwick convincingly demonstrates the commonalities between the two in his *National Communism* (Boulder, CO: Westview, 1983).

9 Talmon, *Myth*, p. 545.

10 *Ibid.*, p. 162.

11 In a similar way, few could have expected (Andrei Amalrik is a distinguished exception) that "taking the lid off" totalitarian communism would lead to national conflicts as bitter and pervasive as have recently occurred in the Soviet Empire (Andrei Amalrik, *Will the Soviet Survive Until 1984?* [New York: Harper and Row, 1970]). The internationalism of Rosa Luxemburg seems an anachronism in the denouement of the USSR.

12 Talmon, *Myth*, p. 162.

13 *Ibid.*, p. 163.

14 Paul B. Henze, "The Spectre and Implications of Internal Nationalist Dissent: Historical and Functional Comparisons," *Soviet Nationalities in Strategic Perspective* (London: Croom Helm, 1985), p. 15.

15 Alexander Gershenkron, *Economic Backwardness in Historical Perspective* (Cambridge MA: Harvard University Press, 1979).

16 Roman Szporluk, *Communism and Nationalism* (New York: Oxford University Press, 1988), p. 223.

17 *Ibid.*, p. 229.

18 Isaac Deutscher, *Stalin: A Political Biography*, 2nd edn (New York: Oxford University Press, 1967), p. 243.

19 They also became the target of nationalist revindications when Gorbachev's *demokratizatsia* policies provided nationalist leaders with the legitimacy to articulate and aggregate their views.

20 Szporluk, *Communism*, p. 51.

21 Walker Connor, *The National Question in Marxist-Leninist Theory and Strategy* (Princeton: Princeton University Books, 1984), pp. 5–20.

22 Hélène Carrère d'Encausse, *Decline of an Empire: The Soviet Socialist Republics in Revolt* (New York: Newsweek Books, 1979), p. 46.

23 Ronald Suny, "The Revenge of the Past: Socialism and Ethnic Conflict in Transcaucasia," *New Left Review*, November/December 1990, no. 184, pp. 5–6.

24 It is significant that there was support among some Marxists for this position. Most notable was Tatar revolutionary Sultan Galiev, who advanced the notion of "proletarian nations," where entire nations on the periphery were thought to be subordinate to the imperialist center. Class and national cleavages on the periphery could be thought to coincide and, following this reasoning, could be cultivated simultaneously. See Alexandre A. Bennigsen and S. Enders Wimbush, *Muslim National Communism in the Soviet Union: A Revolutionary Strategy for the Colonial World* (Chicago: University of Chicago Press, 1979), pp. 41–45.

25 Connor, *National Question*, pp. 45–61.

26 The recognition of the power of nationalism did not only lead to sanction. The power of Russian nationalism was used instrumentally by Stalin (as was organized religion) during World War II. When mass mobilization was necessary in a hurry, Stalin called the citizens to fight for Great Russian nationalism and the *Rodina* (Motherland), not socialism.

27 For a poignant historiographical account of this process, see Robert Conquest, *The Nation Killers: The Soviet Deportation of Nationalities* (London: Macmillan, 1970). Also see Aleksandr M. Nekrich, *The Punished Peoples: The Deportation and the Fate of Soviet Minorities at the End of the Second World War* (New York: W.W. Norton, 1978).

28 It is therefore ironic that mass national identities were strengthened by Stalin's internal passport system, under which citizen nationality was officially reported. The strength of Soviet policies of preference can be clearly seen in the decisions of ethnically-mixed marriage descendants, who have invariably chosen to affiliate themselves with their local titular nationality, irrespective of whether or not they lived in the RSFSR. Given the choice, it was deemed preferable to be Russian only in Russia.

29 Examples of this focus include Robert Conquest, ed., *The Last Empire: Nationality and the Soviet Future* (Stanford: Hoover Institution Press, 1986); Nadia Diuk and Adrian Karatnycky, *The Hidden Nations: The People Challenge the Soviet Union* (New York: William Morrow and CO, 1990); and Bohdan Nahaylo and Victor Swoboda, *Soviet Disunion* (New York: The Free Press, 1990).

30 This scholarship includes Lubomyr Hajda and Mark Beissinger, eds., *The Nationalities Factor in Soviet Politics and Society* (Boulder, Co: Westview, 1990); Gregory Gleason, *Federalism and Nationalism: The Struggle for Republican Rights in the USSR* (Boulder, CO: Westview, 1990); and Graham Smith, *The Nationalities Question in the Soviet Union* (London: Longman, 1991).

31 See, for one notable example among many, the well-documented but none the less insular *Studies of Nationalities in the USSR Series* (published by Hoover Institution Press), a collection of ethnographic "thick descriptions."

32 Stephen Cohen, *Rethinking the Soviet Experience* (New York: Oxford University Press, 1986). Such a framework would also have usefulness in the study of national relations outside and, of course, within the Soviet successor states themselves. The resurgence of nationalism in the post-colonial period was not a phenomenon specific to the Soviet Union, and much as examples for understanding national group relations are usefully drawn from outside the Soviet

Union, so too applications of its methodology should not be confined to its former borders.

33 Max Weber, "Politics as a Vocation," in H.H. Gerth and C. Wright Mills, eds., *From Max Weber: Essays in Sociology* (London: Routledge and Kegan Paul, 1948), pp. 77–78.

34 In an ethnocratic state, when center and titular nationality are more or less synonymous, there are only three relationships: center/titular nationality (A) – non-titular nationality (B); B – A; and B – B.

35 Ernest Gellner, *Nations and Nationalism: New Perspectives on the Past* (Ithaca: Cornell University Press, 1983), pp. 1–7.

36 Anthony D. Smith, *Theories of Nationalism* (London: Macmillan, 1971).

37 Paul Goble, "Imperial Endgame: Nationality Problems and the Soviet Union," paper presented at Washington Nationalities Conference, Washington D.C., November 1990, p. 3.

38 And once again signs of weakness in the power of the center, like anarchy in the international realm, would serve as the catalyst for the competition.

39 That Russian nationalists often derided nationalist movements in these areas as fomented by the KGB (assumedly under Gorbachev's control), in order to undermine the Russian national movement should therefore come as no surprise.

40 This can work in reverse as well. A titular nationality may cooperate with the center because a competitive relationship with a neighboring titular nationality is considered more important. Note that the case is slightly different for the lower-order titular and non-titular nationalities, whose collusionary relationship with the center is *not* temporary because its resolution of the more "pressing" matters (conflict with the dominant titular nationality) necessitates its becoming a first-order titular nationality itself. The relationship then indeed becomes one of liberation from the center, but no longer between center and lower-order titular or non-titular nationality.

41 Determination of which relationship takes precedence in such instances may be conditioned by many factors, including historical, political, and economic motivations. Of course, only analysis of individual cases will clarify the relative importance of motivations in any given case, but once this has been established, fundamental ethnic objectives may be more accurately deduced.

42 Szporluk, 'Dilemmas of Russian Nationalism," *Problems of Communism*, July/August, 1989, pp. 15–35.

43 Significantly, from this perspective union republican nations are considered to be lower-order titular nationalities.

44 Both categories may be aptly titled "empire savers," with the only substantive distinction being *size* of empire (since the RSFSR may hardly be considered a nation), but Szporluk's distinction none the less applies.

45 See Michael Rywkin, *Moscow's Muslim Challenge* (Armonk, NY: M.E. Sharpe, 1986), pp. 94–96.

46 That which existed was generally limited to the intelligentsia, which acted in competition for scarce professional positions. The few exceptions include isolated assertions of linguistic autonomy and anti-Stalinist sentiment during the Brezhnev years.

47 See, for example, Anders Åslund, *Gorbachev's Struggle for Economic Reform*

(Ithaca: Cornell University Press, 1989); Marshall I. Goldman, *Gorbachev's Challenge: Economic Reform in the Age of High Technology* (New York: W.W. Norton, 1987); and Ed A. Hewett, *Reforming the Soviet Economy* (Brookings: Washington DC, 1988).

48 See Albert O. Hirschman, *Exit, Voice, and Loyalty* (Cambridge: Harvard University Press, 1970).

49 Barbara A. Anderson and Brian D. Silver, "Aspects of Soviet Ethnic Demography," unpublished paper. University of California, Berkeley, February 1991.

50 Russians are typically the majority group in these cases, often vastly outnumbering the titular nationality. In 1989 the Buryat population was 70 percent Russian and 24 percent Buryat; in Karelia, 74 percent Russian, 10 percent Karelian; and in Mordvinia, 67 percent Russian, 33 percent Mordvin (see Appendix B).

51 Central Asia is the most gradualistic of the cases, as fundamental national issues there were neither ones of sovereignty or independence. Greater autonomy over economic matters had not so much been demanded as requested. Calls for linguistic, religious, and cultural autonomy were only somewhat stronger. The primary demand has been for help, particularly on the environmental front (in regards to the Aral issue), but also economically. Central Asia, lacking both infrastructure and promising non-Soviet regional alternatives, found themselves reliant upon the continued support of the center. These problems necessitated the immediate attention of all Central Asians; national sovereignty did not assist in their solution.

52 Roma Hadzewycz, "Rukh declares Ukraine's Independence," *The Ukrainian Weekly*, Sunday, November 4, 1990, p. 8. To label this situation republicanism would be a mild overstatement, because these movements undoubtedly gained strength from their ties to specific national groups. None the less, the republican element appears to have had significant influence.

53 Donna Bahry, "Soviet Regions and the Paradoxes of Economic Reform," in Ian A. Bremmer and Norman M. Naimark, eds., *Soviet Nationalities Problems* (Stanford: Center for Russian and East European Studies, 1990), p. 52.

Part II
The Center

Part II
The Career

2 Success and collapse: traditional Soviet nationality policy

VICTOR ZASLAVSKY

The current nationality crisis in the former Soviet Union is probably the most acute manifestation of the general crisis of Soviet-type societies. While the deepening economic crisis has simply destroyed the Soviet Union, the nationality crisis threatens the very survival of the Soviet empire. The rapidity with which Soviet disintegration unfold can only be understood if one takes into account the structural base of the Soviet crisis.

Today Soviet economists unanimously acknowledge that the Stalinist command-administrative system exhausted not only its initially enormous natural resources, but also its developmental potential and even its ability to maintain the status quo.[1] A remarkably high degree of internal stability in the post-Stalin USSR, in which terror and crude coercion declined significantly, depended upon specific conditions and social policies which characterized the period of extensive economic growth. These conditions and policies, often conceptualized in Sovietology as the "social contract" or "social compromise" between the party-state and the populace, included price stability and the absence of inflation, job security and egalitarian income policy, a semi-free labor market and preferential treatment of territorially-based nationality groups.[2] Having secured for a period of time a slow but steady improvement in consumption and general standard of living, this social contract acquired positive connotations for the population and became the basis of Soviet society's normative consensus. This social contract was presented to the population by the powerful ideological and propaganda apparatus "not only as a set of desirable material benefits, but as norms – implicit conventions which have been widely accepted by the public and by the elite as expected and fair rules of the economic game."[3] The economic decline undermined the system's ability to maintain this state of consensus since the rising costs of social policies and arrangements designed to maintain internal stability and legitimacy of the regime could no longer be met. The exhaustion of the extensive growth model and the failure of the highly bureaucratized, centralized, and militarized economy to raise productivity and finance even the most important social policies were, therefore, responsible for the collapse of Soviet nationality policy. Still, this long-standing policy was one of the most successful social

29

policies of the Soviet regime. A thorough understanding of its basic principles and practices is necessary to make sense of the developments which have resulted in the present turmoil. This chapter focuses upon the policy outputs of the Soviet center with regard to nationality issues. It traces nationality policies from Lenin to Gorbachev and shows that while practices have changed, the fundamental principles informing them have largely remained the same. This chapter does not deal with the reaction of targeted nationalities to the centrally-designed process of nation-building – that task is left for the rest of this volume. It serves to examine the logic of the Soviet state and assess its successes and its failures in the sphere of nationality relations.

Marxism-Leninism, nationalism and the formation of the Soviet Union

Soviet nationality policy as the system of theoretical assumptions, established practices, and institutional arrangements which regulate nationality relations in a multi-ethnic state was born of the entire historical development of Soviet society. It is well-known that nationalism and Marxism-Leninism are ideologically incompatible. As Walker Connor pointed out, "nationalism is predicated upon the assumption that the most fundamental divisions of humankind are the many vertical cleavages that divide people into ethnonational groups. Marxism, by contrast, rests upon the conviction that the most fundamental human divisions are horizontal class distinctions that cut across national groupings."[4] This basic attitude towards nationalism as a transitory social phenomenon subordinate to the class struggle, which could be used to achieve some immediate political goals proved instrumental for the Bolsheviks' acquisition of power.

Before the October revolution the right of nations to self-determination became the centerpiece of the Bolshevik program on the nationality question. Lenin, who intended to "combine in one general assault all the manifestations of political opposition, protest, and indignation" to overthrow Tsarism, could not pass up the power of nationalism. The slogan of national self-determination allowed the Bolsheviks to win the support of the numerous national movements which emerged in the various parts of the Russian empire. Lenin's entire nationality program was designed to use nationalist forces to weaken Tsarist authority and later the Provisional government. Having seized power, the Bolsheviks were confronted with the disintegration of the Russian empire, whose breakup into a conglomeration of small national states threatened to undermine the economic foundations of the emergent revolutionary state. Consequently, a drastic reinterpretation of the principle of national self-determination was introduced almost immediately after the October revolution. Already in December 1917 Stalin asserted that the Soviet government could not permit national self-determination to serve as a cover for counterrevolution. Supported by many other leading Bolsheviks, Stalin suggested "to limit the principle of free self-determination of nations by granting it to the toilers and refusing it to the bourgeoisie."[5] This early attempt to replace the principle of national self-determination by that of "proletarian self-determination," even if formally rejected by Lenin, symbolized the purely propagandist character of the famous article preserved in all subsequent Soviet constitutions which declared the Union republics to be sovereign and possessing the right to secede at will from the Soviet Union. The proclamation of the right to self-determination served simply to remove ethnic psychological resistance to the formation of a unitary state.

One of the crucial issues facing the young Soviet government was the development of new forms of political organization for the country's multi-ethnic population. The Bolsheviks, who had vehemently opposed the federal idea before November 1917, turned to federalism as an indispensable instrument for putting together the scattered parts of the defunct empire. Since national states had already emerged in the borderlands, the Leninist government had little choice but to build the new federation on the principle of national-territory autonomy. As a consequence, Soviet Russia became "the first modern state to place the national principle at the base of its federal structure."[6]

Early Soviet policies concerned with state formation were strongly influenced by Stalin's 1913 article "Marxism and the National Question" and especially by Stalin's definition of nation, which included territory as a necessary attribute: "A nation is a historically constituted, stable community of people, formed on the basis of a common language, territory, economic life, and psychological make-up manifested in a common culture."[7] One of the fundamental innovations of federal state formation under Soviet rule was based on the Stalinist linkage of ethnicity, territory, and political administration and enshrined in the idea of national statehood.

The integration of the ethnic periphery into a single state terminated at the end of 1922 with the establishment of the Union of the Soviet Socialist Republics. The concept of national statehood was made an institutional reality by the creation of a federation of ethnoterritorial units organized into an elaborate administrative hierarchy. This complex process had by and large been completed by the end of the Stalinist era. The number of officially recognized nationalities was gradually reduced from more than 190 in the 1926 census to 104 registered in the 1970 census, of which 53 nationalities were grouped into four ranks or categories, each representing a different level of statehood.[8] In this way, the building blocks for the new Soviet federal system were not simply geographic administrative divisions but a collection of national-territorial "states."

Many political scientists viewed Soviet federalism with open scepticism. According to Hugh Seton-Watson's typical judgement,

> the various Soviet constitutions, including that of 1936, have been described as "federal" but the Soviet Union was not a federal but a unitary state. The essential feature of federal government – that the territories should not be subordinate to the central authority but "coordinate" with it – did not apply. Apart from this, the apparatus of the state was in reality dominated by the Communist party, whose organization was strictly centralist.[9]

Indeed, Soviet federalism never granted any economic or political autonomy to the various ethnic groups within their assigned territories. The one-party system, centrally-planned economy, and massive Moscow-based bureaucracy precluded effective federalism. But Soviet leadership preserved and cultivated the federal structure since it performed important, if limited, functions in the maintenance of internal stability. In order to grasp federalism's true meaning, we must first examine the whole system of Soviet nationality policy, of which it always was an integral part.

Traditional Soviet nationality policy: basic principles and practices

Traditional Soviet nationality policy, introduced and elaborated by the Stalinist administration, fine-tuned by Khrushchev and rationalized and routinized during the Brezhnev period, remained in effect for the first two or three years of Gorbachev's rule. Only at the end of the 1980s, when the rising costs of maintaining this policy began to make significant contributions to the crisis in Soviet society, was its sheer inadequacy for the new tasks and objectives fully understood by the Soviet leadership. The basic goals of Soviet nationality policy were similar to those of any modern multiethnic state. First, the state tries to secure its territorial integrity and internal stability by suppressing various nationalist and, especially, separatist movements. Second, the modern state requires "a mobile, literate, culturally standardized, interchangeable population."[10] The process of modernization necessitates the imposition of a standardized, homogeneous, centrally sustained culture on all minority groups. The specificity of Soviet nationality policy was often seen in the regime's dominant ideology which treated nationality as a strictly temporary phenomenon and predicted the rapprochement and eventual merger of different Soviet nationalities in some unspecified future. But attempts at tailoring the practical policy to theoretical conceptions characterized only relatively short periods of Soviet nationality policy which, on the whole, sacrificed utopian ideology to pragmatic considerations. The major tasks of Soviet nationality policy can thus be more realistically defined as mobilizing ethnic populations to accomplish Soviet-style modernization, while maintaining internal stabiity in a multinational country harboring deep ethnic divisions and resentments.

The role of terror and repression. Traditional Soviet nationality policy was uniformly applied to a variety of different ethnic groups. The same socio-economic model, similar institutions, analogous economic methods and industrialization strategy were imposed on all major nationalities of the country. Throughout Soviet history, nationality policy depended upon the state's willingness to suppress, by means of coercion, dissenting groups that opposed the multiethnic state. In Stalin's time, the role of the terrorist-ic central state with its powerful coercive apparatus in brutally destroying both real and imaginary ethnic oppositions is well documented.[11] In the mid-1950s, during his de-Stalinization campaign, Khrushchev reduced con-siderably the use of mass terror in administering Soviet society. Over the subsequent three decades the coercive apparatus, particularly the KGB, had become less harsh and visible, but remained a major instrument of intimidation by "shaping people's perceptions of what could happen to them if they were to overstep the boundaries of acceptable behavior."[12] De-Stalinization obviously expanded the realm of the permissible, but the suppression of nationalist dissent continued unabated, since in Alexander Motyl's words, "the Soviet state has never failed to conceal its extreme hostility to non-Russian nationalism."[13] The central state worked out sophisticated methods of surveillance over indigenous political elites and educated middle classes, ruthlessly suppressing any attempt to propagate the ideal of nationalism or accumulate the resources necessary to the pursuit of independence. The role of the coercive apparatus in implement-ing Soviet nationality policy was thus truly enormous. Still, the impressive internal stability which began breaking down only at the end of the 1980s cannot be explained solely in terms of terror and repression. Most impor-tantly, throughout Soviet history nationality policy depended also on the relative strength of the economy, which provided the resources that made the multiethnic state attractive or at least tolerable to crucial sectors of ethnic populations, and state-engineered stratification which undermined the capacity of major nationalities to act as unified entities in defence of their own interests.

Institutionalization of ethnicity. Among the institutional arrangements responsible for the efficient implementation of Soviet nationality policy, Soviet federal structure and the system of internal passports which register ethnic origin of every citizen merit special attention. In Soviet society eth-nicity became institutionalized on the group level through the estabish-ment of ethnoterritorial organizations linking nationalities and their terri-tories and on the individual level through the introduction of an officially recognized ethnic affiliation for each Soviet citizen.

The emergence of Soviet federalism has been discussed above. In 1990, the Soviet Union remained a federal state composed of fifteen Union republics and dozens of lower-ranking ethnic units. The status of a Union republic was the highest accessible to a Soviet nationality; other forms of statehood, such as autonomous republics, autonomous provinces, and national districts, ranked much lower and their rights and spheres of jurisdiction remained unclear and in many cases uncodified.[14] Clearly, Soviet federalism did not grant economic or political autonomy to the various nationalities within their traditional territories. Rather, Soviet federalism was designed as a means of accommodating major nationalities within a unified multi ethnic state, with Union republics serving as units of central planning and major instruments of personnel policy.

The registration of one's nationality (ethnic origin) on the internal passport was introduced by the Stalinist regime in 1932 and implemented by the mid-1930s. Initially the recorded nationality was chosen on the basis of more or less voluntary self-indication. This measure was justified by the need to guarantee special rights of ethnic minorities, especially their representation in the system of higher education and among the ranks of local officials.[15] After a few years, however, the free choice of nationality or change of the previously registered one were suddenly prohibited. According to the passport regulations, in effect for the past 50 years, a citizen's nationality was registered strictly on the basis of the corresponding entries in the parents' passports, irrespective of culture, mother tongue, religion, or personal preferences. Of course, nationality affiliation is "not a biological but rather a social category which is not determined by birth, but is formed in the process of the individual's socialization and specifically through conscious self-identification."[16] Accordingly, a person's ethnic identity can change in the course of one's lifetime and, even more so, in the course of several generations. The Soviet state, however, kept treating nationality as an ascriptive characteristic determined by birth. As a result, the patterns of ethnic identification in the 1930s determined, once and for all, legally registered nationalities of the subsequent generations. Thus, Soviet bureaucracy obtained a unique instrument of introducing and implementing a specific nationality policy. The registration of nationality in passports helped establish rigid boundaries between nationality groups, served as a main determinant of ethnic self-identification, and provided an objective basis for the policy of preferential treatment of territorially-based nationalities. The institutionalization of ethnicity created the prerequisites necessary for pursuing an ethnic policy which combined divisive measures and integrative techniques to prevent the organization of alliances between neighbouring ethnic groups, to undermine the capacity of any existing ethnic group to act as a unified entity, and to coopt the crucial sectors within each ethnic population into the Soviet regime.

Societal segmentation and integration in Soviet nationality policy. The unquestionable success of Soviet nationality policy in controlling and containing ethnic nationalism largely depended upon the institutional arrangements that produced societal segmentation along the lines of nationality and social class. The divisive aspects of the passport system should be mentioned first, since the bureaucratic registration of one's ethnic origin as a biological category established rigid barriers between different nationalities, preventing processes of ethnic assimilation and change of ethnic identity. Second, the whole federal political-administrative system served as an elaborate structure of ethnic inequality. It divided ethnic groups into those with recognized territory and certain rank in the hierarchy of state formations and those withouts such territory. It organized the former groups into a four-rank hierarchy which determined corresponding amounts of ethnic rights and privileges. Moreover, the borders between ethnic territories were drawn arbitrarily, often in accordance with a divide-and-conquer policy in obvious conflict with historical traditions and existing ethnodemographic conditions. In many regions, especially Central Asia, this policy effectively prevented the emergence of supraethnic groupings and alliances threatening to the unitary state. Also, it should not be forgotten that Soviet nationality policy worked in tandem with bureaucratic arrangements which stratified each nationality by class and territory. Thus, social and geographical barriers between the urban poulation and collective farmers have been in place in each republic for the past half century. Collective farmers were denied internal passports and could not leave the countryside, while urban dwellers had no right to buy or build houses in rural areas. The so-called "system of closed cities," which required a special permission to reside permanently in any of the major urban centers, represented another major divisive measure.[17] It established an important social and territorial barrier between the university graduates, who usually reside in closed cities, and the rest of the ethnic population by perpetuating the privileged access to higher education and middle class positions from one generation of the ethnic middle class to the next. Finally, special mechanisms and practices were developed to control ethnic political elites and make them completely dependent on central authority while depriving them of their ethnic power bases and increasing social distance between them and their ethnic constituencies.

Simultaneously, Soviet nationality policy included a host of integrative techniques instrumental for maintaining internal stability of the multinational empire. From its very inception, Soviet federalism fostered the policy of preferential treatment of the representatives of local nationalities within their own territories with regard to access to higher education and placement into managerial and administrative positions. A special quota system for the indigenous populations in the system of higher education emerged in the 1920s, together with an intensive program of "indigenizing" (*korenizatsiya*) local adminitrations. In the post-Stalin period this policy of preferential treatment of titular nationalities in their own republics was intensified. The basic strategy consisted of the establishment of institutional isomorphism in all Union republics, thus counteracting any ethnic division of labor. All of them obtained identical state, bureaucratic and educational structures, analogous research and development establishments, including republican Academies of Science with comprehensive sets of research institutes, analogous organizations for production and distribution of culture, from the state publishing houses and the ministries of culture and education to the creative unions of writers, artists, architects, and other cultural producers. The goal was to achieve equalized and comprehensive development of each republic pursuing a mild form of redistribution from more to less developed areas. Studies of the Soviet budget and allocation policies have demonstrated that poorer republics, on the whole, had higher rates of investment.[18] Thus, socio-economic development of the republics was always considered a means of the promotion of equality among nationalities and their integration into the Soviet system. Even if this policy of equalization did not realize its professed goal, it created considerable homogeneity in republican social structures. Especially important is the fact that in the 1980s in the least developed republics the number of university-educated specialists – the new middle class of Soviet society – grew considerably, increasingly approaching that of the Russian population.[19] In fact, Soviet nationality policy was to a large extent designed as a class-specific policy aimed at the comprehensive integration of ethnic political elites and educated middle classes into the Soviet regime.

Any social class or group within a given nationality may be permeated with nationalist feelings and separatist aspirations. Ethnicity, once politicized, becomes a fact of life as real as any material concern. To paraphrase Alexander Motyl, it assumes a psychological, almost primordial reality.[20] Nevertheless, different social classes and groups are receptive to nationalist ideas in different, structurally determined ways. The central role of educated classes and indigenous intelligentsias in promoting ethnic mobilization and organizing secessionist movements is well-known. The structural position of educated classes which are the principal bearers of a "shared, literate, educationally-transmitted culture" make them especially receptive to the appeals of nationalism in industrial societies.[21] As Miroslav Hroch put it, "both the old and the new middle classes become the main champions of 'nationalism', both in state-nations and in small nations that experienced the nation-building process."[22] Soviet sociological reearch confirms the conclusions reached earlier in many Western studies that in the USSR, as in other modern industrial multinational states, ethnic political elites and middle classes were the groups primarily responsible for ethnic politicization and most prone to use nationalism as an instrument for competing against other ethnic groups for economic and political privileges.[23]

The policy of preferential treatment of nationalities within their territories was designed to coopt educated and ambitious members of nationalities into the ranks of local political elites and educated middle classes. Since the mid-1950s, most leadership positions and high-ranking posts in practically all the republics belonged to members of local nationalities.[24] Since republican political elites were mainly established by appointment and cooption by central party apparatuses, they remained beholden to the central authority rather than to their ethnic constituences, and thus faithfully followed orders from the center. In addition, a well-developed system of control made attempts at fostering nationalist sentiments and aspirations on the part of local political elites both very risky and unlikely. Moreover, by protecting the educational and occupational interests of the indigenous elites and middle classes, Soviet nationality policy was unusually successful in integrating the groups most receptive to nationalist ideas into the political regime or, at least, in neutralizing their separatist aspirations. Control over higher education was always a crucial aspect of nationality policy. For decades competition for university admission among applicants of various nationalities was regulated by a quota system which accorded considerable preference to the titular nationalities residing in their own republics. Also the central leadership was preoccupied with creating employment for the representatives of ethnic intelligentsias, expanding local bureaucracies, founding republican Academies of Science and research centers, and supporting ethnic union of writers, painters and film-makers. Consequently, the potentially explosive ethnic situation, when educated members of ethnic minorities find their social mobility blocked by the majority group, was by and large avoided. Table 2.1 compiled by Soviet demographers illustrates the triumph of the policy of preferential treatment of indigenous nationalities within their own republics.

In sum, federal structure, nationality registration in the internal passport, preferential treatment of territorially-based nationalities, and protection of the educational and occupational interests of ethnic middle classes and political elites all contributed to the maintenance of stable nationality relations in the USSR. The powerful Soviet coercive apparatus obviously succeeded in suppressing the activities of dissident nationality groups and demoting and punishing those local leaders who tried to develop indigenous power bases. During the Brezhnev period, Soviet institutions demonstrated a seemingly unlimited capacity to combat ethnic nationalism, managing to keep the level of inter-ethnic tensions relatively low. For their part, territorially-based nationalities that preserved a degree of autonomous national existence learned to manipulate Soviet nationality policy to their advantage. Soviet nationality policy was a uniform policy applied to a variety of different ethnic groups. In the period of extensive development and relatively abundant resources, it proved capable of generating a necessary degree of compliance.

Table 2.1. *Ethnic composition of populations at large and administrative-managerial personnel by republics, 1989 (percentages)*

| Union Republics | Indigenous nationality | Proportion of the indigenous nationality in the | |
		Population at large	Administrative-managerial personnel
Russian	Russian	81.5	77.3
Ukrainian	Ukrainian	72.7	79.0
Belorussian	Belorussian	77.9	77.7
Uzbek	Uzbek	71.4	67.6
Kazakh	Kazakh	39.7	39.5
Georgian	Georgian	70.1	89.3
Azerbaijan	Azeri	82.7	93.8
Lithuanian	Lithuanian	79.6	91.5
Moldavian	Moldavian	64.5	49.8
Latvian	Latvian	52.0	63.1
Kirgiz	Kirgiz	52.4	55.1
Tajik	Tajik	62.3	66.3
Armenian	Armenian	93.3	99.4
Turkmen	Turkmen	72.0	71.8
Estonian	Estonian	61.5	82.2

Source: L.L. Rybakovskij and N.V. Tarasova, "Migratsionnyi protsessy v SSSR: Novye yavleniya," *Sotsiologicheskie issledovaniya*, no. 7, 1990, p. 40.

Major defects of Soviet nationality policy

No sooner had the Soviet leadership initiated major reforms than did the inadequacies of Soviet nationality policy for the requirements of economic and political restructuring become evident. Perestroika rapidly laid bare and even intensified certain inherent defects of this policy. First, the traditional policy essentially maintained the status quo in ethnic relations. Although interethnic tensions multiplied, this policy did not address their structural base; rather, it suppressed the symptoms by eroding communities' capacity to act as unified entities. In the conditions of the present economic crisis, the old social contract between the regime and the population was no longer tenable because its political and economic costs could no longer be met. Second, it has become increasingly clear that Soviet nationality policy preserved and often even exacerbated regional inequalities.[25] It could not be otherwise when an essentially uniform policy was applied to very different ethnic groups which found themselves at quite different stages of socio-economic development.

In the 1980s many Soviet analysts began criticizing the uniformity of the old policy stressing both its failure to achieve its proclaimed goal of reducing inter-republic inequalities[26] and its sheer wastefulness.[27] Moreover, the twin policies of nationality registration in the internal passports and preferential treatment of indigenous nationalities within their administrative units became especially counterproductive. These policies proved to be essentially antimeritocratic and resulted in the rise of parasitic attitudes and the diminishing prestige of productive work. Also they created strong dissatisfaction among minorities deprived of their own territories and residents of ethnically alien republics. In many cases it led to the emergence of a potentially explosive ethnic division of labor (the best examples being Tallinn and Tashkent, the republican capitals of Estonia and Uzbekistan), in which members of indigenous nationalities have dominated jobs and professions requiring university education, while migrants, largely Russians, have been overwhelmingly employed as blue-collar workers.[28]

The situation became particularly tense in republics where titular nationalities had been transformed into numerical minorities due to massive influxes of other nationalities, the best examples being Kazakhstan and Yakutiya, where the first cases of ethnic unrest in Gorbachev's era were registered. The dissatisfaction of the indigenous population, which fears for its traditional privileged, and, indeed, its ethnic survival, combines with an acute sense of injustice on the part of the discriminated-against majority. Soviet nationalities relations had, thus, entered a qualitatively new stage in which, as a Soviet ethnographer put it, "ethnic tensions have reached the critical mass level when even an accidental event, only marginally connected with nationalities relations, may lead to a major explosion."[29]

Soviet nationality policy has largely contributed to a reversal of the habitual migrational pattern which characterized the Russian empire since the mid-nineteenth century and continued during the first five decades of Soviet existence. By the end of the 1960s the traditional direction of the Russian migration from the center to the periphery had been reversed when the outflow of Russians from Central Asia, Kazakhstan, the Caucasus, Moldavia and even the Ukraine began.[30] The 1989 census has demonstrated a substantial in-migration into the Russian republic and a corresponding Russian out-migration from the non-Russian republics, except the Baltic ones.[31] At the same time the process of out-migration of the members of non-titular nationalities from the non-Russian republics and their return to the territories of their own republics accelerated as a result of the exacerbation of ethnic tensions.[32] Consequently Soviet nationality policies triggered the process of ethnic homogenization which has been underway in many Soviet republics for the past two decades. They created the preconditions for large-scale ethnic transfers that occurred between Azerbaijan and Armenia, between Central Asian republics and Russia at the end of

Gorbachev's era. Thus, the inextricable link between an ethnic group, its territory and its political administration established and maintained by decades of Soviet federalism has been reinforced by ethnic transfers and the resulting increase of ethnic homogeneity among various nationalities.

Finally, in the 1980s the policy of protecting the occupational interests of ethnic educated classes by co-opting them into swelling bureaucracies had become utterly meaningless, since the conditions in the Soviet labour force, where roughly one person in six holds a bureaucratic job, necessitated strong cuts of bureaucratic personnel. Thus, the Soviet Union provides yet another example of the dialectic of history, whereby the same social arrangements and policies that served for a time as the pillars of internal stability suddenly become counterproductive, leading to instability and profound tension.

This brief analysis of the complex history of Soviet traditional nationality policy leads to the following conclusions. Soviet nationality policy promoted a peculiar process of nation-building. As Ronald Suny points out, much of the story of nation-building, and even nationality formation, for many peoples of the Russian empire belongs more appropriately in the Soviet period than in the years before the civil war.[33] On the one hand, the state imposed formal ethnic cohesion, created practically impenetrable barriers between different ethnic groups, and established an administrative link between individuals and their nationalities. Consequently, in the various republics there emerged such preconditions for independent existence as their own political elites and educated middle classes, their own administratively defined political subunits inhabited by the indigenous populations, and continuous traditions of cultural production in their own literary languages. As popular Russian writer Boris Strugatsky argued, "The republics exhibit the full set of characteristics of independent states that have lost their independence."[34]

On the other hand, the state developed effective mechanisms of controlling the composition and activities of local administrations and preventing any ethnic community from acting as a unified entity in defense of its ethnic interests. By the 1980s, however, the resources necessary for maintaining extensive growth of the Soviet system had been exhausted. In these new conditions, traditional nationality policy, whose success was inextricably linked to a strong central state pursuing the strategy of extensive economic development, proved dysfunctional for the Soviet regime. The rising costs of maintaining this traditional policy made significant contributions to the crisis of Soviet society. Its dismanting, therefore, became one of the most urgent, if belatedly acknowledged, tasks on the reformist agenda.

As it has been justifiably noted, "Mikhail Gorbachev originally placed the nationalities issue at the very bottom of his agenda and did not even raise the need for a reevaluation in nationalities policy until he was almost two years in office."[35] During his period in power Gorbachev was oscillating between his original aim of reforming the Soviet economy and that of preserving the Soviet Union as a political entity. Taking into account the legacy of Soviet nationality policy, however, it is not surprising that Gorbachev's persistent attempts to reconcile the transition to democracy and a market based economy with the preservation of the territorial integrity of the Soviet Union were to prove futile. In all multiethnic Soviet-type societies, universal ethnic mobilization and strong separatist movements in the most developed republics have been an inevitable reaction to the profound systematic crisis. Under these conditions the progressive weakening of the central state made Soviet disintegration inevitable.

Notes

I am indebted to Professors Judith Adler, Robert Brym, and Volker Meja for help with this chapter. I am also grateful to the editors of *Daedalus* for permission to reprint, in modified and abridged form, a part of my "Nationalism and Democratic Transition in Postcommunist Societies," no. 2 (Spring 1992), pp. 97–121.

1 Stanislav Shatalin, "Ekonomika krivykh zerkal," *Ogonek*, no. 20 (1990); E. Yasin, "Problemy perekhoda k reguliruemoj rynochnoj ekonomike," *Voprosy ekonomiki*, no. 7, 1990.

2 George Breslauer, "On the Adaptability of Soviet Welfare-State Authoritarianism," in Karl Ryavec, ed., *Soviet Society and the Communist Party* (Amherst: University of Massachusetts Press, 1978); Seweryn Bialer, *Stalin's Successors, Leadership, Stability, and Change in the Soviet Union* (Cambridge: Cambridge University Press, 1980); Victor Zaslavsky, *The Neo-Stalinist State, Class, Ethnicity and Consensus in Soviet Society* (Armonk, N.Y.: Sharpe, 1982).

3 Peter Hauslohner, "Gorbachev's Social Contract," *Soviet Economy*, 3:1, 1987, p. 58.

4 Walker Connor, *The National Question in Marxist-Leninist Theory and Strategy* (Princeton: Princeton University Press, 1984), p. 5.

5 Iosif Stalin, *Sochineniya* (Moscow: Politizdat, 1946), vol. 4, pp. 31–32.

6 Richard Pipes, *The Formation of the Soviet Union, Communism and Nationalism, 1917–1923* (Cambridge, Mass.: Harvard University Press, 1954), p. 112.

7 Iosif Stalin, *Marxism and the National Question* (New York: International, 1942), p. 12.

8 V.I. Kozlov, *Natsionalnosti SSSR. Etnodemograficheskij obzor* (Moscow: Statistika, 1975).

9 Hugh Seton-Watson, *Nations and States: An Inquiry into the Origins of Nations and the Politics of Nationalism* (Boulder, CO: Westview Press, 1977), p. 312.

10 Ernest Gellner, *Nations and Nationalism* (Ithaca: Cornell University Press, 1983), p. 46.

11 Roy Medvedev, *Let History Judge. The Origins and Consequences of Stalinism*, rev. and enlarged edn (New York: Columbia University Press, 1989); Robert Conquest, *The Great Terror: A Reassessment* (Oxford: Oxford University Press, 1990).

12 Donna Bahry and Brian Silver, "Intimidation and the Symbolic Uses of Terror in the USSR,' *American Political Science Review*, 81:4, 1987, p. 1067.

13 Alexander Motyl, *Sovietology, Rationality, Nationality. Coming to Grips with Nationalism in the USSR* (New York: Columbia University Press, 1990), p. 157.

14 G.Ch. Guseinov and D.V. Dragunskii, "A New Look at Old Wisdom," *Social Research*, vol. 47, no. 2, Summer 1990.

42   *Victor Zaslavsky*

15 B.T. Shumilin, *Passport grazhdanina SSSR* (Moscow: Znanie, 1976).
16 Kozlov, *Natsionalnosti* . . ., p. 256.
17 Zaslavsky, *Neo-Stalinist State*, chs. 2, 6; S.G.Kordonsky, "Sotsialnaya struktura i Mechanizm Tormozheniya," in F.M. Borodkin, L. Ya Kosals, R.V. Ryvkina (eds.), *Postizhenie: Sotsiologiya, Sotsialnaya Politika, Ekonomicheskaya Reforma* (Moscow: Progress, 1989), pp. 36–51.
18 Stephen White, "The Supreme Soviet and Budgetary Policy in the USSR," *British Journal of Political Science*, vol. 12, part 1, pp. 75–94; Donna Bahry, *Outside Moscow. Power, Politics, and Budgetary Policy in the Soviet Republics* (New York: Columbia University Press, 1987).
19 Ellen Jones and Fred Grupp, "Modernization and Ethnic Equalization in the USSR," *Soviet Studies*, vol. 36, no. 2, 1984; Yu. Arutyunyan and L. Drobizheva, "Nekotorye osobennosti kultury i nekotorye aspekty sotsialnoj zhizni sovetskogo obshchestva," *Voprosy istorii*, no. 7, 1987.
20 Alexander Motyl, *Will the Non-Russians Rebel? State, Ethnicity, and Stability in the USSR* (Ithaca: Cornell University Press, 1987), p. 23.
21 Ernest Gellner, "The Dramatis Personae of History," *East European Politics and Societies*, vol. 4, no. 1, 1990, pp. 131–132; Gellner, *Nations and Nationalism*.
22 Miroslav Hroch, "How Much Does Nation Formation Depend on Nationalism," *East European Politics and Societies*, 4:1, 1990, p. 115.
23 Yu. Arutyunyan, "A Concrete Sociological Study of Ethnic Relations," *Soviet Sociology*, vols. 3–4, 1972–73, pp. 328–348. Also, Victor Zaslavsky and Robert Brym, *Soviet-Jewish Emigration and Soviet Nationality Policy* (London: Macmillan, 1983), p. 98.
24 Bialer, *Stalin's Successors*, pp. 214–216.
25 A. Illarionov, "Ekonomicheskij potentsial i urovni ekonomicheskogo razvitiya soyuznykh republic," *Voprosy ekonomiki*, no. 4, 1990.
26 Yu. Ginter, M. Titma, "Sravnitelnyj analiz sotsialnogo razvitiya soyuznykh respublic," *Sotsiologicheskie issledovaniya*, no. 6, 1987.
27 D.I. Zyuzin, "Realnye proekty za chuzhoj schet," *Sotsiologicheskie issledovaniya*, no. 2, 1988; V.I. Kozlov, "Osobennosti etnodemograficheskikh problem v Srednej Azii i puti ikh resheniya," *Istoriya SSSR*, no. 1, 1988.
28 A.V. Kirkh, P.E. Yarve and K.R. Khaav, "Etnosotsialnaya differentsiatsiya gorodskogo naseleniya Estonii," *Sotsiologicheskie issledovaniya*, no. 3, 1988.
29 S.V. Cheshko, "Natsionalnyj vopros v SSSR: sostoyanie i perspektivy izucheniya," *Sovetskaya etnografiya*, no. 4, 1988, p. 62.
30 A.S. Bruk and V.M. Kabuzan, *Migratsionnye protsessy v Rossii i SSSR*, vol. 1 (Moscow: INION, 1991), pp. 108–112.
31 Ann Sheehy, "1989 Census Data on Internal Migration in the USSR," *Radio Liberty Report on the USSR*, 1, 45, 1989.
32 A.S. Bruk and V.M. Kabuzan, *Migratsionnye* . . ., pp. 111–112.
33 Ronald Grigor Suny, "Nationalist and Ethnic Unrest in Soviet Union," *World Policy Journal*, vol. 6, no. 3, 1989.
34 Boris Strugatsky, "Zhit' interesnee chem pisat," *Literaturnaya Gazeta*, April 10, 1991, p. 9.
35 Lubomyr Hajda and Mark Beissinger, "Nationalism and Reform," in L. Hajda and M. Beissinger, eds., *The Nationalities Factor in Soviet Politics and Society* (Boulder, CO: Westview Press, 1990), p. 306.

3 Russia: confronting a loss of empire

JOHN DUNLOP

Since 1987, when Mikhail Gorbachev's programs of glasnost and democratization began to set off chain reactions of convulsive political change, ethnic Russians have been a people in quest of an identity. During the seventy years of communist rule, most Russians had come to accept the regime's attempt to identify their interests as a people with those of the USSR as a whole. This identification had been reinforced structurally: unlike the other fourteen union republics, the Russian Soviet Federated Socialist Republic (or RSFSR for short) had deliberately not been given many of the institutions enjoyed by the other republics; there was, for example, no Russian KBG, no Russian MVD, no Russian Academy of Sciences, and no television channels or radio stations geared specifically at the interests of ethnic Russians. Strikingly, there was not even a Russian Communist Party, while all the other republics possessed their own party organizations.

The obvious aim behind this denial of structural parity to the Russian Republic was to bind Russians, the linchpin ethnos of the Soviet Union, as closely as possible to the USSR as a whole. There is evidence that the regime was to a considerable degree successful in achieving this goal. Soviet nationalities specialist Yurii Arutyunyan has noted that, "[the] concepts of 'Union' and 'Russia' in the minds of Russians is one and the same . . ."[1]

This conjoining of the concepts "Russian" and "Soviet" was further emphasized by the fact that some twenty-five million Russians lived in the minority republics. This migration of Russians to the periphery had served to dilute the political and economic clout of the titular peoples of the other republics. In the Russian Republic, on the other hand, Russians lived compactly, comprising 81.5 percent of the population, thereby making Russia the third most ethnically homogeneous republic in the union after Armenia and Azerbaijan. In the words of two Estonian scholars, this vast movement of Russians to the periphery "was a demographic policy specifically directed from the center, whose purpose was the formation of a nationally mixed population in every region of the Soviet Union."[2] In Estonia, they report, the number of Russians increased from 23,000 in 1945 to 475,000 in 1989. The aim behind the regime's encouragement of such migration was to

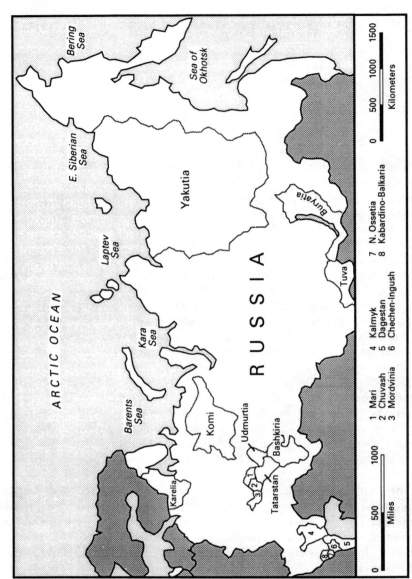

Map 3.1 Russia

create a supra-ethnic "Soviet people" who would speak Russian but be ethnically and culturally mongrelized.

An empire which is not an empire

Western commentators have frequently applied the term "Russian empire" both to pre-revolutionary Tsarist rule and to the post-revolutionary Soviet state. This imprecise use of terminology serves to skew and to distort the position of Russians under both the Tsars and the Soviets. The nationalities specialist, the late Hugh Seton-Watson, was wont to underline his conviction that the Tsarist empire should not be regarded as an ethnic Russian empire. "The government of the Russian Empire," he stressed, "was based on the principle of autocracy. All Russian subjects owed allegiance to the Tsar, who was responsible only to God. Provided that they loyally obeyed him, they enjoyed his protection regardless of whether they were Russian by speech or religion."[3] It was only toward the end of the nineteenth century, Seton-Watson notes, during the reigns of Alexander III and Nicholas II, that the Tsarist government began to adopt a conscious policy of Russification. "The previous policies," he writes, "had been made in the name of a monarch responsible to God. Russification was a policy made in the name of the Russian nation. It assumed that Russians were superior to the other subjects of the tsar . . ."[4]

If the Tsarist empire cannot, except for its closing years, be termed a Russian empire, much less can the Soviet empire be so considered. As Carl Linden points out, "the [Soviet] party-state in its strict conception acts not in the name of those it rules but as a proxy of the future 'communized' humanity freed of political rule and no longer separated into nation-states. By its ideology the Soviet party-state is the revolutionary replacement of the Russian nation-state, not its continuation."[5] However, in practice, as Linden notes, considerations of *Realpolitik* often required the Soviet regime to tap the energies of Russian patriotism as a "secret additive" to its power. This was especially true during Brezhnev's long reign, which witnessed a marked decline in the mobilizing power of the official ideology. During the Brezhnev years, an ideologically illicit "Russian imperial nationalism" was covertly used to prop up a decaying Marxism-Leninism.

If the Soviet Union cannot legitimately be termed a "Russian empire," neither can Russians be called an "imperial people." As Alain Besançon commented in 1983, the position of Russians in the USSR differs in important ways from, say, the position of the English or the French in the British and French empires. "To have an empire," Besançon explained, "one must have a privileged people, an essentially military means of conquest, and limited goals. The Russian people has no privileges. It has 'advantages' certainly, as the surest ally of communism, and party leaders are often drawn from its ranks, even in the national republics." However, Besançon went on, "These advantages [of the Russians] are not rights. Moreover, they are compensated for by heavier obligations, exemption from which is considered by the Russians to be a privilege of the non-Russian nationalities. A Russian who enjoys privileges as a Communist owes his privileges to his communism, not to his Russianness."[6]

With the exception of the Central Asian Muslims, Russians in the Soviet Union did not live noticeably better than did the titular peoples of the minority republics. Debilitating poverty, wretched roads, and environmental degradation are the norm in the Russian Republic as they were throughout the USSR. The Russian national religion, Orthodox Christianity, was as zealously repressed as say, Judaism and Islam. Russian patriotic thought was carefully monitored and, where deemed necessary, suppressed by a watchful censorship. Some Russian nationalist spokesmen, such as Vladimir Osipov, editor of the well-known *samizdat* journal *Veche*, found themselves undergoing long prison sentences for preaching "the Russian ideal."

However, while they lived badly and were not an "imperial people" in the Western sense of that term, ethnic Russians were encouraged by the regime to take pride in the fact that they belonged to a "great power." As Milovan Djilas observed in 1988: "It's true that the ordinary Russian bears the main burden of empire, without sharing its blessings. But the fact is: almost every Russian, lowly or elevated, embraces with enthusiasm the idea of Russian aggrandizement and takes for granted that he has to make sacrifices for it."[7] In a perverse sense, therefore, if Djilas is correct, imperial pride took the place of economic well-being for many ethnic Russians.

Russians witness a fragmentation of empire

During the years 1990 and 1991, we seemed to be witnessing an almost textbook case of the collapse of an empire. The multi national Tsarist Empire – only 45 percent of whose populace were ethnic Russians – had, as is well known, been on the verge of breakup in 1914. Through a combination of coercion, cunning, flexibility, and considerable luck, the Bolsheviks had been able to render this dying empire, albeit with somewhat altered borders, viable for another seventy years, and indeed to expand its direct influence into Eastern Europe and Afghanistan, with its indirect influence spreading throughout the world. In hindsight, we can see that this vast empire began to suffer from degeneracy and "imperial indigestion" during the Brezhnev period. The "bleeding wound" of Afghanistan served gradually to sap the fading imperial will of the Russian people at the same time as the emergence of the Solidarity movement in Poland represented a mortal threat to continued Soviet hegemony in Eastern Europe.

At home, in the USSR, a complementary process was at work. As the

Soviet specialist in inter-republican migration, Viktor Perevedentsev, has noted, a sudden break (*prelom*) in migration patterns became observable in the mid-1970s.[8] Up until then, there had been a marked net outflow of Russians to the other republics; around 1975, this pattern reversed, and a net inflow into the RSFSR became noticeable. To cite Perevedentsev's figures, during the years 1966–1970, the Russian Republic experienced a net outmigration of 598,000 persons; during the period 1971–1975, the figure was 195,000. In the years 1976–1980, by contrast, Russia experienced a net inmigration of 725,000; during the period 1979–1988, the net inflow was 1,767,000. Central Asia, on the other hand, which until the mid-1970s had been a recipient of large inmigration, began to witness a population outflow. Thus during the years 1976–1980, Central Asia (excluding Kazakhstan) experienced a net outmigration of 245,000; for the years 1979–1988, the figure was 850,000. The comparable figures for Kazakhstan were 414,000 and 784,000. From being a "donor" republic, the RSFSR had become the largest "recipient" republic in the Soviet Union.

The gradual loss of Russian "imperial will" during the draining war with Afghanistan was therefore accompanied by a dramatic end to ethnic Russian penetration into the periphery. Yurii Arutyunyan of the Institute of Ethnography in Moscow believes that this dramatic outmigration from the periphery was due, in significant part, to the fact that the "socio-professional" status of Russians in the minority republics was steadily declining. "In Tbilisi," he reports,

> the Russians presently find themselves with lower socio-professional status than the indigenous population. For a long time, they have essentially not competed with the Georgians, who perform more qualified and prestigious work. In Tallinn, the coefficient of occupational prestige for Russians and the indigenous groups are equal, because of the high competitive abilities of the Russians and Estonians. In Kishinev, radical changes have been observed: in the 1970's, the Moldavians had lower occupational prestige than the Russians, but this difference evened out by the 1980's . . . In Tashkent, the Uzbeks in the 1970's were far behind the Russians in prestigious occupations; towards the 1980's the difference was evened out . . .[9]

Losing their competitive advantage *vis-à-vis* the titular peoples of the periphery was a factor powerful in inducing Russians to contemplate returning to their home republic.

The tumultuous events of 1987–1991 came as a profound shock for ethnic Russians living in the periphery, whose numbers were already being depleted by significant outmigration. Suddenly, many of them found themselves deemed "foreigners" in what they had considered their own land. The following letter from Dushanbe, where some 190,000 Russians live, captures the sense of panic and indignation which came over many Russians living in the periphery during the late 1980s:

Dear comrades, mothers and fathers, brothers and sisters!
The Russian-languge populace of the capital of Tadjikistan, the city of Dushanbe, appeals to you!
Agitated by the outrages of fanatical crowds, by the bloodletting, by the blind hatred, and by the pillaging, we appeal to you for help! The lives of children, women, and old men are under threat! The compromising tactics of the [Soviet] government and its fear to take decisive action to halt the disorders assist the raging of anarchy and of religious [i.e., Muslim] fanaticism.[10]

Or there is this letter describing the fate of ethnic Russians living in the republic of Azerbaijan:

And now Russians have become refugees in their own country [note the implied assumption that Azerbaijan is Russian]. When has this ever happened?! Perhaps only during the time of the Great Fatherland War . . . Our gratitude to the military! They evacuated the civilian population from Baku, both Russians and mixed families.[11]

The unexpected headlong collapse of the Soviet Empire, and, with it, of the historic Tsarist Empire during the period 1987–1991 came as an agonizing surprise to Russians living in the periphery as well as to those in the RSFSR. The fast-moving breakup of the empire placed Russians before a stark choice which historian Roman Szporluk has aptly described as one between "empire saving" and "[Russian] nation-building."[12] It was a choice which most Russians, including Mikhail Gorbachev and Boris Yeltsin, had never expected to have to make.

Gorbachev and the Russian Republic

Perhaps no Russian has been more taken by surprise by the lightning collapse of the "inner" Soviet empire than the Soviet president and Communist Party general secretary. From the time of his accession in 1985, Gorbachev had repeatedly shown himself to be blind and insensitive to ethnic issues. An ardent "Soviet patriot," Gorbachev fought hard to preserve the "Russian"/"Soviet Union" identification in the minds of Russians which had served as vital cement for the unitary Soviet state during the pre-perestroika period.

Once glasnost and democratization had begun to loosen things up, Gorbachev found himself in an unexpected squeeze between two groups which thoroughly detested one another but for whom, for different reasons, the political and economic autarchy of the Russian Republic was a high-priority desideratum. The first group was a conservative alliance of neo-Stalinists, National Bolsheviks, and conservative Russian nationalists who, in a sense, wanted to resurrect policies which had obtained during the reigns of Tsars Alexander III and Nicholas II. The decaying official ideology of Marxism-Leninism was to be boosted by potent doses of Russian imperial nationalism. As for the Russian Republic, members of the conservative coalition insisted that it be granted the same institutions – and especially a Russian Communist Party – as were enjoyed by the minority republics.

Another group, who were sworn opponents of the conservatives, also emerged to champion the cause of Russian autarchy. This was a coalition of so-called "democrats," whose standard bearer was, of course, Boris Yeltsin, and who advocated turning the RSFSR into an economically and politically sovereign republic, with the USSR becoming a confederation of fully self-governing republics. (The conservative coalition, by contrast, believed that Russia should suppress the separatist leanings of the periphery, by force if necessary.) Throughout his period of rule, Gorbachev attempted to counter the agendas of these two powerful coalitions. Contrary to the wishes of the conservatives, he struggled to maintain the traditional structural asymmetries, whereby the RSFSR was denied institutions – such as its own Academy of Sciences – enjoyed by the other republics. Like Brezhnev before him, Gorbachev wanted to preserve the "Russian/USSR" linkup in the minds of ethnic Russians. Contrary to the goal of the increasingly powerful democrats, he struggled to maintain the USSR as a unitary state, permitting only a modest and largely cosmetic devolution of power to the republics.

An important Party Central Committee plenum on the nationalities question which was held in September 1989 showed the extent to which Gorbachev was determined to resist the encroachments of Russian autarchy. The plenum's platform stoutly resisted the thesis that the RSFSR should be granted its own communist party, advocating instead the resurrection of a body which had existed under Khrushchev: a bureau for RSFSR affairs at the USSR Party Central Committee.[13] Russia, it emerged, was to be denied the powerful post of first party secretary of the Russian Republic.

In an interview published in *Izvestiya*, Aleksandr Vlasov, a close Gorbachev ally who had been selected to chair the RSFSR Council of Ministers and, in May, 1990, ran unsuccessfully against Yeltsin for the post of chairman of the Russian Supreme Soviet, defended the continued existence of such structural asymmetries.[14] The RSFSR, he said, should be given a Secretariat for Russian Affairs at the All-Union Central Trade Union Council and a Bureau for Russian Affairs at the All-Union Komsomol. These changes fell short of establishing parity with the positions of the minority republics, which possessed their own trade union and Komsomol organizations.

Another close Gorbachev ally, Central Committee secretary Yurii Manaenkov, vigorously defended the maintenance of structural asymmetries between the position of Russia and of the other fourteen republics. Manaenkov pointed to the immense size of the RSFSR and its large population (146 million inhabitants) as justification for special treatment. The fact that there were 10.6 million Communist Party members living in the RSFSR also constituted, he said, grounds for a special approach. "The formation of a Russian Communist Party. . .," he warned, "could strengthen the centrifugal forces in the CPSU and, obviously, in the country as well . . . As we know, V.I. Lenin stood for a federation of peoples but repudiated a federation within the party. The duty of communists is not to admit any divisions on national grounds."[15]

Despite vigorous and determined efforts on the part of Gorbachev and his followers, they were unable to plug the dike against the rising waters of Russian autarchic sentiment. In 1990, over their objections, the conservative alliance brought into existence a Russian (*Rossiiskaya*) Communist Party, under the leadership of outspoken neo-Stalinist tribune, Ivan Polozkov. In the same year, Russia also gained its own trade union organization, Komsomol, and Academy of Sciences.

Once Boris Yeltsin had succeeded in achieving election as chairman of the RSFSR Supreme Soviet – in late May, 1990 – and in declaring the republic's sovereignty, Gorbachev was forced grudgingly to acquiesce to the Russian Republic's gaining the trappings of a "normal" Soviet republic – its own KGB, MVD, and State Committee for Defense and Security; its own television channel and radio station, as well as newspapers officially published by the Russian Republic; and, finally, the activization of a previously dormant and largely symbolic RSFSR Foreign Ministry. These developments succeeded in bringing Russia into a state of rough ethnic "parity" with the other union republics.

In addition to struggling hard against the emergence of Russian autarchy, Gorbachev and his allies consistently sought to fragment the unity of the Russian Republic. The draft Communist Party platform on the nationalities question had, for example, proposed that the RSFSR be divided up into large autonomous economic regions.[16] In the above-cited interview with *Izvestiya*, RSFSR prime minister Aleksandr Vlasov elaborated upon this scheme. New territorial formations, he stated, should take over certain of the functions of the RSFSR Communist Party *obkoms*. The first such region to be established, he said, would probably be the Far Eastern Economic Region, which would unites the Primorskii and Khabarovsk *krais*, as well as the Amur, Kamchatka, Magadan, Sakhalin, and Chita oblasts. Similar large economic regions, he said, should be formed in Eastern Siberia, Western Siberia, the Urals and in Central Russia. Each region would be headed by a deputy chairman of the RSFSR Council of Ministers.

The proposed economic restructuring of the RSFSR drew sharp criticism from Russian *obkom* secretaries, who understandably feared a diminution of their power and prerogatives, and from conservative Russian nationalists, who believed that a chopping up of the Russian Republic into autonomous economic units would serve to weaken the cohesiveness of the republic and possibly to undermine its very existence (which may have been Gorbachev's intention all along).

The party platform on the nationalities issue had also called for strengthening of the position of the autonomous formations within the union republics. Most of these formations were located in the RSFSR, where there were sixteen autonomous republics (or ASSRs), five autonomous oblasts, and autonomous districts. Like the plan to divide Russia into autonomous economic regions, this Central Committee plan to beef up the autonomous formations appeared to be aimed at fragmenting the unity of Russia.

Once Yeltsin had gained election as RSFSR chairman in May of 1990 and Russia had declared her sovereignty in June, the Gorbachev "center" began actively to encourage the Russian autonomous formations to declare their full sovereignty from the RSFSR. This strategy was presumably pursued to weaken the power of Yeltsin and of the democrats around him. In the words of one Yeltsin supporter, RSFSR people's deputy Oleg Rumyantsev, executive secretary of the RSFSR Constitutional Commission: "[Gorbachev] would have earned a place in Russian history as a great reformer had he not made his principal error, the error of tearing Russia apart. Russia does not forgive such transgressions, for Gorbachev bears a great political blame for the anti-Russian direction of his politics."[17] Rumyantsev notes that "even prior to the first [RSFSR] Congress, a law conflicting with the RSFSR was drafted [by the center] to proclaim all autonomous areas located on the territory of the Russian Republic as subjects of USSR rule."

In this case, too, Gorbachev appears to have failed in a determined effort to fragment the unity of Russia. Among the autonomous formations of the RSFSR, only Tatarstan refused officially to participate in the elections for the RSFSR president, in June, 1991, and only it refused to sign the union treaty as a part of the RSFSR. The Soviet president's concerted attempts to fragment the Russian Republic were no more successful than his frenetic efforts to preserve the unity of the USSR.

Boris Yeltsin and Russia

The leader and living symbol of the Russian democratic forces has been Boris Yeltsin, a former high-ranking party official, who channeled his uncommon energy, personal courage, and considerable political savvy into a position rivaling, then surpassing, that of Gorbachev in terms of authority and power. Yeltsin's election as RSFSR president in June, 1991 gave him the popular legitimacy that Gorbachev lacked. In a high-stakes contest, Yeltsin used his extraordinary popularity with ethnic Russians, as well as with the other peoples of the USSR, to force repeated concessions from the center.

The assumption of power in the Soviet Union's largest republic by a dynamic maverick who had officially broken with the communist party and with its legitimizing ideology served to move the breakup of the "inner" Soviet empire along at a blistering pace. The Russian Republic's declaration of sovereignty in June, 1990 was the first important nail which Yeltsin drove into the coffin of the USSR, and his conclusion of a Confederation of Independent States with other Republics in December, 1991 buried the USSR for good.

One significant result of Yeltsin's election as head of the Russian Republic was that it induced Russians to begin to see the RSFSR as a discrete political and economic entity, something apart from and opposed to the USSR. In 1989, at the first USSR Congress of People's Deputies, conservative Russian nationalist writer Valentin Rasputin had attracted attention when he had exclaimed, "perhaps it is Russia which should leave the [Soviet] Union . . ."[18] These words had been uttered carpingly, and their intention had been to underline the absurdity of such a development. One year later, Russia had declared its sovereignty and a separate political existence for Russia no longer seemed such an absurdity.

In directly challenging Gorbachev and the center, Yeltsin for the first time embossed the dichotomy "Russia/USSR" upon the minds of contemporary Russians. In a series of pitched battles with the center, Yeltsin, as had been noted, gradually acquired for Russia institutions already enjoyed by the other republics – a Ministry of Internal Affairs, television channel, and so forth. In May of 1991, after a crippling miners' strike, the center grudgingly agreed to transfer control of the mines in the Kuzbass, Rostov, and Komi regions to the jurisdiction of the Russian Republic. Each of these political victories served to advance the cause of Russian autarchy.

In addition to acquiring for Russia the trappings of a normal Soviet republic, Yeltsin also began to sign a number of treaties and economic agreements with the other union republics. In December, 1990, for example, a full year before the Confederation of Independent States, he signed an important treaty with the Ukrainian Republic in which the following was agreed to:

> The High Contracting parties
> —recognize each other as sovereign states . . .
> —protect the rights of their citizens residing on the territory of the other party;
> —recognize and respect the territorial integrity of the Russian Federation and the Ukraine within the existing boundaries in the USSR.[19]

It will be noted that this signed agreement between the RSFSR and Ukraine explicitly recognized the existing boundaries separating the two republics. Given the fact that the USSR was in the process of fragmenting into sovereign republics, the question of boundaries took on added importance. Unlike Yeltsin and his democratic allies, a number of ethnic

Russians, as we shall see, believe that the current borders separating the RSFSR and Ukraine, as well as those dividing Russia and other republics, are unfair and historically unjustifiable. They believe that the RSFSR represents a truncated entity which can in no way be considered the legitimate heir of prerevolutionary Tsarist Russia.

If his recognition of the other republics and of their extant borders got Yeltsin into hot water with some Russians, it understandably earned him the gratitude and admiration of many representatives of the minority republics. Referring to the January 11, 1991 treaty signed between the RSFSR and Estonia, two Estonian scholars have written: "This treaty is historically significant because it is the first bilateral agreement made between Estonia and her Eastern neighbor on the basis of equal rights after the loss of Estonian independence."[20] In May of 1991, Andrei Kozyrev, foreign minister of the Russian Republic, made the new relationship "official" when he formally accepted the accreditation documents of Estonia's newly arrived representative to the RSFSR, Evgenii Golikov.[21] In addition to signing agreements with the other republics, Yeltsin early on also upheld their right to secede from the Soviet Union if that should be the will of their populace.

Yeltsin's approach to the minority peoples of the RSFSR, who comprise approximately 18.5 percent of the republic's population, has been to be as accommodating and flexible as possible: "the autonomous [formations of the RSFSR]," he maintained in March of 1991, "can take as much sovereignty as they can administer. We can agree to all of that. But they will have independently to answer, of course, for the well-being of their people. We make one condition: they will have to take part in a federation treaty with Russia. I underline: we will not let anyone pull Russia down."[22] On the symbolic level, Yeltsin scored points with RSFSR minorities, and especially Muslims, by appointing a dynamic Chechen, Ruslan Khasbulatov, as his deputy chairman.

What is Yeltsin's view of the position of the twenty-five million Russians living outside the Russian Republic? "It is the duty of Russia and of its Supreme Soviet and leadership," he observed in March, 1991,

> somehow to help them. But understand me: It is impossible to defend people with tanks. After that, their lives would be more complicated. It is necessary to put our relations with those republics on a juridical foundation, one of international rights, which we are presently doing. In that case, any fact of discrimination against the Russian populace [on the part of another republic] can be juridically resolved, and we can apply sanctions against this or that republic or state. For example, we have concluded treaties with Latvia and Estonia, and they are now amending their laws in a number of instances . . .[23]

Given this changing situation, Yeltsin believes that Russians living in the periphery must choose what is most convenient for them: "If they want to return to Russia," he pledges, "then we will create proper conditions for them there." To which he adds: "Incidentally, in our treaties with the [other] republics we provide compensation [to Russians] for loss of property incurred in the process of leaving that republic . . ."[24]

To summarize, Yeltsin's role in recasting and redefining the role of ethnic Russians within the "inner" Soviet empire has been pivotal. By officially recognizing the sovereignty and the present boundaries of the other republics, he contributed *de facto* to rendering Russians living in those areas "foreigners." From then on, Russians in the periphery had to decide whether to become, say, Latvian or Uzbek citizens, or to emigrate back to Russia. By opting decisively for Russian "nation-building" and by firmly rejecting "empire saving," Yeltsin helped deal a death blow to the world's last major empire and also liberated Russians so that they can get on with the task of solving their monumental economic and social problems.

The view from a revived Russian foreign ministry

Under Brezhnev, the post of RSFSR foreign minister had been a symbolic one, since the Russian Republic's interests had been wholly subordinated to those of the USSR as a whole. In the fall of 1990, a young thirty-nine-year-old specialist in international affairs, Andrei Kozyrev, was appointed to the post of RSFSR foreign minister, and he immediately began to elaborate upon Yeltsin's view of a new role for Russians in a revamped confederation. In his numerous writings and public statements, Kozyrev has taken note of the fact that the tendency in Western Europe in recent decades has been toward integration, not disintegration. The task at hand, he believes, is to bring about a similar process of integration on the territory of the former unitary Soviet state, on the basis of full sovereignty for each constituent republic.

"Usually the opponents of this process," Kozyrev observes, "point to the fact that the [present] republican borders inaccurately represent the ethnic make-up of the population." His rejoinder to this argument: "Let this be the case. But does this mean that the republics must now carry on endless territorial disputes with one another? Germany and France conducted wars for centuries over Alsace and Lorraine until they finally understood the principle of a civilized resolution of an ancient conflict. They simply made the border conditional."[25]

Kozyrev expresses a firm conviction that a sovereign Russia has a good chance of reconstituting the present union, or at least a major part of it: "as Russia learns to stand on its own," he wrote in a piece which appeared in *The New York Times*, "a democratic Russia will become a national center of gravity for the other sovereign republics . . ."[26] The new treaties and agreements which the RSFSR concluded with such republics as Ukraine, Belarus, Moldova, and Kazakhstan were, he maintains, intended to provide "an alternative to disintegration." *De facto*, the new agreements laid "the basis for a new union."[27]

One wonders whether Kozyrev's views on reintegration may not represent wishful thinking. Could the union in fact be reconstituted on the basis of granting full political and economic sovereignty to its members? Aleksandr Tsipko, deputy director of the Institute of International and Economic and Political Research of the USSR Academy of Science, is one who holds that it cannot. "If the Federation Council will rule the country," he predicts, "then, of course, the country will once again be ruled by the head of the largest republic, that is, by Russia."[28] Russians like Kozyrev, Tsipko believes, are suffering from "the inertia of imperial thinking." Not all the republics which sought full independence from the USSR would in the future opt for reintegration with Russia, and for the specific reason that Tsipko cites. Indeed, one wonders whether in the long run the paths of the USSR's three Slavic and its six Muslim republics lie in the same direction. Writing in the journal *Foreign Policy*, Graham Fuller, former vice chairman of the US National Intelligence Council, observes that

> In the wake of Gorbachev's revolutionary recognition of long-suppressed national yearnings for greater autonomy, about 50 million Soviet Muslims will soon be reentering the broader Muslim world, creating an entire new calculus of Muslim power and regional blocs . . . Afghanistan, Iran, and Turkey may well be competing for allies in the Muslim reserve of Soviet Central Asia, dramatically altering the weight and influence they have wielded in the Middle East.[29]

Finally, it appears to be far from certain that even the three Eastern Slav republics – Russia, Ukraine, and Belarus – will hold together over the coming decades.

The "hardliners" and Russia

Together with the Gorbachev "center" and the Yeltsin "democrats," the so-called hardliners represent a third major political force impacting the future of the Russian Republic. With strong representation in such elite institutions as the KGB, the party bureaucracy, the military command, and the Soviet military-industrial complex, this group has been in a position to attempt to impose its will on the Russian Republic and on the union as a whole. In January, 1991, the hardliners seem to have played the key role in attempting a *putsch* in the Baltic and they were, of course, supporters of the August, 1991 coup. There is, however, as has been mentioned, a basic contradiction in their position. On the one hand, they were vehement champions of the unity of the Soviet state; on the other hand, paradoxically, they were ardent defenders of Russian autarchy, a stance which *de facto* served to weaken the very cohesion of the USSR which they sought to preserve.

An example of the "empire saving" obsession of the hardliners is the open letter which a number of them wrote to Boris Yeltsin, in his capacity as chairman of the RSFSR Supreme Soviet, in January, 1991.[30] The authors of this truculent letter included such well-known conservative Russian nationalist writers as Valentin Rasputin (who had served, at Gorbachev's request, as a member of the now-defunct Presidential Council), Vasilii Belov, and Vladimir Krupin (chief editor of the journal *Moskva*), and National Bolshevik publicists Aleksandr Prokhanov, Eduard Volodin, and Karem Rash. The letter's signatories assailed Yeltsin for supporting the desire of the Baltic republics to secede from the USSR. Underlining the "historical rootedness of Russia in the Baltic lands," the authors maintained that Yeltsin's primary task as head of the Russian Republic was to safeguard ethnic Russians and Eastern Slavs living in the periphery.

Even worse than Yeltsin's perceived sins against the unity of the Soviet Union was, the authors believed, his conniving in the breakup of Russia itself. "Only a politician indifferent to the fate of the Fatherland," they wrote scornfully, "could hand out willy-nilly free economic zones and sovereignties on the territory of Russia, dismembering the Russian state . . ." And they concluded sternly: "Taken as a whole, your [i.e., Yeltsin's] actions can be simply defined as the disintegration of the USSR and the destruction of Russia, neither of which was created by you, and it is not up to you to decide their fate."

For Russian nationalists like Valentin Rasputin and National Bolsheviks like Aleksandr Prokhanov, Russia and the USSR were the same thing. In such a reading, Latvia and Georgia, say, are as much a part of "Russia" as are the RSFSR cities of Moscow and Khabarovsk.

Another example of the "empire-saving" mentality characteristic of this group is an article by a certain Aleksandr Fomenko which appeared in *Literaturnaya Rossiya* in March, 1990.

> An empire [Fomenko wrote] is a multi-national centralized state which is sufficiently strong and well-organized (for example, the British empire at the time of its flowering, or the present-day 'democratic empire' of the USA). It guarantees to its subjects a clear-cut set of rights and, naturally, demands that they fulfill certain specific obligations. In such a state, snipers do not as a rule fire on passers-by, peaceful dwellers are not turned into refugees, and neighboring provinces, while they do not possess 'sovereignty,' also do not conduct military actions against one another. What is wrong [with such an empire]?[31]

In his polemic, which concentrated on the Baltic dimension of the Soviet nationalities problem, Fomenko emphasized that Russians and other Slavs have lived in the present Baltic region for a millennium. For him, the Baltic was therefore *ipso facto* Russian soil. He noted that the city of Yur'ev, now Tartu, in Estonia was founded in 1030 by Prince Yaroslav the Wise of Kiev. The Baltic lands, Fomenko contended, were too small to remain independent; they would either be ruled by Russia, Germany, or Poland.

(Implicit in these remarks is a belief that neither the Germans nor the Poles have undergone any changes in the postwar period.)

In the eyes of the hardliners, thus, the Soviet Union and Russia were the same thing, an indivisible entity that had to be preserved, by force if necessary. Minority separatist leaders like presidents Landsbergis of Lithuania or Gamsakhurdia of Georgia were seen as violent enemies of Russia who had to be removed from office. Some hardliners also advocated that the fourteen minority republics be abolished and replaced by American-style states which would belong to a "Pan-Russian Republic." In economics, some of them opposed all market reform; others would countenance a "Pinochet model" or "South Korean model" of authoritarian modernization. In summary, it should be clear that the hardliners sought to replace the Soviet empire, which was rooted in Marxism-Leninism, with a resurrected Russian Empire, such as the one that began to emerge in the Tsarist period during the reigns of Alexander III and Nicholas II. The bankruptcy of such a strategy was forcefully pointed out by Alain Besançon in 1983: "Once the ideological magic [of Marxism-Leninism] has been destroyed," he wrote,

> there would be only one source of magic left – the imperial or colonial legitimacy of the Russian people in a world that today is entirely decolonized. This anachronistic legitimacy would immediately stimulate the resistance of the non-Russian nations, who would call forth their own legitimacies, necessitating military occupation. The Russian people is not sufficiently populous for that task.[32]

The failed quest for a Russian Popular Front

While powerful popular fronts emerged in all of the minority republics in the USSR, a comparable organization did not emerge on Russian soil. In retrospect, it seems clear that the "empire saving"/"nation-building" split among contemporary Russians served to block the emergence of such an organization.

An aborted attempt to form an RSFSR Popular Front occurred in July of 1989, when delegates from nearly fifty Russian cities and towns journeyed to the provincial city of Yaroslavl' for a two-day conference. According to a report which appeared in *Moscow News*, the delegates were unable to come to agreement concerning the character of the proposed popular front.[33] One of the hotly debated issues was reportedly whether the proposed front should have a "Russo-centric" or "democratic" character. Since they were unable to reach agreement, the delegates decided to put off holding a constituent conference for the front.

In October, 1989, the organizers made a second attempt, once again in Yaroslavl'. One hundred and sixteen delegates arrived from forty-one cities and towns in the RSFSR. Representatives from fourteen local popular fronts in Russia were in attendance.[34] Once again, the "empire savers" and "nation-builders" were unable to come to a meeting of minds. According to a report published in the Riga-based Russian language newspaper *Atmoda*, "The adherents of the faction which called itself patriotic spoke in favor of remaining a great power and of the salvation of Russia, one and undivided."[35] The "patriots" who were in attendance also called for a holding back of "separatist" passions in the Soviet Union, i.e., agitated for a retention of the "inner" Soviet empire. The effort to found a Russian Popular Front therefore foundered on deep divisions separating ethnic Russian "empire savers" and "nation-builders."

Solzhenitsyn's program of Russian "nation-building"

In late 1990, three months after the Russian Republic had declared its sovereignty, two major Soviet newspapers, *Komsomol'skaya pravda* and *Literaturnaya gazeta*, published Nobel prizewinner Aleksandr Solzhenitsyn's programmatic brochure *How Shall We Reconstitute Russia?* in a print-run of over twenty-five million.[36] Given its huge readership, the brochure inevitably served as a catalyst for ethnic Russians to begin thinking about the future of the Soviet empire.

On the subject of the future of the USSR as a unitary state, Solzhenitsyn sided decisively with Yeltsin and the democratic "nation-builders" against Gorbachev and the hardliners. The Soviet Union, he contended, had no future as a single state. Centrifugal developments and separatist tendencies had, he believed, proceeded to a point where the union could be held together only at the cost of enormous bloodshed. An additional factor, he noted, was that Russians had been so debilitated by seventy years of communist rule that they simply lacked the strength to maintain an empire. "We have to choose firmly," Solzhenitsyn declared, "between an empire that first of all destroys us [i.e., ethnic Russians] ourselves, and the spiritual and bodily salvation of our people." He noted that Russia became stronger once it had cut Poland and Finland loose and that postwar Japan surged in vigor after abandoning its expansionist dreams.

Unlike Yeltsin and the democrats, Solzhenitsyn believed that Russia herself should take the initiative in disbanding an empire that was sapping her strength and in fact killing her. He consequently urged that eleven of the Soviet republics be cut loose from Russia whether they wanted this or not. He held that Russia should concentrate on resuscitative "nation-building" uncluttered by debilitating alliances or confederations with former Soviet colonies.

While Yeltsin and the democrats were prepared to recognize the present boundaries separating Russia and the other republics, Solzhenitsyn, for his part, wanted to redraw some of those boundaries if that should prove to be the will of the populace, as expressed through plebiscites. Thus in the case of the Muslim republic of Kazakhstan, he believed that the republic's northern tier, which is heavily settled by Russians, should be ceded to Russia, while its southern part, largely populated by Kazakhs, should be free to choose to remain with Russia or to go its separate way. (Angered over Solzhenitsyn's views, crowds of ethnic Kazakhs reportedly staged burnings of those Soviet newspapers which carried the text of his brochure.)

With regard to the Eastern Slav republics of Ukraine and Belarus, Solzhenitsyn expressed a hope that their populations would choose to remain in union with their Russian brethren. He proposed the formation of what he calls a Pan-Russian Union (*Rossiiskii soyuz*) to accomplish this purpose. (Yeltsin's advisor on nationalities' questions, RSFSR congresswoman Galina Starovoitova, noted that the term "Slavic Union [*Slavyanskii soyuz*]" would be preferable for what Solzhenitsyn had in mind, "otherwise there is discrimination in the very title."[37]) Aware that separatist sentiment had been growing in Ukraine, especially in the republic's western regions, Solzhenitsyn stated categorically that the people of Ukraine should not be held in union with Russia by force. Rather, he contended, the populace should be free to express its will through the vehicle of referendums, on an oblast by oblast basis. Implicit in Solzhenitsyn's comments was a belief that Ukraine was likely to split, with its western regions voting for independence and its eastern regions electing to remain together with Russia. In Belarus, in his view, separatist tendencies were not strong at present.

As for the non-Russian peoples of the RSFSR, Solzhenitsyn argued that those autonomous regions, such as Tatarstan, whose historical borders are fully enveloped by the Russian Republic, will have to share the future fate of the Russian people, though their ethnic, economic, and religious needs should receive maximum attention. The Russian Council of Nationalities – one of the few worthy Soviet institutions in Solzhenitsyn's opinion – should, he believed, serve as a forum for the enunciation of such needs. Those minority peoples of the RSFSR who enjoy external borders could, in his view, secede from Russia if that should prove to be the will of their populace expressed through a plebiscite.

Solzhenitsyn took pains to warn that the dismemberment of the Soviet Union should not occur chaotically, "like the Portuguese fleeing from Angola," but rather in an orderly fashion carefully prepared by specialists. Particular attention, he emphasized, should be paid to ensuring the rights of all minority peoples, including ethnic Russians living in the Soviet periphery.

To conclude, Solzhenitsyn's anti-imperial model for the reconstitution of Russia had, of course, nothing in common with the vision of a unitary state promulgated by Gorbachev and the hardliners. It also, however, differed in significant ways from Yeltsin's concept of a "democratic" confederation of sovereign republics. Solzhenitsyn believed that such a body would likely serve to bog Russia down in imperial residue and would therefore slow down or prevent the recovery of her health. The answer, Solzhenitsyn contended, is for Russia fairly and democratically to adjust her borders with the neighbouring republics and then get on with the business of "nation-building' unencumbered by deleterious alliances.

Several authoritarian "nation-building" programs

Following in the wake of Solzhenitsyn's brochure, there have emerged other programmatic statements by ethnic Russians which, like the Nobel laureate's proposals, express a willingness to accept the loss of much of the current Soviet "inner" empire, but with an adjustment of the present borders. Certain of these statements favor an authoritarian, rather than democratic, resolution of the border disputes.

Areas within the USSR in which Russians live compactly have served as one source for such statements. The March, 1991 issue of *Put'*, the newspaper of the Russian Christian Democratic Movement, for example, carried a letter by A.N. Los', chairman of the Russian Society of Crimea, in which the author argues that the Crimea, which, he claims, was "unlawfully" given to Ukraine by Khrushchev in 1954, be returned to the Russian Republic. "Seventy percent of the population of Crimea," Los' writes, "is made up of Russians, 24% of Ukrainians, and 6% of Crimean Tartars. Of the 24% who are Ukrainians, more than 90% have named Russian as their native language." And he concludes: "One would think that the question of returning Crimea to Russia should automatically be posed."[38] It should be noted that on January 2, 1991, the Crimean electorate voted 93.3 percent to reclaim that region's pre-1945 status as an autonomous republic, but this time within the Ukraine.[39] The Ukrainian government accepted this decision on the part of the Crimean voters.

North-east Estonia, an area where Russians live compactly, represents another point of tension. In early 1991, the city of Narva, the main urban center in the region, proposed that it be declared a free economic zone. If approved, this play would tie Narva's industry, energy plants and raw materials into an economic conglomerate outside the control of the Republic of Estonia.[40] Some Estonians viewed this move as the first step toward the attempted secession of north-east Estonia.

The January, 1991 issue of the newspaper *Put'* published an open letter which was signed by forty-three employees of the Laboratory for Theoretical Physics at the Combined Institute for Nuclear Research in Dubno.[41] This letter strongly protested Yeltsin's decision to recognize the present borders separating Russia and Ukraine. "These borders," the authors maintain, "are historically unfounded. In the Russian Empire, a distinction was made between Little Russia [i.e., the Ukraine proper], on the one hand, and the New Russia region [i.e., the oblasts of Nikolaev, Odessa,

Kherson, and Dnepropetrovsk] and Tavriya [i.e., the Crimea] on the other. The latter two areas were taken from the Turks on the strength of Russian arms . . ." The authors advocate that New Russia and the Crimea be given back to Russia.

In May, 1991, there took place the constituent congress of the so-called "Russian Party of the RSFSR," a conservative Russian nationalist organization. According to Russian Radio, the new radio station of Yeltsin's Russian Republic, the party's draft program calls for the rebirth of the state of Russia, which is to be made up of the present RSFSR, plus the predominately Russian areas of the other republics: the Crimea; the left bank region of the Dniester in Moldova; the northern tier of Kazakhstan, including the city of Alma Ata; and northern Kyrgyzstan, including the city of Frunze (Bishkek). The party's program also calls for the creation of Russian autonomous formations in the other republics; for a unitary state structure in the RSFSR, without autonomous formations; and suggests the repatriation of all Jews from Russian territory.[42] While representing an aggressive and even racist program – i.e., its position on the Jews – the document is interesting as a pioneering conservative Russian nationalist statement which implicitly acquiesces to a loss of those Soviet territories in which Russians do not live compactly: the entire Baltic region; the entire Caucasus; most of Central Asia, Ukraine and Moldova, and even, apparently, all of Belarus. This program therefore may signal a new realism on the part of conservative Russian nationalists. It also demonstrates, graphically, that the Russian empire is in the process of being redefined.

Russian public opinion on the question of retaining an empire

Before the advent of glasnost, Western analysts had little hard data at hand with which to assess the opinions of ethnic Russians living in the Soviet Union. To fathom the workings of the Russian mind, analysts were reduced to such arcane pursuits as scrutinizing the favorite novels of Russians; examining the comment book of an exhibit given by a popular Russian nationalist artist; and dissecting the films to which Russians flocked in great numbers.[43] Due to a lack of trustworthy information, Western observers at times succumbed to a temptation to exaggerate the significance of such lurid developments as the emergence on the political scene of a violently anti-Semitic organization, called Pamyat, in May of 1987. Some Western commentators speculated that Pamyat might represent the authentic voice of ethnic Russians in the USSR, and they warned gravely about the specter of Russian neo-Nazism.

Once the Soviet press began to publish the results of scientific polls – and this commenced in the fall of 1989 – it soon became clear that Pamyat no more represented the voice of ethnic Russians than did, say, the Ku Klux Klan speak for most Americans. Thus, for example, a poll taken in

May of 1990 by the All-Union Center for the Study of Public Opinion (or
VTsIOM for short) showed that Pamyat and similar extremist groups
enjoyed the support of not more than 1–2 percent of the RSFSR populace.[44] This snapshot of Russian sentiment was further confirmed by the
results of the March, 1990 elections, and of the subsequent runoffs, to the
RSFSR Congress of People's Deputies and to local Russian soviets, which
demonstrated conclusively that there was little public support among
Russians for the racist views of the extreme right.[45]

What about the opinions of present-day Russians concerning the
breakup of the "inner" Soviet empire? The polls show persuasively that
ethnic Russians are growing accustomed to the fragmentation of the
empire and that they, by a significant margin, refuse to countenance the use
of force to hold it together. A rapid "deimperialization" of the Russian
psyche has been occurring.

To demonstrate the speed of this shift, one need merely cite the results of
a poll which was conducted in the Russian Republic by VTsIOM in the fall
of 1989, and then contrast its results with two subsequent polls taken in the
RSFSR in May and September of 1990. In the 1989 poll, the results of
which were published in the weekly magazine *Ogonek*, 63.4 percent of the
RSFSR citizens contacted gave a high priority to preserving "the unity and
cohesion of the USSR."[46] By contrast, only 10.6 percent of Armenians, 10.2
percent of Balts, and 30.9 percent of Ukrainians accorded it a high priority.
This poll therefore showed that "empire saving" sentiment remained
strong among Russians in the fall of 1989.

Six months later, in May of 1990, shortly before Yeltsin was elected
chairman of the RSFSR Supreme Soviet, VTsIOM conducted a new poll of
1,517 persons in twenty areas of the RSFSR.[47] This poll yielded markedly
different results from the one in 1989. On the question of what the future
relations of the RSFSR to the "center" should be, for example, the
respondents held:

18% – that relations should remain the same as at present;
35% – that the economic and political rights of Russia should be expanded but
that the final say in all questions should remain with the "center";
43% – that Russia should receive political and economic independence (up to
and including leaving the USSR);
4% – other.

It seems clear that a major shift in Russian public opinion had occurred.
For more than 43 percent of RSFSR respondents, the bonds conjoining
"Russia" and "the USSR" had been severed.

Another intriguing result of this poll was that, it emerged, growing
number of ethnic Russians were prepared to countenance the granting of
added political clout to the autonomous formations of the RSFSR:

20% – stated that the power of the autonomous regions in the RSFSR should
remain the same as at present;

57% – stated that the economic and political rights of the autonomous regions should be broadened, but that the final say in all questions should remain with the RSFSR as a whole;

20% – stated that the autonomous regions should receive economic and political independence (up to and including leaving the RSFSR);

3% – other.

The responses to this question seemed to demonstrate that there was considerable popular support within the RSFSR for the position embraced by Yeltsin, namely, that the autonomous formations be offered broad self-rule in exchange for their remaining members of the Russian Republic.

A poll taken by VTsIOM four months later, in September, 1990, showed an even more pronounced shift in public attitudes.[48] This poll contacted 1,458 persons residing in twenty-five population points within the Russian Republic. Here is what the respondents felt concerning the proper relationship of the RSFSR and the "center":

Should the organs of the Soviet Union have the right to revoke or halt the decisions of the Russian Federation?
They should have the right – 23%
They should not have that right – 52.5%
Difficult to answer – 24.5%

Should the organs of the Russian Federation have the right to revoke or halt the decisions of the organs of the Soviet Union?
They should have that right – 48.1%
They should not have that right – 21.9%
Difficult to answer – 30.2%

On questions which concerned the position of the autonomous formations within the RSFSR, the respondents were of the following opinion:

What variant of the organization of the Russian Federation seems preferable to you?
One historically formed state with special rights for the national-territorial formations – 28.6%
A federation in which the national-territorial formations, regions and oblasts enjoy full rights – 47.8%
Difficult to answer – 23.7%

The autonomous formations should have the right to leave the Russian Federation if a majority of their populace should favor it
Yes – 55.9%
No – 27.8%
Difficult to answer – 16.3%

On their own territory, the laws of the autonomous formations should take precedence over the laws of the Russian Federation
Yes – 26.5%
No – 46.6%
Difficult to answer – 26.8%

This September 1990 poll, thus, offered strong support for Yeltsin's policies of pursuing sovereignty for the Russian Republic and of offering a broad degree of self-rule to the autonomous formations within the RSFSR. The respondents, as can be seen, were even prepared to let the autonomous formations secede from Russia, if their populace expressed such a preference through referendums.

Russians on the use of force to retain the "inner" empire

The protracted, bloody war in Afghanistan appears, as we have seen, to have gradually drained ethnic Russians of a willingness to support the use of Russian lives to preserve the so-called "outer" Soviet empire. By the beginning of the 1990s, this sentiment had spread to the issue of the forcible preservation of the "inner" Soviet empire. When, for example, the central authorities attempted to call up reservists in southern Russia for use in Azerbaijan in January of 1990, there occurred a revolt on the part of the reservists' mothers and families, and an organization called "mothers against mobilization" came into existence.[49] In August of the same year, the newspaper *Izvestiya* reported that conscripts' mothers had rallied in the Russian provincial city of Perm' to protest the failure of the commandant of the local military district to meet with them. The mothers had been demanding that their sons serve only in the RSFSR and not be sent to the Caucasus or to Central Asia.[50]

In January of 1991, when the "center" orchestrated a *putsch* against the lawfully elected Baltic parliaments and their presidents, similar anti-imperial sentiments emerged among ethnic Russians.[51] On January 16, just three days after "Bloody Sunday" in Vilnius, the polling organization VTsIOM contacted 962 persons living in thirteen cities of the RSFSR.[52] Their reaction to the attempted coup was:

Do you approve or do you condemn the actions of the troops?
Approve – 29%
Condemn – 55%
Difficult to answer – 16%

In Moscow and Leningrad, as it was still known, which represented the political "wave of the future" for much of the rest of the RSFSR, the reaction was even more decisive. Less than 15 percent of Leningraders came out in support of the troops' actions, while in Moscow the figure was 15.4 percent.[53]

Another important indicator is the feelings of young Russians, of the so-called "upcoming generation." In early 1991, the magazine *Reader's Digest* asked the Institute of Sociology of the USSR Academy of Sciences to conduct an RSFSR-wide poll of the attitudes of young Russians aged 18 to 25.[54] On the critical question of whether or not the minority Soviet republics should be permitted to secede from the union, the young Russians who were contacted felt as follows:

Yes – 70%
No – 19%
Undecided – 11%

The findings of such polls appear to indicate a marked willingness on the part of present-day ethnic Russians to let those republics who want to leave the USSR do so. It might be asked, however, how such results tally with those of the March, 1991 referendum, in which approximately 71 percent of RSFSR voters reportedly voted to preserve the union. (Approximately the same percentage, roughly 70 percent, voted to institute the post of president of the RSFSR, i.e., supported Boris Yeltsin and his agenda.)

A first point which should be made is that the language in which the referendum was couched was deliberately vague. Voters were asked: "Do you consider necessary the preservation of the Union of Soviet Socialist Republics as a renewed federation of equal sovereign republics, in which the rights and freedom of the individual of any nationality will be fully guaranteed?"[55] This language was notably ambiguous and did not overtly contradict the "Yeltsin model" of a renewed confederation of fully sovereign republics. A second point to be made is that there may have been tampering with the vote in parts of the Russian provinces. One Soviet academic with whom I discussed this question told me that, in his opinion, the vote count in large Russian cities was probably accurately tabulated but that in the provinces, where conservative party bureaucrats retain great power, "it is a different matter altogether."

One notes that in the more politically advanced areas of the Russian Republic the referendum did quite poorly. In Boris Yeltsin's home base of Sverdlovsk city, for example, only 34.4 percent voted for Gorbachev's "renewed federation," while in both Moscow and Leningrad the figure was only slightly above 50 percent. This was hardly a ringing endorsement of the Soviet president and of his policies.

The views of Russians living in the periphery

Like the views of ethnic Russians living in the core Russian Republic, the attitudes of Russians in the non-Russian periphery have been changing with considerable rapidity, and in a direction favorable to the interests of the titular peoples of the minority republics. In the republic of Estonia, for instance, where 475,000 Russians make up the bulk of the non-Estonian populace, polls taken in 1989 and 1990 showed considerable changes in attitude (see table 3.1):[56]

By early 1991, when the regime attempted a coup in the Baltic, ethnic Russian sentiment had shifted even more decisively in the direction of sympathy for the independence of the Baltic republics. This shift was politically significant, inasmuch as Russians comprise 34% of the population of Latvia and 30.3% of the population of Estonia. (By contrast, they make

Table 3.1. *Preferences concerning the future political status of Estonia (%)*

	Estonians		Non-Estonians	
	1989	1990	1989	1990
	April/Sept.	Jan./May	April/Sept.	Jan./May
The maintenance of the status quo	2 2	0 0	54 37	20 21
Estonia must stay in a reformed Soviet Union (confederation)	39 31	15 2	25 47	52 46
Estonia should be an absolutely independent state	56 64	81 96	5 9	17 26
Unable to answer	3 3	4 2	16 7	1 7

up only 9.4% of the population of Lithuania.) In a critical February, 1991 plebiscite of the populace of Latvia, 73.6% of those voting supported Latvian independence. Since only 54% of Latvia's population was ethnic Latvian, this meant that hundreds of thousands of Russians had to have supported the Latvians in their bid for secession. A similar result obtained in the Estonian referendum, with 77.8% of those voting supporting independence for the republic.[57]

During approximately the same time frame, in January, 1991, *Moscow News* published the result of a poll of 1,005 ethnic Russians living in nine minority republics and in one autonomous formation of the RSFSR, which had been taken in November and December of 1990.[58] The poll was conducted by the polling organization VTsIOM. Published under the heading "Do the Russians Want to Flee?" the poll offered a useful snapshot of ethnic Russian sentiment in the Soviet periphery (see table 3.2):

One notes that in Central Asia (excepting Kazakhstan) and in Georgia approximately a third or more of ethnic Russians wanted to be repatriated to Russia. In Estonia, Western Ukraine, and Kazakhstan, the percentage of Russians desiring to return to the RSFSR stood at 20 percent or higher. These figures suggest that the derussification of the periphery will continue at a rapid pace in coming years; indeed, in certain republics, the process could snowball and result in "Russian flight" from areas of Central Asia and the Caucasus. According to Soviet ethnographer Yurii Arutyunyan, an outmigration of Russians from Moldova and the Baltic became observable

Table 3.2. *Do the Russians want to flee?*

Are you on the whole satisfied or dissatisfied that you live in precisely this republic?

Republic	% satisfied	% dissatisfied	% difficult to answer
Estonia	51	19	30
Latvia	75	7	18
Western Ukraine	36	21	44
Georgia	62	22	16
Azerbaijan	86	6	10
Kazakhstan	73	11	16
Kyrgyzstan	56	4	40
Tadjikistan	61	25	14
Uzbekistan	64	11	25

Do you have the desire to leave for Russia or would you like permanently to reside in this republic?

Republic	% leave for Russia	% remain	% difficult to answer
Estonia	23	50	27
Latvia	16	65	19
Western Ukraine	26	44	31
Georgia	37	36	26
Azerbaijan	5	68	27
Kazakhstan	20	63	17
Kyrgyzstan	31	42	26
Tadjikistan	37	38	25
Uzbekistan	38	36	26

during 1990 and 1991; Russians, increasingly, were coming "home" to the RSFSR.[59] The net result of this migration process is, of course, the demise of the Soviet Union as a unitary state. The devolution of power to the republics corresponds objectively to a retreat of Russians from the periphery.

The August coup and after

If the entire Gorbachev period witnessed a rapid succession of dramatic events, then high drama continued in the Russian Republic in the second half of 1991. In June, the republic's bid for full sovereignty received a significant boost when Boris Yeltsin bested five opponents and was elected president of the RSFSR, with 57.3 percent of the vote.

After months of bitter rivalry, Yeltsin and Gorbachev had succeeded in

April of 1991 in coming to rough agreement concerning the political and economic shape of a future Union of Sovereign States. The scheduled signing of the union treaty, which was set for August 20, precipitated the failed coup of August 18–21. That political earthquake, in turn, set off powerful aftershocks which would likely be felt for years.

Like the Bolshevik *putsch* of 1917, the failed August coup appears to constitute a critical twentieth-century turning point. In its immediate aftermath, the Communist Party was outlawed, the KGB was disassembled, and the Soviet "center" was marginalized to a point of irrelevancy. The Ukrainian vote for full independence on December 1 nailed down the lid on the coffin of what had until recently been the USSR.

The death throes of the Soviet center required that the Russian Republic step in and gradually assume many of its functions. This development, however, served to strain relations with the minority republics, which clearly suspected that the new confederation of sovereign states being championed by Yeltsin and his team was in fact a "mask" for increased ethnic Russian political and economic control. The prospects for a viable confederation appeared therefore to be dim at best.

Similarly, Yeltsin's expressed hope that the minority peoples of the RSFSR would prove to be satisfied with real autonomy ran into serious obstacles in the post-coup period. The Chechens declared their full independence from Russia, and Yeltsin had to back down from an unwise declaration of emergency rule in Checheno-Ingushetia. Tatarstan, too, began to take steps toward achieving complete independence. The sole realistic democratic approach to this thorny dilemma appeared to be that counselled by Yeltsin's inter-ethnic affairs adviser, Galina Starovoitova: Yeltsin, she said, must stick to his original policy of being willing to grant as much autonomy to the autonomous regions as they wanted to assume. If that meant full independence, so be it. In the long run, Starovoitova argued, this enlightened approach would rebound to Russia's benefit.

The headlong breakup of the historic Russian and Soviet empires has understandably served to shock and bewilder many present-day Russians. Writing in the no. 45, 1991 issue of the reformist weekly, *Moskovskie novosti*, Sergei Razgonov, for example, reflected despairingly:

> Let us total up the losses. We have given away the Baltic, ceded Crimea, and we are going to sell the Kurile Islands . . . Lord, will we really once again be reduced to the size of Vladimir-Suzdal' Rus' or of the Serpukhovsk princedom? No, no, I am not weeping for the empire, although, of course, it is painful that it will soon not be easy to take a stroll along Tallinn's Vyshgorod, to sit with friends in the cafes of Tiflis, or to warm oneself on the beaches of Koktebl' . . .

And Razgonov continued his lament:

> We [Russians] are no longer one-sixth of the earth's surface . . . But we continue to carry within ourselves one-sixth of the globe – from Riga to Shikotan. It is a

scale we have become accustomed to. Ah, how difficult it is to part with it . . . From that former Homeland, we will be required to emigrate, all of us, to the last man.

This disoriented sense of loss experienced by contemporary Russians as they cast about for a post-imperial national identity can, of course, serve as a breeding ground for extremist currents and ideologies. In the Russian presidential election in June, 1991, a charismatic proto-fascist demagogue, Vladimir Zhirinovskii, came in a surprising third with 7.8 percent of the vote. Zhirinovskii's message was and is a crudely simple one: ethnic Russians should take back the empire and put the minority peoples in their place. Economic disintegration and gnawing remorse over the loss of empire could provide fertile soil for extremist activists like Zhirinovskii, publicist Aleksandr Prokhanov, and television journalist Aleksandr Nevzorov.

Consequently, one must hope that the pro-democracy force in Russia, aided by perceptive and far-sighted Western statesmen and businessmen, will be able to find a way out from under the rubble of a collapsed communist system. A failure to do so could threaten the interests of the West as much as it would those of Russians themselves.

Conclusion

The tumultuous processes which resulted from Gorbachev's accession and his programs of glasnost and democratization have, for the first time in seventy years, required ethnic Russians consciously to define their relationship to the "inner" Soviet empire. As the various polls, plebiscites, and elections we have examined show, ethnic Russians, with each passing month, were increasingly resigned to a loss of empire. Faced with a choice between "empire saving" and "nation-building," Russians were firmly opting for a resuscitative program of nation-building. In decisive numbers, they opposed the use of force to preserve the crumbling Soviet state. It was time, they appear to believe, for Russia to get on with the task of solving its own severe economic, social, demographic, and spiritual problems. The long-term question concerning Russians, as James Billington has put it, "boils down to the question of whether [they] can find a non-Leninist and nonchauvinist identity for themselves: a way of feeling good about themselves without feeling hostile to others."[60] Together with the perceptive observer of contemporary communist societies, Milovan Djilas, one suspects that Billington's question can be answered in the affirmative. Referring to the Soviet Union's imminent loss of empire, Djilas comments:

We are talking about the natural expiry of an unnatural and tyrannical regime which is bound to come, as surely as the British and French empires had to face their demise when the time was ripe. The Russian people would benefit the most. They would gain a free and more prosperous life and yet remain, undoubtedly, a great nation ... I firmly believe that a reduced but self-confident, opened-up democratic Russian state would induce much less brooding in the Russian people and make them a happier race ..."[61]

Paradoxical as it may seem, the loss of the historic Tsarist and Soviet Empires could lead directly to the rebirth of Russia as a major Eurasian power with a vibrant economy and cultural achievements which would be the envy of the rest of the world.

Notes

1 From Yu.V. Arutyunyan, "The Russians Outside Russia," unpublished paper presented at an international colloquium, sponsored by the Feltrinelli Foundation of Milan, on "Underdevelopment, Ethnic Conflicts, and Nationalisms in the Soviet Union," held in Cortona, Italy, on May 16–18, 1991.

2 From Aksel Kirch and Marika Kirch, "Russians as a Minority in Contemporary Estonia," unpublished paper presented at Cortona conference.

3 Hugh Seton-Watson, *The New Imperialism* (Chester Springs, PA: Dufour Editions, 1961), p. 23.

4 *Ibid.*, pp. 30–31.

5 Carl A.Linden, *The Soviet Party-State: The Politics of Ideocratic Despotism* (New York: Praeger, 1983), p. 95.

6 Alain Besançon, "Nationalism and Bolshevism in the USSR," in Robert Conquest, ed., *The Last Empire* (Stanford, CA: Hoover Institution Press, 1986), pp. 10–11.

7 "Djilas on Gorbachov," *Encounter*, October, 1988, p. 7.

8 From Viktor Perevedentsev, "Mezhrespublikanskie migrantsii naseleniya SSSR," unpublished paper presented at Cortona conference.

9 Yu.V. Arutyunyan, "The Russians Outside Russia." Here and subsequently, I have tampered with the English versions of the papers presented by Soviet participants in the Cortona conference. The aim has been to make the English more grammatical and readable.

10 In *Literaturnaya Rossiya*, September 28, 1990.

11 In *Sobesednik*, no. 6, 1990.

12 See Roman Szporluk, "Dilemmas of Russian Nationalism," *Problems of Communism*, July–August, 1989, pp. 16–23.

13 For the text of the platform, see *Pravda*, September 24, 1989, pp. 1–2. For an informative discussion of the debates preceding the Central Committee plenum, see Gail W. Lapidus, "Gorbachev and the 'National Question': Restructuring the Soviet Federation," *Soviet Economy*, July–September, 1989, pp. 201–250.

14 For the interview, see "Interesy Rossii," *Izvestiya*, September 1, 1989, p. 3.

15 In *Pravda*, November 9, 1989, p. 2.

16 The draft platform was published in *Pravda*, August 17, 1989, pp. 1–2.

17 Oleg Rumyantsev, "Russian Reform: The Democratic Position," unpublished essay, *circa* March, 1991.

18 In *Literaturnaya gazeta*, June 14, 1989.

19 From *Moscow News*, no. 48, 1990, p. 9.
20 Kirch and Kirch, "Russians as a Minority."
21 Announced on "Russian Radio," May 12, 1991.
22 In *Komsomol'skaya pravda*, March 14, 1991, p. 2.
23 *Ibid.*
24 *Ibid.*
25 In *Novoe vremya*, no. 9, 1991, p. 91.
26 From *The New York Times*, November 25, 1990, p. E11.
27 In *Stolitsa*, no. 6, 1991, pp. 6–7.
28 See "Spor o Rossii," *Novoe Vremya*, no. 13, 1991, p. 7.
29 Graham Fuller, "The Emergence of Central Asia," *Foreign Policy*, no. 78, Spring, 1990, p. 50.
30 In *Sovetskaya Rossiya*, January 19, 1991.
31 In *Literaturnaya Rossiya*, March 16, 1990, p. 4.
32 Besançon, "Nationalism," p. 11.
33 See *Moscow News*, no. 29, 1989, p. 2.
34 See the account in *Moskovskie novostie*, no. 44, October 29, 1989, p. 2.
35 In *Atmoda*, November 27, 1989, p. 6.
36 The text of the brochure appeared in the September 18, 1990 issues of *Komsomol'skaya pravda* and *Literaturnaya gazeta*. For an analysis and for a discussion of Russian reactions, see my essay "Solzhenitsyn Calls for the Dismemberment of the Soviet Union," *Report on the USSR*, December 14, 1990, pp. 3–4.
37 In *Literaturnaya gazeta*, October 3, 1990, p. 4.
38 See A.N. Los', "Referendum po-bol'shevitski," *Put'*, March, 1991, p. 2.
39 Radio Free Europe/Radio Liberty, *Daily Report*, January 3, 1991.
40 Radio Free Europe/Radio Liberty, *Daily Report*, May 2, 1991.
41 See "Narodnym deputatam RSFSR," *Put'*, January, 1991, p. 10.
42 In Radio Free Europe/Radio Liberty, *Daily Report*, May 21, 1991.
43 See Klaus Mehnert, *The Russians and Their Favorite Books* (Stanford, CA: Hoover Institution Press, 1983); Vladislav Krasnov, "Russian National Feeling: An Informal Poll," in Conquest, ed., *The Last Empire*, pp. 109–130; and "Two Films for the Soviet Masses," in the collection of my essays, *The New Russian Nationalism* (New York: Praeger, 1985), pp. 60–74.
44 For the poll, see *Moskovskie novosti*, no. 20, 1990, p. 9.
45 On the March, 1990 elections, see John B. Dunlop, "Moscow Voters Reject the Conservative Coalition," *Report on the USSR*, April 20, 1990, pp. 15–17.
46 See *Ogonek*, no. 43, 1989, p. 4.
47 See *Argumenty i fakty*, no. 21, 1990, pp. 2–3.
48 See *Moskovskie novosti*, no. 40, October 7, 1990, p. 9.
49 On the January 1990 events, see "V Krasnodare posle mobilizatsii," *Komsomol'skaya pravda*, January 28, 1990, p. 1.
50 In *Izvestiya*, August 14, 1990.
51 On the attempted *putsch*, see John B. Dunlop, "Crackdown," *The National Interest*, Spring, 1991, pp. 24–32, and "The Leadership of the Centrist Bloc," *Report on the USSR*, February 8, 1991, pp. 4–6. See also "Litva–yanvar' 1991: Otchet gruppy nezavisimykh voennykh ekspertov soyuza 'Shchit'," *Russkaya mysl'* (Paris), February 22, 1991, special appendix, pp. i–iv. Excerpts from the "Shchit" report appeared in *Moskovskie novosti*, no. 9, March 3, 1991, p. 10.

52 For the results of the poll, see *Komsomol'skaya pravda*, January 18, 1991, p. 1.
53 *Moskovskie novosti*, no. 4, 1991, pp. 8–9, and "Russian Radio," January 22, 1991.
54 In *Reader's Digest*, March, 1991, pp. 49–54.
55 Ann Sheehy, "Updated Fact Sheet on Questions in March 17 and Later Referendums," Radio Liberty Report via *sovset'*, March 14, 1991.
56 In Kirch and Kirch, "Russians as a Minority."
57 See *The New York Times*, March 5, 1991, p. A3.
58 The poll appeared in *Moskovskie novosti*, no. 4, January 27, 1991, p. 12.
59 From Yu.V. Arutyunyan, "The Russians Outside Russia."
60 In *The Washington Post*, January 22, 1990, p. A11.
61 In *Encounter*, November, 1988, p. 30.

Part III

The "new" Eastern Europe

4 Ukraine: the politics of independence

BOHDAN KRAWCHENKO

Ukraine was a collossus among the former Soviet republics: with 53 million people it accounted for 25 to 30 percent of the USSR's gross domestic product.[1] But until recently this republic was relatively quiescent. It gave the Kremlin little cause for concern, and was even a stabilizing factor in the trend towards disunion. In 1991, however, the drive for statehood gained steam, and Ukraine's independence was formally achieved after the overwhelming referendum result of December 1991. This chapter considers the reasons for this *volte-face*.

Political leadership and political change

As late as September 1989 the republic was still ruled by an ardent Brezhnevist, Volodymyr Shcherbytsky, the First Secretary of the Communist Party of Ukraine (CPU). The nascent national and democratic movement in Ukraine viewed with envy Moscow's relatively liberal atmosphere. A certain provincial ferocity had always characterized communist rule in Ukraine. As the prominent poet Ivan Drach quipped in June 1989, "In Moscow they clip your nails, but in Kiev they cut your fingers off."[2] The Ukrainian intelligentsia urged Mikhail Gorbachev to end "Ukrainian exceptionalism" and allow the winds of glasnost and perestroika to blow in Ukraine.[3] Shcherbytsky's policy of resisting all measures aimed at political and economic modernization was becoming increasingly untenable since it clashed with Gorbachev's programe. Indeed, Shcherbytsyky's presence in Ukraine was a liability, given the growing radicalization of public opinion in the wake of the Chernobyl nuclear disaster. At the same time, spurred by the example of the Baltic republics, former dissident circles in Galicia pressed for the launching of Ukraine's own version of a people's front, envisaged initially as a movement in support of Gorbachev's reforms. On September 8, 1989 the People's Movement for Restructuring – "Rukh" (the word means "movement" in Ukrainian) held its constituent Congress in Kiev. Two weeks later Gorbachev flew to Kiev to oversee the ouster of Shcherbytsky.

Volodymyr Ivashko, who replaced Shcherbytsky, was an unimaginative but conciliatory apparatchik. Following Gorbachev's example in March

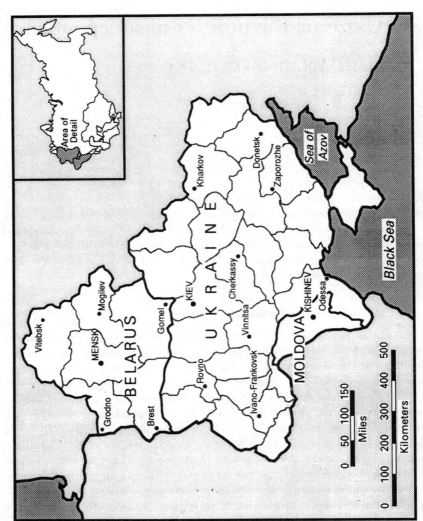

Map 4.1 The "new" Eastern Europe

1990, he was also elected head of the Presidium of the Supreme Soviet. It was during this period that the national and democratic movement in Ukraine made its greatest breakthroughs. The mass actions launched by Rukh were truly impressive. For example, on January 22, 1990, almost one million people formed a human chain from Kiev to Lviv, commemorating Ukraine's 1918 declaration of independence and act of union of Western and Eastern Ukraine. In the March 1990 elections, despite widespread fraud, the Rukh-led opposition electoral bloc gained one quarter of the seats in Ukraine's Supreme Soviet. Since all parliamentary debates were broadcast live on radio and television, the opposition now had access to a national audience and skilfully exploited this opportunity. Having won control of the three oblast regional governments in Galicia, and of city, municipal and rural soviets in many other regions (among them the city of Kiev), the opposition now had at its disposal significant institutional resources which enhanced its ability to carry out mass campaigns.

Political initiative had clearly passed to the side of the opposition. Rukh's membership had grown to over 500,000, and other unofficial groups such as the Ukrainian Language Society, *Zelenyi svit* ("Green World") and Memorial also gained strength.[4] Throughout the summer of 1990 thousands thronged Parliament as it debated the declaration of sovereignty. The document was passed almost unanimously on July 16, 1990. On July 22, 1990, with Kiev still reeling from the drama of the passage of this act, Ivashko ignominiously resigned from all of his Ukrainian posts and moved to Moscow as second secretary of the Central Committee of the Communist Party of the Soviet Union. Lacking charisma he could not interact with the public and quickly became an object of popular derision. Neither did he have the political skill to plot measures to hold the unfolding national movement in check, a weakness which made him lose the support of key sectors of the communist hierarchy in Kiev.

Leonid Kravchuk, a former ideological secretary of the Central Committee of the CPU, replaced Ivashko as head of Ukraine's Parliament. His elevation to this post surprised many. What undoubtedly played a role in his selection was the fact that Kravchuk had earned his spurs as the party's only capable public debater against Rukh, and thus could be expected to keep order in Parliament. The dour and tough industrial administrator Stanislav Hurenko became first secretary of the CPU. A team was thus put into place which could challenge the gains of the national movement.

Indeed, throughout the autumn of 1990, in concert with the major provocations which Moscow unleashed in the Baltics, steps were taken in Ukraine to roll back the challenge to communist authority. Demonstrations near Parliament were banned; troops were massed outside of Kiev; the communist majority in Parliament changed procedures and restricted the opposition's use of the air waves; administrative obstacles were raised to thwart the work of democratically-controlled regional and local soviets; and a radical nationalist deputy, Stepan Khmara, was arrested in a crude provocation. Khmara languished in prison since the communist majority voted to strip him of his parliamentary immunity. Democratic deputies began to wonder who would be arrested next. Ukraine was rife with rumors that direct presidential rule or martial law was about to be imposed. Indeed, instructions on whom to arrest, and what organizations to ban under the terms of a state of emergency, were circulated to reliable functionaries in oblast soviets.[5]

This conservative backlash poured cold water on the euphoria over the adoption of Ukraine's declaration of sovereignty. It appeared that the declaration was destined to remain on paper only. The opposition accused the communists of voting for Ukraine's sovereignty only to surrender it under the terms of a new union accord. (It would look better politically if a 'sovereign' Ukraine signed a new treaty of union.) The nation had been duped.

Resistance to this strategy came from a totally unexpected quarter – Ukraine's students. Their actions captured the public's imagination, forced the resignation of Vitalii Masol, the chairman of the Council of Ministers, and committed Parliament to strict conditions for the signing of a union accord, namely, the prior passage of a constitution enshrining Ukraine's sovereignty.

The student movement which unfolded in the early days of October 1990 carried out some of the most remarkable mass actions Ukraine had ever seen. It began with a small group of hunger strikers who camped on October Revolution square in downtown Kiev. They were quickly joined by hundreds of others and the square was turned into a miniature Woodstock. Post-secondary institutions throughout Ukraine went on strike and an all-Ukrainian student strike committee was formed. On October 16 some 150,000 people marched on Parliament – naval cadets in the front rows with marshalling provided by over one thousand Afghan veterans. The crowd was an unusual conglomerate of social layers – vocational students and punkers, university students and the intelligentsia, workers and white-collar staff. Student leaders addressed Parliament and their demands were broadcast live on radio and television. For the next two days the city was seized with tension. The government refused to negotiate with the student strike committee, and armored vehicles prowled about the city. Yet the students held firm.

On October 18, unexpectedly, a large column of workers from Kiev's largest factory marched on Parliament in suppport of students. They chanted only one word, their factory's name – "Arsenal." Workers tipped the balance. That evening the government reported that it would meet all student demands. Kiev celebrated the victory into the early hours of the morning. The students had stopped the march of reaction in its tracks.[6]

Civil society, state structures, and sovereignty

The events of autumn 1990 were a sobering experience for Ukraine's political elite and hastened the rise of a more moderate leadership, one more willing to seek a *modus vivendi* with public opinion. The systematic mass mobilization that Rukh and other democratic forces had carried out throughout 1989 and 1990 also served as a catalyst in this respect. Public opinion polls showed that the population, young people in particular, had developed a high level of civic involvement. For example, a February 1989 survey of Kiev secondary school students between the ages of thirteen and eighteen found that two-thirds of them had actively participated in the national movement.[7] Through actions such as the Days of Cossack Glory, designed to rekindle historical consciousness in the industrial Dnipro region, millions were awakened to the possibilities and promise of nationhood and independence.

Without painstaking preparatory work – the launching of some 350 unofficial newspapers, the establishment of Hyde Park corners in every major city, rock festivals and conferences, and the communication of a new national message by increasingly bold journalists working in radio, television and the press – it would be impossible to imagine the surprising turn of events which unfolded during the miners' strike of February and March 1991. Echoing students, miners from russified Donbass raised as their first political demand the immediate constitutional sovereignty of Ukraine and the reduction of Moscow's powers to that of a coordinating center of a commonwealth of sovereign states. In the words of Serhii Besaha, the miners' spokesman who addressed Ukraine's Parliament on March 22, 1991, "The political demands raised by the miners require decisive measures on the part of Ukraine's parliament . . . People of freedom-loving Ukraine understand our position: we are in a difficult situation and can get out of it only by Ukraine becoming fully sovereign."[8] The settlement that was reached between the miners and the government once again committed Parliament to acting in earnest on the question of sovereignty. It is important to note that half the population of Donbass is non-Ukrainian. The sector of Ukraine's population most likely to resist state-building measures had been won to a sovereigntist perspective.

The role of Ukraine's "Piedmont" – Galicia – loomed large in all national mobilizations. Donbass miners, for example, were first exposed to ideas of independence by their colleagues on the strike committee from the Lviv-Volyn' coal basin. Part of Austria before 1918, and then of interwar Poland, Galicia had escaped the devastation of Stalinist rule. When the Soviets occupied the area after the Second World War they confronted an active and militant national movement which had penetrated the masses down to the last village.[9] Under glasnost, the national movement there rapidly established hegemony, and spread to other areas of Western

Ukraine (especially Volhynia). Galicia resembles the Baltic republics, except for the fact that unlike in the Baltics there were no "Interfronts" there: Russians account for only 5 percent of the population of Western Ukraine.[10] In the March 1990 elections candidates of the democratic opposition won forty-three out of forty-seven Galician seats to the Supreme Soviet, and were swept into power at the municipal and oblast levels. (In other Western oblasts their success was also impressive. For example, six out of nine seats in Volyn' fell to the democratic opposition.)[11] In Galicia the Communist Party for all intents and purposes collapsed, and an aggressive program of de-Sovietization of public life was undertaken: the removal of visible symbols of Soviet rule (such as Lenin monuments), changes to the school curricula, and the like. A more radical market reform, beginning with serious moves to de-collectivize agriculture, was initiated. During the March 17, 1991 referendum on the fate of the "Union," the three Galician oblasts had their own third ballot which asked voters whether or not they wished Ukraine to be an independent state. Independence received the support of close to 90 percent of voters.[12] Other regions of Western Ukraine were also catching the Galician virus. For example, a March 1991 survey showed that support for the Kiev student hunger strikers among students in Uzhorod, Transcarpathia, was actually marginally higher than among Lviv students.[13]

Western Ukraine has a population of almost 10 million, of whom 5.4 million live in Galicia. But this region plays a role in Ukraine's political life disproportionate to its numbers. Western Ukraine provided a large number of the organizing cadres of the movements in Eastern Ukraine, and Galicia could always be counted on to provide several thousand people to support demonstrations in that region. The institutional infrastructure of Galicia (printing presses, newspapers) was also put at the service of national and democratic forces in Eastern Ukraine, thus circumventing the obstacles raised by the local communist apparatus. Communist officials lamented Galician "messianism" which sought to win the rest of Ukraine to its independentist positions, but were powerless to stop its progress.[14]

It is also important to stress that the Galician experience of democratic rule created space in the imaginations of eastern Ukrainians for the possibility of life without communists, as one Kiev author noted in Ukraine's leading Russian-language newspaper.[15] The Communist Party apparatus was checked from meddling in daily life in many oblasts, which produced much greater freedom and less corruption. That all of this was achieved by the national movement served to identify the national idea with a radical political and social message.

After January 1991 politics in Ukraine entered into a new period, that of primary state-building. Increasingly the power of initiative in the drive for sovereignty moved from the streets into the corridors of state and economic institutions. Of course the foundations for this development lay in the pressure which the new mass movements had exerted on the existing political elite. The partial democratization of the political order which had occurred, and the prospect of imminent elections, forced sectors of the political elite to think seriously about their future. Public opinion polls in Ukraine revealed that the popularity of the party apparatus had sunk to abysmally low levels. A 1989 study, for example, found that the least prestigious occupation that a politician could have is "employee of the party apparatus." This group was preferred by only 4 percent of people surveyed, of whom the vast majority were old-age pensioners. Only 1 percent of young people ranked this profession in first place.[16] In November 1990, Leonid Kravchuk's popularity among Kievans was so low that he did not even figure in the top twenty most popular politicians.[17] But by June 1991, after he had become closely identified with the sovereignty issue, Kiev polls showed him to be the preferred candidate for President of Ukraine. He was chosen by 54 percent of respondents. Hurenko, the first secretary of the CPU, could not even garnish 1 percent support.[18] The party, to quote I. Tarapov, rector of Kharkiv State University, "is gripped by crisis."[19] The party's unpopularity hastened calls for the establishment of an independent Ukrainian Communist Party as a way of marking distance from the Moscow apparatus.[20] The CPU took a partial step in this direction by adopting its own statutes, a move criticized by some hardliners as the beginning of the federalization of the party.[21]

Throughout 1991 state structures gained greater significance and served as the hothouse for a new political class. The Communist Party was never a party in the traditional sense of the word, for a one party system is really a non-party system. The Party was a structure organizing the totalitarian adminstration of the state. The introduction of a rudimentary multi-party system, the removal of party cells from any factories, democratic control of local governments and the separation of powers between the Party and the state served to enhance the role of state structures.[22] Moreover, Parliament began to resemble a real legislature. Unicameral, with a budget twice that of Russia's, Ukraine's Supreme Soviet nurtured a core of professional full-time politicians.[23] Parliamentary commissions, in which the opposition played an active role, took numerous legislative initiatives, while the relationship between party and state became strained. At a session of the Presidium of the Supreme Soviet, Ivan Pliushch, the deputy head, reportedly told Hurenko, "gone are the days when instructors from the Central Committee will tell the Council of Ministers what to do." In most oblasts and cities, the head of the state apparatus wielded more power than the party boss.[24] Emblematic of the balance of forces between the two institutions was the Presidium's decision to strip Hurenko of the use of the state private airplane and give it to Kravchuk instead.

The center of political gravity, therefore, shifted away from the preeminent all-Union structure – the party – towards the Ukrainian state, whose logic of existence was bound-up with an expansion of its prerogatives. This served to factionalize the party elite and draw a sizeable number of its members, namely, enterprise directors, government ministers and the like, into a group popularly called "the centrists" or "communists-sovereigntists." Thus, on many crucial votes in Parliament, over a third of the so-called "Communist majority" could be counted on to vote with the opposition. The break in party ranks proved decisive in the debate on the March 1991 referendum on the new union. Despite the opposition of the party leadership, almost half the communist members of Parliament voted in favour of adopting the second "Ukrainian" question which negated the one formulated by Gorbachev (see below).[25] Communist discipline in Parliament slipped: many communist deputies did not even bother to turn up at CPU Parliamentary faction meetings. The June 16, 1991 gathering, for instance, was attended by only 184 out of 324 deputies

The communists' rapprochement with the opposition was also dictated by their fear of the latter's ability to unleash social unrest on a massive scale. In the face of initiatives such as the establishment of the All-Ukrainian Union of Solidarity Committees of Toilers, a new trade union patterned closely after Solidarity which held its founding congress on June 23, 1991, communists understood the advantages to be had from coopting the opposition. The new trade union supported radical social, political and economic reform, and full Ukrainian independence. The opposition, in turn, felt unprepared to take power, and decided to use this rapprochement to push the new centrists into taking real measures to build Ukrainian statehood.

Politics in a country as diverse and large as Ukraine is a complex matter. The strategy adopted by Ukraine's leadership were not to irritate Moscow with bold symbolic gestures. Rather, it preferred a low-key, incremental approach. The March 1991 referendum on the Union is a case in point. Rather than challenge Moscow's right to hold the referendum in Ukraine, Parliament instead placed its own question on the ballot. Whereas the Kremlin's question asked people to decide whether or not they wished to remain in the USSR on the basis of renewed federalism, the Ukrainian question asked people whether they wished to be part of a Commonwealth of Sovereign States whose Ukrainian membership would be based on Ukraine's declaration of sovereignty. Kravchuk urged people to vote "yes" for both, saying that the first question merely asked "are you for a Union?," whereas the second asked "what kind of Union do you want?"[26] In its massive propaganda campaign the Communist apparatus totally ignored the second question, but to no avail: 70 percent of voters supported the Kremlin's question, and 80 percent Ukraine's question.[27] Kravchuk interpreted this as a mandate to accelerate the process of the "sovereigntization" of Ukraine and the transformation of the Union into a

Commonwealth of Sovereign States with the center playing a loose co-ordinating role.[28]

Throughout 1991 the Parliament had a full agenda, as some sixty laws fundamental to establishing Ukrainian statehood were considered. In the first instance the focus was on creating instruments for independent economic policy. Thus, Ukraine was to nationalize All-Union property by the end of 1991; all external trade was to be placed under the republic's jurisdiction. Ukraine established its own customs service and independent national bank, and the first plans were made to introduce a separate Ukrai-nian currency. Measures were adopted making all USSR Presidential decrees null and void unless they were passed by Ukraine's Parliament. A commission on external and internal security was created as the first step in the formation of a ministry of national defense and a national army.[29] In the area of foreign relations, Parliament passed a resolution instructing the Cabinet to take measures to establish "diplomatic, consular and trade rela-tions with foreign states" in order to implement "the Declaration of State Sovereignty of Ukraine in the Field of External Relations." Ukraine agreed to exchange diplomats with Poland and Hungary, and signed political, economic and cultural treaties with Czechoslovakia, Romania, Bulgaria and Turkey. Indeed the first major diplomatic breakthrough came in June 1991 when, on the basis of a direct bilateral agreement (which by-passed Moscow), Ukraine and Hungary opened consulates. Ukraine was the first Soviet republic to take this measure.[30]

Ukraine's attitude towards the Union accord is an example of its quiet, determined approach. Unlike the first six republics which opted for full independence, Ukraine participated in the talks, but it drove a hard bargain. For example, Ukraine wanted to retain the right to form an inter-nal army, and argued for relatively weak structures at the Union level. (Kravchuk, for example, was opposed to a Union constitution.) The Union government was not to be allowed to raise taxes in Ukraine. Rather, the republic was to fully control taxation, and transfer funds to the All-Union budget to pay for central programs which Ukraine had agreed to. Before any accord could be signed, All-Union property had to be in hands of the republic. These demands, taken in concert with the imminent introduction of Ukrainian currency, were designed to deprive Moscow of the mechanisms of policy implementation. Resisting Gorbachev's haste in con-cluding a new Union treaty, Ukraine dragged out the process. The logic here was that the more sovereign Ukraine became, the stronger its bargain-ing position would be. It also felt that time served to weaken the central government. Such tactics stalled the new Union treaty Gorbachev advo-cated until the time of the coup. In the post-coup political conditions, the treaty became a dead letter.

Thus Ukraine proposed an elaborate process for the signing of the Union accord which would have postponed the act for at least six months.

Ukraine had first to pass its own constitution enshrining its sovereignty, then Parliament was to debate the draft treaty "word by word," then it was to send a delegation to negotiate with other republics and produce a second draft. Only at this point could the accord be signed. Ukraine was insisting that different republics join the Union at different times and under different conditions.[31] Interestingly, the vast majority of communists agreed on the wisdom of this approach. The opposition realized that some kind of treaty had to be signed: one which would begin the process of the *de-montage* (dismemberment) of the Empire, to quote Mykhailo Horyn, a radical oppositionist deputy.

Socio-economic factors and cultural assertion

The drive for independence was motivated by numerous factors, not all of which carried the same weight in different parts of the republic. Overall, however, there was a profound realization that the USSR was disintegrating as a socio-economic and political formation. The centralized bureaucratic system (described as "the monster" by Kravchuk in one parliamentary debate) was seen as a brake on economic and social development and modernization. Moscow had nothing to offer – it was neither a source of technological know-how, nor an international financial center. It was merely an apparatus of repression and control. Neither was Ukraine tied to the center by virtue of its membership in a single, unified market called the USSR. The USSR was never that. Ukraine itself cannot even be considered a single market. Rather, what existed were monopolistic structures, a mono-ministerial branch economy. All talk of economic integration was ludicrous when factory X, thousands of miles away, supplied factory Y with goods which Y could get from an enterprise across the street. In many cases transportation costs were higher than production costs. Territorial, horizontal integration is a precondition of the rational use of economic resources, and of a strategy of market reform. And before Ukraine's economy could be integrated into a larger market, not to speak of the world market, a Ukrainian market had to be first established with all of the institutions of a modern economy – bank, currency, customs service, economic statistics.[32] As for ties with other republics, these had to be developed through bi-lateral treaties. There was no pressing economic reason why Ukraine's exports of meat to oil-producing Tiumen had to be mediated by a Moscow ministry. It is far more efficient to do this directly. (Indeed, starting in 1991 all of Ukraine's food exports to other republics were direct deals which by-passed Moscow.)

In Central and Eastern Ukraine the motor force for independence was socio-economic in nature. It could hardly be otherwise given that decades of Russification had weakened the traditional determinants of a Ukrainian national identity. Moreover, the largest Russian population outside

Table 4.1. *National composition of Ukraine, 1970–1989 (%)*

Year	Total population	Ukrainians	Russians	Jews	Others
1970	47,126,517	74.9	19.4	1.6	4.1
1979	49,609,333	73.6	21.1	1.3	4.0
1989	51,452,034	72.7	22.1	0.9	4.3

Source: *Itogi vsesoiznoi perepisi naseleniia 1970 goda*, 7 vols. (Moscow, 1972–1973), no. 4, table 7; *Chislennost' i sostav naseleniia SSSR. Po dannym Vsesoiuznoi perepisi naseleniia 1979 goda* (Moscow, 1984), table 17; *Vestnik statistiki*, no. 10, 1990, p. 76.

the RSFSR lives in Ukraine (11.3 million in 1989) (see tables 4.1 and 4.2). An analysis of census language data shows that every tenth Ukrainian was acculturated into Russian culture or Russified, and three-quarters of Ukrainians knew Russian (see table 4.3). One-third of the total population of Ukraine gave Russian as their mother-tongue. It should also be noted that language data drawn from the general population census is an unreliable indicator of language use. A comprehensive 1988 survey of parents of first grade students in Kiev found that only 16.5 percent of respondents used Ukrainian in the home, and only 4.7 percent used the language at work. But 92 percent of respondents considered it "extremely important . . . to cultivate and raise the prestige of the Ukrainian language."[33]

As Soviet sociological investigations have pointed out, the system of attitudes on nationality relations depends not so much on cultural orientation, that is, the Russification of an individual's cultural pattern, as on a complex combination of social, economic and cultural interests.[34] The fact of the matter is that Ukraine's economy, its society and environment have been ravaged at the hands of the Moscow center, and this in turn spurred

Table 4.2. *Mother-tongue identification of Ukrainians, 1970–1989*

Year	Total number of Ukrainians	Total giving Ukrainian as mother-tongue (%)
1970	32,283,857	91.4
1979	36,488,951	89.4
1989	37,419,053	87.7

Source: Same as table 4.1: *Perepis' 1970*, vol. 4, table 8; *Perepis' 1979*, table 17; *Vestnik statistiki*, no. 10, 1990, p. 76.

Table 4.3. *Ukrainians' national identity data, 1970–1989**

Year	Unadapted	Adapted	Acculturated	Russified
1970	55.6	35.8	4.3	4.2
1979	37.3	51.8	5.8	5.1
1989	28.2	59.5	7.0	5.2

* Unadapted = unilingual Ukrainian speakers; adapted = Ukrainians who give Ukrainian as their mother-tongue and know Russian; acculturated = Ukrainians who give Russian as their mother-tongue but know Ukrainian; Russified = Ukrainians who give Russian as their mother-tongue and do not know Ukrainian.
Source: Same as table 4.1: calculated from *Perepis' 1970*, vol. 4, table 8; *Perepis' 1979*, table 17; *Vestnik statistiki*, no. 10, 1990, p. 76.

the growth of a movement for independence. The dominance of socio-economic factors in the sovereigntist discourse explains why surveys show that 45–50 percent of Russians in the republic favored Ukraine's independence.[35] Survey data show that support for independence was strongly correlated with a high level of social mobilization (residence in a large urban center, a higher education). These are social characteristics found disproportionately amongst Russians.[36]

The social structure of Ukraine, it should be noted, mitigates against the formation of Interfronts. Unlike in the Baltic republics, the working class in Ukraine is Ukrainian, hence Russian reaction cannot use populist demagogy to whip up sentiment against the intelligentsia who leads the national movement. There is virtually no inter-ethnic conflict in Ukraine. During the referendum on the Union, Russian towns such as Simferopol supported overwhelmingly the republican ballot. The town of Svitlovods'k in Kirovhrad oblast serves as an interesting example in this respect: its population is over 90 percent Russian and is dominated by the scientific intelligentsia. (A major nuclear installation controlled directly by Moscow is located there.) In Svitlovods'k the Gorbachev question on the Union received almost twice as many votes. Paradoxically, it was the rural areas of Central and Eastern Ukraine, the least mobilized (and most controlled) sector of the population, which delivered the largest pluralities for the Union question.[37]

It should be stressed that the success of the national movement in Ukraine in winning the support of minorities is in part explained by the fact that it incorporated and hegemonized the democratic discourse in the widest sense of the word. It is the national movement which has led the battle for the democratization of political structures, the abolition of censorship, and the removal of the most nauseous forms of privilege. In Ukraine, Rukh has also led the fight against anti-semitism.[38] The national movement in Ukraine IS the democratic movement.

The drive for statehood was motivated by a profound realization of just how mismanaged and ravaged Ukraine's economy had been at the hands of the Moscow center. Until 1990, 95 percent of Ukraine's economy was controlled by Moscow, which was responsible for the distribution of over 90 percent of what was produced in the republic. Less than a quarter of Ukraine's national income remained in the republic – the rest was repatriated to the center. Enterprises controlled by Moscow often repatriated 90 percent of their profits.[39]

Moscow's investment and pricing policy discriminated against Ukrainian industry. Consider the case of the metallurgical industry. Ukraine's share of the USSR output of this branch was 54 percent. Yet in the last twenty years Ukraine received only 20 percent of total capital investment in metallurgy in the USSR. Central control also resulted in the total technological economic impoverishment of the coal industry in Ukraine. The All-Union government increased the price of coal in 1990 by 170 percent, except for Donbass, where the price increase was a mere 19 percent. When Fokin reported these figures he said, "I almost choke when I say this."[40] In the case of sugar, Moscow decided to pay Ukraine 48 roubles per tonne – the lowest price in the USSR – whereas the price in Russia was seventy-three roubles. Yet Ukraine's sugar industry is antiquated and starved for new capital investment: 60 percent of sugar refineries operate on pre-1917 equipment. Ukraine did not have its own banking system: the center controlled 120 billion roubles of Ukraine's savings, half of which was until recently lent back to the republic at high interest rates (8 percent on the average). All of Ukraine's hard currency earnings went to Moscow – 30–34 billion roubles annually. Some 113 billion roubles were taken from Ukraine to the center annually, through taxation and profits. Every year 365 million roubles gathered by Ukrainian customs went to the center.[41] No economy can sustain such a drain of funds. This policy had serious consequences in all spheres of life. Expenditures on the development of basic science research per capita in Ukraine was 6.3 roubles, in Russia 25.5; per capita expenditure on culture in Ukraine was 3.8 roubles, in Russia 12.8; per capita investment in housing was 94 and 145 roubles respectively.[42] These and many other statistics received wide publicity and most citizens of Ukraine agreed with Prime Minister Fokin, "Our only hope, our only chance of improving the situation is economic independence."[43]

The environmental devastation of Ukraine at the hands of Moscow is one of the most powerful leitmotifs of independentist agitation. Ukrainians see their nuclear experience as an example of Moscow's environmental imperialism, on a par with dumping toxic waste in Africa. As Serhii Odarych, secretary-general of Rukh observed, "Chernobyl helped us to understand that we are a colony."[44] While Moscow scientists have been known to sell Chernobyl statistics to the West, the Ukrainian health ministry is reduced to begging for local medical statistics.

Chernobyl is but part of the story. Southern Ukraine has been so polluted by industry and mindless land improvement projects that this fertile steppe region now has Ukraine's highest infant mortality and most appalling longevity rates. In Mykolaiv oblast, the average longevity of males has dropped from 65.2 years in 1988 to 63.4 by 1989. Scientists warn of the erosion of Ukraine's gene pool: 46 percent of the republic's secondary school children have experienced chronic illness of one kind or another. Only 5–8 percent of graduates of secondary schools can be considered healthy; 80 percent of pregnant women in Ukraine become ill (ten years ago the figure was 30 percent); 40 percent of pregnant women miscarry. Ukraine's birth rate was the lowest in the former USSR – 13.3 per 1,000 of population.[45]

But at the same time there is a realization that Ukraine has considerable economic and social potential if only it could get control of its resources. Much information has been released on this score. Ukraine has high grade ores and metallurgical coal; it is a large exporter of cement to the Middle East; it exports electric power for which it does not receive a kopeck, and its climatic and soil conditions could support a flourishing agriculture. Kravchuk quoted with pride a German study evaluating all republics of the USSR on the basis of their potential to integrate into the European market. In a scoring based on 100 points, Ukraine took first place with 83 points, Latvia, Estonia and Lithuania obtained 77, the RSFSR 72, Georgia 61 and so forth down to Tajikistan with 18.[46]

The unbelievable economic incompetence of the central government also served to convince the Ukrainian political class that sovereignty is an indispensible component of crisis management. Ukrainian officials complained that the Moscow government was printing money with abandon, causing inflation, through to late 1991, whereas the Ukrainian government was engaged in the impossible task of trying to take out of circulation surplus roubles (800 million roubles were burnt in Ukraine in 1990). Out of desperation, to provide an elementary defense of the domestic consumer market in the face of this mountain of surplus roubles, Ukraine introduced the coupon system, and planned to issue its own currency in 1992.[47]

Gorbachev's and Pavlov's decrees, said one factory director from Dnipropetrovsk, "are ruining our economy."[48] Moscow decided to confiscate the lion's share of enterprises' hard currency earnings, thereby killing all export incentive; it also took 20 percent of enterprises' amortization funds. Moscow decided to slap huge import duties which ruined trade. For these and other reasons, the central government was seen not as an agent of economic reform, but as a cause of the crisis. No one looked to the Kremlin for direction any more. As Fokin said, "The centre is simply losing significance."[49]

A defense of socio-economic interests can have a reciprocal influence on elements of national identity such as language. The development of indigenous culture is a way of bolstering the republic's claim for economic and political independence. When a speaker at a large public rally in Kiev in October 1989 declared, "A sovereign republic needs a sovereign language," he was cheered by the largely Russian-speaking audience.[50]

Decades of Russification have devastated Ukrainian national culture. In the 1988–1989 school year, only 47.5 percent of pupils studied in Ukrainian-language schools. Most large cities of the Donbass or southern Ukraine did not have a single Ukrainian-language school until recently. In 1987 only 14 percent of lectures at Kiev university were delivered in Ukrainian. Only four Ukrainian-language records were produced between 1980 and 1985. Since the mid-1970s, with one exception, all scientific journals in Ukraine were published in Russian. Output of books per capita in Ukraine in 1991 was 0.9, as compared to 12.7 for Russia.[51]

An important part of the drive for sovereignty was the adoption of a program of Ukrainization. Although the Ukrainian language was recognized as the official state language in November 1989, the Masol government "froze the project" and nothing was done until Fokin (a Russian) became Prime Minister.[52] Not surprisingly, the Masol government was toppled by students. Recently, however, 300 Ukrainian-language schools were opened up, as well as several thousand Ukrainian-language classes in Russian schools.[53] The Ukrainian language is being introduced in political and economic administration, and management staff in factories such as the giant Antonov aircraft works are taking intensive Ukrainian-language courses.

As one observer noted, "For the first time since the eighteenth century we see in Ukraine a profound crisis of loyalty to the imperial center."[54] A concomitant of this process has been the legitimation of a Ukrainian national identity. The rediscovery of Ukrainian history and culture has become a mass phenomenon. The three-million strong Ukrainian diaspora and its numerous centers of Ukrainian studies and publishing houses have contributed substantially in this respect.

National identity does not exist *in statu naturae*. It is the product of social learning carried out by agencies such as the media and the educational system. For the first time since the 1920s, these infrastructures are communicating a national message. National identity is also created by leading social groups who elaborate and politicize objective cultural markers. In this respect is should be noted that the impulse for Ukrainian independence was fed not only by the all too obvious failures of the Soviet regime in the socio-economic realm, but also by its successes. In the last half century the republic has developed a modern social structure with a quarter of the employed population having higher or specialized secondary education. Ukrainians predominate in the working class and intelligentsia: they accounted for 73 percent of personnel in administrative organs, 74 percent of the factory and enterprise management, and 67 percent of the

CPU.[55] Ukraine, in short, has a sizeable elite, which, having been trained for responsible positions, is anxious to assume them free of suffocating domination from the center.

In a statement to Ukraine's Parliament, Leonid Kravchuk summarized well the new elite's mission:

> We are proceeding in stages [and] affirming Ukraine's sovereignty in all spheres – economic, social, international, cultural – in all aspects of our life . . . These are the first steps to independent statehood. Some people may not understand this, but this is for real. It is such a pleasure to watch those deputies who are conscious of the fact that they are the creators of an independent state, a state which does not look submissively to the center, and which is not a colony.[56]

Vitold Fokin declared, "The time has come for us to focus our energy, intellect and knowledge for a real rebirth of Ukraine as an independent, economically independent, industrially developed state, which will occupy its rightful place in the international community. This is our historic chance."[57]

Ukraine opposition to a new union treaty and the attainment of independence

Until 1991, "historic chances" to affirm statehood had been few and far between in Ukraine's tortuous past. If we are to believe President Kravchuk, the real opportunity to become an independent country came neither in the anti-Soviet backlash that followed the failed August 1991 coup, nor at the meeting in Minsk on December 7 that created a new Commonwealth of Independent States. The disintegration of the Soviet Union could be traced to "the beginning of the period of perestroika – and we know exactly who the author of this breakup was."[58]

The August coup was, nevertheless, decisive in moving independence forward in Ukraine. For the first two days of the coup Kravchuk appeared hesitant in condemning the Emergency Committee. But as soon as it became evident that the *putsch* was doomed, he went further than the leaders of the other republics: as well as intensifying his anti-Communist rhetoric, he supported a declaration of independence before the Ukrainian Parliament that was quickly passed on August 24, making the country independent contingent upon ratification in a general referendum. In this way Kravchuk showed himself sensitive to changes in public opinion, which had grown considerably more anti-Moscow as the extent of the farcical coup, pitting Gorbachev against his once-trusted lieutenants, became known.

Increasing stimuli in the drive for Ukraine independence came, then, from events taking place in Moscow itself. Belligerent statements from Yeltsin's advisors, including vice-president Aleksandr Rutskoi and press secret-tary Pavel Voshchanov, on what should constitute the frontiers of an independent Ukraine increased local distrust towards Russian rule of any kind. Russian nationalist demagogery from Vladimir Zhirinovsky raised concerns about political leadership in Russia. One article in a Russian newspaper which discussed the option of a nuclear strike on Ukraine should Kravchuk refuse to give up his strategic arsenal did nothing to increase trust in Russia at the critical juncture when Ukraine was contemplating its constitutional future.[59] The Ukraine Parliament's initial proclamation of state sovereignty on July 16, 1990, had not appeared to stir up such Russian backlash to the extent that the post-coup declaration of independence had. Political developments within Russia were to remain of ongoing concern to Ukraine even with independence within grasp. As Kravchuk put it to the Rukh Congress held in late February 1992, "Remember, when there is frost in Russia on Thursday, there will be frost in Kiev by Friday."[60]

Not a small part in Kravchuk's proclamation of independence was played by the diplomatic spadework he carried out in 1991 which, admittedly, was still being overshadowed in the West by Gorbachev's own international skills. In October 1990 Ukraine concluded an important agreement with its onetime overlord, Poland, which recognized the existing border between the two countries. On subsequent official visits to Western states – Germany, France, Switzerland, Canada, and the US – Kravchuk prepared foreign leaders for Ukrainian independence while establishing contacts with Western businessmen and renewing relations with Ukrainian communities abroad. His ability to undertake such extended foreign visits was linked, in turn, to political stability prevailing at home, and, relatedly, the absence of serious unrest among Ukraine's own national minorities.

But it was the country's intransigence in rejecting Gorbachev's proposals for a new Union treaty that may have sealed the fate of the USSR as effectively as the coup tragi-comedy, Yeltsin's own political ambitions, or the breadth of nationalist discontent across the Soviet Union. In October 1991 Kravchuk refused to join eight republic leaders, including Yeltsin, in signing an economic pact. Deputy Prime Minister Masik noted at the time that "The Treaty on an Economic Community still resembles a political document more than it does an economic one."[61] We again observe the determined approach taken by Ukraine to achieving its objectives while avoiding the publicity and tension that came where nationalist mass demonstrations (as in Lithuania) were staged. Yeltsin himself was later to remark on the significance of Ukraine obstinacy in concluding the Union agreement: under conditions of disagreement over state borders, national currencies, national armies, and nuclear weapons, "it would have been criminal to conclude a treaty on a union of republics without Ukraine."[62]

On November 6, Ukraine and Russia – the two largest republics of the

USSR – signed a trade and cooperation agreement. Only then did Ukraine Prime Minister Fokin sign the treaty designed to create an economic community out of the disintegrating Soviet Union. These actions demonstrated Kravchuk's strategy of forging horizontal ties between republics, excluding participation by the center, and opposing a new union. He shared this approach with Yeltsin, of course, which helped bring the two leaders together. But in the way that the Russian leader was unmistakably bent on the destruction of the USSR, Kravchuk's more subtle and seemingly malleable tack made him appear less destructive to even a seasoned politician like Gorbachev.

By the end of November, however, Ukraine's "historic chance" for independence was about to be seized. The State Council of the USSR failed to approve Gorbachev's new Union treaty at a meeting outside Moscow; one newspaper presciently titled its story "Gorbachev's Waterloo at Novo-Ogarevo."[63] Kravchuk made clear his now uncompromising opposition to a Union of Sovereign States as Gorbachev envisioned it: "A confederation and a united state are two incompatible, mutually exclusive things. When will we stop deceiving our own peoples? Half-hearted measures, vagueness, matters left unsaid, endless attempts to evade the tough questions – how long can this go on? I won't participate in this deception."[64]

On December 1, 1991, Ukrainians voted on the question of independence. With a turnout of 84 percent, the proposal received support throughout the country. In Western Ukraine, whose intense political activism has already been remarked upon, over 90 percent of voters favored independence. In industrialized oblasts which were markedly russified such as Donetsk, Dnepropetrovsk, Zaporozhe, and Kharkov, support for independence did not dip below 83 percent. Even in the Crimea, with its ethnic Russian majority and its fairly recent (1954) incorporation into Ukraine, 54 percent cast ballots favoring independence. Rejecting the ethnocentric concept of "Ukraine for Ukrainians," both Kravchuk and Rukh had succeeded in attracting Ukraine's minorities to the notion of statehood. As Kravchuk had put it in an interview with *Izvestia* on the eve of the referendum, "the desire to be the masters in one's own land is ineradicable."[65]

The sense of being masters was appealing to many different peoples living within Ukraine and totalling some 15 million – Russians, Tatars, Poles, Jews – and it signified both national rights and democratic processes. In particular, Ukraine's 1989 language law making Ukraine the official language had also been generous in offering "governmental status" to other languages spoken in areas of ethnic group concentration. None of this suggested, however, that the issue of national minorities had been resolved. Indeed, on the day of the referendum, in two southwestern oblasts – Transcarpathia and Chernovtsky – voters overwhelmingly approved special status for the regions that would enhance local autonomy. Many Hungarians and Romanians are concentrated here, and Ukraine relations with the latter group have been strained for some time over Soviet annexation of northern Bukovina. Spillover of Moldova's conflict with the self-proclaimed Dniester republic could also upset ethnic peace. But more than any other issue, the future of the Crimea could contribute to political instability in Ukraine. Kravchuk repeatedly made clear that the Crimea was to remain in integral part of an independent Ukraine. And in September 1991 the Crimean Supreme Soviet seemingly concurred when it declared "state sovereignty" but within Ukraine. Any action that would upset the ethnic balance in the region would, nevertheless, test the willingness of Russia and Ukraine to cooperate with each other as independent states. The establishment of an independent Crimea might not resolve the issue since both states would likely remain rivals in seeking influence there.

Following the December referendum, then, Ukraine became the largest state in Europe in terms of surface area, fourth largest in population, and highly-ranked in natural resources. Yet, a week after the ballot, Kravchuk met with his Russian and Belarusan counterparts in Belovezhskaya Pushcha outside Minsk and signed the Agreement on Creating a Commonwealth of Independent States. What differentiated this agreement from Gorbachev's Union treaty and why would Kravchuk, so quickly after his referendum and Presidential election victories, wish to conclude a non-bilateral pact?

The Ukraine President made his position clear: "Under no circumstances would Ukraine have signed a Union treaty that presupposed a state within a state. But we have made our idea a reality and signed an interstate agreement – a European model for future political, economic, and societal coexistence." Speaking at an airport press conference after returning from Minsk, he elaborated: "We will do everything we can so that there will never be a center in our lives and so that no center will ever again be in charge of our states."[66]

Subsequent actions taken by Ukraine made evident that the newly-independent state did not feel bound to any supranational authority. Its Parliament recommended no fewer than twelve changes to the Minsk agreement's text. The most significant included expanding Article 6 to read: "The member-states of the Commonwealth will reform the groupings of the Armed Forces of the former USSR stationed on their territory and, creating their own armed forces on the basis of those groupings, will cooperate in ensuring international peace and security." This effectively eliminated any prospects of a unified military by establishing national armies without any unified command structure. At a meeting of the expanded Commonwealth, held in Alma-Ata on December 21, Ukraine joined in an Agreement on Joint Measures with Respect to Nuclear Weapons and pledged to sign the 1968 non-proliferation treaty and, further, remove tactical nuclear weapons from its soil by mid-1992. But at the end of 1991

Ukraine's position on nuclear weapons remained ambivalent. The Ukraine Supreme Soviet announced in October 1991 that the country would adhere to three non-nuclear principles: no acceptance, production, or acquisition of nuclear weapons. It added that "the presence on Ukraine territory of nuclear weapons of the former USSR is temporary."[67] Days after the referendum the Supreme Soviet unanimously adopted a document reiterating that "Ukraine will not be a nuclear power."[68] Yet in an interview with *Izvestia* later in the month, President Kravchuk ingeniously argued that collective responsibility for nuclear weapons signified to him "control over the *nonuse* of nuclear weapons." Accordingly, "we will have nuclear weapons but it will be impossible to launch them."[69] The Russian President could become Commander-in-Chief of strategic forces, Kravchuk conceded, but the inference was that Ukraine would remain in possession of nuclear forces. Regarding conventional forces, Kravchuk's decree of December 13 "nationalizing" army and air force units stationed in Ukraine and the Black Sea fleet in Ukrainian waters had already upset Russian leaders. The fighter jets and aircraft carriers that subsequently were taken out of Ukraine showed disaffection within some of the military as well. Ostensibly it was the oath of loyalty "to the people of Ukraine" that caused misgivings among some ex-Soviet military personnel. But the purpose of setting up a Ukraine national army that seemed to be intended to make of the country a medium-sized European power was of greater concern to many.

Ukraine's Parliament also amended another part of the Minsk agreement that dealt with foreign policy. Rather than, as Article 7 would have it, "coordination of foreign policy is to take place through the common institutions of the Commonwealth," Parliament supported the substitution of "consultations about foreign policy" as the preamble to the article. Only 288 of 367 deputies approved the Commonwealth agreement – sufficient to ratify it but indicating considerable Parliamentary reservations. A number of deputies brought into question Kravchuk's methods and motives: why had he not consulted with Parliament before entering into the agreement? Had he failed to protect the interests of the new Ukrainian state in surrendering authority to the Commonwealth? For some legislators, the new Commonwealth was just a new way that *Moscali* – Muscovites – sought to rule over Ukraine, whether in a paternalistic or exploitative way. But Kravchuk's more assertive position on a Ukrainian army and navy, nuclear forces, the new "second currency," and the Crimea issue seemed to demonstrate again his ability to stave off any criticism of his insufficiently nationalist credentials.

Conclusions

In this chapter we have focused on the process of state-building, undertaken largely within Parliament, and on party coalition building as key stages in the road to independence. We have also examined Kravchuk's leadership in the crucial months that followed the abortive August coup. We noted how his political skills served him well in debating and eventually overshadowing Rukh leaders. These skills were also in evidence during the Presidential election, held the same day as the referendum on independence. Running against two candidates having lengthy apprenticeships as dissidents and just as lengthy prison terms – Vyacheslav Chornovil and Levko Lukyanenko – the former Communist Party ideologist received 61 percent of the popular vote. Kravchuk's electoral campaign emphasized the continuity of the Ukrainian state which he hoped to build on. He referred to early twentieth-century historian and political leader Mykhailo Hrushev'sky as the first president of Ukraine whose mission he intended to pursue, and also described the "thousand-year-old tradition of Ukrainian statehood" that originated in Kievan Rus'.[70]

But if Kravchuk proved an adept leader when a historic opportunity presented itself to Ukraine, a wide array of social and political forces were indispensable to the achievement of statehood. While that objective was achieved peacefully and harmoniously, new problems confronted by Ukraine would test the skills of society and its leaders. By spring 1992 hyper-inflation, the fall in value of the coupon, and political disagreements within Rukh over whether to stand in support of Kravchuk or serve as loyal opposition compounded uncertainties brought about by Ukraine-Russian friction. A political organization called New Ukraine emerged, with an agenda that gave priority to achieving democratic and economic reforms instead of concentrating on state-building functions and what some in the movement saw as symbolic politics. There was nothing unusual about this increase in pragmatic politics after Ukraine had won the hardest battles in late 1991. And it was perfectly conceivable that new political coalitions under new leaders would gain in significance as different tasks had to be achieved in Ukraine. Still, Ukraine's road to independence was unique and it involved political activism and sophistication of leaders and civil society alike. Ukraine's collective decision to split from the former USSR effectively buried that political entity, and its orientation to the successor Commonwealth, and to Russia itself, is just as likely to prove decisive in charting the post-Soviet political landscape.

Notes

1 Bohdan Hawrylyshyn, "Renaissance in Ukraine," *Europe 2000*, vol. 18, November 1990, p. 65.
2 *Literaturna Ukraina*, July 9, 1987.
3 *Ibid.*, June 4, 1987.
4 *Vechirnii Kyiv*, February 18, 1991.
5 *Ratusha*, March 29–30, 1991.

96   *Bohdan Krawchenko*

6 See Solomiia Pavlychko, *A Kiev Diary* (Edmonton: Canadian Institute of Ukrainian Studies, 1991).
7 E.A. Toverovskaia, "Kto on, gorodskoi podrostok?," *Filosofskaia i sotsiologicheskaia mysl'*, no. 1, 1990, p. 88.
8 Session of Ukraine's Supreme Soviet, March 22, 1991.
9 See Ivan L. Rudnytsky, *Essays in Modern Ukrainian History* (Edmonton: Canadian Institute of Ukrainian Studies, 1987), p. 470.
10 *Chislennost' i sostav naseleniia SSSR. Po dannym Vsevoiuznoi perepisi naseleniia 1979 goda* (Moscow: Finansy y Statistika 1984), table 7.
11 *Pravda Ukrainy*, March 13 and 24, 1990.
12 *Za vil'nu Ukrainu*, March 19, 1991.
13 *Molod' Ukrainy*, March 26, 1991.
14 *Radians'ka Bukovyna*, December 27, 1990.
15 *Komsomols'koe znamia*, March 27, 1991.
16 V.S. Nebozhenko, "Vybory – shliakh do demokratii," *Filosofs'ka i sotsiolohichna dumka*, no. 8, 1990, p. 4.
17 *Ukraina Business*, no. 2, January 1991.
18 "Tsentr Vyvchennia hromads'koi dumky – 'Demos,'" typescript, table 12.
19 *Krasnoe znamiia*, December 9, 1990.
20 *Prykarpats'ka pravda*, December 12, 1990.
21 *Ibid.*, December 18, 1990.
22 *Krasnoe znamiia*, December 29, 1990; *Robitnycha hazeta*, January 1, 1990; *Naddniprians'ka pravda*, December 8, 1990.
23 Central Ukrainian Television, February 3, 1991.
24 *Radians'ka Ukraina*, June 14, 1991.
25 *Holos Ukrainy*, no. 4, 1991.
26 Interview with L. Kravchuk on Central Ukrainian Television, March 12, 1991.
27 *Moloda hvardiia*, March 20, 1991.
28 *Holos Ukrainy*, March 29, 1991.
29 "Postanova Verkhovnoi Rady Ukrains'koi RSR. Pro poriadok dennyi ta orhanizatsiiu roboty tret'oi sesii Verkhovnoi Rady Ukrains'koi RSR," February 1991; *Ukraina Business*, no. 23, June 1991.
30 "Deklaratsiia pro derzhavnyi suverenitet Ukrainy. Zovnishn'opolitychna khronika,"typescript, n.d.
31 Chrystia Freeland, "Ukraine and the (Dis-) Union Treaty," typescript, June 1991. See also her report in *Financial Times*, May 30, 1991.
32 Valerii Popovkin, "Suchasnyi stan ekonomiky Ukrainy i shliakhy vykhodu Ukrainy z ekonomichnoi kryzy," Scientific-research Institute of State Planning Commission of the Ukrainian SSR, Kiev, March 2, 1991.
33 S.A. Voitovych, I.O. Martyniuk, "Perspektyvy 'neperspektyvnoi' movy," *Filosofs'ka i sotsiolohichna dumka*, no. 5, 1989, p. 22.
34 See Bohdan Krawchenko, *Social Change and National Consciousness in Twentieth-Century Ukraine* (London: Macmillan, 1985), pp. 216–217.
35 *Vechirnii Kyiv*, February 2, 1991.
36 See H.I. Sovoliev, "Deklaratisiia pro derzhavnyi suverenitetu Ukrainy. Shcho pro nei dumaiut'. Kyiany," *Filosofs'ka i sotsiolohichna dumka*, no. 7, 1990, p. 29. This study found that support among Russians in Kiev for the declara-

tion of sovereignty was marginally higher than among Ukrainians because Russians had higher rates of educational achievement. Most who did not support the declaration felt that it did not go far enough towards independence.

37 Mykhailyna Borodai, "Vidomosti pro rezul'y referendumu SRSR po Ukraini," typescript, March 1991.
38 See *Kyivs'kyi chas*, no. 4, December 1990.
39 Report of First Rukh Congress, *Suchasnist'*, no. 12, December 1989, p. 43.
40 *Radians'ka Ukraina*, February 28, 1991. See also *Vechirnii Kyiv*, March 14, 1991 and *Holos Ukrainy*, April 4, 1991.
41 *Komsomol'skoe znamiia*, June 7, 1991; *Ukraina Business*, no. 7, February 1991; *Literaturna Ukraina*, February 27, 1991.
42 *Vil'ne slovo*, December 13, 1990.
43 *Literaturna Ukraina*, April 5, 1990.
44 *The Economist*, April 17, 1991.
45 *Holos Ukrainy*, March 3, 1991 and Serhii Plachynda's remarkable articles on the environmental crisis in Ukraine published in *Literaturna Ukraina*, March 14 and 21, 1991.
46 *Holos Ukrainy*, April 3, 1991. See also *Literaturna Ukraina*, February 27, 1991.
47 *Holos Ukrainy*, June 5, 1991.
48 *Robitnycha hazeta*, February 26, 1991.
49 *Komsomol'skoe znamiia*, March 16, 1991.
50 Tape of the meeting deposited at the Archives on Contemporary Ukraine, Canadian Institute of Ukrainian Studies, University of Alberta.
51 *Narodnoe obrazovaniie i kul'tura v SSSR* (Moscow, 1989), p. 88; *Literaturna Ukraina*, June 11, 1987; *Holos Ukrainy*, February 2, 1991.
52 *Kul'tura i zhyttia*, February 2, 1991.
53 *Osvita*, January 25, 1991.
54 Iurii Badzio speaking at conference on "Natsional'ne vidrodzhennia – Ukrains'ka perspektyva," Republican Association of Ukrainian Studies, February 16, 1991.
55 *Trud v SSSR* (Moscow: Trud v SSSR i Statistika, 1988), p. 20; *Storinky istorii Kompartii Ukrainy* (Kiev, 1990), p. 485.
56 *Holos Ukrainy*, March 29, 1991.
57 *Vechrnii Kyiv*, March 12, 1991.
58 *Izvestia*, December 11, 1991.
59 The article was published in *Niezavisimaya gazeta*. A Russo-Ukrainian nuclear war over borders or over Ukraine's treatment of its large Russian minority were other scenarios that were considered in a *Reuters* dispatch of December 4, 1991.
60 *Holos Ukrainy*, March 1, 1992.
61 *Holos Ukrainy*, October 18, 1991.
62 *Rossiiskaya gazeta*, December 13, 1991.
63 *Rossiiskaya gazeta*, November 28, 1991.
64 *Izvestia*, November 26, 1991
65 *Izvestia*, November 26, 1991.

66 *Holos Ukrainy*, December 9, 1991.
67 *Izvestia*, October 25, 1991.
68 *Holos Ukrainy*, December 6, 1991.
69 *Izvestia*, December 25, 1991.
70 *Demokratychna Ukraina*, November 26, 1991.

5 Belarus: a long road to nationhood

MICHAEL URBAN and JAN ZAPRUDNIK

The history of the lands that comprise Belarus[1] is a history of political contention. In one epoch or another, Poles, Lithuanians, Russians and – for briefer intervals in wartime – Germans have laid claim to, invaded and exercised dominion over these territories. Relatedly, Belarus's history itself has been an object of contention. As might be imagined, the reconstructions of the past performed by those with aspirations for Belarusan nationhood have contrasted sharply with the interpretations of historical events associated with those written from the perspective of, say, Polish or Russian domination. Whereas the latter would emphasize the inseparable affinity between the Belarusan people and the nation then exercising sovereignty over them, thus justifying the political status quo, the former would highlight the integrity and uniqueness of Belarus, thereby making the case for future independence.

This struggle over Belarus's past has never been sharper than it is today,[2] a fact that reflects the emergence of a powerful nationalist movement in Belarus locked in political combat with the remnants of the Communist regime. In the same way that the historiographic controversy over the past is simultaneously a political contest over Belarus's future, so the outcomes of this political contest in the republic have already altered the terms of debate and narrowed some of the differences between the contending parties. For example, historic symbols of Belarusan nationhood, such as the flag and coat of arms, that long had been outlawed by the communist authorities who, until mid-year 1990, had publicly associated them with fascism, have since been officially recognized.[3]

As this illustration with respect to national symbols – as well as others concerning language and national sovereignty that we discuss below – would suggest, Belarus has only recently completed the long journey to nationhood. However, the political form which its nationhood might take – whether independence or some type of association with neighboring peoples – remains for the moment unclear. Certainly, it will be influenced by a number of diverse factors, not all of which lie within the scope of this study. Our focus falls on what can be regarded as the principal moment, the development of a national consciousness. Reference to Belarus's troubled and often tragic past provides an understanding of how this

99

consciousness has emerged and how it has been retarded. It accounts for the unusual situation in which an identifiable national group that has for centuries occupied a particular territory has only in the past few years begun to exhibit in full the signs of nationhood.

Belarus and the Belarusans

The origin of the name, Belarus ("White Russia"), is obscure. In some accounts it is said to derive from the white complexion of the population or from their white dress.[4] In others it has been traced to an administrative designation for those areas lying beyond the Russian lands that had been required to pay a regular tax to the Tatars during the years of their hegemony in Russia.[5] Whatever the initial derivation of its name may have been, however, Belarus first displayed a number of features of national identity during the period in which it was incorporated in the multiethnic state comprised of the Grand Duchy of Lithuania, Rus' and Samogitia (beginning in 1386), for the Belarusan language then served as the official language of the region's chancellery, courts, diplomacy and literature.[6]

The relative autonomy that Belarus had enjoyed within the Grand Duchy of Lithuania was diminished when the latter entered into political union with the Kingdom of Poland in 1569. Polish influence in the area succeeded in bringing much of the Belarusan Orthodox hierarchy under the authority of the Vatican. The Uniate Church thereby created in 1596 retained the Eastern rite while simultaneously embracing a number of Roman Catholic dogmas.

The subsequent expansion of Muscovy into the area brought Poles and Russians into direct and violent competition for control of Belarus.[7] Both sides regarded Belarus as a constituent unit of their respective states, and accordingly, each side promoted its religious and cultural policies in those areas of Belarus under its jurisdiction.

The partitions of the Polish-Lithuanian Commonwealth effected by Russia, Prussia and Austria in 1772, 1793 and 1795 fully incorporated the Belarusan lands within the Russian empire. By that time, however, the Belarusan nobility had already identified itself with Poland, as evinced by their acceptance of Roman Catholicism and the Polish language. Moreover, strong memories of the historical attachment to Lithuania persisted among the upper strata of the population, which, since the interests and policies of the Lithuanians and Poles had in the past been by no means identical, meant that neither had these strata fully acculturated along Polish lines.

The policy of the tsars in the lands "returned" to the Russian fold aimed at russifying the population and converting them from the Uniate to the Russian Orthodox faith. The inscription on a coin minted under the order of Catherine II summed up the attitude of the empire toward the Belarusan lands: "What was torn away has been returned." Her successors, however, showed themselves more obliging toward Polish interests in Belarus. This was particularly true during the reign of Alexander I (1801–1825), who allowed his friend, the Polish prince Adam Czartoryski, to handle educational policy in the annexed territories. As a consequence of Czartoryski's school reform and the growing prominence of the university at Wilno (Vilnius), the influence of Polish culture in Belarus during this period of Russian rule became even stronger than it had been in the previous epoch.

It was also at the Unviersity of Wilno, as recent research has shown, that "a foundation for Belorussian [Belarusan] national thought" was laid.[8] There, a circle of Uniate professors from the Bielastok region had assembled a collection of ancient documents written in Belarusan that inspired the idea of regaining autonomy for the Grand Duchy of Lithuania and restoring thereby the Belarus language and the Uniate religion to official status within it. The pronounced Polish nationalism among most students and professors at Wilno at this time, however, all but guaranteed an unhappy future for the project. Indeed, by 1830 when rebellion broke out in the western regions of the empire, the insurrection in Belarus evinced a clearly Polish orientation.

The Tsarist government's response to the rebellion was severe. In addition to the physical repression that it visited on the active participants, it introduced a number of measures designed to eradicate "foreign" influences from cultural life. Wilno University was closed. Russian replaced Polish as the language of government and in educational institutions. In 1839 the Uniate Church, to which most Belarusans belonged, was abolished. In the following year, Nicholas I even banned the terms "Belorussian" ["Belarusan"] and "Lithuanian" in reference to the provinces of Vitebsk, Mogilev, Vilna and Grodno, because of the allegedly separatist overtones. At the same time, the laws of the Statute of the Grand Duchy of Lithuania (first published in Belarusan in 1588) were replaced by the Russian code. It was at this juncture that the term *Zapadnaya Rossiya* ("Western Russia"), first made its appearance. According to this appellation and the "theory" of *zapadno-russizm* ("Western Russianism") that accompanied it, those ethnographic distinctions that had set Belarusans apart from Great Russians were purely the product of artificially imposed Polish influences. *Zapadno-russizm* quickly became the secular creed of Orthodox priests, bureaucrats and school officials. Its obvious intention was "to destroy all that could remind anyone of Belorussia [Belarus] and Lithuania as separate national regions with their own historical, cultural, and linguistic traits."[9]

Administrative prohibitions constituted one side of the russification policy. The other concerned appeals to the distant past when, during the era of Kievan Rus', all "Russians" belonged to the same church and used the same written language. But the Romantic thrust of the new historiography also contained implications that cut in the opposite direction. For by reopening – or rewriting, as the case may have been – the pages of the past, the new doctrines rekindled interest in Belarusan history that had only recently been retrieved by the scholars at Wilno University. A famous graduate of this university, the Belarusan-born Polish poet Adam Mickiewicz, articulated this revived historical consciousness while teaching in Paris in his later years:

> The Belorussian [Belarusan] language which is also called Russinian or Lithuanian . . . is spoken by approximately ten million people. This is the richest and purest tongue, ancient in origin and wonderfully developed. During the period of Lithuania's independence grand dukes spoke it and used it in their diplomatic correspondence.[10]

In the middle of the nineteenth century, the idea of a Belarusan national identity began to crystalize among some students at the re-opened university at Wilno.[11] For the time being, however, it was largely connected to the Polish language – the language of instruction at the university – and to the memory of a common polity. Accordingly, the nobility and some segments of the peasantry in Belarus joined the Polish uprising of January 1863. Although the uprising failed, it marked a new stage in the development of a national consciousness. Kastus Kalinowski (1838–1864), the young and dynamic leader of the rebellion in Belarus, succeeded in publishing the first clandestine newspaper in the Belarusan language, *Mužychaja Praŭda* ("Peasants' Truth"). Kalinowski subsequently became one of Belarus's most celebrated national heroes. His words written on the eve of his execution in Wilno – "For I say to you from beneath the gallows, my People, that only then will you live happily, when no Muscovite remains over you"[12] – would inspire succeeding generations of Belarusan nationalists. In the period immediately following the 1863 uprising, however, the national idea languished.

The key to an understanding of why the national movement remained relatively weak throughout the nineteenth century and why its exponents were usually advocates of union with Poland and Lithuania, rather than outright independence, lay in Belarus's social structure. As Thomas Hammond has argued, national consciousness and its attendant political movements arose among the various peoples of East Europe in the context of economic and demographic shifts which concentrated a critical mass of the population in towns whose social and occupational differentiation was sufficient to support an intelligentsia.[13] This intelligentsia would then press for their own group interests, a dominant representation in the civil service and the professions, by championing the vernacular and the national idea against the extant dominion of the respective empires – Russian, German or Austrian – under whose dominion they had fallen.[14] Importantly, the

Table 5.1. *Nationalities of the five Belarusan provinces of the north-western region, 1897*

Nationality	Number	Percent of the area's total population	Number in towns	Percent of given group in towns
Belarus	5,408,420	63.5	137,608	2.6
Jews	1,202,129	14.2	553,997	46.0
Russians	492,921	5.9	185,027	37.8
Ukrainians	377,487	4.5	9,461	2.6
Poles	424,236	4.9	122,785	28.5
Lithuanians	288,921	3.3	5,201	1.7
Latvians	272,775	3.1	3,843	1.4
Germans	27,311	0.3	13,365	48.0
Tatars	8,448	0.1	5,094	61.0
Others	19,658	0.2	7,293	37.0
Total	8,522,306	100.0	1,043,854	12.3

Source: Calculated from V.N. Pertsev, *et al.*, eds, *Dokumenty i materialy po istorii Belorussii, 1900–1917*, vol. 3 (Minsk: Academy of Sciences of the BSSR, 1953), p. 30.

spread of literacy made possible the attraction of a mass following, as emerging national literatures communicated a sense of nationhood to expanding circles of people.

In Belarus, however, the great mass of the native population in the last century remained on the land, leading lives that had been essentially unaltered for centuries. Literacy rates among these Belarusan speakers were, of course, exceedingly low and the language of instruction in the primary schools was itself not Belarus but Russian.[15] In the towns, where a national consciousness may have caught on, Belarusans were vastly outnumbered by Jews, Russians, Poles and other nationalities (as the figures in table 5.1 from the 1897 census would indicate). Moreover, this census revealed that only some 7.3 percent of urban dwellers in these provinces spoke the Belarusan language.[16] Whereas non-Belarusans in the countryside retained their national identities as, say, Poles or Lithuanians, Belarusans commonly referred to themselves simply as "the locals."[17] The identification of the category "Belarusan" with the rural population – poor, backward and overwhelmingly illiterate – was in fact so strong that in the 1906 records of the Russian State Duma where the respective nationalities of the deputies were listed, some from the North-Western Region (Belarus) were described as "peasant-Belarusan" or "Belarusan-peasant."

Nationalist leaders were, of course, acutely aware of these facts. In 1884, for instance, the underground populist journal, *Homon*, noted that:

The Belarusan people, a plebeian nation, are still awaiting the emergence of their intelligentsia. Until now, their talents have served either Polish or Great Russian culture. Mutely but persistently they have protested against the treacherous attempts to polonize or to russify them, and both cultures, forcibly foisted on them, have failed to take root. Piously they have preserved the foundation of their life while awaiting the emergence of their own intelligentsia who would not uproot those foundations but develop and improve them.[18]

In the face of a considerable number of archaeological, ethnographic and philological publications in the latter years of the nineteenth century that attempted to show that Belarus was merely a province of either Poland or Russia, nationally-oriented Belarusan intellectuals began to draw their own conclusions. For example, many such studies portrayed the Belarusan language as a "dialect" of Russian and consequently categorized its speakers as Russian by nationality. However, even while the name "Belarus" remained taboo and the Belarusan lands were known officially as the "North-Western Region," the census of 1897, as we have seen, did enumerate Belarusan speakers in the Region. Consequently, Belarusan intellectuals, such as the academician, Yefim Karski, could call attention to the close link between language and nationality for all the peoples of East Europe and argue that language for the Belarusans had been "an inseparable indicator of the Belarusan nationality during its centuries-old history."[19]

The revolutionary ferment characteristic of the Russian empire at the turn of the century propelled the Belarusan national movement onto a new stage of political activism. In 1902, the Circle of Belarusan National Education was founded by a student group in St. Petersburg. The Circle transformed itself in the following year into the Belarusan Socialist *Hramada* (BSH), a self-professed political party, complete with a program for Belarusan autonomy. With the lifting of the prohibition against publishing in the Belarusan language that followed the 1905 Revolution, the BSH launched a weekly, *Nasa Niva* (*Our Soil*), that grew into a center for a revival of Belarusan national consciousness until its closure in 1915. The *Nasa Niva* movement was led by the brothers, Ivan and Anton Lutskievich – an archaeologist and publicist, respectively – and by two towering figures from the world of letters, Janka Kupala and Jakub Kolas. This movement culminated in the All-Belarusan Congress of 1917 and the proclamation of the Belarusan Democratic Republic on March 25, 1918.

Although Belarus enjoyed a brief period of formal independence (terminated by the Polish invasion in the following year), questions have remained with respect to the maturation of nationhood at this time. On one hand, the existence of a Belarusan government would seem to have owed much to the political convulsions besetting surrounding states and to the presence of German forces in the region when independence was proclaimed.[20] On the other, the movement for independence lacked a mass

Table 5.2. *Belarusan-speaking population of the five Belarusan provinces of the north-western region according to their religion, 1917*

Religion	Number	Percentage
Orthodox	4,384,217	81.0
Roman-Catholic	994,210	18.5
Old-Believers*	25,495	0.47
Lutherans	643	0.03
Total	5,404,565	100.00

* Karski explains this category: "These are mostly Great Russians who use Belorussian elements in their language, but otherwise they generally have not mingled with Belorussians."
Source: Ye.F. Karski, *Etnografischeskaya karta belorusskago plemeni* (Petrograd: Belorussian National Committee of the All-Russian Soviet of Peasant Deputies, 1917), p. 27.

base in the population. Both the indigenous nobility and bourgeoisie were overwhelmingly non-Belarusan. Belarusans made up a sizeable proportion of those in the lower civil service and in the teaching profession, but most of these individuals were new arrivals from the countryside. The great majority of Belarusans on the land had little or no notion of national identity, much less national independence, taught as they had been by their clergies in the Orthodox and Catholic Churches that their religion bound them to either the Russians or Polish nations (see table 5.2 for respective figures). Indeed, only one nationalist delegate from Belarus was elected in 1917 to the All-Russian Constituent Assembly, and he has been described as a disguised Russian socialist.[21] Belarus's path to nationhood, then, has been a longer and in many ways more difficult one than those of surrounding peoples. It would remain for future generations, again beset by contradictory and largely inhospitable circumstances, to advance further along it.

A Soviet Belarus

During the interwar period, the Belarusan lands were divided between Poland and Soviet Russia. The Treaty of Riga (1921), which ended the Russo-Polish War, placed some 38,600 square miles of Belarus – and nearly 3.5 million Belarusans – under Polish sovereignty. In these "western territories," the newly reconstituted Polish state directed an increasingly brutal policy of polonization at the local population, aimed at extirpating all media by which a Belarusan identity might be expressed and sustained. Until broken by mass arrests and political trials that followed Joseph Pilsudski's coup in 1926, the Belarusan Peasant-Workers' Hramada, which numbered at its peak about 150,000 members, had been able to organize the Belarusan population for its self-protection, including armed resistance. When the Hramada was destroyed, the political orientation of the resistance became increasingly radical, with the Communist Party of West Belarus, an organization linked closely to countrymen and communists across the border, assuming a leading role. The Polish authorities enacted even harsher measures in reply and by the end of the 1930s many thousands of Belarusans had suffered imprisonment, fines, confiscation of property, cultural and religious prosecution, and internment in concentration camps.[22]

The approximately 5 million Belarusans under Soviet rule were incorporated into the Belarusan Soviet Socialist Republic (BSSR) that was proclaimed January 1, 1919. By 1926, the BSSR included the Mogilev and Vitebsk provinces, the capital of Minsk and its surrounding districts, and the districts of Gomel and Rechitsa.[23] Initially, conditions here contrasted sharply with the anti-Belarusan measures employed by Poland in the western territories. Throughout most of the 1920s, the new communist state devoted considerable effort to reviving, establishing and developing national cultures. For Belarusans in the BSSR, this meant an unprecedented flowering of nationhood that for the first time reached the masses of people on the land through literary campaigns and official support for the native literature and culture.[24] The Belarusan State University, the first university to be built on Belarusan soil, along with a Belarusan Academy of Sciences were founded in Minsk. Moreover, Belarusans occupied leading positions in government and administration at all levels.

By the end of the decade, however, these policies were reversed. Nationally oriented elites became targets for repression throughout the USSR and the Belarusan experience was typical of this pattern. Belarusans were expelled from important posts in every sector and replaced by non-Belarusans, imported from other parts of the USSR in many cases to fill politically sensitive positions. In similar fashion, a considerable number of Belarusan officials were exported to other regions of the USSR. During the thirties, with the jailing of those accused of "nationalism" and succeeding waves of repression visited on the cultural expression of nationhood, national consciousness perforce moved underground.[25]

Yet, like the proverbial "mole of revolution," the development of this consciousness remained busy, albeit in ways that did not upset the surface of life of Stalinism. The industrialization of Belarus in the thirties drew hundreds of thousands from the countryside to the cities. Whereas Belarusans comprised only about two-fifths of the BSSR's urban population in the mid-twenties,[26] by the end of the forties they had come to represent an overall majority in the urban centres.[27]

The Second World War represented a pivotal experience in the making of the Belarusan nation. Its prelude, the Molotov-Ribbentrop Pact and its secret protocols, incorporated the western territories into the BSSR. When the German armies rolled eastward in 1941, however, they rapidly overran the entire Belarusan Republic and established an especially harsh regime of occupation. Suffice it to say that by the time of liberation, all of the BSSR's cities lay in ruins – in Minsk, only one building remained standing – and that Belarus had lost a quarter of its population to Soviet deportations and executions (1939–1941), the widespread terror practised by the German occupiers, banditry and guerrilla war, and, of course, conventional warfare.[28]

In the face of the prospect of the physical liquidation of the Belarusan nation, a Soviet-sponsored partisan movement became increasingly active in the German zone of occupation. Not only did partisan ranks swell in response to the widespread terror practised by the German invaders, but the leadership of the Belarusan partisans – frequently lacking communication links with their formal superiors in the Soviet armed forces – enjoyed considerable autonomy in staging their operations and in administering those areas that they had liberated.[29]

This wartime experience would prove seminal in shaping postwar politics in the BSSR. On the one hand, the bulk of the former partisan leadership embarked on political careers in the postwar period. Without doubt, their shared wartime experiences contributed a cohesiveness to this group that characterized it as an identifiable faction in Belarusan politics. By the mid-fifties, this faction dominated the BSSR's top party and governmental positions.[30] When their leader, K.T. Mazurau, was rewarded with the office of First Deputy Chairperson of the USSR's Council of Ministers and a seat on the Politburo in 1965 for his participation in the coalition that deposed N.S. Khrushchev, he brought a number of partisans with him to Moscow, thus establishing an influential presence for this faction at the all-union level. On the other hand, the partisans were able to promote at least a limited version of Belarusan national identity within the BSSR. Drawing on their experiences in the resistance, they portrayed the liberation, indeed, the salvation, of Belarus as the result of the heroic *national* resistance of the Belarusan people within the larger framework of the tremendous sacrifice and achievements of the *Soviet* people. This adroitness in the use of symbology – the framing of a national identity in terms not antagonistic to Moscow – was no small achievement during a postwar epoch in which the various peoples of the USSR were officially regarded as "growing together" to form one "Soviet people." Accordingly, the state-sponsored rites and ceremonies commemorating the liberation of the BSSR would feature prominently the contribution of the Belarusan partisans. Along these same lines, Mazurau's successor in the Republic, P.M. Masherau, who would often attend these ceremonies wearing native costume, became the first leader of the BSSR to address his countrymen on solemn occasions in their native tongue.[31]

The period of partisan leadership in the BSSR, which ended definitively with Masherau's death (or, perhaps assassination[32]) in 1980, is also noteworthy on two other counts pertinent to the formation of the Belarusan nation. First, patterns of elite mobility in the USSR demonstrate that the influence of Moscow over recruitment and promotion to important positions in the structures of the party-state had been negligible. Despite the impressive formal powers over key personnel decisions in the BSSR that lay in Moscow's hands, the actual career patterns of officials in the BSSR primarily had been determined by factors indigenous to the Republic, principally, the patronage of former partisans and rival groups. Within the framework of the Soviet order, then, the BSSR had been since the mid-sixties, if not earlier, a self-governing republic.[33]

Second, the postwar economic development of the BSSR has been, by Soviet standards at least, impressive. Minsk, whose industrial base had to be rebuilt from scratch after World War II, numbered among the leading industrial cities of the USSR.[34] Around the Republic, postwar construction of metal-working and machine-building industries had come to form the basis of an agro-industrial complex noted for the production of heavy trucks and agricultural machinery which, along with an integrated potassium mining and chemical fertilizer sector,[35] had enabled the BSSR to become one of the top agricultural producers in the Soviet Union.[36] Again, by Soviet standards, the light industrial sector performed remarkably well, making the BSSR one of the best supplied republics in terms of consumer goods.[37] Demographic changes have, of course, accompanied the Republic's economic growth. Whereas as recently as 1970 only about one-third of the population had resided in cities, the urban-dwelling proportion of Belarus's 10 million inhabitants had nearly doubled by 1985.[38]

These factors – the relative autonomy of the BSSR's political elites in the post-Stalin period and the industrialization and attendant urbanization of Belarus – might be regarded as determining, rather than as casual, forces shaping the development of a national consciousness. That is, in neither case do they exhibit some uni-directional influence pushing either toward or away from nationhood. In general terms, of course, a relatively high degree of self-government might be counted as a positive factor in this respect. Similarly, the emergence of an urban industrial society in recent decades would appear to provide that ingredient so long absent in Belarus's history, namely, an educated majority of Belarusans concentrated in urban areas who would represent for the first time a mass audience potentially receptive to the ideas of nationhood long associated with the cultural intelligentsia.

However, in specific context, these same factors, can have – and, in the case at hand, have had – the reverse effect. Economic development in the BSSR, for instance, seems to have sustained a large measure of conservatism among the Republic's political elites. As one observer, a Belarusan deputy to the USSR's Congress of People's Deputies has noted, a relatively prosperous, orderly and unreformed BSSR had been a living example that "developed socialism" (the shibboleth of the Brezhnev era) had continued to function reasonably well and, therefore, that perestroika was uncalled for.[39] In equal measure, the political faction that replaced the partisans during the early 1980s as the dominant force in Belarusan politics has distinguished itself by its conservatism, earning for the BSSR the sobriquet "Soviet Vendeé," after the 1793 seat of French counterrevolution.[40] This orientation appears to have been shaped by the particular career histories of the group in question, nearly all of whom had been upwardly-mobile industrial workers who launched their political careers in Minsk's leading enterprises.[41] The rapid advancement of their individual careers against the backdrop of the group's success in coming to power in a republic where a palpable degree of material success within the status quo had been maintained would suggest ideal conditions for the development of a conservative orientation in politics.

The politics of nationhood

In the same way that a modern Belarusan identity was forged during the period of partisan resistance when the continued existence of the Belarusan people was at stake, so the broad manifestation of national consciousness in recent years has been fired by three concerns, the measure of whose combined effect has been of equal impact on the fate of the nation. The first of these involved the steady decline of the native tongue as the primary language for ethnic Belarusans in the BSSR, dropping from 80.5 percent in 1970 (already the lowest figure for any of the Soviet republics[42]) to 74.2 percent in 1979.[43] The equally steady rise in Russian language usage among ethnic Belarusans – again, far and away the highest rates among any of the non-Russian republics[44] – and the ongoing decline of schooling and print media in Belarusan, had convinced a sizeable number of the BSSR's cultural elite that the nation faced the very real prospect of linguistic extinction.[45]

On December 15, 1986, twenty-eight Belarusan intellectuals took the first public action on this issue by going over the heads of their superiors in the cultural establishment and addressing a letter of petition to then General Secretary of the Soviet Communist Party, Mikhail Gorbachev. This letter – also signed by a number of rank-and-file workers and subsequently endorsed by the BSSR's Writers' Union – observed that since "language is the soul of the nation," the General Secretary's intervention was now required "to save the Belorussian [Belarusan] people from spiritual extinction."[46] They went on to advise him that "we can now observe a noticeable growth of national awareness" that, in turn, "is provoking a hostile reaction from the bureaucracy," and to argue that the Belarusan language "must be protected by [new] legislation."

The appendix which accompanied this letter – "A Proposal for Radical Improvement of the Status of the Belarusan Language, Culture, and Patriotic Education in the BSSR" – soon took on the character of a general political program for a number of "informal" groups and youth associations that had begun to form in the Republic. On December 26, 1987, more than thirty of these independent groups convened near Minsk and issued "An Appeal of the Initiative Group of the Confederation of Belarusan Youth Associations to Belarusan Youth" which lent a sharp edge to the general desiderata contained in the "Proposal" of the twenty-eight by reconfiguring the standard Soviet concept of "internationalist duty." "The cause of self-determination for the Belarusan youth movement," stated the "Appeal":

> has ripened not only because of internal reasons. We are watched with hope and concern by the peoples of Estonia, Latvia and Lithuania. They are waiting for us to join the formidable wave of national upsurge that is rolling over the Baltic region. In Belorussia's [Belarus's] joining this surge, there is the assurance of the irreversibility of the revolutionary changes in the Baltic republics as well as throughout the entire Soviet Union, which means that it is our internationalist duty to do so.[47]

At its second convention (January, 1989) – held in Vilnius because authorities in the BSSR, already alarmed by the growth and independent direction taken by the youth movement, refused to sanction such meetings – the sixty-six groups now represented in the Confederation of Belarusan Youth Societies issued another "Appeal" which addressed the issues of national renewal, democratization, a multi-party system, economic reform, the formation of all-Belarusan units in the armed services, and language and cultural policy. Moreover, turning the tables on the authorities again (this time with reference to Belarus's hitherto nominal membership in the United Nations), the "Appeal" argued for Belarusan independence and the opening of foreign relations with other countries.

The second issue igniting the nationalist movement has been the discovery by the archaeologist, Zianon Pazniak, that genocidal executions had been carried out by the Soviet regime from 1937 to 1941 in the Kurapaty wood near Minsk. The publication of Pazniak's findings in the Writers' Union weekly, *Litaratura i Mastactva* (June 3, 1988), which documented the existence of over 500 mass graves where lay the remains of an estimated 300,000 innocent victims, mobilized a broad public protest. On June 19, 1988, some 10,000 people marched to the site of the killings to commemorate the dead and demand a full investigation of the tragedy by an independent civil commision. The reply from officialdom was an attenuated inquiry which those outraged by the butchery at Kurapaty regarded as a cover up.[48] Activists therefore created Committee-58 (after the notorious article in the criminal code under which the exterminations had been conducted) to pursue the investigation. At its meeting in October 1988, this group founded the Martyrology of Belarus, a group whose purpose, in the words of the renowned writer and highly-regarded man-of-conscience in Belarus, Vasil Bykau, was "to compile a great martyrology of our losses and our martyrs. This would be laid as a cornerstone in the foundation of our national consciousness, would become an important element of our historical memory."[49] Martyrology's five-member Civic Council included representatives of its four constituent organizations – the BSSR's Union of Cinematographers, Writers' Union, Union of Artists and the editorial board of *Litaratura i Mastactva* – along with Pazniak who was elected president. At its founding meeting, Martyrology established a political organization, the Belarusan Popular Front (BPF), also with Pazniak as president. The BPF's first act, a demonstration drawing 10,000 people on October 30, 1988 which both revived the national custom of *Dziady* (remembrance of the dead) and coincided with USSR's "Day of Remembrance" for the victims of Stalin's terror, was forcibly dispersed by police beatings, dogs, water cannon and noxious gas. Subsequent protests against this violence were dismissed by the BSSR's Procuracy and Supreme Soviet, thus dampening any hopes that the authorities might be open to accommodation and dialogue.[50]

Kurapaty symbolized for the growing national movement a past tragedy for Belarus to which the present regime would respond with only cover ups and repression. The third major concern sparking the movement, the nuclear disaster at Chernobyl, represented a new and immediate danger to the survival of the nation. Although 70 percent of the fallout from Chernobyl had landed on two-fifths of the BSSR's territory and directly threatened the lives of some 2.2 million people, the Republic's authorities took little action to address the crisis except to suppress information and falsely reassure the population that they had no cause for alarm. Everyday life was simply permitted to continue in the contaminated zone, the inhabitants thus compounding their exposure to high-level radiation by ingesting locally raised vegetables, meat and milk containing concentrations of radio-nuclides that exceeded permissible limits many times over.[51]

Focusing on these three threats to the Belarusan people – the gradual loss of the native language, the massacres at Kurapaty and the ruin brought by the Chernobyl disaster – and accusing the communist regime of either agency or complicity in each, the BPF staged a rally in Minsk's Dynamo stadium on February 19, 1989 that drew over 40,000 supporters. This event, which occurred as part of the election campaign to the USSR's Congress of People's Deputies, marked a turning point in the struggle between the nationalist movement and the communist authorities. Inasmuch as the elections allowed for a limited amount of competition,[52] the BPF was able to go beyond the politics of protest and mount a challenge to the authorities that would be decided at the ballot box, rather than by police truncheons or rigged courts. Despite the huge advantages enjoyed by the communists, and the repression employed against their opponents, the BPF contributed to the defeat of at least seven of the BSSR's top officials at the polls and managed to elect eight of its own candidates to the new Soviet legislature.[53]

The battle between the BPF and the regime intensified enormously in the advent of the March 1990 elections to the Supreme Soviet and local soviets in the BSSR.[54] The BPF, which had by now grown to over 100,000 members,[55] formally constituted itself in Vilnius in June 1989 – a venue that at once bespoke the regime's continued hostility to the movement by again refusing it a meeting place in the BSSR and symbolizing the historic bonds between the Belarusan and Lithuanian peoples. In fending off the electoral challenge presented by the BPF, the authorities resorted to a number of devices, many of highly questionable legality, to insure an outcome favorable to themselves. Their control of the nomination process and the commissions formally encharged with monitoring it, meant that hundreds of would-be opposition candidates were arbitrarily refused places on the ballot, while representatives of the regime were easily registered, often in safe rural districts without genuine competition. Candidates' access to the voters – either through the mass media or via face-to-face encounter in meeting halls – was, again, lopsided in favor of those preferred by the regime.

The authorities' coarse manipulations of the electoral process reflected their worry over the situation confronting them. For instance, one survey of public opinion conducted at the outset of the elections found that 90 percent of respondents took a dim view of any candidate associated with the apparatuses of the Communist Party, the Komsomol, the soviets or the trade unions.[56] Moreover, the regime's blatant disregard for procedural regularity and any measure of evenhandedness proved more than their junior partner, the Komsomol, could abide. As election day approached, the Komsomol passed a resolution claiming that the behavior of the authorities had caused the public to lose confidence in the BSSR's leadership and that "the leaders . . . must honestly and in a politically responsible way evaluate their own actions."[57] Additionally, the Komsomol inaugurated a new organization, Democratic Consent, that sought to foster dialogue and cooperation between the opposition and those elements in the party-state who might be committed to perestroika. Although this remained impossible for the moment, the results of the elections fundamentally altered the constellation of political forces in the Republic and increased the chances that at least some elements in the regime might seek some form of accommodation with other elements appearing in the political process.

Although representatives of the nomenklatura fared well as candidates in the essentially non-competitive rural districts where the political culture tended toward passivity, in the larger cities they were decimated at the polls. Given that a number of prominent communists were rejected by the voters, that only about one-quarter of the deputies elected were officials from the party or government apparatuses, and that the largest bloc of successful candidates was composed of intellectuals and technical specialists (many of whom were associated with the BPF), it was already clear when the new Supreme Soviet convened on May 15, 1990 that the old leadership would be unable to command a majority in the legislature, despite the fact that most of the deputies were members of the Communist Party and that regionally-based deputies' groups had been organized by the communist apparatus in an attempt to enforce party discipline in the legislature.[58]

The initial voting in the Supreme Soviet indicated the change that the elections had induced in the BSSR's political life. For the office of Chairperson of the Supreme Soviet, N.I. Dzemiantsei (Dementei), the incumbent, failed on the first ballot. Although he succeeded in the second round, his nominee for First Deputy Chairman, I.G. Moshko (Second Secretary of the Grodno Obkom) encountered such stiff opposition from the legislators that his name was withdrawn before a vote was taken. In his stead, the BPF's candidate, S.S. Shushkevich (then Vice-Rector of Belarusan State University) was elected as First Deputy Chairperson. In like fashion, V.F. Kebich retained his post as Chairperson of the BSSR's Council of Ministers, but the opposition was able to defeat his nominees to the positions of First Deputy Chairperson, Deputy Chairperson, and those to four of the ministries and three of the heads of state committees.

These votes highlighted the fact that although the old authorities had managed to hold on to power, their grip on it seemed far more tenuous than ever before. In a context now ripe for compromise, Dzemiantsei and Shushkevich forged a tactical alliance on the seminal question of Belarus's political future. Abandoning the less flexible members of their respective blocs in the legislature, they reached agreement on what was described in Dzemiantsei's proposal of June 12 to the BSSR's Supreme Soviet as "real political and economic sovereignty [and] the re-establishment of independence for the Belorussian Soviet Socialist Republic."[59] It was left to the legislature to fill out Dzemiantsei's general proposal, and the Declaration on State Sovereignty that was eventually passed on July 27 (henceforth an official holiday in the BSSR known as Independence Day) went considerably beyond the basic conceptions of the supremacy of Belarusan law on Belarusan soil and Belarusan ownership of all economic and natural resources contained in Dzemiantsei's plan. In its final version, the Declaration announced that the BSSR has become a nuclear-free zone, that it was officially neutral in international affairs, that it reserved the right to raise its own army and security forces, as well as establish its own national bank and issue its own currency.[60] Nationhood, so long the dream of Belarusan nationalists, had been proclaimed by the government of Soviet Belarus.

Table 5.3. *National composition of Belarus, 1926–1989*

Nationalities	1926 in 1000's	1926 in %	1959 in 1000's	1959 in %	1970 in 1000's	1970 in %	1979 in 1000's	1979 in %	1989 in 1000's	1989 in %
Belarusans	4,017	80.6	6,532	81.1	7,240	81.0	7,568	79.4	7,897	77.8
Russians	384	7.7	658	8.2	938	10.4	1,134	11.9	1,341	13.2
Poles	98	2.0	539	6.7	383	4.5	403	4.2	417	4.1
Ukrainians	35	0.6	133	1.7	191	2.1	231	2.4	290	2.9
Jews	407	8.2	150	1.9	148	1.6	135	1.4	112	1.1
Others	42	0.9	42	0.4	52	0.6	61	0.7	71	0.9

Source: H.I. Kaspiarovic, "Etnademahraficnyja pracesy i miznacyjanalnyja adnosiny u BSSR," *Viesci AN BSSR. Sieryja hramadskich navuk* (Minsk), no. 5 (1990), p. 83.

Inter-ethnic relations

To date, Belarus has not evinced any of the varieties of inter-ethnic conflict that surfaced in the Soviet Union during the years of perestroika. In part, this may be due to the fact that the indigenous nationality, as indicated in table 5.3, has not been overwhelmed as it has in, say, Estonia and Latvia with a large Russian immigration threatening to displace it as the majority group. But it also has seemed to reflect the traditional pattern of tolerance and goodwill toward other national groups historically associated with the Belarusan people. On the one hand, this has been evident in the nationalist movement. In its official charter, for instance, the BPF defines itself as:

> a mass socio-political movement [with the goal of] creating a society, and renewing the identity, of the Belarusan nation based on the principles of democracy and humanism, securing the conditions for a free and full-fledged development of the cultures of both the majority of the inhabitants and Belarus's national minorities."[61]

Similarly, Vasil Bykau has stressed this same point in his message to the founding congress of the BPF by noting that:

> Our movement for *pierabudova* [perestroika] is national in form and democratic in content. All the nationalities that comprise the Belarusan state will find a place within it. We are not excluding from it our brothers, the Russian people, with whom we share our land and fate, who for a long time have innocently suffered together with us. Nor do we exclude the tragic Jewish nation with whom we have shared the modest fruits of our land during the entire course of our history. The Poles and Lithuanians are our brothers, and we have countless examples of shared and truly fraternal coexistence.[62]

On the other hand, the government has been equally sensitive to the matter of inter-ethnic relations in the Republic. In the preamble to the Declaration of State Soveriegnty, it has reaffirmed "respect for the dignity and the rights of the people of all nationalities who reside in the Belarusan SSR." Moreover, the Declaration itself specifically avoids the privileging of any national group in the Republic. "Citizens of the Belarusan SSR of all nationalities," it reads, "constitute the Belarusan people." And while the January 1990 Law on Languages in the Belarusan SSR does establish Belarusan as the official language of state, it allows for a period of from three to ten years' transition to its use. The Ministry of National Education has also drafted comprehensive plans for schools in which the respective languages of instruction include Russian, Ukrainian, Polish, Lithuanian, Yiddish, and Tatar.[63]

Perhaps as a consequence of sovereignty and Belarus's particular path to nationhood, the concept of the political state – rather than language, as in the past – has become the primary focus of the nation today. To be sure, concerns for reviving and developing the Belarusan language and culture remain much in evidence. Yet instances of Russian language publication and Russian speakers in Belarus endorsing Belarusan independence have also become commonplace. This overall allegiance to the Belarusan state, as well as governmental provisions for protecting minority languages and cultures, suggests that Belarus will continue to avoid the inter-ethnic conflicts that have beset most of the former Soviet republics.

The perspectives on Belarusan sovereignty and independence

The idea of the Belarusan people living in a Belarusan state has developed in the modern period from a project embraced by relatively narrow circles of intellectuals into an established political reality. At the same time, however, defining a concept of sovereignty pertinent to this state has been another bone of contention for organized political forces in the country. Prior to the coup d'etat staged in Moscow on August 19, 1991, it appeared that the government would opt for a limited form of sovereignty and the retention of Belarusan membership in a "renewed" federal union.[64] In this respect, they appeared to have a solid base of support in the population. For example, one poll of 33,000 respondents from all districts of the BSSR had found that "over 80 percent of those questioned condemn separatist attempts but actively support the idea of full sovereignty for the Republic."[65] Others, conducted on the eve of the USSR's March 17, 1991 referendum on a "renewed union," indicated that about four out of five citizens of the BSSR were opposed to secession.[66]

For its part, the BPF had consistently opposed all plans that would establish close political bonds between Belarus and Moscow. Until mid-summer of 1991, they had advocated the creation of an East European

Commonwealth in which Belarus would join Ukraine, Lithuania, Latvia and Estonia. Pazniak, the BPF's Chairman and leader of the opposition in the BSSR's Supreme Soviet, has argued that such a commonwealth would be postulated on both geopolitics and history. Half a millennium of our common history, he has remarked, "tells us much more than 200 years of imperial bondage."[67]

Although this proposal for a commonwealth was discussed at several meetings of Belarusan, Ukrainian and Baltic leaders, little progress toward its realization was recorded. As these negotiations proved fruitless, the BPF modified its approach. In its August "Appeal" to the Belarusan people, it registered its opposition to the draft of a new Union treaty then under discussion and called for independence. Moreover, the BPF argued that the immediate future would be regarded as "a transitional period" and that the BSSR should join with other Soviet republics in "a commonwealth of sovereign states based on principles of confederation in which each state would be sovereign, where there would be no general laws and common organs of power, where common actions would be coordinated, and problems solved collegially on the basis of inter-state treaties."[68]

Although when promulgated, this Appeal may have appeared to have been no more than a rather far-fetched proposal reflecting neither the orientations of the majority of the legislature nor the opinions of most citizens, the coup that was launched in Moscow just five days later changed everything. Not only did the coup attempt succeed in destroying the very union that the plotters had risked all to save, but its result thoroughly discredited the unionist bloc in the BSSR and swung the political balance dramatically toward the position advocated by the BPF. At the extraordinary session of the BSSR's Supreme Soviet on August 24, N.I. Dzemiantsei was forced to resign as Chairman due to his support for the coup.[69] Shortly thereafter, Prime Minister Vechaslau Kebich and his cabinet resigned from the Communist Party citing the complicity of the Party's hierarchy in the coup attempt.[70]

The BSSR's Supreme Soviet returned to session in mid-September. In addition to changing the name of the country to the Republic of Belarus, it passed a battery of laws that initiated the transfer of all armed forces and units of state security on Belarusan soil – excepting strategic nuclear forces – to the jurisdiction of the Belarusan Council of Ministers.[71] The creation of an Armed Forces of the Republic of Belarus was thus emblematic of the radical change affected by the failed coup in the entire political structure of the Soviet Union. There no longer seemed to be any "center" that could hold. Stanislau Shushkevich, who officially replaced Dzemiantsei as Chairman of the Supreme Soviet at this session, reflected this change as well. Although he spoke at the September session in favor of Belarusan membership in a larger union,[72] by December he was meeting with Russian President Boris Yeltsin and Ukraine head Leonid Kravchuk to bury the old union and inaugurate a Confederation of Independent States[73] – a political structure apparently identical to that advocated since August by the BPF. Indeed, the Belarusan delegation to subsequent conferences of the member states of the Commonwealth has not only included representatives of the BPF, but the delegation itself has adopted the BPF's view of the Commonwealth "as a civilized form of transition to independence."[74] While the eventuality of such independence would remain contingent on a myriad of factors and considerations too complex to invite prediction, the remarkable journey to nationhood only recently completed by the Belarusan people would already count as an accomplished fact.

Notes

1 We have employed throughout the terminology recently (19 September 1991) adopted as official: "Belarus" rather than "Belorussia"; "Belarusan" rather than "Belorussian."

2 For examples, see: S. Kurganskii, "Polupravda – ne pravda," *Sovetskaya Belorussiya*, June 7, 1989; V. Korzun, "Po sledam odnoi besedy," *Politicheskii sobesednik*, no. 12, 1989.

3 Mikhail Tkachev, interviewed by Aleksandr Shagun, "Vsadnik s mestom nad gorodom," *Soyuz*, no. 43, October, 1990, p. 9.

4 *Etnahrafija Bielarusi. Encyklapiedyja* (Minsk: Bielaruskaja Savieckaja Encyklapiedyja, 1989), p. 77.

5 Nicholas P. Vakar, *Belorussia: The Making of a Nation* (Cambridge, MA: Harvard University Press, 1956), pp. 1–4.

6 *Encyklapiedyja litaratury i mastactva Bielarusi* (Minsk: Bielaruskaja Savieckaja Encyklapiedyjia, 1984), vol. I, pp. 364–367.

7 P.N. Milyukov, *Natsional'nyi vopros. Proiskhozhdeniye natsional'nosti i natsional'nye voprosy v Rossii* (Prague: Free Russia Publishers, 1925), p. 154.

8 Aleh Latysonak, "Bielastoccyna i narodziny bielaruskaje dumki," a lecture at the Byelorussian Institute of Arts and Sciences in New York, February 23, 1991.

9 Academy of Sciences of the BSSR, Institute of History, *Historyja Bielaruskaj SSR* (Minsk: Nauka i technika, 1972), vol. I, p. 586.

10 A.A. Lojka, V.P. Rahojsa, compilers, *Bielaruskaja litaratura XIX stahoddzia. Chrestamatyja* (Minsk: Vyšejšaja škola, 1988), p. 32.

11 Academy of Sciences of the BSSR, Institute of History, *Historyja Bielaruskaj SSR*, p. 515.

12 Jan Zaprudnik and Thomas E. Bird, *The 1863 Uprising in Byelorussia: "Peasants' Truth" and "Letters from beneath the Gallows" (Texts and commentaries)* (New York: Kreceuski Foundation, 1980), p. 68.

13 Thomas T. Hammond, "Nationalism and National Minorities in Eastern Europe," *Journal of International Affairs*, vol. 20, no. 1, 1966, pp. 9–31.

14 Zygmunt Bauman, "Intellectuals in East-Central Europe: Continuity and Change," *East European Politics and Societies*, vol. 1, Spring, 1987, pp. 171–172.

15 Vakar, *Belorussia*, pp. 34–36.

16 Stephen L. Guthier, "The Belorussians: National Identification and Assimilation, 1897–1970," (part 1), *Soviet Studies*, vol. 29, January, 1977, p. 43.

17 Vakar, *Belorussia*, p. 78.

18 S. Ch. Aleksandrovič, *et. al.*, compilers, *Bielaruskaja litaratura XIX stahoddzia. Chrestamatyja* (Minsk: Vyšejšaja škola, 1971), pp. 193–194.

19 Ye. F. Karski, *Etnograficheskaya karta Belorusskago plemeni* (Petrograd: Belorussian Regional Committee of the All-Russian Soviet of Peasant Deputies, 1917), p. 1.

20 Vakar, *Belorussia*, p. 105.

21 *Ibid.*, p. 97.

22 *Ibid.*, pp. 121–133. On the Belarus Peasant-Workers' Hramada inside Poland, see Aleksandra Bergman, *Sprawy bialoruskie w II Rzeczypospolitej* (Warsaw: Panstwowe wydawnictowo naukowe, 1984), pp. 33–37.

23 Ivan S. Lubachko, *Belorussia Under Soviet Rule, 1917–1957* (Lexington, KY: University of Kentucky Press, 1972), p. 129.

24 Helene Carrere d'Encausse, *Decline of an Empire* (New York: Newsweek Books, 1979), pp. 24–28.

25 Lubachko, *Belorussia Under Soviet Rule*, pp. 111–118; Vekar, *Belorussia*, pp. 146–149.

26 Vakar, *Belorussia*, pp. 141–142.

27 *Narodnoe khozyaistvo Belorusskoi SSR v 1981 g.* (Minsk: Belarus', 1982) pp. 3, 5.

28 Jan Zaprudnik, "Belorussia and the Belorussians", Zev Katz *et al.* eds., *Handbook of Major Soviet Nationalities* (New York: The Free Press, 1975), p. 52.

29 K.T. Mazurov, *Nezabyvaemoe* (Minsk: Belarus', 1984), *passim*.

30 I.M. Ignatenko *et al.*, *Istoriya Belorusskoi SSR* (Minsk: Nauka i tekhnika, 1977), p. 145.

31 One of us learned from a number of Belarusan scholars in December 1988 that although Masherov spoke Belarusan rather poorly, many people were moved by a feeling of national pride by the fact that he had chosen to speak in that language.

32 See Amy Knight, "Pyotr Masherov and the Soviet Leadership: A Study in Kremlinology," *Survey*, vol. 26, Winter, 1982, pp. 151–168.

33 Michael E. Urban, *An Algebra of Soviet Power: Elite Circulation in the Belorussian Republic 1966–1986* (Cambridge: Cambridge University Press, 1989).

34 P.U. Brovka *et al.*, *Belorusskaya Sovetskaya Sotsialisticheskaya Respublika* (Minsk: Glavnaya redaktsiya Belorusskoi Sovetskoi entsiklopedii, 1978), pp. 587–588.

35 *Ibid.*, pp. 134–135; V.P. Borodina *et al.*, *Soviet Byelorussia* (Moscow: Progress, 1972), pp. 82–85, 134–135.

36 N. Matukovskii, "40 tsentnerov i bol'she," *Izvestiya*, September 9, 1987.

37 Brovka *et al.*, *Belorusskaya*, pp. 271–280; Borodina, *et al.*, *Soviet Byelorussia*, pp. 93–95; V.P. Vorob'eva, *et al.*, *Vitebsk* (Minsk: Nauka i tekhnika, 1974), pp. 197–198; V. Ya. Naumenko, *Brest* (Minsk: Nauka i tekhnika, 1977), pp. 123–135.

38 *Izvestiya*, December 16, 1985. The 1989 census recorded a population of 10.2 million in the BSSR and noted continued migration to urban centers. M. Shimanskii, "Kto zhivet v Belorussii," *Izvestiya*, March 13, 1990.

39 Alexander Zhuravlyov, "Not to miss a chance," *Moscow News*, no. 48, December 3–10, 1989, p. 11.

40 This term was initially coined by the Belarusan writer, Ales' Adamovich, in his "Oglyanis' okrest," *Ogonek*, no. 39, September 24–October 1, 1988, pp. 28–30. It has subsequently gained considerable currency throughout the Soviet Union. See, for instance, "Ekho tragedii," *Daugava*, no. 1, 1989; Kathleen Mihalisko, "Georgii Tarasevich – Prime Culprit in 'The Vendee' of *Perestroika*", *Radio Liberty Report on the USSR*, RL 299/89, June 14, 1989, p. 18–20.

41 Urban, *Algebra*, pp. 70–73, 98–135.

42 Stephen L. Guthier, "The Belorussians: National Identification and Assimilation 1897–1970" (part 2), *Soviet Studies*, vol. 29, April, 1977, pp. 272–274; Brian Connolly, "Fifty Years of Soviet Federalism in Belorussia," in R.S. Clem, ed., *The Soviet West* (New York: Praeger, 1975), pp. 114–115.

43 Michael Kirwood, "Glasnost', 'The National Question' and Soviet Language Policy," *Soviet Studies* vol. 43, no. 1, 1991, pp. 68–69.

44 *Ibid.*

45 Roman Szporluk, "West Ukraine and West Belorussia," *Soviet Studies*, vol. 31, January, 1979, pp. 76–77.

46 *Letters to Gorbachev: New Documents from Soviet Byelorussia*, 2nd edn (London: The Association of Byelorussians in Great Britain, 1987).

47 Jan Zaprudnik, "Belorussian Reawakening," *Problems of Communism*, vol. 38, July–August, 1989, p. 27.

48 Adamovich, p. 29; "Ekho tragedii", *Daugava*, 1989.

49 *Press-hrupa "Navina paviedamlaje"* (Minsk), Samizdat (n.d.), p. 2.

50 Evgenii Budinas, "Ternii pravdy," *Vek XX i mir*, no. 3, 1989, pp. 26–31.

51 See, for instance, Vasil' Bykov, "Gumanizm 'nevozmozhno uchredit' . . .," *Znamya yunosti*, February, 1989, p. 3; Ales Adamovich, "Belorussia's Calamity," *Moscow News*, no. 41, October 15–22, 1989, p. 12; Yevgeniya Albats, "The Big Lie", *ibid.*, no. 42, October, 1989), pp. 8–9; Evgenii Konoplya, "Ostorozhno, zona otchuzhdeniya," *Soyuz*, no. 7, February 12–18, 1990, p. 12.

52 On the organizational advantages enjoyed by the Communist Party in the all-union elections of 1989, see Michael E. Urban, *More Power to the Soviets: The Democratic Revolution in the USSR* (Aldershot, UK and Brookfield, VT: Edward Elgar, 1990), chapter 5.

53 Zaprudnik, "Belorussian Reawakening," p. 49.

54 For a full account of these elections, see Michael E. Urban, "Regime, Opposition and Elections in the Belorussian Republic," in Darrell Slider, ed., *Elections in the USSR* (Durham, NC: Duke University Press, forthcoming).

55 Kathleen Mihailsko, "Year in Review: Belorussia," *Radio Liberty Report on the USSR*, RL 583/89, December 15, 1989, p. 21. Mihailsko also points out that the Communist Party of Belorussia had been alone among republic-level communist parties in the USSR in forbidding its members to join a popular front and that the BPF lost a large number of its most active members as a result of this decision.

56 G. Akulova, ". . . Zainteresovany v silnykh Sovetov," *Sovetskaya Belarussiya*, January 7, 1990.

57 Mikhail Shimanskii, "Zayavlenie byuro Tsk LKSM Belorussii, *Izvestiya*, March 1, 1990.
58 V.V. Baranovskii *et al.*, "Ob etike glasnosti i demokratii," *Sovetskaya Belorussiya*, May 19, 1990.
59 N. Dementei, "Zapistak Verkhovnomu Sovetu Belorusskoi SSR o gosudarstvennom suverenitete respubliki," *Sovetskaya Beloruyssiya*, June 20, 1990.
60 "Deklaratsiya o gosudarstvennom suverenitete respubliki," *Sovetskaya Belorussiya*, June 20, 1990.
61 Radio Liberty, Belorussian Service, June 29, 1989. See also Zaprudnik, "Belorussian Reawakening," p. 51.
62 *Litaratura i Mastactva*, July 7, 1989.
63 *Nastaunickaja hazieta* (Minsk), October 10, 1990.
64 See, for instance, the interview given by Dzemiantsei to N. Matukovskii, "Sud'bu ne nazyvayut, a vybirayut," *Izvestiya*, February 14, 1991.
65 Evgenii Babosov, "Effekt bumeranga," *Kommunist Belorussii*, no. 12, December, 1990, p. 46.
66 Three such polls are discussed in M. Shimanskii, "Belorussiya: soyuzy byt'!," *Izvestiya*, March 14, 1991.
67 Z. Pazniak (an interview), "Slach u budučyniu," *Bielarus* (NY: Byelorussian-American Assoc., no. 375, November 1990).
68 *Zviazda*, August 14, 1991.
69 Aleksandr Shagun, "Srazhayas' nasmert', nomenklatura ukhodit so stseny," *Soyuz*, no. 35, August 28–September 4, 1991, p. 9.
70 Radio Moscow, August 28, 1991.
71 *Viedamasci Viarchounaha Savieta Respubliki Bielarus*, no. 30, 1991, pp. 22–27. This transfer was completed in early 1992, "Belarus' primeryaet dospekhi," *Rossiiskaya gazeta*, January 13, 1992, p. 2.
72 The proclamation and Agreement in the Creation of the Commonwealth of Independent States can be found in *Rossiiskaya gazeta*, December 10, 1991, p. 1.
73 *Niecarhovaja Sostaja Siesija Viarchounaha Savieta Bielaruskaj SSR Dvanaccataha Sklikannia (Biuleten)*, no. 2, September 17, 1991, p. 5.
74 See the interview given to Igor Sinyakevich by a member of the Belarusan delegation, Leonid Borshchevskii, "Belorusskaya delegatsiya ser'eznee drugikh otneslas' k peregovoram," *Nezavisimaya gazeta*, December 28, 1991, p. 3.

6 Moldova: breaking loose from Moscow

DARIA FANE

Moldova[1] proclaimed its independence from the Soviet Union on August 27, 1991, in the wake of the failed attempt to overthrow Gorbachev. The ethnic Moldavian population of the republic who fiercely support independence responded with celebrations – thousands danced and sang in the streets. However, the news caused little stir abroad and for the most part was not recognized internationally; only Romania, Lithuania and the independence-seeking Soviet republics of Georgia and Armenia granted recognition to the fledgling. Instead, Moldova's attempt to secede from the Soviet Union brought only increased domestic problems and a sharpening of ethnic tensions within the republic. Two of the republic's ethnic minorities, the ethnic Russians living in the Trans-Dnestr region and the Gagauz, responded with counter-declarations, proclaiming their own independence from Moldova.

Moldova is unique among the Soviet union republics in that it has a counterpart across the border of the same ethnic group and with which the republic was historically united – Romania.[2] For many Moldavians the goal of independence is reunification with Romania. However, unlike the recent reunification of Germany, where the Western portion held economic promise for the East, both Romania and Moldova have dismal economies, ruined by years of communism. Romania's living conditions and political situation are so miserable that even some of Moldova's most ardent nationalists are dubious about casting their lot with Romania at this time.

Moldova's drive for independence and its potential reunification with Romania now pose one of the most serious centrifugal challenges to the center's attempts to maintain some form of Commonwealth. The question of reunification, however, is so controversial that it is polarizing Moldavian society. Its supporters see independence only as a temporary stepping stone on the path to unification, while those who oppose reunification see independence as a goal in itself.

The Kremlin attempted to justify its rule in Moldavia since World War II with the claim that Moldavians are a different ethnic group from the people of Romania. A central postulate of this claim is that the two speak different languages. Glasnost, however, permitted a national awakening throughout the USSR during which the Moldavians began to reclaim their

Romanian heritage and challenge this false postulate. During this period, language issues constituted a central part of the Moldavian national movement, a development that set Moldova apart from the other republics. While Moldavia had existed as a principality for hundreds of years, "Moldavian" as a nationality and language separate from Romania were artificially created by Stalin. Because language was critical to the pretense of a separate nationality, the issue became a vital part of the national awakening.

In August 1989 Moldavia took the lead in language politics, becoming the first Soviet republic to pass a law that declared the language of the indigenous people to be the official language. This law proved to be a turning point in the republic, spearheading rising nationalism for both Moldavians and ethnic minorities who opposed the law. In addition to making Moldavian the state language, the language law reclaimed the Latin script and formally proclaimed that the Moldavian and Romanian languages were one. This law triggered a shift in the republic's political climate which fostered a radicalization of the popular front and witnessed the open emergence of a Moldavian independence movement. The Popular Front now supports reunification with Romania as the eventual goal.

One of the barriers impeding the Romanianization of Moldova is the republic's internal ethnic problems. Moldova is home to five significant ethnic minorities – Russians, Ukrainians, Gagauz, Bulgarians and Jews – in addition to the Moldavians. Relations among these groups are tense, and ethnic violence is a reality. Politically these groups are striving for different goals. As the Moldavians reclaim their Romanian identity and seek to limit ties with Moscow, the other ethnic groups are leaning in the opposite direction, supporting a central authority.

Torn apart on several fault lines, the main ethnic split in the republic is between ethnic Moldavians and Russians, though additional problems divide each of the ethnic groups from the mainstream. According to the 1989 census, Moldavians constitute approximately 64 percent of the republic's 4.3 million population;[3] the five main ethnic minorities constitute: Ukrainian 14 percent, Russian 13 percent, Gagauz 3.5 percent, Bulgarian 2 percent, and Jewish 1.5 percent.

The rise of Moldavian nationalist consciousness triggered responses in the republic's other ethnic groups, and frictions between the nationalities intensified. First the Gagauz and then the Russians and Ukrainians of the "left bank," the strip of land across the Dnestr, proclaimed their own republics. This "secession" was representative of a new model of nationality problems emerging as fragmentation spread in the Soviet Union. This pattern, in which pro-union ethnic minorities rebel against a secessionist republic's majority, is being repeated by other groups, such as the South Ossetians in Georgia and the Poles in Lithuania. Moldova now finds itself confronting ethnic violence and territorial disintegration while it pushes for independence and possible reunification or federation with Romania.

Moldova's history differs from the other Soviet republics. Like the Baltic states it was annexed by the Soviet Union in 1940, a result of the secret Molotov-Ribbentrop pact. However, Moldova's status differs from the Baltics because, while the incorporation of Lithuania, Latvia and Estonia into the Soviet Union was never recognized by the majority of Western countries, the international community did recognize Moldova's forced annexation when Romania ceded Moldavian territory to the Soviets. Thus while the independence of the Baltic states is now recognized and the three were accepted as members of the United Nations on September 17, 1991, Moldova faced greater difficulties in gaining international recognition. Since Moldova had not existed as an independent state at the time of its incorporation into the Union, but rather, as a part of Romania, the question of "one Romanian state" or "two Romanian states" divides the anti-Moscow nationalists.

The independence declaration

The August 19–21, 1991, attempt to overthrow Gorbachev proved a turning point for center–republic relations. For Moldova it was the catalyst that hastened its independence declaration. That declaration was proclaimed by Alexandru Mosanu, president of the Moldovan Parliament, several days later on August 27. The declaration repudiated the Molotov-Ribbentrop pact, invoked both historical rights and democratic legitimacy as the basis for statehood, called on the United Nations to accept Moldova as a full member, and asked the world's governments to recognize its independence.

Steps towards independence

A series of legislative decisions followed the declaration of independence, aimed at untangling the republic's state institutions from those of the center and developing local control over functions that had been performed by Moscow. On the day of the proclamation of independence, the Parliament passed a decree rescinding all articles in the republic's constitution that related to Moldova's membership in the Soviet Union. Simultaneously, a state delegation was appointed to negotiate with the USSR on issues arising from Moldova's secession.

The Moldovan government decided to introduce its own currency, and planned to begin printing money within one year.[4] The republic also decreed on October 30, 1991, the nationalization of all Soviet enterprises in the republic's territory. This decree stipulates taking over these enterprises together with their bank accounts without providing any financial compensation.[5] Among the affected enterprises are the heavy-industry combines in the Russian-speaking region of the Dnestr.

A series of other measures include the Moldavian government's September 11 decision to set up checkpoints on the republic's borders. All customs posts were subordinated to the State Department on Customs Control, and plans were made for a border service. The republic also set up a Ministry of National Security to replace the disbanded KGB.

Breaking Communist Party control

A major part of Moldova's effort to free itself from its Soviet past was its effort to break the back of the local Communist Party. The Communist Party had already lost much of its influence in Moldavia, although party institutions maintained their strength in the Russian-inhabited areas, particularly in the Dnestr region. For the Russians, the party was seen as a stronghold of resistance to Moldavian nationalism, while for radicalized Moldavians it represented an instrument of the occupiers.

The already precipitous decline in Communist Party authority resulting from its anti-nationalist image was further hastened by the removal of party secretary Petr Luchinski and a subsequent split within the party. Luchinski had replaced Semen Grossu as first secretary on November 16, 1989, in the wake of violent demonstrations that stopped the celebration of that year's November 7th revolution day parade. Luchinski enjoyed some success in slowing the party's declining popularity and authority by taking a conciliatory approach toward the demands of the Popular Front. Luchinski attempted to set up the party as a moderating body that could mediate between the social forces in society. He hoped to retain the leading role of the Communist Party in the republic by integrating the various viewpoints;[6] some of the Popular Front's demands were thus incorporated into party policy. Under Luchinski, the party accepted the Moldavian language demands – including the transfer to Latin script – the Moldavian flag, and other symbols of the Moldavian national rebirth. Luchinski even advocated greater contact with Romania, believing that this would forestall calls for unification.

None the less, it was clear in 1990 that the party was in the process of losing its leading role in society. In July, Luchinski reported that 8,000 out of 200,000 Moldavian communists had already quit the party and that this process was gathering momentum.[7] By January, 1991, the party leadership reported that during 1990 more than 25,000 people – 13 percent of its membership – had left the party.[8] Among those who left in 1990 were some sixty parliamentary deputies.

Luchinski was elected to the post of secretary of the CPSU Central Committee, and left the republic for Moscow. Grigori Yeremei was elected to replace him as republic first secretary on February 4, 1991. Yeremei's first weeks in office found him in an unpopular pro-Moscow role because of his support for Gorbachev's proposed Union referendum. He came under fire from nationalist forces that opposed holding the referendum. During Yeremei's brief tenure as party secretary, the party was thus increasingly identified as Moscow's instrument in pushing its policies.

The decline of the Communist Party was hastened by a split which resulted in the formation of the Independent Moldavian Communist Party (IMCP) on April 8, 1991.[9] The new party was established by a democratic wing of the party known as the Democratic Platform. The split is similar to those that took place in the communist parties of the Baltic republics, as mostly Russians and Russified minorities remained loyal to the CPSU. The predominantly-Moldavian IMCP withdrew from the CPSU, and the two wings of the party became embroiled in a struggle over which would be heir to party property in the republic.

On 15 May, 1991, the Popular Front proposed legislation on nationalizing the Moldavian Communist Party's assets which included publishing houses and official structures. The Supreme Soviet, however, voted down a proposal to consider such a draft law. Two factors affected their decision to block the proposal: the influence of the Moldavian Agrarians who supported the Communist Party and the party's promise to give up some property. This concession helped temporarily, even though the party did not specify what property it would give up. That same day, however, the Supreme Soviet did vote to grant legal registration to the breakaway IMCP wing.

The fate of party property was determined days after the failed coup. On August 23, the Moldavian legislature nationalized party property and declared the activities of the party illegal.

Presidential elections

The December 8, 1991, presidential elections further polarized the republic. Not only did the Dnestr and Gagauz republics declare that they would not participate, but the Moldavians themselves were split. The trans-Dnestr declared it would not participate in the elections of a "foreign state." The Gagauz and Dnestr republics not only refused to participate but held their own elections a week earlier, on December 1. The Popular Front set itself in opposition to the Moldavian elections, declaring them illegal. The Democratic Youth Party, which claimed to have 100,000 supporters joined the Front in the boycot. President Snegur denounced these boycotts. Though the motives of the Popular Front's boycott were entirely different from those of the Gagauz and Dnestr, the election campaign created a strange convergence of political interests that led the Front into conflict with Snegur. Consequently, the Front's large bloc in parliament – comprising about 30 percent of the seats – switched to the side of the opposition.

The Popular Front's collision course with Snegur's government further polarized the already fractured republic. The Front organized rallies against Snegur and the elections, supporting unification with Romania. An estimated 10,000 people united on November 3 under the slogan of "No to Presidential Elections in Moldova." The opposition of the Front shifted the election issue to a near-referendum on the question of reunification. Snegur came out in favor of independence but not reunification, while the Front pushed for joining Romania.

Single-candidate elections

Only one candidate, Snegur, was in the presidential race. This was due to two factors – the withdrawal of the other candidates and an election law that appeared as if it were purposely drawn up to eliminate the competition. Originally three candidates entered the contest; in addition to Snegur were Grigori Yeremei, former first secretary of the Moldavian Communist Party, and Gheorghe Malarchuk, the nominee of the Green Party. However, Yeremei and Malarchuk withdrew their candidacies.

The election law was drawn up apparently for the specific purpose of eliminating sections of the competition. One clause of the law banned candidates over sixty years, which cut out A. Moshanu, President of the Parliament. Another clause excluded those who did not have permanent residency in Moldavia during the last ten years. This provision cut out Snegur's most powerful rival, Mircea Druc, a prominent Popular Front leader who had spent much of his time out of the republic.

The Popular Front's main candidates were thus eliminated. Without a candidate to support, the Front chose to boycott, hoping to defeat Snegur by denying him the required majority. The Front further accused Snegur of illegally removing Druc from his position as Prime Minister in order to concentrate power in his own hands.

Establishing foreign relations

As part of its attempt to establish an independent identity, Moldavia began to establish relations abroad. This effort began before the August 1991 declaration of independence, as its June 23, 1990, sovereignty declaration had already announced that Moldavia was to become an independent subject of international relations. Moldavia has sought direct trade relations both with other republics and with foreign countries. In this endeavor, the republic's Ministry of Foreign Affairs is working to ensure the republic's emergence in the international arena. Moldavian Foreign Minister Nikolai Tiu stated that the main task of the MFA was to achieve Moldavia's broad international recognition and argued that this would help attract foreign capital to the republic in order to "reanimate the economy."[10]

Israel was one of the first countries to establish business ties with Moldavia. A cooperative business association known as "Mo-Iz" was formed between Moldavia and Israel, with the participation of more than twenty of Kishinev's large enterprises and cooperatives. A series of protocols on trade and cooperation provide for Israel to purchase red wine and champagne from Moldavia as well as wooden and metal articles, in exchange for a variety of food processing and packing equipment. The association also plans to set up both hard currency and rouble stores to sell a variety of consumer goods. In addition, preliminary agreements were reached with the Mo-Iz Association for construction of a four-star hotel in Kishinev.[11]

Moldavia also established trade relations with Eastern and Western Europe. The Moldavian government held talks with the Hungarian, Polish, and Czechoslovak Consuls General in Kiev and with government delegations from Bulgaria and Romania concerning the conclusion of bilateral trade agreements.[12] In addition, Italian and German firms are participating in joint ventures that Moldova hopes will introduce modern equipment and technology to the participating enterprises.[13] Talks are also under way with Turkey on the mechanics of how to proceed with economic cooperation. Turkey will produce packaging materials for Moldavian juices and wines, which the republic hopes to sell on the world market.[14] Intergovernmental agreements on economic cooperation have even been concluded with such African states as Burkina Faso, Burundi, and Botswana.

Thus far these fledgling contacts are very preliminary. While complete data is not available, it appears that the impact of these agreements is mostly symbolic: establishing relations in order to expand sovereignty. Moldova is particularly interested in developing direct relations with its Eastern European regional neighbors, hoping that these partners can provide suppliers and markets outside the former Soviet net.

Reunification with Romania

The most critical area of Moldavia's foreign policy is its relationship with Romania, and indeed the key question underlying Moldavian politics is the shape of the future Moldavian-Romanian relationship. Although closer cooperation with Romania is the openly articulated goal of Moldavia's government, the question of reunification lurks under the surface. The drive for closer ties has broad-based popular support, and reunification sentiment is growing on both sides of the Prut River.

Reunification is controversial, and the question is currently a polarizing factor in Moldavian society. The Moldavian Popular Front advocates speedy union, rather than independence. One of the Front's most vocal spokesmen has been former Prime Minister Mircea Druc. He views the declaration of independence of Moldova as a first step, with the ideal being

Romania's reintegration. Druc's parliamentary opposition group based their opposition to the December 8, 1991, elections on the argument that elections would institutionalize the presidency, creating a state that acknowledged the consequences of the Molotov-Ribbentrop pact.[15]

While the Mircea Druc brand of pro-unification activism sees independence as a temporary stepping stone to unification, for others independence itself is the goal. This issue has brought Druc and the Popular Front into opposition against the current President Snegur. Snegur supports state independence and opposes unification. However, while during the election campaign Snegur staked his political career on a "two Romanian states" position, earlier interviews indicate that Snegur had done a political flip-flop. In interviews from August 1991, Snegur had expressed the view that independence was only a temporary stage on the way to unification.

The view from Romania

A spillover effect of the 1989 Romanian revolution has been that it reopened the "Bessarabia question." From the end of World War II until 1985, Soviet rule in Moldavia went unchallenged. The advent of perestroika changed the nature of the political dialogue on the Soviet side of the border, but it was also the fall of Ceaucescu in Romania that really permitted the question of reunification to be raised.

The post-Ceaucescu Romanian Government was wary about pressing any claims to Moldavia for fear of antagonizing the Soviets and opening up the possibility of other claims on Romanian territory, specifically Hungarian claims on Transylvania. As Romanian President Iliescu said in a November 1990 interview, "If you start to move one border, there will be a chain reaction, and we have to think intelligently about the problem." Iliescu insisted that Romania was bound by the 1975 Helsinki accords to respect the present borders.[16] In another interview, Iliescu referred to the annexation of Bessarabia as a "historic injustice," but argued that "we cannot afford to take positions which strongly complicate life for the people over there and also relations between our two states."[17] Romania has "no intention of altering the existing borders between the two countries," he told Austrian television.[18]

Former Romanian Prime Minister Petre Roman was less cautious. In a December 1990 interview with *Die Welt* he said that one of his country's tasks was "the struggle for the independence of the Republic of Moldova." During a visit to Chile in March 1990, he was reported to have told journalists that Romania expected to regain the territory of Moldavia from the Soviet Union. The next day, in Brazil, apparently realizing he had gone too far publicly, he modified his statements, arguing that "this should be settled by the Moldovans."

Roman's views on reunification again became the subject of a political flap shortly before he was forced out of office. This time *Romania Libera* reported that in an interview the Vienna-based *Die presse* he stated that Romania is "ready to unite with Moldova, and that all depends on the Moldovan people's will."[19] This remark triggered off repercussions, and Moldovan President Snegur phoned Romanian President Iliescu to request an explanation of the remark.[20] The Moldova press office accused *Romania Libera* of an "erroneous interpretation" of Roman's comments.

Foreign minister Adrian Nastase was more careful in his public statements to focus on Moldova's independence, rather than on reunification. In his September 25 address to the UN General Assembly, Nastase expressed hope that before long Moldova would be internationally recognized as a member of the United Nations. None the less, his comments reflect a belief in eventual unification. When asked about unification in a *Berliner Zeitung* interview in May 1991, he responded, "History will answer this question," but after this coy response, he continued that "if it does not take long, this will be positive."

While the Romanian Government refrained from openly advocating reunification, a spate of nationalist groups were more outspoken in their views on the subject. These special interest lobbying groups were increasingly active in organizing demonstrations in support of unification with Moldavia. The most visible groups pushing the reunification agenda were the Bucharest-Kishinev Cultural Society, the pro-Bessarabia and Bukovina Association, the Vatra Romaneasca ("Romanian Hearth"), and the Stephan the Great-Bukovina Association.

The Bucharest-Kishinev Cultural Society was headed by Gheorghe Gaveila-Copil. During the Gagauz-Dnestr secession crisis in November 1990, the group organized solidarity rallies in Bucharest. It appealed for volunteers to sign up for detachments to fight for the "protection of the territorial integrity of the republic of Moldova." The appeals noted that the volunteer detachments thus formed would not cross the Prut unless expressly requested by the government of the "Republic of Moldova" or the People's Front of Moldova.[21]

The Pro-Bessarabia and Bukovina Association, founded by Nicolae Lupin,[22] has several branches, the main one being in Bucharest. The group believes in the historic right of Romania to rule over Moldavia. The association's first congress took place on November 18, 1990, and adopted a "Declaration of the Romanian People's Right." This declaration asserts the Romanian people's historic right "to be sovereign and exercise its sovereignty" in the territory delimited by the 1918 borders. The association seeks to have the Romanian state officially reject the Molotov-Ribbentrop Treaty.[23]

Increased contacts and cooperation

Following the Romanian revolution, cross-border contact increased dramatically. In early 1990, the border between Moldavia and Romania was opened for private travel for the first time since World War II. In April 1990, Romanian peasants in the border area dismantled the wire fence on their side of the Prut River and urged Soviet Moldavians to do the same. A historic action on May 6, 1990, called the "Bridge of Flowers," opened the border to anyone who wished to cross. Moscow Radio estimated that 200,000 Romanians and 150,000 Moldavians took part.[24]

A series of political rallies and cultural festivals also took place along the border. These events, organized by the Popular Front in Moldavia and pro-Bessarabia societies in Romania, marked a series of anniversaries and became a vehicle for unificationist expressions. On June 24, 1990, about 10,000 Romanians, with neither passports nor visas, many waving flags and chanting "unite," poured across the bridge into Moldavia to mark the 50th anniversary of Moscow's annexation of the republic. Smaller groups from Moldavia crossed into Romania to visit relatives.[25] Other border demonstrations included a "human chain" on June 27 to mark the 50th anniversary of the Red Army's entry into Bessarabia and North Bukovina.

The popular movement increased pressure for official changes in travel requirements. Border guards began to remove the barbed wire fences on the border; by January 10, 1990, TASS reported that the fence had been removed along a 50-kilometer stretch. Simplified border crossing points were set up for residents of the border zones, with a telegram from the other side of the Prut serving as sufficient documentation. Plans were made to open another six border stations at Giurgiulesti, Cahul, Stotanovca, Sculeni, Costesti-Stinca and Lipcani. Further plans were made to repair the Lipcani bridge over the Prut which was damaged during World War II. Opening these six border stations did not proceed according to plan. On November 1, 1991, *Krasnaya Zvezda* reported that the opening was postponed for the second time, perhaps indefinitely, and mused that speculators from both sides would be the ones to benefit from open borders. None the less, the easing of travel restrictions led to a Soviet-Romanian agreement signed on March 11, 1991, formally abolishing visa requirements.

In addition to the increased travel that followed the opening of the border, leadership contacts developed quickly. After counterpart visits, a series of agreements were reached. One of the first agreements concerned communications. In September 1990 the Moldavian minister of information and telecommunications visited Romania.[26] The agreement made possible mutual reception of radio and television programs. Moldova national television began broadcasting Romanian television on October 14, 1990.[27] Then, on November 1, a convention on scientific cooperation was signed between the Romanian and Moldovan Academies of Science.[28]

Trade has also grown rapidly. The two have begun to hold business exhibitions in the hopes of stimulating joint ventures. Some cooperation has been set up in textiles, leather, television manufacture, but the two are still so steeped in socialist economic systems and currencies that they view a barter system the best option for now.[29] As a step toward integrating the economies of the two areas, Moldova and Romania signed an agreement on November 5, 1991 to create a joint Romanian-Moldovan bank.

Relations with Ukraine

A treaty with Ukraine on economic and cultural cooperation for 1991–1995 was announced on January 11, 1991, which agreed to preserve supplies for 1991 at a level no lower than that of 1990.[30] The agreement also specified that if either side introduces its own currency, all transactions will be made under a special agreement.

Economic relations with Ukraine are particularly important, as Moldova traditionally receives most of its energy resources from there. In 1991 deliveries from Ukraine were drastically reduced. Moldova is seeking alternative energy supplies, and has arranged a deal with Romania to process crude oil imported from Ukraine.

Relations with Ukraine, however, pose a special problem because of unresolved territorial claims. When Stalin annexed Bessarabia he partitioned the land, giving a chunk of southern Bessarabia to Ukraine. Assertion of Moldova's claim to this territory is part of the program of the Moldavian Popular Front. The Front's position calls for annulment of the August 2, 1940, decision creating the Moldavian SSR, and the return of Romanian lands transferred to Ukraine.[31]

Ukraine does not agree. On June 28, 1990, people in these areas celebrated the 50th anniversary of their joining the Soviet Union. In the city of Bolgrad, near Odessa, a rally was staged protesting against Moldavia's territorial claims. Several days later, on July 5, 1990, the Odessa oblast local soviet issued a statement stressing that the territory of Ukraine is not subject to redivision, refuting the territorial claims of the Moldavian nationalists.

Independent Ukraine and independent Moldova are likely to become embroiled in a nasty irredentist struggle. Some in Kishinev suggest a settlement in which Moldova relinquishes the trans-Dnestr area, allowing it to join Ukraine in exchange for the regions of South Bukovina lost when the Soviets redrew the borders. The Southern Ukraine – with its access to both the Black Sea and the Danube River – would be a strategic plus for landlocked Moldova. Moldovan president Snegur rejected this plan and said that such a deal was out of the question for the duration of his office.[32] Furthermore, the population of the trans-Dnestr does not want to be part of Ukraine, which has passed an even stricter language law than Moldova.

Relations with the Kremlin

Moldavian opposition to signing the Union treaty advocated by Gorbachev throughout much of 1991 was at the heart of its nationalist political stand. On the eve of the USSR Congress of Peoples' Deputies session to consider the Union treaty, the Moldavian Popular Front organized a popular demonstration at which hundreds of thousands of Moldavians demonstrated against signing the treaty.

The March 17, 1991, Union referendum was a volatile moment in the republic which focused the passions surrounding the contentious Union treaty issue. The republic's polarized politics were expressed along ethnic lines. Despite the Moldavia Parliament's February 19 decision not to hold the referendum, the Dnestr and Gagauz area councils adopted resolutions announcing their intention to do so. Moldavian President Snegur sent an ultimatum to Tiraspol, demanding the annulment of that decision. But Tiraspol held firm, responding that they were proceeding from the "primacy of the laws of the USSR over the laws of republics."

The Communist Party supported the referendum, and the Kremlin sent in reinforcement troops several days before the scheduled vote to make sure polling stations were set up. Of the seven polling stations set up at enterprises in Kishinev, only one was operating by afternoon, the rest having been blocked by militant Popular Front supporters. Servicemen stationed in Moldavia took part at polling stations set up on their bases; Moldavian nationalists claimed fraud – one Moldavian interviewed on TV claimed that he had been allowed to vote eight times on military bases. In the Dnestr and Gagauz areas, the referendum carried by strong majorities.

The independence movement: the centrality of language

The Moldavian language law was a turning point for the republic that moved the Moldavian people forward on the path toward independence. It was a major victory for Moldavian nationalism, but the highly-charged atmosphere surrounding its debate politicized non-Moldavians and polarized the republic. The interests of ethnic groups diverged as the language law promised to affect each community differently. Moldavia was the first of the Soviet republics to initiate language legislation aimed at reinstating its previous alphabet, which reflects the importance of language for Moldavians in reclaiming their national identity. Although the law was passed in August 1989, the history of language tensions is a long one, and the movement for a language law started earlier.

The "Moldavian" language

In 1940 there were virtually no differences between the Romanian spoken on the two banks of the Prut, though there is a detectable Bessarabian regional accent. One of the key tools for the Kremlin in its nationalities policy was asserting that the two were separate languages. To create the differences, Stalin introduced the Cyrillic alphabet, replacing the Latin letters in which Romanian is written, and proclaiming the new variant to be the "Moldavian" language, something apart from Romanian.

Following the annexation of Bessarabia, some Russian loan words were slipped into Moldavian while the Soviets advanced a new theory that the language was Slavonian, or at least one of combined Slavic-Romance origins.[33] Although certain words relating to technology, the party, or the administrative structure took hold, the effort to show that Moldavian was a totally different language from Romanian was basically futile because there was no significant change in grammar or syntax. Official Soviet publications, however, presented a different image, claiming Moldavian as a completely different language with Slavic roots. "The Moldavian language is of Latin origin, but with considerable Slavonic elements," explained a Novosti Press Agency official publication on Moldavia written in 1972.[34]

Soviet nationalities policy always devoted close attention to the question of languages. Like the Russian Empire before it, Soviet authorities had to deal with language problems from the very beginning. By 1917 the Bolsheviks were already aware of the significance of political linguistics in their union. Lenin favored a voluntary union, with free right of secession, and argued for a language policy "which only the nationals in the given republic can compile in any successful manner."[35] However, by the time the nationality question was discussed in April 1923 at the Twelfth Party Congress in Moscow, a Stalinist tendency had taken over, and a policy of greater centrism won out.

Although in principle the Soviet Constitution provided the right of using national languages, linguistic equality was never the goal of Soviet language policy. Soviet long-range linguistic strategy involved three overlapping phases: (1) promoting Russian as a second language, (2) encouraging bilingualism, and (3) substituting Russian for ethnic languages.[36] Thus adoption of Russian and its use by non-Russian populations was the measure of linguistic assimilation in the Soviet Union.

We can divide subjects of a multilingual society like the former Soviet Union into four groups: (1) parochials – who speak only their national language, (2) unassimilated bilinguals – who speak Russian in addition to their national language, (3) assimilated bilinguals – who have switched to Russian as native language but also speak their national language; and (4) assimilated subjects – have Russified by shifting linguistically, speaking only or predominantly Russian.[37]

According to this system, an increasing number of Moldavians were achieving bilingualism, with a declining number falling into the parochial category. While 1989 census figures revealed that only 4.3 percent of Moldavians considered Russian their native tongue, another 53.3 percent said they spoke it as a second language. With 57.6 percent of Moldavians claiming they spoke Russian as either native or second language, the remainder considered themselves "parochials," claiming no ability to speak Russian. The self-proclaimed "parochials" were declining, from 63 percent in 1970, 50.6 percent in 1979, to 42.3 percent in 1989. While a strong majority of Moldavians (95.4 percent) considered their own language their mother tongue, the trend toward increasing bilingualism was very clear.

By comparison, the Ukrainian, Gagauz, Bulgarian, and Jewish populations of Moldavia are far more linguistically assimilated. Seven percent of Gagauz, 18.1 percent of Bulgarians, 36.6 percent of Ukrainians, and 72.9 percent of Jews consider Russian their native language, according to the 1989 census. With respect to those who speak Russian as either a first or second language, 79.7 percent of Ukrainians, 80.3 percent each of Gagauz and Bulgarians, and fully 96 percent of the Jews fall into this category. Thus the majority of the Jews are linguistically Russified, while Gagauz, Bulgarians, and Ukrainians can be considered as bilinguals.

Growth of the language movement[38]

In the summer of 1988 two opposition groups were formed, the Alexi Mateevici Literary and Musical Club and the Democratic Movement in Support of Restructuring. The two movements attracted a large segment of the republic's writers and linguists and became a focal point for articulating the opposition's demands. The language demands focused on three basics: that (1) Moldavian be adopted as the official language in the republic, (2) public recognition be made that "Moldavian" and "Romanian" are one and the same language, and (3) the abandonment of the Cyrillic alphabet be accompanied by a return to Latin script.

At this point the official apparat still vigorously opposed making any linguistic concessions. In the first half of 1988, the chief party ideologist, Central Committee Secretary Nikolai Bondarchuk, argued at a plenum that replacement of the Cyrillic script would effectively render a large segment of the population illiterate, bringing irreparable damage to Soviet Moldavian culture.[39] Other officials argued that the changeover would be too expensive.

The debate on the future of the Moldavian language intensified following the November 1988 publication of the Communist Party of Moldavia theses entitled "Affirming Restructuring through Concrete Actions."[40] The theses dealt with economic matters and language questions. The section on language issues dealt a blow to the aspirations of the opposition, rejecting all three "basics." These theses argued that Moldavian could not be adopted as the state language because this would offend other nationalities; that although Moldavian and Romanian "belong to the same Romance group of languages" and "there is little difference between them," none the less the "Moldavian tongue has its own history, present, and future"; and that transition to the Latin alphabet "would cost billions . . . which would inevitably lead to the disruption of social programs, damage the population's prosperity, have an adverse effect on their spiritual development, and render them illiterate for many years."

After the theses were published, a passionate debate erupted in the republic. For the next month every issue of the party daily newspaper ran pages of arguments on both sides of the question. In this politicized climate, an interdepartmental commission appointed by the republic's Parliament made an in-depth study of the language issue, and released its report on December 28, 1988.

Whereas the theses represented the conservative position toward the language question adopted by the Communist Party, the Parliamentary commission's report represented a victory for the opposition, upholding the three basic demands. It recommended making Moldavian the state language, favored recognizing the identity of Moldavian and Romanian, renounced the concept of two different Eastern Romance languages, and supported the transition to Latin script. The commission's report set the stage for the volatile events of 1989.

On January 26, 1989, the presidium of the Moldavian Supreme Soviet passed a resolution instructing its permanent commissions to come up with a draft language law by March. A preliminary draft was published on March 31, 1989, although soon after the Writers' Union produced an alternative draft. The political climate in the republic shifted rapidly once a draft law was published. Moldavian nationalism grew, and so did the response by the other ethnic groups. Feeling the need to defend their interests, ethnic Russians formed the organization *Yedinstvo* ("Unity").

Work on the language law continued, and an updated draft was prepared for the August 29, 1989, session of the republic Supreme Soviet. Non-Moldavians began preliminary protest strikes in mid-August; on August 16 work collectives in Tiraspol, Bendery, and Rybnitsa held a two-hour warning strike. Strikes heated up after the draft was published on the 20th, as Tiraspol workers went on strike the next day.

Strikes among Russian workers in Moldavia spread and the population took to the streets demanding postponement of the Parliamentary session scheduled to consider the law. On Sunday August 27, enormous crowds demonstrated in Kishinev. In downtown Victory Square, hundreds of thousands, predominantly Moldavians, attended the Popular Front's rally in support of the law. In a separate rally nearby, an estimated 2,000 members of the Russian nationalist group *Yedinstvo* protested against the law. While the numbers at this latter demonstration were smaller than those at the pro-language law rally, this action was a turning point for *Yedinstvo* as well. A third rally with several thousand protesters was held by the Gagauz. Meanwhile, strikes continued in the Russian cities, demanding that the Russian language be given the status of state language along with Moldavian and that it be used as the language of inter-ethnic communication.

Despite the demonstrations, the Supreme Soviet presidium announced on August 27 that the session would not be postponed. The Parliamentary session lasted for three days amidst a highly charged atmosphere of strikes and rallies. At the urging of President Gorbachev, a compromise law was considered. On August 31 the Moldavian Supreme Soviet adopted a language law making Moldavian the republic's official language and reinstituting Latin script. The Popular Front considered the law its first major political victory.[41] Despite a compromise formula included in the law, which declared Russian the language of inter-ethnic communication, strikes at Russian enterprises continued for about a month.

After the passage of the language law, and as Moldavian nationalism grew, many places throughout the republic were renamed. Names with Soviet symbolism were rejected, and original Romanian names were reclaimed, or new names with Moldavian nationalist significance were selected. The Kishinev city soviet presidium decided to rename Kishinev's main avenue, formerly Lenin Prospekt, after the Moldavian ruler, Stephan the Great. The city's center, Victory Square, was renamed the Grand National Assembly Square.[42] Iskra Street reverted back to Bucharest Street, a name it carried during the Romanian era. Villages that had been given Russian names, such as Glaven, Suvorov, and Frunzen, had their old names of Tsarigrad, Aleksandr Ioan Kuza, and Chenusha restored.[43] An amendment was introduced into the republic's constitution on June 5, 1990, which changed the republic's name from "Moldavian Soviet Socialist Republic" to "Soviet Socialist Republic of Moldova."[44] The name was further modified on May 23, 1991, when the Moldavian Supreme Soviet dropped the words "Soviet" and "Socialist" and adopted the official title "Republic of Moldova."

Other symbolic steps were taken toward reclaiming a non-Soviet identity. One such change was the adoption of the state flag on April 27, 1990. The tri-color has the same colors – red, yellow, and blue – as the Romanian flag, but has the coat of arms of the medieval principality of Moldavia, the "auroch's head." in the center. The tricolor flag first reappeared on the streets of Kishinev during the unauthorized demonstrations of March 1989. Within a year, the flag was elevated from a symbol of defiance to state flag.

Further nationalist changes followed. A new law on holidays removed the anniversary of "The Great October Socialist Revolution," November 7, from the republic's calendar of holidays. Orthodox Christmas, celebrated on January 7 and 8, and the Moldovan Language Holiday, August 31, were added.[45] These changes set a separatist tone for the republic, distancing it from elements of its identity in the Soviet era and beginning the switch to a non-communist cultural base.

Challenges to independence

The republic's ethnic minorities

A key challenge to Moldova stems from the demographics of the republic's ethnic mix. Rising Moldavian nationalism caused other ethnic minorities in the republic to stir. The phenomenon of heightened nationalism revealed how divided the nationality groups in the republic are. The tensions that arose in Moldavia following the language law demonstrated deep underlying schisms in society along ethnic lines. Each ethnic group in the republic is now asserting its own nationality claims, challenging the Moldavian authorities.

The Gagauz and a Russian-Ukrainian coalition living across the Dnestr each announced secession from Moldavia and proclaimed their own republics. After the coup, they went one step further and pronounced those republics independent. Current political cleavages within Moldavia for the most part parallel ethnic divisions, and to a large extent ethnicity is politics, with Moldavian radicals and reformers confronting conservative Russians. This is both an ideological confrontation as well as an ethnic one, with conservative forces represented by a coalition of the Communist Party, ethnic Russians, and Gagauz separatists. It is not a purely ethnic split, however, since there are some ethnic Moldavians who remain faithful to the Communist Party, as well as a small number of ethnic Russians who have been involved in the Moldavian Popular Front.

The primary ethnic conflict in the republic is between Moldavians and Russians, but additional problems divide each of the ethnic groups from the mainstream. As mentioned above, according to the 1989 census,

Table 6.1. *National composition of Moldavia, 1897–1989*

	1897	%	1930*	%	1959	%	1979	%	1989	%
Romanian	920,919	46.15	1,610,402	56.03	1,887,000	65.40	2,525,687	63.95	2,790,769	64.37
Russian	155,774	7.81	351,912	12.24	293,000	10.20	505,730	12.80	560,423	12.93
Ukrainian	379,198	19.00	314,211	10.93	421,000	14.60	560,679	14.20	599,777	13.83
Jews	288,168	14.44	204,858	7.13	95,000	3.30	80,127	2.03	65,668	1.51
Gagauz	57,054	2.86	98,172	3.42	96,000	3.30	138,000	3.49	152,752	3.52
Bulgarian	103,492	5.19	163,726	5.70	62,000	2.10	80,665	2.04	87,779	2,02
Others	90,865	4.55	131,099	4.56			58,868	1.49	78,192	1.80
Total	1,995,470		2,874,380		2,854,000		3,949,756		4,335,360	

* Bessarabia.

Moldavians constitute a majority, nearly two thirds (64 percent) of the republic's 4.3 million population, with five main ethnic minorities comprising the remainder: Ukrainian, Russian, Gagauz, Bulgarian, and Jewish. This section will examine each of the five minority groups, their history, and current politics.

Russians: the Dnestr republic

The biggest challenge to the Moldavian leadership comes from the Russian population. Playing the dual role of disaffected minority and representative of Moscow's power, the republic's Russian population was galvanized in the wake of Moldavia's language law. The republic's Russians fall into two main groups: those living in the area that was traditionally Bessarabia and those from the trans-Dnestr area – the "left bank."

Like the Trans-Dnestr Russians, those within the area that was traditionally Bessarabia oppose the nationalist decisions of the Moldavian government. They have organized in several groups to protect their interests. One of these is *"Yedinstvo"* (Unity), a group which first appeared in Moldavia at the beginning of 1989. The *Yedinstvo* International Movement for the Defense of Perestroika (Intermovement) was formed in opposition to the Moldavian language law. According to Intermovement Presidium member Vladimir Solonar, the movement grew out of the realization that the non-Moldavian ethnic groups had to press their own interests.[46]

Intermovement took on the language law issue, pressing for Russian as well as Moldavian as official languages. They did win a compromise in this issue, but they did not appear to have been very effective in other areas of political activism; the Russians of the "left bank," trans-Dnestr region have been far more active.

The largely Russian and Russified Ukrainian population of the Dnestr area has a different history than that of the rest of the republic. This region is not part of Bessarabia and North Bukovina, and was not part of Romania during the interwar period. The trans-Dnestr area was part of the Ukraine until 1940 when it was joined together with the annexed Bessarabia to form the Moldavian SSR. This secessionist region currently accounts for about 900,000 of the 4.3 million people of Moldavia, most of whom settled in the area in the early 1940s.

In August 1989, while the Moldavians were considering the language law, strikes broke out in the left bank area and in Russian enterprises on the right bank. In Tiraspol, where almost 90 percent of its 200,000 people are Russian speakers, a two-hour warning strike was held on August 16, and almost all of the town's factories shut down on August 21 to protest the final draft of the law. Strikes spread, and by August 24, more than fifty factories in Kishinev, Bendery, Rybnitsa, Komrat and other cities had joined the strike started in Tiraspol. By August 29, when the Parliament was considering the law, 80,000 workers were on strike at a hundred factories. The law passed on August 31, and the strikes intensified and continued for over a month, particularly in the Dnestr cities of Tiraspol, Bendery, and Rybnitsa.

After the Gagauz proclaimed themselves an autonomous republic in November 1989, the trans-Dnestr Russians also began to take a secessionist tack. The city of Tiraspol on January 27, 1990, voted to become a self-governing, independent territory, the first vote of its kind concerning a city. It was quickly followed by an announcement from the Russian-dominated city of Bendery that it would do likewise. The vote was organized by the Tiraspol United Council of Labor Collectives (OSTK), the local equivalent of a popular front, headed by V. Rylyakov.

As Moldavian nationalists pulled away from the Kremlin, the Russians of the Dnestr pulled closer, intensifying a deep ideological rift in the republic. The fault line split wider as separatist tendencies grew. Following the Moldavian Supreme Soviet adoption of the tricolor flag as the republic's official symbol in April 1990, the local soviets of Tiraspol, Bendery, and Rybnitsa refused to recognize it, passing a resolution in June rejecting this change. Instead, these cities continued to fly the communist flag of Moldavia SSR over official buildings. The rejection of Moldavian nationalism embraced a reaffirmation of Soviet values. Perhaps inspired by encouragement from the Kremlin, the area announced it was breaking away from Moldavia, proclaiming the Dnestr republic on September 2, 1990.

The newly proclaimed republic declared that only Union laws would be recognized on its territory, suspending legal validity of Moldavian laws adopted since 1989. The Dnestr republic also rejected the Moldavian version of history; in particular it disagreed with Parliament's interpretation of the events of 1940. The Dnestr continued to celebrate "Reunification Day," the June 28 anniversay of the 1941 incorporation of Bessarabia, while the Parliament denounced the annexation and creation of the Moldavian SSR.

Within hours of the trans-Dnestr independence decision, the Moldavian Parliament denounced the secession as illegal and in violation of both republican and Union constitutions. The Parliament dissolved the local soviets in the trans-Dnestr and instituted presidential rule.

After the secessionist Gagauz held their elections on October 28, 1990, the Dnestr republic announced that it too intended to hold elections, setting a November 25 date. Ethnic conflict flared into violence on November 2 when Moldavia's government sent MVD troops to clear roadblocks set up by militants in the Dnestr area. Six people were killed and thirty wounded in clashes between police and armed civilians in Dubossary.[47] Following this bloodshed, tension escalated. Local officials declared a state of emergency, and residents prepared to defend Dubossary, blocking bridges over the Dnestr. Moldavian "volunteer" units traveled down to the right bank of the Dnestr while thousands of Dnestr workers formed defense bands.

Violence swept the Moldavian capital following the November 12, 1990, death of Dumitru Moldovanu, a young Moldavian who was stabbed during an argument with a Russian who had insulted the new flag of the Moldavian republic. His funeral service on November 15 turned into a mass demonstration that triggered a new round of ethnic violence. Gangs of Moldavian youths, sometimes numbering as many as 100–200, roamed the streets of Kishinev, attacking Russian speakers, breaking into cafés, and beating up people who did not speak Moldavian.

Amidst this ethnic tension the Moldavian Parliament resumed its session on November 12; however, the deputies from both the Dnestr and Gagauz regions boycotted. Petr Luchinski, chairman of the Parliamentary reconciliation commission, reported on the commission's work. As a result of talks with the Gagauz, a moratorium was declared on the creation of state structures in the Gagauz republic. In an attempt to diffuse the tension, the Moldavian Parliament on November 21 adopted in the first reading a clause guaranteeing the rights of ethnic groups residing in the republic.

Gorbachev sent Marshal Akhromeyev to the republic on November 22, 1990, with a proposal that the November 25 elections to the Dnestr Supreme Soviet be suspended in order to stabilize the situation. The elections were held none the less, and sixty people's deputies were elected to form a Dnestr Republic Parliament – twenty-five Russians, eighteen Ukrainians, twelve Moldavians, two Bulgarians, one Gagauz, and one Turkmen.[48] The Moldavian Parliament rejected the Dnestr elections,[49] but a new Dnestr parliament was formed which held its first session on November 29, electing Igor Smirnov chairman. After the Dnestr Parliament was formed, the area's politics continued in a pro-Kremlin, anti-Moldavian direction.

In January 1991, following the Soviet crackdown in Lithuania, the Dnestr deputies held a special congress in Tiraspol and condemned Lithuania's "nationalist and anti-Soviet forces" for having "deliberately provoked" the recent clash in Vilnius. The Moldavian parliament had condemned the Soviet use of force. The Dnestr republic also recognized Gorbachev's declaration on joint army-MVD patrols beginning on February 1, 1991, which had been opposed by the Moldavian parliament. And when the Moldavian republic introduced a coupon system on February 21, the Dnestr repealed it. The republic then declared that, effective April 1, 1991, all enterprises in the area would cease making contributions to the state budget, a sum that could amount to 250 million rubles per year.[50] Instead, the Dnestr Parliament proclaimed that the republic would have its own state bank.

Leaders of the Parliament in press interviews cited several reasons for the establishment of the republic. The primary reason was the language law – Dnestr residents, most of whom did not know Moldavian, viewed the law as a threat. Second were actions taken by the Popular Front in calling for renaming the republic the "Romanian Republic of Moldova." This provoked apprehensions that Moldavia would seek to unite with Romania. Some leaders explained the trans-Dnestr secession as "uncertainty about their future and the fear of waking up in another state in the morning."

The Dnestr situation is volatile, and the area's future uncertain. If Moldavia were to reunite with Romania, the Dnestr area would seek to remain inside Russian Ukraine. On October 22, 1991, the Dnestr Parliament appealed to Moscow to recognize it as a member of a renewed Soviet Union, but the demise of the USSR left the Dnestr appealing to a center that no longer existed.

Ukrainians

Many of Moldavia's Ukrainians live in the Dnestr area. According to the 1979 census, of the 5.5 million Ukrainians living outside the Ukrainian SSR, about 10 percent, 561,000, lived in Moldavia. The Ukrainians in Moldavia are a highly Russified group – 37 percent of them consider Russian their native language, and 80 percent speak it. Politically, the Ukrainians have lined up with the Russians, making common cause in the Dnestr area.

Moldavian Popular Front leaders held discussions with the Ukrainian Popular Movement (*Rukh*) leaders at which they agreed to initiate steps in both parliaments to provide native language instruction for Moldavians in Ukraine and Ukrainians in Moldavia and to continue consultations about the disputed territories.[51] The *Rukh* movement encourages Ukrainians in Moldavia to concentrate on the development of Ukrainian culture, schools, and clubs, rather than play the role of Russifiers.[52]

In an effort to win support from the Ukrainian population, Moldavian President Snegur issued a decree providing for state support for Ukrainian cultural life in Moldavia. The February 28, 1991, decree introduced Ukrainian language instruction in schools in the Ukrainian-speaking areas of the republic and initiated Ukrainian language television and radio broadcasts. In the past there were no Ukrainian schools in Moldavia; now they are beginning to open.

Gagauz

The Gagauz are an Orthodox Christian, Turkic-speaking ethnic minority of about 153,000. They live concentrated in a compact region of five districts in the south of the republic. According to the 1989 census, 197,000 Gagauz live in the territory of the former Soviet Union. In addition to the

Gagauz in Moldavia, another 27,000 live in Odessa Oblast – the contiguous part of Ukraine that was formerly part of Bessarabia – where they are mostly concentrated in the Bolgrad rayon. Additional small communities in the North Caucasus and in the Kazakh SSR date from 1908–14 when some of the Gagauz moved there in response to Stolypin's agrarian reform.

There are two main theories about the origins of the Gagauz. The more widely held view is that they are the descendants of Turkic tribes who adopted Orthodox Christianity after moving into eastern Bulgaria in the middle ages. The other theory is that they are Orthodox Bulgarians who became Turkified under the Ottomans, but retained their Christian faith.[53] Whatever their more distant origins, the Gagauz are generally believed to be the descendants of Christians who came to Moldavian territory from northeastern Bulgaria along with Bulgarians fleeing persecution under the Ottoman Empire during and after the Russo-Ottoman war of 1806–12.

The Gagauz Language

While Cyrillic script was introduced to the Moldavians of Bessarabia in 1944,[54] it was not introduced into the Gagauz language until 1957. Theoretically, the Gagauz alphabet was Latin script until then. However, since no books were printed, no newspapers appeared, and no teaching was conducted in Gagauz for the first fifteen years of Soviet rule from 1940–1941 and 1944–1957, it is a somewhat artificial question to debate in what script Gagauz would have been written.[55]

In 1957 the Presidium of the Supreme Soviet of Moldavia decreed that Gagauz be written in Cyrillic script. After a few years, the first books began to appear in cyrillicized Gagauz; first a dictionary in 1959, then poetry collections in 1959 and 1963, and then a collection of short stories in 1966. However, Gagauz did not go far as a literary language.

During this period the Gagauz people were becoming linguistically Russified; many Gagauz were already bilingual and relied on Russian for their literary needs, while others turned to materials in Turkish. The percentage of Gagauz in Moldavia that speak Russian rose from 65 percent in 1970 to more than 80 percent in 1989. With the majority of schools teaching in Russian, most Gagauz can read in Russian, although more than 90 percent of the population considers Gagauz to be their native language.

Thus the Moldavian language law affected the Gagauz directly. In the 1989 census, only 4.4 percent of Gagauz said that they spoke Moldavian. While in earlier years the Gagauz and Moldavians might have made common cause against the Russians, at this point the Gagauz were sufficiently Russified that they sided with the Russians against the Moldavians.

Although to a large extent politics in Moldavia is determined by ethnicity, it was not a foregone conclusion with whom the Gagauz would side. Originally it appeared that the Gagauz and Jews would side with the

Moldavians on the language law. A preliminary draft of the law enshrined Hebrew, Yiddish, and Gagauzi as official minority languages. Had the Moldavian movement been less nationalistic and more political, it might have better courted the ethnic minorities in a coalition of the republic's interests in its confrontation with the Kremlin.

The Gagauz movement for greater autonomy emerged cautiously with the beginnings of glasnost and at first focused primarily on language-related demands. The authorities made small language-related concessions; in 1986 the Gagauz literary weekly *Literatura si Arti* began carrying a cultural page in the Gagauz language, and monthly radio and television broadcasts in Gagauz began.

Although the Moldavian language law made provisions for the Gagauz community, the Gagauz began to mobilize against it, fearing the effects on their cultural and linguistic life. The final version of the language law as passed on August 31, 1989, contains a section providing for use of Gagauz in their compact areas. According to Section 1, Article 2: "In localities where a majority of the inhabitants of Gagauz nationality live, the language for official spheres of life is Gagauz or Russian." Thus many Moldavians concluded that the radicalization of the Gagauz was not really in response to outrage at the language law, but rather was the result of prompting from Moscow.

In any event, with the passing of the Gagauz language law, simmering Gagauz frustrations began to explode. This led to formation of the Gagauzi Movement, *Gagauzi Khalk*. The movement held its first extraordinary congress in Komrat on November 12, 1989. It adopted a resolution creating a Gagauz ASSR (Autonomous Soviet Socialist Republic) within Moldavia and proclaimed November 12 the day of Gagauz rebirth. The Moldavian Supreme Soviet dismissed the proclamation of the Gagauz ASSR as illegal and rejected the idea of autonomous areas on the republic's territory. Like the Moldavians, the Gagauz too proclaimed a new flag, and in Komrat, the national flag of the Gagauz ASSR flew over the city soviet.

After a delay, the Moldavian Parliament eventually took up a discussion of the Gagauz issue in August 1990. It annulled the decisions of the Gagauz congresses at its July 27 session, rejecting the idea of autonomous entities on the republic's territory. The Supreme Soviet also officially confirmed the ideas contained in a report from a Parliamentary commission considering issues of local self-management.[56] That report contained the official Moldavian version of the republic's history, and the history of the Gagauz, whom it declared "not indigenous" and therefore to be viewed as an "ethnic group", not a "nation." Excerpts of that report follow:

Historical documents irrefutably demonstrate that the Gagauz are not indigenous residents of Moldova. The homeland of the Gagauz is Bulgaria, where the nationality and statehood of the Gagauz formed during the 12th–17th centuries, and where a portion of the Gagauz ethnic community still lives today . . . The first Gagauz groups came to the territory of the State of Moldova, along with other trans-Danubian refugees (Bulgars and others) at the invitation of Russian tsarism during the Russo-Turkish War, 1806–1812. It must be emphasized that the Tsar of Russia made such a proposition not only to the Gagauz, since such "invitations" were a reliable mechanism of tsarist policy for creating a national and social base in alien annexed territories within the border zone of the Russian Empire . . . In 1818 these received the status of colonists. . . . According to international law and ethnographic science, if a segment of any people or nation emigrates to inhabit the territory of another people or nation, both the emigrants and their heirs comprise an ethnic group . . . The Gagauz as well as other ethnic groups residing in the Moldavian SSR within the national territory of Moldavians do not have their own national territories within the Moldavian SSR.

Outraged by the conclusions of this report, the Gagauz pushed their demands a step further. On August 19, 1990, a congress of Gagauz announced the secession of the Gagauz inhabited territory from the Moldavian SSR and the formation of a Gagauz republic. The declaration stated that the Gagauz intended to remain a part of the Soviet Union but to separate from Moldavia; the leaders announced their willingness to sign a Union treaty and set the date for elections to the Gagauz Parliament for October 28, 1990.

The Moldavian response showed that republic leaders can be even less tolerant of the aspirations of their ethnic minorities than the Kremlin had been toward the republics. The day after the Gagauz secession declaration, an emergency sitting of the Moldavian Supreme Soviet presidium declared the act unconstitutional, "having no force in law," and annulled all decisions of the Gagauz congress, warning that any attempt to implement them would be viewed as opposition to the law.[57] The following day, August 22, the Moldavian government dissolved the Gagauz national movement, outlawing *Gagauzi Khalk* and repealing its October 1989 registration.[58]

Tension mounted as the date set for Gagauz elections approached. In October busloads of Moldavian "volunteers" traveled to the Gagauz region to stop it from installing its own government after the elections. In Komrat and other Gagauz cities, people dug trenches and created barriers out of bulldozers and trucks, and roads into the area were blocked by militia and cars. Soviet troops were moved in,[59] as busloads of volunteers from the trans-Dnestr who wanted to help the Gagauz also arrived. Large groups were blocked at the border to the Gagauz region by militia troops sent to the area.

Moldavian President Snegur urged the Gagauz to call off the elections, but instead the Gagauz began early balloting. A state of emergency was declared on October 26; public meetings were banned for a two-month period. On October 29, 1990, a compromise was reached; the leaders of the Gagauz movement and representatives of the Moldavian leadership agreed to declare a moratorium on both the Gagauz elections and the Moldavian Supreme Soviet's decision to reject the Gagauz request for autonomy.

By March 1991 a split was apparent in the Gagauz movement. A competition had emerged between Stepan Topal, chairman of the Supreme Soviet of the Gagauz republic, and his political opponent, Leonid Dobrov. The split represented a polarization between forces opposed to any compromise with the Moldavians and those supporting Dobrov's position in favor of a settlement. In May 1991 Dobrov, together with Konstantin Taushanzhi, submitted a plan to the Moldovan Supreme Soviet calling for autonomy and a free economic zone for the Gagauz, but affirming the indivisibility of Moldova.[60]

The conflict between the Moldavians and the Gagauz came to a head when, on August 23, 1991, Moldovan Ministry of the Interior forces arrested the leaders of the Gagauz "Republic," Stepan Topol and Mihail Kenderelian, charging that they had supported the attempted coup against Gorbachev. Moldovan Interior Minister Ion Costas accused the Gagauz leaders of sending a telegram of congratulations to the Committee for the State of Emergency upon their proclamation of taking power.

The Gagauz then met in a national Congress in Komrat, and declared their own independence. Delegates to the Congress issued an appeal on September 2, 1991, to the leadership of Moldova, demanding the release of their leaders and proposing the creation of a confederation of three republics: Moldova, the Gagauz and the Dnestr republics. The Congress formed a commission, headed by Georgiy Kalchu, which was authorized to hold talks with the Moldovan government.

Jews: a vanishing community

Jews currently form about 1.5 percent of Moldavia's population, but in 1897 Jews formed almost 12 percent of the population of Bessarabia. They would be more numerous in Moldavia today, at least an estimated 10–15 percent, if so many had not been killed during World War II. In addition, Bessarabia has lost significant portions of its Jewish population to several waves of emigration. And because of looser exit requirements since perestroika, a steady stream of departures has taken a further toll on this shrinking community.

Jewish communities in Southern Bessarabia date back to the sixteenth century. After the Russian annexation in 1812, Bessarabia was included in the "Pale of Settlement" and many Jews settled there from other parts of the Pale. The number of Jews in Kishinev grew rapidly; from 10,509, or 12.2 percent of the population, in 1847, to 50,237, or 46 percent of the city's population in 1897.[61] At that point the majority of Jewish children attended traditional *cheder* schools that taught religious subjects and although most could read Hebrew Bibles, the 1897 census showed that only 27.8 percent of Jews over age ten could read Russian.[62]

The problems of the Jews in Bessarabia became known worldwide as the result of the Kishinev pogroms. The first of these took place during Easter weekend, April 6–7, 1903; both Russians and Moldavians participated in the violence. Agents of the Ministry of the Interior and Russian officials of the Bessarabian administration were apparently involved in its preparation; the local police chief had authored some of the most virulently anti-Semitic articles to appear in the local paper. According to official statistics, forty-nine Jews were killed, more than 500 wounded, 700 homes looted and destroyed, and 600 businesses and shops looted. Material losses amounted to 2,500,000 gold rubles, and about 2,000 families were left homeless.[63]

Many Jews decided to flee as a result of the pogroms. From 1902 to 1905, the Jewish population in Kishinev dropped from around 60,000 to 53,243 as thousands emigrated to the United States. The second Kishinev pogrom took place on October 19–20, 1905. It began as a protest against the Tsar's declaration of August 19, 1905, but deteriorated into an attack on the Jewish quarter. A wave of pogroms swept Bessarabia; three towns and sixty-eight other localities were affected; 108 Jews were killed.[64]

When the Soviets annexed Bessarabia in June 1940, it had a Jewish population of about 300,000.[65] During the following year of Russian domination, all Jewish institutions were closed down and the Zionist movement outlawed. In March 1941 many activists of the various Jewish movements were arrested and exiled to Siberia.[66]

During the war period from 1941–1944, the interests of the Jewish community were very different from that of the Moldavian majority. When Hitler attacked the Soviet Union, the Romanians agreed to join. On June 22, 1941, German and Romanian troops crossed the border, and within a few weeks Bessarabia was restored to Romania. For the Moldavians, the Romanian move was a liberation that pried them loose from Soviet domination. But while Soviet control had been difficult for the Jews, rule by Romania – an Axis ally aligned with Hitler – meant a harsher fate. Deportations of the Jews from Bessarabia began immediately. They were uprooted from their villages and driven hundreds of miles eastwards in conditions of hardship and violence.

On July 17, 1941, German and Romanian forces occupied Kishinev together with units of Einsatzgruppe D, the mobile killing units which were responsible for northern Bukovina and Bessarabia. In a single week five thousand of Kishinev's Jews were murdered.[67] The first major ghetto was set up in Kishinev on August 4, 1941; another was formed three days later at Tighina. By the time the concentration of Jews into a ghetto was completed, about 10,000 had been slaughtered.

On September 3 a killing "action" took place in Dubossary. About 600 elderly Jews were removed from their houses and driven into Dubossary's eight synagogues, which the Germans surrounded and set on fire. All died an agonizing death.[68] Two mass graves in Dubossary were subsequently found to contain the bodies of 10,500 Jews from Dubossary and the vicinity.[69] This type of "action" took place in other towns as well.

In September most of the Jews of Bessarabia and Bukovina were evacuated to Transnistria; in the course of two months almost 120,000 were transported in cattle trucks to a site close to the Dnestr, and from there they were force-marched in convoys to the other side of the river.[70] Many perished en route.

By 1942 about 185,000 Jews were in the Transnistria area,[71] concentrated in camps. Conditions were abysmal. There was no food distribution and, according to survivors, the inmates of Pecsara camp had no clothes, having sold them all for food; in several camps the Jews were eating grass.[72] When the Soviets reoccupied Bessarabia in 1944, only a few were still alive.

Recent ethnic tensions between Moldavians and Russians leave the Jewish community in a quandary. The Moldavians tend to see the Jews as "Russian-speakers," while the traditional Russian anti-Semitism that permeates the area leaves the community shut out from both sides. Many Jews fear that as hostility between Moldavians and Russians intensifies, they will be cast as the eventual scapegoats. The republic's history of pogroms and holocaust has left a scar that is deeply ingrained in the historical memory of Moldavia's Jewish community. As a result, many see emigration as the best solution.

Glasnost has loosened the requirements for emigration, and a substantial number are leaving. Comparing the census figures for 1979 and 1989, one sees a drop in Jewish population from 80,000 in 1979 to 65,700 in 1989, due largely to the ongoing flow of emigration. According to a statistical report published by the Moldovan visa department, 15,230 Jews emigrated in 1990, and the departure rate rose to 10,640 during the first six months of 1991. Thousands more have applied for exit visas but are held back by long waits for exit permission from UVIR.[73] In the last two years more than 30,000 Moldavian Jews, almost half the republic's remaining Jewish population, have either applied to emigrate or already left.[74]

At the same time that glasnost has permitted more emigration, it has also allowed the Jewish community greater freedom to organize, and thus Moldavia's Jewish community is also experiencing a cultural revival. Groups such as the "Hebrew Culture Society" and the Jewish coop *Menorah* have been able to register officially and function openly. There is some revival of interest in attending synagogue, although greater numbers are turning to Jewish cultural events than religious events.

However, now that there is greater freedom of religion, a small group is reclaiming their religious roots, and traditional observance can be found again in Kishinev; a Hassidic rabbi and follower of the Lubavicher Rebbe, Reb Zalman Leib, was recently named Chief Rabbi of Kishinev and Moldavia. Originally from Kishinev, he had emigrated to Israel after World War

II, but he returned to Moldavia a year ago to work at the local synagogue. He has since set up a religious school (*yeshiva*) with a small group of students, as well as classes for women and a children's choir.[75] A *shochet* (ritual butcher) is available to provide kosher meat for the community, and a young apprentice is being trained. While synagogue attendance is growing, the years of Soviet atheism so damaged Jewish religious consciousness that traditional religious observance still attracts few people.

Bulgarians

Bulgarians live in compact communities in southern districts of Moldavia and in Ukraine. According to the 1989 census, of the 378,790 Bulgarians living in the USSR, 23 percent (87,779) are found in the southern Bessarabian districts of the Moldavian SSR. A far larger number, 62 percent (232,784), live in the adjacent areas of Ukraine, which were annexed by the Soviet Union in June 1940.

Bulgarian sources, however, give a much higher figure for the number of Bulgarians living in the Soviet Union. In a recent interview Aleksandur Milanov, spokesman for the Bessarabian Society and Chairman of the Bulgarian Translators' Union in Sofia, argued that many Bessarabian Bulgarians are registered as other nationalities – the majority are probably sufficiently assimilated to list themselves as Russians. At a 1988 symposium on national minorities held in Budapest, a figure of 2.2 million Bulgarians in the Soviet Union was circulated, with about 600,000 Bessarabian Bulgarians living in Ukraine and Moldavia.

Like the Gagauz, the Bulgarians arrived in Moldavia in the eighteenth and early nineteenth centuries. After the Russian annexation of Bessarabia in 1812, numerous Gagauz and Bulgarians took refuge from the Turks and settled there. The Bulgarian population in Moldavia was 61,652 according to the 1959 census, 73,776 in 1970, 80,665 in 1979, and 87,779 in 1989. The population figures appear to reflect primarily natural population growth and a higher-than-average birth rate, rather than in-migration, although there was some migration from the Bessarabian districts in Ukraine into Moldavia.[76]

Slower to be politicized than the other ethnic groups in Moldavia, the Bulgarians have now begun forming a national movement, and like the Gagauz and the Russians and Ukrainians of the Dnestr, they too may end up declaring autonomy.

The Bulgarians are troubled by Moldavian nationalism and the language law. About a hundred Bulgarian students were suspended from the university in Kishinev because they failed the Moldavian language exam.[77] Their nationalist organization, "The Saints Cyril and Methodius Voluntary Society to Promote the Development of Soviet Bulgarian Culture," was formed in Bolgrad soon after perestroika began;[78] its focus has been on the language problem. Use of Bulgarian has declined, and it is not taught in schools. In an attempt to improve the situation, optional Bulgarian language lessons were introduced in thirteen schools in Bolgrad district.

Soviet Bulgarians held their first congress in May 1991 in Bolgrad (Ukraine) and formed the "Association of Bulgarians in the Soviet Union." According to Soviet press reports, the association intends to work for the revival and promotion of Bulgarian culture and intends to establish a program for the opening of Bulgarian schools.

The Bulgarian community is highly Russified; according to the 1989 census more than 80 percent speak Russian. Although 79 percent of Moldavia's Bulgarians claimed Bulgarian as their first language, and only 18 percent claimed Russian as their first language, more than 62 percent said they speak Russian as a second language. Moldavian national television does broadcast some programs in Bulgarian.

For many years there was little contact between the Bulgarians of Moldavia and those in Bulgaria. Now, a small party in Bulgaria, the Fatherland Party of Labor (FPL; its leaders claim 4,600 registered members) has taken up the banner of Moldavia's Bulgarians. They are making arrangements to bring 550 Moldavian Bulgarian families to Bulgaria as temporary residents, to be settled in the region of Khaskovo in southeast Bulgaria.[79]

Facing an uncertain future

Moldavian politics is held together by a fragile balance of forces, with segments of the population bent on independence, and the republic's leadership trying to handle two secessionist regions. Ethnic politics has erupted into violence several times, and tension is further heightened by the lines of secessionist antagonism that have been drawn. The republic is facing fragmentation and the possibility of territorial realignment as it confronts a future outside the Soviet Union.

The Romanian unification issue will remain controversial, and a strong possibility exists of eventual reunification with Romania. While the leaderships on both sides of the Prut have been hesitant about supporting this step, popular movements will likely escalate their agitation until reunification takes place. That, in turn, would produce the ethnic backlash whose origins have been explored in this chapter.

Notes

The views expressed in this chapter are those of the author and do not necessarily reflect US government policy or the official position of the US Department of State.

1 The republic parliament on June 5, 1990, amended the constitution to change the republic's name from "Moldavian Soviet Socialist Republic" to "Soviet Socialist Republic of Moldova," modifying the pronounciation to reflect its name in Romanian. A further amendment on May 23, 1991, changed the

republic's name to "Republic of Moldova." This chapter will use the name "Moldova" to refer to republic events taking place after the declaration, but, will use "Moldavia" when referring to historical events. To avoid confusion, this chapter will continue to use the traditionally accepted designation in English, "Moldavian," when referring to the people or the language.

2 The autonomous republic (ASSR) of Tuva had historically been united with Mongolia, though it was the independent state of Tannu-Tuva at the time of its incorporation into the Union in 1944.

3 Moldavia's 4.3 million people live in an area of only 13,000 square miles, giving the republic the highest population density in the Union: more than 300 persons per square mile.

4 Moscow Interfax; October 28, 1991; 2138 GMT; as monitored by FBIS.

5 *Izvestia*; October 30, 1991, p. 1, as translated by FBIS.

6 Interview with author, February 25, 1990; Kishinev.

7 Moldavian First Secretary addresses news conference; Moscow Tass in English, July 9, 1990, as monitored by FBIS.

8 Telegraphic Agency of the Soviet Union in Russia 1518 GMT, January 11, 1991; translated by BBC Summary of World Broadcasts, January 30, 1991. SU/0983/B.

9 Reported by Moscow TASS in English, April 1991, 1536 GMT and 1936 GMT, monitored by FBIS.

10 Moscow TASS in English, October 30, 1991, 1338 GMT refers to Foreign Minister Tiu interview with newspaper *Sfatul Tarii*.

11 "Moldavia establishes contacts with Israeli Businessmen," *Izvestiya*, August 2, 1990, p. 2; translation in FBIS-SOV-90-153, August 8, 1990, p. 83.

12 "Moldavia to Conclude Trade Agreements with Hungary, Czechoslovakia," RFE/RL Daily Report, no. 26, February 6, 1991, p. 7.

13 From the Vremya newscast, July 12, 1990, 1700 GMT; translated in FBIS-SOV-90-135, July 13, 1990; "Moldavia Begins Forming Foreign Trade Ties," p. 83.

14 TASS Interview Moldavian Foreign Minister, Moscow TASS in English, 1243 GMT, September 24, 1990.

15 Interview with *Romania Libera*, reported by Bucharest Rompres in English, October 31, 1991, 1223 GMT; as monitored by FBIS.

16 Reuters, November 27, 1990.

17 Interview with the Munich-based *Süddeutsche Zeitung*, November 2, 1990 issue.

18 Reported by TASS in English, November 1, 1990, 1515 GMT, referring to an interview on Austrian television telecast October 31, 1990.

19 Reported in *Romania Libera* in Romanian, September 25, 1991, p. 1.

20 Reported in *Adevarul* in Romanian, September 28, 1991, p. 6.

21 *Flacara*, November 4–10, 1990, p. 15.

22 Bucharest Rompres in English, 1344 GMT, November 29, 1990, as monitored by FBIS.

23 *Ibid.*

24 FBIS, Moscow Domestic Service, May 8, 1990.

25 API press release, June 24, 1990.

26 *Adevarul*, in Romanian, September 5, 1990, p. 3.

27 Moscow domestic service in Russian, 2100 GMT, October 13, 1990, as monitored by FBIS.

28 Bucharest Rompres in English, 1344 GMT, November 1, 1990, as monitored by FBIS.
29 Statements by Moldovan Deputy Prime Minister Constantin Tampize in an interview with the Romanian daily *Dimineata*, reported by Bucharest Rompres, October 18, 1991.
30 Moscow World Service in English, January 11, 1991, 2200 GMT, as monitored by FBIS.
31 *Izvestia*, July 3, 1990, p. 2, translated in FBIS, reports on the Popular Front of Moldavia's Congress, which passed a resolution calling for the annulment of the August 2, 1940, decision.
32 *Adevarul* in Romanian, September 19, 1991, p. 8.
33 Nicolas Dima, *Bessarabia and Bukovina: The Soviet-Romanian Territorial Dispute* (East European Monographs: Boulder; distributed by Columbia University Press, New York, 1982), p. 96.
34 *Moldavian Soviet Socialist Republic* (Moscow: Novosti Press Agency Publishing House, 1972), p. 20.
35 Lenin's Memorandum on the National Question, dictated from his bed on December 31, 1922, originally published in *Sotsialisticheskii vestnik*, December 1923, pp. 13–15, translation based on the version in the fourth edition of Lenin's *Works*; V.I. Lenin, *Sochineniia* (Moscow, 1957), XXXIII, pp. 553–559, reprinted in Richard Pipes, *The Formation of the Soviet Union: Communism and Nationalism 1917–23* (Cambridge: Harvard University Press, 1964), pp. 282–287.
36 Vadim Medish, *The Soviet Union* (New York: Prentice Hall, 1990), p. 57.
37 Dima, *Bessarabia and Bukovina*, cites Brian D. Silver, "Methods of Deriving Data on Bilingualism from the 1970 Soviet Census," *Soviet Studies*, vol. XXVII, no. 4 (October 1975).
38 Except where otherwise indicated, information in this section was pieced together from daily news reports from the local newspapers, and from numerous translations in FBIS; these news items are not individually noted.
39 Bondarchuk's statement was reported by the writer Gheorghe Malarciuc in *Literatura si arta*, June 16, 1988, p. 3, and cited by Vladimir Socor in RFE/RL March 24, 1989, "Soviet Moldavia: A Breakthrough on the Alphabet Issue?"
40 See Jonathan Eyal, "Soviet Moldavia: History Catches Up and a Separate Language Disappears," RFE/RL Report on the USSR, February 24, 1989, pp. 25–29, for a more complete discussion of the politics surrounding the party theses.
41 Interview with Yuri Roshka, Popular Front Leader, Kishinev, February 24, 1990.
42 Moscow Television News Service program, August 23, 1990, 1200 GMT, translated in FBIS-SOV-90-156, "Moldova Presidium Announces Place Name Changes," August 23, 1990, p. 97.
43 Supreme Soviet decree of July 27, 1990 published in *Sovetskaya Moldavia*, August 1, 1990, translated in GBIS-SOV-90-159, August 16, 1990, "Moldavia Restores, Alters Former Settlement Names," p. 82.
44 Text of Supreme Soviet law passed June 5, 1990, published in *Sovetskaya Moldavia* on June 10, 1990, translated in FBIS-SOV-90-143, "Amendments to Moldavian Constitution Published," July 25, 1990, p. 107.
45 TASS in English, December 25, 1990, 1744 GMT, reprinted in FBIS.

46 Interview with author, Kishinev, February 1990.
47 Moscow TASS in English, 1715 GMT, November 2, 1990, reprinted in FBIS.
48 Moscow TASS in English, 1152 GMT, November 27, 1990, reprinted in FBIS.
49 Text of the November 27 "Decree of the Moldova SSR Supreme Soviet on the Invalidation of the Elections to the So-Called Dnestr Moldavian Soviet Socialist Republic" was published in *Sovetskaya Moldova* on November 28, 1990, and reprinted in FBIS-SOV-91-018-S, January 28, 1991.
50 Preliminary calculations published by *Krasnaya Zvezda*, April 4, 1991, p. 3; translated in FBIS-SOV-91-066, April 5, 1991.
51 RFE/RL Daily Report no. 197, October 16, 1990, p. 5: "Moldavian and Ukrainian Movements Confer."
52 Interview with *Rukh* chairman, Ivan Drach; Kiev Domestic Service in Ukrainian, 12 November 1990; FBIS, plus information from author's discussions with Rukh leader, Mikhail Horyn.
53 "Cultural Concessions but No Autonomy for Gagauz," Radio Liberty Research, RL 456/87, by Ann Sheehy, November 12, 1987.
54 In the Moldavian ASSR – a small area with few Moldavians which roughly corresponded to the trans-Dnestr and was then part of the Ukraine – Cyrillic was introduced earlier.
55 A discussion of Gagauz script appears in Michael Bruchis, *Nations-Nationalities-People: A Study of the Nationalities Policy of the Communist Party in Soviet Moldavia* (East European Monographs: Boulder; distributed by Columbia University Press, New York, 1984), pp. 8–10.
56 The full text of the Moldavian Supreme Soviet Decree as well as the Commission reports were published in *Sovetskaya Moldavia*, August 5, 1990, pp. 3–4, and translated by FBIS in SPRS-UPA-90-051; September 5, 1990, "Decree on Gagauz Autonomy" and "Commission Report on Gagauz Autonomy," pp. 26–29.
57 Text of the Supreme Soviet decree published in *Sovetskaya Moldova*, August 22, 1990, pp. 1, 3, translated in FBIS-SOV-90-181, "Moldavia Issues Decrees Against Gagauz Movement," September 18, 1990, p. 65.
58 Full text of the August 22 decree was published in *Sovetskaya Moldova*, August 23, 1990, p. 1, and translated in FBIS-SOV-90-181, September 18, 1990, "Calls for Movement's Disbandment," p. 67.
59 It appears that both army and MVD troops were used, despite the denial by Commander of the Interior Ministry troops in the area, Colonel Shatalin, that there were army units in Komrat; in an interview with a TASS correspondent Shatalin said there were only MVD troops to whom the Armed Forces had given some of their automatic weapons and armored equipment. Broadcast Moscow Domestic Service, 1400 GMT, October 29, 1990, as translated by FBIS-SOV-90-209, "Shatalin Denies Units in Komrat," October 29, 1990, p. 94.
60 Interview with Leonid Dobrov in *Nesavisimaya Gazeta*, June 20, 1991, p. 3; as translated is FBIS-USR-91-015, July 19, 1991, "Dissent in Gagauz Movement Observed," p. 56.
61 "Kishinev," *Jewish Encyclopedia*, p. 1,064.
62 "Bessarabia," *Jewish Encyclopedia*, p. 706.
63 "Kishinev," *Jewish Encyclopedia*, p. 1,066.
64 "Bessarabia," *Jewish Encyclopedia*, p. 706.

65 Raul Hilberg, *The Destruction of the European Jews*, New York: Holmer and Meier, 1985, p. 486, calculates that the 1930 census figure was 307,340, including 92,492 in Bukovina and 204, 858 in Bessarabia. From 1930 to 1940 the population probably increased to about 330,000. However, Southern Bukovina was not transferred to the Soviets, hence the 1940 total for the transferred provinces of Bessarabia and North Bukovina must have been about 300,000.

66 "Kishinev," *Jewish Encyclopedia*, p. 1,067, based on the 1897 census.

67 Martin Gilbert, *The Holocaust, A History of the Jews of Europe during the Second World War*, New York: Holt Rinehart and Winston, 1986, p. 172.

68 *Ibid.*, p. 188.

69 "Transnistria," *Jewish Encyclopedia*, p. 1,330.

70 Leni Yahil, *The Holocaust: The Fate of European Jewry, 1932–1945*, New York: Oxford University Press, 1990, p. 345.

71 Nora Levin, *The Holocaust: The Destruction of European Jewry, 1933–1945*, New York: Schocken Books, 1973, p. 576.

72 Eugene Levai, "Martyrdom"; quoted by Raul Hilberg, "The Destruction of the European Jews," *op. cit.*, pp. 495–496.

73 As of February 1990, UVIR in Kishinev was processing only twenty people a week, while thousands were on line, according to information from one local informant who had applied for an exit visa, but was still waiting for an appointment with UVIR.

74 "Ethnic Enmity Governs a New Soviet Republic," *New York Times*, October 7, 1990, p. A8, quotes Aleksandr Brodsky, chairman of the Jewish Cultural Association

75 "Izbran Glavnii Rabbin"; *Molodoj Moldavii*; February 25, 1991, p. 2.

76 Dima, *Bessarabia and Bukovina: The Soviet-Romanian Territorial Dispute*, pp. 81–82.

77 Sofia Faks in Bulgarian, May 17, 1991, p. 4, translated by FBIS.

78 Moscow Tass in English, 1640 GMT, June 24, 1990, FBIS.

79 Sofia BTA in English, 1747 GMT, January 15, 1991; as published by FBIS-EEU-91-011, January 16, 1991, "Fatherland Party Helps Bessarabian Bulgarians," p. 10.

PART IV

The Baltics

7 Lithuania: nationalism in the modern era

RICHARD KRICKUS

Introduction

Lithuanian nationalism has its roots in a deep and abiding commitment to the Lithuanian language, culture, and territory, to the Roman Catholic Church, and to a shared history seared by centuries of oppression. These communal bonds have produced a Lithuanian identity which has been variable over the centuries, depending upon time and circumstance. But the disparate economic and political factors that have shaped it are secondary, not primary, in understanding the Lithuanian national revival as it has developed since the early nineteenth century.

This ascriptive thesis clashes with Marxist-Leninist and liberal social theory; both of these theories claim that ethnic self-awareness is derivative of economic circumstances. It also is at odds with explanations of Lithuanian nationalism that stress the overriding influence of Soviet policies and institutions.

Ethno-nationalism and social theory

In their treatment of nationalism, both Marxist and liberal social theorists posit that ethnic values and affiliations will expire in the crucible of modern society. The Marxist interpretation of nationalism, Walker Connor argues, has taken many different forms, but it rests on the assumption that in a socialist commonwealth, "parochial," "nationalistic" impulses will be superseded by universalistic norms.[1] Mainstream Western social theory see much the same thing happening, and here, too, economics is deemed pivotal – that is, in the crucible of the market place, "economic man" will replace "ethnic man."[2]

Note that in both cases there is a normative component to this assessment; that is, insofar as ethno-nationalism persists in the modern world, it is "bad." From the classical Marxist perspective, it is false consciousness since it prevents workers from gaining a true proletarian consciousness. In the Western case, it is pernicious because it is seen as the basis for intergroup conflict and bloody wars between nations.

157

Map 7.1 The Baltics

Given the worldwide influence of both intellectual traditions, even seemingly benign interpretations of nationalism are fraught with negative connotations. Nationalism often is described as being "pre-modern" and a remnant of "traditional society"; that is, as the source of social upheaval in the modern world.[3] Even with current reassessments, it remains common practice for political writers and policy makers to use the word "nationalism" in a pejorative fashion.

Lithuanian nationalism and the Soviet setting

Those who claim Lithuanian nationalism is the product of policies and institutions unique to the Soviet Union have proffered a number of disparate explanations.

1. Mikhail Gorbachev asserted that economic stagnation was the basis for nationalism in Lithuania and would expire as the Soviet Union resolved the problems for which Brezhnev's calamitous economic policies were responsible.
2. Russian chauvinism, which Lenin warned his colleagues about before and after the Bolshevik Revolution, was a second explanation commonly cited. Ethnic equality was the solution to it.
3. Widespread discontent associated with authoritarian rule was a third explanation and democracy the appropriate prescription.

Phillip G. Roeder, however, holds that expressions of nationalism in the former USSR generally are confined to two approaches. The first is the "primordialist paradigm" that "sees ethnic identities as one of the givens of social existence, shaped by historic memory, language, religion, and geographic compactness."[4] The second, "instrumentalist," paradigm "sees ethnic identities as contingent and changing self-ascribed roles. The politicization of ethnicity and protest are goal-oriented behaviors – often focused on pursuit of socioeconomic gain."[5]

From this last perspective, ethnic mobilization is just another asset that a group employs to improve its political and economic place in society. Instrumentally oriented elites manipulate primordial impulses to achieve pragmatic outcomes, political privileges, economic advancement and the like. This analysis of ethnic mobilization has been influenced by American political science with its emphasis on interest group behavior.[6]

"The prevailing paradigm in Sovietology," Roeder contends, "has been primordialist." But, "[t]here is little evidence to suggest that it is the relative strength of their primordial sentiments" that accounts for high levels of political protest on the part of some nationalities in the USSR. He concedes that "the paradigm might be 'saved' by claiming that assertiveness of ethnic leaders in the Baltic . . . is evidence of the relative levels of ethnic awareness in these lands." But "the concept of relative levels of national consciousness is not a predictor of politicized ethnicity or part of a causal relationship; it is, rather, a description or definition."⁷ In other words, explanations using the primordial paradigm are irrelevant or, at best, of secondary importance.

Writing before the breakup of the USSR, Roeder perceives limits to the instrumentalist paradigm also. It does not "explain the willingness of some counterelites such as [Lithuanian leader, Vytautas] Landsbergis to sacrifice socioeconomic benefits for symbolic issues of self-expression."⁸ Phenomena which neither paradigm explains can best be illuminated by an assessment of Soviet federalism. In this connection, the Soviet strategy to control and neutralize ethnopolitics has been three-fold:

(1) creating within each ethnic homeland an indigenous cadre assigned a monopoly over the mobilizational resources of the community, (2) constraining the behavior of this new ethnic cadre by creating an incentive structure that deterred the expression of unsanctioned, particularly primordial ethnic agendas, and (3) assigning the cadre the responsibility for creating an ethnically distinct stratification system within official institutions and for impeding the emergence of alternative ethnic entrepreneurs outside these institutions.⁹

Roeder concludes that in practice, however, the Soviet strategy, which rests on "socialist federalism" and "indigenization," backfired. Non-Russian party cadre exploited Soviet federalism to achieve rewards at the center's expense. None the less, federalism provides the key to understanding nationalism in the USSR because it is through Soviet institutions and policies that latent nationalistic impulses became manifest.

Lithuanian nationalism before the Soviet era

Developments leading up to the Lithuanian restoration of sovereignty and events since then suggest that powerful and enduring ascriptive phenomena, language, culture, history, and religious life are the primary bases of Lithuanian nationalism. As Harold Isaacs has written, an ethnic group's language, culture, and shared historical experiences (the components of what he calls "basic group identity") are vital to the psychic and social well-being of its members. An individual's identity, personality, and value system are shaped by group affinities, religious beliefs, and other phenomena that sociologists on both sides of the old Iron Curtain have deemed "premodern."¹⁰

Encounters with (Soviet) Russia over the past fifty years have profoundly shaped expressions of Lithuanian nationalism, but deep and abiding emotional attachments predating the Bolshevik Revolution are of first, rather than second, order importance. The Lithuanian national revival from the early nineteenth century to World War II, activities of dissenters during the Soviet era, the appearance of Sajudis, the efforts to restore Lithuanian sovereignty, and the responses to the abortive January

13, 1991 coup, all support the existence of a single powerful common bond
– a shared national identity.

Aside from the persistence of a powerful ethnic common bond, recent
developments in Lithuania indicate that nationalism there cannot be dis-
connected from a quest for democracy, for political pluralism as it is
manifested in Western liberalism. An effort to explore the relationship
between the two, however, is beyond the scope of this study and must be
addressed at another time.

The roots of Lithuanian nationalism in the modern era: 1800–1940

Language and culture

The Lithuanian national revival began early in the nineteenth century at
a time when the Romantic celebration of language and folk culture was
spreading throughout Europe. By this point, the Lithuanian gentry, intelligentsia, and clergy had become Polonized, reflecting a close association
with the larger Polish state since the fourteenth century. The intimate
relationship between Polish and Lithuanian culture was not, however,
altogether one-sided. The words of Adam Mickiewicz, Poland's nineteenth-century national poet, are illustrative: "Litwo! Ojczyzno moja!"
(Lithuania! My Fatherland!).[11] More recently, two contemporary Poles, the
Noble poet laureate Czeslaw Milosz and Pope John II have expressed
similar sentiments, underscoring deepseated, positive feelings toward Lithuania among many contemporary Poles.

In 1795, the Polish-Lithuanian political association ended with the third
partition of the Polish-Lithuanian Commonwealth. Although living mainly
under Russian rule (a small part of Lithuania went to Prussia), the Lithuanians did not break free of Polish cultural influences, and there was a
danger that the Lithuanian language would eventually disappear altogether. But early in the nineteenth century, Lithuanian gentry, influenced
by German linguists, began to study their mother tongue and Lithuanian
history and culture. Later, Russian philologists would become mentors to a
new generation of Lithuanians seeking to resurrect their ancient culture.
What attracted foreigners to the Lithuanian cause was the uniqueness of
the Lithuanian language and the belief that this ancient tongue faced
extinction.[12]

After the January insurrection of 1863, Russian authorities sought to
reduce Polish cultural influence over the Lithuanians. Provisions were
made for them to study in Russian universities. Jonas Basanavicius, one of
the founding fathers of the Lithuanian revival and the publisher of *Ausra*
("Dawn"), the first Lithuanian newspaper, would be lured to the University
of Moscow with a scholarship.[13]

But the Tsarist Russification campaign was heavy-handed. Among other things, the Russians banned Lithuanian materials published in Latin script and dictated that Cyrillic script be used instead. Latinized Lithuanian publications were smuggled by Lithuanian nationalists into areas dominated by the Russians (Lithuania Major) from East Prussia (Lithuania Minor). Among their number was the grandfather of Lithuania's future president, Vytautas Landsbergis. Gradually, the leaders of the Lithuanian cultural revival realized that the cause was doomed without a political agenda. Here again, a common language played an important part in the political mobilization of the Lithuanian people.

Throughout the Lithuanians' history, their language has been both a curse and a blessing to them. By denying them easy access to intellectual achievements, such as the promulgation of political and economic liberalism, occurring elsewhere in Europe, it was a curse. Yet, it was also a blessing because it sustained a profound sense of national identity and solidarity even in the face of German, Polish, and Russian political and cultural hegemony.

By the second half of the nineteenth century, Lithuanian had fallen into disuse among the educated elements of society who used Russian or Polish as their preferred tongue. In the last quarter of the nineteenth century, it was from the common folk that a new wave of intellectuals, often the first in their families to attend a university, began to appear. They would provide the leadership needed to mobilize the peasants who had been the repositors of Lithuanian national life for centuries.

Roman Catholicism

Embracing Catholicism in the fourteenth century, the Lithuanians were the last people of Europe to become Christians. Afterwards, they earned a reputation for their devoutness, but by the time of the national revivals much of the clergy had become Polonized. While the peasants spoke Lithuanian at home and their children used Russian in school, all Catholics attended mass where Polish was the primary language. Given the "Polish caste" of the Church, many secular nationalists, like Jonas Sliupis, saw the Church as a barrier to the national revival.[14]

In 1908, however, devout Catholics established the *Ateitis* ("Futurist") Movement. Its members embraced an ideology that merged Catholicism with nationalism. Comprised of students, clergy, and former priests, the movement secured a devoted following in Lithuania after independence. *Ateitis* was later outlawed in Lithuania as the country fell to authoritarian rule between the two world wars, but it was resurrected in North America where the association between Catholicism and Lithuanian nationalism became firmly fixed.

Mass and religious instruction were conducted in Lithuanian, and, through Church-affiliated social and cultural associations Lithuanian-Catholic youngsters learned about their national history and culture. As immigrants in a foreign land, the secular/religious schism that divided their relatives in the old country was a luxury the Lithuanian-American community could ill afford. Moreover, those Lithuanians who resided outside of homogeneous Lithuanian neighborhoods saw the Catholic Church as a positive affiliation, conferring status upon poorly educated, working people with low self-esteem. Along with organized labor and urban political machines, the Church was a vital part of the trinity of Catholic, white ethnic power for much of the twentieth century. But that trinity eventually attenuated the impact of nationalism among the first wave of Lithuanian immigrants.[15]

The diaspora

After the 1863 insurrection, Lithuanians left their homeland in search of new economic opportunities abroad. Most of them emigrated to the United States with an estimated 508,000 emigrating between 1867 and 1914. Among an additional 200,000 to 300,000 migrants, who identified themselves as Poles or Russians, a large number were conceivably ethnic Lithuanians.[16] Chicago became a magnet for Lithuanian immigrants and, by the turn of the century, about 100,000 Lithuanians resided there, making it the largest Lithuanian city in the world.

The American-Lithuanians would play a significant role in the Lithuanian revival. The United States was a refuge for many nationalist leaders who were hounded under the Russian Empire, and they continued their work in the New World until the collapse of the Romanov dynasty and the emergence of an independent Lithuania in 1918. With American funds gleaned from the slim earnings of working people, the Lithuanian language and culture were sustained in the diaspora. Books and other publications in Lithuanian were published in the US and transported back home.

In 1905, American representatives attended the Grand Vilnius Congress (*Seimas*) which attracted 2,000 Lithuanians from all corners of the globe. It passed resolutions supporting the Lithuanian language and culture and called for an independent Lithuanian state. In 1915, Lithuanian-Americans would establish an information center in Geneva and lobbied the allies for Lithuanian national self-determination. After Lithuania achieved independence, Americans provided economic assistance, arms, and manpower as Lithuania fought Polish, Soviet-Russian and Lithuania-Bolshevik enemies. An estimated 20,000 to 30,000 Lithuanians returned to an independent homeland between the two world wars, but they returned to a country which would be dominated by leaders who never were exposed to a democratic political culture.[17]

A Lithuanian state

As the twentieth century approached, some leaders in the Lithuanian national revival realized that their language, culture, and national life were at risk as long as the Lithuanians did not live in a sovereign state of their own. They were surrounded by three powerful neighbors with well-defined cultures, and all of them had designs on Lithuanian territory. It was in the face of similar circumstances that other small nations of Europe, the Basques and Tyrolians, never attained political independence.

But the Lithuanians enjoyed an advantage over other mini-nations of Europe, for they once had a state of their own. Appearing as early as the thirteenth century, Lithuania was at one time a mighty empire covering much of what is today Belarus Ukraine, and parts of the Caucasus. Later it would join in a union with Poland, eventually become a junior partner, and, still later, lose its political sovereignty altogether.

On the eve of the twentieth century, the Lithuanians had concluded that the best they could hope for politically was autonomy within a Russian federation. With the Russian revolution and Germany's defeat (the Kaiser's armies had occupied Lithuania in 1915), they believed that an independent Lithuania was within their grasp. The Germans had established a Lithuanian State Council (*Taryba*) hoping one day to absorb Lithuania, but the *Taryba* provided the Lithuanians with a semi-independent political institution. It declared Lithuanian independence on February 18, 1918.

The Entente remained skeptical about the viability of a Lithuanian state and feared it would become a puppet of Germany, but the Lithuanians demonstrated their resolve in resisting the efforts of their powerful neighbors to subjugate them. In 1919, Britain provided *de facto* recognition, strengthening Lithuania's bid for sovereignty. A year later, Lenin signed a treaty with Lithuania renouncing, forever, any claims on Lithuanian territory. In 1922, the US extended diplomatic recognition, and Lithuania was admitted to the League of Nations that same year.

From the outset, the new state was confronted with serious minority problems. About 20 percent of the population was not ethnic Lithuanian. The two largest minority groups were the Jews, with a population of 200,000 to 300,000, and the Poles, who numbered about 150,000.[18]

Ezra Mendelsohn has observed that the Jews in Lithuania were the most "Jewish" of their brethren in East-Central Europe largely because the mainstream culture was poorly defined, the indigenous intelligentsia was small, and most Lithuanians were peasants.[19] By contrast, many Jews had become secularized in Poland and Russia as they were attracted to large and viable cultures in both societies. For these reasons, and because anti-Semitism in Lithuania was not as strong as in other East European countries, the Jews supported an independent Lithuania and, through their international contacts, actively fought for its establishment. Fearful of

Polish control of Vilnius, the Jews also supported the Lithuanians in their quest to regain their ancient capital.

Istvan Deak writes that in return:

> ... the new democratic regime granted special rights to all ethnic minorities, and thus also to the Jews. A ministry of Jewish affairs was set up in Kovno (Kaunas) as well as a Jewish national council. Jews served in the Lithuanian administration, in parliament (where they were free to address their audience in Yiddish), and as officers in the army. Street signs in Hebrew characters were permitted in Kovno. In 1919 both the minister of Jewish affairs and the deputy foreign minister were well-known Zionists.[20]

But after Polish forces seized Vilnius in 1920, the Lithuanians lost about one-third of what they assumed would be their Jewish population. By 1921, the government began to restrict Jewish rights, and the Jews suffered economically as the government subsidized their Lithuanian competitors.

In 1940, the Jews took comfort in the Soviet occupation of Lithuania, less because of their love of the Russians or attachment to Marxism, but, rather, out of fear of the Nazis. In the process, they earned the enmity of the Lithuanians who deemed them traitors. When the Germans occupied the country, some Lithuanians collaborated with the Nazis in the extermination of all but 10 percent of the Lithuanian Jewish population.[21]

Relations with the Poles were severely strained from the outset. In 1918, Poles in Lithuania, preferring association with Poland, refused to join the *Taryba* and a year later, fearful of Polish fifth-columnists, the Lithuanians denied the Poles a place in the government. After the units of the Polish army seized Vilnius, forcing the Lithuanians to establish a "provisional" capital in Kaunas, and engaged in a Polonization campaign, enmity towards the Poles never subsided. For much of the inter-war period, Polish-Lithuanian relations did not exist, and the two were on the brink of war on more than one occasion. Ironically, Lithuania would get Vilnius back in 1939 as a result of the Molotov-Ribbentrop Pact, the very treaty that would seal its fate as an independent country.

The Lithuanians would lose their democracy on December 17, 1926, in a military coup which had been conducted on behalf of the small Nationalist Party (Tautininkai). Many of the founding fathers of Lithuania belonged to the party, such as Jonas Basanavicius, Antanas Smetona and Augustinas Voldermaras, but it faded after independence. The Christian Democrats became the nation's largest party, and it drew its support from the country's predominately Catholic and rural population. Smetona was elected president by a rump parliament in 1927 (the left-wing parties had bolted), and afterwards he ruled by decree. In face of mounting economic problems, religious/secular and ethnic divisions, powerful enemies on its border, and a society barren of a pluralist political culture, Lithuanian democracy was doomed.[22]

The Soviet era: July, 1940 – March, 1990

In July 1940, Lithuania was forcefully annexed by the USSR as a result of secret protocols to the 1939 Molotov-Ribbentrop Pact and a phony people's revolution. President Franklin Roosevelt refused to recognize the annexation, but Stalin ignored the snub. In face of his drive to liquidate political, intellectual, and religious leaders, thousands of Lithuanians fled the country. A second migration occurred with the Nazis' occupation of Lithuania in 1941, and a third with the return of the Red Army and Soviet occupation several years later. Altogether, an estimated 30,000 to 50,000 Lithuanians died resisting the two Soviet occupations. The Lithuanian partisan movement ("forest brethren") was not suppressed until 1953. Several hundred thousand Lithuanians were imprisoned in labor camps where many perished. Most who had survived Siberian and northern Russian exile returned home in the 1950s, about 50,000 men, women and children.[23] With bitter hatred of the Soviets, many would resist Soviet rule, albeit in an unorganized fashion and without much effort. Their sentiments were shared by the vast majority of their countrymen and women. Few families escaped brutal Soviet deportations or confrontations with Soviet authorities. In subsequent years, all would suffer political and religious persecution.

Unlike the earlier, economic migrants, Lithuanians fleeing German and Russian oppression were well-educated and secure in their language and culture. Largely professionals, government functionaries, and intellectuals, the second wave of migrants thought of themselves as "exiles," not "immigrants," and they formed organizations in Displaced Persons' (DP) camps to sustain a Lithuania in exile with the intent of one day returning to their homeland. About 35,000 of them would settle in the United States and another 15,000 in Canada.[24] In addition to the formation of political organizations, they would form language (Saturday) schools for their children and cultural and social associations to guarantee that their national language and culture would be sustained in the diaspora through the intermarriage of their offspring. The ATEITIS movement would become a powerful force among the second migration giving impetus to the linkage between Lithuanian nationalism and Catholicism in North America.

In contrast to its sister Baltic republics, Lithuania enjoyed a large and homogeneous population throughout the Soviet era. After Armenia, it was the second most homogeneous of the USSR's republics, and after the Georgians and Armenians, the Lithuanians were the third least likely to change their ethnic identity.[25]

With post-war industrialization, Lithuania's labor requirements were primarily met with indigenous manpower. As Lithuanians left the countryside for the city and more of them attended university, they acquired skills to fill positions that Russians had occupied in other republics where rates of urbanization and university training were low.[26] None the less, the number of Russians who found employment in the Republic grew. In mixed Russian-Lithuanian marriages, however, children generally identified with the Lithuanian parent. This phenomenon reflected ethnic homogeneity and the strength of Lithuanian national feeling.[27]

Unlike Estonia and Latvia, Lithuania was not afflicted by a large number of Russified Balts who had lived in the USSR between the wars and returned with the Red Army. Looking at the 1991 landscape, for example, unrepentant Leninists like the late Boris Pugo, who Gorbachev would turn to in 1990 as he sought to crush the Baltic independence movements, and Colonel Viktor Alksnis, a leader of the hardline Soyuz faction in the Congress of People's Deputies, leap to mind.

Longevity in office allowed the Lithuanian party chief, Antanas Snieckus (1940–1974), to build his own personal machine and to manipulate strong nationalist sentiments to his advantage.[28] Although the Lithuanian party would grow at a faster pace than the CPSU as a whole, by "1984 the percentage of party members in the population of Lithuania (5.25%) was still below the corresponding USSR average (6.75%)."[29] Many Lithuanians were opportunists and joined the party to acquire privileges associated with membership in it. But they retained a strong sense of being Lithuanian and rejected the designation "Soviet."

Snieckus's successors were two cautious and unimaginative bureaucrats; Petras Griskevicius who took over in 1976, and Ringaudas Songaila who replaced the latter in 1987. Neither man, nor the party intellectuals of their ilk, embraced Gorbachev's reforms. On the contrary, these apparatchiks adopted harsh measures in the hope of crushing the Catholic human rights movement and displays of resistance on the part of other dissidents.[30]

For most of the Soviet era, the only overt displays of protest against Soviet-Russian rule emanated from outside the party and the established intellectual community. The dissidents included people like Antanas Terleckas and Viktoras Petkas who were imprisoned for "anti-Soviet" activities. In 1978, they formed the Lithuanian Freedom League (*Lietuvos Laisves Lyga*) although it did not surface until a decade later. The League's goal was full and complete independence for Lithuania.

The Lithuanian resistance relied upon common folk for support years before a substantial number of intellectuals challenged Soviet hegemony. Indeed, in 1972, when Kaunas theater director Jonas Jurasas was fired for refusing to produce plays that "the center" could approve of, he stated that many of his old friends, members of the Lithuanian intellectual community, avoided him. But he was welcomed by what he called "invisible people," ordinary men and women who persisted in their resistance to Moscow.[31]

The first and most impressive sign of organized mass resistance to Soviet rule materialized with the Catholic human rights movement. Stalin had attempted to destroy the Catholic Church in Lithuania because of its association with Lithuanian nationalism. He outlawed all religious orders and closed and demolished churches. Those clergy who escaped execution were exiled or denied opportunities to perform their pastoral duties. Stalin's draconian policies forced priests and nuns to conduct religious activities in private homes and other places undetected by his agents.

The Kremlin's policies toward the Church varied after Stalin's death. At times, the authorities adopted greater tolerance toward it while on other occasions they resorted to oppressive policies. The Catholic human rights activists argued that the Soviet and Lithuanian constitutions provided for freedom of conscience but that the country's Catholics were being denied religious liberty. By the mid-1960s, devout Catholics feared that the Soviet's anti-religious campaign was slowly destroying organized religion in Lithuania and intimidating the faithful. Emboldened by the Prague Spring, the activities of Russian dissidents like Andrei Sakharov, and protests by Jewish and other ethnic activists, they decided to fight back. They circulated petitions, wrote letters demanding that their religious rights be honored, and resisted the orders of superiors that they kow-tow to communist authorities.[32]

It was only after their protest was brushed aside that they began publishing in 1972 the samizdat, *Chronicle of The Catholic Church* in Lithuania, documenting the government's illegal anti-Catholic campaign. In spite of persistent KGB efforts to halt publication, including numerous arrests, the incarceration of people in mental institutions, and mysterious deaths, the *Chronicle* was never silenced.

In contrast with the Russian dissident movement at that time, the Lithuanian Catholic activists had attracted mass support for their cause. People from all walks of life, rural and urban, young and old, workers and scholars, lent their support to it. In a two-year period in the early 1970s, over 50,000 Lithuanians courageously signed petitions protesting the government's religious persecution. In 1979, 149,000 Lithuanians signed a petition demanding that the Mary Queen of Peace Church in Klaipeda be returned to its congregation.

On several occasions, militant Catholics, workers, and students took to the streets, and in the spring of 1972 several protest suicides occurred. The self-immolation of a young nationalist, Romas Kalanta, a Komsomol member whose father was a communist, had a particularly profound, traumatic impact upon Lithuanians in all parts of the country and among people from all groups and points of view. After the young martyr killed himself in a Kaunas park, muted discontent was channeled into purposeful public resistance to state oppression. Afterwards the anniversary of Kalanta's death was occasion for public protests against Soviet rule, and he became a symbol for both Catholic and secular anti-Soviet militants alike.[33] His martyrdom helped link people who previously thought they had little in common and often were at odds with one another. It is believed, for example, that some of the first protest documents produced by Catholic priests to reach the West were carried out by emigrating Lithuanian Jews.[34]

After the 1975 Helsinki Accords, intellectuals began to protest human rights violations, although their numbers were small. Following the lead of activists in the Soviet Union, the Lithuanians formed a Helsinki Watch group. Its membership included people like the Lithuanian scholar and poet Thomas Venclova, who came from a prominent "communist" family, and more traditional opponents of the regime like Viktoras Petkas. It included as well, a Catholic priest, Karolis Garuckas, and a Jew, Eitan Finkelstein. Russian dissidents like Sergei Kovalev and Andrei Sakharov assisted the Lithuanians. Sakharov, in particular, legitimized the Lithuanians' claim that they had been illegally incorporated into the USSR when he joined Baltic activists in Moscow protesting the Molotov-Rippentrop Pact. Sakharov signed "A Statement of Russian Democrats," which proclaimed, "Lithuania, Estonia and Latvia have been annexed into the Soviet Union . . . essentially as a result of the occupation of the Baltic States by the Red Army."[35] The Helsinki group, however, declined in effectiveness as a result of the arrest, death, and emigration of its members.

Sajudis

The Helsinki Watch Group was the first indication that intellectuals were prepared to overtly protest Soviet rule. Aside from occasional protests from people like Jurasas, intellectuals and academics remained silent, fantasizing that the Soviet Union would be destroyed in a war with the West or, faced with mounting internal contradictions, self-destruct. Vytautas Landsbergis said that intellectuals of his generation "were concerned to last until then, to await the fall, so that at least some would survive" to witness that development. But in the meantime, they would remain on the sidelines and not overtly challenge Soviet rule.[36]

By the early 1980s, a growing number of people in the Lithuanian establishment, party elite, and intellectuals feared that their language, culture, and homeland were at risk. Writers and teachers voiced concern that in the face of Russification policies the Lithuanian language would slowly die. Educators and historians resented teaching children and publishing material that distorted Lithuanian history. College students organized to salvage the nation's historical monuments and other treasures that were being neglected or bulldozed to build ugly Soviet structures. And just about everyone was appalled at the ecological destruction that the Soviets had visited upon their beloved *Tevyne* ("homeland"). After the Chernobyl meltdown, ecological concerns exploded into open protest when planned additions to the nuclear power plant at Ignalina were announced. Everyone was mindful of the fact that Russians ran the installation in an area (Snieckus) where large concentrations of them lived. Environmental protest, in the minds of many Lithuanians, was inextricably linked to hostility toward Russian hegemony.

Growing but diffuse resistance to Soviet rule did not become organized until 1988, with the founding of Sajudis, the Lithuanian Reconstruction Movement (*Lietuvos Persitvarkymo Sajudis*).[37] The courage and determination of the Catholic activists and others who risked careers, freedom, and even their lives to protest Soviet rule did not go unnoticed by intellectuals and communist leaders who feared that Lithuania and its language and culture were at risk. It also was apparent that the party hardliners were not moving against dissidents with the same confidence that they had displayed only a year earlier. Clearly, some had grave doubts about the ability of the regime to survive in the face of mounting economic problems and popular disgruntlement.

It was against this backdrop that public displays of protest on the part of the Freedom League contributed to the birth of Sajudis. On August 27, 1987, for example, Terleckas and a former nun, Nijole Sadunaite, organized a gathering in Vilnius to protest the Molotov-Ribbentrop Pact. On February 16, 1988, they commemorated the 70th anniversary of Lithuanian independence and several weeks later condemned Stalin's purges and deportations. The authorities reacted by harassing the demonstrators, arresting leaders, and intimidating sympathetic bystanders. But the demonstrators were not cowed, and they regrouped and took to the streets after each effort to stop them.

The Lithuanian *apparat* resisted Gorbachev's reforms, but it was deeply troubled by Gorbachev's actions. They were particularly bothered by his release of dissidents from prison who were then given access to the media and other forums to throttle the system, boldly publicizing the flaws of the command economy and the CPSU's shortcomings. Andrei Sakharov's release, in December 1986, was especially shocking to them as was Moscow's toleration of a popular front movement in Estonia. Perhaps even more disquieting was the visit in August 1988 of Alexander Yakolev, then Gorbachev's right-hand man and the undisputed godfather of perestroika, who told Songaila that national consciousness had to be accepted as a fact of life. He even mentioned the confrontation between Nikola Mitkin, the Russian second-secretary of the LCP, and the Lithuanian writer Vytautas Petkevicius over the issue of Lithuanian nationalism. Petkevicius said, "Isn't it a paradox? I know three languages, and am a nationalist. And he who calls me that knows one – Russian – even though he has lived in the republic for more than a decade. But he is an internationalist!"[38]

The reformers in the party and among the intellectual community proceeded cautiously but were provoked by Songaila when he ignored Gorbachev's recommendation that delegates to the 19th CPSU Conference seek popular approval for their candidacies. The *apparat* further fueled open displays of opposition when it announced that "central ministry authorities had unilaterally decided to speed up the expansion of giant chemical industries in" several areas that were "already choking from pollution."[39]

It was against this backdrop of grievances that intellectuals and scholars at the University of Vilnius formed an "Initiative Group" in June 1988. Among the original founders of Sajudis were many leading communists, such as Bronius Genzelis, Antanas Buracas, Romualdas Ozolas, and Kazimiera Prunskiene. But they were joined by others who had spurned party membership, like the music professor, Vytautas Landsbergis, whose family had played a vital role in the Lithuanian revival and whose wife, Grazina, had been a Siberian deportee.

On June 14, Sajudis and the Freedom League, although in separate groups, gathered in old town Vilnius's Gediminas Square to commemorate the 1941 mass deportations. The groups were separated by a broad ideological chasm. Many of the long-time dissidents viewed Sajudis as a communist-dominated organization whose leaders could not be trusted.[40] The League would boycott the 1990 elections to the Lithuanian Supreme Soviet even though most Lithuanians by that time believed Sajudis was a patriotic movement and serious about independence.

Members of Sajudis, in turn, considered Terleckas *et al.*, to be extremists, cranks, and anachronisms from the past. Close association with such people could play into the hands of the *apparat*, which was trying to discredit Sajudis in the eyes of moderate Lithuanians and Moscow. At this point, many members were not altogether comfortable with an association with Catholic clergy who, in turn, remained wary of Sajudis.

On June 24, Sajudis again held a rally with delegates to the 19th Party Conference at the square, which fronted Vilnius Cathedral. It had been closed to worshippers for years. Twenty thousand people gathered there; among them was Algirdas Brazauskas, a Central Committee Secretary. This gathering would promote the political futures of both Sajudis and Brazauskas.

The founding congress of Sajudis was held October 22 through October 24, 1988. What has been called the Second Great Vilnius Seimas was attended by supporters from abroad and throughout the Soviet Union; e.g. leaders from the diaspora like Vytautas Bieliauskas, who was the president of the World Lithuanian Community, and Yuri Afanas'ev, who represented the Russian democrats. For two days, Lithuanians throughout the country watched with amazement as the proceedings were televised. At one point, Antanas Buracas interrupted the proceedings and astounded the gathering and TV audience when he announced that the Cathedral on Gediminas Square would be returned to the Catholic Church.[41] At this point, doubts about Sajudis on the part of many Catholic clergy and faithful vanished. The Conference was concrete proof that Sajudis was as deeply committed to a Lithuania free of Moscow's domination as most ordinary people were. The fact that the *apparat* could not prevent the gathering was further evidence that their power was in decline.

Lithuanians who had vainly resisted Soviet rule, and others who were searching for leaders to mobilize the nation into a powerful opposition movement, had found what they were looking for in Sajudis. It provided well-educated, talented, well-connected leaders who could forge popular, but heretofore inchoate, protest into organized opposition.

By this time, Moscow was having second thoughts about supporting Sajudis. Alexander Yakovlev characterized talk about independence among the organization's members as unrealistic. But in February 1989, after attempts by party hardliners to coopt Sajudis failed, the organization called for the full restoration of Lithuanian sovereignty and, a month later, won thirty-six of Lithuania's forty-two seats in the Soviet Union's Congress of People's Deputies.

This was a stunning victory, especially as hardliners in the LCP tried to obstruct Sajudis's campaigning. Access to the media and printing materials were restricted but to no avail. The *apparat*'s inability to prevent the first, albeit limited, expression of popular will for almost fifty years, and the appearance of Sajudis and reformed communist delegates at the Soviet Union's Congress of People's Deputies, further emboldened the people and disheartened the *apparat*. Of course, Brazauskas hoped that he would ride the tidal wave of mass mobilization that Sajudis had generated, and he used his influence to block efforts to deny Sajudis candidates electoral success.

Meanwhile, his fortunes soared when, with Moscow's help and Sajudis's support, he was selected the LCP's first-secretary in October 1988. A year later, he was at the helm when the party broke with the CPSU, excepting a rump-group, and joined Sajudis in demanding independence for Lithuania. Some Lithuanians believed he was under instructions to take such actions in the hope of coopting the militants in Sajudis who proposed immediate independence. It is not unlikely that Gorbachev concluded that the outer empire in Eastern Europe would have remained intact had men like Brazauskas ruled there. Lithuania, however, was in the "inner", not the "outer" Soviet-Russian empire, and it was not clear how much maneuvering room Gorbachev would grant Brazauskas.

On the eve of the 1990 elections, many Lithuanians were convinced that Gorbachev had crafted a strategy to place Brazauskas in the top spot in the new Lithuanian Supreme Soviet. Polls indicated that he was the most popular figure in the country even though he was the head of the party that had served the hated center. A high school teacher in Ukmerge, a provincial city seventy kilometers north of Vilnius, told a visiting American scholar that "Brazauskas is not like the rest of them. He listens to people . . . he even treats his critics with respect. Besides, he knows how to work with Moscow and through his step-by-step approach, he can bring about independence. Eventually.''[42]

The Sajudis leadership looked for support abroad and the diaspora would play a critical role here. Young Canadians and Americans of Lithuanian descent worked for Sajudis as translators, press aides, and liaisons with the Western media. Lithuanian organizations in North America provided fax machines, computers, and financial assistance to Sajudis. The Brooklyn-based Lithuanian Information Center established a press office for the organization. Later the Center's small but talented staff would plan and help advance US trips for Prunskiene and Landsbergis, and provide translators for them in meeting with President Bush and the US Congress. All the while, it kept the American media and scholars abreast of developments in Lithuania.

A team of foreigners who had been invited to witness the elections were puzzled by the casual attitude which the Sajudis leadership displayed on election eve, especially in face of efforts on the part of party hardliners to sabotage the campaigns of Sajudis candidates by restricting access to paper, printing shops and, most important of all, the media. But they could be cavalier about the election; some had the support of party bureaucrats, and they all knew that the vast majority of the people were behind them.[43]

Sajudis-backed candidates won about 80 percent of the seats to the Lithuanian Supreme Soviet on February 24 and in follow-up elections two weeks later. Landsbergis was selected chairman of the newly established Lithuanian Supreme Council, the single most powerful body in the new Republic of Lithuania. Prunskiene (who like many other communists was supported by Sajudis) was chosen Prime Minister. Brazauskas, along with Ozolas, became Deputy Prime Ministers.

On March 11, the first freely elected republic government in Soviet history gathered in Vilnius and proclaimed the restoration of a sovereign, independent Lithuanian state. The new government moved quickly because it wanted to present Gorbachev with a *fait accompli* before he acquired new presidential powers which the Lithuanians feared he would use to crush them. It was hoped, moreover, that this bold step would force the West to recognize the new government in Vilnius.[44] Landsbergis, however, indicated early that he expected Lithuania's exit from the USSR to be gradual. Economic relations with the USSR would remain close, and Lithuania was prepared to grant the Soviets the right to maintain military installations in the country.

Gorbachev proclaimed the action illegal and said that, while the republic had the right to secede, it would have to follow a three-step process before it broke cleanly with the USSR. It included a two-thirds "yes" vote in a republic-wide referendum, a five-year waiting period to sort out disparate economic claims, and, finally, approval of the Soviet

Parliament. Landsbergis replied that Lithuania had been illegally incorporated into the USSR and, hence, Soviet law did not apply to it.[45]

To Vilnius's dismay, the US government asserted that it could not extend formal diplomatic recognition to Lithuania until the new government had physical control of its territory, a prerequisite to recognition. This reaction clearly strengthened Gorbachev's hand, and, in April, he imposed an economic embargo upon the recalcitrant republic. It lasted until late June, when Landsbergis called a moratorium on Lithuania's independence declaration as a precondition for ending the embargo and beginning discussions with Moscow.

Bloody Sunday: the abortive coup

In October 1990, Prime Minister Nikolai Ryzhkov met with a Lithuanian delegation and said that the Molotov-Ribbentrop Pact had nothing to do with Lithuania's annexation into the USSR in 1940. "It was," the Prime Minister said, "the result of a people's revolution."[46] This was Joseph Stalin's interpretation of Baltic annexation, and the fact that Ryzhkov resorted to it indicated that Moscow had no intention of negotiating its differences with Vilnius. Gorbachev had decided upon force to resolve his dispute with Landsbergis whom, it was rumored, the Soviet president disliked personally.

Lithuania had become a bellwether for independence movements throughout the USSR, and Gorbachev seemed to think that, if the recalcitrant Lithuanians could be crushed, more faint hearted nationalists in other republics would comply with Moscow's demands. By this time, Gorbachev probably realized that he could not compel the Lithuanians to renounce their independence by dangling economic inducements before them.

At the 1990 Washington Summit, the Gorbachev entourage proclaimed that ethnic strife in the Soviet Union rested on economic stagnation, and it would fade as perestroika put the economy back on a firm footing. Gorbachev, in several meetings, had told the Lithuanians that he was relying upon the Baltic states to lead the other republics toward economic reform, but he lost his composure and resorted to hostile rhetoric and threats, reminiscent of his predecessors, when the Lithuanians asked about independence.[47]

During Landsbergis' December, 1990 visit to Washington highlighted by a meeting with President Bush, the Lithuanian delegation displayed grave misgivings about the near future. They said Moscow would launch a crackdown against them as the American-led coalition was poised to remove Saddam Hussein's forces from Kuwait. The invasion of Hungary in 1956, during the Suez Crisis, was seen as a historical precedent.[48] The White House revealed little about the Bush-Landsbergis meeting, but the Lithuanians hoped it would serve to dissuade Gorbachev from applying the mailed fist against them lest he alienate the Americans. Bush urged Landsbergis to seek a resolution to his crisis with Gorbachev and mentioned a referendum as a possible way out. The Lithuanians left Washington dismayed. Their pessimism was not unfounded.

On January 8, 1990, Prime Minister Prunskiene's feud with President Landsbergis, who was unyielding in his country's drive for independence while she favored a more conciliatory approach, culminated in her resignation when the two clashed over a price hike. That same day, Prunskiene had sought, but did not receive, assurances from Gorbachev that force would not be used against Lithuania. Reports of Soviet troop movements to and within Lithuania appeared over the next several days, punctuated by threats from Gorbachev that the Lithuanians had to stop breaking the law.

About 1.30 am, January 13, 1991, Soviet paratroopers and KGB forces surrounded the Vilnius TV tower and the nearby TV station with the expectation that the crowds guarding them would flee in face of small arms fire and body-crushing tanks. These assaults were part of a series of steps that would precipitate a declaration of presidential rule from Moscow and the eventual replacement of the democratically-elected Lithuanian government with Lithuanian communists who remained loyal to the CPSU. These Lithuanian communists had formed the so-called Committee for the Salvation of Lithuania, but, with the apparent exception of the LCP's ideological chief, Juozas Jermalavicius, the committee's members remained a secret.

That day, fourteen people were killed (another victim would later die), hundreds wounded, and three went missing. Within a week, five people would be killed in Riga in a similar confrontation.

> A careful study of available information indicates that the violence in Lithuania and Latvia in January was in fact the result of a failed coup, an unsuccessful Soviet attempt to overthrow the pro-independence governments of the Baltic republics and to establish direct presidential rule by Mr. Gorbachev. The plan appears to have been drafted in Moscow with Gorbachev's approval and carried out by the Soviet military establishment at the instigation of local Communist party chiefs, who gave the party and military leaders in Moscow misleading assurances it would work.[49]

Gorbachev had refused to take a phone call from Landsbergis two days prior to Bloody Sunday, and he offered condolences to the victims' families only after he encountered intense pressure from abroad. He had hoped to neutralize criticism of the coup by claiming that the Lithuanians had broken the law on numerous occasions. He, and the Soviet media in the weeks leading up to Bloody Sunday, had paid special attention to draft resistance there. It was only a matter of time, observers were led to believe, before "the generals" lost their patience and resorted to force.

But Gorbachev hoped to sully the reputation of Landsbergis and his colleagues by playing up a theme to which pro-Soviet Russian and Polish commentators in Lithuania frequently resorted to; that is, human rights violations against the republics' minorities. Spokespersons for the mysterious "National Salvation Committee" had made similar charges.

Ethnic Russians and Poles in Lithuania number approximately 9 and 8 percent, respectively, of the republic's 3.7 million population. The Russian population falls into two groups. The first is comprised of members of the military, KGB, and other security bodies along with managers of All-Union institutions and large industrial enterprises. Few of these people speak Lithuanian, they send their children to Russian schools, live in Russian ghettos (e.g. Snieckus), and plan to return to Russia.

In the second group are people who are attracted to Lithuania's relatively high living standards, who socialize with Lithuanians, and are among those Russians, about 34 percent, who speak Lithuanian.[50] Many of them harbor concerns about the discrimination they might suffer in an independent Lithuania, but most of them have supported (and some even belong to) Sajudis. They were deeply moved by Bloody Sunday and, like the Archbishop Khrisostom of the Russian Orthodox Church who joined Landsbergis in the parliament building when it was considered to be a target of a military attack, many of their number who previously opposed independence have since sided with the Lithuanians.

The Polish community, for the most part, is concentrated in and around Vilnius and Salcininkai, in eastern Lithuania. Many Poles have supported Sajudis, and several of them were elected to the Supreme Council in 1990. One of their number is Czeslaw Okinczyc, who is the vice-chairman of the Council's foreign affairs commission. Okinczyc, the publisher of a Polish-language newspaper, delivered an impassioned speech before the parliament in Warsaw during the January crisis and has been accused by some Poles in Lithuania of being "pro-Lithuanian." By contrast were those Polish apparatchiks who remained linked to the Soviet system and supported the August *Putsch*. They had hoped to exploit their people's fears about an independent Lithuania in order to undermine the new government and enhance their stock in Moscow.

Poles in Lithuania are not without grievances. They claim that their schools are poorly funded, that only a tiny number of their young people attend university, and that social services in their communities are shortchanged. Poles also have expressed outrage about being denied access to the Vilnius Cathedral by their Lithuanian counterparts. And citing the passage of a law declaring Lithuanian the official language, some Polish leaders have demanded political autonomy for their communities.[51]

Early on the government in Warsaw gave Landsbergis and his colleagues high marks for their approach to the "Polish problem." And representatives from both countries have met in an effort to resolve the complaints of Poles in Lithuania.

Lech Walesa was outspoken in his praise of the government in Vilnius, and his former colleagues in Solidarity who have since parted company with him, Adam Michnik, Bronislaw Geremik and Jacek Kuron, travelled to Vilnius in a gesture of support for Lithuanian independence.[52]

The coup in Vilnius was designed to remove Landsbergis and his colleagues from office, to crush the will of the people, and to demoralize democrats in Russia and separatists in other republics who had been challenging Gorbachev. It failed on all counts. In wake of Bloody Sunday, Landsbergis's popularity soared. The courage and steadfast leadership he provided during the bloodletting had a calming effect on his people.[53] It gave them strength to stand in place and not run from their tormentors; and to peacefully resist them with song, and not resort to violence which would provide the pretext that the paratroopers were firing upon a "violent mob."

It is noteworthy that none of the members of parliament deserted the cause but, like Landsbergis, remained in the building even though a lethal assault on it was deemed imminent. The single possible exception to this statement involves the mysterious disappearance of the newly appointed prime minister, Albertas Simenas, over the Bloody Sunday weekend.

The trauma of the massacre helped seal a bond between the people and their leaders. It enabled Lithuanians of all backgrounds to forget their past differences and work toward Lithuanian independence together. For example, Antanas Buracas, a Sajudis founder and former member of the USSR Supreme Soviet, and Viktoras Petkus, the Freedom League activist who boycotted the 1990 elections, have become co-directors of a new Lithuanian human rights organization. After the January incident, polls indicated that a significant number of Poles and Russians in the country supported Lithuanian independence.[54]

As Gorbachev feared, developments in Lithuania had consequences for the rest of the USSR, for, immediately after Bloody Sunday, the democrats in Russia who had become demoralized and whose ranks were wracked by bitter in-fighting caught a second wind. In taking to the streets to protest Bloody Sunday, and in demonstrations against Gorbachev, they refused to be intimidated by police and troops. Events in Lithuania forced the hard-liners to acknowledge that it was not at all clear whether troops would fire upon large crowds of civilians in future confrontations or join the demonstrators. The failed coup of August 1991 demonstrated that these fears were justified.

Conclusions

What we are witnessing in Lithuania is the confluence of two compelling forces in the modern era, the quest for national self-determination and democracy. It will be some time before the precise relationship between the two can be determined, i.e., how much weight should be given to nationalism on the one hand, and democracy on the other. But the Lithuanian people seem to be demanding a democratic, independent Lithuania, not a society marked by pre-World War II authoritarianism or post-war totalitarianism.

One litmus test of the maturity of Lithuanian nationalism clearly will be the treatment afforded the country's Russian and Polish minorities. In this connection, the prospects are hopeful. Czeslaw Okinczyc criticized the Lithuanian government for not moving immediately after the March 11 declaration to meet some of the Polish communities' grievances, and he later protested the dissolution of two raion councils in heavily Polish areas of eastern Lithuania. But he said that Lithuania's minority law was the "most progressive in Europe," and relations between Warsaw and Vilnius have not been permanently harmed by the incident.[55] Meanwhile Lithuania and Yeltsin's Russia have signed an agreement guaranteeing minority rights for Lithuanians and Russians in both republics. And most ordinary Russians residing in Lithuania will claim that they remain there even though the country is now independent.[56]

None the less, in Lithuania, political, social and cultural fissures, which had been latent under Soviet rule, may now become manifest. Like the East European countries which only recently have achieved independence, the Lithuanians must build a civil society, and that task may be as challenging as the drive for independence.

Notes

1 Walker Connor, *The National Question in Marxist-Leninist Theory and Strategy* (Princeton: Princeton University Press, 1984).
2 Joane Nagel, "The Ethnic Revolution: The Emergence Of Ethnic Nationalism in Modern States," *Sociology and Social Research*, vol. 68, no. 4, July, 1984, pp. 417–734.
3 Some Western scholars have praised twentieth-century communism for destroying ethno-nationalism; for example, Eric Hobsbawm, *Nations and Nationalism since 1780* (New York: Oxford University Press, 1990). This has prompted Jeremy R. Azrael to remark: "This, however, is clearly giving credit to those who are most to blame for creating and fueling what eventually became an explosion waiting to happen." See his chapter, "The Soviet 'Nationality Front': Some Implications for U.S. Foreign and Security Policy," in Michael Mandelbaum, ed., *The Rise of Nations in the Soviet Union* (New York: Council on Foreign Relations Press, 1991), p. 101.
4 Philip G. Roeder, "Soviet Federalism and Ethnic Mobilization," *World Politics*, vol. 43, no. 2, January, 1991, p. 228.
5 *Ibid.*
6 It also has been influenced by ethnic relations in the United States where all but the native Americans and some Mexicans belonged to secondary ethnic groups.

That is, unlike primary ethnic groups, who reside in their traditional homeland (Lithuanians, Armenians in the USSR), secondary ethnic groups live outside their homeland, such as Americans of Lithuanian descent in the US.

7 Roeder, "Soviet Federalism," p. 229.
8 *Ibid.*, p. 230.
9 *Ibid.*, p. 203.
10 Harold Isaacs, *Idols of the Tribe* (New York: Harper and Row, 1975).
11 Stephen R. Burant, "Polish-Lithuanian Relations: Past, Present, and Future," *Problems of Communism*, vol. 40, May-June, 1991, p. 67.
12 Antanas J. Van Reenan, *Lithuanian Diaspora; Konigsberg to Chicago* (Lanham, NY: University Press of America, 1990).
13 Alfred E. Senn, *Jonas Basanavicius* (Newton, MA: Oriental Research Partners, 1980).
14 Jack Stukas, *Awakening Lithuania* (Madison, NJ: Florham Park Press, 1963).
15 For a discussion of the elements of a white ethnic sub-culture in the United States, see Richard J. Krickus, *Pursuing the American Dream* (New York: Anchor Press, 1976).
16 Stukas, *American Dream*, p. 149.
17 Alfred Eric Senn, *The Emergence of Modern Lithuania* (New York: Columbia University Press, 1959), pp. 220–232.
18 Jerzy Ochmanski, *Historia Litwy* (Wroclaw: Ossolineum, 1982), pp. 320 and 321. In 1923, a large number of Germans joined Lithuania when Lithuanians occupied Memel (Klaipeda).
19 For a concise treatment of Jews in Lithuania, see Ezra Mendelsohn, *The Jews of East Central Europe between the World Wars* (Bloomington: Indiana University Press, 1983), pp. 212–239. For a discussion of the Holocaust in Lithuania, see Avraham Tory, *Surviving the Holocaust: The Kovno Ghetto Diary* (Cambridge, MA: Harvard University Press, 1990).
20 Istvan Deak, "Surviving the Holocaust: The Kovno Ghetto Diary," *The New York Review of Books*, November 8, 1990, p. 54.
21 The crime is so horrible and unspeakable that it is difficult to discuss it objectively, but Mendelsohn makes an effort to do so:

> The coming of Communism, a calamity for Lithuanian nationalists, was welcomed by the left-wing elements within Lithuanian Jewry, whose importance within the small Lithuanian Communist Party has already been described. Having little support among the Lithuanian population, the new regime encouraged, at first, Jewish support, and a sizable number of Jewish leftists rose to positions of prominence in areas previously closed to them – the state apparatus, the army, the judiciary, and so forth. The Soviets therefore established a pattern which would be followed, after World War II, in the satellite states of Eastern Europe. The prominence of some Jews in the communist regime . . . was a disaster for the entire Jewish community." (*The Jews*, pp. 238–239)

22 V. Stanley Vardys, "The Rise of Authoritarian Rule in The Baltic States," in Vardys and Romuald J. Misiunas, *The Baltic States in Peace and War* (University Park, PA: Penn State University Press, 1978), pp. 68–72.
23 For a discussion of the deportations during the war and immediately after it, see Romuald J. Misiunas and Rein Taagerpera, *The Baltic States; Years of Dependence 1940–1980* (Berkeley, CA: University of California Press, 1983).
24 Lithuanian Information Center, Washington, DC.

25 Barbara Anderson and Brian Silver, "Some Factors in the Linguistic and Ethnic Russification of soviet Nationalities," in Lubomyr Hajda and Mark Beissinger, eds., *The Nationalities Factor in Soviet Politics and Society* (Boulder, Co: Westview Press, 1990), p. 119.
26 Gertrude E. Schroeder, "Nationalities and the Soviet Economy," in Hajda and Beissinger, eds., *Nationalities Factor*, pp. 43–71.
27 Romuald J. Misiunas, "The Baltic Republics," in Hajda and Beissinger, eds., *Nationalities Factor*, p. 206.
28 *Ibid.*, p. 207.
29 *Ibid.*, p. 209.
30 V. Standley Vardys, "Lithuanian National Politics," *Problems of Communism*, vol. 38, July-August, 1989, pp. 54–55.
31 Interview, Jonas Jurasas.
32 For a comprehensive treatment of the *Chronicle* and the role of the Catholic Church during the Soviet era, see V. Stanley Vardys, *The Catholic Church, Dissent and Nationality in Soviet Lithuania* (New York: Columbia University Press, 1978).
33 *Ibid.*
34 Interview, Father Casimir Pugevicius.
35 Richard J. Krickus, *The Superpowers in Crisis* (New York: Pergamon-Brassey's, 1987), pp. 44–47.
36 Interview with Vytautas Landsbergis in *The Lithuanian Review*, vol. 1, May 11, 1990.
37 For a detailed discussion of the formation of Sajudis see Alfred E. Senn, *Lithuanian Awakening* (Berkeley, CA: University of California Press, 1990).
38 *Ibid.*, p. 111.
39 Vardys, "Lithuanian National Politics", p. 56.
40 Interview, Viktoras Petkus.
41 Senn, *Lithuanian Awakening*, p. 225.
42 Anonymous interview in Ukmerge.
43 The author was invited by Sajudis to witness the February 1990 elections in Lithuania.
44 All of the Sajudis leaders and staff members I spoke with were convinced the Bush Administration would recognize an independent Lithuania if the Sajudis state elected enough of its candidates to the Lithuanian Supreme Soviet to restore the state which had been crushed in 1940.
45 Interview, Vytautas Landsbergis.
46 Interview, Lionginas Vazilauskas.
47 Interview, Bronius Genzelis.
48 Interview, Rolandas Barysas.
49 Jeri Laber, "The Baltic Revolt," *The New York Review of Books*, March 28, 1991, p. 60.
50 Riina Kionka, "Are The Baltic Laws Discriminatory?", *Report on the USSR*, April 12, 1991, p. 22.
51 Interview, Czeslaw Okinczyc.
52 For a comprehensive discussion of Polish-Lithuanian relations see Burant, "Polish-Lithuanian Relations."
53 Interview, Lowry Wyman.

54 See Riina Kionka, "Baltic Laws."
55 Interview with Okinczyc. For a discussion of the dispute over the dissolution of the rayon councils, see Richard J. Krickus, "Lithuania's Polish Question," *Report on the USSR*, November 29, 1991, pp. 20–23.
56 In a discussion with Russian workers at the Ignalina Nuclear Power plant in Snieckus in the summer of 1991, I was told that many of their brethren opposed independence for Lithuania, but if it occurred the vast majority would choose to live there.

8 Latvia: origins, evolution, and triumph

NILS MUIZNIEKS

The Soviet central government recognized the independence of Estonia, Latvia, and Lithuania on September 6, 1991, thereby formally bringing to an end fifty-one years of Soviet rule in the Baltic republics. This was the second time Moscow recognized the Baltic states this century; the first recognition came under Lenin, when the Soviet Union signed peace treaties in 1920 renouncing "forever" all claims to Baltic territory. "Forever" lasted but twenty years, as Stalin annexed the Baltic states in 1940. The rebirth of the Baltic states, then, signifies the reversal of the consequences of World War II for the Balts and a return to the status quo ante. Below, I trace the origins, evolution, and triumph of the political movement that culminated in the second incarnation of the Latvian state.

A broad-based Latvian nationalist movement emerged soon after Mikhail Gorbachev assumed power in 1985 and initiated liberalizing reforms in the Soviet Union. Diverse groupings coalesced into a Popular Front in 1988 that sought to promote perestroika and the decentralization of authority from Moscow. In short order, however, the movement came to espouse the more radical goals of democracy and the restoration of independence. The goal of independence came to have virtually unanimous support among ethnic Latvians and substantial backing among the other nationalities in the republic. The neutrality or support of non-Latvians was critical for the movement's success: Latvians constituted only 52.0 percent of the 2,666,567 inhabitants of the republic in 1989. Russians comprised the bulk of the remainder with 34.0 percent, followed by Belarusians with 4.5 percent, Ukrainians with 3.5 percent, and Poles with 2.3 percent.[1]

The impetus for independence was varied. For Latvians fearful of demographic minoritization due to Slavic immigration, independence signified control over Latvia's borders and the ethnic composition of the population. Representatives of all nationalities could agree on the desirability of separation from the Soviet social order, based on the Communist Party and central planning, and the creation of a new order, founded on democracy and the market. For many, faith in the viability of an independent Latvia rested on the memory of the 20 year period of independence between the two world wars. The contemporary movement has been imbued with the historical memory of this era and the violence that attended its closing.

Latvia before Soviet power

A modern Latvian national consciousness emerged only in the latter half of the nineteenth century when the territory of Latvia was a province of the Russian empire. Baltic German barons held the leading political and economic posts, and the vast majority of Latvians were peasants. The small but active Latvian intelligentsia considered the Baltic German nobility to be its primary adversary. Many Latvian activists welcomed the erosion of Baltic German control over provincial life that was a consequence of the crown's policy of Russification after the 1880s. By 1905 national development had brought Latvians to the point of demanding autonomy within the Russian empire. Widespread peasant and worker unrest that year evoked harsh punitive expeditions by the imperial army, leading a large part of the intelligentsia to begin formulating more far-reaching political goals.[2]

World War I and the collapse of the Russian Empire provided the opportunity for the proclamation of an independent Latvian state in 1918. The 1920 peace treaty with the Soviet Union guaranteed the new state's integrity. The government of the new Republic of Latvia soon gained international recognition, pursued a neutral foreign policy, and became a member of the League of Nations.[3] In domestic policy, Latvia was notable for its radical land reform, rapid economic growth based on agricultural exports, and progressive welfare system. From 1920 to 1934, Latvia had a parliamentary democracy in which the Social Democrats were the largest single political party. As in much of Eastern Europe during that era, however, the Great Depression engendered social tensions and political polarization that set the stage for authoritarianism. Karlis Ulmanis, one of the founders of Latvia, engineered a bloodless coup in 1934 and ruled through the bureaucracy and the army until World War II. The mild authoritarianism of Ulmanis's regime contrasted starkly with developments to the East, where Stalin was brutally pursuing policies of collectivization, forced draft industrialization, and political terror that took millions of lives.

From independent state to Soviet republic

The signing of the Molotov-Ribbentrop Pact by Nazi Germany and the Soviet Union on August 23, 1939, marked the beginning of the Soviet encroachment on Latvia's sovereignty. A secret protocol of the pact placed Latvia, along with Estonia and Lithuania, in the Soviet sphere of influence. Soon thereafter, the three Baltic governments submitted to growing Soviet intimidation and signed mutual assistance treaties allowing Soviet bases and troops on their territories. As in postwar Eastern Europe, the presence of Soviet troops was followed by terror and rigged elections. The hand-picked Baltic governments soon tendered requests to join the Soviet Union, which were quickly granted in August of 1940. The following months witnessed coordinated campaigns of Sovietization in all three Baltic republics, capped by massive deportations. On one night alone – June 14, 1941 – over 15,000 individuals were deported from Latvia to the Gulag. Total population losses stemming from deportations, massacres, and unexplained disappearances during the first year of Soviet occupation have been estimated at 35,000.[4]

When German forces attacked the USSR and invaded the Baltic republics at the end of June in 1941, many Latvians welcomed them at least passively. The Latvian stance stemmed not from any widespread sympathy with the Nazis, but rather from a sense of relief that further Soviet terror would be halted and hopes that the new invaders might permit the restoration of independence. Nazi Germany had no interest in restoring Latvia's independence; rather, the new occupiers sought to use Latvia's human and economic resources for its own purposes. While many Latvians suffered under Nazi rule, some also participated in one of the darkest chapters of Latvia's history: collaboration with the Nazis in exterminating most of the local Jewish population.[5]

The return of the Soviet army in 1944 led over a hundred thousand people to flee for the West. Thousands more resisted, either fighting alongside the retreating Germans or engaging in guerilla warfare. As the Red Army destroyed all resistance, the Soviet authorities reintroduced their own distinctive brand of terror. In 1945–1946, an estimated 60,000 people were deported from Latvia, to be followed by about 50,000 more during collectivization in 1949.[6] The armed guerilla resistance was wiped out by the early 1950s, though passive resistance continued for years. The extreme violence employed to cow the Latvians into submission continues to shape ethnic relations and popular attitudes towards the period of Soviet rule in the region to this day.

Some Russians in Latvia came to brand any anti-Soviet sentiment among the Latvians as a manifestation of fascism. Many Latvians, on the other hand, came to associate the brutality of communism in its Stalinist guise with Russians. It must be remembered that Stalin manipulated Russian nationalism for his own purposes, elevating it to a core systematic value.[7] The alien ethos of the new regime in Latvia was intensified by Soviet cadres policy. Those members of the Latvian elite that had not fled to the West or perished in the Gulag were little trusted by the authorities. The Communist Party of Latvia was miniscule when the Soviets arrived, numbering less than 1,000 in 1940 and perhaps 5,000 in 1945.[8] These factors pushed the authorities to import Russians and Soviet-born or

Table 8.1. *Industrial production in Latvia, 1960–1988 (percentage of total production value, in 1982 prices)*

	1960	1970	1980	1985	1988
Heavy industry	31.6	41.9	49.3	53.5	54.7
Light industry	33.8	27.0	23.4	20.4	19.3
Food industry	34.6	31.1	27.3	26.1	26.0

Source: Latvijas PSR Valsts Statistikas Komiteja, *Latvija Sodien: Socialekono-misku Aprakstu Krajums* (Riga, 1990), p. 74.

Soviet-educated Russified Latvians to fill the leading posts in society. The latter group, known as *latovichi*, usually spoke no Latvian and, but for their names, were indistinguishable from Russians. Thus, embedded in the Leninist political system was an ethnic hierarchy, with Russians or Russified *latovichi* ruling over the indigenous Latvians.

Latvia under Khrushchev and Brezhnev

From 1957 to 1959, during the Khrushchev thaw, "national communists" briefly gained the upper hand within the leadership of the Communist Party of Latvia. Led by Deputy Chairman of the Council of Ministers Eduards Berklavs, this group attempted to slow the influx of Slavic settlers into Latvia, promote native cadres, expand the use of the Latvian language in the educational system and in party affairs, and increase republican autonomy in the organization of the economy. This attempt to put a Latvian face on communist rule was quelled in the summer of 1959 and soon thereafter, when Berklavs and nearly 2,000 other officials were purged.[9] The purge in Latvia was part of a broader crackdown in nationalities policy that begin in the latter half of 1958 and continued for several years.[10] The 1959 purge was a turning point in postwar Latvian history, for it was followed by almost 30 years of economic irrationality, extensive migration, and Russification. Many Latvians associate the subsequent era and its pathologies with the leadership of two *latovichi*: Arvids Pelse and Augusts Voss.

From 1960 to the late 1980s, the republic's leadership and central authorities subjected Latvia to the rapid growth of heavy industry for which the republic's supply of labor, raw materials, and consumption patterns were unsuited. Table 8.1 shows the dramatic increase in the percentage of industrial production accounted for by heavy industry and the concomitant decline in the share for the light and food industries. The increasing weight of heavy industry in the Latvian economy was the result of the rapid development of the machine-building, metallurgical, chemical,

Table 8.2. *Percentage of all industrial workers in Latvia, 1960–1988, employed in different categories of work*

	1960	1970	1980	1985	1988
Machine construction and metal work	26.4	33.3	39.4	39.9	39.9
Light industry	23.0	21.6	19.2	18.3	17.6
Food industry	14.6	13.4	11.9	12.1	12.3

Source: Latvijas PSR Valsts Statistikas Komiteja, *Latvija Sodien: Socialekonomisku Aprakstu Krajums* (Riga, 1990), p. 74.

and petrochemical industries. Another measure of the evolution of the economy can be had by examining the sectoral distribution of employment in industry.

Table 8.2 shows the rapid increase in the production of employment in machine construction and metal work and the concomitant decline in the sectors of light and food industry. Latvia's share of the total Soviet output of several categories of machine products became very high. In 1988, the republic produced 100 percent of all railroad passenger cars and streetcars, 18 percent of all diesels and diesel generators, 19 percent of all buses, 17 percent of all farm machine loaders, and 58 percent of all mopeds of the entire Soviet Union.[11] The sectors of machine construction and metal work are highly labor intensive, employing 39.9 percent of all industrial workers in 1988, but producing only 27.7 percent of the total value of industrial production.[12] The construction of such labor intensive industries in labor-short Latvia necessitated the importation of labor from other republics.

After the 1959 purge, the rate of migration into Latvia from other republics soared. While a large part of the influx was offset by an outflow, net immigration from 1951 to 1989 numbered over 400,000, as can be seen in Table 8.3 below. The scale of the migration flow eventually led many Latvians to conclude that Moscow was attempting to dilute the Latvian population or assimilate it altogether. Moreover, the steady influx of immigrants put a great strain on the infrastructure and social services in Latvia, accentuating the housing shortage and leading to tensions between Russian immigrants, who often viewed themselves as *Kulturtrager*, "economic benefactors," or "liberators,"[13] and the Latvian population, which felt its proprietary rights were being ignored.

The regime itself was heavily staffed by immigrant Russians, especially after the 1959 purge. Data on the nationality composition of the Latvian Communist Party were never published before the Gorbachev era, undoubtedly because of the embarrassing under-representation of Latvians. When the figures were finally published, the reasons for secrecy

Table 8.3. *Migration flows into and out of Latvia, 1951–1989 (thousands)*

	Arrived	Departed	Net immigration	
			Total	avg. per year
1951–1960	—	—	75.0	7.5
1961–1970	471.3	325.5	145.8	14.6
1971–1980	538.1	435.9	102.2	10.2
1981–1985	255.6	213.5	42.1	8.4
1986	54.5	43.3	11.2	
1987	56.9	40.7	16.2	
1988	52.3	41.1	11.2	
1989	38.0	35.7	2.3	

Source: Latvijas PSR Valsts Statistikas Komiteja, *Latvija Sodien: Socialekono-misku Aprakstu Krajums* (Riga, 1990), p. 32; Juris Dreifelds, "Latvian National Consciousness and Group Demands," in George W. Simmonds, ed., *Nationalism in the USSR and Eastern Europe in the Era of Brezhnev and Kosygin* (Detroit: University of Detroit Press, 1977), p. 141.

became clear: on January 1, 1989, well before the CPL crumbled, Latvians accounted for only 39.7 percent of the 184,182 party members and candidates, less than the Russian share of 43.1 percent.[14] A portion of the Latvian total was accounted for by *latovichi*, thus rendering the number of home-grown Latvians even smaller. If earlier estimates of the nationality composition for previous years are accurate, the Communist Party of Latvia did not have Latvian majority since the late 1940s or early 1950s, if ever.[15]

The Russian-dominated Communist Party of Latvia carried out a social policy that was, in many realms, discriminatory against Latvians and the Latvian language. Issues of language use in the Soviet context and elsewhere are often infused with ethnopolitical meaning, because they affect economic opportunities and group status. If the regime favors one language, those who are native speakers have a competitive edge in the economy. Moreover, as Donald Horowitz has noted, "the status of the language denotes the status of the group that speaks it."[16] By this measure, Russians have occupied a position of superior status to the Latvians, leading to considerable resentment among the latter. When the taboo on discussion of nationality conflicts was destroyed during the Gorbachev era, Latvians strongly voiced their sense of grievance, highlighting education and language policy as particularly sore points.

While a comprehensive survey of education policy falls beyond the purview of this chapter, a few examples should suffice to demonstrate the general thrust of the discriminatory measures despite the regime's formal commitment to bilingualism. Before changes at the end of the 1980s, Latvian-language schools required four to six hours of Russian-language study each week, while Russian-language schools required only two hours of Latvian study. Latvian high school students were required to take a final exam in Russian, while Russians faced no such requirement in Latvian.[17] Teachers of the Russian language in rural schools had salaries 15 percent higher than those of teachers of Latvian.[18] Beginning in 1975, doctoral dissertations had to be translated into Russian in Latvia and the other non-Russian republics, otherwise they could not be approved.[19] Educational policy perpetuated asymmetric bilingualism – a feature of daily life that was particularly galling for Latvians.

Only 21.1 percent of the Russians claimed knowledge of Latvian in the 1989 census; the corresponding figures for the other large minorities were even lower except for the Poles, of whom 22.8 percent claimed to know Latvian. 65.7 percent of all Latvians, on the other hand, claimed knowledge of Russian.[20] This asymmetry in language knowledge caused considerable resentment among the Latvians, particularly in light of the fact that many Russian-speakers did not learn even rudimentary Latvian after many years of residence in the republic. Adding insult to injury, Russians were known to demand that Latvians speak a "human language" (i.e. Russian) and not the language of "dogs" and "fascists" (i.e. Latvian).[21] Though the regime never used such terminology, it did politicize the language issue, often making the knowledge of Russian and willingness to speak it a sign of political loyalty.

Discontent with hyperindustrialization, Slavic immigration, Russification, and other pathologies of communist rule in Latvia could not be openly voiced before the era of glasnost in the late 1980s. Indeed, the few dissidents that raised the banner of nationalism or democracy during the 1970s were harshly repressed.[22] Unlike their Lithuanian counterparts, Latvian dissidents lacked an organizational base such as the Catholic Church. Open resistance was rare. Despite the pressures outlined above, there was little assimilation among Latvians, but some acculturation. Though many Latvians claimed knowledge of Russian in 1989, 97.4 percent considered Latvian their native language. That same year, over 95 percent of all Latvians in the Soviet Union resided in their titular republic.[23] The large population of non-native immigrants in the republic, however, led to a relatively high proportion of mixed marriages, indicating an erosion of Latvian group boundaries. About 20 percent of all marriages involving a Latvian are mixed marriages – one of the highest shares for the titular nationality of any union republic.[24] The overwhelming majority of Latvians, however, neither assimilated nor actively joined the ranks of the dissidents.

A more common response appeared to be either a turn to consumerism or cultural activism. Latvia and its Baltic neighbors consistently had the highest relative levels of consumption per capita of all the union republics,[25] a feature that might have blunted some political dissatisfaction during the Khrushchev and Brezhnev years. While some Latvians might have turned to consumerism, others sought refuge from the pressures for political conformity in culture. By the mid-1970s, the vibrant Latvian cultural scene led some Western observers to detect in Latvian efforts to protect and extend their cultural values a "conscious commitment to nationalism."[26] While some of Latvia's cultural output had political undertones, there is little evidence that most cultural activity exemplified more than an affirmation of humanistic values against the dead hand of communist ideology. Ultimately, any judgements about the political significance of consumerism or cultural activism during the Brezhnev years fall in the realm of speculation. Other than the economic and demographic data, the only "hard" evidence about the state of the Latvian nation before perestroika comes from interviews with emigres.

One study conducted in the early 1980s asked respondents about their perception of trends in the "power of the local nationality" in the non-Russian republics. Of the respondents mentioning the Baltic republics, 59 percent perceived the power of the Baltic nationalities to be decreasing, as Russians immigrated more, held the decisive positions in society, and imposed their culture on natives. The perception of decreasing power in the Baltics contrasted sharply with the perceived gains or stable positions of other republican nationalities.[27] It was only under Gorbachev that circumstances would permit Latvians to act to recoup their power position and voice their grievances about Soviet policy in Latvia since World War II.

Latvia at the dawn of the Gorbachev era: 1985–1987

One of Gorbachev's first moves as general secretary was to accelerate the personnel changes begun under Andropov as a means of breaking up entrenched republican machines and reasserting central control in the periphery after the "benign neglect" of the Brezhnev years.[28] In Latvia, the post of first secretary had already changed hands in 1984 with the accession of Boris Pugo, the former KGB chief in the republic. Far-reaching personnel turnover in Latvia was implemented in the first two years of Gorbachev's reign with the passing away and retirement of many beneficiaries of the 1959 purges. Key changes in 1985 included the rise of the moderate Latvians Anatolijs Gorbunovs and Janis Vagris to the posts of Central Committee secretary for ideology and chairman of the Presidium of the Supreme Soviet, respectively.[29] While Gorbachev was reasserting central control on personnel matters, he was loosening control in other realms by reducing official coercion and advocating glasnost.

The impact of glasnost in Latvia, as in the other Baltic republics, was profound. When Gorbachev legitimized a reevaluation of history, especially that of the Stalin era, he unwittingly gave Baltic activists the sanction to question the circumstances of the Soviet annexation of the Baltic states, and thus, the legitimacy of Soviet rule. Glasnost in Latvia was given a boost from outside actors when a conference on US–Soviet relations organized by the Chautauqua Institution, the Eisenhower World Affairs Institute, and the USSR–USA Society, took place September 15–19, 1986, in Jurmala, Latvia. The town-hall type conference featured speeches in which American representatives reaffirmed their government's non-recognition of the Soviet annexation of the Baltic republics. Though the US stance was condemned by Soviet officials, it was quietly welcomed by many Latvians, who were heartened to learn that the outside world still remembered them.[30] Since the American delegation included several members of Latvian descent, the conference also marked the first involvement of the emigre community in the political changes in Latvia.

Soon after the conference ended, glasnost became a political resource for unofficial activists for the first time. In Latvia, as in many areas of the Soviet Union, one of the first issues to elicit mass protest was environmental destruction. Why the environment became an early focus of discontent throughout the Soviet Union is not difficult to divine. The Chernobyl disaster and the slow official reporting on its effects evoked outrage and suspicion that the authorities were covering up other health hazards as well. From a political point of view, environmentalism was a relatively safe topic. It could be portrayed as a matter of efficiency and the rational employment of resources – technical, not political, problems. Moreover, the environment could bring together activists of widely divergent ideological inclinations: nationalists decrying the rape of their native soil and technocrats concerned with economic rationality.

In Latvia the specific issue that elicited a popular outcry was the construction of a hydroelectric dam on Latvia's most cherished river, the Daugava. Popular mobilization against the project was sparked when journalist Dainis Ivans and writer Arturs Snips published an article criticizing the project in a mid-October 1986 issue of a popular Latvian-language cultural weekly. In the following months, a debate about the project raged in the weekly, and grass-roots activists organized meetings and a letter-writing campaign against the project. Over 30,000 people of all nationalities signed letters protesting the dam – an astounding achievement for that period. The public outcry led the Latvian Council of Ministers to set up a commission to review the project, which was finally cancelled in the summer of 1987.[31] Though nationalism was not a driving force in the controversy, the campaign was a critical experience of empowerment for many activists. It was, for example, the political baptism of Dainis Ivans, who was later elected president of the Popular Front.

Public activism against the dam coincided with the emergence of several independent associations, some of which had distinctly political and nationalist agendas. A small group of mostly young, Latvian countercul-ture activists that had been organizing expeditions to repair old churches and monuments since 1983 coalesced into the Environmental Protection Club (VAK) in 1987. In many ways, VAK resembled Western green move-ments, with their holistic approach to the environment, inclusiveness, and aversion to structure and bureaucracy. VAK lent a political coloring to ecological activism by linking it to democratization. The group's manifesto stated that "democratization is not a dessert that will be brought to us on a platter from Moscow. Democratization will have to be won by struggle in every factory, farm or office . . ."[32] At the outset, however, VAK was tame in comparison to another grouping that emerged at about the same time – Helsinki '86.

Formed in July 1986 by three Latvian workers in the city of Liepaja, Helsinki '86 was the first openly nationalist unofficial organization to appear in Gorbachev-era Latvia.[33] Small in membership and harshly re-pressed by the regime, Helsinki '86 wrote letters to the regime, appeals to the West, and assorted memoranda. It called for the restoration of Latvia's independence, an end to the Sovietization and Russification of Latvia, and adherence to international covenants on human rights. Denied access to the media, the group reached only a limited audience through the circula-tion of *samizdat*. In the summer and fall of 1987, however, Helsinki '86 created shock waves throughout Latvia by organizing demonstrations in the heart of Riga at the Monument of Freedom, a symbol of Latvia's independence. The "calendar demonstrations" were organized to publicly commemorate the anniversaries of key events in Latvian history: the depor-tations of June 14, 1941, the signing of the Molotov-Ribbentrop Pact on August 23, 1939, and the declaration of Latvia's independence on Novem-ber 18, 1918. Despite the detention of several organizers and official harass-ment, thousands participated, attesting to the latent support for nation-alism among the Latvian population.[34]

Though several Helsinki '86 activists were exiled to the West and those remaining in Latvia were to play only marginal roles in subsequent events, the group was extraordinarily influential during the gestation period of a Latvian nationalist movement in 1987. The group provided a heroic example by facing down fear, repression, and official threats to openly advocate nationalist goals. It articulated numerous demands that would later gain wide currency: the elevation of Latvian to the status of state language, the end to non-native immigration, the end to discriminatory practices against Latvians, and, ultimately, the restoration of Latvia's independence. Both Helsinki '86 and VAK pioneered the use of nonviolent demonstrations, petition campaigns, appeals to international law, and the delegitimation of Soviet rule by filling in historical "blank spots" – tactics that came to be employed by the broader Latvian nationalist movement in following years.

Groups such as Helsinki '86 and VAK, however, could not attract a mass following in the absence of media coverage. Composed primarily of working class youth and elements from the counterculture, they were short on skilled professionals and political savvy but rich with enthusiasm and courage. Though some links between these "informal" groups and the creative intelligentsia had been forged during the campaign against the hydroelectric dam in 1986–1987, it was only in 1988 that the intelligentsia jumped on the nationalist bandwagon.

The emergence of a mass nationalist movement: 1988

At the beginning of 1988, the intelligentsia took the lead in reexamining and commemorating the historical events that occasioned the demonstrations of the previous summer. In early March, the creative unions established two commissions to rehabilitate victims of Stalinism. More significantly, the creative unions organized an official demonstration at the end of the month commemorating the 1949 deportations. Official sanction for the ceremony opened the floodgates of popular participation, and some 25,000 people attended the ceremony.[35] Soon thereafter, the Latvian intelligentsia followed the example of its Estonian counterpart, which had already begun to engage in political activity outside the confines of the Communist Party.[36]

The Latvian creative intelligentsia entered the political arena at an expanded plenum of the Writers' Union on June 1–2 devoted to "Pressing Problems of Soviet Latvian Culture on the Eve of the 19th CPSU Conference."[37] The most prominent theme in the speeches of the participants of the plenum was the perceived threat of Latvian ethnic annihilation. The sense of looming disaster was highlighted in numerous speeches decrying the demographic situation, in which unregulated migration into the republic and a low (in some years, negative) birth rate augured the minoritization of Latvians in their ancestral homeland. The demographic crisis, in turn, was portrayed as having led to a cultural crisis in which the Latvian language had been forced out of many spheres of public life by the Russian language. Finally, the same hypercentralized economic system that had channelled immigrants into the republic was creating an ecological disaster with increasingly adverse effects on the health of the population, Latvian and non-Latvian alike.

The speakers at the plenum touched upon extremely sensitive topics, going far beyond officially prescribed norms of glasnost. One of the most controversial speeches was given by Mavriks Vulfsons, a veteran political commentator, who openly questioned the official myth of a socialist revolution in the Latvia of 1940 and called the events an "occupation." Many speakers condemned Russian chauvinism and the privileged status of Russian in Latvia – an issue of extreme political sensitivity. Several speakers, among them liberal communists and non-Party members, openly criticized the former Communist Party leadership as the cause of current ills and the current leadership for being conservative and incapable of facing the challenges of the day. While the plenum served as a forum for the pent-up grievances of almost fifty years, the most significant result was the resolution passed by the participants.[38]

The primary theme of the resolution was the demand for decentralization and "sovereignty." In the realm of economics, the resolution called for republican self-financing and local control over the natural resources of the republic. In defense matters, it suggested the desirability of territorial military formations and military training in the Latvian language. As a "sovereign" member of the Soviet federation, Latvia should also be able to participate in the international arena as a member of the United Nations, UNESCO, the Olympics, and in other fora. "Sovereignty" would also entail the creation of republican citizenship, a badge of the union republics' heightened political status, as well as a measure that would facilitate a more practical task: the "strict regulation and control of migration processes" into the republic. While decentralization was portrayed as being in the interests of all of Latvia's inhabitants, the resolution unequivocally demanded priority status for Latvians. The Communist Party of Latvia and the government of the Latvian SSR were urged to consider one of their main tasks to be "the preservation and renewal of the Latvian nation." Moreover, pointing to the precedents of Georgia, Armenia, and Azerbaijan, the resolution recommended that Latvian be granted the status of state language. National demands were accompanied by liberal democratic ones, such as the demand to halt censorship, guarantee the inviolability of postal and other forms of communication, separate the legislative and executive branches of government, and support the nomination to leading posts of non-Party members.

The plenum witnessed the first moves towards the creation of a new political organization, as an initiative group led by journalist Viktors Avotins circulated a document arguing the need for a "democratic popular front of Latvia."[39] The plenum's resolution, however, omitted mention of the front. This marked the start of a complicated game of cat-and-mouse by the Communist Party, the creative intelligentsia, and the informal groups. The Party was on the defensive thereafter.

On June 18, CP head Boris Pugo called a crisis plenum of the Central Committee. The minutes of the stormy plenum[40] reveal a Party leadership that was deeply divided, dominated by conservatives, fearful and suspicious of the activism in society. Representatives of the media came under repeated criticism. For example, CPL second secretary Vitaly Sobolev angrily confronted Janis Leja, the head of Latvian television and radio, with the questions: "Do you not think that the three days of propaganda which Latvian television made for the Writers' Union meeting poured oil on the fire? Was it necessary?" Several participants expressed outrage at Mavriks Vulfsons' speech at the Writers' plenum, with one local party secretary calling it "political prostitution." Pugo and other speakers noted with some concern the "consolidation" of the forces of the informal groups and the increasingly "political," "nationalist," and "anti-Soviet" character of their activities. The KGB chairman accused Radio Free Europe of "seeking to provoke the creation of a national front." The proceedings of the plenum were not published in Latvia, but the general thrust of the meeting became common knowledge, driving together the intelligentsia and the informal groups.

On June 21, another appeal to form a front signed by representatives of both the informal groups and the creative intelligentsia was circulated, but was not published because it featured such controversial signatories.[41] This appeal, with more "mainstream" signatures beneath it, finally found its way into the press a month later.[42] The various writers, journalists, and academics who had been discussing plans for a front then coalesced into a single organizing committee that worked out of the Writers and Artists Unions and tapped the expertise of lawyers, economists, and other professionals.[43]

While the Party leadership had initially viewed the stirrings towards a popular front with alarm, it quickly moved to regain the initiative after the crisis atmosphere of its June 18 Central Committee plenum. Party chief Boris Pugo made an uncharacteristically liberal speech at the 19th Party Conference in Moscow at the end of June, echoing some of the demands raised at the Writers' meeting.[44] After an early August visit to Latvia by Politburo member Aleksandr Yakovlev,[45] the Party leadership in Latvia apparently decided to stop resisting the inevitable and take a more active role in influencing events. The first president of the Popular Front, Dainis Ivans, later recalled that "in August, in many factories, the Party committees urged workers to join the TF [Popular Front]; many of these tried to disrupt work at the first Congress."[46]

At the same time, leaders of the informal groups, especially of Helsinki '86 and VAK, remained suspicious of the establishment intellectuals and the liberal communists organizing the popular front during the summer. Some of the more radical members of the informal groups had already formed "Latvia's National Independence Movement" (LNNK) in late June with the aim of promoting complete independence.[47] The removal of the signatures of radicals from the June 21 appeal aroused suspicions among the leaders of VAK, prompting them to move towards the creation of another front – an "informal Popular Front" to unite all the informal groups.[48]

Despite the maneuverings of the leadership of the CPL and the suspicions of the radicals, the initiative led by the creative intelligentsia rapidly gathered force. By September 20, 2,300 Popular Front local chapters had formed with over 80,000 members.[49] Faced with this groundswell of activism, the republican leadership moved to defuse popular discontent. On September 29, the Supreme Soviet declared Latvian the state language and legalized the long-banned independence-era national flag.[50] On the eve of the Front's founding congress, Moscow intervened to shuffle the republic's leadership in preparation for more trying political times. Boris Pugo was promoted to head the Party Control Commission in Moscow, Janis Vagris became first secretary of the CPL, and Anatolijs Gorbunovs became the chairman of the Supreme Soviet.

On October 8–9, over 1,000 delegates representing more than 110,000 dues-paying members of over 2,300 local chapters convened in Riga for the founding congress of the Popular Front of Latvia (LTF). The social composition of the delegates, almost all of whom were Latvians, was as follows: 20 percent engineers and mechanics; 16 percent teachers and professors; 16 percent factory workers, construction workers and drivers; 3 percent journalists; 3 percent cultural workers and 2 percent artists.[51] About one-third of the delegates were Communist Party members, though representatives from Helsinki '86, VAK, LNNK, and religious groups also participated alongside the creative intelligentsia.[52] At the congress, the informal Popular Front merged into the LTF, though its members remained the voice of radicalism within the ranks of the larger organization. While the congress featured speeches that sometimes went beyond those at the Writers' plenum to demand Latvia's complete independence, more important were the passage of the statutes, programs, and several resolutions.[53]

The program incorporated the demands contained in the resolution of the Writers' plenum, expanded upon them, and set out additional demands. It placed the Front more clearly in competition with the Communist Party, stating that the LTF "does not recognize as democratic the monopoly rights of any political organization to rule society and public life." Political sovereignty, according to the program, entailed the republic's right to veto central legislation affecting its interests. Economic sovereignty would permit Latvia to issue its own currency after a shift to republican self-financing on January 1, 1990. On the subject of nationality relations, the program demanded that a law be passed guaranteeing Latvians a majority vote in representative bodies at all levels. Moreover, the program called on the Latvian government to promote the voluntary return of immigrants (in the parlance of nationalists, "victims of Stalinist national policy") to their places of origin – a demand bound to raise the hackles of immigrant Slavs. Though the program and resolutions strongly asserted Latvian prerogatives, they also supported the right of all nationalities to cultural autonomy (including minority-language schooling), and called for the convocation of a Nationalities Forum to air ethnic grievances.

Janis Peters, the influential head of the Writers' Union, turned down the presidency of the Front and nominated Dainis Ivans for the post. Ivans, the thirty-three-year-old journalist who rose to prominence in the campaign against the hydroelectric dam, won the endorsement of the Congress to become the prime spokesman for the new organization. The congress also elected a 99-member Governing Council, which, in turn, elected an 18-member board to run the day-to-day affairs of the Popular Front.[54] The board came from diverse backgrounds: most members were Latvian, several were Russian, and one was Jewish. It contained prominent radicals such as Eduards Berklavs, the "national communist" purged in 1959 who had recently joined LNNK, and Ints Calitis, a dissident active in VAK. It also featured several party members, including the editor of the Latvian-language Komsomol daily. Most were skilled professionals or representatives of the creative intelligentsia. In theory, all major decisions required approval by the Governing Council. In practice, the board and its staff were to become the key actors in formulating policy, maintaining contacts with local chapters, and dealing with the republic's leadership.

The Popular Front ascendant

The newly appointed state and Party leaders had attended the founding congress as observers. Afterwards, Communist Party first secretary Janis Vagris held a joint new conference with Popular Front president Dainis Ivans in which both men pledged cooperation between their organizations.[55] However, several days later, the Central Committee issued a statement criticizing some of the anti-Soviet and secessionist calls at the congress and expressing concern about the underrepresentation of Russian-speakers in the Front and in its leadership.[56] Indeed, one of the most serious challenges facing the leadership of the Front was to attract the support of the non-Latvian population of the republic.

The overwhelming majority of the Front's estimated 200,000–300,000 members, perhaps as many as 90 percent, were Latvians.[57] Though the leadership and program of the Front were relatively moderate, anti-immigrant sentiment was strong among the membership of the Front at large. Even progressive Russian-speakers could be expected to have strong qualms about the Front, whose program was based on liberal nationalism and the priority of the Latvian nation. The Russian-speaking masses could not be expected to yield their privileged status on language issues and the like without a fight. Ethnic polarization had begun with the Writers' plenum, as Russian-speakers heard the pent-up grievances of Latvians for the first time. The process of polarization appeared to accelerate soon after the founding of the Popular Front, when word began to spread about the emergence of a Russian-dominated "International Front of the Workers of the Latvian SSR," or Interfront for short.[58]

The leadership of the Popular Front moved quickly to fulfill promises of supporting minority cultural autonomy and fostering interethnic dialogue. In November and early December 1988, the Popular Front helped to initiate eighteen National Cultural Associations (for Jews, Ukrainians, Belarusians, and others).[59] Then, in cooperation with the Communist Party leadership, the Popular Front helped to organize a Nationalities Forum in early December. The forum provided an opportunity for all groups to air their grievances, and the participants passed three resolutions expressing support for Latvia's sovereignty, concern about the ecological situation, and support for the efforts of minority groups to preserve their cultures.[60] From the perspective of the Popular Front's leadership, a key accomplishment was the support of minority groups for political sovereignty and economic autonomy – key planks in the Front's program.

The efforts of the Popular Front to garner the support of non-Latvians were not completely successful, as many Russian-speakers remained passive or outright hostile towards the Popular Front. Those in the latter category assembled for the founding congress of the Interfront in early January 1989.[61] The Interfront cast itself as the defender of the Russian-speaking population, though it was never to attract more than a vociferous minority of conservative Communist Party members, workers and managers in the military-industrial complex, and retired military officers. The Interfront's aim was to oppose any changes that threatened the formerly privileged status of Russian-speaking immigrants. The Interfront stoked fears that republican sovereignty and the erosion of Communist Party rule would leave Slavic immigrants in the position of second-class citizens under the resurgent Latvians. The Interfront, with its Brezhnev-era rhetoric, was more an object of ridicule than concern for most Latvians in late 1988 and early 1989.

A greater challenge to the Popular Front was posed by Moscow's proposals in late October 1988 to limit democratic changes and the rights of the republics through constitutional reform. The Popular Front moved rapidly to coordinate with its Estonian and Lithuanian counterparts a letter-writing campaign against the proposed amendments. This was the first instance of what was to become extensive cooperation between the three Baltic movements. By the end of November, Latvian Supreme Soviet chairman Gorbunovs reported receiving about a million signatures against the changes, demonstrating the depth of the Front's support.[62] Assisted by the Popular Front's legal experts, Gorbunovs successfully lobbied Moscow to change several points in the draft document.[63]

The spring 1989 elections to the Congress of People's Deputies provided the Popular Front with another opportunity to test its popular support and to gain access to the halls of power in Moscow. The Front engaged in a lively electoral campaign, successfully promoting the election of reformist communists and of several of its own more moderate leaders. Electoral success was the product of both an effective campaign and ethnic gerrymandering: some rural Latvian-dominated electoral districts contained 28,000 voters while multiethnic urban districts contained 150,000 voters each.[64] Once in Moscow, the Front's deputies, in cooperation with their counterparts from Estonia and Lithuania, succeeded in pushing through the creation of a special commission on the Molotov-Ribbentrop Pact in the Congress. But Baltic deputies would soon become disillusioned with the Congress and the new USSR Supreme Soviet because majorities of both these institutions were hostile towards Baltic aspirations.[65] While some of the Front's moderate leaders were in Moscow promoting the republic's sovereignty, those who remained in Latvia were promoting a more radical agenda.

Towards Latvian independence

While the Front's initial program called for "sovereignty" within the Soviet Union, many Front activists and informal groups wanted full independence. Throughout the spring of 1989, the leaders of the Front were subject to many pressures: criticism from Helsinki '86, VAK, and LNNK on the Front's ambiguous position on independence; the growing radicalization of the Front's rank and file; the example of the more assertive Fronts in Estonia and Lithuania; and the criticism of emigre groups, which had always espoused full independence. The Front was losing the political initiative. A turning point appeared to be the widely publicized congress of LNNK on May 28, at which the goal of independence was firmly set out and widely publicized in the Latvian media.[66] Three days later, those leaders of the Popular Front who were not in Moscow issued an appeal to the membership of the Front calling for a discussion of complete independence for Latvia.[67] The appeal presented the moderates, who were in Moscow, with a *fait accompli*. Even the Popular Front's president, Dainis Ivans, had not been informed of the decision to issue the appeal.[68] Once issued, the appeal could not be easily retracted, and the goal of independence was soon ratified by local chapters of the Front and the Governing Council.

With the decision to support independence, the Front aligned itself with the more radical informal groups, complicated relations with the Communist Party, and set itself on a collision course with Moscow. The conflict with Moscow first came to a head with the "Baltic Way" demonstration of August 23, 1989 – the fiftieth anniversary of the signing of the Molotov-Ribbentrop Pact. The three Baltic popular fronts mobilized nearly 2 million people to form a human chain stretching from Tallin through Riga to Vilnius.[69] This mass action was meant to demonstrate to Moscow and the world the lack of legitimacy of Soviet rule in the Baltic. Three days later the CPSU Central Committee issued a statement harshly criticizing the three Baltic movements and their leaders.[70]

The leaders, however, were generally more moderate than the membership at large. Their room for maneuver was constrained, not only by their own program and radicalized membership, but also by the more militant groupings on their political flanks who were quick to cry "Betrayal!" at the first sign of compromise by the Front. The informal groups had coalesced into a militant pro-independence "Citizens' Movement" over the summer that was pushing for a rapid break with the Soviet Union and the disenfranchisement of immigrants. By the beginning of 1990, this new movement gathered 900,000 signatures of people who wanted to be citizens of an independent Latvia, in effect, carrying out an unofficial referendum.[71]

Another factor that facilitated the radicalization of the Latvian and other Baltic movements was the example of the East European revolutions of late 1989 and early 1990. That the East European states could go their own way without Moscow intervening must have raised doubts in the minds of some Baltic activists about Gorbachev's willingness to use force to preserve the internal empire. When the newly elected Lithuanian Supreme Soviet declared independence on March 11, 1990, Moscow's reaction was relatively mild, and throughout the Baltic region there were strong hopes for a negotiated path to independence. The imposition of an economic blockade on Lithuania on April 18 was a sobering reminder that Moscow had other means of pressuring the Baltic republics. However, candidates supported by the Popular Front ran on a platform of independence during the elections in March and April. The Front's opposition was in disarray, and the Communist Party of Latvia split along national lines into pro-Soviet and pro-independence factions in early April.[72] When the final results of the elections were counted, candidates supported by the Front had trounced conservative communists and representatives of the Interfront.

On May 4, 1990, over two-thirds of the Latvian Supreme Soviet voted for the reestablishment of an independent state. In the hope of avoiding the fate of Lithuania, the Latvian declaration was a conditional one, calling for a "transitional period" of indeterminate length leading to complete independence from the Soviet Union.[73] The electoral success of pro-independence forces was striking in view of the demographic situation in Latvia: pro-independence candidates won the votes of not only an overwhelming number of Latvians, but also those of many non-Latvians.

In late 1990 and early 1991, the new Latvian government made little headway on economic and political reforms because Moscow used its economic and military power to obstruct most changes. The government of Latvia, in cooperation with those of Estonia and Lithuania, sought diplomatic support from the West and negotiations with Moscow. For over a year, the Baltic governments had little success on either front. The issue of Baltic independence generated divisions and controversy within Western governments, which responded timidly for fear of undermining Gorbachev. Non-recognition of the Soviet annexation of Latvia and other Baltic states after World War II did not translate into immediate support for the attainment of *de facto* independence. Calls for negotiations with Moscow fell on deaf ears, as Gorbachev had thrown in his lot with the conservatives.

Within Latvia, the pro-Soviet movement caused some instability. Though this movement represented only a small minority of the non-Latvian population, it had substantial support from the armed forces. On repeated occasions, Moscow tried to intimidate pro-independence forces with shows of force by the army and special MVD "black beret" troops.[74] The tactic backfired, steeling the resolve of independence advocates and pushing non-Latvians into the pro-independence camp. When the Latvian government held a plebiscite on independence on March 3, 1991, 73.68 percent of the voters opted for independence, a figure that included a large number of Russians.[75]

The conservative turn in Moscow came to a head in August 1991, when leaders of the Communist Party and the security organs carried out a short-lived coup. At the height of the coup attempt, the Latvian and Estonian governments declared full independence, thereby ending their "transitional periods" and aligning themselves with Lithuania.[76] The failed coup emasculated the Soviet central government and boosted the influence of Yeltsin, whom the Balts had supported since his ouster from the Politburo in 1987. When the resurgent RSFSR recognized Baltic independence on August 24, numerous Western countries followed suit. Recognition by the central Soviet government on September 6 was almost an anti-climax.

Prospects

At the end of 1991, a whole range of issues concerning the end of Soviet rule was being negotiated by the Latvian and Soviet governments: the status of the Slavic settler community, the timetable for withdrawal of Soviet troops, economic arrangements, Latvia's obligations with regard to past international agreements signed by the Soviet Union, and more. There appeared to be a willingness on both sides to come to mutually acceptable agreements, though many in Latvia appear to have unrealistic expectations about a rapid Soviet troop withdrawal and the possible "repatriation" of Slavic settlers to Russia proper. Conflicts within Latvia both among Latvians and between Latvians and Russians are bound to surface during the process of "deoccupation." The prospects for peaceful resolution of these conflicts appear positive, given the past lack of bloodshed in the region, the emergence of political pluralism and a vibrant independent press, and the severing of links between the local pro-Soviet movement and Soviet security forces.

The Latvians and their Baltic neighbors now confront the constraints of economic dependence on Russia and the other former Soviet republics and the uncertainties of living next door to a large, unstable country. Economic ties between Latvia and Russia are bound to remain close, as Latvia imports the lion's share of its energy resources and raw materials from the East. Since most Latvian manufacturers cannot yet compete in the world market, they will be forced to continue targeting the Russian market for the time being. Though the small size of the Baltic economies means they will be affected by the continued deterioration of the Russian economy, it also means that radical marketizing reforms and aid from the West will have a proportionately larger beneficial impact.

Conclusion[77]

With their attainment of independence, Estonia, Latvia, and Lithuania have broken all the rules. Rule number one: violence and war are the midwives of new states. As the Balts defied Moscow, students of ethnic conflict urged them to "stay put," pointing to the bloody civil wars that generally erupt from territorial secessions. Students of history noted that the final disintegration of the great European land empires took place in the aftermath of world war. The Baltic nationalist movements triumphed without violence, despite the numerous provocations of the pro-Soviet movement and Soviet security forces. Rule number two: territorially contiguous secessions generally fail. Only one secession in the post-war era – that of Bangladesh from Pakistan – had been successful. If history were any guide, the Baltic independence movements would be suppressed by Moscow or moderate their demands due to economic dependence.[78] The cost of suppression proved too high for Moscow, and the collapse of the Soviet economy only enhanced the appeal of independence. Rule number three: the international community is profoundly hostile to the fragmentation of one of its member states.[79] Some analysts have gone so far as to argue that the conservative nature of the interstate order constitutes a "regime" that is self-sustaining and brooks few challenges.[80] The special legal position of the Baltic states and Western non-recognition of the Soviet annexation set the Baltic republics apart from other republics in the Soviet Union and garnered the Baltic movements international support for independence.

Notes

I would like to acknowledge the support of the Albert Einstein Institution during the writing of this chapter.

1 *Lauku Avize*, March 23, 1990.
2 For a cogent examination of developments in Latvia in this period, see Andrejs Plakans, "The Latvians," in Edward C. Thaden, ed., *Russification in the Baltic Provinces and Finland, 1855–1914* (Princeton: Princeton University Press, 1981), pp. 207–284.
3 For a history of interwar Latvia, see Georg von Rauch, *The Baltic States: The Years of Independence, Estonia, Latvia, Lithuania, 1917–1940*, trans. Gerald Onn (Berkeley and Los Angeles: University of California Press, 1974).
4 Romuald J. Misiunas and Rein Taagepera, *The Baltic States: Years of Dependence, 1940–1980* (Berkeley and Los Angeles: University of California Press, 1983), p. 41.
5 For an overview of the period of Nazi occupation, see *ibid.*, pp. 44–68. See also Frank Gordon, *Latvians and Jews Between Germany and Russia*, trans. Vaiva Pukite and Janis Straubergs (Stockholm: Memento, 1990).
6 Deportation figures cited in *ibid.*, pp. 70, 96.
7 Seweryn Bialer, *Stalin's Successors: Leadership, Stability, and Change in the Soviet Union* (New York: Cambridge University Press, 1980), p. 23.
8 Cited in Misiunas and Taagepera, *The Baltic States*, table 6, p. 282.
9 See *ibid.*, pp. 134–141, and Juris Dreifelds, "Latvian National Consciousness and Group Demands Since 1959," in George W. Simmonds, ed., *Nationalism in the USSR and Eastern Europe in the Era of Brezhnev and Kosygin* (Detroit: University of Detroit Press, 1977), pp. 136–156.
10 See Bohdan Nahaylo and Victor Swoboda, *Soviet Disunion: A History of the Nationalities Problem in the Soviet Union* (New York: The Free Press, 1990), pp. 130–137.
11 Latvijas PSR Valsts Statistikas Komiteja, *Latvija Sodien: Socialekonomisku Aprakstu Krajums* (Riga, 1990), p. 81.
12 *Ibid.*, p. 74.
13 See Rasma Karklins, *Ethnic Relations in the USSR: The Perspective From Below* (Boston: Allen and Unwin, 1986), p. 53.
14 *Padomju Latvijas Komunists*, no. 6, June 1989, p. 29.
15 See the estimates for various years published in Misiunas and Taagepera, *The Baltic States*, pp. 281–284.
16 Donald L. Horowitz, *Ethnic Groups in Conflict* (Berkeley and Los Angeles: University of California Press, 1985), p. 219.
17 *Literatura un Maksla*, no. 28, July 1, 1988.
18 *Latvijas Tautas Fronte, Gads Pirmais* (Riga: Latvijas Tautas Fronte, 1989), p. 196.
19 *Literatura un Maksla*, no. 28, July 1, 1988.
20 *Natsional'ny Sostav Naseleniya, Chast' II* (Moscow: Gossudarstvenny Komitet Po Statistike, 1989), pp. 85–86.
21 See *Latvijas Tautas Fronte, Gads Pirmais*, p. 188, and *Literatura un Maksla*, July 1, 1988.
22 For a survey of dissent in Latvia, see Ludmilla Alexeyeva, *Soviet Dissent: Contemporary Movements for National, Religious, and Human Rights* (Middletown, CT: Wesleyan University Press, 1985), pp. 97–105.
23 *Natsional'ny Sostav Naseleniya, Chast' II*, pp. 85, 101.
24 Latvijas PSR Valsts Statistikas Komiteja, *Latvija Sodien*, p. 29.

25 See, e.g., the data in Gertrude E. Schroeder, "Nationalities and the Soviet Economy," in Hajda and Beissinger, eds., *The Nationalities Factor*, table 4, p. 51.

26 Janis John Penikis, "Latvian Nationalism: Preface to a Dissenting View," in Simmonds, ed., *Nationalism in the USSR and Eastern Europe in the Era of Brezhnev and Kosygin* p. 159.

27 Karklins, *Ethnic Relations in the USSR*, p. 81.

28 For an overview of personnel changes at the dawn of the Gorbachev era, see Thane Gustafson and Dawn Mann, "Gorbachev's Next Gamble," *Problems of Communism*, vol. 36, July–August 1987, pp. 1–20.

29 For a summary of the personnel changes in 1985–1986, see Romuald J. Misiunas and Rein Taagepera, "The Baltic States: Years of Dependence, 1980–6," *Journal of Baltic Studies*, vol. 20, no. 1, Spring 1989, pp. 66–67.

30 For the proceedings of the conference, see Edvins Berkos *et al.*, eds., *Jurmalas Dialogi* (Riga: Avots, 1987). See also Dzintra Bungs, "After the Jurmala Conference: Imperfect Glasnost'," *Radio Free Europe Research*, Baltic Area Situation Report (hereafter, cited as RFER BA SR), no. 8, December 9, 1986.

31 For a review of the entire incident, see Nils R. Muiznieks, "The Daugavpils Hydro Station and Glasnost in Latvia," *Journal of Baltic Studies*, vol. 18, no. 1, spring 1987, pp. 63–70.

32 *Staburags*, no. 1, January–February, 1988, p. 5. For an overview of VAK's activities, see Juris Dreifelds, "Latvian National Rebirth," *Problems of Communism*, vol. 38, no. 4, July–August, 1989.

33 For an overview of the membership and goals of the group, see Dzintra Bungs, "One-and-a-half Years of Helsinki 86," RFER BA SR, no. 2, February 16, 1988.

34 For a *samizdat* account of the June 14 demonstration, see *Auseklis* (Riga), no. 1, September, 1987, pp. 7–10. For an overview of the latter demonstrations, see Dzintra Bungs, "The Latvian Demonstration of 23 August 1987," RFER BA SR, no. 7, October 28, 1987, and "A Survey of the Demonstrations on November 18," RFER BA SR, no. 9, December 18, 1987.

35 On the emergence of public activism on the part of the intellectuals, see Dreifelds, "Latvian National Rebirth," p. 83.

36 See Toomas Ilves, "The People's Front: the Creation of a Quasi Political Party," RFER BA SR, no. 5, May 20, 1988.

37 The speeches of the participants were published in *Literatura un Maksla*, no. 24, June 10, no. 25, June 17, no. 28, July 1 and no. 29, July 8, 1988.

38 The resolution is printed in *Literatura un Maksla*, no. 24, June 10, 1988.

39 See the speech by Valdis Steins in *Atmoda*, no. 24, June 12, 1989. The original document has not been published and is only available in *samizdat* form.

40 The minutes have yet to be published in Latvia. Excerpts were published in the Swedish newspaper *Dagens Nyheter*, October 16, 1988, translated in *Foreign Broadcast Information Service*, October 21, 1988, pp. 59–64.

41 See Dzintra Bungs, "People's Front Planned," RFER BA SR, no. 7, July 13, 1988; see also the speech by Janis Ruksans in *Latvijas Tautas Fronte, Gads Pirmais*, p. 64.

42 See the interview with Dainis Ivans, the first president of the Popular Front and

a signatory of the June 21 appeal, *Jurmala*, October 20, 1988, for an account of the machinations surrounding the appeal. See also Dreifelds, "Latvian National Rebirth," p. 84.

43 *Ibid.* See also the comments by Peters at the founding Congress of the Popular Front in *Latvijas Tautas Fronte, Gads Pirmais*, pp. 10, 13.
44 For a text of Pugo's speech, see *Pravda*, July 1, 1988.
45 See Dzintra Bungs, "Yakovlev in Latvia: An Exercise in 'Socialist Pluralism,'" RFER BA SR, no. 9, August 26, 1988.
46 *Atmoda*, October 2, 1990.
47 See Dzintra Bungs, "New Group for Latvian Independence Formed," RFER BA SR, no. 7, July 13, 1988.
48 See the interview with Valdis Turins, the former vice president of VAK, in *Briva Latvija* (Munster, FRG), October 24, 1988.
49 *Padomju Jaunatne*, September 22, 1988.
50 *Cina*, September 30, 1988.
51 Ojars Rozitis, "The Rise of Latvian Nationalism," *Swiss Review of World Affairs* (Zurich), 38, no. 11, February, 1989, p. 26.
52 Dreifelds, "Latvian National Rebirth," p. 85.
53 The congress speeches, resolutions, statutes and program have been published in *Latvijas Tautas Fronte, Gads Pirmais*.
54 For lists of members of the Council and board, see *ibid.*, pp. 231–233.
55 *Padomju Jaunatne*, October 11, 1988.
56 *Ibid.*, October 15, 1988.
57 These figures are cited in J. Brolish, "Perestroika i natsional'nye protsessy v sovetskoy Latvii," *Chto delat'* (Moscow: 1989), p. 183.
58 See *Sovetskaya Latviya*, October 20, 1988; see also *Cina*, October 30, 1988, for an interview with two Interfront spokesmen.
59 See *Latvijas PSR Tautu Forums, Foruma Orgkomitejas Specializlaidums* (Latvian SSR Nationalities Forum, Special Publication of the Forum Organizing Committee), December 10–11, 1988, pp. 2–3.
60 For speeches by prominent delegates to the Forum and the texts of the resolutions, see *Latvijas PSR Tautu Foruma Materiali* (Riga: Avots, 1989).
61 For an overview of the Interfront, see Nils R. Muiznieks, "The Pro-Soviet Movement in Latvia," *Report on the USSR*, 1, no. 34, August 24, 1990.
62 *Padomju Jaunatne*, November 24, 1988.
63 See Dreifelds, "Latvian National Rebirth," pp. 87.
64 Valerii A. Tishkov, "An Assembly of Nations or an All-Union Parliament?" *Journal of Soviet Nationalities*, 1, no. 1, Spring 1990, p. 113.
65 See Nils R. Muiznieks, "The Evolution of Baltic Cooperation," *Report on the USSR*, 2, no. 6, July 6, 1990.
66 See Dreifelds, "Latvian National Rebirth," p. 88.
67 For the text of the appeal, see *Atmoda*, June 5, 1989.
68 Author's interviews with Dainis Ivans and other Front leaders in Riga, June 1989. This version of events is similar to that in Dreifelds, "Latvian National Rebirth," p. 88.
69 See Dzintra Bungs, "Balts Mark 50th Anniversary of Molotov-Ribbentrop Pact," RFEF BA SR 8, September 11, 1989.
70 For a text of the statement, see *Pravda*, August 27, 1989.

71 See Nils R. Muiznieks, "The Committee of Latvia: An Alternative Parliament?," *Report on the USSR*, 2, no. 29, July 20, 1990.
72 See Dzintra Bungs, "Latvian Communist Party Splits," *Report on the USSR*, 2, no. 17, April 27, 1990.
73 *Cina*, May 5, 1990.
74 See Muiznieks, "The Pro-Soviet Movement in Latvia."
75 Voter turnout was 87.57 percent. *Diena* (Riga), March 5, 1991, p. 1.
76 For English-language texts of the declarations, see *The Baltic Independent* (Tallinn), August 30–September 5, 1991, p. 3.
77 This section draws heavily on an article I published in *Khronika*, vol. 2, no. 1, September 1991 (the newsletter of the Berkeley-Stanford Program in Soviet Studies), Berkeley, entitled "The Future of the Baltic States."
78 See Horowitz, *Ethnic Groups in Conflict*.
79 See Lee C. Buchheit, *Secession: The Legitimacy of Self-Determination* (New Haven: Yale University Press, 1978), pp. 16–42.
80 For an in-depth treatment of this issue, see Alexis Heraclides, "Secessionist Minorities and External Involvement," *International Organization*, 44, no. 3, Summer 1990, pp. 341–379.

9 Estonia: a plural society on the road to independence

CYNTHIA KAPLAN

Estonia's national awakening began during the middle of the nineteenth century and culminated in the birth of the Republic of Estonia in 1918. The cultural, economic, and linguistic phenomena associated with Estonian nationalism conform to the European model of the emergent nineteenth-century and early twentieth-century nation state.[1] Although Estonian independence ended in August 1940 when it became a Union Republic of the USSR, Estonian national sentiment survived. The secret codicil of the Molotov-Ribbentrop Pact of 1939 decided the fate of Estonians for over fifty years, but it could not provide a basis for the legitimate exercise of power. Perestroika did not give rise to nationalism. Perestroika provided a venue in which national goals and aspirations could be articulated and defined. How national sentiment defines political goals and methods is a process reflective of the nature of Estonian society, the interaction of political leaders in the context of competition for political authority and power, the environment shaped by Moscow, the actions of other national groups in the Soviet Union, and the response of the outside world.

The role of nationality in the political process can only be understood in the context of the basic characteristics which define Estonia and those living on its territory. Estonia is neither homogeneous, nor a heterogeneous "melting pot" of hyphenated nationalities. It is a plural society in which ethnic groups, primarily Estonians and Russian speakers (mostly Slavs) live separate lives defined by language, education, jobs, occupational structures, and attitudes. The degree to which this is a function of past state policy versus group preference remains impossible to determine. However, to miss this central feature of Estonian existence is to ignore a critical factor shaping interaction between ethnic Estonian aspirations and relations with its non-titular national groups and the center.[2]

Plural society

The pre-Soviet period

Historically, Estonians lived with Germans and Russians who formed the upper levels of urban society through the nineteenth century. Estonians

206

constituted the peasantry, but with industrialization and the growth of commerce during the nineteenth century, they began to increasingly live in cities.[3] Given low birthrates, Estonian society has always been particularly sensitive to in and out migration. During the republican era (1918–1940), Russians slightly increased their proportion of the population. In 1934, Russians reached 8.2 percent of the total population, while Germans had declined to 1.5 percent. Estonians living in traditionally defined areas (Estland and northern Livland as opposed to areas added as a result of the 1920 Treaty of Tartu) rose to 92.9 percent.

On the eve of World War II, Estonia remained a rural society with 67.2 percent of the population residing in the countryside. However, Estonians had assumed important roles in the industrial and commercial sectors of the economy.[4] "In 1936, 84 percent of all industrialists were Estonian and 59 percent of the value of urban commercial transactions was in Estonian hands.[5] The urban population by 1934 was overwhelmingly Estonian (85.5 percent).[6] Due at least in part to Protestantism, Estonians enjoyed high literacy rates despite their rural background. As noted by Toivo Raun, Estonia was among the most homogeneous of the Eastern European states to emerge after World War I.[7] The period of independence produced a nation state in which, for the first time, Estonians enjoyed access to both the political and social hierarchies of the state.

Political structure: pre-Gorbachev

As was true throughout the Soviet Union, the Communist Party in Estonia dominated the state. This meant not only control over policy making and implementation, but also over *nomenklatura*.[8] On the mass level, native Estonian membership barely maintained its majority during the 1980s.[9] In the Central Committee and Politburo, however, native Estonians were a distinct minority. Leadership cadres were drawn primarily from non-native Estonians (those from outside of Estonia) and Russians. Johannes Käbin, a non-native Estonian, led the party in Estonia for over three decades. Over time, he acted as an intermediary representing local interests to Moscow. Upon his retirement in 1978, he was replaced by another non-native Estonian, Karl Vaino, who favored centralization and showed little sympathy for local and ethnic interests.[10] Policies during these years often led to conflict with Estonian intellectuals, those who were to become the new political leaders of Estonia. This period epitomizes nationality policies associated with a view from Moscow. Only in 1988 did a native Estonian, Vaino Väljas, become First Party Secretary.[11] Thus, the pinnacle of political power before perestroika remained outside the purview of native Estonians. Differences in access to political and economic power and authority based on nationality typifies plural societies.

The political consequences of World War II not only destroyed the Republic of Estonia, but had a dramatic effect on the nature of Estonian society. The influx of migrants from other areas of the Soviet Union contributed to a heterogeneous population living on the territory of Estonia. The political domination of the center translated heterogeneity into a pattern of separate societies, a plural society.

Demographic structure

Within the post-1939 borders before the war, 92 percent of the population was ethnically Estonian.[12] The changes produced by the war, incorporation into the Soviet Union with its concomitant immigration of Estonians living in the USSR and the exiling of Estonians make precise estimates difficult, but by 1950 the Estonian proportion of the population had dropped to approximately 76 percent.[13] The demographic situation stabilized during the 1950s, but turned against the Estonians during the 1960s and 1970s when industrialization planned by Moscow attracted Slavic migrants. Migration into Estonia declined through the 1980s, but the low birthrate of Estonians contributed to the continuing fall in the percentage of the republic's Estonian population. According to the 1989 census, they comprised 61.5 percent with Russians accounting for 30.1 percent.[14] Entire areas of northeast Estonia are now Russian, with the capital, Tallinn, almost evenly divided between Estonians and non-Estonians. Given their low birthrates and an age structure weighted toward the elderly, Estonians fear becoming a minority in their own country and with that, eventual assimilation. Demographic shifts alone, however, cannot produce a plural society. None the less, rapid changes in population patterns shape the dynamic of ethnic relations.

The economy

The structure of Estonia's economy also contributed to the formation of the postwar plural society. Industrial growth after World War II in Estonia was the highest in the USSR.[15] These growth rates continued to exceed Soviet averages until the 1970s.[16] Much of the industrial growth was planned centrally and required augmentation the workforce, i.e., the migration of workers, most frequently Slavs. Before 1964, industry was directed locally, but "by 1969 about 40 local and Union-wide command centers were involved."[17] In 1980, 28 percent of industrial output was administered directly by all-Union ministries in Moscow and 60 percent by Union-republic ministries under central control.[18] The consequences of this centrally controlled growth was the migration to Estonia of Slavs who then worked in large factories directed by Russians with almost exclusively Slavic workforces. Frequently, these industries were defense-related. Estonians tended to be employed at smaller enterprises in the light industrial sector or involved in primarily white-collar work.[19]

The economic draw of jobs in an area with one of the highest standards of living in the USSR was evident. Of non-Estonians, 57 percent were born outside of Estonia, with 40 percent born in Russia.[20] Among "non-Estonians born outside of Estonia 60 percent had lived in the country over 15 years."[21] The period of economic expansion matches the influx of migrants.

The geographic concentration of the population is in large cities where there was industrial growth.[22] In the Northeast cities of Narva and Kohtla-Järve, Russians constitute 85.1 and 60.4 percent of the populations respectively. The countryside in general, and even rural hinterlands surrounding cities inhabited predominantly by Russians, remains almost exclusively Estonian.[23]

Data on the economic branch of employment clearly reflect the consequences of planned economic growth. In a survey of almost 7,000 residents of Estonia conducted during January through February 1991, ethnic segmentation by occupation is clear. Among those employed, Russians accounted for 52.3 percent of those in industry as compared to 35.5 percent of Estonians. Among all employed Russians, those in industry accounted for slightly over 40 percent, while Estonians accounted for only 13.2 percent of Estonians employed. In agriculture, Estonians dominated with 87.3 as compared to 7.8 percent of Russians. As a percentage of all employed Estonians, those working in agriculture accounted for approximately 31 percent. Russian agricultural workers accounted for only 5.8 percent of the entire employed population.[24]

Geographic and economic concentration by ethnic group promoted separate societies in which either Estonians or Russian-speakers dominated. Even in mixed areas such as Tallinn, jobs and housing are frequently segregated. Housing patterns are a consequence of special provisions provided for migrants. This policy is at least perceived to be at the expense of Estonians who wait long years in queue. Both the physical separation and the perception of unequal treatment shape the lives of Estonians and Russians on the territory of Estonia.

Language

The case for a plural society, of course, depends not only on the patterns of residence and employment, but also on knowledge of language and education. The issue of language – the knowledge of Estonian by non-Estonians – is, along with citizenship, the most serious dispute between the Estonian and Russian speaking communities. Among the Estonians interviewed in my survey of citizen participation in politics in Estonia (CPE), 85 percent knew Russian while approximately 37 percent of the Russian

Table 9.1. *Knowledge of the Estonian language by Russians, 1991*

Born/length of residence	Percentage of Russian respondents who know Estonian (%)
Born in Estonia	59.3
Entire life in Estonia	60.0
Majority of life in Estonia	31.6
Half of life in Estonia	22.8
Quarter of life	19.8
Several years	9.0

Source: Survey on Citizen Participation in Politics in Estonia. Random Sample = 6,884. Conducted: January–February 1991. Number of Russians in Sample = 2,025

respondents stated that they knew Estonian. Of course, these figures cannot provide the proficiency of the respondent's knowledge.

Length of residence in Estonia is clearly related to knowledge of the Estonian language. Knowledge of Estonian drops precipitously between those who were born or lived their entire lives in Estonia and those who migrated after childhood. This suggests that migrants, even those who have spent the majority of their lives in Estonia, have failed to learn Estonian. Without official intervention, migrants have been able to live using Russian within enclave communities or in their communications with Estonians. Granted that Estonian is a particularly difficult language to learn, none the less, migrants who do not know Estonian remain isolated from the cultural and mass communication networks of the Estonian community.[25] Furthermore, the extensive use of Russian has heightened the sensitivity of Estonians on the issue of ethnic survival.

If we turn to those respondents who are employed in industry, the knowledge of Estonian among Russians declines to 29.6 percent, whereas 98 percent of Estonian workers knew Russian. Needless to say, few Estonians engaged in agriculture claimed to know Russian. The general perception that Russians do not know Estonian and that a difference exists between those Russians who were born or have lived their entire lives in Estonia from those who have migrated more recently appears confirmed.

Another social division reflective of social stratification is based on occupation. If we define members of the intellectual classes as including those employed in the fields of science, mass communications, art, culture, and education, once again social differences emerge. Among Estonians employed 15.5 percent would fall into the category of "intellectual" (using the above definition) as compared to 9.5 percent of the Russian population. If the field of education is excluded, we find Estonian "intellectuals" fall to

Table 9.2. *Education among Estonians and Russians, 1991*

Level of education	Estonians	Russians
Less than completed secondary*	24.0%	14.0%
	(1,016)	(88)
Completed secondary	21.5	19.4
	(919)	(122)
Specialized secondary	32.6	54.5
	(1,381)	(343)
Higher education	21.8	12.0
	(925)	(76)

* Secondary education for Estonians is 11 years and for the Russian population is 10 years. This also means that higher education for the Estonian population equals a total of 16 years of education and for Russians 15 years.
Source: Survey of Citizen Participation in Estonia.

6.7 percent of the employed Estonian population and Russians to 2.7 percent. This tends to substantiate the stereotype often noted by Estonians that the Russian population lacks a humanistic intelligentsia.[26]

Given the reasons for migration, we would expect a large skilled and semi-skilled Russian working population and a smaller humanistic elite. The lack of the latter is often cited as a reason for the relatively weak leadership of more democratic forces in the Russian community. Perhaps this is an excuse offered by Estonian activists, but social differences clearly do exist. These differences tend to support the image of a differentially stratified society in which Estonians and Russians live in both horizontally and vertically stratified communities.

A final factor separating the two ethnic communities is education (see table 9.2). Educational levels among the Estonians and Russians reflect their respective occupational structures. More Estonians have higher education than Russians. The number of Russians with specialized secondary education necessary for skilled and semi-skilled jobs in industry, however, exceeds the Estonian.

To summarize, evidence tends to support the existence of horizontal stratification by ethnic group. Within each community, as would be expected in a plural society, vertical stratification differs. Occupational and educational differences were confirmed. These characteristics reflect the influx of a Slavic workforce necessitated by centrally planned industrial development. The migration which transformed a relatively homogeneous pre-World War II society into an increasingly heterogeneous society has reached the point of tipping the demographic and linguistic balance against the titular nationality. The fact that migration and its consequences were

the product of non-Estonian decision-makers intensified Estonian intellectuals' dissatisfaction with the nature of the state. The tensions arising
from the plural nature of society and the absence of autonomous control
over the country's future shape the nature of Estonian political life.

The politics of autonomy and self-determination

Estonian national aspirations arose in the context of economic autonomy and environmental concerns against a backdrop of cultural reassertion. The first goals were policy-oriented goals which could be negotiated
between a reformist center and an Estonian reformist movement and state.
Indeed, initially Gorbachev appeared to view Estonia as a perfect venue in
which to demonstrate the success of economic reform and perestroika.
How did within-system pressure for change become transformed into a
political movement aimed at independence?

Demands for economic autonomy first made in 1987 began a complex
political process within Estonia and between Estonia and Moscow which
ultimately resulted in demands for independence. The mass public played
an important role through demonstrations and its electoral participation.
Demonstrations and other political activities clearly centered around issues
of nationality. Voting preferences, for example, closely reflect nationality.[27] Yet the public's role could not determine the goals and methods of
political organizations and movements. Support for political ideals and
against symbols of the past may give impetus to political movements and,
in the context of a competitive electoral system, may shape opportunity
structures, but the masses alone cannot determine the course of political
events. The political agenda is the product of elites associated with political organizations. In Estonia, the political agenda arose through jockey-
ing for position between Estonian political organizations during competitive elections held in March 1989 (Congress of Peoples' Deputies),
December 1989 (local elections in Estonia), February 1990 (Congress of
Estonia), and culminated in the March 1990 elections to the Supreme
Council of Estonia.[28] The political agenda was also affected by interaction
with the center – Moscow. An additional factor in the political equation
was the position taken by the non-Estonian Russian speaking community,
which only partially supported Moscow's positions.

The political agenda moves from economic to national goals

The political process began in earnest with the formation of the Popular
Front of Estonia (PFE), a mass movement in support of perestroika. It was
established in October 1988 (officially registered in January 1989) in connection with the economic self-management program.[29] The PFE was an
umbrella organization coordinating the political activities of other organi-

zations. The General Program of the Popular Front of Estonia (October 1988) called for the "dismantling of the state-oriented administrative system," the formation of a Soviet Union based on the principles of confederation, the decentralization of power and making soviets into "competent decision-making bodies," and the adoption of self-management for Estonia.[30] In response to political and potential electoral challenges posed by radical (Estonian) and conservative/orthodox (non-Estonian) organizations, the PFE, in the fall of 1989, decided to support a policy calling for an independent Estonia outside of the Soviet Union.[31] Independence was pursued through a transitional stage in which negotiations between the Supreme Council of Estonia and the Soviet government in Moscow were to occur. The PFE correctly perceived its major vulnerability – popular support for independence was aroused by the radical forces. The growing tension with conservative/orthodox forces intensified nationalist desires for independence. Although initially an offer of a confederation of sovereign states by Moscow would have been seriously considered, by the December 1989 elections the national momentum had moved towards independence.

The radical Estonian organizations, such as the Estonian Heritage Society, Estonian National Independence Party, and the Union of Christian Democrats, sought the restoration of the former Republic of Estonia through elections to a successor parliamentary body to that of the Republic, the Congress of Estonia. The Supreme Council of Estonia was viewed as a temporary instrument through which policies could be implemented.[32] The clearly nationalist position assumed by these organizations placed not only independence on the political agenda, but also focused attention on nationalist issues, such as language and citizenship.

The orthodox/conservative political organizations, the Intermovement (established July 1988), and the United Council of Labor Collectives (OSTK, established November 1988) were set up in response to the PFE. Along with the Communist Party of Estonia (ideologically based on the platform of the CPSU), it provided the organizational leadership of the non-Estonian Russian speaking community. The Intermovement led by factory directors and retired military officers supported the indivisibility of the Soviet Union and defended socialism.[33] The OSTK focused more on the economic welfare of the Russian speaking population. By the spring of 1991, it appeared that OSTK supporters began to favor an autonomous Estonia within a Soviet confederation.

In the context of local elections (December 1989), the Estonian political center had to move toward independence if it was not to lose support. The Russian speaking organizations had boycotted these elections but returned to the political arena for the March 1990 elections to the Supreme Council of Estonia, realizing that authority resided increasingly in Tallinn.

Moscow's ability to exercise authority in the periphery had dramatically declined. In part, this was due to the collapse of the Communist Party of Estonia. The CPE initially supported autonomy in a confederation and economic self-management. It also stressed equal rights, intended to appeal to the non-Estonian population. As the Communist Party began to lose its popularity among Estonians, tension rose between members who wished for greater autonomy and independence and those who favored a federal structure. A split became inevitable. At the March 1990 20th Congress of the CPE, a split occurred with the creation of an independent party, predominantly Estonian, and a Russian party organization supporting Moscow.[34] With the exception of the best known CPE leaders, communist candidates were unsuccessful in the competitive elections. The independent CPE saw a role for itself as an intermediary between the politics of Estonian nationalism and those of the center. Yet, as a result of electoral failure, Moscow could not easily exercise power through the Estonian Supreme Council in which the Popular Front forces dominated.[35] For Moscow to act, it would have had to pursue an extra-parliamentary policy which would create a crisis. In the case of Estonia, it tried to avoid this.

The growing strength of nationalism was made clear during the elections. Organizational support took second place during elections to the politics of ethnicity (i.e., independence) and personality.[36] Personal competition for power contributed to dissension on the Estonian political scene. Dissatisfaction with leaders of the Popular Front, who formerly were associated with the Communist Party of Estonia, contributed to the near collapse of the Estonian government in the winter of 1990. This discontent, however, was focused more on style than substance.

The election of the Supreme Council of Estonia made possible the pursuit of the nationalist agenda. In particular, this meant the call for, and drafting of, electoral, citizenship, language, and migration laws. Residency requirements for candidacy and voting effectively disenfranchised recent immigrants to Estonia.[37] The citizenship law was hotly contested. For those on the right (radicals), residence in Estonia during the republican period or the inheritance of citizenship from republican citizens was the preferred basis for citizenship. However, the decision as to who was to be an automatic citizen without formal application had to await the passing of a new constitution. Many Estonian intellectuals believed that a referendum for independence and the determination of the type of state an independent Estonia should be was the purview solely of ethnic Estonians. Using this logic, other national groups could later gain citizenship or could become resident aliens enjoying complete human and economic rights, but lacking political rights. When the human rights issue was raised, Estonians often cited the model 1925 laws which promoted community organization based on ethnicity. None the less, the non-Estonian community continued to view new citizenship laws as threatening. Ultimately, the issue of citizenship was to be decided in the new constitution of the independent Republic of Estonia.

A language law making Estonian the official state language and requiring those involved in occupations with public contact to know Estonian was passed in 1989.[38] However, the enforcement of this law was difficult. Although the study of the Estonian language grew dramatically, the ability of those required to pass language exams was somewhat disappointing; accordingly an extension was granted to them[39] A migration law which allowed the Supreme Council of Estonia to set immigration quotas also proved unenforceable.

The language and citizenship issues were divisive and, against a backdrop of calls for full independence, made compromise with the center difficult. These issues clearly address the tension inherent in the nature of Estonia's plural society. As economic reform stalled in Moscow, the non-Estonian community had time to become more accustomed to the idea of Estonian independence. At any rate, with little prospect of effective economic assistance from Moscow, non-Estonian attitudes began to change.

Political attitudes

As might be expected, the political attitudes and historical memory of the Estonian and non-Estonian communities differ. The Estonian flag and the Molotov-Ribbentrop Pact evoke differing emotions among Estonians and Russians. The most critical attitude, however, is identification with the state. Andrus Saar, in conducting the International Values Survey in Estonia, explored the issue of ethnic and state identification.[40] When asked what regions they identified themselves with (home town, Estonia, the Soviet Union, Europe, or the world),

> 37 percent of the non-Estonians associate themselves above all with Estonia, followed by home town (32 per cent) and finally, the Soviet Union (21 percent) ... Only a decade ago the non-Estonians determined themselves first of all as citizens of the Soviet Union, followed by home town and the world.
>
> The Estonians associate themselves above all with Estonia (67 per cent) and only then with their actual neighbourhood (30 per cent).[41]

These changes in identification are reflective of changing political attitudes towards the status of Estonia. Saar noted that already in 1990

> 42 percent of the non-Estonians give priority to the option where the republic would figure as an independent entity within the composition of the Soviet Union ... 35 percent of the non-Estonians would [prefer] a union treaty between sovereign Union republics, and finally, 16 per cent would like to see Estonia as a sovereign independent state. It is quite natural that the majority of respondents among Estonians are in favour of the option mentioned last (87 per

cent), but there is also a considerable number of people in favour of a union treaty (11 percent), while 1 per cent of respondents would like the present status to be continued.[42]

The above figures showed a shift from the 56 percent of Estonians and 5 percent of Russians who supported total independence in April 1989.[43]

These changes found further confirmation in the results of the referendum held in Estonia on March 3, 1991. Almost 83 percent of the eligible voters participated in the referendum with 77.8 percent supporting an independent Estonia. Even in Russian speaking districts of Tallinn a majority of voters favoured independence.[44] In predominantly non-Estonian areas, the option of sovereignty within a confederation was offered. In Kohtla-Järve 65 percent, Narva 79 percent and in Sillamiae almost 90 percent preferred the sovereignty option. In areas of non-titular nationalities, those for complete independence accounted for 65.7 percent in districts of Tallinn, 25.5 percent in Narve, in Kohtla-Järve approximately 46 percent, and in Sillamiae 40 percent (turnout in Sillamiae was only 27 percent).[45] These figures both confirm a shift in opinion among non-Estonians and differences within this population reflecting the ethnic isolation of the Northeast and its particular economic concerns. The centrally sponsored referendum held on March 17, 1991, had a turnout rate of only 23 percent, clearly avoided by most of the non-Estonian population.[46] Perhaps, the rise in nationalist demands made by Estonians at first intimidated the non-Estonian population, but later led to a reassessment of their interests. Such a change strengthened the bargaining position of independent-minded Estonian politicians with Moscow. Sovereignty for many non-Estonians was directly linked to economic autonomy. If this goal in non-Estonian areas was not to be supported by the Supreme Council, then the danger that residents of these areas would refocus their demands towards Moscow increased. The non-Estonian community needed leaders who could act on their behalf and who were willing to negotiate with Estonian leaders. Before the August 1991 coup, this was not always the case.

Estonian policies: Moscow, the Baltic region, and the world

New Estonian leaders sought a legal and measured means through which to detach their state from the USSR. Even the formal declaration of republic sovereignty in November 1988 and its restatement by the Supreme Council in March 1990 called for a transition period during which the laws of the Estonian state would be suspended in favor of those of the USSR. The attempt was to find a legal, non-violent means while at the same time remaining firm. After initially participating, Estonian representatives changed their status to observers from a foreign country at the Supreme Soviet of the USSR, but were active in consulting with democratic forces.

They did not participate in union treaty discussions held in the spring of 1991, nor in the negotiations over an economic crisis program.

After a certain degree of euphoria connected with a sense of empowerment embodied by the flying of the Estonian flag and the formal recognition of the existence and illegality of the secret codicils to the Molotov-Ribbentrop Pact, Estonians began to realize that their desire to be part of Western Europe might not lead automatically to Western assistance. Overtures to the Nordic countries and observer status at European meetings did not lead to large grants in aid. Only Iceland and Denmark were forthright in their immediate legal recognition of Estonia's independence. Although the United States sympathized with the desires of the Baltic states, it was unwilling to take actions which might undermine Gorbachev. The Bush administration, on the whole, continued to see US interests associated with the short-run political stability of the Soviet Union. Western Europeans, especially the Germans, were preoccupied with the needs of Central and Eastern Europe. Increasingly, Estonian intellectuals recognized that they had to negotiate their independence with Moscow. It is with Moscow that the majority of Estonian trade is conducted after independence. Needless to say, witnessing the violence in Lithuania and Latvia and the economic blockades contributed to a more realistic view of Estonia's future.[47] None the less, the official procedures provided by the USSR Supreme Soviet were unacceptable. Although negotiations were thought to be necessary, there remained among Estonians on the right strong sentiment that any talks would endanger the legal argument that Estonia is an occupied country. Of course, the procedures provided by the USSR Supreme Soviet also made eventual seccession extraordinarily difficult to obtain.

Although a Baltic Council for the coordination of policy existed, Estonian methods towards the realization of independence from Moscow still differed from those of its neighbors. In part, this reflected differences in the structure of the ethnic communities in each of the Baltic states. Lithuania with only a 20 percent non-native population was able to take more extreme actions which in Estonia would be an immediate cause of civil unrest. The unintended consequences of such actions, of course, might have included vigilante groups calling for central intervention leading to violence. Latvia, whose native population was in an even more precarious position than that of ethnic Estonia, has had a different relationship with its Russian population. This was due to the relative stability of its non-Latvian population. As a consequence of greater communication and non-immigrant status, non-Latvians associate their future with the Republic of Latvia in a way that, until recently, was untrue of non-Estonians. The absence of communication indicative of separate ethnic communities has made the cooperation between ethnic groups more difficult in Estonia than in Latvia. However, it can be argued that attitudinal changes among non-Estonians made cooperation easier.

Although speculative, the background of the new political leadership in the Baltic states may also have fostered different methods and approaches toward Moscow. The absence of political experience of some leaders may have made them more strident. By contrast, previous experience in the Communist Party and other official organs may have fostered unnecessary reticence. The latter was the case in Estonia. Nevertheless, Baltic leaders managed increasingly to present their case for independence and aid to the West as a united front. Their ability to economically and politically coordinate their policies reinforced their position as a special region illegally incorporated into the Soviet Union.

The process of informal negotiations over independence was interrupted by the August 1991 coup. With the failure of the coup in Moscow, Estonia proclaimed its full independence and received legal recognition by the international community and the USSR. The conservative/orthodox organizations of the non-Estonian community and the Communist Party of Estonia were disbanded. The issue of citizenship became part of a new negotiating process, the writing of the new constitution for the Republic of Estonia.

National aspirations in Estonia were not the product of perestroika and glasnost. The Republic of Estonia remained a meaningful social memory in the minds of Estonians. The Gorbachev era presented the opportunity for pursuing long repressed goals through the policies of glasnost and economic reform and, later, through the declining authority of the regime itself. The nature of the Estonian demands reflects an internal political process of competing groups on the right and center as they began to assess public support in the political arena. The presence of a large, distinctive non-Estonian population contributed to both the political agenda and the methods adopted in pursuit of autonomy and independence. The existence of a plural society in Estonia, a result of post-World War II policies, played a pivotal role in shaping ethnic relations and state policies within Estonia and between Estonian leaders and Moscow.

Notes

1 See Toivo U. Raun, *Estonia and the Estonians* (Stanford: Hoover Institution Press, 1987), pp. 57–111.
2 Plural society does not mean that Estonians and other national groups living in Estonia never have personal, social, or job related contacts.
3 Raun, *Estonia*, pp. 51–53, 71–74, 90–91, and 129–133.
4 *Ibid.*, p. 131.
5 *Ibid.*, p. 132.
6 *Ibid.*, p. 131.
7 *Ibid.*, pp. 130–131. *Eesti arvudes 1920–1935* (Tallinn: Riigi Statistika Keskbüroo, 1937), p. 26 cited by Raun, *Estonia*, p. 130.
8 *Nomenklatura*, a system of certification for employment based on both expertise and political reliability, provided a means of control for the party.

9 See Raun, *Estonia*, pp. 190–193 and Romuald J. Misiunas and Rein Taagepera, "The Baltic States: Years of Dependence, 1980–1986," *Journal of Baltic Studies*, 20, no. 1, 1989, p. 70.

10 See Raun and Rein Taagepera, "Estonia in September 1988: Stalinists, Centrists and Restorationists," *Journal of Baltic Studies*, 20, no. 3, 1989, pp. 277–278.

11 Väljas was born in 1931 on the Estonian island of Khiiumaa. He entered the CPSU in 1952. He completed a Candidate of History degree at Tartu University where he was active in the Young Communist League. From 1955 to 1961, he was the first secretary of the TSK LKSM Estoniia and was involved in party work from 1961, becoming a secretary of the Central Committee CPE in 1971. In 1980, he served as ambassador in Venezuela and Nicaragua.

12 Romuald J. Misiunas and Rein Taagepera, *The Baltic States: Years of Dependence 1940–1980* (Berkeley: University of California Press, 1983), pp. 272–273.

13 Taagepera, "Baltic Population Changes," p. 47, cited by Raun, *Estonia*, p. 182.

14 "Estonia and Latvia Most Vulnerable to Soviet Migration," *Homeland*, September 27, 1989. The article cites data from the 1989 census published in *Rahva Hääl*, September 19, 1989.

15 See Raun, *Estonia*, pp. 175–176.

16 Raun, *Estonia*, p. 199.

17 Misiunas and Taagepera, "The Baltic States," p. 218.

18 *Nòukogude Eesti saavutusi*, p. 21; Järvesoo, "Postwar Economic Transformation," p. 143; *Soviet Estonia: Land, People, Culture* p. 143; and *Narodnoe khoziaistvo ESSR 1980*, p. 80, cited by Raun, *Estonia*, p. 198.

19 See Kh.L. Taliga, "O dinamike national'nogo sostava trudiashchikhsia ESSR v 1970–1980-kh gg.," in R. Veermanno, ed., *Sotsial'nie protsessy nakanune perestroiki* (Tallinn: AN ESSR, 1989), pp. 136–154, and A.V. Kirkh, P.E. Iarve, K.R. Khaav, "Ethnosotsial'naia differentsiatsiia gorodskogo naseleniia Estonii," *Sotstiologicheskie issledovaniia*, May-June, 1988, no. 3, p. 33.

20 This material comes from a survey conducted in Estonia as part of the International Values Survey carried out by the Mass Communication Research and Information Centre in cooperation with the Estonian Academy of Sciences, Institute of Philosophy, Law and Sociology Institute. The sample contained 1,010 adults selected "according to the ethnic model of the Estonian population." Andrus Saar, "Inter-ethnic Relations in Estonia," *The Monthly Survey of Estonian and Soviet Politics*, November-December, 1990, p. 13.

21 *Ibid.*, p. 13.

22 Katus, p. 13.

23 See Raun, *Estonia*, p. 207. Raun relies on evidence from Rein Taagepera, "Size and Ethnicity of Estonian Towns and Rural Districts, 1922–1979," *Journal of Baltic Studies* vol. 13, 1982, 101–127.

24 These data are drawn from a research project studying citizen participation in politics in Estonia. The sample included 6,884 respondents drawn from a clustered, stratified sample using random selection of respondents. The questionnaire was adapted from the survey of Sidney Verba, Norman Nie, Kay Schlozmann, and Henry Brady used in a study of participation in America. The adaption and fielding of the survey was conducted by the author, Andrus Saar (Saar Poll, Tallinn, Estonia), and the Institute of Philosophy, Sociology, and Law, Estonian Academy of Sciences.

25 Toomas Hendrik Ilves, "Reaction: The Intermovement in Estonia," in Jan Arveds Trapans, ed., *Toward Independence: The Baltic Popular Movements* (Boulder, Co: Westview Press, 1991), p. 75.
26 Kirkh, Iarve, and Khaav, "Ethnosotsial'naia . . .," p. 33.
27 This observation is based on the unpublished research of Tiina Raitviir, Vallo Saar, and Oleg Samorodni, "Elections in Estonia 1989–1991: From the Territorial Aspect," presented at the Conference on the Sunset of Socialism in the Baltic States, Suurupi, Estonia, May 14–15, 1991.
28 For a detailed analysis of the electoral process see Cynthia S. Kaplan, "Elections in Estonia," in Darrell Slider, ed., *Elections in the USSR* (Durham: Duke University Press, forthcoming).
29 Edgar Savisaar, *Narodnyi kongress: Sbornik materialov kongressa Narodnogo fronta Estonii 1–2 Oktiabria 1988 g.* (Tallinn: Periodika, 1989), p. 20.
30 "General Programme of the Popular Front of Estonia," *The Popular Front of Estonia*, pp. 13–14.
31 *Popular Front of Estonia: Election Platform* (published in English, n.d., n. p.), p. 6. The election platform was published in Russian in *Molodezh' Estonii*, 20 October 1989. Citations are from the English version. Radicals considered Estonia independent and occupied and supported the Congress of Estonia, a non-state sponsored body. Radical groups included: ERSP, the Estonian National Independence Party, part of EMS or the Estonian Heritage Society and EKL, the Estonian Christian Union. Orthodox groups included the Russian, conservative and orthodox groups: Intermovement, Joint Council of Labor Collectives, the Soldiers-Internationalists, and the Strike Committees. *Election Platform* (in English), p. 1. A third group with whom the Popular Front stated a wish to collaborate included those pursuing economic and ecological programs, the ERL, the Estonian Green Movement, TKL, the Union of the Workers Collectives (Estonia), Central Union of the Estonian Farmers, and professional unions. *Ibid.*, p. 5.
32 See Rein Taagepera, "A Note on the March 1989 Elections in Estonia," *Soviet Studies* 42, no. 2 (April 1990), pp. 334–335 and Oleg Samorodnii, "Baltiiskii put'," *Raduga*, no. 12, 1989, p. 51.
33 See Samorodnii, "Baltiiskii put'," p. 49.
34 See, "XX s"ezd Kompartii Estonii," *Molodezh' Estonii*, March 24, 1990. Although Russians from the Northwest initially joined the independent Communist Party of Estonia, they were later to break with it and rejoin the pro-Moscow group. Herbert Vainu, "Independent Communist Party of Estonia," *The Monthly Survey of Estonian and Soviet Politics* April, 1991, pp. 16–22.
35 For an assessment of parliamentary factions, see Rein Toomla "Parliamentary Factions of the Supreme Council of the Estonian Republic," *The Monthly Survey of Estonian and Soviet Politics*, November-December, 1990, pp. 1–4.
36 This was an observation made by many of the Estonians and some of the Russians with whom I have spoken during trips to Tallinn, Estonia in December 1989, March 1990, and June 1990. Andrus Saar, the director of the Mass Communication Research and Information Centre, notes that the electorate did not select candidates for the Supreme Soviet of Estonia based on parties or political organizations. "Vashe menenie, abonent?" *Molodezh' Estonii*, March 23, 1990.

37 A new law passed by the Estonian Supreme Soviet in August 1989 stipulated that voters be eighteen years of age, be Estonian citizens, and live for either two years in the electoral district or five years in the republic. However, it was suspended for the December 1989 local elections. On November 17, 1989 a new law on elections for the Supreme Soviet of Estonia was passed. The law gave residents of Estonia the right to vote, reduced the number of Supreme Soviet seats from 284 to 105, permitted candidates to run only as individuals and stipulated that they live or work in their electoral districts, and reserved four seats for the Soviet armed forces. Candidates had to live in Estonia ten years and be twenty-one years of age.

38 *Zakon o iazyke Estonskoi SSR i sviazannye s ego primeneniem materialy* (Tallinn: AN Estonii, 1989).

39 This material is drawn from an interview in May 1991 in Tallinn by the author with Mart Rannut, General Director, State Department of Language.

40 See Andrus Saar, "Inter-ethnic Relations in Estonia," *The Monthly Survey of Estonian and Soviet Politics*, November-December, 1990. pp. 12–15. The sample had 1,010 adult respondents.

41 *Ibid.*, p. 14.

42 *Ibid.*, p. 14.

43 The number of Estonians supporting Union Republic status dropped from 2 percent to zero. Among Russians those supporting republic status dropped from 54 percent to 16 percent. The major shift among Russians living in Estonia occurred among those who favored Estonia within a new confederation (April 1989, 25 percent; June 1990, 48 percent). The data are the results of a poll conducted by Mainor, an organization associated with the Popular Front. "Independence vs Confederation: Results of June Poll," *The Estonian Independent*, July 25, 1990. A summary of published survey results on attitudinal differences can be found in Ilves, pp. 71–83.

44 "Referendum: Podvedeny itogi," *Molodezh' Estonii*, March 5, 1991.

45 "Sekretari TsK KPE o referendume," *Molodezh' Estonii*, March 6, 1991.

46 *RFE/RL Daily Report*, no. 55, March 19, 1881.

47 These observations are made on the basis of extended conversations in Estonia during six trips from December 1989 through May 1991.

Part V
The Transcaucasus

10 Azerbaijan: search for identity and new partners

SHIREEN HUNTER

Introduction

One of the most significant – albeit unintended – consequences of Mikhail Gorbachev's reform policies was the upsurge of ethnic and cultural particularism, drive for political independence, and the rise of a variety of popular movements throughout the USSR.

In the Baltic republics, Georgia, and Armenia, from the beginning popular movements have had a clear nationalist focus, politically and culturally. They also have had a clear sense of their external orientation, which is toward Europe and the West.

In the Muslim republics, by contrast, the enhanced ethnic and cultural particularism and self-assertion has led to confusion among the people and the elite regarding their national self-identity and the direction of their external ties. Indeed, these republics are torn between several poles of cultural and political attraction.

Greater freedom of cultural expression, plus the diminution in Russia's political and cultural threat, have revived old ethnic, cultural, and territorial rivalries and conflicts. They have led to a reinterpretation, and often distortion, of geographic and historical facts and events with the clear purpose of forging a new sense of national identity. The result has been increased risk of intra- and inter-republic hostility and conflict.[1]

The loosening of bonds between the republics and the central authority in Moscow, and the complete dissolution of the Soviet Union, have brought the question of how different republics would relate to their immediate neighbors and to the broader international community to the fore. The latter is of great importance to the neighboring states and to the extra-regional powers, including the great powers. No clear patterns of interaction between the Muslim republics and their neighbors have yet emerged. Nevertheless, the entire Soviet Asia has become the focus of regional and international competition for influence.

It is clear, however, that the Muslim republics' relations with the outside world, in particular with their neighbors and other Islamic countries, will expand. It is also clear that outsiders would be keenly interested in the evolution of these republics' external relations, and they would try to affect

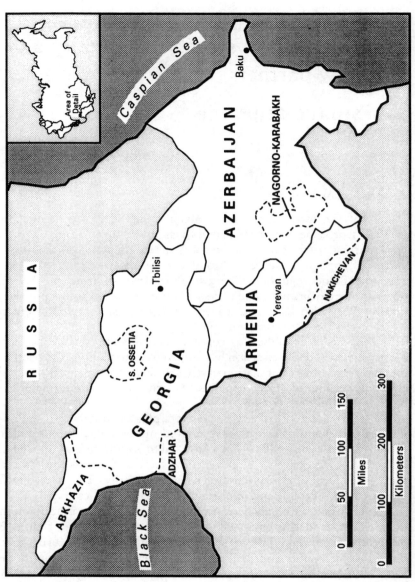

Map 10.1 The Caucasus

their characters. In particular, with growing interaction between these republics and Muslim states, the dynamics of Middle East politics would affect the outsiders' views of events in these republics, and would influence their approach toward them. The great powers, notably the United States, would be keenly interested in the pattern of relations which could emerge between these republics and their neighbors, especially in such sensitive regions as Transcaucasia. This interest is natural because the character of these relations would affect regional politics, including regional balances of power far beyond the region's immediate vicinity. For example, the United States and Western countries would want to see Turkey's position as a Western NATO ally enhanced in this region and in Central Asia, and that of Iran contained.

How these new interactions would affect these republics' internal developments and the shape of regional politics in Central and Southwest Asia are still hard to predict. What is clear is that their impact in both areas would be significant.

The impact would be most dramatic if these republics were to gain full independence and have no mediating center, and somewhat less important if they were to remain within the Commonwealth – even if very loose – with Russia and other Slavic republics. This would be so because even within a loose confederal structure the central authority in Moscow would have some influence over issues of foreign relations. In this case, in all likelihood, Moscow's priorities and its policy *vis-à-vis* the neighboring states would have considerable influence in determining the character of their relations and not merely the latter's own proclivities.[2] The Commonwealth of Independent States, if it can achieve a unified military force, could reduce the risk of intra- and inter-republic conflict. But the Soviet Union's dissolution and the proliferation of national armies has increased the risk of such conflicts, as well a conflict between these republics and their neighbors. This is so because new states often use foreign enemies to foster their national unity.

Paradoxically, the chance for regional cooperation could also increase as the newly independent and economically weak republics seek to replace the Russians with new economic partners.

The Soviet Republic of Azerbaijan provides an excellent case from which to observe the evolution of these diverse and often contradictory forces and their interaction as they shape this country's self-image and its perceptions of its surroundings and its own place in it.

Azerbaijan's historic legacy, its mixed ethno-cultural makeup, its sectarian divisions, and the multiplicity of its minorities make the task of developing a new national identity and charting a new course for the country outside the context of the Soviet Union a challenging, and potentially destablilizing, process.

The same characteristics offer opportunities for the republic to forge new and satisfying ties with its two big neighbors, Iran and Turkey, but they also entail risk of conflict, especially with Iran.

A more problematic issue for the republic would be the future of its relations with neighboring Armenia, with whom it has been locked in a long and bloody conflict. Indeed, the dynamics of Azerbaijan's relations with Armenia could also affect the course of its relations with Iran and Turkey.

Azerbaijan's developments would have implications beyond its borders. An excessively pan-Turkist cultural policy and irredentist philosophy would increase the risk of regional conflict involving Iran and Turkey, in addition to Azerbaijan. However, an approach which drew on all aspects of Azerbaijan's rich and multi-faceted cultural heritage could become a catalyst for new thinking on regional ties and an impetus to broader regional cooperation involving Iran, Turkey, and perhaps even other Transcaucasian republics.

Azerbaijan's experience would also have implications for other Muslim republics. In short, developments in Soviet Asia would have ramifications for a vast region stretching from the Black Sea to the Persian Gulf. Thus, while Soviet republics' ties with the new Commonwealth, and even Russia alone will remain of key importance, other regional ties may very well become more significant. Therefore, rather than merely chronicling recent events, political changes, and similar issues, it is more important to analyze the process of nation-building in Soviet Asian republics in its historical and cultural context, and in light of current dynamics of regional and international politics. It is also important to analyze the scope and character of ties which are developing between these republics, their neighbors, and other states. It is equally important to see how these republics' neighbors view their developments and their impact on their own security and interests.

Perhaps even more important is a critical look at many of the currently accepted definitions of ethnicity, territories, borders, etc. and how they have evolved as they apply to Soviet Asia. The history of this region was frozen sometime in the mid nineteenth century. Then the Communists tried to write a new history and ethnography for it. What is currently happening is the resumption of history, but with all the baggage of Soviet historiography. How this resumption of history would unfold is what would determine the future of these regions and their neighbors.

Where is Azerbaijan?

In January 1990 a number of Soviet Azerbaijanis tore down border posts on the Soviet-Iranian frontier. The impression was then created that the world was witnessing something akin to the crumbling of the Berlin Wall, which heralded the reunification of the two Germanies.[3]

The nationalists of Azerbaijan's Popular Front (APF) and others tried to convey such an image to international observers. They called for the reunification of the so-called "Northern" and "Southern" Azerbaijans. They attributed the separation of the two regions to a historic conspiracy between Tsarist Russia and Iran in 1808 under the terms of the Treaty of Gulistan.[4]

In addition to wanting reunification, Soviet Azerbaijani nationalists – official and non-official – have a very extensive notion of the territorial confines of what they call "Southern Azerbaijan." According to them, the territory of so-called Southern Azerbaijan extends as far as central Iran.

Some ultra nationalists go even further than the idea of pan-Azerbaijanism, and argue in favor of a pan-Turkist approach *vis-à-vis* Iran. They say that Soviet Azerbaijan's goal should be to unite all of Iran's Turkic-speaking population.[5]

The inaccuracy of the notion of two Azerbaijans divided as a result of imperial conspiracies is beyond any doubt for any objective and impartial historian. The history of Russo-Iranian wars and the character of the treaties signed between the two states and the fact that the Treaty of Turkmanchai (1828) is known in Iran as the "Shameful" (*Nangin*) treaty shows that there was no deal struck between Iran and Russia at Azerbaijan's expense. Rather, the separation of the current territory of Soviet Azerbaijan from Iran was a clear consequence of Russia's imperial expansion. This is not to suggest that these lands – or rather, their local feudal lords, or at least some of them – may not have wanted independence from Iran, although most of them fought on Iran's side during these wars.[6] It is merely to point to the hollowness of the theory of Russo-Persian conspiracy.

In November 1919, the Azerbaijan delegation at the Paris peace conference presented to the Iranian delegation – which was not admitted to the peace conference – the text of a treaty envisaging close economic and political ties between the two countries, including the sphere of foreign relations.[7] However, realizing that Iran was not capable of protecting them against the Russians, in Article 6 of the proposed treaty the Azerbaijanis said that they needed the same kind of help that the British were supposed to give Iran in the context of the 1919 Anglo-Persian treaty, which would have made Iran a virtual British protectorate. Thus, Azerbaijan was willing to accept conditions that the Iranians rebelled against, for the Iranian parliament defied Britain and refused to ratify the treaty.

Consequently, nothing came out of these Iran-Azerbaijan contacts. These points are noted here in order to balance the thesis of the universal appeal of pan-Turkism to the Azerbaijanis at the time, and the inevitable gravitation of Azerbaijan toward Turkey. Moreover, even prominent figures of Azerbaijan's pan-Turkic movement had before dabbled in other ideologies and had tried an Iran-oriented strategy.

For instance, Mohammad Amin Rasul-Zadeh, the president of the

Musawat Party, was first a socialist and a member of the socialist-oriented "Himmat" Party. He spent many years in Iran and published a newspaper in Tehran called *Iran-e-Now* ("New Iran"). It was only after being expelled from Iran for his leftist ideas that he went to Turkey and became an ardent pan-Turkist.[8] The fact is that historically two principal poles of attraction, Iran and Turkey, have existed for this region. Moreover, more than mere ethnic or cultural affinity, practical considerations of which partner could be more helpful has determined the political orientation of Azerbaijani intellectuals and political activists.

Thus, the facts behind the creation of the 1918–1920 republic and its philosophy are somewhat different from the myth that surrounds its creation and currently acts as a historic point of reference for Azerbaijani nationalists and their vision of the future.

When the republic of Azerbaijan was first created in 1918, their choice of name was not welcomed by the Iranian Azerbaijanis, even those who had their own grievances against the central government in Tehran. For example, according to Ahmad Kasravi, the anti-center movement in the Iranian Azerbaijan under the leadership of Mohammad Hussein Khiabani toyed with the idea of changing the name of the Iranian province to Azadistan ("The Land of Liberty"), so as not to be confused with or subsumed under the new republic.[9] This also disputes the notion promoted by some recent writers that the creation of a republic of Azerbaijan led to the outpouring of pan-Azerbaijanist sentiments in Iran.[10] Later events revealed it was spurious as the Soviet Union and the Iranian leftists used the notion of one Azerbaijan being separated artificially in order to promote separatist tendencies in the Iranian Azerbaijan. The best example of this policy were the efforts of the Soviet Union in 1945 to set up an autonomous government in the Iranian Azerbaijan through the manipulation of the presence of Soviet troops in that region.

It was also after the Sovietization of the region and, in particular, in the Stalinist period that first the words "Northern" and "Southern" Azerbaijan became common in Soviet commentary. Moreover, the Democratic Party of Azerbaijan and the Communist Party of Soviet Azerbaijan began to promote the thesis of the oppression of southern Azerbaijanis by what they called "chauvinist Persians."[11] In later years, long before the Soviet reform movement and the rise of nationalist groups, communist leaders of the Soviet Socialist Republic of Azerbaijan talked about the reunification of the two Azerbaijans. For example, the head of the Azerbaijan KGB, Gaidar Aliev, who later became a member of the Politburo, said in 1983 that he hoped that the two Azerbaijans would be united during his lifetime.

Even today many of the most extreme irredentist claims toward the Iranian Azerbaijan emanate from those within the Soviet Azerbaijan national movement that are Iranian-origin leftists. For instance, a prominent exponent of this view is Rasul Siamek, one of the leaders of an unofficial organization in Soviet Azerbaijan called *Birlik* ("Unity"). He is from Iran and was a member of the leftist guerrilla group in Iran called *Fedayan-e-Khalgh*, which is still engaged in clandestine activities against the current regime in Tehran.[12]

It is no secret that the Soviet Union consistently followed a dual track policy toward Iran, namely, good relations at state level and clandestine infiltration through leftist forces. Historically, the Soviet Azerbaijan Communist Party and the local KGB played important roles in devising and conducting policy toward Iran.[13]

The Azerbaijan Communist Party remained influential after 1989, first aided by the presence of Soviet troops, then, by acquiring a nationalist garb. Changes in the leadership have resulted from factional competition within the Communist Party and not because of the elimination of its influence. Thus, beneath the new rhetoric many of the old mindsets and attitudes toward internal and external issues still affect outlook and policy in Azerbaijan even after the departure of President Mutalibov.

Moreover, popular movements in Soviet Azerbaijan did not develop exactly the way they did in other republics. Certainly the so-called Azerbaijan Popular Front, particularly those elements who are allowed to be active, is not fully representative of the range of popular views in the republic. Additionally, there is a widespread suspicion that there has been a deal between elements of the Communist establishment and certain activists of the Popular Front. Thus, what they say does not necessarily represent the views of all Azerbaijanis or even the majority.

In fact, despite the prominence that the Popular Front acquired in 1989 and 1990, making it seem today to be very powerful, it is very difficult to determine what it exactly is beyond a collection of individuals who came together in November 1988, many of whom have since drifted apart. There are indeed some political parties in Azerbaijan, such as the Social Democrats and the Yeni Musavat, but none is under the APF umbrella.[14]

I have described the historical background that will to a great extent determine the dynamics of Azerbaijan's relations with Iran. The persistence of the Soviet Azerbaijani leadership in the view of themselves and the Iranian Azerbaijan as one land and one people divided by imperial machinations and as a result of Russo-Iranian collusion would almost certainly lead Iran to respond. Iran will begin to refute these theses more vigorously and will emphasize the historical differences between the two regions as well as the Iranian dimension of the region's background and culture. It may even begin to promote a pan-Iranist or pan-Islamic thesis to counter pan-Turkic themes promoted by the Soviet Azerbaijanis and certain circles in Turkey.

But depending on conditions within Iran, in particular the ability of the central government to meet the economic, social, and cultural aspirations of its people, the above thesis could gain popularity in the Iranian Azerbaijan.

In that case, separatist movements could develop in Iran seeking unification with Soviet Azerbaijan. This type of movement, if supported by the Soviet Azerbaijan, could lead to armed conflict with Iran.

It is clearly logical for the Soviet Azerbaijanis to want to promote the thesis of geographic, historic, and ethnic unity of the region and the notion of Russo-Iranian conspiracy. The unification of the two regions would enhance the economic and political position of the new unit by expanding its size and increasing its resources. In the more immediate future, Soviet Azerbaijanis make no secret that they want to use the Iranian Azerbaijan expatriate community in order to promote their position in Europe and in the United States, and to attract their capital. However, so far they have not been very successful. In the future, too, if Iran's economic and political situation improves and the process of privatization and the opening of the economy continues, and the regime continues to woo the exiles back home, most Azerbaijani investors are likely to go back home to Iran rather than try operating in a society that in the last seventy years has lost much of its mercantile and entrepreneurial skills and is likely to be politically unstable for some time.

However, there is an even more immediate and pressing reason for this historic revisionism. The Soviet Azerbaijanis, by focusing on foreign enemies, are trying to foster a separate national identity for themselves. This is clearly admitted in conversations with Azerbaijani intellectuals once their thesis is challenged with valid historic arguments. Whatever the motives behind this policy, the achievement of this goal will not be easy and its political costs could be very high. Although not clearly spoken, it is clear that in talking about unification the Soviet Azerbaijanis see themselves as the leader and the senior partner in a united Azerbaijan, although in order to attract the Iranians, they proclaim that Tabriz would be the capital of the new state. There is a thinly disguised – and hardly justified – sense of superiority among Soviet Azerbaijanis, or at least the Baku intellectuals, *vis-à-vis* the Iranian Azerbaijanis. This attitude, however, shows lack of understanding of the Iranian Azerbaijanis' characteristics. It is doubtful that the Iranian Azerbaijanis in Tabriz would want to replace Tehran's authority with that of Baku, even if the nominal capital was Tabriz. Even within Iranian Azerbaijan, local differences are significant. These differences are even more pronounced with Soviet Azerbaijan beyond the immediate border villages. The long period of Russification and recent trends toward what could be called "Turkeyization," as opposed to mere Turkification, have made even the two dialects vastly different.

Moreover, while some Iranian Azerbaijanis may want greater autonomy and even independence from Tehran, it is unlikely that, with few exceptions, they would like to be subsumed in some sort of confederation under the Russians or to become a cultural satrapy of Turkey. In this regard, too, the Iranian Azerbaijanis' proud and independent nature and the rather disdainful attitude of the Russians, and even certain Turkish intelligentsia, toward them as rough and unrefined would act as significant barriers. Beyond the secular, a-religious intellectuals, religious affinity with other Iranians would continue to affect the masses' attitude. Such schemes could only succeed in two cases: (1) a collapse of central authority in Iran; (2) profound regional and international changes leading to a total redrawing of regional maps. The latter development, however, almost inevitably would also mean the disintegration of Turkey, as well as Iraq and perhaps others.

It is in the recognition of these facts that in the last year, officially the current government of the republic and even the APF have toned down their nationalist rhetoric. There is no more talk of immediate reunification. There is not even talk of setting a timetable for reunification. Rather, the thesis now promoted is that of "one people living within two states." This diminution in the nationalist and irredentist rhetoric is partly due to the fact that popular reaction in the Iranian Azerbaijan to calls of unification were subdued. True, some Iranian Azerbaijani intellectuals, both in Iran and abroad, are receptive to such ideas.[15] Many of them, however, are motivated by their opposition to the current Islamic regime rather than separatist feelings. Consequently, as one member of the Academy of Sciences of Azerbaijan SSR told me, many Soviet Azerbaijanis began to say that before making unification a principal goal they should first find out if the Iranian Azerbaijanis want to unite with them.

There has also been a greater realization on the part of Soviet Azerbaijani leadership of differences between the two people. Indeed, an official of the so-called *Vatan Jamiyati* (The Homeland Association), an organization predating perestroika, with the goal of attracting Iranian Azerbaijanis told me that the two people first need to become reacquainted with one another before talking about unification.

Another reason has been the realization by Soviet Azerbaijanis that unification may not necessarily mean the separation of the Iranian Azerbaijan and its joining with the Soviet republic. Rather, there may be the risk that at least some Soviet Azerbaijanis, particularly those speaking Iranian dialects, may want to join Iran. In fact, a Soviet academician admitted to me that in places like Lankaran, and heavily Shi'a border areas, most people would like to join Iran. Moscow's influence, which is concerned about its own relations with Iran, also contributed to the lowering of nationalist rhetoric. Moreover, as long as there was a chance to keep most of the Union together, it seemed that Moscow would try its best to keep Azerbaijan within the Union, even if other Transcaucasian republics such as Armenia and Georgia became independent.[16] But a united and thus expanded Azerbaijan may be less easily persuaded to remain within the new Commonwealth.

In the meantime, however, Moscow cannot openly repudiate this thesis.

Moreover, it may hope that it would be able to keep an expanded Azerbaijan in its orbit. However, after the acceleration of the process of the Soviet Union's disintegration following the failed right-wing coup of August 1991, this point has been made moot. With Azerbaijan becoming completely independent the campaign for reunification with the Iranian Azerbaijan could begin in earnest again. Whatever transpires in the future, it is clear that the issue of historic confines of Azerbaijan will acquire more than academic interest.

Ethnic and cultural legacy and composition

Azerbaijan's ethnic, sectarian, and linguistic composition and the character of its cultural legacy also contribute to its problems of defining a new national identity, and determining the nature of its relations with its neighbors.

Azerbaijani nationalists are proud of their ancient history and often refer to that. Meanwhile, most of them insist on the pure "Turkicness" of Azerbaijan, both ethnically and culturally, throughout its history. It is important to make a distinction between the Soviet Azerbaijan and the Iranian Azerbaijan. From ancient times, after the massive introduction of Iranian people into the region, and until the introduction of Arab and Turkic elements in later centuries, the Iranian Azerbaijan has been ethnically solidly Iranian. In ancient times, however, Albania or Eran or what is now Soviet Azerbaijan had had a more mixed population, including some of the Iranian family of Indo-Europeans.[17] Another difference is that the area that is now Soviet Azerbaijan historically has been more vulnerable to migratory pressures, including those by Turkic tribes. Most historians agree that the gradual Turkification of Azerbaijan began in the tenth or eleventh century. Prior to that, for nearly 3,000 years, in addition to indigenous inhabitants, particularly in Soviet Azerbaijan (the people of the Caucasus), the dominant ethnic group in the region was the Iranian branch of Indo-European tribes.

The rise of rival Safavid and Ottoman empires in Iran and what is now Turkey in the fifteenth and sixteenth centuries accelerated the Turkification trend. While the Safavids were Iranian, their court was heavily influenced by Turkic elements. Thus, while disputed, the theory that many Azerbaijanis are linguistically Turkified Iranian people has merit. Certainly their physical characteristics are more similar to Iranian people than to other Turkic people such as the Turkmen, Uzbek, Kyrgyz, etc. Thus, the current thesis of Soviet Azerbaijani nationalists that Azerbaijan has always been one hundred percent Turkic is not valid. It is, of course, to be noted here that extreme pan-Turkists in Turkey, and in Soviet Azerbaijan, believe that such ancient people as the Sumerians, Chaldeans, Iranian Parthians, and even Kurds and Medes, were Turk. And they date the existence of Turkic people in Central Asia, Asia Minor, and elsewhere to 5,000 years before the birth of Christ.[18] However, even some of the Soviet Azerbaijani nationalists in private admit to these historic inconsistencies and recognize the more mixed ethnic and cultural background of their country, including the existence of a strong Iranian element.

The reason for emphasizing Turkic purity, it was explained to me by a Soviet Azerbaijani political scientist, is political expediency. The nationalists believe that this attitude is justified in order to forge a strong Turkic national identity. Other issues, including conflict with Armenia, are also manipulated for the same purpose.[19] Moreover, being fully aware of the strength of Soviet Azerbaijan's ties with Iran, this attitude is partly aimed at preempting and preventing potential attraction toward Iran. Officials of the current government of Soviet Azerbaijan, which is still dominated by the old Communist establishment, albeit in a nationalist garb, sanction this policy. Until the developments following the failed coup of August 1991, and in view of the close link between the Azerbaijani leadership with the center, so, it appeared, did Moscow. Similarly, such views also suit Western proclivities which want Turkey to emerge as the strongest influence in Azerbaijan.

Therefore, views which challenge this ultra-Turkic nationalist theory of history are not openly aired. But there are some indications that such views exist. According to the chairman of the political science department of the Academy of Sciences of Azerbaijan, only 3 percent of people in Azerbaijan hold the view that the ethnic and historic origins of Azerbaijan is connected with that of other Iranian peoples.[20] There is some reason to believe that there may be a much larger number of people who support this view. For instance, according to the same academician, there is a widespread campaign of insult and discredit in Soviet Azerbaijan aimed at the Iranian Azerbaijani historian-scholar Ahmad Kasravi, a prominent proponent of the Iranian origins of Azerbaijan's history and culture. The main charge against Kasravi is that he was an Iranian nationalist and a pan-Iranist. This creates the suspicion that Kasravi's views may be more popular than admitted openly. Otherwise, such a campaign seems fruitless and mean-spirited.

What is important for the future of Azerbaijan is how its people will choose to define themselves irrespective of historical facts or the precise ethnic mix of the population. If these people see themselves as pure Turks or predominantly Turk or Turkified, then that is what they will be. If they develop a different vision of themselves, then that view would mold their self-identity. Nevertheless, manipulation of these facts by various groups inside the country, in the region, and even by outside powers would have an impact on the evolution of the Soviet Azerbaijanis' self-image. For example, an official policy of Turkeyization through more extensive cultural contacts with Turkey, reform of language, and the propagation of cultural pan-Turkism through the mass media, would deeply affect the self-perception of the next generation. A different policy would have a different impact. Irrespective of the ultimate outcome of this search for national identity, the exaggeration of one aspect of the regional and popular culture could in the process become highly divisive.

These issues are also noted here because of their implications for the future character of the republic's relations with its neighbors. For example, overemphasis on Turkic purity would certainly complicate efforts to create closer ties with the Iranian Azerbaijan.

A culturally pan-Turkic policy on the part of Soviet Azerbaijan is likely to be jarring to most Iranian Azerbaijanis. This would be particularly the case if Soviet Azerbaijan were to become a cultural satrapy of Turkey. There is already a trend in this direction, at least in Baku. The efforts to rid Azerbaijan's Turkic dialect of Persian words and the introduction of modern Turkish idioms and, in general, a vast increase in Turkey's cultural influence from music to writing there will make communication between the two Azerbaijans more difficult. This is so because the modern Turkish and the Azerbaijani Turkic dialect are not mutually understandable, particularly to non-educated people, or at least not easily.

Past efforts on the part of separatist movements in the Iranian Azerbaijan, most notably that of the Democratic Party of Azerbaijan sponsored by the Soviet Union in the 1940s to impress a Turkic character on the region by, among other things, instituting instructions in the Turkick dialect, did not succeed.

Admittedly part of this failure was due to the anti-religious and socialist character of the movement which offended the masses' religious sensibilities. But a large part of the Azerbaijani intelligentsia – including some leftists – were also against the anti-Iranian dimension of the Party's ideology.[21] Therefore, barring widespread disaffection of the Iranian Azerbaijanis from the rest of the country, which is not very likely although not inconceivable, the current emphasis on the part of Soviet Azerbaijani nationalists and leadership on ultra-Turkic nationalism coupled with pan-Turkic tendencies is likely to deepen the barriers between the two Azerbaijans rather than bring them closer together.

Moreover, these attitudes would make the development of a distinct "Azerbaijani" identity with both its Turkic and Iranian dimensions more difficult. The failure to develop such an identity, in turn, could alienate other ethnic groups within Soviet Azerbaijan since the population of this republic is not solidly Turkic. There are, for example, Iranian-origin people with special Iranian dialects called "Tati" and "Taleshi," as well as Kurds and Dagestanis. In the Iranian Azerbaijan, a large part of the Western Azerbaijan is inhabited by non-Turkic, Indo-European, Iranian-origin Kurds and hence, ethnically and linguistically part of Kurdistan.

These ethnic diversities further illustrate the unrealism of the notion of "Northern and Southern" Azerbaijans forcibly separated that now must be reunited.

The Communist regime was responsible for a systematic reinterpretation of the region's history and culture.[22] It downplayed Azerbaijan's links with Iran and emphasized the differenes between them, hoping eventually to incorporate the Iranian Azerbaijan into the Soviet state. This policy also fit neatly into the overall Soviet strategy of developing separate territorial and cultural entities out of its Asian possessions, as well as its effort to fragment neighboring Iran, since it believed this would make its Sovietization easier.

Today Azerbaijan is bedevilled by this legacy. Indeed, many of the same methods of historical revisionism are used by the current leadership and nationalist leaders. But their unwillingness to come to terms with the realities of their past and to recognize their cultural *duality* is likely to complicate their problems of defining their cultural and political identity and developing positive ties with their neighbors. The Azerbaijanis certainly have the option of repudiating the Iranian dimension of their origin and culture. But they cannot both lay claim to an ancient and vast culture and deny its historic characteristics.

Religion: factor for unity or division

Historically, religious proclivities of the local population have played important roles in determining the political directions of the regions now incorporated in the Iranian and Soviet Azerbaijans. The principal line of religious divide in the region is that between the Sunni and the Shi'a Muslims. The Iranian Azerbaijan is solidly Shi'a, with the exception of many of its Kurdish inhabitants who are Sunnis. The Soviet Azerbaijan also has a strong Shi'a majority. Estimates as to the percentage of Shi'as versus Sunnis vary somewhere between 75 to 85 percent in favor of the Shi'as.

Historically, religion has been a principal factor in this region's identification with Iran. In what is now the Soviet Azerbaijan, pro-Ottoman tendencies in the past and pro-Turkish tendencies now have been strongest among the Sunni population or those without strong religious beliefs. By the same token, pro-Iranian tendencies have always been strongest among the Shi'as. However, to assume, as some Western scholars have done, that religion was the only reason for the Azerbaijanis' identification with Iran is incorrect. Iran's relations, for example, with southern Iraq, which is also overwhelmingly Shi'a but mostly Arab or Arabized, illustrate that religious affinity is not enough to bind different people together. Similarly, the Shi'as of Turkey – known as the Alawis – do not identify with Iran despite religious affinity. Rather, it has been the combination of religious bonds and other affinities that has been the reason for Azerbaijan's closeness with Iran.

During the events of winter 1989–1990 that saw an outpouring of nationalist and autonomist sentiments, Soviet authorities, including Mikhail Gorbachev himself, blamed disturbances on "Muslim fanatics." He accused Iran of igniting the fires of fundamentalist fervor and warned it to stay out of the republic's affairs. The reaction of Azerbaijani nationalists to these accusations was negative and tinged with anger. They, in turn, accused the Soviets of wanting to turn Western opinion against the Azerbaijanis in their conflict with Armenia by accusing them of fundamentalism. Since then, both the Soviet Azerbaijani authorities and the National Front leaders have strenuously tried to downplay religious dimensions of the republic's popular movements.[23]

Certainly there is no valid evidence which would support the accusations made by the Soviet authorities that the Azerbaijan national movement was a religious fundamentalist movement. However, the playing-down of the Islamic element by both governmental authorities and National Front personalities also seems exaggerated. As long as there are no truly democratic politics in Soviet Azerbaijan, it would be extremely difficult to ascertain the strength of different tendencies in the republic. Indeed, Azerbaijan's political scene since the stationing of Soviet troops in the republic in January 1990 has been characterized by a compromise between segments of the old Communist establishment and elements of the National Front. This became quite clear during the October 1990 parliamentary elections. Many political parties and tendencies existed clandestinely but were not allowed to operate freely.

Islamically oriented groups, including pro-Iranian groups but also pro-Turkish Islamists such as the followers of the Yeni Musavat Partesi also exist, but mostly in clandestine form.[24] An opinion poll taken in Baku in early 1990 showed that only 3.8 percent of Baku's population favored the establishment of an Islamic republic and only 18.9 percent favored full integration into the Islamic world. However, 76.7 percent favored establishing conditions and institutions which would satisfy the religious feelings of Muslims and 97.0 percent welcomed the opportunity to learn more about Islamic culture.[25]

The point to be stressed here, however, is that Baku – like many other capitals – is not typical of the rest of the country. This is partly due to the fact that in the last 150 years there has been a large influx of foreign ethnic and religious elements into Baku. Moreover, secularization is always stronger in urban centers. Indeed, it is believed that religious feelings are very strong outside of Baku and especially in the villages.[26] Therefore, it is conceivable that a republic-wide poll would have shown a more balanced breakdown between Islamic and other orientations among the population.

What is clear is that there is growing interest in religion in the republic and many mosques are reopening. Azerbaijani authorities want to gain control over the direction of this movement and influence it. For example, they intend to translate the Koran into Azeri Turkic dialect and probably control religious instruction. There is a fear that interest in religious instruction would direct Azerbaijan Muslims toward Iran because of Shi'ism, particularly now that holy Shi'a cities of Iraq have been destroyed. Turkey, here too, seems to be taking a lead by sending Turkish religious instructors to the republic. Even the Saudis are funding Egyptian instructors in Azerbaijan. The Iranians are not totally absent from the scene either.[27] How the religious element would play in the process of molding Azerbaijan's national identity and its political orientation is not clear. What is clear is that religion would affect the attitude of many Azerbaijanis to their surroundings and especially to their two neighbors with whom they have so many affinities. However, it would be only one factor, and perhaps not the most important one, in this process.

Modernization and requirements of development

As in most Muslim lands, the quest for modernization and development has been a significant force in what is now Azerbaijan independent over the last century and a half. In the nineteenth century, those Azerbaijanis that welcomed Russian rule felt that by associating with Russia they would have a better chance of developing a modern economy and society. The same considerations were partly responsible for the growth of pro-Ottoman tendencies among certain Azerbaijan intellectuals. As Iran's economic and political decline accelerated in the nineteenth century and the perception of Ottoman Turkey as the most advanced of the two Muslim states grew, coupled with the fact of Turkey having a foothold in Europe, the number of Soviet Azerbaijanis leaning toward Turkey also grew. After the Bolshevik revolution, too, those Soviet Azerbaijanis who preferred to remain within the new Soviet state, rather than join Turkey or Iran, did so because they viewed the Russians as the more advanced.

The issue of development and modernization has also been a central issue in Soviet Azerbaijan, and in the attitude of the Soviet Azerbaijanis toward their ties with Moscow, their neighbors, and the outside world. The Azerbaijani government and intelligentsia want to move closer to those who could best help them develop their economic and technological base. Thus, until the failed coup, although the Soviet economy was in shambles, many did not see much better alternatives to continued economic links to Moscow. Even after the coup, and despite showing greater reluctance to sign any new economic union treaty, Azerbaijan did not burn its economic bridges to Moscow. The greater attraction toward Turkey among many Soviet Azerbaijani intellectuals is also partly due to their perception that Turkey has made great strides in economic development, not merely because of their pan-Turkism or ethnic affinity. By contrast, Iran's political and economic problems over the last ten years make it not a very attractive partner for development. Another consideration is access to Europe and to the West in general. This consideration also favors Turkey since it is viewed as a conduit to the West.

Moreover, the Azerbaijanis want to develop a positive image which could help them in their conflict with the Armenians. The Western countries, especially the United States, have made no secret of the fact that they would like to see Turkey emerge as the dominant influence in Soviet Asia from the Caucasus to Central Asia.[28] They feel that as a secular pro-Western state, the Turkish presence would enhance Western influence. Some Western countries feel this may compensate Turkey for not being invited to join Europe.

However, the inconclusive result of the Turkish parliamentary elections of November 1991, growing problems of the Turkish economy, the increasing threat of Kurdish separatism, and divisions within the Turkish polity on how to deal with this problem cloud Turkey's future. Should Turkey's economic and political problems worsen, it would affect its leadership aspirations in Azerbaijan and in Central Asia.

What is clear is that imperatives of economic development and modernization would have a very important impact on the orientation of Soviet Azerbaijanis. These considerations may even prove more significant than that of ethnic, linguistic, religious, and other bonds in deciding the nature of their regional links.

Balancing the two neighbors

As we have observed, the nationalist rhetoric and the general culture trend in Soviet Azerbaijan is distinctly pan-Turkic and pro-Turkish. The majority of Azerbaijan intellectuals and National Front leaders make no secret that they see Kemalist Turkey and Mustapha Kemal as the model to be emulated. Some of them have even talked about the possibility of creating a confederation with Turkey which later could extend to the Central Asian Republics. This view was, for instance, expressed by a number of APF members including Ebulfez Aliev in an interview published in the Turkish daily *Miliyet* on July 16, 1990. However, pro-Turkish tendencies are strongest in Baku and within the intelligentsia. There is some evidence that in border areas with Iran and among the more religiously-oriented rural population, pro-Iranian sentiments are stronger.

In the last two years a number of agreements on economic and commercial cooperation have been signed between Turkey and the Azerbaijan SSR. In addition, direct air links between Istanbul and Baku have been established. There has recently been talk of building a bridge over River Aras in order to facilitate communication with Turkey.[29] Telecommunication linkage has also expanded. Yet, while Turkey is emerging as the favored partner, ties with Iran are not ignored.

Indeed, similar economic and commercial agreements have been signed with Iran.[30] In addition to wanting to maximize their economic gains, the authorities do not want to antagonize Iran. Thus there is a desire to at least keep a semblance of balance between the two neighbors. Moreover, the authorities realize that antagonizing Iran would hamper their plans of intensifying contacts with the Iranian Azerbaijan and thus reduce the chances of a future unification of the two regions. Moreover, given Azerbaijan's problem with neighboring Armenia and even possible tensions with Georgia, it cannot afford to engender Iranian hostility as well.

The question of balancing ties is not limited only to economic and political areas and extends even to cultural issues. For example, during the debate over changing the current cyrillic alphabet into either the Arabic or Latin script, in addition to the intrinsic merits of the two, the impact on relations with Iran and Turkey was also considered. Concern was expressed that in the case of choosing Arabic script, Iran's cultural influence might become overwhelming, and in the case of Latin, that of Turkey. The debate was finally settled in favor of Latin, hence favoring Turkey. But in making their choice, the Azerbaijanis had also had their future ties with the West in mind.

Nevertheless, in late 1991 there were signs of greater willingness on the part of Soviet Azerbaijanis to allow a more visible Iranian cultural presence. Particularly significant has been the agreement between the two countries that allows Iran to set up a ground satellite station in Baku's Radio and Television Company which would enable Soviet Azerbaijanis to receive Iranian television. They have also agreed to jointly produce programs in both Persian and in Azerbaijani dialect, including a 90-minute weekly program. If these programs are implemented, they would go a long way to restore the current imbalance in Turkey's favor.[31]

In addition to trying to balance their two big neighbors and cultural kin, the Azerbaijanis are trying to expand their direct ties with other countries as part of their drive to enhance their independent national identity and international personality. Thus diplomatic relations were established with Egypt, a trend likely to extend to other Muslim countries. But Azerbaijan has even reached agreements with Israel on economic and technical cooperation. This is a positive development. The more independent the republic becomes in these matters, the better it is to have constructive relations with many states in the region, thereby mitigating the fear of becoming dominated by one or the other.

Views from Ankara and Tehran

As could be expected, events in Soviet Asia have been keenly followed by both Iran and Turkey. The attitude and approach of each country to events in that area have been determined both by their historic ties and by their current domestic conditions and aspirations, as well as the dynamics of international politics.

The events of 1989–1990 in Soviet Azerbaijan faced both Turkey and Iran with their first serious policy test *vis-à-vis* the Soviet Muslims' popular movements. Turkey's immediate response to disturbances in Azerbaijan was extremely cautious and well in accord with the Kemalist principles of Turkish foreign policy. For example, asked about Turkey's view of events in Soviet Azerbaijan, President Turgut Ozal of Turkey said Turkey was concerned solely with its own internal problems and that the Azerbaijan crisis was an internal affair of the Soviet Union. He further added that Turkey did not nurture aspirations of a Turkish empire that would encompass the Turkic republics of the Soviet Union. Rather, Turkey would continue to follow Ataturk's policy of non-entanglement in foreign disputes and the principle of "Peace in the Homeland; Peace in the World."

More importantly, Ozal stressed the differences between the Azerbaijanis and the Turks. He said the Azerbaijanis are Shi'as and although Azerbaijani dialect is close to Turkish they are separate. Ozal also committed the ultimate sin from the perspective of pan-Turkists in Turkey and in Azerbaijan by saying that the Azerbaijanis, being Shi'as, were more a concern of Iran.[32] Ozal's speech created an uproar in Turkey and strong ripples in Baku. Ozal's rival politicians attacked him. Erdal Inonu, the leader of the socialist party, said Ozal's reference to the Sunni-Shi'a split was causing rifts between Turkey's citizens of different denominations. Suleiman Demirel, the leader of DYP and prime minister of Turkey, said that Ozal's statement ignored the secular principles upon which the Turkish republic was founded. Bulent Ecevit, leader of the DSP, accused Ozal of irresponsibility in pushing the Soviet Azerbaijanis toward Iran.[33]

There were also demonstrations in Ankara and Istanbul demanding a more active Turkish role in Azerbaijan. Since then, Turkish policy toward Azerbaijan, and in general *vis-à-vis* Soviet Asia, has changed and has become more activist with tinges of pan-Turkism, at least of a cultural type. To begin with, Ozal sent his wife Semra to Azerbaijan to reassure the Azerbaijani leaders that Turkey was not indifferent to their situation. And following that, contacts both at official and unofficial levels between Turkey and Soviet Azerbaijan increased dramatically, including a visit by President Turgut Ozal in the spring of 1991.

This changed Turkish attitude reflected a gradual but fundamental shift in Turkey's foreign policy orientation reflecting both domestic developments in Turkey and international changes, especially the end of the Cold War. A discussion of changes in Turkish foreign policy is beyond the scope of this study. Thus only certain essential points pertinent to this study will be noted here.

The first point is that in the last few years Turkey has been going through a process of reassessing its foreign policy orientation and some of its essential ideological underpinnings. This reassessment has been a result of two developments: the end of the Cold War and the dimming of Turkey's hopes of joining Europe.[34] Many of Turkey's foreign policy moves, including its growing activist policy toward the Middle East, highlighted by the high Turkish profile during the Persian Gulf War of January–March 1991, as well as its activism in the Caucasus and Central Asia, derive from this factor.

The end of the Cold War has reduced Turkey's importance to the West as the southern flank of NATO. Events in Eastern Europe have further reduced Turkey's chances of joining Europe as the EC would give priority to accommodating the newly democratic East European countries, as well as others such as Austria and Sweden, before considering Turkey.

Given the fact that orientation toward Europe and eventual integration in it were the underpinnings of Turkey's Kemalist foreign policy, the recent changes inevitably test their continued validity. It is in recognition of these facts that Turkish officials from President Ozal to the Turkish foreign minister have been saying that Kemalism has done its part and that Turkey needs new principles to guide its foreign policy.[35]

Thus, rebuff by Europe has led to a growing interest in other Turkic and Islamic people. Domestically, many Turks now contend that the Europeans and the Westerners in general are anti-Turkish.[36] They argue that Turkey should look elsewhere for partners. Indeed, a mild form of pan-Turkism is becoming stronger in Turkey as the lines between "Turkish" and "Turkic" are increasingly blurred and Turkey sees itself as the model, protector, and spokesman for all Turkic people.[37] Turkey also sees the Soviet Muslim republics with their large Turkic populations as promising export markets for a growing Turkish industry. Thus, it is expected that Turkey will try to maximize its assets and will pursue an activist policy in Azerbaijan. A sign of this new, more aggressive policy of implanting Turkish influence in Azerbaijan was the Turkish government's recognition of Azerbaijan's independence which the latter declared after the failed coup. Reportedly, competition with Iran was another factor: Turkey did not want Iran to be the first to recognize Azerbaijan.[38]

As noted earlier, this greater Turkish role is also favored by the West so long as Turkey's orientation remains secular and pro-Western. No doubt, Turkey is legitimately entitled to a significant economic, political, and cultural role in Soviet Azerbaijan and other Muslim republics. The challenge for Turkey and for these republics is that this goal should be pursued in a way that does not exacerbate ethnic and sectarian divisions in these areas or threaten legitimate interests and territorial integrity of other countries, notably those of Iran.

Events in Soviet Azerbaijan presented Iran with a different and more acute set of dilemmas. Burdened by a longer association with the area, Iran would have a more difficult time managing the Azerbaijani issue. When the Azerbaijan crisis erupted in January 1990, Iran was in a delicate position in terms of its domestic politics and in its international relations.

Domestically, the factional power struggle and positioning for the post-Khomeini period was at its peak as the Ayatollah Khomeini's health waned. The war with Iraq had ended in a ceasefire, leaving chunks of Iranian territory under Iraqi occupation. And the country was economically devastated, militarily weak, and in the grips of an intense political debate about the mistakes of its revolutionary decade.

Internationally, the controversy over the Ayatollah Khomeini's edict in 1989 that the Indian-born British author Salman Rushdie should be killed on charges of apostasy against Islam in his book *Satanic Verses*, had created the worst crisis in Iran's relations with the West since the time of the American hostage crisis. The effects of this crisis were still affecting Iran–West relations in 1991.

The only positive element in Iran's foreign relations at the time was the improvement of relations with the Soviet Union, which had culminated in the then-speaker of the Iranian Parliament Ayatollah Al-Akber Hashemi Rafsanjani's trip to Moscow in June 1989.

Thus the eruption of the Azerbaijan crisis presented Iran with a difficult dilemma: if it were to take a high profile in defense of the Azerbaijanis it would risk scuttling all recent improvements in ties with the Soviet Union; and if it responded too coolly, it would jeopardize future ties with the Azerbaijanis.

In addition, understandably, Iran was concerned about the ramifications of events in the Soviet Azerbaijan for its own security and territorial integrity. Iran was also concerned about possible Soviet military action against itself. The official attitude of the Iranian government was cautious and based on the principle of respect for every country's independence and territorial integrity and support for the legitimate aspirations of Azerbaijani Muslims.[39]

Unofficially, however, opinion on how to respond was divided, with some segments advocating a more activist policy in support of Azerbaijani Muslims.[40] However, the Iranian government did not succumb to these pressures and continued its low-key policy. This attitude of the Iranian government was manipulated by the ultra pan-Turkists in Soviet Azerbaijan and projected as the modern-day version of historic Russo-Iranian collusion to thwart Azerbaijan's aspirations for unity and independence.

After the relative stabilization of the situation in Azerbaijan, the Iranian government tried to expand and consolidate relations with the republic. Apart from economic agreements between the two countries, the Iranian government and unofficial bodies were using cultural and religious affinities to cement ties and to prevent a Turkish monopoly of the republic's cultural scene. Cultural societies in Iran and in Baku have been set up, entitled "Nezami Associations" after the great Persian-Azerbaijani poet Nezami Gandjavi. A conference commemorating Nezami's 850th anniversary was held in Tabriz, the capital of the Iranian province of Eastern Azerbaijan in June 1991, attended by experts on Persian literature from the region and the world. Religious leaders from Iran also visited the republic and there are Soviet Azerbaijani students in the theological schools in Ghom. However, the Iranians are still cautious in completely opening up the borders.

What is clear is that Iran will be keenly interested in the evolution of events in the republic and their implications for its security. Iran, at least at this point, does not have any irredentist aspiration toward the region and is more concerned about the Soviet Azerbaijan's irredentist claims toward its own territory. Its principal objective is to have a presence there and to prevent the emergence of ultra pan-Turkic tendencies which could expand to Iran and its Turkic minorities.

However, growing Turkish activism has raised concerns in Iran. The Iranian press has been saying that by failing to take a more activist attitude toward Azerbaijan, the government is allowing Turkey to implant its power there and to turn it into a NATO base which could be used against Iran.[41] Thus, in the immediate future, Iran may try to raise its profile there. In December 1991, the Iranian Foreign Minister Ali Akbar Velayati visited Baku and reached new agreements with Azerbaijan. He denied the charges made in an *Izvestia* article that Iran was against Azerbaijani independence.[42]

Let us briefly consider the issue of Armenia and how it would play in Turkish-Azerbaijani relations. The Armenian leaders, largely because of pressure by the West, are seeking to improve ties with Turkey.[43] But, as at the popular level, anti-Turkish sentiments are strong. Too close Turkish-Azerbaijani relations would affect Armenia's efforts to improve ties with Turkey. Iran, by contrast, has been a safe haven for Armenians fleeing Ottoman repression since the nineteenth century.[44] Iran, therefore, can play the Armenian card in its competition with Turkey. In fact, the Armenians, although circumspect in their rapprochement with Iran, have been keen on creating airlinks with Iran, as well as a land bridge over the Aras River.[45]

Also Russia's interest and stake in Azerbaijan would act as a balance against Turkish or Iranian domination of the republic's economic and cultural life. A cooperative relationship with both Turkey and Iran would best serve Turkey's interests economically, culturally, and politically, and would enhance its independence in these domains.

A promising note in this regard is the request of Soviet Azerbaijan to join the Economic Cooperation Organization (ECO) which groups Iran, Turkey, and Pakistan. It may lead to expansion of this organization and eventually perhaps include other Soviet Muslim republics.[46]

Azerbaijani-Armenian relations: is reconciliation possible?

In terms of fundamental issues of national identity and culture, the evolution of the nature of Azerbaijan's relations with its two Muslim neighbors, Turkey and Iran, are more important than any other relations that the republic may develop with other countries.

But in terms of immediate prospects for Azerbaijan's security, political stability, and economic growth and prosperity, relations with Armenia are the most significant. The nature of Azerbaijan's relations with Armenia – a small, land-locked, and isolated Christian community – would also have a considerable impact on the character of its relations with the West.

Thus, a repeat of the killing of Armenians in Baku in January 1990 would adversely affect Western opinion and its willingness to help Azerbaijan economically. Continued conflict, or even worse, outright war, would prohibit foreign investors from moving into Azerbaijan, thus dimming its prospects for rapid economic development. Continued conflict with Armenia would also undermine Azerbaijan's bargaining position *vis-à-vis* its two large neighbors. In terms of Azerbaijan's domestic political evolution, continued conflict with Armenia would further undermine any chances, which are already slim, for the development of democratic institutions in the near future.

The current Azerbaijani leadership, which has strong authoritarian tendencies, would use the conflict with Armenia and the external threat to the republic's territorial integrity in order to justify undemocratic rule. More dangerous would be that the Armenian-Azerbaijani conflict over Nagorno-Karabagh could lead to their over-militarization, much as the Indo-Pakistan dispute over Kashmir led to the militarization and nuclearization of the Indian subcontinent. If this were to happen, the implications would go far beyond the two republics and would destabilize neighboring areas as well.

Nagorno-Karabagh and the roots of the Armenian-Azerbaijani dispute

The focus of the recent Azerbaijani-Armenian dispute has been conflicting territorial claims in regard to the mountainous region of Nagorno-Karabagh, a small autonomous area, part of Azerbaijan, but with an overwhelmingly Armenian population. Despite a reduction in the region's Armenian population, the Armenians have a 70 percent majority in this area.

But other factors beyond territorial grievances have contributed to mutual animosity. The genesis of the Karabagh dispute dates to the early period of the establishment of control by the new Bolshevik regime over the Tsar's possessions in the Transcaucasus, and the beginning of the process of carving territorial states out of them.

Initially, on June 3, 1921, the Bolshevik regional bureau awarded Karabagh to Armenia as part of delimiting the boundaries of local governments. But on July 5, 1923, the bureau reversed this earlier decision and gave the region to Azerbaijan.[47] This change of policy was justified in part on the grounds that Azerbaijan was in better economic condition and, therefore, the Armenians of Karabakh would be in a better position economically. However, Azerbaijani protests and also concern for Turkey's preference to have common borders with Azerbaijan were other important factors in this change of heart. But the latter factor was more significant in the Soviet decision to give the area of Nakichevan, with its large Armenian minority, and which is physically separated from Azerbaijan by Armenian territory, to Azerbaijan with the status of an autonomous republic. This change of heart over Karabakh on Moscow's part was never accepted by the Armenians, and they have requested the unification of the Nagorno Karabakh Autonomous Oblast (NKAO) with Armenia.

Communal tensions between the Azerbaijanis and the Armenians have been an endemic problem in this region since the arrangements of 1923, and became progressively worse since the early 1960s. For example, in 1968, clashes between the Armenians and the Azerbaijanis broke out in Stepanakert, capital of the NKAO, triggered by the alleged killing of an Armenian pupil by an ethnic Azerbaijani teacher and the authorities' failure to charge him with murder.[48]

In the 1970s, Armenian activism with strong nationalist undercurrents, both in NKAO and in Armenia, increased. These activists demanded the unification of the region with Armenia, thus exacerbating communal tensions and finally leading to an increase in the number of Armenian-Azerbaijani clashes in 1977.

Similar trends became even stronger in the early 1980s, accompanied by a rapid rise in the number of underground Armenian political groups. But increasing Armenian nationalism accelerated rapidly in 1987 with glasnost and perestroika.[49]

Increased Armenian nationalism, coupled with the opportunities offered by glasnost, resulted in turn in an outpouring of Azerbaijani nationalism. Indeed, it has been argued that intensified Armenian nationalism, crystallized in the claim to Karabagh, finally overcame official and popular apathy in Azerbaijan and led to the development of popular and nationalist groups.[50] Through 1988, protests, demonstrations, and strikes multiplied in NKAO and in Armenia, all aimed at gaining the unification of the region with Armenia.

A particularly important watershed in the worsening of Azerbaijani–Armenian relations and growing bitterness between the two peoples was the anti-Armenian riots in Sumgait, an industrial city near Baku on February 28–29, 1988, by the Azerbaijani youth. These riots resulted in extensive property damage and large numbers of dead and wounded, with estimates varying according to Soviet or dissident sources.

Similar attacks were made by Armenians on Azerbaijani communities and villages. Rising tension between Azerbaijanis and Armenians also resulted in large migration of peoples from each republic. These refugees, especially the Azerbaijani refugees in Baku, became a major contributor to the worsening relations between the two peoples, increased nationalist passions, finally leading to the large-scale massacre of Armenians in Baku in the winter of 1990, and the introduction of Soviet military forces to Baku in January.

Since that time, while there has not been anything resembling what happened in Baku, Azerbaijani-Armenian clashes have continued and all efforts at reconciliation, including those engineered by Boris Yeltsin, President of the Russian Federation, and Nursultan Nazarbayev, President of Kazakhstan on September 21, 1991, failed to resolve the problem. The crash of a helicopter on a peace mission in November 1991 carrying officials from Azerbaijan, Kazakhstan, the KGB, the Defense Ministry, and the Russian Republic's parliament, was blamed by Azerbaijan on the Armenians.[51] The outlook for a quick resolution of this problem is not promising. Rather, with the Soviet Union's disintegration and the rush by both Armenia and Azerbaijan to form national armies, the risk of outright war between the two republics has increased.

The principal culprit: religion, ethnicity, or the legacy of Soviet imperialism and mismanagement?

While the dispute over the territory of Nagorno-Karabagh is the immediate and most tangible cause of Armenian–Azerbaijani conflict, other factors have also contributed to this problem. During the crisis of January 1990 and the massacre of Armenians in Baku, many Western observers, especially journalists, referred to religious and ethnic differences between the Azerbaijanis and the Armenians as the underlying causes of conflict between the two peoples.

No doubt these factors are important, but nevertheless, undue emphasis on them, especially religion, should be avoided. In fact, the case of the Armenian communities in neighboring Iran, including the Iranian Azerbaijan, proves that religious differences have never been an insurmountable obstacle to peaceful and even friendly coexistence.

Since the Safavid times in Iran, Armenian communities have lived in safety in that country. Admittedly, non-Muslims do not enjoy equal rights with Muslims in Islamic societies run by Islamic law. But they enjoy protection and freedom to practise their faith. In secularized Muslim societies, they enjoy equal status with other citizens. This was increasingly the case in Iran under the secularizing influence of the Pahlavis.

The situation worsened after the Islamic revolution as Islamic law and morality was enforced with greater rigor. But there was no gross violation of the Armenian community's rights, at least not more than those of other Iranians who did not fit the Islamic mold promoted by the new government.

In short, the main problem has never been religion but the lack of democracy. Thus, religious abuses that the Armenian community in NKAO suffered, such as the destruction of churches, especially during the period that Gaider Aliev was the KGB boss of Azerbaijan, were the consequence of anti-religious dimensions of Communism and not the anti-Christianism of Islam.[52]

The ethnic factor is more important, given the identification of Azerbaijanis as "Turks," and in view of the unhappy experience of the Armenian community in Ottoman Turkey even before the tragic events of 1915, which is imprinted on their collective consciousness as wilful genocide.

But again, this factor should not be exaggerated. Certainly the linguistically Turkified Iranian Azerbaijanis have lived peacefully with the Armenians. Even in Kemalist Turkey inter-communal relations have improved. Nevertheless, the Armenians' historic memory of suffering at the hands of the "Turks" colors their present attitudes. Thus every Azerbaijani-Armenian conflict acquires dimensions which go beyond what is justified by the specific incident as they merge with this collective consciousness of Armenian suffering.

Ethnic animosity steadily increased following the introduction of Russian power and the relative favoring of the Armenians as fellow Christians. Thus even in earlier times, envy and disparity in social and economic conditions have been more important than mere ethnic differences.[53]

Repressive policies adopted by Communist regimes only exacerbated these tensions. These policies, plus the manipulation of inter-ethnic conflict both by the local Communist leadership and central power in Moscow in the battle between reformers and hard-liners, as well as the center's vacillation and confusion during the early part of the crisis in 1988 and Gorbachev's desperate and inept efforts to keep a crumbling union together, have been principal culprits in exacerbating Azerbaijani–Armenian animosity.[54]

Indeed, some observers have gone so far as to accuse the communist establishment in Azerbaijan of complicity with hard-liners in Moscow in provoking the worst of Azerbaijani–Armenian clashes, namely those in Sumgait in 1988 and in Baku in 1989–1990. These riots were supposed to show the dangers of perestroika and glasnost, and thus discourage the central government in Moscow from pursuing them. In January 1990, attacks against the Armenians were allegedly provoked in order to pave the way for the introduction of the Russian army to Baku in order to crush the Azerbaijani independence movement. This move at the time was viewed as pro-Armenian by the Azerbaijanis. They maintained that undue influence of the Armenians within the Moscow establishment was the reason for this move. It is very difficult to ascertain the veracity of these charges. But there seems to be enough circumstantial evidence to support the thesis that some degree of manipulation by local and central authorities was indeed involved, both in the Sumgait and Baku events.

Certainly the attitude of the central government toward the issue of Nagorno-Karabagh and the conflicting claims of Azerbaijan and Armenia since 1987 largely depended on the two republics' positions on the issue of independence or remaining within the union. Thus, when by August 1990 Armenia seemed to be moving toward independence while Azerbaijan indicated that it was willing to remain in the union, the central government began to shift toward a more pro-Azerbaijani position. Thus during the Azerbaijani–Armenian clashes which took place in May 1991, Soviet troops and Azerbaijani forces cooperated against the Armenian militia.

The immediate cause for these clashes was Soviet efforts to disarm Armenian militia which the republican government had promised to do but had not been able to complete. But the Armenians accused the central government of using this pretext to punish Armenia for having failed to sign the new Union Treaty, and thus sided with Azerbaijan.[55]

Others related this to the intra-leadership conflict in Azerbaijan between Mutalibov and Hasan Hasanov, the Azerbaijani equivalent of a Prime Minister. The Karabagh issue has been manipulated by various factions and groups in Azerbaijan in efforts to gain power and influence.[56]

But perhaps more than any factor other than political repression and economic stagnation, the inherent inconsistencies of the notion of "socialist internationalism" and its contradiction with the nation-building policies of Soviet leadership which began under Stalin have contributed to current difficulties not only in Azerbaijan, but also in other parts of the Soviet empire. The essence of socialist internationalism was that class interests and loyalties rather than ethnic and religious particularisms and allegiances would constitute principal bonds among people in a socialist society. But a socialist society cannot be created overnight. Not only the old socioeconomic and political structures have to be dismantled, but people must be cured of their religious and nationalist and ethno-centric proclivities.

This goal was supposed to be achieved by what the Soviets called "internationalist education." Even as late as 1987–1988, Gorbachev blamed the outpouring of nationalist sentiments and ethnic violence throughout the empire on the government's laxness in internationalist education. The fact, however, is that ethnicity and religion have proven stronger forces of group identification than class.

Moreover, in a paradoxical way, the Soviet policy of carving out separate territorial and cultural entities of ethnically, culturally, and religiously interpenetrated Asian possessions of the Tsar have contributed to a heightened sense of ethnic and cultural particularism. This increased sense of separateness has sown the seeds of future conflicts.

In Central Asia, for example, because of the Communists' nation-building strategies, suddenly the mixed Turko-Iranian-Islamic culture of the region has become divided into Tajik, Uzbek, and Kyrgyz. Together with historic falsification practised by the new system, the legacy of this policy has been ethnic and cultural conflict and unrealistic irredentist claims by these new entities toward their neighbors. The best example of this is the fabrication of the notion of Northern and Southern Azerbaijans.

In addition to this process of state- and nation-building, which accentuated ethnic and religious particularism rather than fostering socialist internationalism, Soviet policies, such as playing one ethnic group against another, forced displacement of ethnic groups, such as the transfer of Shi'a Meshketian Turks to predominantly Sunni Uzbekistan. Drawing of borders without adequate concern about ethnic and linguistic factors – such as leaving the Persian-speaking Tajiks of Samarkand and Bukhara in Uzbekistan – also contributed to ethnic and cultural rivalry and animosity. In the case of NKAO, the fate of the region was not decided on the basis of its ethnic composition nor on the principle of national self-determination.

As long as the central government pursued a total policy of repression, these feelings were kept beneath the surface. But as soon as the lid was lifted under glasnost, to Gorbachev's utter surprise these feelings came pouring out.

Economic stagnation, environmental damage, and other socioeconomic shortcomings of the Soviet system further exacerbated ethno-cultural animosity. In fact, the Azerbaijani–Armenian conflict over Karabagh, in addition to its obvious territorial dimensions, has been affected by all these factors. Probably under a truly open multicultural and economically prospering system the Karabagh Armenians' desire for unification with Armenia would have become much less intense, if not totally eliminated. Moreover, if inter-republic cultural and other contacts and cooperation had been kept at a high level, the Armenians would not have felt separated from their kin and thus would not have seen any need for territorial reunification.[57]

In the more recent past, the same lack of understanding of the forces of ethnicity by the Soviet leadership, especially Gorbachev, contributed to the mishandling of the Armenian-Azerbaijani conflict. Indeed, a constant complaint in the Soviet Union and abroad was that Gorbachev had no understanding of the nationalities problem nor any real interest in it, nor any clear plans to deal with it.[58]

It seems that the Soviet leadership was stunned to find out that the Soviet Union was nothing but a colonial empire, and that as soon as opportunity was offered, the non-Russian people would express their anti-colonial sentiments in an upsurge of nationalist feelings.

Thus, Gorbachev's statement that by expressing nationalist feelings and their desire for independence, the Armenians were stabbing at the heart of perestroika was the direct result of this lack of awareness. In addition, as noted before, the central government's efforts to hold the union together without at the same time completely reverting to the repressive methods of the past, despite occasional use of military power, led to a policy of inconsistency and vacillation on the NKAO issue, as indeed on the entire nationality problem.

The result was the exacerbation of the conflict and growing animosity by both the Armenians and the Azerbaijanis toward the Russians and the central government in Moscow.

What the above implies for the future of Armenian–Azerbaijani relations is that the current status of Karabakh is untenable. It is very unlikely that an overwhelmingly Armenian area could remain under Azerbaijani jurisdiction. However, there are no easy alternatives to the current situation either. For instance, neither the return of NKAO to Armenia, nor a repatriation of the Armenian population, are plausible alternatives. The so-called Baku Plan mediated by Yeltsin and Nazarbayev envisaged keeping the area as part of Azerbaijan but also holding free elections and granting NKAO complete self-rule. But so far these plans have not been implemented. Indeed, it seems increasingly unlikely that either Moscow or other Asian Republics could find a peaceful solution to this problem. Thus, some kind of international – including perhaps United Nations – mediation and intervention appear necessary.

However, once the NKAO dispute is settled, and after a period of healing, there is no viable reason why Azerbaijan and Armenia cannot live in peace, if not in total amity. To achieve this goal, however, in addition to resolving the Karabagh problem, care should be taken not to exacerbate the Armenians' feelings of being encircled. An irredentist, pan-Turkic policy on the part of Azerbaijan would do just that, exacerbate the Armenians' feelings of encirclement and being alone. Viewed in this light, the policy of overly promoting Turkey as the main influence in Azerbaijan could backfire, even with recent efforts of the Armenian leadership to improve ties with Turkey.

Post-August 1991 coup developments and outlook for the character of Azerbaijani government

The communist establishment in Azerbaijan was never comfortable with perestroika and glasnost. However, they manipulated these issues, and even more so the Karabagh problem, in their internal in-fighting. This in-fighting and manipulation first led to the dismissal of Kamran Bagirov and his replacement by Abdul Rakhman Vezirov, and then the dismissal of Vazirov and the coming to power of Ayaz Mutalibov. Moreover, following Moscow's military intervention in Baku, the Azerbaijanis, including the leadership, developed a strong dislike of and resentment toward Gorbachev's person, although for a variety of reasons, including concern over Karabagh, they maintained reasonable ties with Moscow.

Thus, when the coup attempt took place in August 1991, the Azerbaijani leadership was pleased. Indeed, Azerbaijan's president Ayaz Mutalibov, who at the time was visiting Iran, expressed his satisfaction at Gorbachev's dismissal.[59] He later denied that he had done so. But these denials did not satisfy opposition forces. On September 5, Moscow Radio broadcast a report that Mutalibov had survived an assassination attempt and blamed the Azerbaijan Popular Front for it. But this was denied by Azerbaijani sources.[60]

Indeed, Ayaz Mutalibov managed to consolidate his power and be elected as president in the election on September 8 in which he ran unopposed. The only other candidate, a Social Democrat once affiliated with APF, Zardusht Ali Zade, withdrew his candidacy at the last minute.

Azerbaijan moved quickly to declare its independence as it became clear by early 1992 that the Soviet Union was no more and that the so-called "Commonwealth of Independent States" did not have much chance of replacing it. The disintegration of the Soviet Union intensified the power struggle within the Azerbaijani leadership. It also led to the flaring up of the conflict with Armenia over Nagorno-Karabagh. In fact, the problem of Nagorno-Karabagh and the Azerbaijani power struggle became inextricably linked together.

Conscious of the fact that with the end of the Soviet Union they were left to themselves to settle the Karabagh issue, the two sides took measures which led to fierce fighting in the winter and spring of 1992. In January, Azerbaijan decided to bring Karabagh under its direct jurisdiction, an act which contributed to the flaring up of conflict. During the fighting the Azerbaijanis suffered serious reverses and a large number of Azerbaijanis were killed by the Armenian forces, particularly in the Khojali and Agdarn villages. These reverses convinced the Azerbaijan Popular Front and the opponents of President Ayaz Mutalibov to force him out of office. In view of the fragmented nature of the APF and the divisions within the old communist establishment after Mutalibov's removal, the future of Azerbaijan's leadership became very clouded. Elections were scheduled for June 1992 and it surprised many that they were held. While various factions proceeded with developing their separate militia, a development which did not augur well for Azerbaijan's stability, elections provided citizen participation through a non-violent outlet. The man elected to the presidency, APF leader Abol Fez Ilcibey, promised to regain Nagorno-Karabagh for Azerbaijan.

The Azerbaijani leadership crisis made resolution of the Karabagh problem more difficult by making it extremely hard for any Azerbaijani leader to be flexible. In fact, one of the charges against President Mutalibov was that he was too flexible on this matter. As a result, throughout spring 1992, various mediation efforts by Iran, the CSCE, and the United Nations to solve this problem did not yield any results.

Another consequence of the heightened Karabagh crisis and Azerbaijan's leadership problems was a more interventionist Turkish policy *vis-à-vis* Azerbaijan, partly in view of APF's pro-Turkish and pan-Turkist tendencies, whereas Mutalibov was more even-handed in regard to relations with Azerbaijan's two big neighbors. Turkish leaders such as Turgut Ozal and Mesut Yilonaz openly advocated a more active and intrusive Turkish policy on the issue of Nagorno-Karabagh.

In sum, as was noted earlier in this essay, the rapid disintegration of the Soviet Union brought to the fore Azerbaijan's many contradictions and divisions. Consequently, on the eve of its independence, the new republic's future seemed very uncertain.

Conclusions

Soviet Azerbaijan and its people are going through a process that many of the new nations of the Third World experienced during the 1960s and 1970s known as the process of nation-building. In doing so, they are trying to rediscover their past. In this exercise, they are burdened by the Soviet legacy of historic falsification, forced Sovietization, and Russification.

What they discover about their own history and cultural roots is often incompatible with their current and future vision of themselves. Thus, some of the Azerbaijani intellectuals are engaging in historic revisionism of their own and are reinterpreting history in order to fit their present goals.

Historic revisionism, romanticism, and even mythification of one's history is a practice that all nations engage in to varying degrees. But in the case of Soviet Azerbaijan, if pushed too far, it could create serious problems for them in their external ties.

This search for identity and efforts at nation-building are happening in a highly controlled atmosphere within a narrow elite. Popular debate on these issues and the range of participants are limited. Thus, whatever its outcome, it may not be very lasting. In this process, Azerbaijan is feeling the impact of several aspects of its ethnic, linguistic, cultural, and religious composition. The people are divided as different groups feel the pull of one factor (religion) or another (language) to, at times, vastly different degrees.

Moreover, there are extremist tendencies within different groups which further complicate problems of nation-building and increase the risk of fragmentation along sectarian and other lines. Azerbaijan's problems of defining its self-identity are exacerbated by the presence of two large neighbors which have a great stake in the outcome of this search for identity, and with both of whom the republic has long-standing ties and affinities.

In relating to its neighbors, not only must Azerbaijan be careful not to antagonize them, but also not be overwhelmed by them. This danger would be more serious if Azerbaijan were to go too far in self-Turkeyization. Given the language factor, such a policy could lead to a loss of a distinct Azerbaijani identity. Given the linguistic difference with Iran, such a risk is less great, but not non-existent.

Of even more immediate significance for the country's future prospects for stability and economic growth is its relations with Armenia. Without reaching some kind of *modus vivendi* with Armenia, Azerbaijan may end up exhausted by a conflict which would sap its economic resources, lead to over-militarization, and delay its democratization and political maturation.

Given where it is located, Azerbaijan will in time be drawn into regional and international politics. Outsiders will have a growing interest in the outcome of this process and will try to influence it.

Last, but certainly not least, the outcome of this process and Azerbaijan's future would be affected by what happens to the Commonwealth of Independent States. Total elimination of the Russian presence would in all likelihood sharpen the republic's many contradictions and divisions. It could even increase the risk of outside interference and enhance the danger of its fragmentation. Or Azerbaijan might become embroiled in an irredentist adventure against Iran which almost certainly would increase the risk of regional conflict.

Ironically, if the Commonwealth holds together it could help give Azerbaijan a chance to pursue the process of nation-building under more stable conditions and to develop a new, broad-based, and realistic synthesis of its multi-faceted history and culture, a synthesis which would form the basis of a distinct Azerbaijani culture and identity, a necessary underpinning of a more independent and confident Azerbaijani political system.

It would also allow Azerbaijan to develop more constructive and mature relationships with its neighbors based on mutual respect for their respective interests. Under the best circumstances, such relations could be the basis for new and expanded forms of regional economic and cultural cooperation.

In short, nation-building in Azerbaijan is likely to be a lengthy, difficult, and potentially destabilizing process. Its dynamics and outcome will affect the republic itself, as well as the neighboring states and even beyond. It entails potential both for positive developments and for conflict. Which of these potentials is more likely to materialize cannot be foreseen.

Notes

1 On renewed ethnic and cultural rivalries in Central Asia, see Ann Sheehy, "Tadjiks Question Republican Frontiers," *Radio Liberty Research*, August 11, 1988, p. 15. Also see Akbar Tursonzad, "Zaban Peyvand e-Aslha va Nalseha" (Language: The Bond Among Peoples and Generations), an unpublished paper in Persian by Tajik author and member of Tajikstan Academy of Sciences. Territorial conflicts exist between Uzbek and the Kyrgyz.

2 Currently Moscow's desire not to antagonize Iran and at the same time prevent too close a rapprochement between Soviet Azerbaijan and Iran, while encouraging better ties between the republic and Turkey, greatly influences the attitude of Soviet Azerbaijanis toward their neighbors.

3 On the unfolding of events in Soviet-Iranian borders, see various issues of Foreign Broadcasting Information Services *FBIS/MES* January/February 1990.

4 Bakhtiar Vahabzadeh, one of the pan-Turkic leaders of the APF, develops this theme in his poem called "Gulistan," after the name of the Russo-Iranian treaty. See also Audrey L. Alstadt, "Azerbaijanis Reassess Their History," *Report on the USSR*, vol. 1, no. 23, August 18, 1988, pp. 18–19.

5 Such opinions were expressed to me by a number of Azerbaijani academics during a visit to Baku in the autumn of 1990. In their vision, a large part of north and north-eastern Iran where Turkmen tribes live should be joined with the two Azerbaijans.

6 On Russo-Iranian wars, see R.K. Ramazani, *The Foreign Policy of Iran: A Developing Nation in World Affairs: 1500–1941* (Charlottesville: University Press of Virginia, 1975). Some of these lords chose the Russian side, but this was mostly for personal ambition rather than anti-Iranianism. Among those who chose the Russian side were relatives of the Qajar kings of Iran who were fighting the Russians.

7 See Firuz Kazemzadeh, *The Struggle for Transcaucasia 1917–1921* (Birmingham: Temple Press, 1951), pp. 229–230.

8 See Alexander Benningsen, "Pan-Turkism and Pan-Islamism in History and Today," *Central Asian Survey*, vol. 3, no. 3, 1985, p. 48.

9 See Ahmad Kasravi, *Tarikh-e-Hedjdah Saleh-e-Azerbaijan* (The Eighteen Year History of Azerbaijan) (1353/1974), Tehran: Amir Kabir Publishing, p. 874.

10 On this view, see Tadeusz Swietochowski, *Russian Azerbaijan 1905–1920* (Cambridge: Cambridge University Press, 1985).

11 For instance, on the third anniversary of the official creation of the Democratic Party of Azerbaijan, the Communist Party of Azerbaijan sent a congratulatory telegram and praised it for struggling to free "the southern part of our homeland that for years has been suffering under the cursed hands of Persian chauvinists . . ." For the text, see *Azerbaijan*, no. 18, September 1948. See also, David B. Nissman *The Soviet Union and Iranian Azerbaijan: The Use of Nationalism for Political Penetration* (Boulder, CO: Westview Press, 1987).

12 See Mirza Michaeli and William Reese, "The 'Birlik' Society in the Azerbaijani Democratic Movement," *Report on the USSR*, vol. 1, no. 35, September 1, 1989, pp. 30–31.

13 On Soviet-Iranian relations, see Shireen T. Hunter, *Iran and the World: Continuity In A Revolutionary Decade* (Bloomington, Indiana: 1990), pp. 79–96; also Professor R.K. Ramazani's works on Iran's foreign relations.

14 For example, a young Soviet Azerbaijani, in talking to me, asked rhetorically why is it that some APF leaders are in jail and others are active. After the reforms of Mikhail Gorbachev and greater freedom of expression, a variety of so-called informal groups from environmentalist to cultural societies and groups closer to political parties emerged in Soviet Azerbaijan. The following are some of these groups: Birlik, Dirchalish ("Rebirth"), Kyzylbash, all which wanted independence and unification of the two Azerbaijans. Other groups included the Azerbaijan Green Party, the Azerbaijan Social Democratic Party, Yeni Musavat Partesi, etc. But the Azerbaijan Popular Front was not the result of a coming together of these groups. Rather, it was an assembly of certain individuals, most of them prominent writers. Thus, as Mark Saroyan has put it, "The APF's formation did not reflect an attempt to build a coalition between organizations that had already worked out their own respective programs and concerns on political, economic, cultural, and environmental issues." Rather, it was an association "attempting to accommodate varying interests and political orientations of diverse individuals." As a result, it was not really a body representative of all trends in the republic. See Mark Saroyan, "The Karabakh Syndrome and Azerbaijani Politics," *Problems of Communism*, vol. XXXIX, no. 5, September/October 1990, p. 22. See also: Mirza Michaeli, "Formation of Popular Front in Azerbaijan," *Radio Liberty Research*, December 9, 1988.

15 A prominent Iranian pan-Turkist is Javad Heiat who publishes the "Varliq" in Azerbaijan Turkic dialect in Tehran. There is an Azerbaijani cultural foundation in Frankfurt created by Iranian Azerbaijanis. Similar groups are emerging in the United States.

16 For example, according to Geihun Molla-Zade, a political scientist at the republic's Academy of Sciences, Moscow believed Azerbaijan must stay in the union. "Perhaps Armenia and Georgia can go. But Azerbaijan, its oil, the border with Iran, the Caspian Sea, the cotton, it won't be given up easily . . ." See "Carrot and Stick: Communism Keeps Azerbaijan in Two," *Washington Times*, June 11, 1991, p. 49.

17 The number of non-Iranian people was large in what is now Soviet Azerbaijan and Dagestan. But what is now the Iranian Azerbaijan was solidly Iranian. However, the Iranian branch of Indo-Europeans was also numerous in the above regions. For example, according to Bakikhanof, the "Oss" whence currently the name of "Ossetia" in Georgia were Iranian people. He says "their language still has old Persian words. They call themselves 'Irooni' and their country 'Iroonstan.'" Then he says that in the colloquial pronunciation of the name "Iran," in Iran too it is "Iroon." See *Gulestan-E-Eram*, op. cit., p. 7, more detail p. 3.

18 See, for example, the works of Ziya Gokalp such as *Turkculugan essaslari* (Istanbul, 1952); also the accounts of the Second Congress of Turkish History held in Istanbul in 1943. However, most historians and geographers dispute this view. Most agree that major Turkic influx into Central Asia began in the sixth century AD. The "pan-Turanists" have an even larger vision of what constitutes the homeland of the Turks. They include the Magyars and Finno-Ugrians, also, as Turks. However, the thesis that historic Turan was Turkic is not correct. The legend has it that Fereidoun, the Iranian founder of the "Kian" dynasty, divided his kingdom among this three sons: Salm (also written as Sarm), Tour, and Eradj (Erak). Salm's kingdom was known as Sarman (in

Avesta, the Zoroastrian holy book, it is referred to as Sairima), Tour's realm as Touran, and Eradj's was Iran.

The conflicts that emerged between Iran and Touran and are chronicled in Shahnameh were mostly because the Iranians became sedentary, highly developed agricultural societies, while most of Touranians remained nomadic. For a discussion of these issues and excellent documentation, see Enayatollah Reza, Azerbaijan va Eran (Albaina-e-Ghafghaz) (Azerbaijan and Eran or Albania of Caucasus). Tehran: Entesharat-e-Iran Zamin 1360 (1980–81), pp. G3-III.

19 See Saroyan, "The Karabakh Syndrome and Azerbaijani Politics," pp. 14–29.

20 See Eldar Namazof. "Taking the Path of Renewal," unpublished paper, Baku, 1990.

21 For example, a prominent Iranian leftist, Dr Taghi Erani, a native of Azerbaijan, in the 1930s suggested the forced elimination of the Turkic dialect and linguistic Persianization of the region.

22 On aspects of this Russian policy, see Mark Saroyan, "Beyond the Nation-State: Culture and Ethnic Politics in Soviet Transcaucasia," *Soviet Union/Union Sovietique*, vol. 15, no. 23, 1988; also, Ronald Suny, "The Revenge of the Past: Socialism and Ethnic Conflict in Transcaucasia," *New Left Review*, no. 184, November/December, 1990.

23 See Elizabeth Fuller, "The Nemat Panakhov Phenomenon – As Reflected in the Azerbaijani Press," *Report on the USSR*, vol. 1, no. 7, February 17, 1989, especially the following: "Questioned about the significance of green Islamic flags and portraits of Khomeini, Panakhov dismissed them as marginal. ". . . For all of Panakhov's attempts to play down the Islamic element, its significance should not be underestimated" (p. 4). Also William Reese, "The Role of the Religious Revival and Nationalism," *Radio Liberty Research*, December 5, 1988, pp. 1–3. However, what worried Western observers about Khomeini posters was not so much its Islamic dimension, but rather its significance as to the existence of pro-Iranian tendencies in Azerbaijan. In fact, in addition to Khomeini's portraits, pictures of the last Persian king of the region, Fath Ali Shah Qajar, were also hoisted in demonstrations.

24 Islamic groups exist in underground fashion and at times under the cover of Sufi Brotherhoods. The only open group is the non-political group "Tubeh" (repentance). See also "Islam Revival Stirs in Azerbaijan," *Christian Science Monitor*, 30 October, 1990. While full of historic inaccuracies reflective of the current thesis on the region discussed here, it gives a flavor of the role of religion in the area.

25 See Eldar Namazaf, "Path of Renewal."

26 See, "Isalm Revival Stirs in Azerbaijan." Many of the rural population are also pro-Iran. The above article noted that "some talk of Iran as their own."

27 See "Musavi-Ardebili Delivers Friday Prayers Sermon," *FBIS/MES*, April 22, 1991, pp. 52–55. He is a native of Iranian Azerbaijan. He discussed the issue of Soviet Azerbaijan's ties to Iran and Turkish efforts to propagate Wahabism there.

28 See Graham Fuller, "The Emergence of Central Asia," *Foreign Policy*, no. 87, Spring 1990, pp. 49–67.

29 See various issues of *FBIS/Europe* on Turkey. There is talk of creating a permanent Turkish economic and cultural center in Baku. With Turkey's recognition of Azerbaijan, Turkey will open an embassy there.

30 See various issues of *FBIS/MES*, Iran.
31 On the visit of Soviet Azerbaijan's prime minister to Iran, see *FBIS/MES*, June 11, 1991, pp. 50–51.
32 On Ozal's statement, see "Flas Ulke Oluruz," *Cumhuriyet*, January 19, 1990.
33 See "Ozal Ozur Dilesin," *Cumhuriyet*, January 20, 1990. Also on what Turkey should do about Azerbaijan, see Husseyin Mumtaz, "Turkiye Ne Yapmali" (What Should Turkey Do), *Turk Yurdu*, vol. 32, Nisan (April) 1990. For a more pan-Turkist account, see Ayvaz Gokdemir, "Azerbaycan Hitabesi," *Turk Yurdu*, vol. 31, Mart (March) 1990.
34 See Shireen T. Hunter, "Turkey's Foreign Options," *Middle East International*, no. 400, May 17, 1991, pp. 18–19.
35 See "Ozaldan Batiya Kurt Sozij," *Cumhuriyet*, September 25, 1991.
36 For example, in the face of Western criticism of Turkey's handling of Kurdish refugees, such sentiments were expressed. One Turkish columnist wrote that "Western countries simply do not like Turkey. A time will come when we will see this more clearly. It is a truth that the Crusaders' wars continue." See "Turks Angry as Kurd Aid Backfires," *New York Times*, May 17, 1991, p. A-8.
37 For example, Turkish press are referring to Iraqi Turkmen as Turkish.
38 See "Recognition of Azerbaijan Will Set a Model for Other Republics," *Turkish Times*, December 1, 1991, p. 3.
39 For example, in a letter to the then-Soviet Foreign Minister Eduard Shevardnadze, Iran's foreign minister emphasized Iran's "adherence to the principle of non-interference in other nations' affairs." See "Velayati on Helping Resolve Azerbaijan Crisis," *FBIS/MES*, February 8, 1990.
40 For example, a large number of deputies in Iran's parliament asked for a more activist policy in favor of Azerbaijani Muslims. See various issues of *FBIS/MES*, Winter/Spring 1990.
41 See "Iran and Soviet Azerbaijan Sign Memorandum of Understanding on Economic, Cultural and Political Cooperation," *Keyhan*, December 4, 1991.
42 "Armenia, Casting Wary Eye on Azerbaijan, Seeks Closer Ties with Turkey," *New York Times*, November 14, 1991, p. A-42.
43 In the seventeenth century, Iran's Safavid king Shah Abbas the Great gave sanctuary to the Armenians in Isphahan, the Safavid capital. They built a church and a community which they call Jolfer after a border town in Iranian Azerbaijan.
44 See "Armenian Seeking Closer Ties with Turkey."
45 See *Middle East Economic Digest (MED)*, vol. 35, no. 24, June 2, 1991, p. 13.
46 On the background to the Karabakh problem, see *The Karabakh File* (Zoryan Institute, Cambridge, MA, 1988) and various issues of *Radio Liberty Research* in 1988.
47 On the killings, see *Soviet Nationalities Survey*, "Special Issue: Crisis in the Caucasus" (United States Department of State, no. 15, August 22, 1988, p. 1.
48 *Ibid*.
49 See Saroyan, "The Karabakh Syndrome."
50 On Yeltsin and Nazarbayev's efforts, see: "Yeltsin in Azerbaijan," *New York Times*, September 22, 1991, p. 10; on the crash, see "Missile Suspected in 'Copter Crash," *Washington Post*, November 22, 1991, p. 42.
51 On Gaidar Aliev's mistreatment of Armenians, see "Special Issue: Crisis in the

Caucasus," *Soviet Nationalities Survey*, United States Department of State, Bureau of Intelligence and Research, no. 15, August 22, 1988, p. 10.

52 See Ronald Suny, "The Revenge of the Past: Socialism and Ethnic Conflict in Transcaucasia," *New Left Review*, no. 184, November/December 1990. See also Saroyan, "The Karabakh Syndrome."

53 On Gorbachev's vacillation, see Mark Saroyan, "Trouble in the Transcaucasus," *Bulletin of the Atomic Scientists*, vol. 45, no. 2, March 1989, p. 18.

54 On the pro-Azerbaijan tilt, see "Armenians and Azerbaijanis Clash in Two Soviet Villages," *Christian Science Monitor*, May 7, 1991, p. 5.

55 On Mutalibov-Hasanof rivalry, see *ibid.*

56 On the Armenians' cultural grievance, see Saroyan "The Karabakh Syndrome."

57 On Gorbachev's lack of understanding of nationality problems, see Ludmilla Alexeyeva "Unrest in the Soviet Union," *Washington Quarterly*, vol. 13, no. 1, Winter 1990, pp. 63–77. Also, Quentin Peel, "Dagger at Heart of Perestroika," *Financial Times*, January 18, 1990, p. 17.

58 See Elizabeth Fuller, "The Azerbaijani Presidential Election: A One Horse Race," *Report on the USSR*, vol. 3, no. 37, September 13, 1991, p. 14.

11 Armenia: the nation awakens

NORA DUDWICK

In a speech to the Armenian Parliament in October, 1990, Levon Ter-Petrosian observed that the "Armenian people finally woke up from its delightful slumber" to realize the realities of its situation.[1] In his comment, Ter-Petrosian, now president of Armenia, was using one of the most popular tropes of nationalism.[2] Nineteenth-century nationalist discourse defined the development of vernaculars and the exploration of folklore which formed the first phase of European nationalism as the "'rediscovering' of something deep-down always known."[3] Metaphors of awakening, rediscovery, and regeneration, all of which appear with frequency in Armenian public discourse, are apt for conceptualizing national sentiment in Armenia, for which, despite an unbroken presence of nearly 3,000 years on the Armenian plateau in Asia Minor, "history has been a broken trail."[4]

The formation of the Armenian People

It has yet to be ascertained whether Armenians originated in western Asia Minor or whether they were among the native inhabitants of the highlands of eastern Anatolia. Nor is it known where the term "Armenia," or the indigenous term, "Hayastan" originates,[5] although Greek and Persian sources refer to "Armina" and "Armenians" as early as 500 B.C.[6] The Armenian tribes were first recognized around 600 B.C., with the collapse of the wealthy kingdom of Urartu, centered in Van (in present-day Turkey).[7] Whether Urartu was primarily Armenian, with a small ruling elite from a different ethnic stock, is today a contentious issue for Armenian historians eager to prove that Armenians were indigenous to eastern Anatolia. Articles on Armenia's relation to the kingdom of Urartu periodically appear in the local press.[8] Politically, early Armenia was made up of feuding dynastic principalities, a pattern which continued throughout the medieval period, making Armenia a prey to larger neighboring empires. At the same time, this pattern probably ensured the survival of a distinct ethnic identity since part of Armenian territory continually maintained some autonomy and thereby resisted assimilationist pressures.[9]

The adoption of Christianity as the state religion at the beginning of the fourth century, and the creation of a phonetic, thirty-six character alphabet a century later under Church sponsorship, played a major role in maintaining a distinctive Armenian identity, for "in a real sense, Armenians did not even fully become 'Armenians' until they acquired their own distinctively Armenian religion . . ."[10] In A.D. 451, at the Battle of Avarayr, St. Vardan Mamikonian and his 696 men died resisting the Persian Empire's attempt to impose Zoroastrianism on the Armenians. Today, Armenians commemorate this date as a reminder of their willingness to martyr themselves for their Christian faith. What is significant, however, is that for the early chronicler of this event, it was not just a religious conflict. According to Elishe, Vardan and his men fought the Persians to defend their traditional customs and way of life, evidence that a sense of distinctiveness already existed among Armenians some 1,500 years ago.[11] After the sixth century schism between the Armenian and Byzantine churches, Armenia formed a distinct cultural unit between the Classical west and the Persian east.[12] Split between the Persian and Roman (and later, Byzantine) empires by the end of the fifth century, Armenians continued to enjoy relative autonomy despite rendering nominal fealty to their imperial rulers.[13]

Waves of invasions by Turkic tribes from Central Asia in the eleventh century, followed by the Mongol invasions of the thirteenth and fourteenth centuries, stimulated Armenian migration to cities throughout Europe, Russia, and the Middle East. By the end of the fifteenth century, the Ottoman Turks had established themselves in Constantinople, and were extending their power into Anatolia. The Ottoman Empire ruled religious minorities through their religious leaders; thus, the Patriarch of the Armenian Apostolic Church became the functional head of the Armenian community, or *millet*. The Church became the single most important institution of Armenian life within the Ottoman Empire,[14] and "from the fifteenth to the late nineteenth century, whoever led the Church spoke for what there was of the nation."[15]

A sixteenth-century treaty with the Persian Empire divided Armenia into a western portion under Ottoman hegemony and an eastern portion under Persian hegemony. The new boundary transformed Armenia into a perpetual theater of war, as military campaigns, pillage, deportations and famine during the following centuries accelerated the depopulation of the Armenian hinterland, ultimately turning Armenians into a minority in their homeland.[16] In contrast to the impoverishment of the Armenian heartland, a prosperous commercial bourgeoisie developed in the urban diaspora. It was among these communities that a nationalist consciousness first developed. Now permanent "outsiders," Armenians turned their attention to the plight of the distant but longed-for homeland. In these cities, they were also exposed to the revolutionary and nationalist currents which began to sweep Europe in the eighteenth and nineteenth centuries. As in Europe, nationalism among Armenians developed unevenly among social groups and regions, beginning with a purely cultural and literary phase, which led to a militant campaign for the "national idea."[17]

The first awakening

The "prehistory" of Armenian nationalism can be dated to the sixteenth century, when an Armenian cultural renaissance began in the diaspora. The use of the printing press by Armenian commercial entrepreneurs led to a stream of publications in Armenian, including the first printed Armenian Bible (Amsterdam, 1666), and the first journal of Armenian affairs (Madras, 1794). All these publications disseminated European Renaissance learning among Armenians.[18] A very significant factor in the Armenian cultural awakening was the rediscovery and republication of Armenian classical religious, literary and historical texts by the Mekhitarist monks, an Armenian Benedictine order founded in Venice in the eighteenth century.[19] The Mekhitarists' efforts were aimed at the culturally backward Armenian communities of the Ottoman Empire, "but they were careful not to transform cultural views into political trends."[20] Historical and mythological Armenian heroes who had resisted foreign domination were offered to Armenians primarily as sources of pride and spiritual values. The concept of the "nation," however, remained cultural rather than political and within the Ottoman Empire, where the bulk of the Armenian population still formed an impoverished, semi-literate, often Turkish-speaking mass, the "nation" as a self-conscious entity consisted primarily of the *millet*'s clerical and wealthy classes.[21]

Following the Mekhitarists modification of the ancient literary language, *grabar*, Khatchatour Abovian popularized a radically modified vernacular with the publication of his novel, *Wounds of Armenia*. This vernacular subsequently became the medium of an increasingly nationalistic literary revival in which appeals were made to Armenians in the Ottoman empire to "wake up . . . from your death-inviting slumber of ignorance, remember your past glory, mourn your present state of wretchedness and heed the example of other enlightened nations . . ."[22]

In the mid-nineteenth century, cultural practices, as summed up by the conception of "nation," gradually displaced religion as the guarantor of ethnic identity for a new Armenian middle class of doctors, lawyers, writers, teachers, and small manufacturers, who challenged elite control over social and political life in the *millet*.[23] This new liberal class achieved a limited democratization of the *millet* administration, which turned its attention to spreading literacy and enlightenment among the Armenian population. But most liberals focused their efforts within Constantinople, for as one liberal editor wrote, "the Patriarch is there, the progressive and educated elements of the nation are there. In one word, the great strength of the nation is there."[24]

The growth of cultural nationalism in the urban centers contrasted with the lack of national consciousness in the rural hinterland, where the very concept of "Armenia" had been lost for the mass of Armenians until it was rediscovered and reinvented by intellectuals in the nineteenth century.[25] Sentiment in the countryside consisted of "the simple attachment to a land invested with historical and spiritual significance," and the goal of the peasantry was the creation of an environment which allowed them to preserve traditional norms.[26] In contrast, the cultural awakening in the cities stimulated a new generation of educated provincial Armenians, such as the self-taught clergyman from Van, Mkrtich Khrimian, who in his concern for the welfare of the masses "began a shift in Armenian political thought from an abstract nationalism to a concrete populism . . ."[27] By redefining patriotism as love of the fatherland, the nation was linked to particular territory, a further step in the development of a political program.

Despite the *millet* reforms and the guarantees for Armenian security which the European powers forced the Ottoman Empire to make after the Russo-Turkish war of 1877–1878, the economic and political situation in the provinces steadily deteriorated. The war had devastated the Armenian countryside, and the Sultan's repression against the Armenians for their perceived pro-Russian orientation and increased politicization resulted in the massacres of 1895–1896, which took 300,000 Armenian lives.[28]

By the early nineteenth century, the annexation of the Crimea and Eastern (Persian) Armenia by Russia introduced new security and prosperity to the Russian Armenians.[29] As in the Ottoman Empire, a new generation of secular, nationalist intellectuals emerged by mid-century. Their socialist and revolutionary ideology had a profound impact on the programs of the Armenian political parties. Although two of these parties, the Hunchak party (Geneva, 1887), and the Dashnak party (Tbilisi, 1890) were founded outside Armenia proper, their efforts were directed primarily at the six eastern provinces of the Ottoman Empire, where most Turkish Armenians lived. Their programs were radicalized by increased oppression and large-scale massacres in the Ottoman Empire and the example of the successful Balkan resistance movements. Ultimately, the parties' dearth of manpower and economic strength, the lack of active support from internecine conflicts, and a futile reliance on assistance from the European powers, contributed to the failure of the nineteenth-century revolutionary movement to secure its aims.[30]

The 1915 genocide

The Armenia liberation movement came to an abrupt halt during World War I, when the Ottoman Empire took the opportunity to rid itself of its troublesome Armenian population. In the organized slaughter which peaked between 1915 and 1917, between one and 1.5 million Armenians

Table 11.1. *Distribution of the Armenian population, 1988*

Soviet Union	4,600,000	Latin America	100,000
Armenia	3,100,000	Canada	50,000
United States	750,000	Balkans	
Middle East & Libya,		(Bulgaria, Greece, Romania)	50,000
Egypt, Ethiopia	475,000	Australia	25,000
Western Europe	400,000	Far East	12,500
Iran	140,000	Africa	5,000

Source: adapted from Claire Mouradian, *De Staline à Gorbatchev* (1990), p. 169. Where she has provided a range of figures I have averaged them to produce a single estimate for a given region.

were executed or died on death marches across Turkey.[31] Refugees poured into Russian Armenia, where they constituted at least one fourth of the population by the beginning of the twenties.[32]

It is impossible to exaggerate the significance of this event for contemporary Armenian thinking, both in Armenia and in the diaspora. The genocide virtually eliminated Armenians from nine-tenths of their historical homeland in eastern Anatolia, leaving them only the small, mangled territory in the Russian Caucasus. Throughout the Middle East, Europe, and North America, it created new or vastly enlarged diasporan communities where the memory of the genocide served as a virtual "charter of identity," even among families who had not directly experienced it.[33] Since then, Armenians have repeatedly sought an official acknowledgement of the genocide by Turkey, which in recent years has poured a significant amount of money into a sophisticated denial.[34] In the aftermath of the genocide, Armenians were willing to see the Soviet Union as its bulwark against traditional enemies, or at least, as the lesser of two evils. This perception partly explains Armenians' acceptance of Soviet authority, as well as the relative lack of anti-Sovietism among many diasporan Armenians.

With the collapse of central power which followed the October Revolution in 1917 and the withdrawal of Russian troops from the Transcaucasus, Armenia, Azerbaijan, and Georgia declared independence. In 1918, the

> Armenian republic began its existence under the leadership of the Dashnak Party, on about 4,500 square miles (12,000 square kilometers) of bleak rugged terrain, crammed with refugees, devoid of the bare essentials of life, and surrounded by hostile forces ... it became the "Land of Stalking Death," as famine, contagion, and exposure swept away nearly 200,000 people during the ensuing year.[35]

During the war with Turkey, harvests had decreased by 40 percent, the land under cultivation by a third, and industrial production had almost ceased. The Turkish invasion and occupation of 1918 left 200 villages and half the vineyards in the Ararat valley in ruins.[36] By 1919, the republic was overwhelmed by almost 300,000 refugees, resentful at failures of the East Armenian leadership; new refugees poured in daily from the North Caucasus and Azerbaijan.[37]

Sovietization

Sovietization of the republic occurred "as a measure of last resort by the defeated, discouraged, and disintegrating Dashnak government of independent Armenia," which signed away its powers on December 2, 1920.[38] According to a British eyewitness, "people were amazed, incredulous, but for the most part apathetic. Anyhow, they thought it would be better to have the Russians back and to lose their independence than to be massacred by the Turks."[39]

The primary aim of the new Soviet Armenian leadership was to restore agricultural productivity to pre-war levels. By 1926, agricultural production had reached 71.5 percent of its prewar level, and 90 percent of prewar sown land was again under cultivation. By the end of the twenties, a number of irrigation projects had been completed and twenty electric stations had been constructed.[40] Industrial production proceeded slowly during this period and unemployment remained high throughout the 1920s, with the bulk of the population (82.1 percent) still living in the countryside.[41]

The Armenian peasantry was collectivized in the 1930s, despite a vigorous resistance from 1930 to 1934 led by traditional village leaders and occasionally supported by rural Communists. The most widespread form of resistance was the slaughter of livestock and the cutting down of mulberry trees in silk producing areas.[42] Between 1928 and 1935, industry's share of total production increased from 21.7 to 62.1 percent.[43] After 1950, however, investment in industry increased, especially in the energy and chemical industries (later to become a target of ecological protest), and per capita income in Armenia rose 162 percent between 1960 and 1978, as compared to an all-Union average of 149 percent.[44] By 1975, only 20 percent of the labor force worked in agriculture and forestry, with 38 percent of the labor force in industry, and 42 percent in services. With two-thirds of the population living in cities and towns, Armenia had completed the transition from an agrarian to an urban, industrialized society.[45]

This transformation has without doubt been a source of legitimation for the regime. For many Armenians, after the genocide, economic development took on a "patriotic and quasi-mystical value" as the embodiment of the Armenian people's resurrection, and thereby, as a justification for the system.[46] Indeed, some middle-aged Armenians in Yerevan recall that people were pleased at the growth after World War II; they had jobs, food to eat, and were optimistic about getting ahead through hard work.[47]

Exploring the limits of nationalism

Overall, the relationship between the Armenian population and the Soviet regime between 1920 and 1990 can best be characterized as ambivalent and shifting, depending on what period and which social groups we are considering. Attitudes ranged from the sincere conviction, especially among first-generation communists, that they were indeed building a new society, to the opportunism of new local elites whose status depended on their support for the regime, to the disaffection, even hostility, among many Turkish Armenian refugees,[48] repatriates, and the tens of thousands of families affected by Stalin's purges.[49]

The Armenian Church never became the focus of dissident nationalism, but rather, played a cautious and accommodating role in relations with the Soviet state. It had already lost many of its social and educational functions, as well as its influence among the intelligentsia, before Sovietization, although the peasantry remained devout.[50] But it retained a national significance for Armenians because of its role in providing leadership and preserving Armenia's scholarly and literary heritage through centuries of statelessness. And for people living in an environment where medieval churches and carved stone crosses are almost a part of the natural landscape, Christianity, history and "the nation" are not easily compartmentalized.[51]

Throughout the Soviet period, Armenians continued to push at the boundaries of permitted nationalism while still conforming to Soviet requirements of "national in form, socialist in content." Paradoxically, nationalism in the Soviet Union was unintendedly encouraged by the status of "the nation" as the only domain in which a limited contestation of political issues was allowed, as long as these issues were couched in the idiom of culture. Defense of the "nation" – whether of the Armenian language, Church, cultural heritage, or history – was simultaneously an attempt to heal the physical and psychic trauma of the genocide and a means of protecting local interests and traditions. Armenians living outside their titular republic, however, have not always been able to maintain a strong sense of national identity; these communities have thus been characterized by high rates of intermarriage and loss of ethnicity.[52]

The institutional framework of nationalism

Initially, Soviet authorities encouraged the staffing of local government with Armenians and the development of the Armenian Communist Party. By 1929, 94.9 percent of total government staff were Armenian,[53] although throughout the twenties a significant portion were recruited among Armenians living outside the republic.[54] By the end of 1933, 89.2 percent of local Party members were Armenian. Thus, up until 1936, "ambitious youths did not have to cease being Armenian, they had to become Soviet Armenians."[55]

During this time, Armenia acquired the structures of national statehood and a network of cultural institutions. Yerevan State University opened in 1921,[56] an Armenian affiliate of the Academy of Sciences was founded in 1935, followed by museums displaying the historical and cultural patrimony: the Museum of History; Erebuni Museum, the Matanadaran, the repository of Armenian manuscripts; the Miasniakian Library, and several art museums. The Academy of Sciences became autonomous in 1943 and expanded, along with scientific facilities such as Biurakan Observatory, which took on a nationalist significance as a result of the international reputation of its director, the astronomer Victor Hambartsumian.[57]

The centralization of authority under Stalin in the thirties drastically reduced the autonomy of Armenia's government and Communist Party. The Great Purge began with the mysterious death in 1936 of the Armenian first secretary, Aghasi Khanjian. None of the sixteen members of the Bureau of the Armenian Party's Central Committee of 1936 still held their posts in 1937, and of the eleven new members, only two were still in office by March, 1940.[58] In Armenia, the purges destroyed two generations of intellectuals, and replaced the remaining old Communists and the second generation of Communist Party leadership with "apparatchiks" rather than revolutionaries, controlled by and dependent on the center.[59] By 1947, "Armenians were required to be more than Soviet Armenians; they had to be Armenian Soviets."[60]

Yet strong political and economic centralization cannot be equated with absolute central control, and national republics come to wield power to the extent that they were responsible for implementing central directives.[61] The zig-zag policy toward nationalism in Armenia since the 1920s reflects the paradox that achievement of centrally-determined policies depended on the abilities of local leaders to mobilize local populations, which they could best accomplish when perceived as responsive to local interests. The high degree of nativization in the post-Stalin period (in 1964, Armenians made up 91.8 percent of Party membership, but only 88 percent of the population),[62] combined with the republic's ethnic homogeneity, created a "palpable native cast" to the local bureaucracy's perception regarding its own welfare and that of the republic.[63] During the 1960s, a movement toward greater economic decentralization allowed the Armenian government to increase its independence from Moscow and solidify local support by making concessions to local nationalism. Installed in 1974 as First Secretary after an essentially local career, Demirjian, like his predecessor, Anton Kochinian, was able to manipulate national feelings and strong traditional networks of mutual assistance to solidify his personal position.

Table 11.2. *National composition of Armenia, 1979–1989*

	1979		1989	
	(thousands)	%	(thousands)	%
Armenians	2,725	89.7	3,076	93.7
Azerbaijanis	161	5.3	41	1.4
Russians	70	2.3	51	1.6
Kurds	51	1.7	65	1.8
Others	30	1.0	50	1.5
Total	3,037	100.0	3,283	100.0

Source: from Mouradian, *De Staline à Gorbatchev* (1990), p. 165.

What's in a name?

Language in Armenia has been a way of describing and arguing about political issues, including Russian cultural hegemony and Moscow's political control. Armenian enlightenment figures of the nineteenth century recognized the symbolic significance of language; in the first Armenian vernacular grammar, published in 1866, the impoverished, Turkified state of Armenian vernacular speech served as a metaphor to describe the "incursions and devastations" occurring under the Ottomans.[64] Language remains an emotive issue for Armenians, who consider the Armenian language, an archaic branch of Indo-European, and its unique alphabet, to be one of the factors responsible for their long survival as a distinct ethnic entity. Even in Turkophone Armenian communities of the Ottoman Empire, it was not uncommon for Armenians to write Turkish using the Armenian alphabet.[65]

The new Soviet government encouraged the use of the Armenian language in administration and education, using it as the "transmission belt" for disseminating Marxist-Leninist ideology and Soviet policies.[66] Yet, Armenian had to withstand a number of assaults. In the thirties, an attempt to Latinize the Armenian alphabet rallied intellectuals, who defeated this measure as well as a later attempt to Cyrillicize it.[67] A Terminological Committee formed to "modernize" Armenian introduced Russian scientific, political, and governmental terms into the lexicon, even when equivalent Armenian terms already existed. By 1955, this policy was reversed, and new terms were drawn from *grabar* (Classical Armenian) or even Western Armenian, once condemned as bourgeois.[68] Rules were further liberalized in the sixties, and political terms could once again be expressed in Armenian.[69]

In the 1930s, the hours of Russian-language instruction in the schools climbed steadily, displacing Armenian,[70] and the number of Armenian children in Russian schools increased due to parents' concern that their children's career mobility would be blocked by inadequate mastery of Russian. In 1927, 98.5 percent of pupils in Armenia were attending Armenian schools;[71] by 1987, this decreased to 75 percent.[72] Even members of the Armenian Writers' Union enrolled their children in Russian schools.[73] This trend was deeply disturbing to many Armenian cultural figures, who accused local party elites of alienation from their own culture and national interests.[74] The poet, Gevork Emin, asserted that the republic's schools were graduating pupils who spoke neither Armenian nor Russian fluently,[75] and an ethnographer claimed that the fact that most Armenian children entered the Russian-language classroom with no prior knowledge of Russian impeded learning and even emotional development.[76] Delegates to the 1981 Congress of the Armenian Writers' Union warned that the increased voluntary use of Russian posed a serious threat to the vitality of the Armenian language and culture, and that an ever-growing number of pupils were enrolling at Russian schools since the adoption of the requirement that dissertations must be submitted in Russian.[77]

The issue of bilingualism had often been manipulated by the Party to secure local legitimacy. Demirchian, one of the longest-serving first secretaries skilled at exploiting local sentiments and public anxieties, declared in a speech that every pupil must "acquire a perfect knowledge of his native language, its riches and peculiarities . . ."[78] Nevertheless, in 1987, the popular poet, Silva Kaputikian, noted that the position of Armenian in the republic was diminishing every year, even within strictly local institutions, to the point where parents hesitated to send their children to Armenian schools.[79]

Interpreting the past

Even sharper battles over nationalism have been fought in the arenas of literature and historiography as Armenian writers and scholars worked to construct a past which ratified and legitimized national claims and aspirations. After the creation of a Soviet Armenia, the intellectual and cultural establishment undertook the task of firmly establishing the Armenian historical claim to its territory. A toponymic reform replaced Turkish and Russian place-names with Armenian names, effectively erasing from popular memory the fact that Muslims had formed a majority of the region's population until the last half of the nineteenth century.[80]

Expressions of grief over the genocide, nostalgia for the lost territories in Western Armenia, and pride in Armenia's unique cultural heritage were allowed a limited expression as long as the progressive historical role of Tsarist Russia and the Soviet Union in Armenian history was acknowledged. An introduction to a 1946 collection of patriotic Armenian literature, for example, links the achievement of the Armenians' age-old desires for independence and freedom to the establishment of Soviet Armenia.[81]

During the twenties, well-known Armenian writers, composers, and artists living outside the republic were invited to work in Armenia. The first decade of Soviet power saw a cultural renaissance, a period that "would later be looked back upon fondly as a period of relative freedom and great creativity."[82] In the thirties, many writers were arrested on charges of nationalism, and an entire generation of Armenia's most talented writers, including Axel Bakounts and the poet Eghishe Charents, perished in Stalin's purges.[83] During World War II, however, limited concessions were made to harness Armenian nationalist feelings to the war effort; a 1941 *Izvestia* editorial praised "the talents of the Armenian people . . . (and) their centuries old culture."[84] Armenian folk literature was collected and published, and performances of Armenian folk music and dancing organized.[85] During the war, the Church also "began to enjoy a respite from Soviet persecution, if not from Soviet control."[86]

After the war, the campaign against nationalism began anew as contemporary Armenian writers were condemned for "idealizing the historical past" and popular nineteenth century authors such as Raffi banned for their "bourgeois nationalism."[87] Following Stalin's death, censored works were republished and writers rehabilitated, some, such as Charents and Bakounts, posthumously. Historical themes appeared with increasing frequency in literature, and monographs were published on the ancient, medieval and early Soviet periods of Armenian history.

The exploration of diasporan themes, especially the Western Armenian experience, signalled a shift from "national consciousness based on the identification of the nation with a specific territory" to one based on "a more inclusive conception of ethnic experience unfettered by political borders."[88] This new construction of nationality on the basis of ethnic and cultural practices sought to incorporate Armenian diasporan communities into a single Armenian nation. This trend is exemplified by literature on the genocide. The first major work, John Kirakosyan's *The First World War and the Western Armenians*, was published in 1965, followed in the late 1970s and 1980s by a spate of studies under Kirakosyan's sponsorship.[89]

Crossing the boundary: dissident nationalism in Armenia

In the post-Stalin era, Armenia has been characterized by a "complex interplay" between official nationalism, the highly regulated expression of "national pride, patriotic sentiments, a certain glorification of the past," and the dissident nationalism of public protest and unsanctioned political organizations.[90] To the extent that Armenian demands were directed at Turkey, they were not perceived as threats to Soviet hegemony. On the contrary, Armenia remained "a 'loyal millet' within the Soviet Socialist world."[91]

Nevertheless, in contrast to the intellectuals' protests, which were confined to the realm of culture, radical dissent arose among a small group of people born toward the end of the Stalin era into working class or lower middle class families.[92] Many of these families had originated in Turkish Armenia, and the national question was inextricably bound up with their personal fate. Human rights issues were often instrumentalized to serve the "Armenian Cause" (Armenian irredenta) in a system where the only authorized political space was the national, and where the heavy burden of the Armenian past and the ongoing reality of the national question made it difficult for young Armenians to think politically in universalistic terms.[93] For the most part, their activities received little attention or support among the Armenian diaspora.

The first known Armenian group with a nationalist agenda, the Union of Patriots, appeared in 1956 at Yerevan State University.[94] It was followed in 1963 by the Union of Armenian Youth, which continued for three years.[95] The National Unification Party (NUP) formed in Yerevan in 1966, called for an independent Armenia which would include Western Armenia, Nakhijevan[96] and Karabagh. The leaders were arrested in 1968, and the nineteen-year-old Parouir Hairekyan took over leadership until his arrest in 1969.[97]

Despite the small numbers involved in radical protest, it was during the sixties that the first massive outbreak of national feeling occurred in Yerevan. On April 24, 1965, as public officials, representatives of the Armenian Apostolic Church, and delegates from the diaspora gathered in the Spendarian State Theater of Opera and Ballet to commemorate the fiftieth anniversary of the Armenian Genocide, an estimated 100,000 people gathered outside, demanding the return of Armenian lands seized by the Turks and asking for Soviet assistance.[98] The demonstration was broken up by the militia, and many of the student-age participants spent a few days in jail, among them, future leaders of the Armenian national movement (ANM).

It is evident that the national issue had already become the focus of considerable student activity. Vaskan Manoukian, one of the ANM leaders, says that it was at this time that the idea of independence was born among Armenian youth.[99] In March 1967, for example, thirty-two students were expelled from the university for nationalist, anti-Soviet activity.[100] At Yerevan State University in the 1970s, a group of reform-minded Komsomol members attempted to democratize university policies by engineering the election of popular candidates.[101]

As a result of the 1965 demonstrations, the first secretary of the Armenian Communist Party, Yakov Zohrabian, a member of Khrushchev's team, popular for his perceived honesty and sympathy for national issues, was replaced. His successor, Kochinian, launched a criticism of Armenian nationalism but authorized the first monument to the Armenian Genocide, an imposing structure which thereafter allowed yearly commemorations to be channeled toward a precise and institutionalized space.[102] In the following years, additional monuments were erected to heroes of the Armenian liberation struggle and the battle against the Turkish Army, in a similar effort to assuage and defuse national feelings.[103]

In 1977, the Armenian Helsinki Watch Group was founded to monitor compliance with the Helsinki Accords and to work for Armenian membership in the United Nations; membership included a few of the NUP's founders. An announcement made by the group in June, 1977, described civil rights violations in Armenia and enumerated the "anti-nationality policies of the central and republic governments," the destruction of national customs and language, the privileging of Russian over Armenian schools, linguistic Russification, and finally, the ongoing violation of the Karabagh Armenians' civil rights. By February, 1978, with its members in prison and awaiting sentencing, the group had been crushed.[104] The ensuing investigations tried to discredit the NUP and the Armenian Helsinki Watch Group by linking them to an explosion which occurred in the Moscow metro, January 8, 1977. Three young workers, including a former NUP member (rehabilitated in 1986), were tried secretly in Moscow and executed in 1979.[105] The early eighties saw continuing arrests and trials for the dissemination of *samizdat* urging independence for Armenia.[106]

The Karabagh movement

In February, 1988, in response to activism among the Armenians in Nagorno-Karabagh, the largest demonstrations since 1965 erupted in Armenia. In Nagorno-Karabagh, a concerted movement developed around the single goal of attaching the oblast to Armenia. In Armenia, the protests of support transformed into a movement with a broad agenda of democratic and cultural demands. The goal of independence was first articulated much later in the movement, and even then, with ambivalence. In effect, while Armenians in Nagorno-Karabagh used Gorbachev's slogans of perestroika and glasnost to legitimize their struggle to join Armenia, those in Armenia used the Karabagh issue to further their struggle for perestroika and glasnost.[107]

Historically, Nagorni Karabagh[108] was one of the few regions in Eastern Armenia to preserve a certain degree of autonomy, ruled by local Armenian princes who offered fealty to Muslim khans. But

> while Armenian cultural and economic activity flourished in this region, it also became an important site of Muslim intellectual and political development. More than Baku, it was this mountainous area that served as the focal point of emerging Azerbaijani identity . . .[109]

Nora Dudwick

Table 11.3. *Population of Nakhijevan and Nagorno-Karabagh, 1914-1979*

	1914	1926	1959	1970	1979
Nakhijevan					
Armenians	53,700	11,300	9,500	5,800	3,400
Azeris	81,300	93,600	127,000	189,700	229,700
Nagorno-Karabagh					
Armenians	170,000	117,000	110,000	121,100	123,100
Azeris	9,000	13,600	18,100	27,200	37,200

Source: from Mouradian, *De Staline à Gorbatchev* (1990).

After annexation by Russia in the early nineteenth century, Nagorni ("mountainous") Karabagh, along with Zangezur and most of present-day Azerbaijan, was incorporated into a single province. Despite Nagorni Karabagh's largely Armenian population, the construction of roads and rail lines bound it ever more tightly to Baku, and Armenian workers streamed from Zangezur and Nagorni Karabagh to work in the thriving Baku oil industry.[110]

When Armenia and Azerbaijan became independent republics in 1918, Zangezur, Nakhijevan, and Nagorni Karabagh became the objects of bitter contention between the Armenian, Azerbaijani, and Ottoman armies. After Sovietization, Nakhijevan and Nagorni Karabagh were made part of Azerbaijan, despite militant Armenian resistance, and in 1923, most of Nagorni Karabagh was organized into the Nagorno-Karabagh Autonomous Oblast, comprising an area of 1,700 square miles, and separated from Armenia by a narrow corridor.[111] As a result of the ethnic-territorial basis of the Soviet federal structure, local cultural minorities such as the Armenians in Azerbaijan found themselves treated as factually non-indigenous, and excluded from republic-based cultural development.[112]

Resistance never completely died in Nagorno-Karabagh, but after Stalin's death, the Karabagh Armenians began to protest more openly, sending hundreds of letters, petitions, and delegations to Moscow. They complained about the systematic economic underdevelopment and steady erosion of cultural rights in the oblast. A petition addressed to Khrushchev in 1964 details the transfer of local enterprises to regions lying outside the oblast, and the neglect of agriculture, industry, roads, water and energy supplies.[113] Three years later, an appeal to the Soviet authorities and the Armenian people refers to the "hundreds of requests to the Central Government in Moscow and to the government of Azerbaijan" regarding the harassment, murder, and imprisonment of Armenians in Nagorno-Karabagh.[114] Additional protests noted the unavailability of Armenian instructional and cultural materials, lack of facilities for receiving television broadcasts from Armenia, and the appropriation of Armenian historic and cultural achievements.[115] As a result of exclusion from the Party and loss of employment, many protesters were forced to leave Nagorno-Karabagh.

Elsewhere in Azerbaijan, without even the nominal institutional structures of oblast-based cultural autonomy, Armenians either lived in monoethnic villages, or found a *modus vivendi* in the city with their Azerbaijani neighbors. Most notably in Baku, they became part of an ethnically mixed, Russian-speaking elite which regarded itself, in the words of Armenian refugees from Baku,[116] as exemplifying the "new Soviet person" whose primary affiliation was to the "internationalist" city of Baku.

Pressures for change built up throughout 1987. Prominent Armenians such as Zori Balayan, a writer for *Literaturnaya Gazeta*, the historian Sergei Mikoyan (son of Anastas Mikoyan), and Abel Aghabekian, Gorbachev's economic advisor, publicly expressed optimism regarding an imminent resolution of the Karabagh problem. On October 18, 1987, the day after the demonstration against environmental pollution,[117] hundreds of Armenians gathered in Yerevan to protest recent clashes which had occurred in the Armenian village of Chardakhlu, located in Azerbaijan, and to call for Nagorno-Karabagh's attachment to Armenia. Meanwhile, in both Armenia and Nagorno-Karabagh, signatures were gathered on a petition supporting this demand.[118] These activities culminated on February 20, 1988, when, after a week of strikes, deputies to the Nagorno-Karabagh oblast soviet voted to request that Nagorno-Karabagh join Armenia.[119]

1988 and after

News of the events unfolding in Nagorno-Karabagh was disseminated at a February 18 ecology demonstration protesting the planned construction of a new chemical plant just outside Yerevan. The following day, people gathered at the Spendarian State Theater of Opera and Ballet in a demonstration of support. During the course of the week, the number of demonstrators increased exponentially when Moscow refused to consider border changes and branded the demonstrators as "nationalists" and "extremists." The students, teachers, and intellectuals who made up the demonstrations in the first days were soon joined by blue collar workers and agricultural workers from the countryside. The crowds dispersed after one week at the urging of Zori Balayan and Silva Kaputikian, who returned from discussions with Gorbachev and Alexander Yakovlev in Moscow with guarded assurances of a favorable outcome.

No one who participated in this first week of demonstrations will forget the almost transcendental mood of solidarity, even elation, that gripped the men and women who stood for hours in the freezing February cold, listening to a succession of speakers from Armenia and Nagorno-Karabagh. The memory of these days later took on an important mobilizing role as the proof and symbol of Armenians' ability to act in concert.[120] The massive demonstrations also provided tangible evidence for the impotence of the authorities, who were unable to provide responsive leadership but unwilling to suppress the movement by brute force.

Leadership and strategy

In Nagorno-Karabagh, Party and government leaders played an active role in articulating the population's grievances and in organizing their resistance. In Armenia, an informal advisory role was played by prominent intellectuals, many with personal or familial origins in Karabagh. Strategy and tactics were formulated by what came to be known as the "Karabagh Committee," an informally organized, fluid group of writers, teachers, and scientists, mainly consisting of men in their thirties and forties, few with Party affiliations.

While demonstrations in Yerevan came to a temporary halt in March, 1988, a network of committees sprang up at industrial enterprises, institutes, university departments, and schools to disseminate accurate information and to organize collective actions if necessary. The Karabagh Committee achieved enormous credibility with the population during their frequent "informational" meetings which resumed a few months later, and also received *de facto* recognition from local Party authorities, with whom they held periodic negotiations.

In the immediate aftermath of the disastrous earthquake of December 7, 1988,[121] as the Karabagh Committee was organizing relief efforts, eleven members were arrested and transferred to prisons in Moscow by the Armenian authorities, now headed by first secretary Suren Harutiunian,[122] in a last-ditch effort to retrieve their own crumbling legitimacy.[123] For the next six months, the most salient aspect of political life in Armenia was their detention, which itself triggered further protests and political organization. They were released without charges six months later, in May, 1989, virtually sanctified in the eyes of most Armenians. Under their leadership, the dozens of groups, parties, and political activists who had entered the political scene since February, 1988, came together in autumn, 1989, to form the Armenian National Movement (ANM).

In Armenia, the Armenian National Movement brought together three groups with distinct, but overlapping agendas: those interested in democratic reforms in an all-Union context, those exclusively concerned with the Karabagh issue, and a broad, middle group, interested in all political and cultural issues affecting the "nation." The movement also mobilized a vast reservoir of discontent among a population fed up with official cant and hypocrisy, pervasive corruption, severe environmental pollution, and the declining standard of living. Ordinary people in Armenia greeted Gorbachev's call for reforms with enthusiasm, but few changes were apparent by 1988, aside from an increased freedom to express criticism. Demirjian, ensconced in a web of corruption, proved more orthodox than Moscow in his resistance to liberalization.[124]

Initially, Armenians believed that if they produced sufficient documentation to back their historic claim to Nagorno-Karabagh,[125] the injustice of its inclusion in Azerbaijan, and the discrimination suffered by the Karabagh Armenians, then Moscow would resolve the problem in the spirit of glasnost and perestroika. Moscow's steadfast refusal to consider border changes, the failure of the Armenian authorities to support national demands, sharp attacks from the central press, and silence from the local press directed the movement's activities toward a parliamentary struggle. By spring, 1990, ANM-sponsored candidates had been elected to the Armenian parliament, and Levon Ter-Petrosian, one of the Karabagh Committee members, was elected president of the Parliament. This marked the end of Communist Party power in Armenia.

Violence in Azerbaijan

During demonstrations in Yerevan, in February 1988, Armenian rioting broke out in the depressed industrial city of Sumgait (not far from Baku), home to 16,000 Armenians out of a total population of 250,000. Of the thirty-two people killed, twenty-six were Armenians, hundreds of Armenians were injured, and many apartments were sacked and burnt.[126] This shocking event provided additional impetus for political organization in Armenia. In November 1988, new outbreaks of anti-Armenian violence occurred in Azerbaijani cities and towns as local authorities offered little protection. This set off a two-way flood of refugees, as Armenians fled from Azerbaijan, and Armenia's 160,000-strong rural Azeri population fled to Azerbaijan. While acknowledged incidents of harassment and violence occurred in Armenia, their extent remains a contentious issue.[127] A year later, with a new outburst of violence in Baku, Azerbaijan's remaining Armenian community (outside Nagorno-Karabagh) fled the republic and Baku was occupied by Soviet troops.[128]

Within Azerbaijan, the Karabagh question became the symbol of challenge to Azerbaijan's territorial integrity and sovereignty. Armenian activism triggered formation of an Azerbaijani Popular Front, which put forth a platform calling for democratic reforms along with reassertion of control in Nagorno-Karabagh. Faced by lack of grass-roots support, and the rigid refusal of the Communist Party to engage in even limited discussion, the Front adopted an increasingly nationalistic, anti-Armenian program[129] In 1989, hoping to crush Armenian activism, it organized a rail blockade of

Nagorno-Karabagh and Armenia. The blockade failed to counter Armenian demands, but seriously disrupted reconstruction in the earthquake ravaged regions of Armenia, and put Nagorno-Karabagh and adjacent Armenian-populated districts in a virtual state of siege. The blockade continued on-and-off through 1990 and 1991, with Armenians occasionally instituting "counterblockades" of Nakhijevan.

In Nagorno-Karabagh, Armenians continued work stoppages and protests. In January, 1989, Moscow replaced the local organs of government with a "Special Administration Committee" headed by Arkady Volsky; although initially welcomed by the Armenian population, the Committee failed to halt tensions in the oblast. Moscow replaced it less than a year later with a military administration which Armenians accused of supporting Azerbaijan's attempt to reassert control of the oblast. As inter-ethnic violence continued, groups of volunteers from Armenia came to help defend villages in Nagorno Karabagh,[130] but the violence escalated in a series of attacks, ambushes, and the taking of hostages on both sides. In April, 1991, specially-appointed Azerbaijani militia, aided by Soviet Army troops, began violently deporting Armenians from their villages under the pretext of searching for armed Armenian militants. Armenians concluded that Soviet troops were supporting the Azerbaijanis in return for their promise to sign the proposed union treaty. In 1991, several attempts to negotiate the conflict failed, and in the first months of 1992, Nagorno-Karabagh remained a site of virtual war, with an escalating number of casualties reported weekly as Armenians recorded military successes.

Nation and state

By autumn, 1991, Armenians had made up their minds on the question of independence. In their September 21, 1991 referendum, they voted in favor of withdrawing from the Soviet Union. When the Union collapsed, however, Armenia joined the new Commonwealth of Independent States. The Armenian leadership must now create a functional governmental structure, a national ideology able to mobilize people's energies for the difficult period ahead, and a strategy for coping with the Karabagh conflict and the republic's acute economic problems.[131]

Armenian leaders also speak about the importance of creating a feeling of "statehood" among their people. As a sovereign state, Armenia must now rethink its relation with the diaspora. The Karabagh Movement described itself as a pan-Armenian movement with relevance for both local and diaspora Armenians. The new leadership has called upon the diaspora for assistance in building a new state, but feels that eventually "the core (e.g., independent Armenia) will be assisting the Armenians of the dispersion."[132] Diasporan Armenians have been invited to participate in the economic and political restructuring; several now hold high government posts. Likewise, diasporan political parties have established themselves in Armenia.

The new power alignments have caused tensions, however, as traditional diasporan agendas come into conflict with the requirements of state-building. Friction arose, for example, when the government decided to seek diplomatic and commercial relations with Turkey. The reality of Armenia's border with Turkey reconciled most local Armenians to this strategy, but some sections of the diaspora accused the government of betraying what has become over the years a focal point of diasporan identity – the Armenian Cause.

How Armenia defines her responsibilities for the "nation" will affect the role she plays in the Karabagh conflict. In Armenia, some people viewed the government's cautious approach tantamount to abandoning Nagorno-Karabagh.[133] In fact, the population's attitude is ambivalent: the Karabagh Armenians are heroes as long as they remain in their villages at the "front," but those who voluntarily leave or advocate compromise are criticized for betraying the common homeland. Many Armenians fear that if Azerbaijan succeeds in driving Armenians from Nagorno-Karabagh, they will next attack Zangezur. However, others privately question whether holding on to Nagorno-Karabagh is worth the sacrifice of lives and the disruption it has caused in Armenia. Yet, the ideals and values at the core of Armenian identity, such as martyrdom in the defense of nation and faith, exert subtle limits on the strategic options available to the government. This ideal is reinforced at the public funerals in Yerevan honoring the men killed in Nagorno-Karabagh, where speakers compare their deaths to the martyrdom of St. Vardan Mamikonian.

Since 1988, Armenian language and culture are experiencing a revival, to the point where some Russian-speaking Armenians feel discomfort. Dozens of new journals and newspapers have appeared in Armenian, and Armenian-language education has been made mandatory for Armenian children. Aided by gifts from the diaspora, the Armenian Apostolic Church is expanding its activities: it has reopened churches, ordained new priests, and organized parish youth groups. Reconstructing the nation also involves erasing the signs of the Soviet period: monuments of Russian and Armenian Communists have been removed, and a new toponymic reform has replaced their names on streets and squares, and in cities, towns and villages throughout the republic. It is interesting to speculate as to how the Armenia of the future will reshape its past.

Concepts of democracy, social justice, human rights, ecology, and cultural regeneration are terms which figure in a public discourse where visions of Armenia's future vie for dominance. The position represented by the president and his close advisors reflects the traditional Armenian conception of her "civilizing mission." This Armenia is firmly oriented toward Europe and principles of the Enlightenment. Other groups propose a national ideology constructed around the defense of Armenian society, biologically conceived as an organism which must be protected from degradation by avoiding contact with alien influences.[134] This is an ideology of cultural isolation and of the subordination of individual rights to the welfare of an abstract whole.

Now that Armenians are constructing a state, the national ideology which prevails will help define the character of her external relations and the political rights available to her own citizenry. The prevailing ideology will influence Armenia's ability to integrate the tens of thousands of Russian speaking, "Turkified" Armenian refugees from Azerbaijan, and the extent to which the cultural development of ethnic minorities will be protected and encouraged. Ultimately, the guiding philosophy of the new state will interact with the practical exigencies of political and economic restructuring to determine the extent to which cultural variation and diversity find encouragement in Armenian society.

Notes

I would like to thank the International Research & Exchanges Board for their research support, and Aram Nigogosian and Asia Lerner for their critical comments on an earlier draft of this chapter.

1 The speech is translated and reprinted in Gerard J. Libaridian, ed., *Armenia at the Crossroads: Democracy and Nationhood in the Post-Soviet Era* (Watertown, MA: Blue Crane Books, 1991), p. 115.
2 Benedict Anderson, *Imagined Communities: Reflections on the Origin and Spread of Nationalism*, revised 2nd edn (New York: Verso, 1991), p. 195.
3 *Ibid.*, p. 196.
4 Ronald Suny, "Some Notes on the National Character, Religion, and Way of Life of the Armenians," unpublished paper presented at the Lelio Basso Foundation conference, Venice, October 18–20, 1985, p. 3.
5 Christopher J. Walker, *Armenia: The Survival of a Nation*, revised 2nd edn (New York: St. Martin's Press, 1990), p. 20. This is a good, overall introduction to Armenian history, 1800–1900. This revised edition also includes a brief discussion of the Karabagh movement.
6 Herodotus, Strabo, and Xenophon describe Armenia's wealth of flocks, natural products, metals, precious stones, and the fame of her soldiers. For a discussion of classical references to Armenia, see Robert W. Thompson, "The Armenian Image in Classical Texts," in Richard G. Hovannisian, ed., *The Armenian Image in History and Literature* (Malibu, CA: Undena Publications, 1981), pp. 9–25. See also David Marshall Lang, *The Armenians: A People in Exile*, (London: Unwin Paperbacks, 1988, new edn), pp. 39–48.
7 The Urartian fortress, Erebuni, just outside Yerevan, gives the city its name.
8 The philologist, Raphael Ishkhanian, known in Yerevan for his efforts to increase the use of Armenian in the public domain and outlaw Russian-language schooling for Armenian children, has published a number of articles on this theme.
9 Ronald Suny, *Armenia in the Twentieth Century* (Chico, CA: Scholars Press, 1983), p. 4.

10 Suny, "Notes," p. 6.
11 The dating of Ełishe's history of Vartan is controversial. Soviet Armenia scholars consider him a contemporary of Vardan, while Robert W. Thompson places his account toward the end of the sixth century. See his commentary in Thompson (translator), *Ełishe. History of Vardan and the Armenian War* (Cambridge MA: Harvard University Press, 1982), pp. 1–53.
12 Cyril Toumanoff, *Studies in Christian Caucasian History* (Washington: Georgetown University Press, 1963).
13 Walker, *Armenia*, p. 21.
14 Khajig Tölölyan, "The Role of the Armenian Apostolic Church in the Diaspora," *Armenian Review*, vol. 41, no. 1–161, Spring 1988, p. 56.
15 *Ibid.*, p. 57.
16 According to Armenian Patriarchate figures of 1882, there were 2,660,000 Armenians in the Ottoman Empire, of whom 1,630,000 lived in the six eastern vilayets. According to Walker, these estimates are probably too high. Nevertheless, most sources agree that Armenians formed about a third of the population of Eastern Anatolia by the end of the nineteenth century, although in many regions they were the largest single minority. Walker, *Armenia*, pp. 95–96.
17 Eric Hobsbawm, *Nations and Nationalism Since 1780* (Cambridge: Cambridge University Press, 1990), p. 12.
18 Henry Jewel Sarkiss, "The Armenian Renaissance, 1500–1863," *The Journal of Modern History*, vol. 9, no. 4, December 1937, pp. 437–438.
19 *Ibid.*, p. 441.
20 Gerard J. Libaridian, "Nation and Fatherland in Nineteenth Century Armenian Political Thought," *Armenian Review*, vol. 36, no. 3, Autumn 1983, pp. 71–90.
21 *Ibid.*, p. 71.
22 Quoted from the liberal Armenian newspaper, *Hayastan*, published in Constantinople, *ibid.*, p. 76.
23 Until the emergence of a liberal middle class, the *millet* was dominated by an oligarchy of bankers, rich merchants, and government officials known as the *amira* class.
24 Libaridian, "Nation and Fatherland," p. 78.
25 Suny, "Notes," p. 4.
26 Libaridian, "Nation and Fatherland," p. 87.
27 *Ibid.*, p. 79.
28 Walker, *Armenia*.
29 Ronald Suny, "The Formation of the Armenian Patriotic Intelligentsia in Russia: The First Generations," *Armenian Review*, vol. 36, no. 3, Autumn 1983, p. 25.
30 This paragraph is based on Louise Nalbandian's *The Armenian Revolutionary Movement: The Development of Armenian Political Parties through the Nineteenth Century* (Berkeley: University of California Press, 1967), one of the definitive works on the Armenian revolutionary movement. See also Anaide Ter Minassian, *Nationalism and Socialism in the Armenian Revolutionary Movement* (Cambridge MA: The Zoryan Institute, 1984); this short monograph covers the period 1885–1914.
31 Exact mortality figures are difficult to determine because of uncertainties in the pre-1915 census figures for Armenians in the Ottoman Empire. For a thoughtful

282 *Nora Dudwick*

discussion of this issue, refer to Daniel Panzac, "L'enjeu du Nombre: La Population de la Turquie de 1914 à 1927," *Revue du Monde Musulman et de la
Méditerranée*, vol. 50, no. 4 (1988), pp. 45–67. Panzac estimates the number of
casualties at about 900,000.

32 Mark Saroyan, "Beyond the Nation-State: Culture and Ethnic Politics in Soviet
Transcaucasia," *Soviet Union/Union Soviétique*, vol. 15, nos. 2–3 (1988),
p. 222.

33 See Jenny Phillips, *Symbol, Myth and Rhetoric: The Politics of Culture in an
Armenian-American Population* (New York: AMS Press, 1989), for an
extended discussion of this theme, based on her field research.

34 See the collection of articles in Richard Hovannisian, ed., *The Armenian Genocide in Perspective* (New Brunswick, NJ: Transaction Books, 1987) for an
introduction to this discussion.

35 Richard Hovannisian, "Caucasian Armenia Between Imperial and Soviet Rule:
The Interlude of National Independence," in Occasional Paper No. 99, Kennan
Institute for Advanced Russian Studies (1980), p. 4. The definitive works on the
Armenia republic are Hovannisian's *The Republic of Armenia: The First Year,
1918–1919. Vol. 1* (Berkeley: University of California Press, 1971) and *The
Republic of Armenia: From Versailles to London, 1919–1920, Vol. 2* (Berkeley:
University of California Press, 1982). A third volume is forthcoming.

36 Hovannisian, "Caucasian Armenia," p. 13.

37 *Ibid.*, p. 14.

38 Suny, *Armenia in the Twentieth Century*, p. 41.

39 *Ibid.*, p. 41.

40 Mary Kilbourne Matossian, *The Impact of Soviet Policies in Armenia* (Leiden:
E.J. Brill, 1962), p. 57.

41 *Ibid.*, pp. 58–59.

42 *Ibid.*, pp. 107–108.

43 *Ibid.*, p. 116.

44 Gertrude Schroeder Greenslade, "Transcaucasia Since Stalin – the Economic
Dimension," Occasional Paper No. 101, Kennan Institute for Advanced
Russian Studies (1980), table 1.

45 Suny, *Armenia in the Twentieth Century*, p. 75.

46 Claire Mouradian, *De Staline à Gorbatchev. Histoire d'une république soviétique: l'Arménie* (Paris: Editions Ramsay, 1990), p. 105.

47 This conversation occurred during the context of my field work in Yerevan,
conducted over four visits between 1987 and 1991.

48 Matossian, *Impact*, p. 61.

49 Approximately 200,000 Armenians entered Soviet Armenia as refugees after
1921, as "repatriates" after World War II, mainly from the Middle East and
Europe, and as migrants from other Soviet republics. See Hovik Meliksetian,
Hayrenik-Spiurki Arnchutiutnere ev Hayrenatartsutiune: 1920–1980 tt.
(Yerevan: Yerevan State University, 1985) for figures on the repatriation. An
English-language summary is provided pp. 455–458. The postwar climate of
hardship and distrust led to hostility toward the immigrants, many of whom
left Armenia when emigration subsequently became possible. In June, 1949,
Armenians in Armenia, Georgia, and Azerbaijan with suspected Dashnak con-
nections were arrested and deported to the Altai region; many returned to

Armenia after Stalin's death. According to popular accounts, there were many repatriates among the deportees.

50 Matossian, *Impact*, pp. 90–91.
51 See Mouradian, *De Staline à Gorbatchev*. She devotes a full chapter to the role of the Armenian Church in Soviet Armenia, pp. 361–403.
52 Suny, *Armenia in the Twentieth Century*, p. 77.
53 Matossian, *Impact*, p. 42.
54 *Ibid.*, p. 46.
55 *Ibid.*, p. 133.
56 A university had actually been founded at Leninakan in 1920, during the period of the republic.
57 Mouradian, *De Staline à Gorbatchev*, p. 239.
58 Matossian, *Impact*, p. 156.
59 Mouradian, *De Staline à Gorbatchev*, p. 90; Suny, *Armenia in the Twentieth Century*, p. 91.
60 Matossian, *Impact*, p. 163.
61 Gregory Gleason, *Federalism and Nationalism: The Struggle for Republican Rights in the USSR* (San Francisco: Westview Press, 1990), p. 55.
62 Mouradian, *De Staline à Gorbatchev*, p. 87.
63 Gleason, *Federalism*, p. 87.
64 Ruben Adalian, "Theory and Rationality in Armenian Thought: Arsen Aytenian's Analysis of the History of the Armenian Language," *Sunderdruck aus Handes Amsorya* (1987), p. 650.
65 Claire Mouradian, "Nation, réalités et fantasmes: Le Cas Arménien," *Raison Présente*, no. 86, 1988, p. 122.
66 Matossian, *Impact*, p. 38.
67 Mouradian, "Nation," p. 122.
68 *Ibid.*, pp. 122–123.
69 Mouradian, *De Staline à Gorbatchev* p. 193.
70 Mouradian, "Nation," p. 127.
71 *Ibid.*, p. 127.
72 These figures were provided to me in March, 1991, by Ruben V. Sarkissian, an education specialist at the Armenian Ministry of Education.
73 Mouradian, *De Staline à Gorbatchev*, p. 197.
74 O.L. Zakarian, "Neskol'ko Zamechanii o Natsional'nom Yazike i Dvuyazichii," in L.A. Abramyan, G.R. Simonian *et al.*, eds., *Natsional'nii Voprosi Novoye Mishleniye* (Yerevan: Yerevan State University, 1989), p. 188.
75 Elizabeth Fuller, "Armenian Writers' Congress Focuses on Language Teaching," *Radio Liberty Research*, RL 242/81, June 18, 1981, p. 2.
76 Hambartusm Galstian, "Nekotorie Aspecti Arm'ano-russkogo Dvuyazichiya (po materialiam Etnosotziologicheskogo Obsledovaniya Naseleniya Yerevan)," *Sovetskaya Etnografiya*, no. 6, 1987. According to his figures, Armenian-Russian bilingualism in Armenia as of 1979 was 34.6 percent overall, and 57.1 percent in Yerevan. More than 20 percent of Yerevan Armenians speak Russian with greater fluency, and Russian is the home language for 11 percent of Armenian families in Yerevan.
77 Fuller, "Armenian Writers," p. 2.
78 *Ibid.*, p. 2.

79 Silva Kaputikian, "Our Motherland – Large and Small," *Armenia Today*, no. 5 (103), 1987, p. 13. This article is translated and condensed from the original, which appeared in *Pravda*, May 7, 1987, 2nd edn, pp. 3, 6.

80 According to George A. Bournoutian, Armenians formed a majority in Eastern Armenia until the mid fourteenth century, when Turkic tribes settled in the region. Until the Russian annexation of the Erevan khanate (which is somewhat larger than present-day Armenia) in 1828, Armenians constituted less than 20 percent of the population, with Muslims (Persians, Kurds, and Turkic tribes) comprising over 80 percent. The subsequent departure of Muslims and influx of Armenians after the annexation brought Armenians up to 50 percent of the population by 1832. See his *Eastern Armenia in the Last Decades of Persian Rule, 1807–1828: A Political and Socioeconomic Study of the Khanate of Erevan on the Eve of the Russian Conquest* (Malibu, CA: Undena Publications, 1982), pp. 73–74.

81 Quoted in Matossian, *Impact*, p. 166.

82 Suny, *Armenia in the Twentieth Century* p. 50.

83 See Matossian, *Impact*, chapter 8. See Marzbed Margossian and Jack Antreassian, eds., *Across Two Worlds: Selected Prose of Eqhishé Charents* (New York: Ashod Press, 1985) for an overview and assessment of nationalist and revolutionary themes in Charents's work.

84 Matossian, *Impact*, p. 165.

85 *Ibid.*, p. 164.

86 *Ibid.*, p. 162.

87 *Ibid.*, p. 167–168.

88 Mark Saroyan, "Beyond the Nation-State," p. 227.

89 *Ibid.*, p. 228..

90 Ronald Suny, *Armenia in the Twentieth Century*, p. 78.

91 *Ibid.*, p. 78.

92 Mouradian, *De Staline à Gorbatchev*, p. 274.

93 *Ibid.*, p. 268.

94 *Ibid.*, p. 253.

95 Ludmilla Alexeyeva, *Soviet Dissent: Contemporary Movements for National, Religious, and Human Rights* (Middletown, CT: Wesleyan University Press, 1985), p. 123.

96 Nakhijevan was once home to a mixed population of Armenians and Muslims, but after its (contested) incorporation into Azerbaijan as an Autonomous Republic, its Armenian population sharply declined, a fate Armenians fear for Karabagh.

97 Hairekyan ultimately spent seventeen years on and off in detention, before his exile from the Soviet Union, and his return in 1989 to take up a seat in the Armenian parliament, where today he heads an opposition party. See "Secret Political Trials in Soviet Armenia," *The Armenian Review*, vol. 31, nos. 3–123, 1979, pp. 309–365, for a *samizdat* transcript of Hairekyan's trials.

98 Suny, *Armenia in the Twentieth Cnetury* p. 78. Alexeyeva, *Soviet Dissent*, p. 123.

99 See the interview with Vasken Manoukian by Louise Simone, "A Discussion with Vasken Manoukian," *AGBU News*, vol. 1, no. 2, June 1991, p. 11.

100 Mouradian, *Impact*, p. 258.

101 One of these, Ashot Manucharian, later a leader of the ANM, was voted first secretary of the university Komsomol, but removed after several weeks on a technicality.
102 Mouradian, *Impact*, p. 288.
103 *Ibid.*, p. 321.
104 In "Documents: 'The Armenian Public Group' and The 'Helsinki Accord'" in *The Armenia Review*, vol. 31, nos. 4–124, April 1979, pp. 418–429.
105 Mouradian, *Impact*, pp. 266–268.
106 *Ibid.*, pp. 266–268; Alexeyeva, *Soviet Dissent*, p. 132.
107 This formulation was suggested by my colleague, Levon Abrahamian, an anthropologist at the Armenian Institute of Ethnography and Archaeology. See L.A. Abramian (*sic*), "Chaos and Cosmos in the Structure of Mass Popular Demonstrations," *Armenia Review*, vol. 29, no. 2, Fall 1990, p. 71.
108 "Nagorni Karabagh" refers to the region, which includes several Armenian-populated districts outside oblast boundaries. "Nagorno-Karabagh" refers to the official administrative unit, the Nagorno-Karabagh Autonomous Oblast. However, the conflict has drawn in the districts lying outside oblast boundaries.
109 Richard Hovannisian, "Nationalist Ferment in Armenia," *Freedom at Issue* (November-December 1988), p. 30.
110 *Ibid.*, p. 30.
111 *Ibid.*, p. 33.
112 Mark Saroyan, "The Karabagh Syndrome in Azerbaijani Politics," *Problems of Communism* (September-October, 1990), pp. 3–4. This article provides an insightful analysis of the Karabagh conflict from the Azerbaijani perspective.
113 Gerard J. Libaridian, ed., *The Karabagh File: Documents and Facts on the Question of Mountainous Karabagh 1918–1988*, (Cambridge, MS: The Zoryan Institute, 1988), pp. 44–46.
114 *Ibid.*, pp. 47–48.
115 Complaints range from physical neglect of Armenian historical monuments, to the Azerbaijani attribution of Armenian churches and carved stone crosses to the Caucasian Albanians, whom the Azerbaijanis claim to be forebears of the modern Azerbaijani people. These complaints are detailed in G. Galoyan and K.C. Khudaverdian, eds., *Nagornii Karabakh, Istoricheskaya Spravka* (Yerevan: Armenian Academy of Sciences, 1988). See also B.S. Mirzoian, "Nagornyi Karabakh," *Soviet Anthropology & Archeology*, vol. 29, no. 2, Fall 1990, pp. 12–33.
116 From several interviews I conducted in Yerevan between 1989 and 1991.
117 In the 1980s, provoked by growing public alarm over the effect of pollution from Armenia's many chemical plants, radioactive leaks from the nuclear power station, and a sharp drop in the level of Armenia's largest lake, Sevan, an ecology movement coalesced and attracted many intellectuals who later became active in the Karabagh movement.
118 According to Elizabeth Fuller, "Moscow Rejects Armenian Demands for Return of Nagorno-Karabagh," from *Radio Liberty Research* RL 91/88, February 29, 1988, p. 2, 75,000 signatures were gathered. According to Fuller, the petition was organized by Robert Nazaryan, one of the organizers of the Armenian Helsinki Watch group; see "Armenians Demonstrate for Return of

Territories from Azerbaijan," *Radio Liberty Research*, RL 441/87, October 20, 1987, p. 2.

119 Christopher J. Walker, ed., *Armenia and Karabagh: The Struggle for Unity* (London: Minority Rights Publications, 1991), pp. 121–122. Walker's account provides a detailed description of the first period of the movement. See also Christopher J. Walker, *Armenia: The Survival of a Nation* (New York: St Martin's Press, 1990, revised 2nd edn), especially chapter 11, and C. Mouradian, *De Staline à Gorbatchev*, chapter 9. Gerard Libaridian's report, "The Question of Karabagh: An Overview" (Cambridge, MA, June 1988), prepared for the Zoryan Institute, is a very perceptive interpretive account of the movement's political, social, and cultural significance. My account here is also based on my own observations and interviews in Armenia, 1987–91.

120 For a fuller description of this phase of the movement, see my earlier article, "The Karabagh Movement: An Old Scenario Gets Rewritten," *Armenian Review*, vol. 42, no. 3/167, Autumn 1989, pp. 63–70. For a discussion of the unique cultural features of the Armenia protests, see the articles by Levon Abrahamian, "Archaic Ritual and Theater: From the Ceremonial Glade to Theater Square," *Soviet Anthropology & Archeology* vol. 29, no. 2, fall 1990, pp. 45–69, and "Chaos and Cosmos in the Structure of Mass Popular Demonstrations (The Karabakh Movement in the Eyes of an Ethnographer)," in the same issue, pp. 70–86.

121 The earthquake virtually levelled two major cities and hundreds of villages. According to official casualty estimates, 25,000 people died; many Armenians believe that up to 50,000 may have perished. The earthquake increased people's bitterness toward the Communist authorities, blamed for the shoddy highrise construction in the area of known seismological activity, and for the ineptness they subsequently exhibited in organizing relief.

122 Karen Demirjian and his counterpart in Azerbaijan, Bagirov, were both replaced in May, 1988, for failing to keep the brewing crisis under control.

123 Those arrested were: Alexander Hakopian, Babken Araktsian (now chairman of Armenia's Parliament), David Vardanian, Hambartsum Galstyan (currently mayor of Yerevan); Samvel Gevorkian, Raphael Ghazarian, Samson Ghazarian, Vazgen Manoukian, Ashot Manucharian, Vano Siradeghian, Levon Ter-Petrosian and ex-member Igor Mouradian, one of the first leaders of the movement in Armenia. All of these men remain active in the new Armenian government, where most of them hold posts.

124 For an account of criticisms of Demirjian shortly before his removal, see Barry Holland, "Armenia: Demirchyan in the Stocks," *Soviet Analyst*, vol. 17, no. 3, February 10, 1988, pp. 2–4.

125 Armenians and Azerbaijanis have each argued their primacy in Nagorno-Karabagh based on their relationship to the region's indigenous inhabitants, the Caucasian Albanians (no relation to the Balkan Albanians). For an elaboration of this dispute, see my paper, "The Case of the Caucasian Albanians: Ethnohistory and Ethnic Politics," *Cahiers du Monde russe et soviétique*, vol. 31, nos. 2–3, April-September 1990, pp. 377–384.

126 See Samuel Shahmuratian, ed., *The Sumgait Tragedy: Pogroms Against Armenians in Soviet Azerbaijan. Vol. 1, Eyewitness Accounts* (Cambridge, MA: Zoryan Institute and New Rochelle, NY: Aristide D. Caratzas, 1990). This is

the first of a projected three-volume series, and was compiled by the editor from hundreds of taped interviews with survivors of the pogrom.

127 See, for example, the account by Robert Cullen, "A Reporter At Large (Armenia and Azerbaijan): Roots," in *The New Yorker*, April 15, 1991, pp. 55–76.

128 The timing of the troops' entry into Baku remains contentious. Although troops were stationed just outside Baku, they did not receive orders to shoot until most of the violence had run its course, at which time they entered, killing over a hundred Azerbaijanis in the process. It has been acknowledged by some Soviet authorities that troops entered to prevent an anti-Soviet take-over of authority in Azerbaijan. See, for example Igor Beliaev, "Baku: Before and After," *The Literary Gazette International*, vol. 1, issue 3, no. 1, March 1990, pp. 6–7.

129 See Saroyan, "Beyond the Nation-State." Also, see Cullen, "Reporter."

130 Armenians have been deported from the region of Nagorni Karabagh, that is, from villages lying outside the oblast boundaries as well as in Nagorno-Karabagh proper.

131 In addition to the economic problems common to all the former Soviet republics, Armenia is faced with reconstruction of earthquake damaged zones, an energy crisis due to the long-standing Azerbaijani blockade of fuel and gasoline, and most recently the closing of the nuclear power station.

132 From an interview with Vasken Manoukian, printed in *The Armenian Weekly*, January 5, 1991, p. 9.

133 See, for example, Aram Ohanian's "Report from Yerevan: Armenia at War!" *Armenian Reporter International*, vol. 25, no. 11, December 21, 1991, p. 18.

134 In the last few years, a number of articles have appeared in the Armenian press, defining the "organic" qualities of the nation. Representative examples are Armen Lalayan, "Natsiya – Organism," *Epokha*, no.6, February 1991, and by M. Shakhsuvaryan, "Natsii Bili, Est' i Budut," *Epokha*, no. 7, February 1991.

12 Georgia: a failed democratic transition

STEPHEN F. JONES

From "enemies of the people" to "members of traitors' families," the wheel of terror rolled on toward the "enemy nations."

Eduard Shevardnadze on the Stalinist terror.
The Future Belongs to Freedom, 1991

The transition from communism to democracy in Central Europe and the USSR highlights the continuing legacy of Soviet political culture. The collapse of communism has led, in many cases, to quasi-democratic hybrids led by pseudo-democratic chauvinists. States such as Serbia, Croatia and Slovakia have returned to the right-wing authoritarianism of the Second World War. New leaders, many of them ex-apparatchiks, have established the legislative and institutional framework for pluralist democracy, but have failed to break old habits of Soviet paternalism. They have replaced the "cognitive monopoly" of communism with a morally fervent nationalism, and the majority of the population, inexperienced in civic politics and under-going tremendous political and economic anxiety, loudly support these new ethnic hegemonies.[1] In the context of today's crisis, the often violent history of these multi-ethnic societies has made the recovery of national identity and the rehabilitation of memory a dangerous challenge to democratic development. The problems of state-building and what Giuseppe di Palma calls the "crafting of democracy" are magnified in an ethnically segmented society like Georgia.[2] Questions concerning the distribution of power among the different ethnic groups have been transformed into a challenge to the new state's legitimacy and a test of its commitment to democratic change.

Georgia is the latest, but not the last, demonstration of the tension between liberalism and nationalism, between majority and minority rights. The impact of perestroika and the breakdown of central control has transformed Georgian nationalism from a force for liberation and democratization to one of ethnic hegemonism and anti-pluralism. In particular after the accession to power of Zviad Gamsakhurdia's authoritarian nationalist government in October 1990, Georgia began to resemble Andrei Sakharov's description of the republic as a "little empire."[3] The atmosphere of national chauvinism undermined the qualities of tolerance, consensus and compromise so necessary to multi-ethnic cooperation and pluralism.

Table 12.1. *National composition of Georgia, 1926–1989*

	1926		1939		1959		1979		1989	
	Pop. in 1000s	% of total pop.	Pop. in 1000s	% of total pop.	Pop. in 1000s	% of total pop.	Pop. in 1000s	% of total pop.	Pop. in 1000s	% of total pop.
Total	2,677	100.0	3,540	100.0	4,044	100.0	4,993	100.0	5,443	100.0
Of whom:										
Georgians	1,788	66.8	2,174	61.4	2,601	64.3	3,433	68.8	3,787	70.1
Armenians	307	11.5	414	11.7	443	11.0	448	9.0	437	8.1
Russians	96	3.6	308	8.7	408	10.1	372	7.4	341	6.3
Azeris	144	5.4	188	5.3	154	3.8	256	5.1	307	5.7
Ossetians	133	4.2	149	4.2	141	3.5	160	3.2	164	3.0
Abkhaz	57	2.1	57	1.6	63	1.5	85	1.7	95	1.8
Greeks	54	2.0	85	2.4	73	1.8	95	1.9	100	1.9
Others	118	4.4	165	4.7	162	3.9	144	2.9	212	3.1

Source: This data is taken from Ann Sheehy, "Data from the Soviet Census of 1979 on the Georgians and the Georgian SSR," *Radio Liberty Research 162/80*, p. 10. V. Jaoshvili, *Sakartvelos Mosaxleoba XVIII–XX Sauk'uneebshi*, Tbilisi, 1984. *K'omunist'i*, January 13, 1990, p. 2.

Both the Georgian opposition and the ethnic minorities now found themselves threatened by a new political paternalism acting in the name of national freedom. The Georgians' dream of liberation following the fall of Soviet power, and the prediction of many Sovietologists that the structural and social changes in the USSR over the last twenty years would inevitably lead to pluralism, have been overturned.

The Georgian route to nationalist authoritarianism should be seen in the context of the political and economic chaos brought on by the union's collapse. Many Georgians saw a strong hand as both acceptable and necessary. But in Georgia's case, the authoritarian tendencies, which are apparent in all the former republics, took on a virulent form. Among the numerous factors which can explain this situation, this chapter shall concentrate on three: Georgians' relations with their minorities, the Soviet civic and political legacy, and the personality of Zviad Gamsakhurdia.

Georgian–minority relations

The pre-Soviet period

Georgia is a complex multi-ethnic state (see table 12.1). Georgian–minority relations, although characterized by mutual prejudice and national stereotypes, have on the whole been peaceful. Notable exceptions to this occurred in 1918–1921, when Georgia was independent, in the 1970s, when Moscow's economic and political control declined in the republic, and again today, when Georgia is fighting for political and economic survival. Moscow's weakening influence has almost always coincided with an economic or social crisis. While there is not necessarily a direct causal relationship between the decline of Moscow's power and the rise of ethnic conflict in Georgia, the economic and social disruption which accompanied Moscow's decline has had a measurable impact on traditional power relationships between ethnic groups.

In 1918, Georgia regained its independence from the Russian empire.[4] For three years until 1921, when Georgia was reincorporated into the Soviet state, Georgia's moderate socialist leaders established a polity based on universal suffrage, popular participation and public contestation for power. The conditions were hardly propitious for democratic development. Georgians were at war with the Turks, the Volunteer Army and the Armenians. They were subject to an economic blockade by the Allied powers, faced problems of internal Bolshevik subversion, and after rapidly emptying the government treasury, experienced economic chaos and hyperinflation. None the less, the Georgian socialists established a democratic legislature, a quasi-independent judiciary, and tolerated competing non-socialist interest groups and organizations.

Initially, Georgia's minorities, who numbered 30 percent of the total population, were given special status and one quarter of the Georgian Parliament's seats. Abkhazia was granted autonomy.[5] By 1919, however, after a number of revolts in non-Georgian areas, inspired in the Georgians' view by the Bolsheviks, relations with the minorities soured. When a Constituent Assembly replaced the parliament in 1919, minority quotas were removed. The Georgian socialists, fighting for their state's physical survival, turned to Georgian nationalism as a source of legitimacy and political mobilization. A Georgianization program was launched in the schools and government administration, and the Georgian Social Democratic party, which was overwhelmingly Georgian, became the sole source of political patronage and power. In this situation, the Armenians, Ossetians, Abkhazians and other minorities, who had organized their own national soviets in 1917–1918, began to fear they would be locked into a position of permanent inferiority.

Social and economic resentments, combined with a newly discovered national consciousness that local Bolsheviks exploited, led to a series of armed conflicts with the Georgian National Guard.[6] The revolts in non-Georgian areas, which entered Soviet mythology as resistance to Menshevik oppression, have become part of today's competing ethnic histories. The Georgian suppression of the June 1920 revolt in Ossetia is interpreted by Ossetians as part of a Georgian strategy aimed at national genocide.

They regard this period as comparable to the struggle of Armenians in Nagorno-Karabakh against the Azerbaijanis.[7] In contrast, the Georgians view it as the first attempt by Ossetians to seize Georgian territory and break up the Georgian state. Ossetian and Georgian newspapers have further Inflamed the current conflict by reprinting 1920 reports of the fighting between Ossetians and Georgians which highlight the atrocities and reinforce brutal national stereotypes.[8] The similar conflicts between Abkhazians and Georgians in 1918–1921 have become historical lessons of ethnic incompatibility for both sides.

The ethnic conflicts of 1918–1921, which extended to Muslim districts in Ajaria and Armenian districts in the south, underlined the weakness of Georgian democracy. Although the Georgian government could legitimately claim it was fighting for the integrity of the new state, its methods – occupation, military governors and military tribunals – reflected an inability to incorporate ethnic minorities into the political system. Arguably, if economic conditions and the threat of invasion had not been so pressing, and if the government had had a less corrupt and more effective civil administration, these ethnic disputes might have been resolved in a more democratic manner. As it was, the experience of Georgian rule reinforced the minorities' alienation from the new Georgian state and led Georgians to view the minorities as a potential "fifth column." This situation has been repeated today, although the Russians are no longer Bolsheviks. But the consequences for pluralist democracy are as threatening now as they were in 1918–1921.

The Soviet period

After 1921, the conflict between national rights and political pluralism in Georgia was transformed into a struggle over power sharing between territorially defined ethnic groups. In 1922 and 1931, the Ossetians and Abkhazians gained Autonomous Region and Autonomous Republic status respectively.[9] Policies of affirmative action gave them limited protection from Georgian dominance. Under the stewardship of Lavretii Beria, from the 1930s onwards Georgian minorities were pressured to assimilate into the majority Georgian population.[10] In the 1930s, when other non-Russians had their alphabets "Cyrillicized," the Abkhazians had theirs "Georgianized" and all native language schools in Abkhazia and South Ossetia were closed.

After Stalin's death, most minority rights were restored, but the loosening of central control combined with increasing Georgian hegemony in the republic's political and cultural life reawakened minority anxieties over their demographic and cultural decline. Georgians occupied positions of power in Tbilisi, dominated the informal structures of the second economy, and controlled republican networks that ensured professional advancement and wealth. Both Abkhazian and Azerbaijani minorities accused Tbilisi of deliberately neglecting the non-Georgian areas of the republic and of forcing them, as socially and linguistically disadvantaged minorities, to accept inferior jobs.[11]

In the 1970s, party boss Eduard Shevardnadze's anti-corruption campaign and his attacks on 'half-baked' nationalism increased minority anxieties as their own ethnic networks of mutual support and self protection came under scrutiny. Shevardnadze admits in his autobiography that in the 1970s and 1980s "inter-ethnic friction had broken out in virtually all the regions in Georgia," and between 1972–1979 more than fifty resolutions of the Georgian Central Committee and the Georgian Council of Ministers addressed the economic and cultural concerns of minorities in Abkhazia and South Ossetia and local Georgians in Ajaria.[12] The most public case of ethnic conflict under Shevardnadze occurred in Abkhazia.[13] Since the 1950s a conflict had smoldered between Georgian and Abkhazian historians concerning the ethnic identity of Abkhazia's first settlers. In the 1950s and 1960s, some Georgian historians publicly challenged the view that Abkhazians were indigenous to Abkhazia, suggesting that they had settled in later centuries, displacing the original Georgians.[14]

The drafting process of the 1978 "Brezhnev" constitution brought the Abkhazian-Georgian conflict to a head. In December 1977, 130 Abkhazian intellectuals sent to the CPSU Central Committee and the Supreme Soviet of the USSR a litany of complaints about political and cultural discrimination by Georgians. They demanded the secession of Abkhazia from Georgia and its union with the RSFSR.[15] This letter was followed in 1978 by demonstrations, petitions, the defacement of Georgian signs and monuments. Moscow installed a new Abkhazian party leadership in April and coordinated with Tbilisi a package of concessions ranging from economic investment in the region to increased publishing and broadcasting in the Abkhazian language. In 1979, the Sukhumi Pedagogical Institute was transformed into an Abkhazian State University and quotas were established to increase the number of Abkhazian students in higher education.[16]

These conciliatory measures did not go far enough to relieve Abkhazian anxieties over Georgian hegemony. Abkhazian demands for the constitutional right to secede and the removal of Georgian as a state language in Abkhazia were rejected. The Georgians were anxious to protect their own minority status within the USSR. They had secured their own concessions as a result of dramatic protests in the spring of 1978 against Moscow's attempt to remove Georgian's status as a state language. A series of resolutions, following a barrage of articles in the Georgian press, called for more comprehensive instruction in the Georgian language and the systematic publication of materials promoting the development of Georgian.[17] In this context, pro-Abkhazian measures only intensified Georgian resentments.

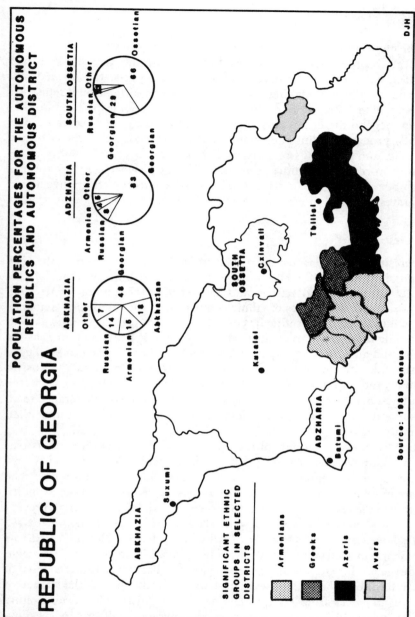

Map 12.1 Georgia

As the plurality in Abkhazia, (see figure 12.1), Georgians claimed they were suffering reverse discrimination. And the Abkhazians, regardless of their political gains in leading party and government posts, remained demographically insecure, making up only 15.1 percent of their own republic's population in 1979. They are still unable to take school instruction in Abkhazian beyond the fifth grade. Moscow continued to use Georgian cadres as their primary conduit of economic and political control in the Georgian republic, and Georgians retained their monopoly over the republic's cultural, historical and political symbols. Like the Quebecois, who are in a much better demographic situation, the Abkhazians felt affirmative action programs were not enough to prevent their eventual cultural extinction.

Perestroika

Perestroika and glasnost intensified ethnic anxieties in the republic. The economic crisis and the absence of central power, the emergence of ethnically based political parties and the rehabilitation of bitter national memories raised th stakes of ethnic competition. The minorities' demands for cultural and educational equality and for greater political and economic representation challenged the Georgians' belief that they, as the titular and autochtonous group in the republic, were entitled to privileged status and control. Stimulated by a history of foreign invasion, Russification, and traditionally weak demographic representation in the republic's periphery, Georgians' deep national insecurity encouraged them to support nationalist policies designed to protect majority, rather than minority, rights.

Central to the programs of the myriad of Georgian parties and associations that have emerged since 1988 are demographic concerns and Georgianization of the republic's administrative and cultural institutions.[18] The Communist Party of Georgia, before it was ousted from power in multiparty elections in October 1990, was no exception. In an attempt to prevent its political marginalization, it published a draft *State Program for the Georgian Language* in December 1988 which advocated an increased role for Georgian instruction in all republican schools, including a Georgian language test for entry into higher education.[19] This was a threat to most of the minorities, who spoke Georgian badly, if at all. Just as the change of the *lingua franca* from Latin to German in the Austro-Hungarian empire led to an explosive reaction among the literate non-German speaking populations, so the loss of Russian as a state language in Georgia seriously threatened the non-Georgian minorities. Other measures included programs for the promotion of Georgian history and the defense of historical monuments, a law restricting immigration, and the institutionalization of previously unofficial Georgian national holidays.[20] The creation of republican military units, comprising only Georgians, and the resettlement of Georgians in areas dominated by the minorities, must have seemed particularly threatening. Although Georgian state-building was understandable, in an atmosphere of growing chauvinism, fanned by the slogan "Georgia for the Georgians," the minorities felt extremely insecure.

After the election of Zviad Gamsakhurdia's Round Table-Free Georgia Bloc in October 1990, minority access to economic and political power was virtually eliminated. Although Abkhazians retained *ex officio* posts in the Georgian Council of Ministers, the Supreme Soviet Presidium and the Committee for the Supervision of the Constitution, the new parliament contained almost no minority representation, except through the opposition communist party. Nationalist arguments for special treatment on the basis of prior settlement, history, or by dint of numbers became the new language of Georgian politics, and censuses, borders and toponyms took on new meaning. Attempts by ethnic minorities to carve out spheres of cultural or economic sovereignty were perceived by the Georgian government as a challenge to its people's spatial and social homogeneity. The government elaborated a theory of minority rights based on the assumption that members of minorities with a relatively recent history of settlement in Georgia, such as the Ossetians or Azerbaijanis, qualified neither for an inalienable right to residence in the republic nor to equal status with the dominant ethnic group.[21] These ideas bore a striking resemblance to those of Lajos Kossuth, who argued that non-Magyar minorities had no right to nationhood because they lacked historical personalities.[22]

During discussion of the citizenship law in the summer of 1990, Gamsakhurdia proposed that eligibility be limited to those residents whose forebears lived in Georgia before the annexation of 1801. The citizenship law which eventually took effect in June 1990 was less discriminatory, granting citizenship to all those who were "permanent residents" with a legal source of support. But the electoral law which had passed nine months earlier prevented all regionally based parties in the republic from registering for the elections, effectively disenfranchising non-Georgians who wished to vote for ethnically based parties. As a result, non-Georgians either boycotted the elections in October or voted for the Georgian communist party which was seen as the best protection for minority groups.[23]

The new Georgian government based much of its ethnic policy on the distinction between "indigenes" and "settlers". The abolition of the South Ossetian autonomous region by the Georgian government in December 1990, which has led to a bitter war between Georgians and Ossetians, was justified by the latter's "settler" status. The Georgian government asserted that Ossetians only began to arrive in Georgia in the nineteenth century and that they were illegally granted an autonomous region by the Bolsheviks in 1922 as a reward for their anti-Georgian activity during the civil war of 1918–1921. The Georgian President, Zviad Gamsakhurdia, called on South Ossetians to return to their "real" homeland in neighboring

North Ossetia. The flight of Ossetian refugees from the region since the war began there in December 1989 has largely completed this agenda.[24] By autumn 1991, the Azerbaijanis had begun to leave in large numbers, and the Russian Dukhobors in Bogdanovka have already returned to Russia. In an agreement between Daghestan and Georgia reminiscent of the forced population exchanges following World War II in Poland and Czechoslovakia, the Avars from northeastern Georgia have been exchanged for Georgians living across the border in southern Daghestan.[25]

But the drive for ethnic homogenization and the promotion of Georgian hegemony has come at great cost. In July 1989, before the war in Ossetia began, bloody clashes over Abkhazian education rights in the Autonomous Republic's capital of Sukhumi left fourteen dead and over 500 wounded.[26] Armenians and Azerbaijanis clashed with Georgians over rights to land and cultural monuments. The Georgian Muslims, known as Ajarians, protested the new government's Christianization program, including its encouragement of mass baptisms in Muslim areas and the appointment of Georgian Orthodox priests as government officials. They strongly resisted the attempted removal of Ajaria's autonomous status. The few Georgian electoral blocs and parties, such as "Democratic Georgia" and "Accord, Peace and Renaissance," which took a more moderate line toward the minorities and proposed constitutional provisions for the protection of their rights and incorporation into the political system, received no electoral support. There was no Georgian equivalent of the Hungarian state patriot Count Stephen Szechenyi, who put up a long struggle against the ethnic patriot, Lajos Kossuth, and his ethnically discriminatory minorities' program in Hungary.[27]

In this situation, the Ossetians and Abkhazians began to organize themselves. With overwhelming support, the Ossetian popular front *Adamon Nykhas* ("Popular Shrine") and its Abkhazian equivalent, Aidgilara ("Unity") used the existing soviet structures to promote regional control and express dissatisfaction with their exclusion from power. In August 1990, the Abkhazian Supreme Soviet, with a bare quorum, declared its state sovereignty. A few weeks later in September, the South Ossetian regional soviet declared a South Ossetian Democratic Soviet republic.[28] The South Ossetian Soviet was abolished in December 1990 but continued its illegal existence and in December 1991 proclaimed the region's independence. The Abkhazian Supreme Soviet continued its "war of laws" with the Georgian parliament. Predictably enough, in September 1991, it attempted to extend the writ of its own procuracy over that of the Georgian republic. The Georgian constitution, in keeping with the Soviet model, kept the procuracy highly centralized under the Georgian Procurator General's control.

The new government's single-minded pursuit of Georgianization alienated the vast majority of the republic's population who is neither Georgian nor Christian. No attempt was made, with the exception of a system of power sharing devised in Abkhazia in August 1991, reminiscent of the Lebanese approach before the civil war, to incorporate non-Georgians into the representative bodies of the republic.[29] The new constitution devotes only ten short articles to the autonomous republics and restricts their rights in innumerable ways, leaving them with almost no recourse against a powerful center and President. Decisions of the autonomous republics' higher bodies must be verified, and may be challenged or rejected by a host of institutions and bodies in Tbilisi.[30] The persistent exclusion of the minorities from real power stymied the development of democracy in Georgia. The philosophy of majority rights has encouraged a siege mentality where any opposition to Georgian hegemony is seen as a threat to national unity and to the state's interests.

The Soviet legacy

The problems of transition

In the elections of October 1990, every Georgian party trumpeted the virtues of political pluralism and the free market. Zviad Gamsakhurdia's coalition, the Round Table-Free Georgia bloc, presented a program which hardly differed from that of its opponents. It called for independence, a multiparty system, the sanctity of law, a market economy, and guarantees of civil rights such as freedom of religion and the independence of the media. On the other hand, in common with the opposition, the program also advocated laws to strengthen Georgian majority rights: more restricted immigration, laws defending the sovereignty of the Georgian language, and a new citizenship law with a narrower definition of prerequisites. But overall, the program, with its call for human rights' guarantees based on UN declarations, could not be called authoritarian.[31]

The election campaign in October was peaceful. Based on a mixed system of proportional and majority representation, Gamsakhurdia's bloc received 155 of the 250 Supreme Soviet seats. The Communist Party of Georgia, which received sixty-four seats or 29.6 percent of the vote, formed the only significant opposition. The Popular Front, which presented a program almost indistinguishable from Gamsakhurdia's, but was represented by more mainstream intelligentsia figures, came a poor third with twelve seats.[32] Although the coloring of the new Supreme Soviet was radical nationalist in composition, the new government under Prime Minister Tengiz Sigua, formerly Director of the Metallurgy Institute in Tbilisi and Chairman of the moderate Rustaveli society, comprised a number of former government officials and academics and was technocratic rather than ideological in character.[33] A law of transition was passed which envisaged a gradual and negotiated path to independence. In the euphoria of victory and with the full support of the newly elected Supreme Soviet, Gamsakhurdia's government began the relatively uncomplicated process of deconstruction. All references to "socialism" were removed from the constitution, the supremacy of all-Union law was ended, the republic's name was changed, the hymn and flag were replaced, civil and criminal codes were amended, the draft into the Soviet army was annulled and the provincial party bodies removed. Throughout, any action taken against Moscow was greeted with unanimous acclaim.[34]

But the construction of a democratic state was a more difficult process. Robert Dahl, writing twenty years ago, concluded that a country which had "little or no experience with the institution of public contestation and political competition and lacks a tradition of toleration toward political oppositions" was unlikely to develop a democratic system quickly. Neither was it likely to endure. Giuseppe Di Palma suggests that an analysis of structural preconditions is a poor historical guide to successful transitions to democracy, but agrees that economic instability, a hegemonic nationalist political culture and the absence of a strong and non-dependent middle class – all characteristics of Georgia – would impede a transition to democracy.[35] The Soviet past has left Georgians without constituencies, institutions and practices conducive to a pluralistic power structure. Unlike their counterparts in post-authoritarian regimes such as Spain and Greece, where autonomous societies and institutions had been allowed to develop, the Georgian leaders were forced to use exclusively, as Benedict Anderson calls it, "the wiring of the old state."[36] The danger, as Alexander Yakovlev points out, is that a country then begins to regenerate "in itself the vices of the past in new wrappings."[37]

In Georgia, the Soviet legacy seems to have had a particularly strong influence on the young state. That debilitating legacy – official nationalism, distrust of one's opponents, paternalism, hegemonism, censorship, the personalization of politics, and a corrupt and unaccountable bureaucracy – were all passed on, virtually unaltered, to the new regime. A politically unsophisticated population distrustful of institutions and inexperienced in the mechanisms of "checks and balances" and managed conflict, and rebouding from seventy years of Russian oppression, supported Gamsakhurdia's single-minded drive for unity and independence. This despite a program that putatively rejected all association with the former Soviet state.[38]

Relations with the opposition

Democracy above all else requires mutual trust and shared principles of political behavior, but both the Georgian government and its opponents proved incapable of establishing a normative framework of political competition. Opposition to Gamsakhurdia fragmented. The most vociferous opposition groups developed in the National Congress, a body elected in the fall of 1990 as an alternative national forum to the Supreme Soviet. Dominated by the National Democratic Party of Gia Chant'uria and the National Independence Party of Irakli C'ereteli, two young nationalist dissidents imprisoned in the 1980s, the National Congress mobilized supporters onto the streets and organized hunger strikes to protest Government policies. Initially, Congress leaders, who dubbed themselves "the irreconcilables," took a more radical stand than Gamsakhurdia on relations with the USSR. They called for a more rapid move to secession and demanded the expulsion of Soviet occupation troops (how it was not clear). Gamsakhurdia, who after much pressure, agreed to the presence of Soviet troops in South Ossetia, was accused of collaboration with Moscow. But after the October elections to the Supreme Soviet, these groups were increasingly marginalized. However, taking advantage of the government's increasing authoritarianism, the "irreconcilables" success-fully redefined themselves as defenders of democracy. When the para-military organization *Mkhedrioni* ("Horsemen"), which was allied to the National Congress, was disbanded by force in February 1991 with the help of Soviet troops and its leader, Jaba Ioseliani, imprisoned without trial, it only served to bolster the new-found image of these groups as persecuted democrats.[39]

Parliamentary opposition was ineffective. The Georgian Communist party, undergoing an internal crisis since its defeat at the polls in October 1990, was extremely defensive. The deputies were expelled from the Supreme Soviet after the August coup and its remaining property nation-alized. The other parties were too small to have any influence. The Round Table-Free Georgia Bloc representatives were docile until the September 1991 events (see below), and needed no party whip to vote en bloc for government legislation. The upper levels of the professional intelligentsia, while critical, were intimidated by the cultural monopolism of Gamsak-hurdia's ministries. They were regularly insulted by the President as "a false intelligentsia" with links to the communist "mafia." Deprived of their traditional role as *vox populi*, they were isolated by the new political hege-mony.[40] They continued to snipe at the government in the press and give interviews to Western correspondents, but were heavily outnumbered by journalists and writers prepared to defend Gamsakhurdia, his policies, and his image.

That situation changed dramatically in August 1991 after Gamsakhurd-ia's ambivalent response to the coup and demotion of the National Guard.[41] A parliamentary opposition led by a number of Gamsakhurdia's former allies from the Round Table-Free Georgia Block created Charter '91, a group of at least forty-nine deputies. It linked up with the extra-parliamentary opposition, disgruntled ministers, military commanders, and resentful intellectuals, to form a coalition which finally overturned

Gamsakhurdia's government by force in January 1992. They accused Gamsakhurdia of economic mismanagement, hostility to the Western powers, crude manipulation of personnel, disrespect for the law and suppression of the opposition.

Throughout Gamsakhurdia's period in office, relations between opposition and government were characterized by intense animosity and an absence of consensus. Unable to shed the policies of direct action, civil disobedience, ultimatums and violence which had been so successful in the final years of communism, the bloody battle for power in December 1991 was a culmination of the boycotts, strikes, occupations, rallies, and physical threats that had been the resort of all parties during the previous year. Gamsakhurdia, with overwhelming support in the Supreme Soviet and among the electorate, had seen no need to compromise or respond to opposition constituencies. At the time, as Robert Dahl might have put it, the costs of not incorporating the interests or anxieties of opposition groups had seemed insignificant.[42] Gamsakhurdia dismissed the extra-parliamentary opposition as "criminals" and "bandits," and characterized his five Presidential opponents in May 1991 as unworthy.

But in some sense Gamsakhurdia was right. The opposition had had no social base. It had been unable to mobilize any real challenge to Gamsakhurdia's one-party hegemony. Gamsakhurdia had received 87 percent of the popular vote for the Presidency in May 1991. His nearest rival, V. Advadze, had received 240,243 votes compared to Gamsakhurdia's 2.5 million.[43] This dramatic unevenness of power forced the opposition into extreme and demonstrative exhibitions of resistance. The Congress parties refused to disarm their para-military organizations or vacate occupied government buildings, and they constantly disrupted civil life with street barricades and long rallies. These parties, like Gamsakhurdia, had failed to make the transition to accommodation and gradualism. They were wedded to fixed principles inherited from their moral crusade against communist oppression. Impatient at being consigned to an insignificant and permanent minority status for at least five years (the term of the Supreme Soviet), they were unable to accept the notion of democratic choice and uncertain outcome, a quality essential to a competitive political market.[44]

By the winter of 1991 both government and opposition had become trapped in an escalating cycle of both verbal and physical assault. The language used by most parties, repeated in the predominantly pro-government press, resembled the hysterical phraseology of the 1930s. "Enemy of the people," "traitor to the nation," or "bandits" were common appellations. Gamsakhurdia's call to his supporters in September 1991, after some anti-government demonstrators had been killed by loyal National Guard troops, was typical:

> The Kremlin's infernal machine has been activated with the help of Georgian traitors based in Moscow. I urge the Georgian people to rise up and destroy

those traitors . . . I am ready to go to the people and, through rallies and demonstrations, to arouse the Georgian people and smash all our enemies . . .[45]

The government daily *Sakartvelos Respublik'a* ("The Republic of Georgia") ran a column entitled "Agents of the Kremlin in Georgia" which indiscriminately attacked all forces in the opposition, from the "irreconcilables" to liberal intellectuals. At a meeting in March 1991 between representatives of the liberal intelligentsia and the government, a university professor commented that the atmosphere of emnity and the language of extremism now helped her understand how the terror of the 1930s began.[46]

The new legislative program

Gamsakhurdia's new government, in its legislative program and constitution, pirated the model of Western style pluralism. It passed liberal laws on citizenship, set up a system of local self government (the *sakrebulo*) and strengthened the independence of the judiciary by extending judges' terms to ten years and banning any party membership among them.[47] In December 1990, a law on the status of deputies guaranteed them parliamentary immunity and substantial rights to question and supervise the executive, and in August 1991, laws on political associations and the freedom of the press were passed restricting government controls.[48] From spring 1991 onwards, a whole series of new laws expanded the sphere of personal ownership and laid the basis for private commercial activity. In particular, legislation authorized the sale of government business and government owned housing.[49] By autumn 1991, a "Rechstaat" guaranteed, on paper at least, the division of powers, public contestation, a multiparty system, and a free press. A Committee for the Supervision of the Constitution was established, with members elected for ten years, to overrule any laws which transgressed the constitution.

This impressive legislative activity gave rise to many problems. The laws were often flawed by omission or too much vagueness, and betrayed a continuing concern for tight regulation by government. The law on political associations, for example, made it relatively easy for the Ministry of Justice to refuse registration to party organizations. Apart from requiring a long list of information on finances, expenditure and the nature of the party's internal organization, the Ministry could refuse registration if the organization interfered "with the normal working of state organs." The Procurator General could ban a party for three months if, among other things, it "crudely broke its own rules." The law on the press was also hazy. Newspapers could be taken to court "for malevolently using freedom of the press, (and) spreading facts not corresponding to reality . . ." or for printing "false and unchecked information, and conscious disinformation . . ." Ostensibly laudable, such vague formulations encouraged arbitrary and inequitable enforcement.[50]

The constitution, amendable by a two thirds majority of the Supreme Soviet, remained heavily "interventionist," despite enormous improvements in defense of civil rights. A whole section was devoted to the spiritual and aesthetic welfare of its citizens, in which the state stipulated equal relations between spouses, and emphasized motherhood and the filial duties of children.[51] But more significantly, the new constitution continued the legacy of strong state regulation in the economy and a powerful executive branch. The laws on the Prefecture and the Presidency, passed in February and April 1991 respectively and subsequently incorporated into the constitution, severely restricted the representative bodies in the regions (the *sakrebulo*) and center. The prefects, described as the supreme regional powerholders, were directly responsible to and appointed by the President and the Supreme Soviet. They had enormous powers over the locally elected *sakrebulo* and could dismiss it, with the Supreme Soviet's consent, at any time. They controlled most of the regional budget and all local appointments, which allowed them to build up personal networks. They rapidly acquired a reputation for corruption and played a crucial role in getting busloads of Gamsakhurdia's supporters to Tbilisi in September, 1991, when the government was besieged by anti-government demonstrations.[52]

The Presidential system dominated the legislatures of the center and Autonomous Republics in similar fashion. Many of the President's powers, such as appointment and dismissal of the cabinet and its Prime Minister, were to be taken "with the agreement" of the Supreme Soviet, although it was unclear whether the legislature had veto rights. The President could cancel any resolutions or orders of the cabinet. His rejection of a bill could be overturned by a two thirds vote in the legislature, but he could then call a referendum or dismiss the Supreme Soviet after "consulting" his Prime Minister and the Chairman of the House. There was no limitation on the number of terms he could serve and he could be removed only on charges of treason by three quarters of the assembly vote. As Commander in Chief, he had personal control over the National Guard and other military appointments, and could declare various degrees of Presidential or emergency rule, during which time the legislature did not need to be consulted at all. The President was advised by a Presidential Council, but had the power to issue both decrees and instructions without consulting anybody. He could also suspend the force of laws, decrees and instructions of the legislative and executive organs of the Autonomous Republics.[53]

The rule of law?

Georgian democracy was undermined less by legislative flaws than by the selective way in which these laws were interpreted. Thus despite a relatively liberal press law, the government maintained its monopoly over the media by controlling paper supplies, personnel appointments, and by intimidating and closing opposition papers. By the winter of 1991, there were only two or three independent newspapers. Oppositionist papers like *Molodezh Gruzii* ("Young Georgia") and *Axalgazrda Iverieli* ("Young Iverian") were closed down, allegedly due to paper shortages. Those with the largest circulation, such as *Sakartvelos Respublik'a*, *Eri* ("Nation"), and *Svobodnaia Gruziia* ("Free Georgia") were declared official government newspapers, and like almost all others, including the formerly liberal *Lit'erat'uruli Sakartvelo* ("Literary Georgia"), became supine followers of government policy.

Television, under the management of a Gamsakhurdia appointee, cancelled outspoken critical programs. *Sagamos Shvidobisa* ("Good Evening"), a popular current affairs program, for example, was axed in the spring of 1991 after it implied Georgia was moving toward totalitarianism. During the Presidential elections, despite a law stipulating equal airtime for all candidates, Gamsakhurdia enjoyed much more exposure. After the August coup, when Gamsakhurdia was attacked on all sides for alleged collaboration with the State Committee for the State of Emergency, some Georgian journalists were arrested, Russian newspapers temporarily banned, and foreign correspondents physically attacked.[54] In September 1991, when the coverage of opposition demonstrations was censored and broadcasts from Moscow were not aired, 189 TV journalists struck in protest. In a letter to the government, they accused the TV management of "Bolshevik like methods," called for an end to the "dictat" of the Department of Georgian Radio and TV, including the removal of its General Director, and the establishment of an alternative channel for the opposition.[55] The *casus belli* of the split in Gamsakhurdia's Round Table ranks in September, when forty-nine deputies abandoned the government benches in protest, was the President's refusal to allow TV coverage of parliamentary debates on the shooting of anti-government demonstrators on September 2. Significantly, when Tengiz Sigua and Tengiz Kitovani, Gamsakhurdia's former Prime Minister and Commander of the National Guard respectively, organized direct action against the government in late September, the TV studios were the first buildings they occupied.

Restrictions on the press were accompanied by an increasingly tight hold on executive power. The KGB was trasnformed into a National Security Department in August 1991 and in September, as part of an attempt to concentrate executive power within a streamlined Cabinet of Ministers, it became a Ministry. Along with the Ministry of Justice and the Ministry of Defense, it was made directly subordinate to the President. The units of the National Guard which had not defected to Tengiz Kitovani were put under Presidential control on September 9.[56] In the following weeks, Gamsakhurdia established a National Security Council with wide ranging emergency powers, suspended the law on political associations,

304 *Stephen Jones*

and declared a state of emergency in Tbilisi.[57] None of these measures were ratified, as required by law, by the Supreme Soviet. Thus ended any pretension that body might have imagined about its capacity to resist the Presidential will. Gamsakhurdia had forced all channels of power under his control.

The Supreme Court, which had already proved its loyalty to Gamsakhurdia by approving the legally dubious decision to expel the sixty-four communist party members from the Supreme Soviet in August, and the Committee for the Supervision of the Constitution provided no resistance to cynical abuse of the law. They failed to prevent the arrest of opposition leaders, and in November they did not protest when the term of imprisonment without charge was extended to nine months if necessitated by the case's "complexity" or "special circumstances."[58]

The Gamsakhurdia factor

A survey of successor states to the former Soviet Union suggests that the Soviet legacy, combined with economic chaos, has almost uniformly encouraged authoritarian tendencies. In the case of Georgia, a major factor has also been the figure of Zviad Gamsakhurdia. Born in 1939 into the family of Konstantin Gamsakhurdia, one of the most popular Georgian novelists and a staunch patriot, Zviad was brought up, in his own words, to recognize Georgia as an "enslaved state."[59] A specialist in American literature, he rapidly became one of Georgia's best-known dissidents. In 1974 he was a co-founder with Merab Kost'ava and Viktor Rtc'xiladze of the Georgian Initiative Group for Human Rights, and in 1976 of the Georgian Helsinki Watch Group. After publishing a series of *samizdat* journals and campaigning on issues of corruption in the Georgian church, Russification and the plight of national monuments, he was arrested in April 1977 for anti-Soviet propaganda, but released in June 1979 after a televised retraction. On his return, he continued his dissident activities and became a leading figure in the Georgian nationalist movement. The death of Merab Kost'ava in a car accident in October 1989 left Gamsakhurdia the most popular leader of the Georgian nationalist movement.[60]

Gamsakhurdia is a complex figure. His actions must be seen in the context of a fanatical commitment to Georgian independence. His deeply expressed religious feelings, for example, are less metaphysical than part of a nationalist ideology that views the Georgian Church as the embodiment of Georgian nationhood. Despite a constitutional provision separating church and state, Gamsakhurdia openly promoted the Christianization of the republic. He deliberately undermined Islam among Georgians in Ajaria, and appointed a priest to the prefecture of Axalcixe, a heavily populated Muslim area.[61] His writings and speeches are infused with a Messianic vision of Georgia's future. His most popular work, *Sakartvelos*

Sulieri Missia ("Georgia's Spiritual Mission") depicts Georgian Christianity as a militant ideology in defense of the nation, but at the same time as a source of Georgia's "special spiritual purpose" to mediate between East and West.

This work, which was eulogized in the government press as "a new stage in Georgian culture and science", reminds one of the fantastic pseudo-racial concoctions of nineteenth century pamphleteers. It is a jumble of mythological theories, taken as fact, depicting Georgia as the embodiment of "ancient spiritual wisdom" and the source of a powerful "proto-Iberian culture" which spread throughout the Ancient world. At one stage, he points out that Japhet, son of Noah and the mythological ancestor of Georgians, is identical to Jupiter, "the planet of the white race."[62] This pamphlet, typical of the nationalist's mind with its search for past glory and distinctiveness, reveals an intellectually superficial, but dangerously naive and irrational personality. There is not a trace of scepticism in the work. Georgia is a superior culture. The consequence of this deeply held ethnocentrism was a policy aimed at the limitation of the smaller and inferior cultures which shared Georgian historical territory.

Gamsakhurdia's other characteristics, unfortunate in a man with so much support, are a sense of paranoia, a conspiratorial frame of mind, virulent anti-communism and a tendency to self-glorification. The first three might be traced to his own experiences in the Soviet Union when he was constantly persecuted by the KGB. His speeches ubiquitously refer to foreign agents, traitors and conspiracies hatched by his "enemies" in Moscow. Colleagues who broke with Gamsakhurdia became traitors, and critical intellectuals became Moscow's tools. Tbilisians who supported the opposition were "cruelly deceived." A key conspirator against both Gamsakhurdia and Georgia (the two presumed identical by Gamsakhurdia) was Shevardnadze who Gamsakhurdia alleged masterminded the "civil junta" which finally overthrew his government in January 1992.[63]

Gamsakhurdia viewed himself as the last in a long line of Georgian national heroes, all of whom, in his words, have embodied "sacrifices on the altar of the fatherland." The struggle for Gamsakhurdia was between "good and evil." If he were removed, Georgia would become "the victim of total anarchy, and Georgia's existence, its future in general, will be in question." Comparing himself to De Gaulle, Gamsakhurdia argued that a strong Presidency corresponded to the "historical laws and characteristics" of the Georgian people, and that it was the only means for Georgia's salvation.[64]

The above is not intended to suggest that Gamsakhurdia was directly responsible for the authoritarianism and violence in Georgia. He was, after all, elected by 87 percent of those who voted in the Presidential elections. His "dictatorial tendencies" were not perceived as a threat by most Georgians, who did not take part in the fighting which finally ousted him. There may be an argument, which cannot be developed here, that Georgian political culture contributed just as much to the paternalism and violence which characterized Gamsakhurdia's reign as the Soviet legacy.[65] But Gamsakhurdia's paranoia, his refusal to enter serious dialogue with the opposition and his manipulation of the law, undoubtedly contributed to an atmosphere in which mutual accommodation and trust were rejected.

Conclusion

Georgia illustrates many of the problems we have seen elsewhere in post-totalitarian societies. It shows that free elections do not always produce democracy, that there are subtler factors – historical, structural and psychological – that determine its success or failure. But Georgia's path to authoritarianism was not inevitable. The legacy of statism, the popular distrust of institutions, and the lack of a legal culture, were not insurmountable obstacles. There were alternative strategies that might have ensured a less bloody transition. As Giuseppe Di Palma has so elegantly phrased it, "crafting" a democracy is possible even in the most difficult of situations. The error of the Georgian government lay primarily in the exclusion of social groups and parties from the state building process and in the failure to establish rules of political behavior. In January 1992, a new Military Council came to power. The question is whether its members have learnt that accommodation and incorporation are the premises on which all democracies have to be built.

Notes

I wish to thank Professor Edwina Cruise and Dr. Tatuna Grdzelidze for their comments and suggestions on a previous draft of this article.

1 For discussion of the problems faced by ex-communist regimes in the transition to democratic change, see Giuseppe Di Palma *To Craft Democracies: an Essay on Democratic Transitions*, and the series of articles in the October 1991 issue of *World Politics* (vol. 44, no. 1), devoted to "Liberalization and Democratization in the Soviet Union and Eastern Europe." The theoretical context of this article draws much from both these sources.

2 Di Palma, *Democracies*.

3 See the interview with Andrei Sakharov in *Ogonek*, no. 31, 1989, p. 27.

4 Georgia declared its independence on May 26, 1918 after brief participation in a Democratic Federal Republic of Transcaucasia from April 1918. For a short outline of this period, see Stephen F. Jones "Transcaucasia: Revolution and Civil War," in H. Shukman, ed., *The Blackwell Encyclopedia of the Russian Revolution* (Oxford: Basil Blackwell Ltd., 1988). See also Firuz Kazamzadeh *The Struggle for Transcaucasia (1917–1921)* (Oxford: George Ronald, 1951).

5 For the national breakdown in Georgia during this period (1897 census figures) see V. Jaoshvili *Sakartvelos mosaxleoba XVIII–XX saukuneebshi* (Mecniereba: Tbilisi, 1984), p. 112. Abkhazia was formally granted autonomy in February

1921, on the eve of the collapse of the Georgian republic. The Abkhazian National Soviet had only limited opportunities of self-rule before then.

6 The most significant in Ossetian districts were in March 1918, December 1919 and June 1920. In Abkhazian districts, the National Guard was constantly involved in suppressing nascent revolts, particularly in the spring and summer of 1918.

7 For the Ossetian point of view, see *Osetino-Russkaia tema etnoperestroechnykh urokov* (Pichidzhen, 1991). See especially pp. 38–41. The Georgian view of Georgian-Ossetian relations is expressed in A. Menteshashvili, *Iz istorii vzaimootnoshenii Gruzinskogo, Abkhazskogo i Osetinskogo narodov* (Znanie: Tbilisi, 1990), pp. 65–80.

8 See for example *Sakartvelos Respublik'a*, no. 40, February 28, 1991, p. 4; no. 41, January 3, 1991, p. 4.

9 In fact, the Abkhazian republic was initially granted "treaty status" in 1921 as an independent republic associated with Georgia. Its change of status in 1931 represented a demotion.

10 See Darrell Slider, "Crisis and Response in Soviet Nationality Policy: the Case of Abkhazia," *Central Asian Survey*, vol. 4, no. 4, 1985, pp. 51–68.

11 *Ibid.*, and Elizabeth Fuller "The Azeris in Georgia and the Ingilos: Ethnic Minorities in the Limelight," *Central Asian Survey* vol. 3, no. 2, 1984, pp. 75=86. See also her "Marneuli: Georgia's Potential Nagorno-Karabagh?," *Radio Free Europe-Radio Liberty Research Bulletin* (henceforth *RFE-RL*), 477/88, pp. 1–5.

12 Elizabeth Fuller "Large-Scale Measures to Improve the Teaching of the Georgian Language," *RFE-RL*, 157/80, p. 2. See also *Kommunisticheskaia partiia Gruzii v rezoliutsiiakh i resheniiakh s"ezdov, konferentsii i plenumov Ts.K.*, vol. 4, 1972–1980 (Sabchota Sakartvelo: Tbilisi, 1980), pp. 898–901.

13 Slider, "Crisis." See also Elizabeth Fuller "Kapitonov on Nationality Relations in Georgia," *RFE-RL*, 125/78, pp. 1–5, and *Kommunisticheskaia partiia Gruzii, ibid.*, pp. 795–804, 881–886, 888–891.

14 Extracts from these disputes in the 1950s and 1960s are included in *Mat'iane* (Tbilisi, 1989), pp. 3–49. *Mat'iane* was the journal of the Georgian Helsinki Group led by Zviad Gamsakhurdia, and is biased. It contains a section from Georgian historian Pavle Ingoroqva's book *Georgi Merchule*, published in 1954, which suggests Abkhazians have been in the region for only 300 years. Abkhazians claim they have been there two millenia.

15 Slider, "Crisis." See also Ronald G. Suny, "Georgia and Soviet Nationality Policy," in Stephen Cohen, Alexander Rabinowitch and Robert Sharlet, eds., *The Soviet Union Since Stalin* (London: Macmillan, 1980), pp. 200–226.

16 Slider, "Crisis."

17 Ann Sheehy, "The National Languages and the New Constitutions of the Transcaucasian Republics," *RFE-RL*, 97/78, pp. 1–12; Elizabeth Fuller "Manifestations of Nationalism in Current Georgian-Language Literature," *RFE-RL*, 106/80, pp. 1–6; Fuller, "Eduard Shevardnadze Speaks on Recent Achievements in Georgian Literature and on the State of the Georgian Language," *RFE-RL*, 146/80, pp. 1–2.

18 See, for example, the programs of the National Democratic Party (*Gouchagi* [Paris], no. 18, 1989, pp. 33–37) and the program of the Georgia Union for National Justice (*Uc'xebani* [Tbilisi] no. 1, October, 1988).

19 *K'omunist'i*, November 3, 1988, pp. 2–3. A later version was published in August 1989 which added the language requirement. I have not been able to obtain a copy of the second version, but was informed of the new stipulation by a reliable informant.

20 For the Georgian History state program, see *K'omunist'i*, August 2, 1989, pp. 2–3; the law on immigration is in *K'omunist'i*, November 26, 1989, p. 1.

21 Numerous examples of this view can be found in the speeches of President Gamsakhurdia. See, for example, his speech justifying the abolition of South Ossetia's regional autonomy in *Sakartvelos Republik'a*, December 12, 1990, pp. 1, 4.

22 See Benedict Anderson's discussion of the Hungarian case in *Imagined Communities: Reflections on the Origin and Spread of Nationalism*, revised edn (London: Verso, 1991), pp. 101–111.

23 Those parties which attained seats in the new Georgian Supreme Soviet elected in October 1990, were as follows:

Round Table-Free Georgia Bloc	155 deputies (53.95%)
Georgian communist party	64 deputies (29.57%)
Georgian Popular Front	12 deputies (1.93%)
Democratic Georgia	4 deputies (1.65%)
All-Georgian Rust'aveli Society	1 deputy (2.32%)
Liberation and Economic Rebirth	1 deputy (1.46%)
Independents	9 deputies

The remaining parties, which shared the rest of the vote between them, failed to receive any seats. In Abkhazian and Ossetian districts, there was a boycott or very low turnout. The Georgian communist party did particularly well in the southern periphery in Armenian and Azeri districts, and in the rural districts of Ajaria. For full details on the election results, see *Axali Sakartvelo*, November 16, 1990,p. 3 and *Zaria Vostoka*, November 9 and November 14, 1990.

24 In 1989, there were 164,000 Ossetians in Georgia. Sixty five thousand of them lived in South Ossetia. Reports have suggested 50,000 to 100,000 refugees. These numbers may include Georgians, and Ossetians outside South Ossetia, but it is likely that the largest proportion are Ossetians from South Ossetia. On refugee estimates, see *Foreign Broadcast Information Service Daily Report: Soviet Union* (henceforth *FBIS-SOV*), 91-214, p. 71 and 91-217, p. 73.

25 "Avars Leave Georgia," *Moscow News*, no. 21, May 26–June 2, 1991, p. 4.

26 For reports on Abkhazian events, see *Current Digest of the Soviet Press* (henceforth *CDSP*), vol. 41, no. 29, 1989, pp. 14–16. See also *K'omunist'i*, July 18, 1989, pp. 1–3 and July 19, 1989, p. 3.

27 For discussion of the conflict between these two Hungarian figures, see Hugh Seton-Watson, *Nations and States: An enquiry into the origins of nations and the politics of nationalism* (London: Methuen, 1977), pp. 161–163.

28 For a review of the events in South Ossetia, see Elizabeth Fuller, "The South Ossetian Campaign for Unification," *Report on the USSR* no. 49, 1989, pp. 17–20, and "South Ossetia: Analysis of a Permanent Crisis," *Report on the USSR*, no. 7, 1991,pp. 20–22.

29 The "Law on Introducing Changes into the Abkhazian ASSR Law on Electing Deputies to the Abkhazian ASSR Supreme Soviet," which was introduced in

August 1991, guaranteed ethnic quotas in Parliament, with each ethnic group voting for its own "ethnic" deputies. The elected posts in the Supreme Soviet, were also ethnically reserved. *FBIS-SOV*, 91-176, p. 80, 91-186, pp. 59–60. For a discussion of the similarities with the Lebanese system, see D. Horowitz, "Ethnic Conflict Management for Policymakers," in Joseph Montville, ed., *Conflict and Peacemaking in Multiethnic Societies* (Lexington, KY: Lexington Books, 1989), p. 126.

30 See chapters 7 and 8 in *Sakartvelos respublik'is k'onst'it'ucia* as amended until October 1991 (no publisher, pp. 63). The author has a copy.

31 For an English translation of the program, see "The Election Block (*sic*) 'Round Table-Free Georgia,' Political Platform." The author has a copy.

32 For a report on the conduct and result of the elections, see *Report on the Supreme Soviet Election in Georgia*, November, 1990. Prepared by the Staff of the US Commission on Security and Cooperation in Europe.

33 For the cabinet appointees and their backgrounds, see *Zaria Vostoka*, November 23, 1990, p. 2.

34 For these early laws and amendments, see *Axali Sakartvelo*, nos. 2 (15 November), 4 (16 November) 7 (22 November), 1990.

35 Robert A. Dahl, *Polyarchy and Opposition: Participation and Opposition* (New Haven: Yale University Press, 1971), p. 208. Di Palma, *Craft*, p. 3.

36 *Ibid.*, p. 160.

37 This quotation is cited in Julie Wishnevsky, "Russia: Liberal Media Criticize Democrats in Power," in *RFE/RL Research Report*, vol. 1, no. 2, p. 6.

38 Benedict Anderson notes that "even the most determinedly radical revolutionaries always, to some degree, inherit the state from the fallen regime" (*ibid.*, p. 159).

39 For more detailed discussion of these groups and the National Congress, see Stephen F. Jones, "Glasnost, Perestroika and the Georgian Soviet Socialist Republic," in *Armenian Review*, vol. 43, nos. 2–3, Summer/Autumn 1990, pp. 127–152.

40 For Gamsakhurdia's derisory assessment of Georgian intellectuals, see his press conference, reported in *Sakartvelos Respublik'a*, no. 38, February 26, 1991, p. 1.

41 For Gamsakhurdia's response to the August coup before its outcome was clear, see *Sakartvelos Respublik'a*, no. 163, August 21, 1991, p. 1. Although not forceful and aggressive in his condemnation of the coup leaders, Gamsakhurdia appealed to the West to support the forces of democracy in the USSR, and in particular, to help the republics threatened by "military aggression." The National Guard was demoted from its independent status and placed under the control of the Georgian Ministry of Interior.

42 Dahl's first axiom on successful democratization was that "the likelihood that a government will tolerate an opposition increases as the expected costs of toleration decrease." Gamsakhurdia viewed the opposition as fragmented and powerless. The costs of its suppression initially looked like a good risk. Dahl, *Polyarchy*, p. 15.

43 For the Presidential election results, see *FBIS-SOV*, 91–159, p. 48.

44 For discussion of this point, see Di Palma, *Craft*, pp. 40–43.

45 *FBIS-SOV*, 91-176, p. 77.

46 For a report of this highly revealing meeting, in which members of the university community in particular condemned the new "atmosphere of fear" created by the government, see *Tavisupali Sakartvelo*, March 22, 1991, p. 2.

47 *Sakartvelos respublik'is k'onst'it'ucia*, chs. 21 and 22. See also *Sakartvelos Respublik'a*, no. 19, December 29, 1990, p. 3.

48 For the draft law on the status of deputies, see *Sakartvelos Respublik'a*, no. 16, December 25, 1990, p. 1. For the law on political associations, see *Sakartvelos Respublik'a*, no. 160, August 14, 1991, p. 4. For the draft law on the press, which was passed on 30 August, 1990 almost unchanged, see *Sakartvelos Respublik'a*, no. 20, December 30, 1990, p. 1.

49 See, for example, *Sakartvelos Respublik'a*, nos. 155–156 (8 August), 181 (18 September), 211 (30 October), and 214–215 (2 November) 1991, for laws on privatization and de-monopolization.

50 *Sakartvelos Respublik'a*, no. 160, August 14, 1990, p. 4, and *ibid.*, no. 20, December 30, 1990, p. 1.

51 *Sakartvelos respublik'is k'onst'it'ucia*, chs. 5 and 6, pp. 10–19.

52 For the powers of the prefects, see *ibid.*, chs. 17 and 18, pp. 51–53. See also *Sakartvelos Respublik'a*, no. 24, February 5, 1991, p. 3.

53 *Sakartvelos respublik'is k'onst'it'ucia*, ch. 13, pp. 40–45. See also *Sakartvelos Respublik'a*, no. 90, April 16, 1991, p. 1.

54 *FBIS-SOV* 91-177, pp. 88–90, 93; 91-178, p .93; 91-204, p. 70; 91-181, pp. 75–77. Tengiz Sigua in an interview in mid-November suggested two government emissaries were sent to Moscow on the eve of the coup to make a deal with the leaders (*Gouchagi*, Paris, no. 26, December 1991, pp. 15–16). I am grateful to Tat'una Grdzelidze for the information about TV programming.

55 *Sakartvelos Respublik'a*, no. 194, October 5, 1991, p. 4.

56 *FBIS-SOV*, 91-174, p. 89; 91-175, p. 93; 91-190, pp. 66–67.

57 *FBIS-SOV* 91-214, p. 72; 91-186, p. 59. *Sakartvelos Respublik'a*, no. 185, September 24, 1991, p. 1.

58 *Sakartvelos Respublik'a*, no. 213, November 1, 1991, p. 1.

59 *FBIS-SOV* 91-007, p. 82.

60 For a biography of Gamsakhurdia, see *Sakartvelos Respublik'a*, no. 89, May 8, 1991, p. 1.

61 *Sakartvelos Respublik'a*, no. 51, March 15, 1991, p. 2.

62 *Samshoblo* no. 22, November 1990, pp. 4–5.

63 *FBIS-SOV*, 91-191, p. 78; 91-196, pp. 69–70. For the ultimate expression of this paranoia, see the government declaration of September 25, "Message to the Georgian People and to the States and Peoples of the World," which names film directors, journalists and political leaders in Tbilisi and Moscow as members of an anti-government plot. This declaration, which was rejected by the majority of Gamsakhurdia's own parliamentary followers, was probably the first step in Gamsakhurdia's plan to launch mass arrests among the opposition. See *Sakartvelos Respublika*, no. 186, September 25, 1991, p. 1.

64 *FBIS-SOV* 91-205, pp. 66–69.

65 This is an argument put forward by Professor Ghia Nodia of the University of Tbilisi. See his "The Political Crisis in the Republic of Georgia," presented at the Kennan Institute, Washington, October 25, 1991.

Part VI
Central Asia

13 Kazakhstan: a republic of minorities

MARTHA BRILL OLCOTT

Introduction

Kazakhstan is the only former Soviet republic in which the titular nationality is a minority population. This fact, more than any other, has limited the scope of the Kazakh's national revival, and is sure to influence the course of Kazakh politics as Kazakhstan develops as an independent state.

According to the 1989 census, Kazakhs constituted 39.7 percent of the population, although Kazakhstan's officials maintain that they are now about 42 percent of the republic's residents. But regardless, Russians and Ukrainians (43.6 percent combined) still outnumber the Kazakhs.[1]

For most of the Soviet period, Kazakhstan's leaders declared that they were proud of the republic's demographic makeup because, home to over a hundred different nationalities, it was truly multinational. Even in 1992, republic president Nursultan Nazarbaev used most public occasions to praise Kazakhstan's multinational character, offering the republic an opportunity to build a demographic society based on notions of equality before the law.

Political stability has been preserved in Kazakhstan, in large part because this republic was part of a much larger multi national state. This relationship certainly provides one reason why Nazarbaev was a strong proponent of the perpetuation of the union, second only to Mikhail Gorbachev in his enthusiasm for this cause.

When the August 1991 coup failed, it was Nazarbaev who introduced plans for a new "union" government to the Supreme Soviet of the USSR.[2] After the new Commonwealth of Independent States was announced, it was Nazarbaev's defection that sealed Gorbachev's fate. It was only then that Kazakhstan declared its independence.

The enormous popularity of Nursultan Nazarbaev, head of the Kazakhstan since June 1989, has been a source of political stability in his republic. But the dissolution of the USSR into smaller nation-states, the trend that neither Nazarbaev nor Gorbachev was able to reverse, makes the long-term stability of independent Kazakhstan problematic.

313

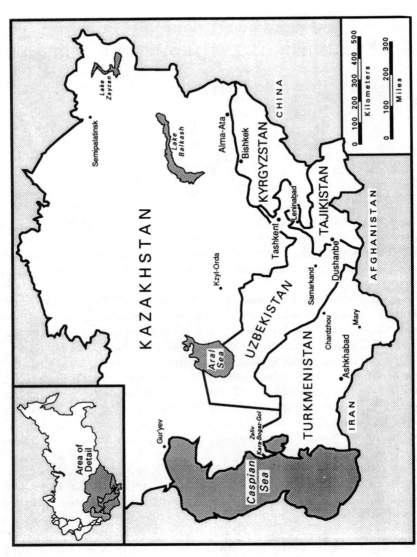

Map 13.1 Central Asia

Whose homeland?

Kazakhs and Russians share many goals for the future. There was strong common support for Nazarbaev's economic program – the introduction of private property and a free market – and both groups seem to harbor hesitations about turning agriculture over to exclusively private cultivation.

Both groups also support the idea of sovereignty for Kazakhstan. But the future path for Kazakhstan society polarizes the two groups. Is it a multinational society, an ethnic hybrid of Kazakhs and Russians, or a Kazakh homeland? Up to 1992, Nazarbaev managed to avoid confronting this issue by alternatively asserting that it was all three.

Much of the problem stems from the history of Kazakhstan's unification with Russia and the different opinions among Kazakhs and Russians regarding its origin. Although there were Russian settlers in the region before the revolution, most Russians living in Kazakhstan came to the republic themselves or are descended from Soviet-period settlers. The Russians still consider Kazakhstan, and particularly the northern part of the republic, to be a part of Russia. This territory, in their opinion, was voluntarily ceded to the Russian Tsars by Kazakh Khans seeking Russia's protection.

The Kazakh version is somewhat different. They do not dispute the basic facts. Abdul' Khayr, Khan of the Small Horde, swore an oath of loyalty to Anna Ionona in 1731, and Khan Ablai of the Middle Horde swore his loyalty to Russia's ruler in 1740.[3]

Soviet historians consider 1731 as the date of the "voluntary unification" of the Kazakhs and Russian peoples because the Kazakh Khans never regained full control over the territory of the Small Horde (northwestern Kazakhstan up to the Ural river). However, Kazakh historians argue that Abul' Khayr intended this alliance to be a shortlived, strategic one.[4]

Certainly, this result did indeed describe the consequent Russian relations with the Middle Horde (whose territory was found in north-eastern Kazakhs around the Irtysh river). Khan Ablai spent the next forty years playing off the Russians and the Chinese in an effort to protect his territory from invasion without fully sacrificing his sovereignty.

Ablai never fully succeeded, and some forty years after his death a series of Russian forts and Cossack outposts stretched across his territory. This first expansion was achieved peacefully. However, in the 1840s, when the Russians moved southward (into the remaining territory of the Middle Horde and that of the Great Horde), they encountered considerable armed resistance – led by Ablai's grandson, Kenisary Qasimov. In the 1860s, there was also fighting in western Kazakhstan when Russia used troops to annex that territory (which belonged to the Small Horde).

The existence of armed opposition, Kazakh historians now claim, is proof that their territory was conquered, and not voluntarily annexed.[5] In fact, for most of the Soviet period, a law declared documentation of the conquest a treasonous act for Kazakhs.

However, for local Russians, Kazakhstan is often understood as an extension of the Siberian frontier. The term Kazakhstan (land of the Kazakhs) was not used during the colonial period. Then Kazakh territory was divided between two administrative districts, the Steppe region, and Turkestan (which included the Kazakh lands of Semirech'e and Syr Darya).

Kazakh land, the colonial administration hoped, would help solve Russia's land problem. Thus, they pursued an aggressive policy designed to achieve the settlement of the nomads and so free up their pasture land for European homesteaders. Between 1906–1915, slightly more than a million Europeans came to farm in the area.[6]

After the revolution, when the boundaries of the Kazakh republic were being drawn up, the northernmost part of the Steppe territory was attached to two Siberian oblasts, and the rest, plus most of the former *guberniias* of Syr Darya and Semirech'e, became an autonomous part of the Russian Federation (briefly as an autonomous oblast, then from 1924–1936 as an autonomous republic). Finally, in 1936, Kazakhstan was awarded full union republic status.

Most of Kazakhstan's non-Kazakh residents came to the republic during the Soviet period. Russians and Ukrainians came in two waves; as deported kulaks in the 1920s and 1930s, and as virgin lands "enthusiasts" in the 1950s. The kulaks were dispersed throughout the republic. The virgin lands settlers were dispatched to the six northern oblasts. Even today, Kazakhs still constitute a small minority in these oblasts.[7]

Kazakhstan also has a considerable population of other deported nationalities. Volga Germans, Crimean Tatars, and Koreans were all forcibly settled in the region just prior to and during World War II.[8] In addition to these groups there are also indigenous minority communities, the Uzbeks, Dungans and Uighurs being the most numerous.[9]

The Kazakhs also believe themselves to be aggrieved. They claim that their colonial overlords – both Russian and Soviet – followed deliberately discriminatory policies designed to leave the Kazakhs a minority in their own republic. This has been an oft repeated theme during the years of glasnost, and an officially sanctioned one since Kazakh poet Olzhas Suleimenov's impassioned speech at the First Congress of Peoples' Deputies in June 1989.

In this address, the head of Kazakhstan's Union of Writers offered a litany of the wrongs done to the Kazakhs: forced settlement at the end of the nineteenth century, political repression on the eve of the revolution, famine during the civil war, near annihilation by Stalin in the 1930s, the final disruption of their traditional culture with the invention of the virgin lands in the 1950s, and finally, systematic poisoning of their environment by the Soviet military industrial complex over the forty year post-war period. These wrongs, he stated, cost four million lives and for this the Kazakh people must receive compensation.[10]

The Alma Ata uprising

Despite their deep sense of grievance against the legacy of Russian and particularly Soviet rule in their republic, the Kazakhs proceeded cautiously in posing their demands during the first three years of Gorbachev's rule.

The aftermath of the public disturbances of December 17, 1986 provided reason for such timidity. These public protests began the day after the announcement of Dinmukhammad Kunaev's retirement as first secretary of Kazakhstan's Communist Party and his replacement by Gennadi Kolbin, former Russian first secretary of Ulianovsk oblast.

The disturbances have been shrouded in controversy ever since. Official press accounts at the time called them the work of disturbed and rowdy nationalist youth.[11] Nationalists maintain that they were an official provocation that turned a spontaneous but peaceful public demonstration into a violent one.[12] Official sources claim two deaths, unofficial estimates range from 58 to over 250.[13]

Kazakhstan under Moscow's control

The result of the uprising on political life in Kazakhstan garners a far clearer consensus. Gennady Kolbin used the unrest to focus his campaign against the remnants of Kunaev's political organization, accusing the Kunaev-led Communist Party of having been lax in its efforts to convey "internationalism" to the citizens of the republic (in a January 11, 1987 plenum).[14]

The following plenum, in March 1987, was devoted almost exclusively to the flaws of Kunaev's leadership and that of his circle.[15] In August 1987, the conclusions of these two plenums were incorporated in a Central Committee of the CPSU resolution "On the Work of the Kazakh Party Organization in the Internationalist and Patriotic Education of Workers."[16]

Kunaev's dismissal, though, did not provoke a thorough-going purge of the party, in large part because of the successful Moscow-sponsored campaign against the Kunaev organization which preceeded the Kazakh party leader's dismissal.[17] Most of those fired by Kolbin were personal proteges of Kunaev. But numerous republic figures who remained on the job were subjected to public critiques of their behavior. The educational establishment was especially chastised, for educational practices giving Kazakhs unfair advantages in the admission process.[18]

For the most part, the threat of dismissal and public disgrace had its intended effect. Most prominent Kazakh figures in the Communist Party became frightened of demonstrating a "Kunaev-like" leadership style; they refrained from doing anything that might be construed as nationalist.

Nursultan Nazarbaev, then Chairman of the Council of Ministers, was effectively the republic's senior Kazakh politician. He had been sharply critical of his former mentor during the year prior to Kunaev's dismissal. Now he went further. He implied that the Alma Ata riots were a violent outburst of destructive nationalism that grew naturally out of the corrupt leadership style of the Kunaev era.[19]

Olzhas Suleimenov, the official nationalist *bête-noire* of the Kunaev period,[20] had gone out onto Brezhnev (now Republic) square during the December disturbances to try and quell the demonstrators with assurances that Kazakhstan's new leadership would protect their national rights.[21] By January, he too was writing sharp criticisms of policies that had led to the lack of "a true sense of national pride and dignity" that had fueled the demonstrations which he was now deploring.

This stance, though, did not insulate him from harsh criticism at the March 1987, Kazakhstan Central Committee plenum. He replied with a speech that he asked be withheld from the public record.[22] Following the plenum, Suleimenov himself became the object of an official party investigation.[23]

Clearly, the pressure on Kazakh intellectuals and politicians led them to publicly misrepresent their real feelings in order to survive politically. Nazarbaev and Suleimenov's subsequent writings about the December uprising, when Moscow toleration of public criticism was substantially expanded, is at odds with their 1987 versions of the same events. Suleimenov now spoke of the uprising as the first major pro-democracy rally of the Gorbachev years, while Nazarbaev claimed that it developed in response to the anti-democratic selection of Kunaev's successor – during an eighteen minute plenum of the Kazakhstan's CP central committee![24]

Certainly the anti-Kunaev crackdown, led by Kolbin but orchestrated in large part in Moscow, shaped the development of party politics throughout Kolbin's tenure in Kazakhstan.[25] Kazakhstan's party leaders felt effectively barred from developing political programs favouring *any* particular national community in the republic. Thus, Communist Party politicians were effectively precluded from endorsing Kazakh claims for special rights as the republic's titular nationality. At the same time, the Party had to be careful not to discriminate against the Kazakhs.

Nevertheless, the Alma Ata uprising, and the crackdown it produced both on the streets of Alma Ata and later in the halls of power, stimulated the development of Kazakh nationalism. Everybody with any connections to Alma Ata knew that the government was lying, that regardless who was at fault, the protests over Kunaev's dismissal were far larger than reported and far more peaceful. Moreover, they knew that the casualty figures were also far higher than reported. Thus, the Kazakh sense of victimization by Moscow (and consequently by Russians) continued to deepen during Kolbin's time in office.

Generally, though, Russians were unable to identify with the psychological impact of the Alma Ata uprising on the Kazakh population. Many Russians, at least initially, felt far more sympathetic toward the Kolbin regime precisely because it promised to regulate the "unhealthy" aspects of nationalism. This attitude especially reflects that of Russians in the northern part of the republic, living far from the rumors, who had little basis to dispute the official version of events. This difference in perceptions only drove the Kazakhs and Russians further apart.

The Kolbin regime, in an effort to demonstrate that it was not "anti-Kazakh," wound up further exacerbating the gulf between the two communities. Kazakhstan's Communist Party, with Moscow's approval, called for the improvement of Kazakh language education in the republic. Initially, in 1987, this endeavour proceeded quite tenuously. Kolbin stressed the absence of trained cadres to improve Kazakh language education and the slow process of the introduction of Kazakh as an administrative language.[26] But by early 1989, Kazakhstan Communist Party officials were calling for a shift of resources to train more Kazakh language teachers so that these goals would be realizable.[27]

None the less, only limited resources were devoted to this goal; Russians felt little pressure to learn Kazakh. In general, despite the Kazakh party organization's sense of alienation from Kolbin, his presence introduced no real rift between the Russian and Kazakh communities in the republic.

Given the Communist Party's tight control over public discussion under Kolbin, "informal" organizations were slow to develop in Kazakhstan. The first groups chartered were involved with ecology and the problem of rewriting Kazakh history, but they had little public visibility while Kolbin was still in power.[28]

The one possible occasion for conflict, the 1989 election campaign for deputies to the new USSR Congress of People's Deputies, was well orchestrated by Kazakhstan's Communist Party and ethnic issues never surfaced in the republic press.[29]

However, Kolbin's final days in the republic were spent putting down an unexpected ethnic disturbance – fighting between North Caucasian oil workers and Kazakhs in the western Kazakhstan town of Novy Uzen. The oil facility that had brought the North Caucasians, mostly Lezgins, to the area had been closed down, turning the one-time boom town into an economically depressed area. The disturbances began on June 16, 1989 and the curfew was lifted on July 7, 1989.[30]

Nazarbaev takes command

On June 22, 1989, Nursultan Nazarbaev was appointed to replace Gennadi Kolbin as first secretary of the Communist Party of Kazakhstan. His appointement was met with approval by the Kazakhs, and he quickly earned the confidence of the Russian population as well.

Nazarbaev demonstrated himself to be a skilled politician. He was able to bridge the gaps between the republic's two major nationalities during a period of rising nationalism, and achieved this compromise while remaining personally loyal to Soviet President Mikhail Gorbachev and his program of reform.

Nazarbaev understood that Kazakhstan had to become more explicitly the homeland of the Kazakhs, but he recognized that the heightened visibility of Kazakh culture, language, and history should not alienate the republic's large Russian and European population. Nazarbaev sponsored legislation that made Kazakh the state language of the republic. Passed in August 1989, the bill took effect on July 1, 1990, and provided for a graduated program for increasing Kazakh language instruction in republic schools and shifting the conduct of local and republic level government business into Kazakh.

A timetable was set up for oblasts and rayons to shift to Kazakh, depending upon the percentage of Kazakhs who lived in the territory. Regions that were over 70 percent Kazakh would have to shift immediately after the law took effect. Areas where the Kazakhs made up under 50 percent had until the end of 1994 to act.[31] Russian-speaking citizens were assured access to Russian language services. Nevertheless, government officials would have to be competent to function in either language.

The Russian population, especially those who lived in northern Kazakhstan, began immediately to lobby for changing the language legislation. They took issue with the provision that Kazakh language fluency was set as a requirement for high school graduation effective 1992 and with the shift to Kazakh as a mandatory administrative language.

In September and October 1990, the language issue became fused with the debate over sovereignty for Kazakhstan; Russian legislators agreed to approve the government sovereignty bill only after securing a commitment that the language legislation would be modified. The education issue was effectively handled by giving local officials discretion to create their own competence tests for graduation. In September 1990 a compromise on the administrative language was struck. Areas that were overwhelmingly Russian would only have to provide Kazakh language services by January 1, 1995; they had until January 1, 2000 to switch to a fully bilingual administration.

Nazarbaev also took up the cause of Kazakhstan's national communists who were purged during the Stalin era. A Kazakhstan central committee commission examined the files of all those who had been arrested. In July 1989, they made public their decision to posthumously rehabilitate all major revolutionary period and early Soviet leaders who had been arrested.[32] However, the government proceeded cautiously in evaluating the historic role that was played by these men. An Association of Local Historians was founded in November 1989, chaired by Manash Kozybaev, director of the Institute of History, Archeology and Ethnography of the Academy of Sciences of Kazakhstan. It was to review the contribution of such figures as Ali Khan Bukeikhanov (1869–1932) and Mir Yakup Dulatov (1885–1935), who had been active in the anti-Bolshevik Alash Orda government.

Kazakhstan's political establishment was far less tentative about taking up the question of rewriting the history of the collectivization in Kazakhstan. Kozybaev, with full approval of the Kazakhstan Communist Party leadership, published a series of articles revealing publicly for the first time that millions of Kazakhs died at the regime's hand during the early 1930s. Blame, though, was placed on Moscow and on local Russians, and a series of archival documents was published to demonstrate how Kazakh members of the Communist Party had been against Moscow's strategy for collectivization.[33]

As the Kazakhs began to review their history, the Russians began to rethink theirs as well. It was a scholar in Moscow, Victor Kozlov of the Institute of Ethnography of the USSR Academy of Sciences, that first raised the question of Kazakhstan's northern boundaries and Russia's historic right to Eastern Kazakhstan, in an article published in *Istoriia SSSR*.[34]

Kozlov later claimed that he was arguing hypothetically. But with or without his, and later Solzhenitsyn's, prodding, it was inevitable that Russian cossacks and Russian descendants of other pre-revolutionary homesteaders would raise the border issue.

Many of these Russians joined together in an informal group, the "Organization for the Autonomy of Eastern Kazakhstan," which successfully sponsored candidates for election in local and city soviets in the five northern oblasts.

Informals, such as Kazakhstan's branch of *Edinstvo* ("Unity"), were viewed as potentially disruptive by the Nazarbaev region, and these groups found their access to the press and other media severely restricted. The same was true of Kazakh informals like *Zheltoksan* ("December," after the Alma Ata uprising) or *Azat* ("Freedom"), whose programs were more nationalistic than Nazarbaev was prepared to tolerate.[35]

Informal organizations that were supportive of regime goals like *Kazakh tili*, the Kazakh language society, or the Nevada-Semipalatinsk Anti-Nuclear movement, enjoyed far more support. The Nevada-Semipalatinsk movement, in particular, came to play a key role in the republic. This organization, headed by long-time Kazakhstan Communist Party central committee member and Writer's Union head Olzhas Suleimenov, was quasi-governmental in makeup. But its demands to shut the nuclear test-site at Semipalatinsk and remove the ecological hazards that forty years of nuclear testing had caused, were very popular ones.

Thus, the movement gave the population a chance to feel involved in the new mass politics of glasnost and perestroika but channeled and supervised its involvement. Moreover, the widespread public support for the movement gave Kazakhstan's government a safe club to use in pressuring Moscow for decisions that were of benefit to the republic.

None the less, Nazarbaev was a very cautious politician throughout this period. He defended the Gorbachev program for having "a strong center and strong republics" and endorsed the idea of "self-administration and self-financing" of republics as a sufficient measure to bring this about.[36]

It was only as a response to the July 1989 miners' strike, which spread from Vorkuta and Kemerova to Karaganda, that he went further to call for partial control of the republic's mineral resources. The demand itself, coupled with increased salary and benefits, was enough to get the miners back to work.[37]

One of the greatest demonstrations of Nazarbaev's virtually complete control of political life in Kazakhstan came in the March 1990 elections of a republic Supreme Soviet. Kazakhstan was one of the few republics which still "reserved" seats, a quarter of the legislature, for representatives of "public organizations".

This decision strengthened the already firm hold of Kazakhstan's Communist Party on the electoral process. In fact, none of the republic's informal organizations ran their own slate of candidates. Of those chosen to serve in Kazakhstan's Supreme Soviet, 94.4 percent were Communist Party members, and the new legislature included fifty-one senior party workers among its 360 members.[38]

President Nazarbaev of Soviet Kazakhstan

One of the first acts of the new legislature, on April 24, 1990, was to elect Nursultan Nazarbaev the first president of Kazakhstan. In his maiden address as President, Nazarbaev pledged himself to advance the cause of "Kazakh self-finance and self-administration."[39] However, Russia's Supreme Soviet vote for sovereignty in June 1990 changed the political environment in the USSR. Nazarbaev was soon forced, as was Gorbachev himself, to go beyond the existing program of perestroika and embrace the cause of republic sovereignty.

The sovereignty issue in Kazakhstan was an extremely controversial one, mobilizing the Kazakh and Russian population in opposition to one another unlike any previous issue. To Russians, Kazakhstan was an extension of Russia, and while Moscow effectively ran the whole country, it did not matter that Russians lived outside the confines of the RSFSR. To live in Kazakhstan did not restrict their sense of Russian identity.

However, the draft version of the sovereignty bill clearly did. It demanded that they formally recognize Kazakhstan as the Kazakh's homeland. This acknowledgement, in turn, meant that the Kazakh language, Kazakh culture, and Kazakh history would be granted a special place.[40]

The Kazakhs were also displeased with the initial versions of the sovereignty bill. They felt that the Kazakhs were ceding too much control by granting that Kazakhstan was a multi-national republic with full guarantees for each major nationality to use its national language in all spheres of public life and with equal rights to preserve its culture. Kazakhs had been persecuted in their own republic and their language and culture had been fated for extinction. Their resurrection and preservation required that they be given privileged status.

Beginning in mid-August 1990, both Kazakh and Russian nationalists began to regularly demonstrate near Kazakhstan's parliament building to try to advance their cause. As the demonstrations grew in size and emotion, Nazarbaev began to attack the informal organizations, the Kazakh *Azat* ("Freedom") and the Russian *Edinstvo* ("Unity"), and began to call for strict control of the activities of informal organizations in the republic.[41]

Probably coincidently during this period, Aleksandr Solzhenitsyn published a lengthy essay in the Soviet press dealing with the revival of Russia, which among other things advanced the proposition that northeast Kazakhstan was a part of historic Russia and should, in a just settlement, be transferred to it.[42] The Solzhenitsyn essay simply added further fuel to what was already growing pro-secession sentiment in parts of northern Kazakhstan. It also sparked a newspaper campaign defense of the republic's existing boundaries by a number of prominent historians.[43]

There was further confusion introduced into the middle of the sovereignty debate. On September 28, 1990, the Supreme Soviet commission investigating the Alma Ata riots for nearly a year published a summary of its official report.[44] The head of the commission, Mukhtar Shakhanov, a prominent poet and a USSR Supreme Soviet deputy, had long before made public his displeasure with Nazarbaev's conduct at the time of the uprising and during the commission's investigation.[45] Now, the commission publicly accused several senior members of Kazakhstan's Communist Party, as well as the senior CPSU officials in Moscow, of criminal activities at the time of the uprising. Neither Nazarbaev nor Gorbachev were accused of complicity but their behavior was implicitly criticized. Thus a shadow was cast over Nazarbaev's honesty and reliability as a political leader at precisely the time when he needed to muster wide public support.

However, on October 25, 1990, a compromise version of the sovereignty bill was passed. The republic sovereignty decree was almost as pro-Kazakh as the original. But rather than stressing Kazakhstan as the Kazakh homeland, it described the Kazakhs as the first among the republic's nationalities. However, this final draft was also more emphatic about stressing the equal legal rights of all citizens, regardless of nationality.[46]

The ability of the government to pass a sovereignty bill was never in question. The Supreme Soviet of Kazakhstan was filled with loyal party members, and they would have obeyed a call to tow the party line. However, Nazarbaev understood that the move away from Communist Party domination of formal political life in the republic demanded that he achieve consensual agreement.

Eventually he was able to attain this consent. However, in the process, not just Nazarbaev but also the leaders of Kazakhstan's various informal groups all became sensitized to the fragility of the political consensus that bound together the republic's two main ethnic groups. This experience seems to have hardened Nazarbaev's conviction that a new basis had to be worked out for holding together the Soviet republics, for Kazakhstan would find it hard to define a stable basis for independent statehood. Nazarbaev became a staunch defender of a "yes" vote in the March 17 referendum on the continuation of a Soviet Union, although he did modify the wording of the resolution that appeared on the ballot in Kazakhstan to strengthen the sovereignty of the republic.[47]

Nazarbaev became a forceful advocate of the "Novo-Ogareva" agreement, between Gorbachev and the republic leaders, to draw up a new union treaty of sovereign republics. Throughout spring and summer 1991 Nazarbaev vigorously defended the premise that the transition to a market economy must be based on preserving the USSR as "a single economic space."[48] However, Nazarbaev demanded ever-expanding economic authority for the republic including partial control of its mines and other mineral wealth, which Moscow ceded to him in June.[49]

Nazarbaev became an increasingly more visible political figure in Moscow throughout this period. His forceful defense of the need for a new union treaty, more steadfast than that of any other republic leader, gained him a great deal of press, television, and radio attention. This attention, in turn, increased Nazarbaev's popularity within Kazakhstan.

It did not, though, slow the development of a Russian separatist movement which had come to center around a revived Cossack presence in Ust-Kamenogorsk and Uralsk. Once the USSR's ban on the Cossacks was lifted, Kazakhstan's Cossacks, like those of Russia, had begun to organize as well, and Kazakhstan's press began to cover their activities.[50] Their increasingly more public presence stimulated the republic's academic establishment to once again launch a public defense of Kazakhstan's current borders on historical as well as pragmatic grounds.[51]

However, the Russian revival strengthened Nazarbaev's position among Kazakh non-party politicians, especially those of *Azat*, whose popularity also began to grow during this period. They accepted Nazarbaev's premise that to undermine his position was to undermine the overall political stability of the republic.

With Gorbachev's political credibility in such visible decline, Nazarbaev took great pains to work out his earlier political differences with Boris Yeltsin. Yeltsin paid a well publicized trip to Kazakhstan in mid-August. On August 16, 1991 Yeltsin and Nazarbaev signed an agreement of cooperation between the two republics, which was predicated on the recognition of existing republic boundaries.

Moreover, in their joint press conference, Yeltsin supported Nazarbaev's position that planned celebrations of the four hundredth anniversary of the formation of the Cossacks were a provocation against Kazakhstan's sovereignty. The Uralsk History and Culture Society and the *Vozrozhdenie* ("Rebirth") group had invited Cossacks from the Don, Kuban, North Caucasus, the Urals and southern Siberia to gather under the Russian flag for a September 14–15 celebration in their city.[52]

The post-coup world

The August coup occurred before the account of this press conference was even published. The coup itself did not have an immediate resonance in Kazakhstan. Nazarbaev sought to remain neutral during the first twenty-four hours of Gennadi Yanaev's three day tenure as acting-President. His first appeal called for unity and warned the population not to respond to possible acts of provocation.[53] This, however, was soon followed by condemnations of the unconstitutional seizure of power.

Both the coup and the rapid collapse of the Soviet state seem to have caught Nazarbaev by surprise. As a result, there was a certain inconsistency in his position in the two weeks which immediately followed the coup.

At first, at the emergency session of the USSR Supreme Soviet, like the rest of the republic leaders Nazarbaev supported the idea of preserving the USSR as a loose confederation.[54] Moreover, the task of introducing the new plan that had been agreed upon by Gorbachev and the republic leaders was passed on to Nazarbaev.

However, by the time the USSR Congress of People's Deputies met a week later, Nazarbaev was again supporting the USSR remaining a federation, albeit a looser one than had been specified in the pre-coup versions of the union treaty.[55] Furthermore, Nazarbaev hosted the republic leaders in Alma Ata on October 1, 1991, in an effort to try and work out a new agreement in an atmosphere unhampered by Gorbachev's presence.[56] Though in the end his efforts failed as well, Nazarbaev remained a consistent proponent of the union until December 10, 1991, two days after the Commonwealth of Independent States was formed in Minsk. Only then did Kazakhstan's Supreme Soviet prepare a declaration of independence, which was passed on December 16, 1991.

Certainly Nazarbaev's interest in preserving the union was partly the product of fears about the vulnerability of Kazakhstan's northern border. Within days of the coup, a press aide to Yeltsin stated Russia's possible claim to north-east Kazakhstan. Yeltsin disavowed the statement and even sent his vice-president to Alma Ata to reaffirm Russia's commitment to the preservation of the Russian-Kazakhstan border.[57]

None the less, the border issue remained a live one. Despite Yeltsin's and Nazarbaev's agreement, the four hundredth anniversary of the Cossacks was celebrated in Uralsk as originally scheduled. The only change was that demonstrators from the *Azat*, *Zheltoksan*, and Nevada-Semipalatinsk movements staged large protests near the Cossack gathering, purportedly arriving in Uralsk on trains provided by Nazarbaev. Moreover, public opinion polls done after the coup showed declining popularity for Nazarbaev in the Russian-dominated northern oblasts.[58]

However, the aftermath of the coup also provided Nazarbaev with an opportunity to consolidate his position. In Kazakhstan, as elsewhere, the Communist Party was disbanded. Nazarbaev had never fully managed to control many of the local party networks. These party networks, in turn, had dominated the elections to the new rayon and oblast soviets.

Once the party was disbanded, Nazarbaev was able to dismiss local officials whose personal loyalty he did not command. He also moved quickly to appoint a new Prime Minister (Sergei Tereshchenko, a Kazakh-speaking Russian from Chimkent in southern Kazakhstan) and Vice-President (Erik Asanbaev, previously Chairman of the Supreme Soviet).[59]

Nazarbaev himself won an enormous vote of confidence in the republic's presidental elections that were held on December 1, 1991. Though he ran unopposed (the leader of *Zheltoksan* failing to get the 100,000 petition signatures necessary for him to appear on the ballot), Nazarbaev got over 98 percent of the vote, with over 80 percent of all eligible voters having cast their ballots.

However, Nazarbaev was less successful in creating a political structure to support his government and his program of economic reform. On September 7, 1991, when the Communist Party was dissolved, a new Socialist Party was created to replace it. But Kazakh politicians and party members were reluctant to join the new organization, leaving it dominated by Russians and assimilated Kazakhs.

In an effort to rectify this, Nazarbaev sponsored the creation of a Popular Congress of Kazakhstan, which was formally constituted on October 7, 1991. Olzhas Suleimenov and Mukhtar Shakhanov were named co-chairmen of the party, which, though open to all nationalities, was intended to be a Kazakh-dominated organization.

Neither organization was able to generate a broad popular following. But the presence of both these officially-sponsored parties was sure to slow the development of independent mass political parties. Moreover, it appeared to be Nazarbaev's intent that they did so. In a number of television interviews, he was expressed his belief that Kazakhstan's population is not yet politically mature enough to maintain a demographic party-based pluralistic system.[60]

The nature of the previous Communist Party in Kazakhstan may explain this view. In many ways there were two communist parties: the republic party – whose power was drawn from the oblast party organizations; and the party that was represented in the large industrial enterprises of the republic – whose leaders were closely tied to the all-union party organization in Moscow.

The Kazakhs dominated the republic party, and Russians who participated actively became absorbed in the various clan and regionally based networks that dominated the different oblasts. But Russians dominated the economy. Those who were active in the management of most large industrial enterprises answered directly to USSR ministries, and they were insulated from direct intervention by Kazakhstan's Communist Party by these ministries and by the CPSU Central Committee bureaucracy in Moscow.

By 1992 Kazakhstan's Communist Party, the CPSU and the USSR ministry system had vanished. All the cumulative authority that they exercised in Kazakhstan has now vested in Kazakhstan's government. Kazakhstan became an independent country, and its government has inherited the function of both regulating and liberating its economy.

This government's authority was generally the reflection of the will of one man, Nursultan Nazarbaev. Nazarbaev talked of the need to create a civil society in Kazakhstan, one in which all the republic's citizens, regardless of nationality, would feel equally well-served by the government. But he showed no signs of knowing how to achieve this, and for now at least no one really knows the definition of Kazakhstani citizenship.

Nazarbaev hoped that the creation of a free-market economy would give both Russians and Kazakhs a shared commitment to the future well-being of the republic. Nursultan Nazarbaev has been a very popular leader. Russians and Kazakhs both accept the legitimacy of his government. So the political climate in Kazakhstan is relatively calm.

However, the economic transition from a republic that is part of a centrally-planned economy to an independent country with a free-market economy is sure to be difficult. Nazarbaev, of course, recognized this and hoped that the strain of the transition could be lessened through the preservation of a single all-union economy. Now Kazakhstan must go it alone, increasing Nazarbaev's burden.

Nazarbaev may not be popular indefinitely; regardless, he must eventually pass from the scene. Unless steps are taken soon to institutionalize a basis for a civil society in Kazakhstan, when Nazarbaev's popularity fails or when he leaves office a sharp increase in inter-ethnic tensions seems inevitable. As the history of the Gorbachev period highlights, promises of economic recovery are not an effective source of political stability.

Notes

1 *Soiuz*, no. 32, August 1990.
2 *Kazakhstanskaia pravda*, August 27, 1991.
3 For details see Martha Brill Olcott *The Kazakhs* (Stanford: Hoover Institution Press, 1987), esp. chapter 2.
4 *Kazakhstanskaia pravda*, May 16, 1991.
5 The well known Kazakh historian E. Bekmakhanov was sent to a labor camp for merely *implying* that Kenisary Kasimov was a hero, in his *Kazakhstan v 20-40 gody XIX veka* (Alma Ata, 1947).
6 *Kazakhskaia SSR. Kratkaia entsiklopediia* (Alma Ata: Glavnaia redakstiia sovetskaia entsiklopediia, 1985), vol. 1, p. 323.
7 Kazakhs comprise 27.2 percent of the population of East Kazakhstan, 28.9 percent of Kokchetav, 22.9 percent of Kustain, 18.6 percent of North Kazakhstan, 28.5 percent of Pavlodar and 22.4 percent of Tselinograd oblast. *Ekonomika i zhizn*, no. 5, 1990, p. 70.
8 Collectively these groups make up just under ten percent of the population. The Volga Germans accounted for 5.8 percent of the population according to the 1989 census, but there has been considerable out-migration since then. *Soiuz*, no. 32, August 1990.
9 However, collectively they account for less than three percent of the population. *Soiuz*, no. 32, August 1990.
10 *Kazakhstanskaia pravda*, June 8, 1989.
11 *Kazakhstanskaia pravda*, December 19, 1991.
12 *Turkestan*, no. 1, February, 1990.
13 See *Pravda*, December 18–21, 1986; the fifty-eight deaths by the MVD are in addition to these two. They are mentioned in *Literaturnaia gazeta*, no. 48, November 28, 1990, p. 11. Kazakh informants who have read the complete text of the Shakhanov Commission report on the Alma Ata riots claim that they admit to 268 deaths. The full version of the report has yet to be published. The summary of the report is found in *Kazakhstanskaia pravda*, September 28, 1990.
14 *Kazakhstanskaia pravda*, January 11, 1987.
15 *Partinaia zhizn' kazakhstana*, no. 4, 1987, pp. 17–33.
16 *Partinaia zhizn'*, August 15, 1987, pp. 6–11. A translation of this document is found in Martha Brill Olcott, ed., *The Soviet Multi-national State* (Armonk, NY: M.E. Sharpe, 1990).
17 For details see Martha Brill Olcott, "Gorbachev, The National Problem and Party Politics in Central Asia," in Dan Nelson and Raj Menon, eds., *Assessing Soviet Power* (Lexington, KY: Lexington Books, 1988), pp. 69–93.

18 See Kolbin's address of January 7, 1987 (*Kazakhstanskaia pravda*, January 9, 1987) and the report of the Central Control Commission of the CPSU (*Kazakhstanskaia pravda*, February 14, 1991).

19 *Kazakhstanskaia pravda*, March 16, 1987; *Kazakhstanskaia pravda*, March 17, 1987; "Istselenie," *Druzhba narodov*, no. 9, 1987, pp. 195–209.

20 Suleimenov had been a major cultural figure in the republic since the early 1960s. He achieved "notoriety" in 1976 with the publication of *Az i ia*, an attempt to present "Igor's Tale" from a Turkic viewpoint. Attacked by the full force of the USSR's academic establishment, he survived with a brief public recantation and a great deal of support from Kunaev.

21 Interviews with bystanders of the December 1986 demonstrations, May 1990.

22 Those who read Suleimenov's speech, which circulated in "tamizdat" among Alma Ata's college students, report that it was obsequious in its apologetic tone.

23 *Soversheno sekretno*, no. 9, 1990, pp. 22–23.

24 For examples see Suleimenov's twenty-eighth CPSU Congress address, *Kazakhstanskaia pravda*, July 8, 1990; see also the interview with Nursultan Nazarbaev which appeared in *Kazakhstanskaia pravda*, June 8, 1990.

25 No one has offered "proof" of Moscow's orchestration. But the best evidence of it is that Kolbin received a "safe landing" after his replacement as first secretary by Nazarbaev. He was named head of the Committee of People's Control, where he remained until the end of the formal life of the CPSU.

26 *Kazakhstanskaia pravda*, February 18, 1987.

27 *Pravda vostoka*, February 26, 1989.

28 The Kazakhstan Social Committee for Ecology and the Aral and Balkhash Problems was founded in November 1987, and the Truth History Education Society (*Aqiqat*) was founded in 1988. The Nevada-Semipalatinsk movement was founded in March 1989 and the December (*Zheltoksan*) Movement in May 1989; both these would later play a very active role in the republic. For a list of Kazakhstan's Kazakh informals see JPRS-UPA-028, *JPRS Report. Soviet Union*, May 23, 1991, pp. 30–32.

29 For details see Martha Brill Olcott, "Kazakhstan" in Darrell Slider, ed. of an as yet untitled volume on the elections to be published by Duke University Press, 1992.

30 *Kazakhstanskaia pravda*, June 18–23, 1989.

31 *Kazakhstanskaia pravda*, August 25, 1989.

32 *Kazakhstanskaia pravda*, July 26, 1989, and December 9, 1989.

33 *Partinaia zhizn' kazakhstana*, no. 6, 1990, pp. 85–90.

34 V.I. Kozlov, "Natsional'nyi vopros: paradigmy, teoriia i politika," *Istoriia SSSR*, no. 1, 1990, pp. 3–21, see especially pp. 11–12.

35 As late as September 1990, Nazarbaev was complaining of the dysfunctional role played by these organizations. *Kazakhstanskaia pravda*, September 9, 1990.

36 *Daily Report. Soviet Union*. FBIS-SOV-89-107, October 27, 1989, as translated from *Sovetskaia Rossiia*, October 19, 1989.

37 *Izvestiia*, July 21, 1989.

38 *Kazakhstanskaia pravda*, April 25, 1990.

39 *Kazakhstanskaia pravda*, April 25, 1991.

40 *Kazakhstanskaia pravda*, October 11, 1991.
41 *Kazakhstanskaia pravda*, September 12, 1991.
42 *Komsomol'skaia pravda*, September 19, 1990.
43 *Kazakhstanskaia pravda*, October 2 and 4, 1990.
44 The report itself became a classified document.
45 *Literaturnaia gazeta*, no. 5, 1989, p. 14.
46 *Kazakhstanskaia pravda*, October 28, 1991.
47 *Izvestiia*, February 13, 1991.
48 *Daily Report. Soviet Union*, FBIS-SOV-91-116, June 17, 1991, pp. 101–103, a transcription of Central Television broadcast from June 14, 1991.
49 *Radio Liberty on the USSR*, August 9, 1991, pp. 13–15.
50 *Kazakhstanskaia pravda*, June 20, 1991, and *Kazakhstanskaia pravda*, August 3, 1991.
51 *Kazakhstanskaia pravda*, May 16, 1991. This article was in answer to one that appeared in *Literaturnaia Rossiia*, March 8, 1991.
52 *Kazakhstanskaia pravda*, August 21, 1991.
53 *Kazakhstanskaia pravda*, August 19, 1991.
54 *Kazakhstanskaia pravda*, August 29, 1991
55 *Daily Report. Soviet Union*, FBIS-SOV-91-170, September 3, 1991, pp. 28–29. Stenographic account of September 2, 1991 Concress of People's Deputies proceedings.
56 *Kazakhstanskaia pravda*, October 2, 1991.
57 *Daily Report. Soviet Union*, FBIS-SOV-91-169, August 30, 1991, p. 125, a translation of a Russian Radio broadcast of August 29, 1991.
58 *Komsomol'skaia pravda*, September 4, 1991.
59 *Soiuz*, no. 44, 1991, p. 8.
60 *Vremiia*, December 2, 1991.

14 Uzbekistan: from statehood to nationhood?

GREGORY GLEASON

As the first popularly elected parliament in the history of Uzbekistan convened its opening session in the spring of 1990, it faced a key question.[1] At issue was the establishment of a new political post – the "Presidency of Uzbekistan." According to advocates of the new office, creating the post of presidency would combine the dignified and efficient aspects of government in the republic, concentrating authority, simplifying government, and uniting the peoples of Uzbekistan. It would make Uzbekistan, they argued, a more rationally governed "sovereign republic" within the USSR. The supporters of the presidency prevailed; the post of President of Uzbekistan was established in March 1990. In retrospect, however, the way this success was proclaimed may say less about the strengths of Uzbekistan's new "presidential system" than about the resilience of various parties in Central Asia's fairly ancient coalition politics.

The lengthy parliamentary decree creating the presidency managed, in its very first two lines, to announce the establishment of the Presidency and then immediately add the caveat that this "does not change the legal position and does not limit the jurisdiction of the Karakalpak Autonomous Soviet Socialist Republic."[2] The assertion of the legal rights of the ethnic minority population of the Karakalpak ASSR *vis-à-vis* the ethnic Uzbek majority of Uzbekistan was obviously a deliberate and carefully calculated political move. It made abundantly clear the fact that this new political office was accepted by the minority Karakalpak population only on the premise that their rights not be limited by its establishment. Even more revealingly, it held that this fact would need to be stated in such a public and visible way that there could be no "reinterpretation" of jurisdictional boundaries at a later date.

Such political maneuvers as these illustrate a basic feature of the politics of Central Asia, namely that *Central Asian politics is the outcome of a highly complex and variegated process in which groups are continually contesting for power, frequently competing for advantage, and sometimes cooperating for mutual advancement.* The purpose of this chapter is to describe and explore the recent intergroup politics of the largest Central Asian republic, Uzbekistan, by employing this basic feature of Central Asian politics as a guiding premise.[3]

This premise may seem a bit trivial at first appearance, but for analyzing politics in Uzbekistan it deserves a close look for three reasons. First, it calls attention to the role of groups. Groups, not individuals, are the key actors in Uzbekistan's politics. The size and importance of these groups vary. More important, the origins of the groups differ. Some are ethnically defined groups, with their origins in extended families, tribes or clans. Others are regionally defined. Still others are "interest groups" in the sense that they represent members of economic or professional sectors with similar interests. Of course, political decisions in Central Asia, like political decisions anywhere else, are often in the hands of particular individuals. But groups in Uzbekistan have a qualitatively different role than they have in other parts of the USSR or in other countries. Moreover, the way in which the groups come into competition, contestation and cooperation is qualitatively different in Uzbekistan than it is in many other areas.

Second, this basic feature of Central Asian politics stresses the *complexity and heterogeneity* of the groupings in Uzbekistan rather than their homogeneity. It is important to bear this in mind precisely because it is so easy to slip into the convenient "Euro-centric" categories of conventional political analysis. Take, for instance, the idea that Muslim fraternal unity links the different groups of Central Asia against Moscow. This proposition was widely accepted among Western students of Soviet Central Asia. It encouraged us to expect the continuing rise of separatist sentiment within Central Asia. During the first five years of perestroika, however, the contestation between Uzbekistan and Moscow was less intense than the contestation among the groups of Uzbekistan. Moreover, as the outcome of the national referendum on the union of March 1991 demonstrated, the support among Uzbekistan citizens for the cohesiveness of the Soviet federal union far exceeded the support for the union, for instance, among Muscovites.

The third reason that this guiding premise is important is that it calls attention to the fact that the complex groups of Uzbekistan intereact as *coalitions* rather than as nations as such. Expectations of strong "pan-Turkic nationalist" sentiment led us to expect not only the rise of separatism but also that differences among the ethnic groups of Uzbekistan were less salient than differences between Europeans and Central Asians. However, with the erosion of party unity, central control, and the anti-Moscow coalition among Central Asia's native groups, the emergence of differences among the groups quickly transformed the political landscape in Uzbekistan in ways not expected by many Western scholars and analysts. The only way to interpret the dynamics of nationalism in Central Asia is to recognize that "national identity" of the groups in Central Asia is qualitatively different than it is, for instance, for Europeans.

National identity in Central Asia appears to have a paradoxical character to it because it seems to be both stronger in some respects and weaker in other respects than the national identity of Europeans. In some respects it is correct to conclude that national identity in Uzbekistan in recent years has been strong. The sense of belongingness to an ethnic collectivity – a "nation" – in Uzbekistan not only influenced preferences in terms of life styles, prayers, or traditions; it also influenced calculations about the most vital human quality of all – the expectation of the future. Calculations of an ethnic group's life chances and expectations for the future played a major role in suffusing national identity in Central Asia with a sense of urgency that by some measures exceeded that of any other region in the USSR. The crudest measure of national identification – the propensity toward nationalist-inspired violence – makes this point tragically and bluntly. The Sumgait riots in the Azerbaijan republic in February 1988 took thirty-two lives, while the riots in Uzbekistan's Fergana valley in May and June of 1989 took 112. The ethnic violence in Abkhazia in Georgia in July 1989 took twelve lives, while the violence in the city of Osh in the Fergana valley in June and July of 1990 took 320 lives.

But in other respects the national identity of members of Uzbekistan's groups often continued to be quite weak. In the European borderland regions of the USSR, many national groups have a cohesive identity based on a common language, common traditions, and a common historical experience. There is a clear sense in the minds of group members of the glory and sufferings the national group has endured in the past and, by implication, the promises and challenges that await the group in the future. By way of comparison, Uzbekistan's national groups are much less clearly defined, cohesive, or even self-conscious. The "national groups" involved in the violent clashes over land disputes in Uzbekistan's Andidzhan oblast, for instance, were scarcely able to distinguish themselves from one another. Since the ethnic Kyrgyz which clashed with ethnic Uzbeks were not physically distinguishable from one another and spoke languages that were closely related, many of the rioting youths donned red or black armbands to distinguish their side from the other side in the fracas. The arm bands offered testimony to the fact that in this area of the world national identity is both extraordinarily intense and difficult to define. It is most useful, therefore, to view national identity not as some essential quality of the groups themselves, but rather to see identity in terms of the consequences that it has for behavior. It is best understood, therefore, as coalition behavior. Coalitions are held together by common purpose, not by essential fraternity. When common purposes change – as they did in Central Asia during the past five years with the weakening of the control of the center – the coalitions themselves begin to change.

Drawing attention to the fact that *complex groups* interact in terms of *coalitions* in Uzbekistan, this chapter lends an interpretation to recent Uzbekistan politics. The chapter offers answers to four key questions of Uzbekistan politics. First, it describes how different cultural communities and groups play key roles in contemporary Uzbekistan affairs. Second, it analyzes what mechanisms these groups use to influence the political system. Third, it evaluates the relations among the various key groups and between the groups and external actors. Finally, the chapter discusses the implications of this analysis with particular emphasis on the changes that followed the failed political coup of August, 1991. Following the collapse of the central Soviet government economic and political ministries after the attempted coup, the republics – not the central Moscow government – became the key units of Soviet politics. Many of the republics very quickly assumed separate trajectories, revealing long-suppressed internal political agendas.

A typical pattern of group development starts with a common people, united by common traditions, common experiences, a common language and a common vision of the future. Only after a "nation" has come into being – and often only then through the efforts of some heroic statesman, a Napoleon or Bismark – is the nation molded and forged into a sovereign state. In contrast to this typical pattern, Uzbekistan came into being as a "state" before it existed as a nation. Uzbekistan's statehood was created for political purposes by the fledgling Bolshevik regime. The development of a national Uzbek consciousness only came afterward. The principal goal of this article is to suggest the importance of this historical sequence of events for the future of an "independent" Uzbekistan.

Uzbekistan: nation and state

The substance of modern nationhood in Uzbekistan owes much to the historical influence of Marxist ideology on Central Asian political development during the past seven decades. The Marxist interpretation of history stresses that "nations" – the ethnic collectivities of like-minded who see themselves as belonging to the same fraternal community – are little more than a temporary by-product of capitalist economic relations. Among Marxists, Lenin in particular emphasized that nations were transitional social formations. Lenin the theoretician was convinced that nations would eventually lose their importance at the same time that class consciousness among the workers increased. But Lenin the tactician also realized that nationalism had a great appeal in the popular psychology. To harness this popular appeal, Lenin agreed to the idea of granting national groups "autonomy," "self-government" and "national statehood" within the new socialist order that he established after the Russian revolution. Lenin's plan was to recognize nations by granting them federal rights within the Soviet system of government.[4] Hence the emergence of the principle of "national-statehood" (*natsional'naia gosudarstvennost'*). This principle lies at the foundation of the Soviet state Lenin designed, despite the fact that for theoretical reasons Lenin had always been antagonistic to federal solutions.

Lenin's tactical compromise was successful in many parts of what later became the Soviet Union, for it enabled him to attract the support of nationalist groups to the aims of the Revolution. In Central Asia, however, nations, and thus nationalism, did not exist. No working class existed. The political institutions that existed were subordinated to the Khanates rather than to institutions of a popularly-based republic. The intellectuals drew most of their inspiration from Koranic teachings. The peasants tended to identify with a particular tribe, valley or oasis rather than with some large national group.

In an effort to make reality conform to the principles of the ideology, Soviet policy in Central Asia embarked upon the creation of nations. National categories would be created, it was reasoned, and national groups would emerge to fill these categories. The borders of the Central Asian republics, on the basis of Marxist ideological presuppositions, were artificially imposed during the early years of Soviet power. At the turn of the century, the political map of Central Asia had been divided into three major Khanates, each one of which was associated with oasis and river agriculture: Kokand, Khiva, and Bukhara. The golden days of prosperity associated with the ancient Central Asian "Silk Road" had long since faded. Gone too was the mythic age of enlightened rule by benign despots. The Emirs governed as unenlightened but all-powerful petty tyrants. The political landscape was dominated by struggles between the Emirs of Bukhara and Khorezm, among the feuding local "revolutionary" factions, and among the internally divided Russian settler population.[5] The territorial borders of these oasis societies were challenged by the influence of the Tsarist government as it expanded into Central Asia in the competition with the British empire over regional influence in the heart of Asia. What the British and Russian troops encountered was groups of sedentary peoples, who called themselves "sarts" along the oases valleys and nomads in hills and deserts. The sarts later became known as the Uzbeks and the nomads as the Turkmen, Karakalpak or Karakyrgyz.

Now, with the coming of the new ideology, a major goal was to create the appropriate "states" for Central Asia. At first, Moscow, absorbed by the Civil War, could do little in Central Asia. By the spring of 1920, Moscow's attention returned to Central Asia. A plan for redistricting was worked out by the "Turkcommission." Lenin reviewed the Turkcommission's report and concluded that the "political map" of Turkestan needed to be redrawn to contain three primary units, "Uzbekia, Kirgizia and Turkmenia."[6] Lenin thought it necessary, as well, to "specify in a detailed fashion how these three would be combined into one group."[7]

The First Congress of Soviets, meeting in Moscow in December 1922, adopted the Union Treaty. The Treaty recognized the Turkestan Autonomous Soviet Republic as a part of the RSFSR, one of the four original republics of the Soviet Union.[8] The Bukharan Peoples' Republic and the

Khorezm Peoples' Republic were both still outside of the union, ostensibly because they were not "socialist."[9] They were soon to be brought inside the socialist structure. As two Central Asian writers assert, Lenin and the other communists "never considered the Bukharan and Khorezm Peoples' Republics to be permanent government structures for the peoples of Central Asia."[10]

In 1924, Moscow's attention returned to the subject of redistricting in Central Asia. A major land reform was enacted.[11] A number of party meetings raised the issue of the optimal design. An idea surfaced that there should be a "Central Asian Federation" consisting of Kyrgyz, Uzbek, and Turkmen republics as well as Karakirgiz (Kyrgyz)[12] and Tajik autonomous oblasts.[13] On June 12, 1924 the RCP(b) CC Politburo issued a resolution "On the National Redistricting of the Republics of Central Asia." According to two notable Uzbekistan scholars, the criteria for redistricting included: consideration of the local ethnic make up; irrigation district management authority; economic specialization of the regions; the suitability of urban areas for the management of agricultural areas; and the distribution of the ethnic groups.[14] A resolution passed at the October 27, 1924 meeting of the Central Executive Committee of the USSR provided for the redivision of the Turkestan ASSR according to the "principle of self-determination of nationalities" into: the Uzbek Soviet Socialist Republic (within which was included the Tajik Autonomous Soviet Socialist Republic); the Turkmen Soviet Socialist Republic; the Karakyrgyz Autonomous Oblast (incorporated into the RSFSR); and the Kyrgyz Autonomous Soviet Socialist Republic (also incorporated into the RSFSR).[15] The new Uzbek government formalized the arrangement on December 5, 1924, with the passage of a "Declaration of the Revolutionary Committee of the Uzbek Republic."[16] A number of major border changes affecting the Uzbek republic followed, but the principle of the ethnic Uzbek control of Uzbekistan was firmly established at this point.[17]

The First Congress of Soviets of the Uzbek SSR, in February 1925, passed a "Declaration on the formation of the Uzbek Soviet Socialist Republic," chose a Central Executive Committee, and approved the Council of Peoples Commissars for the Uzbek Republic. On May 13, 1925, the Third Congress of Soviets of the USSR officially incorporated the Uzbek and Turkmen republics into the USSR, bringing the number of republics in the union to six. At this point, the redistricting was technically completed. By 1926, the Uzbek SSR (not including the area that later became Tajikistan) had a population of 5,272,800, about 66 percent of whom were ethnic Uzbeks.[18]

Over the years of Soviet power, because of party control, the artificiality of the borders, and the fact that most decisions, ultimately, rested on the shoulders of someone in Moscow rather than someone in the provinces, the inter-republican and inter-ethnic group borders in Central Asia had little significance. As the president of Uzbekistan, Islam Kärimav, recently lamented "During all the years of Soviet power, Uzbekistan, in reality, was not a state."[19]

Control over political institutions

Although the republican borders and intra-republican delineations (such as the Karakalpak Autonomous Republic) were artificial creations and enjoyed none of the "national-statehood" supposedly guaranteed them in successive Soviet constitutions, the administrative jurisdictions that these borders introduced did eventually gather a great deal of importance. Political boundaries do not only represent territorial divisions on a map, they also represent structures of political authority and systems of reciprocal exchange. Uzbekistan's political boundaries became the basis for formal political institutions. These formal political institutions were originally in the hands of Moscow's power brokers. But, over the years of Soviet power, such institutions as the local party organizations, the economic ministries and the related production agencies, the Uzbek cultural and scientific establishments, the agricultural organizations, the construction organizations and the educational institutions increasingly were captured by local interests. With the advent of perestroika and political reform at the center, the formal Central Asian political borders have acquired a real significance.

The core of Uzbekistan's politics today is the contestation for the control of these institutions by different groups. How have these groups competed in the past to control resources? Given the agricultural orientation of the Uzbekistan economy, the key resource was control over land. Ethnic Uzbeks fared very well in the division of land in the original districting of Central Asia. They captured the most agriculturally productive region in Central Asia, the Fergana valley. In addition, they gained the watersheds and the associated irrigated agricultural areas of the Chirchik river (which runs through Tashkent), the Zerafshan river (which runs through both Samarkand and Bukhara), and the Surkhan-Doria (a major feeder of the Ama-Doria).

The Uzbeks did not succeed in claiming the main water course of the Ama-Doria downstream from the southern Soviet border and upstream from Urgench. This area went to the Turkmen. The Uzbeks later claimed the fertile Khivan oasis areas around Urgench, even though this area was landlocked within the area acknowledged to belong to the Karakalpak. The Kazakhs received the valuable agricultural lands along the Syr-Doria below Chardara. The Russians had relatively close relations with the Kazakhs. The Russians, therefore, may have insisted that the lower Sir-Doria valley not be considered within the core of Central Asia. The big losers in the division were the Tajiks and Kyrgyz. The Tajiks

Table 14.1. *National composition of Uzbekistan, 1989 (principal nationality groups)*

		percent of total
Total	19,810,077	
Uzbek	14,142,475	71.00
Russian	1,653,478	8.30
Tajik	933,560	4.70
Kazakh	808,227	4.00
Tatar	467,829	2.30
Karakalpak	411,878	2.00
Kyrgyz	174,907	0.80
Ukrainian	153,197	0.70
Turkmen	121,578	0.60
Jew	65,493	0.03
Armenian	50,537	0.02
Azerbaijan	44,410	0.02

Source: *Pravda Vostoka*, June 15, 1990, p. 3.

received national statehood in the form of an autonomous republic in the far south. But the large numbers within Uzbekistan received little. The Kyrgyz were given the grazing lands but gained little of the prime agricultural land of the Fergana valley.

Early Moscow policy emphasized "korenizatsiia" (nativization) of cadres. The motivation of this policy was the assumption by Moscow officials that the local administration needed local support which could most easily come from local leaders who were recognized as representing the interests of the locals. In Uzbekistan this policy came by 1928 to be identified as "Uzbekizatsiia" although this was more a slogan than a policy.[20] The fact remains, however, that the Turkic-speaking Uzbek majority managed to use nativization to gain a privileged position within the republic. The power establishment of the Khiva oasis in the Fergana valley was relegated to a provincial status as was the Persian-speaking power establishment of the Samarkand and Bukhara oases. Over the years, the Uzbek majority increased their share of the minority group by gradually accumulating the Turkic-speaking tribal groups and assimilating them in the Uzbek "nation." By the early 1990s, the Uzbeks comprised more than 70 percent of the Uzbekistan population.

At the commanding heights of Uzbekistan's leadership, "nativization" meant that natives would rule, but they would do so in accordance with Moscow's designs. This implied a certain contract between the local officials and their Moscow patrons. The first class of Central Asian surrogate leaders who adopted this contract were men like Akmal Ikramov who became the Uzbek party first secretary and Faizulla Khodzhaev who became the Uzbek republic's first prime minister.[21] Both men cooperated with Moscow in part from ideological commitment and in part from self-interest. The careers of both men ended tragically in the purges of 1937. Both have since been rehabilitated. This generation of initial leaders was succeeded mainly by appointees from the center. During the Second World War, a substantial Slavic immigration took place as war industries were transported to Central Asia. Slavs assumed many of the key administrative and political posts during this period. The postwar generation saw a reestablishment of local leadership. A rapid series of leaders in Uzbekistan followed the accession to power of Nikita Khrushchev. Then first secretary of the Communist Party of Uzbekistan, Amin Irmatovich Niyazov, was demoted in December, 1955, just months after Khrushchev became first secretary of the CPSU. Niyazov was transferred to a minor republican ministry in Uzbekistan.[22] His replacement, Nuriddin Akramovich Muk-hiddinov, who was Chairman of the Uzbekistan Council of Ministers under Niyazov, served for two years as Secretary before being brought to Moscow as a Secretary and member of the Presidium of the CPSU Central Committee, where he remained until the XXII CPSU Congress in 1961. His successor, Sabir Kamalovich Kamalov, had served as Chairman of the Uzbekistan Council of Ministers before being appointed first secretary of the CPUz late in December, 1957. Kamalov's tenure as CPUz First Secretary lasted just over a year. He was ousted from his party post in March, 1959, for "mistakes" in party work.[23] The CPUz first secretary's mantle was then handed to Sharaf Rashidov who retained it until his death in 1983.

Rashidov's death coincided with the accession to power of Yuri Andropov in Moscow. Andropov initiated an anti-corruption campaign throughout the USSR. But the efforts to root out corrupt officials in Central Asia were especially enthusiastic. The personnel changes in Uzbekistan started with investigations into the "cotton affair."[24] As Moscow investigators conducted a routine investigation into embezzlement in Uzbekistan cotton procurement agencies, they discovered what to them seemed a labyrinthine network of political corruption.[25] The campaign that had begun as an effort to catch a few local criminals mushroomed into Central Asia's most extensive political purge. Between 1984 and 1987, some forty of sixty-five party secretaries in UzSSR were replaced.[26] Over 260 new secretaries of city and district party committees were elected. One-third of all the chairmen and vice-chairmen of oblispolkoms were changed. The result of the purge was that an entirely new generation of Central Asian officials was installed. By the late 1980s, Uzbekistan's managerial elite was the youngest in the union; some 45 percent of party comittee secretaries were under forty. Eventually the most powerful official in Uzbekistan, the

Table 14.2. *Oblasts, UzSSR*

	Territory (sq. km)	Date of formation	Population (1/89)
UzSSR	447.4	1924	19,906,000
Karakalpak ASSR	165.5	1936	1,214,000
Andizhan Ob.	4.2	1941	1,728,000
Bukhara Ob.	143.2	1938	1,141,000
Dzhizak Ob.	20.5	1973	(discontinued)
Kashkadarin Ob.	28.4	1964	1,594,000
Namangan Ob.	7.9	1967	1,475,000
Navoi Ob.		1982	(discontinued)
Samarkand Ob.	24.5	1938	2,778,000
Surkhandarin Ob.	20.8	1941	1,255,000
Syrdaryn Ob.	5.1	1963	1,316,000
Tashkent Ob.	15.6	1938	2,157,000
Fergana Ob.	7.1	1938	2,153,000
Khorezm Ob.	4.5	1938	1,016,000

Source: Narodnoe khoziastvo Uzbekskoi SSR, 1979 (Tashkent: Statistika, 1980), p. 6; *Ezhegodnik, Bol'shaia Sovetskaia Entsiklopedia* (Moscow: BSE, 1988); *Pravda Vostoka*, March 29, 1989.

Uzbek Communist Party first secretary, Inomzhon Usmankhodzhaev, was removed by the scandal. Eventually, he was sentenced to twelve years in jail.

The "cotton affair" not only resulted in death sentences for local Central Asian kingpins, but implicated numerous local and regional officials in a web of political corruption leading from the Central Asian cotton plantations to the heights of political power in Moscow. Among those toppled by the affair were Nikolai Shchelokov, a former Minister of Internal Affairs and his first deputy, Yuri Churbanov, a son-in-law of the late Leonid Brezhnev. The notoriety surrounding the trial made the two special investigators who broke the case popular heroes in Russia.[27] It also made them among the most hated figures among Central Asian circles where the anti-crime campaign was seen as an ethnic Russian backlash against local Central Asian gains.

As perestroika got underway in Uzbekistan then, the internal political situation was "tense." The native party and administrative apparatus had just suffered the worst personnel purge in Uzbekistan's history. There was gathering public anxiety over declining standards of living in the republic. There were bitter conflicts between Moscow administrative officials – both party and government – and the local officials in Uzbekistan.[28] Moscow officials saw the republic of Uzbekistan as the most economically inefficient, difficult to manage, and politically corrupt of the Soviet republics. Uzbekistan officials saw the Moscow administrative elite as having reneged on promises to aid the republic through changes in water policy, assistance for the unemployed, measures to alleviate ecological disasters, and increases in prices for agricultural goods and primary commodities.

A turning point was the first USSR Congress of Peoples' Deputies in the spring of 1989. Uzbek officials spoke out publicly, levelling forthright criticism at the center. The Deputies from UzSSR voiced criticism of policies toward the republic, focusing on the regionalization of the Central Asian economy. Rafik Nishanov decried the "monstrous" cotton monoculture of the region as having brought "Uzbekistan not only to an economic standstill, but produced mass ecological decay and mass illness."[29] Tulepbergen Kaipbergenov bemoaned the state of the Aral Sea, saying that his presentation was "not to cry over the Aral; the Aral needs water, not tears."[30] Kaiperbegenov called for a reduction of the land sown to cotton and pleaded that the Aral Sea be proclaimed an "ecological disaster" zone.

Political reform in Moscow meant a political reform in Uzbekistan as well. The last hurried session of the old Uzbek republic Supreme Soviet, meeting for only two days, passed a series of amendments and decrees that paralleled the changes in the USSR electoral changes that were passed in December 1988. New draft elections laws, one for republican elections and one for local elections, were introduced and then, following a brief discussion period, were spirited through the Uzbek Supreme Soviet on October 20, 1989. The next day a new language law naming Uzbek as the government language of the republic was passed.[31] The last decrees issued by the departing parliament were the resolutions establishing the timing of the republican and local elections.[32] Both the republican and local elections were set for the same day, February 18, 1990. The representation ratio was set at one deputy for each 19,900 voters.

The most important aspect of the election in the Uzbek republic was the nomination process. It is also the aspect of the election on which we have the least reliable information. Individuals only had the right to nominate candidates from within recognized organizations or institutions. Some groups, for instance the "informals" (*neformaly*), were thereby effectively excluded from participation. The voter turnout in the general election was high, especially in the rural areas.[33] 9,385,740 people, or 93.5 percent of the eligible voters, cast ballots.[34] The initial round of voting on February 18, 1990, selected 368 deputies. In the first election, 386 of the districts filled their seats.[35] These deputies' names were printed in *Pravda Vostoka* on February 22 and 23, 1990.

By the time the new Supreme Soviet convened its first session on March 24, 1990, only the first and second round of elections had been completed.[36] According to the public anouncements, 463 of the deputies were sworn in at the new session.[37]

Table 14.3. *Uzbek Soviet Socialist Republic Peoples' Deputies, February 18, 1990, first ballot*

500	electoral districts
174	districts had only a single candidate
177	district had two candidates
149	districts had three or more candidates
1,094	candidates altogether
93.5	percent of voters participating
386	deputies chosen

The republican and local elections in the Uzbek republic changed the landscape of local politics. Groups that had previously lobbied through informal networks now found that taking their message to the public was another method of advancement. However, it is not clear that the substance of local politics changed appreciably or quickly with this political reform.

One good example of the continuity in Uzbekistan politics is the outcome of the all-union referendum on whether to retain the USSR in the form of a "renewed union of sovereign states." During the campaign period, the idea of staying with the union received broad support from

Table 14.4. *Results of the USSR federal referendum within the Uzbek Soviet Socialist Republic*

	Registered voters	% "for"	% "against"
Uzbek SSR	10,287,938	93.7	
Karakalpak ASSR	584,208	97.6	1.8
Andizhan	903,734	94.0	4.6
Bukhara	845,237	96.1	3.1
Dzhizak	360,035	94.8	4.3
Kashkadarin	760,051	94.6	4.2
Namangan	756,947	91.7	6.9
Samarkand	1,114,339	93.5	5.4
Surkhandar	602,816	97.6	1.8
Syrdar	282,928	95.4	3.9
Tashkent	1,144,617	92.8	6.0
Fergana	1,130,981	94.3	3.5
Khorezm	500,199	97.1	2.1
Tashkent City	1,273,846	88.1	10.5

Source: *Savet Uzbekistani*, March 21, 1991.

such groups as the Uzbekistan republican Soviet of Women and many Moslem clerics. Both before and after the referendum, the overwhelming majority of local economists and technical specialists spoke in favor of retaining the Union.[38] In the referendum itself, Uzbek voters virtually unanimously voted in favor of retention of the union.[39]

If the results of the referendum came as a surprise to many who expected more secessionist sentiment from Central Asian voters, this should serve as an indication that we need to explore the reasons for apparent support for the Soviet regime within Uzbekistan. One approach to this question is to analyze the situation in terms of the coalitions of local groups.

Uzbeks, "Turkestanis" and Slavs

The increased nationality tensions in Uzbekistan moved the party authorities to take exceptional measures to see how they had got out of step with social and political processes. In 1990, the Communist Party of Uzbekistan organized a "man on the street" conference to put questions about nationality problems to typical Central Asian citizens. Asked to respond to the question what accounts for the increasing inter-ethnic tension, a welder from Tashkent responded that the differences in the occupations of the various national groups accounted for much of the animosity. V.V. Tregubov, (a Russian), claimed that the local (native) population worked mainly in commerce and trade. In Uzbekistan, Tregubov said, the working class was worse off than the agrarian class. The blue collar workers – the supposed backbone of the Soviet state's popular support – was suffering more than the peasants and "pre-socialist" workers of the Central Asian fields. He added that it was painful to hear people say to him as a Russian: "This is our republic, our language, and all outsiders should just leave."[40] Tregubov's comments touch on three key points about inter-ethnic relations in Uzbekistan: (1) how the Uzbeks have occupied a socio-occupational niche; (2) how the Uzbeks have treated other national groups in Uzbekistan; and (3) how the Russians have fared during the transition to local control initiated by perestroika.

The cotton scandal offers an illustration into how the local populace works within relatively closed and informal authority structures. Local farmers and mid-level managers began to seek ways of finessing the demands of the central planners. They began to embezzle from the cotton procurement agencies by reporting exaggerated or wholly fictitious cotton deliveries. Since every inflated figure was then passed on to the next official in the production and transportation cycle, great numbers of officials were drawn into the network of collusion. While some of the over-reporting was attributed to such things as spoilage and theft, much of it could only be covered up if it was condoned by local officials. In the words of one local official in Central Asia, "the Sovkhoz deceived the *raion*, the *raion* deceived the *oblast*, the *oblast* deceived the republic, and the republic tricked the whole government."[41] The network of deception reached from low-level farm managers to the highest level officials in the political and economic organizations throughout Central Asia. As the network of collusion spread, officials in the cotton textile processing centers of Ivanovo and Moscow were drawn into the network.

One of the most important explanations for the ability of one group to dominate another is that dense personal networks, not the formalized rules and regulations of the Soviet bureaucracy, are what determines outcomes in Uzbekistan. These personal networks are manifested in clan-type relations among groups with familial ties or at least something that they can claim is family resemblance. Ascriptive rather than meritocratic criteria serve to determine whether a bargain is struck, a job is given, or a promotion is gained. These dense personal networks involve the creation and maintenance of communication hierarchies which are separate from the formal and official lines of communication. Under such circumstances, common language, tradition, and cultural practices become the basic currency of social communication and economic advancement. The majority group naturally tends, under these circumstances, to attract the majority of resources to its sphere of activity. In Uzbekistan, 37 percent of the republic's industrial production is concentrated in the traditional stronghold of the Uzbeks, the Tashkent oblast. Yet Tashkent oblast only occupies 5 percent of the territory of the republic and houses only 27 percent of the republic's population.

The other minorities encounter socio-occupational grading as a result of some concentration of opportunity, even when no deliberate discrimination is involved. Moreover, many of the minority groups are essentially migrants to the area. These groups include the Meskhetian-Turks from Georgia, the Tatars from the Crimea, the Germans from the Volga region, the Koreans from the Soviet Far East, and the Finns from Karelia.

One way for a minority group member to avoid the trap of being a second class citizen is to ensure that the life chances of one's minority group are not diminished because of cultural and linguistic isolation. In the USSR, groups would try to maintain their language and traditions through gaining government allocations to pay for education, facilities, and cultural maintenance. Since, until recently, the only way to concentrate the resources necessary for cultural maintenance was to garner government support, self-determination in the restricted sense of maintaining cultural autonomy meant that the government officially recognize a group and deliberately set out to protect its interests. Thus the process of cultural maintenance was a highly politicized one. Even though the situation is changing with the on-going process of *razgosudarstvlenie* (de-governmentalization), groups still lobby to protect themselves within the traditional categories.[42] The Karakalpaks, for instance, decided to follow the example set by many other "national-territorial" groups in the USSR by proclaiming late in 1990 the sovereignty of the Karakalpak Autonomous Soviet Socialist Republic.[43]

One of the most bitter topics of inter-group relations is the question of the role of the former colonial "occupiers" – the Russian-speaking population. Many Uzbeks feel that the time has come that the traditional despoilers of their native lands be repaid by being asked to leave or make restitution.[44] In contrast, many Russian-speakers see the old pro-imperial order as their only protection. Fear for the future is convincing many of them to leave Uzbekistan.[45] 1990 was a year of debate among many Russians whether the time had come for a return to the "Russian homeland."[46]

The Russian-speaking population tends to be concentrated in the administrative and industrial occupational sectors. Many of these jobs are not sought after by Central Asian natives, and thus the occupation competition does not bring the groups into conflict. Furthermore, there is a sense, at least among Central Asia's native elite, that the technical specialists from the European USSR are valuable to Uzbekistan. The Uzbek political commentator Timur Pulatov even argued in 1990 that, if the trend were not reversed, in two to three years the technologically advanced production sectors in Central Asia would experience a "catastrophic shortage of technological specialists," leading to reduced commercial activity, a growth of poverty, and ultimately, to the "Angolicization" of the Central Asian economy.[47]

The difficult situation of the Russian-speaking population in Uzbekistan was underscored late in 1989 with the passage of the new law on the official language in Uzbekistan. Article 5, which calls for a transition from Russian to Turkic, is not to come into effect for eight years. Not everyone thinks that the transition of a native language standard will be damaging to the position of the Russians. As one commentator noted, when the local groups have returned to their native languages they will tend to be separated from one another. "The Russian-speaking population will strengthen their position because the means of communication between different speaking republics naturally will be Russian."[48] And there are good reasons to believe that it may take much longer than that to result in substantial change. Language use patterns are not easily determined by legislative acts. Currently, instruction is conducted in a variety of languages in Uzbekistan; not only Uzbek but also Russian, Karakalpak, Tajik, Turkmen, Kyrgyz and Kazakh are taught in schools located in areas in which there are compact populations of these groups. In addition, according to some reports, the emphasis on some minority languages is increasing; in 1988–1989 academic year Tatar was taught in sixty schools, by 1989–1990 it was taught in seventy-six. Korean was taught only in four schools in 1988–1989; the following year it was taught in seventeen.[49]

Large numbers of the Russian-speaking population began leaving the Central Asian republics after the nationalist-inspired riots in the city of Fegrana in summer, 1989, in Dushanbe in February, 1990, and in Osh in summer, 1990. The psychological atmosphere of uncertainty was so great that many Russians, when confronted with the new language law, with what they view as systematic discrimination in employment, and with the collapse of Moscow's ability (or even willingness) to aid them in the event of local hostilities, simply have chosen to leave. Islam Kärimav appealed for Russians not to leave. Many intellectuals have issued public appeals.[50] The *Birlik* organization and other public organizations in Uzbekistan have appealed for people not to leave. Perhaps the most ironic and cruel aspect of the situation is that many of the Russian-speaking members of the population of Uzbekistan were born there and, were it not for the current political climate, would not seriously entertain moving back north to Russia. Under international law, birth in a country typically confers citizenship. But, for the time being, the situation in Uzbekistan does not appear to be subject either to domestic or international law.

Uzbekistan and the "Union"

On a more formal level, the relations among the groups of Central Asia have tended, under the influence of the diminishing power of the center, to become much more contractual in nature. The initiatives of Kazakhstan's adroit political leader, Nursultan Nazarbaev, encouraged the conclusion of a series of bilateral and multilateral agreements among the Central Asian republics. The most important was the "Announcement of the Leaders of the Uzbek, Kazakh, Kyrgyz, Tajik and Turkmen SSRs" which followed the leaders' summit in the summer of 1990.[51] The "Announcement," which essentially affirmed that Central Asia was one cultural unit but many political entities, was followed by a series of implementing decrees and agreements.[52] In their response to the weakening of the center, then, the Central Asians initially drew close to one another, acting as a bloc in most deliberations.

Kazakhstan President Nursultan Nazarbaev had gone on record early as supporting the new Union Treaty as a way of attaining "horizontal connections" among the republics. This, he argued, would strengthen the economic functioning without return to the old command system. Uzbekistan's President, Islam Kärimav, seemed to play little brother to Nazarbaev's efforts. Early opposition came not from the Central Asian delegations but from the machinations of the Russian delegation and from the determination of the Baltic delegations to avoid the restoration of the old system at all costs.

In the spring of 1990 a committee was established to draft the new Union Treaty.[53] Gorbachev's goal for this first version of the treaty was to combine the self-sufficiency, independence and sovereignty of the republics with an effective center. He maintained that the union should be held together by "mutually advantageous economic relations in an all-union market." Gorbachev wanted to maintain eight key policy spheres under the control of the central government: (1) defense and state security; (2) foreign policy, trade, and customs; (3) human rights; (4) a unified monetary policy, prices, and standards; (5) energy supplies; (6) transportation; (7) environmental regulation; and (8) scientific and technical progress.[54] He underscored the importance of maintaining some key all-union economic institutions, in particular the concept of a "single economic field."[55] The draft was approved by the USSR Parliament's upper house, the USSR Supreme Soviet, on December 3, 1990, and was introduced into the lower house, the Congress of People's Deputies, at the December 17, 1990, opening session. Latvia's delegation refused to attend the Congress. Estonia's delegation attended, but marched out in protest on the first day.

Anticipating a renegotiation of the basic contract, all of the republics – including the Central Asian republics, still acting basically as a bloc – quickly reformulated their negotiating positions in the form of declarations of sovereignty. By the end of 1990, each of the Soviet republics had passed legislation on sovereignty. The provisions of the declarations varied widely. For instance, the resolution of the Russian republic, adopted on June 11, 1990, allowed the center to retain control of defense, state security, aviation, communication, transportation, energy, and space. Other areas of policy were retained by the republic. In contrast, the Ukrainian declaration, adopted on July 15, 1990, went further in asserting the right to establish an independent Ukrainian militia and security force.

In the face of these centrifugal pressures, Gorbachev countered with the promotion of a new contract, one which gave substantially more responsibility to the republics. The draft of the treaty was negotiated in the spring of 1991. Nine republics agreed to sign the treaty. Since the "center" – that is, the Moscow government – was also a key player, the agreement was referred to as the "Nine-plus-One" agreement. Uzbekistan joined the other republics of Central Asia in the "Nine Plus One" agreement signed in Moscow on April 23, 1991.[56] The agreement solidified support for the retention of the Union even given the unwillingness of Latvia, Lithuania, Estonia, Moldova, Georgia, and Armenia to affirm the Union. The treaty itself was dubbed the "Novo-Ogarev" treaty, bearing the name of Gorbachev's private residence in the outskirts of Moscow.

The Novo-Ogarev treaty reduced the role of the Moscow government and included some truly revolutionary propositions. For instance, the document did not recognize the concept of "Union property," assigning all conventions of property ownership to the republics. The treaty limited all-union functions to five areas: (1) defense and state security; (2) defense-related industry; (3) a unified energy system; (4) a single communication system; (5) a single transportation system; (6) and a system of scientific and technical progress and cosmic research. All other functions, including met-allurgy, machine building, industrial equipment production, and agri-culture, were to be returned to the republics. The nine republics gave further support to the economic plan that Gorbachev announced just before meeting with the Western "Group of Seven" economic ministers in July 1991. The Novo-Ogarev document was scheduled to be signed on August 20, 1991 in Moscow. The August *putsch* in Moscow, however, took place on the day before the planned signing ceremony. The political situation changed overnight after the *putsch*. The republics became the key actors in the system.

Immediately following the coup attempt, Boris Yeltsin and Nursultan Nazarbaev joined efforts in urging the establishment of an economic union on the assumption that the political union was too difficult and too conten-tious to negotiate. The announcement of the "High Leaders" of September 2, 1991, outlined the basic objectives of the new agreement.[57] With the idea of an economic association at the forefront, emphasis shifted quickly away from the idea of political union to the concept of a minimal economic community. On October 2, 1991, negotiations began in Alma-Ata, at the invitation of the Nazarbaev. The key issues of negotiation were: (1) the currency and banking system; (2) the management of the existing, centra-lized economic infrastructures; (3) the restoration of trade and commercial connections between enterprises; (4) improving public attitudes and encouraging work habits and labor discipline; and (5) establishing unified external customs arrangements. Important questions remained unad-dressed; for instance, issues of the graduated introduction of market prices, the commercialization of economic relations for enterprises on different republics' territory, the deficits of the republican budgets, maintenance of the social welfare systems, and the problem of the interruption of trans-shipment of goods through republican territory were simply put off in the haste to affirm some economic continuity. The new "Treaty of Economic Association" was signed on October 18, 1991.[58] All of the Central Asian Muslim republics signed the agreement.[59]

Uzbekistan and "Turkestan"

Given the collapse of the Moscow government, Uzbekistan moved quickly to reconfigure its internal political structures. After a period of hesitation on whether to support the GKPCh (the coup committee), the Kärimav government began taking steps to consolidate its powers. Kärimav resigned from the CPSU on August 23, 1991. On August 26, 1991, the Ministry of Internal Affairs and the KGB were both nationalized and legally subordinated to the Uzbekistan President. The property of the Uzbek Communist Party was nationalized on August 30, 1991. The Uzbek party itself changed its form, becoming officially the People's Democratic Party of Uzbekistan in September 1991. And the republic was declared an independent and sovereign state on September 1, 1991. On September 7, Kärimav signed a decree ordering the creation of a national defense force for the country. The sequence of events was so swift and sure that it surprised many Russians, particularly those in Moscow, who saw Uzbekistan as rapidly transforming itself from the most conventional of republics into a "loose caboose."[60]

Yet the speed and drama of Uzbekistan's transformation must be measured in terms of the problems it is facing. Uzbekistan finds itself in a difficult position principally for three reasons: the nature of the republic's economy; the transboundary problems with its immediate neighbors; and the emerging pressures of the post-Soviet political configuration.

Uzbekistan's economic development has been shaped by Moscow's assumption that regional specialization was required for achieving economies of scale. Moscow's goal in economic development policy, accordingly, was to emphasize the role of Uzbekistan as a primary commodity supplier.[61] The collapse of the Soviet economy, therefore, left Uzbekistan in a precarious position. In June, 1990, the Uzbek republic passed a law "On the formation of a Government Committee of the Uzbek SSR on foreign trade and external contacts."[62] The law asserted the republic's right to conduct an independent foreign economic policy. But the law also emphasized the role of the Uzbek government in coordinating all economic, commercial and scientific-technical relations with foreign countries. The law was essentially designed to create an export-led "para-statal" organization to promote trade. If Uzbekistan, and more generally, all of the Central Asian republics have not been very successful in promoting development strategies, it is largely because of a lack of business expertise and the difficulty the republics have maintaining access to large Middle Eastern, European, and Pacific Rim markets.

The collapse of the Soviet commercial infrastructure had two immediate results in Uzbekistan. First, it deprived the Uzbeks of markets for Uzbekistan's goods. In the long run, this is to be welcomed, but in the short run it is highly destructive. Uzbekistan retaliated quickly. Government instructions were reportedly circulated to the cotton ginning stations in early October, 1991, to prohibit shipments of cotton fiber to Russia.[63] The central collapse also cut Uzbekistan off from traditional suppliers. Since Uzbekistan cannot quickly substitute for the wide range of commodities and manufactured goods that were provided by the northern republics of the USSR, Uzbekistan found itself facing a hard currency crisis. Apparently without a formal announcement, Uzbekistan seized control of the republic's gold mining enterprises in early November, 1991, in an effort to begin to generate its own hard currency.[64]

Uzbekistan has a variety of common interests with its immediate neighbors, but it also has many grounds for disagreement. To date, the Central Asian efforts to resolve these disagreements have also resulted more in "joint statements" than in joint deeds. For instance, the agreement between the Uzbek and Kyrgyz republic was signed on March 15, 1991 in Osh, the site of violent riots between armed gangs from the two ethnic groups, to under-score the new spirit of cooperation between the two peoples.[65] Yet the responsibilities for promoting "internationalism" and ethnic mutual understanding devolve directly to the republic and not to any inter-republi-can institution. Similarly, Uzbekistan concluded an agreement with its southern neighbor, Turkmenistan, resulting in a commercial treaty and a statement, at least in principle, of the need to resolve water and land con-flicts along the republics' lengthy common border.[66]

It is finding solutions to these "common problems" that will no doubt be the biggest challenge for Uzbekistan and its neighbors. Despite all the cultural similarities of the Central Asian states, despite all of the formal agreements that have been reached, and despite the clear common advan-tage in solving the area's transnational problems, many old conflicts have not only gone unresolved but have acquired a new urgency given the increase in republic authority and the diminished ability of the center to act as a mediating force. Two of the transborder problems are particularly acute. The first is the issue of the legitimacy of existing territorial frontiers. The second is the question of the use of the region's natural resources.

Territorial disputes have long been a source of problems among the Uzbeks and other groups of Central Asia. Today, many of these disputes have become grounds for "secessionist" and "irridentist" sentiment within Central Asia. For instance, there is currently strong and potentially powerful sentiment in favor of the following: secession of Karakalpakia from Uzbekistan;[67] separation of a part of the Mangyshlak oblast of Kazakhstan and its addition to Turkmenia; separation of the part of the Tashauz and Chardzhua oblasts on the Amu-daria from Turkmenia and their addition to Uzbekistan; separation of the northern part of the Bukhara oblast from Uzbekistan and its addition to Karakalpakia; separa-tion of the south-eastern part of Karakalpakia and its addition to the Khorezm oblast of Uzbekistan; the separation of the southern part of the Chimkent oblast of Kazakhstan and its addition to Uzbekistan; the separation of the Zeravshan valley of Uzbekistan and its addition to Tajikistan; and separation of the Surkhandarin valley of Uzbekistan and its addition to Tajikistan.

These irridentist problems are intensified by the competition for resources and the artificiality of the borders. A good example is the Khorezm oasis. The oasis had been a single oasis under one government for hundreds of years. Within the Soviet period, it was broken up between Karakalpak ASSR, Khorezm oblast of Uzbekistan, and the Tashauz oblast of Turkmenistan. The regions are physically quite close. The distance between the administrative centers of the area is negligible. From Urgench to Tashauz is seventy kilometers. From Urgench to Nukus is 150 kilometers. From Tashauz to Nukus is ninety kilometers. Since, for a long time republican borders were not determinative, the splitting up of the old oasis did not have a great deal of significance. Within the new-found authority of the republican legislatures to exert final authority upon their territory, however, the jurisdictions are suddenly extremely important. To achieve "self-sufficiency," each of the republics now is attempting to develop its own water management system. As a consequence, the republics are triplicating the water and electrical system of the area so that they do not have to be the victim of what one critic called the "administrative-bureaucratic ambitions" of the other governments.[68]

The solution to the problems of economic regionalization, transborder conflict, and inter-ethnic strife is seen, in the eyes of some Central Asians, in the formation of an all-embracing political concept – the creation of a greater Turkestan. This idea has been around for a long time, but only in 1991 was the idea openly discussed as a political possibility. As one *Nezavisimaia gazeta* reporter put it, "the question of the creation of a union of the five Central Asian republics was swirling around the halls of the capitals of the republics" during the July 1991 meeting of the Presidents.[69] After the coup attempt, the feeling intensified. As Goga A. Khidoiatov, a historian at Tashkent State University observed in October, 1991, "The country we call the Soviet Union is gone. I dream to live in a time that we will form a United States of Asia."[70] But the seriousness of a political union has to be understood in terms of a very complex situation. A founding leader of the Uzbekistan *Birlik* informal movement and a leader of the opposition in Uzbekistan's parliament, Muhammad Salih, expressed the yearnings for the near mythical idea of Turkestan unity, saying[71]

> Ten years ago I spoke out for the unification of Turkestan – I even wrote poems about it – and my position hasn't really changed. The difference is that today I don't speak about a unified Turkestan as a realizable goal. In the future, it might be possible to create a Turkestani federation or confederation based on economic ties . . . Without Kazakhstan we can't live – that much is certain. Kazakhstan also can't live without us, and the same can be said of all the Central Asian republics.

Despite such rhetorical expressions of a yearning for Turkic unity, the real interests of the republics are sure to make such union implausible. There are two reasons for this. One is that, at least for the time being, the logic of the situation in the former USSR favors decentralization. The other is that if the Uzbeks ever took the lead in actively promoting a union of Turkestani people, they could not but be seen by others as seeking regional political hegemony. In other words, such an effort would be easily seen more as a "Greater Uzbekistan" than as a "Greater Turkestan."

"Authoritarian democracy" and modernization in Uzbekistan

Such pressures are surely one reason for the status-quo oriented character of the contemporary Uzbek political order. Under the old order, Uzbekistan was frequently referred to by Russians as a last *"zapovednik kommunizma"* ("communist preserve").[72] The republican-level nationalization of political and economic resources that took place in Uzbekistan immediately following the coup prompted many Russian observers to conclude that a dictatorship had been established in Uzbekistan.[73] Certainly the Uzbek government has been guarded and generally cautious if not adverse to the implementation of Moscow-style reforms. The government's caution stems from three key factors: (1) the traditional political culture in Uzbekistan; (2) the nature of the various political and economic difficulties facing the republic; and (3) the political style of the Kärimav government.

The continuing high profile of the former communist party officials as well as the results of the elections and the union referendum in Uzbekistan give ample evidence that the political culture of Uzbekistan is substantially different from that of the European parts of the Union. The Russians may insist that patterns of "Khanstvo" based upon unquestioning respect for elders, deference to authority, and the perceived "impoliteness" of public criticism make democracy impossible in Uzbekistan.[74] But the style of "authoritarian democracy" that has surfaced in Uzbekistan is definitely different from party-led totalitarianism of the past.

The resurgence of Islamic tradition is also playing an increasingly important and generally conservative role in Uzbekistan's affairs. The Deputy Director of the Spiritual Directorate of Muslims of Central Asia and Kazakhstan, Kazi Zakhidzhan, recently explained the grounds for Soviet patriotism among the Islamic faithful of the Soviet Union.[75] The Mufti of Tashkent, Muhammad Sadiq Yusupav, was elected in 1989 to the USSR Congress of Peoples Deputies. He played a role in restoring calm in Fergana after the riots. The official Islamic establishment also favored the retention of the union during the referendum campaign. Those Islamic organizations which sponsor more rapid change have been isolated by the authorities in Uzbekistan. For instance, the "All-union Islamic Party of Renewal" was allowed to register as a party in Moscow, but the branch in Uzbekistan was declared illegal and its meetings were broken up. The Renewal Party, according to its leaders, urges restraint and the avoidance of violence in disputes involving national differences.[76]

Kärimav's government has acted quietly to restore many of the officials who lost their positions and influence in the purge of the mid-1980s.[77] The initial attempts at rehabilitation were modest.[78] But in 1991 the momentum gained so much steam that there was open discussion of "nostalgia for a strong hand".[79] On the other hand, Kärimav's government acted to energetically exclude competing political groups from gaining influence. The

Birlik movement was allowed to exist, but its efforts met with much more official opposition than informal movements elsewhere in the USSR.[80] One finds openly entertained conclusions such as that of a 1990 sociological survey that "given the growth in the activity of the 'informals' in the national and democratic movements . . . all the official political and social institutions will have to work with them in the future."[81] Still, the government used legislative means and the media to counter the growth of informals. The 1991 law on "informals" was strongly status-quo oriented. It gave legal sanction to organizations which promote development, cultural exchange, and mutual understanding, while it outlawed organizations which promote territorial change and political parties which are based on religion.[82]

The Kärimav government moved forward on meeting the single most important challenge of Uzbekistan's economy, the reduction of the republic's dependence on cotton agriculture. Cotton cultivation was once officially beyond the realm of public criticism. After 1987 this changed dramatically. A ringing indictment of the cotton monoculture was published in the first number of the literary journal *Druzhba narodov* in 1990 and even reprinted later in the year in the pro-cotton technical journal of the Uzbek state planning committee *Zhizn' i ekonomika*.[83] But the Uzbek government well recognizes that as long as a major retreat is not sounded on Uzbekistan's cotton cultivation, the problems of land and water are sure to increase. Shortly after he was elected Uzbekistan President, Kärimav told a party plenum:[84]

> We already today have dozens of conflicts over land and water, including those in Fergana, Samarkand and Bukhara. Hundreds of people, stirred up by demagogues from different "informal" organizations, in the presence of striking passivity and helplessness of the local authorities come to the Central Committee imploring that we solve their problem at the expense of their neighbor.

The political potential of such internecine conflict is illustrated by reports that Komsomol volunteer activists formed "water posses," making night raids along borderland irrigation canals to combat water poaching by other nationality groups.[85]

The perspective from Tashkent was not a salutary one. Kärimav's government was hemmed in by opposing trends. The population increases. The government is running a deficit. If cotton cultivation is curtailed to diversify agriculture, revenues will fall. Worse, unemployment on the farms will worsen; Uzbekistan has more than a million unemployed on the farms today.[86] Soviet economists urged the "redistribution of labor resources between the city and village" to prevent catastrophe.[87] Yet there is little employment opportunity in the cities either. For these reasons and despite rhetorical effusions to the contrary, the government continues to rely on cotton as the staple of Uzbekistan's agriculture. To break with cotton cultivation would be to consign the republic to utter poverty and social crisis. Of course, this does not resolve the water crisis in Central Asia. For this reason, the republic, along with the other republics of Central Asia, have focused renewed efforts on revitalizing the scheme to divert northern flowing rivers to Central Asia.[88]

As pressures for political and economic reform build, the Kärimav government is faced with a difficult dilemma. From Tashkent's perspective, the "Moscow solution" of political liberalization only created a new, more uncertain, and in many ways less attractive situation. The "Beijing solution" of economic but not political change would only promise to defer the inevitable. Kärimav's strategy seemed to favor a third choice, a form of "authoritarian democracy" that is top-down, carefully engineered, limited, and consonant with the area's cultural traditions. Uzbekistan is now a state. If this third choice is to succeed, Kärimav – or his successors – will have to discover the magic formula for creating a nation to go along with it.

Notes

Research for this article was made possible with the help of the United States Institute of Peace, the Hoover Institution at Stanford University, and the University of New Mexico. The author gratefully acknowledges this assistance.

1 In the last two years, the political institutions of the former USSR have changed substantially. Conventions of popular usage of political terminology will no doubt change as well though perhaps more slowly. "Ozbekistan" is the Latin transliteration of the Uzbek language name for Uzbekistan. The more familiar variant, "Uzbekistan," is the Russianized verison. With the passage of the Uzbekistan's "Law on Languages" in December 1989 declaring Uzbek to be the official language of the republic and with Uzbekistan's Declaration of Independence of August 31, 1991, the practice of transliterating from Uzbek to Russian to English is no longer justified. In deference to established patterns of usage, however, many of the terms used in this article derive from the Russianized versions of Uzbek words. The exceptions are the names of key political figures such as Islam Äbdughanievich Kärimav (Islom Abduganievich Karimov), Uzbekistan's current president. These names are transliterated directly from the Turkic languages. Transliterations are from either the Russian according to the Library of Congress system or from the Uzbek according to the system presented in Edward Allworth, *Nationalities of the Soviet East: Publications and Writing Systems* (New York: Columbia University Press, 1971).

2 *Pravda Vostoka*, April 4, 1990, p. 1.

3 Our understanding of the "laws of motion" of Central Asian politics is still too rudimentary to allow us the confidence necessary to test general hypotheses in any rigorous, scientific understanding of that term. As is increasingly becoming clear with the emergence of forthright discussions of some areas of decision making in Central Asia, the "Moscow-centric" interpretations of much former political analysis of Central Asian affairs were not so much wrong as they were superficial. What they described, often, was what for political reasons it was

expedient for the Central Asians to have believed about them. A good argument can be made that our general theorizing about politics in Central Asia should proceed less from the presuppositions and methods of Soviet Studies than from the methods and approaches of Middle Eastern studies.

4 See Gregory Gleason, *Federalism and Nationalism: The Struggle for Republican Rights in the USSR* (Boulder, Co: Westview Press, 1990), chapter 2.

5 For an account of the main contests between the local groups and the Russians, see Michael Rywkin, *Moscow's Muslim Challenge*, revised edn (Armonk, NY: M.E. Sharpe, 1990), chapter 2.

6 V.I. Lenin, *Polnoe Sochinenia*, vol. 41, p. 436. A suggestion that Lenin attached a great deal of importance, if only unconsciously, to the unifying aspect of the common Turkic language, was the notable omission of the Persian speaking group, the Tajiks. Lenin, it should be noted, had never been in Central Asia and thus had to rely upon his lieutenants' accounts for descriptions of the political situation there.

7 V.I. Lenin, *Polnoe*, vol. 41, p. 436.

8 The republic had four oblasts: the Zakaspiiskaia oblast (roughly today's Turkmenistan); the Ferganskii oblast (roughly today's Fergana valley as well as the Tadzhik SSR); the Semirechinskaia oblast (today's southern Kazakhstan and Kyrgyz SSR); and the Syrdarinskaia oblast (covering most of today's Uzbek SSR and parts of the Kazakh SSR along the Syr-Daria river).

9 Mysteriously, Soviet historical sources are remarkably inconsistent in the identification of the political units of the early period. For instance, sources will refer frequently to the "Khorezm Peoples Republic" but use the appreviation "KhPSR." Some sources, indeed, in the same article refer to it variously as the "Khorezm Soviet Peoples Republic" and the "Khorezm Peoples Soviet Republic." See Sh. Z. Urazaev, "Uzbekskoi sovetskoi natsional'noi gosudarstvennosti – 60 let," *Obshchestvennye nauki v Uzbekistane*, no. 5, 1984, pp. 3–8, esp. p. 4.

10 A. Agzamkhodzhaev and Sh. Urazaev, "Natsional'no-gosudarstvennomu razmezhevaniiu respublik Sovetskoi Srednei Azii – 60 let," *Sovetskoe gosudarstvo i pravo*, no. 10, 1984, pp. 25–33, at p. 26.

11 On the land and water reform in Central Asia, see Frank A. Ecker, "Transition in Asia," Ph.D. dissertation, University of Michigan, 1952.

12 Russians for some time previously had referred to the Kazakhs as Kyrgyz and to the Kyrgyz as Karakyrgyz.

13 Agzamkhodzhaev, p. 30.

14 A. Agzamkhodzhaev and Sh. Urazaev, "Natsional'no-gosudarstvennomu . . .," p. 29. James Critchlow examines the argument that Faizulla Khodzhev's support for the land reform was lukewarm in light of his nationalist as opposed to internationalist leanings. See James Critchlow, "Did Faizulla Khojaev Really Oppose Uzbekistan's Land Reform," *Central Asian Survey*, vol. 9, no. 3, 1990, pp. 29, 41.

15 Agzamkhodzhaev, p. 31.

16 Khodzhaev, vol. II, p. 415.

17 Two border changes which are critical and should be mentioned are the 1924 subordination of the Karakalpaks to the RSFSR and the 1929 transformation of the Tajik Autonomous Republic into a union-republic. The Karakalpaks

were switched to Uzbekistan subordination with the adoption of the Stalin Constitution of 1936. The Karakalpak Autonomous Republic declared sovereignty on December 14, 1990. For a discussion, see "S. Nietullaev, "Trudnyi put' k soglasiiu," *Pravda Vostoka*, April 4, 1991, p. 3.

18 See Lee Schwartz, "Regional Population Redistribution and National Homelands in the USSR," in Henry R. Huttenbach, *Soviet Nationality Policies: Ruling Ethnic Groups in the USSR* (London: Mansell Publishing Company, 1990), p. 133.

19 See A. Alimmov and A. Mursaliev, "Nas uchili prygat' cherez kapitalizm," *Komsomol'skaia pravda*, March 3, 1991, p. 1.

20 See Bernard V. Oliver, "Korenizatsiia," *Central Asian Survey* vol. 9, no. 3, 1990, pp.77–98.

21 For a description of the various ideological gradations within this group see the chapter "Muslim National Communism," in Alexandre Bennigsen and Chantal Lemercier-Quelquejay, *Islam in the Soviet Union* (London: Pall Mall Press, 1967), pp. 101–119.

22 Niyazov had been First Secretary of the CPUz since 1950. After his demotion he was appointed Minister of Communal Economy, a ministry which was abolished just over a year afterward. He later served for a short period as an agricultural secretary of the CPTu. The data on Niyazov and the other personalities discussed here are taken from a number of sources, the most useful of which is Grey Hodnett and Val Ogareff, *Leaders of the Soviet Republics, 1955–1972* (Canberra: Australian National University, 1973). Additional data is from various editions of *Who's Who in the U.S.S.R*, compiled by the former Institute for the Study of the USSR (Austria: Intercontinental Book and Publishing Company, Ltd.), Herwig Kraus, compiler: Herwig Kraus, "The Composition of Leading Organs of the CPSU, (1952–1982)," Supplement to the Radio Liberty Research Bulletin (Munich: 1982); Directory of Soviet Officials, Volume II, Union Republics (US State Department, June, 1966); various editions of *Directory of Soviet Officials, Volume III: Union Republics* (National Foreign Assessment Center, US Government, Washington, DC); and the author's own files.

23 See Sh. Ziiamov, *Kadrovaia politika KPSS v deistvii*, (Tashkent: Uzbekistan, 1980), pp. 24–25.

24 See Gregory Gleason, "Nationalism or Political Corruption? The Case of the Cotton Scandal in the USSR," *Corruption and Reform*, vol. 5, no. 2, 1990, pp. 87–108.

25 See Ann Sheehy, "Major Anti-Corruption Drive in Uzbekistan," *Radio Liberty Research Bulletin*, RL 324/84, August 30, 1984, pp. 1–17; James Critchlow, "Further Repercussions of the 'Uzbek Affair'," *Report on the USSR*, vol. 2, no. 18, 1990, pp. 20–22.

26 This figure is cited by I. Usmankhodzhaev, *Partiinaia zhizn'*, no. 1, January, 1986, pp. 28–33.

27 The investigators, Telman Gdlyan and Nikolai Ivanov became so popular for their anti-corruption campaigns that they were elected to the Congress of People's Deputies in the Soviet Union's first free elections in March 1989. The two continued to assert that there was evidence to implicate other high-ranking officials, including Egor Ligachev, who, as a Politboro member, was a chief execu-

tive official in the USSR. Amid the growing political ferment in 1989, the charges of corruption in high places garnered Gdlyan and Ivanov widespread public support among the Soviet citizenry and, as well, many powerful enemies. The two were eventually accused of having used illegal methods for gathering testimonies and evidence. In April 1990, the USSR Supreme Soviet opened a debate over whether to revoke Gdlyan and Ivanov's immunity to prosecution. The multiple ironies of the situation were summed up by one commentator who said of Gdlyan that we do not know whether to call him "Knight of Law and Order" or the "Evil Genius of Perestroika" (Savchenko).

28 The citizens of Uzbekistan, as the citizens of many other areas in the USSR, ponder the significance of their republic's name. It is a multinational republic. But many of its names, in Uzbek, in Russian, in Tajik as in English tend to give precedence to the dominant ethnic group. Is it "Uzbekistan?" Is it the "republic of Uzbekistan?" The "Uzbek republic?" Or the "Uzbek SSR?" In the eyes of Uzbekistan's citizens, it is inaccurate and often very misleading to refer to the republic's citizens as "Uzbeks" unless one refers specifically to the ethnic group. "*Ozbekistanlar*" ("Uzbekistanis") sounds contrived. A good solution has not yet been reached.

29 "Vystyplenie deputata Nishanova, R.N.," *Pravda Vostoka*, June 2, 1989, p. 2.

30 *Pravda Vostoka*, June 1, 1989, p. 1.

31 Both laws were passed on October 20, 1989. The text of the laws was published in *Pravda Vostoka* on October 24 and 25, 1989. See "O vyborakh narodnykh deputatov Uzbekskoi SSR," *Pravda Vostoka*, October 24, 1989, and "O vyborakh deputatov mestnykh sovetov narodnykh deputatov Uzbekskoi SSR," *Pravda Vostoka*, October 25, 1989.

32 These decrees were passed on October 19 and 20, 1989, respectively. See *Pravda Vostoka*, October 21, 1989, p. 1.

33 Some questions were raised with respect to high voter turnout. One newspaper reporter observed that the reported turnouts of over 98 percent in some areas were surely fictitious. As he put it in terms that Uzbekistan's citizens could easily appreciate, "even if they sold meat and oranges at the voting booths you couldn't get that kind of turnout." I. Khisamov, "My vybiraem, nas vybiraiut," *Pravda Vostoka*, March 3, 1990, p. 2.

34 This is a high voter turnout by cross-national comparative standards. In comparison with previous Soviet elections, however, it is low. The turnout for the 1987 local elections in Uzbekistan, for instance, was 99.84 percent. See *Pravda Vostoka*, June 27, 1987, p. 1.

35 In one of the districts, the candidate was apparently disqualified and the election was not held.

36 This was the first session of the twelfth convocation.

37 The reader will note that this figure does not correspond with the election return data presented in the official election outcomes. These would set the total number of elected deputies at 460.

38 See Anvar Agzamkhodzhaev, "Na chem stoit soiuz," *Pravda Vostoka*, April 16, 1991, p. 3.

39 The referendum on the Soviet federal principle was held on March 17 in most of the USSR. In Uzbekistan, 9,830,782 ballots were counted. 9,196,848 voted in favor. Thus only about 6 percent of the votes were in favor of withdrawal from

the union. The referendum returns were reported in Soviet Uzbekistoni, March 21, 1991.

40 "SSSR – Nash obshchii dom," Kommunist Uzbekistana, no. 12, 1989, p. 56.

41 L. Kurin, "Trudnye liudi v trudnom raione," Pravda Vostoka, April 16, 1986, p. 2.

42 See, for instance, an appeal for more social expenditures on behalf of Uzbekistan's half million Tatars. M. Malikov, "Tatary v Uzbekistane," Pravda Vostoka, April 2, 1991, p. 3.

43 The resolution on sovereignty of December 14, 1990, asserts that the Karakalpak government holds all rights, prerogatives, and authorities not delegated to central political institutions.

44 See Shakhimarden Kusainov, "Eta zemlia nam Bogom dana," Munosabat, no. 1, January, 1990, pp. 7–8.

45 For a discussion of this theme, see Sergei Tatur, "Vmeste podnimat' Uzbekistan," Zvezda vostoka, no. 1, 1991, pp. 3–17.

46 "Bezhentsy v Rossii: Chto dal'she?" Pravda Vostoka, November 28, 1991, p. 3.

47 Timur Pulatov, "Dogonim i peregonim Angolu!" Moskovskie novosti, no. 14, October, 1990, p. 7.

48 Alisher Il'khamov, "Vozmozhno li 'Uzbekskoe chudo' ili Rynochnaia ekonomika s vostochnym litsom," Zhizn i ekonomika (Tashkent), no. 11, 1990, p. 7.

49 G. Shirmatova, "Kul'turno-nravstvennye problemy garmonizatsii mezhnatsional'nykh otnoshenii," Kommunist Uzbekistana, no. 2, 1990, p. 65.

50 For instance, "My ne smozhem zhit' drug bez druga," Pravda Vostoka, November 6, 1991, p. 1.

51 "Zaiavlenie rukovoditelei Uzbek SSR, Kazakh SSR, Kirgiz SSR, Tadzhik SSR i Turkmen SSR," Kommunist Uzbekistana, no. 8, 1990, pp. 56–58.

52 "Soglashenie ob ekonomicheskom, nauchno-tekhnicheskom i kul'turnom sotrudnichestve Uzbekskoi SSR, Kazakhskoi SSR, Kirgizskoi SSR, Tadzhikskoi SSR i Turkmenskoi SSR," Sovetskaia Kirgizia, June 26, 1990.

53 Although provisions of the treaty had been under public discussion for months, the final draft form of the new treaty was not published until late in 1991. For a text, see Izvestiia, November 24, 1990, p. 1.

54 Grigorii Revenko summarized these goals in an interview. A summary of Revenko's comments appeared in Report on the USSR, August 3, 1990, p. 28.

55 These remarks were made by Gorbachev at the televised press conference of August 31, 1990 on Moscow TV, channel 1. Transcribed in "USSR Today: Soviet Media News and Features Digest," compiled by Radio Liberty Monitoring, 706.01, August 31, 1990.

56 The text of the Joint Declaration was widely published in the USSR. See "Sovmestnoe zaiavlenie," Pravda, April 24, 1991, p. 1.

57 "Announcement of the President of the USSR and the High Leaders of the Union Republics" (Izvestiia, September 2, 1991).

58 Formally known as Dogovor ob ekonomicheskom soobshchestve suverennykh gosudarsty.

59 The republics which signed the agreement were: (1) The Republic of Armenia; (2) Belarus'; (3) Kazakhstan; (4) Kyrgyzstan; (5) Russia; (Rossiia); (6) Republic of Tadzhikistan; (7) Republic of Turkmenistan; and (8) Republic of Uzbekistan. The states that did not sign the Treaty of Economic Community agreement

were: (1) the Baltic States (Estonia, Latvia, Lithuania); (2) Azerbaijan; (3) Georgia; (4) Moldova; (5) Ukraine. Note that several of the republics changed their formal titles at this point, no longer regarding themselves as constitutent republics but as separate states.

60 "Otsteplennyi vagon," *Izvestiia*, September 13, 1991, p. 3.

61 On the theoretical background of this economic specialization, see Gregory Gleason, "The Political Economy of Dependency under Socialism: The Asian Republics in the USSR," *Studies in Comparative Communism*, vol. 24, no. 4, 1991.

62 The law was passed on June 12, 1990. See Anvar Khamidovich Rasulev, "Proryv na vneshnii rynok," *Zhizn' i ekonomika*, no. 10, 1990, pp. 54–57.

63 As reported by the "News Program" of "TV Russia." Transcribed in *USSR Today: Soviet Media News and Features Digest*, October 3, 1991 (880/661).

64 See *USSR Today: Soviet Media News and Features Digest* RFE/RL Research Institute, November 3, 1991 (1000/39).

65 See "Soglashenie mezhdu pravitel'stvom Uzbekskoi SSR i pravitel'stvom Respubliki Kyrgyzstan ob ekonomicheskom i kul'turnom sotrudnichestve na 1991–1995 gody" and "Dogovor o druzhbe i sotrudnichestve mezhdu respubliki Kyrgyzstan i Uzbekskoi SSR," *Pravda Vostoka*, March 19, 1991, p. 2.

66 See "Dogovor o druzhbe i sotrudnichestve mezhdu Turkmenskoi Sovetskoi Sotsialisticheskoi Respubliki i Uzbekskoi Sovetskoi Sotsialisticheskoi Respubliki," and "Soglashenie mezhdu Pravitel'stvom TuSSR i Pravitel'stvom UzSSR ob ekonomicheskom i kul'turnom sotrudnichestve na 1992–1995 gody," *Turkmenskaia Iskra*, April 23, 1991. For a description of the water distribution problems of Central Asia, see Gregory Gleason, "The Struggle for Control over Water in Central Asia: Republican Sovereignty and Collective Action," *Report on the USSR*, vol. 3, no. 25, June 31, 1991, pp. 11–19.

67 In November, 1991, an international organization, *Khalyk-mali*, was registered in Karakalpakia as a political party. Its goal was to politically organize for a "Free Karakalpakia."

68 B. Babadzhanov, "Esli navesti mosti," *Ekonomika i zhizn'*, no. 2, 1990, p. 11.

69 Vitalii Portnikov, "Turkestan poiavitsia osen'iu?" *Nezavisimaia gazeta*, July 27, 1991.

70 Edward A. Gargan, "In Central Asia, Many Dream of Union Under Islam's Flag," *The New York Times*, October 11, 1991, p. 1.

71 Annette Bohr, "Inside the Uzbek Parliamentary Opposition: An Interview with Muhammad Salih," *Report on the USSR*, vol. 2, no. 46, November 16, 1990, pp. 18–22 at p. 20.

72 See A. Alimov and A. Mursaliev, "Nas uchili prygat' cherez kapitalizm," *Komsomol'skaia pravda*, March 3, 1991, p. 1.

73 A. Karpov and A. Protsenko, "Diktatura v Srednei Azii: Tadzhikistan, Uzbekistan, dalee – vezde?" *Izvestiia*, September 25, 1991, p. 1.

74 The traditions of deference appear to be under increasing criticism. Reports circulated in Russia that the Uzbekistan Supreme Soviet held a no confidence vote on Kärimav's leadership in early October, 1991. Kärimav was moved to offer a formal denial that this took place. "Zaiavlenie press-sluzhby Prezidenta Respubliki Uzbekistan," *Pravda Vostoka*, October 4, 1991, p. 1. On traditions of deference to authority, see Gregory Gleason, "Fealty and Loyalty: Informal

Authority Structures in Soviet Asia," *Soviet Studies*, vol. 43, no. 4, 1991, pp. 613–628.

75 S. Bagdasarov, "My – za armiiu. Byli i budem!" *Krasnaia zvezda*, April 10, 1991, p. 3.

76 Vladimir Kazakov, "Gotovy k dialogu," *Literaturnaia Rossiia*, March 8, 1991, p. 10. Also see "*Moskovskie novosti*, no. 10, March 10, 1991, p. 2.

77 See the article R. Rakhmanov, M. Istmatov, Sh. Ubaidullaev, "Nespravedlivost," *Pravda Vostoka*, April 20, 1991, p. 2.

78 Ann Sheehy, "Dismissed Uzbek Officials Fight Back," *Radio Liberty Research Bulletin* RL 403/85, December 4, 1985, pp. 1–5.

79 B. Tashmukhamedov, A. Pulatov, Sh. Ismatullaev, "Nostal'giia po 'khoziainu'," *Izvestiia*, April 5, 1991, p. 1.

80 On the genesis of the *Birlik* (Unity) organization, see Bess Brown, "The Public Role in Perestroika in Central Asia," *Central Asian Survey*, vol. 9, no. 1, pp. 87–96.

81 B. Musaev, "Chto meshaet konsolidatsii," *Kommunist Uzbekistana*, no. 10, 1990, pp. 51–57 at p. 54.

82 For a text of the law, see "Ob'obshchestvennykh ob"edineniiakh v Uzbekskoi SSR," *Pravda Vostoka*, February 26, 1991, p. 2.

83 Sabit Madaliev, "Chernyi tsvet khlopok," *Zhizn i ekonomika*, no. 8, 1990, pp. 47–52, and no. 9, 1990, pp. 55–60.

84 I.A. Kärimav, "Doklad I.A. Kärimava na plenume TsK Kompartii Uzbekistna 23 Marta 1990 goda," *Kommunist Uzbekistana*, no. 5, 1990, p. 28.

85 See Iskander Khisamov, "Voda kak prichina pozhara," *Literaturnaia gazeta*, January 16, 1991.

86 For a discussion of Uzbekistan's agricultural employment problems, see Gregory Gleason, "Marketization and Migration: The Politics of Cotton in Central Asia," *Journal of Soviet Nationalities*, vol. 1, no. 2, 1990, pp. 64–96. Also see Iemat Khushev and Petr Shcherbak, "Tak Mif ili real'nost'?" *Zhizn i ekonomika*, no. 8, 1990, pp. 6–11.

87 N. Smirnova, "Trudnye zaboty obshchego doma," *Ekonomika i zhizn'*, no. 2, 1990, p. 16.

88 For the position that "there is no alternative to the revival of the transbasin water transfer, see S. Ziiadullaev, "Skupoi platit dvazhdy," *Pravda Vostoka*, February 9, 1991, p. 2, and V. Antonov, "Chto daet novoe postanovlenie?" *Pravda Vostoka*, April 3, 1991, p. 3. Ziiadulaev is an influential economist and chair of a USSR Academy of Sciences commission on regional problems in Central Asia. Antonov is the General Director of "Vodoproekt" of the Ministry of Amelioration and Water Economy of the Uzbek SSR.

15 Tajikistan: ancient heritage, new politics

MURIEL ATKIN

As the Soviet regime underwent reform and then collapse in the Gorba-chev era, the inhabitants of Tajikistan grappled with their particular version of the problems of nationality politics that affected the Soviet Union as a whole. After decades during which the Soviet regime defined and regulated national identity in ways which were often restrictive and sometimes demeaning, Tajiks, like members of other nationalities, sought to take control of the interpretation of their own nationhood. This affected not only the Tajiks' ethnic awareness but also relations between Tajikistan and neighboring republics, the Soviet central powers, and foreign coun-tries. At the same time, many of the issues that concerned the Tajiks, including the low standard of living and exasperation with communist hard-liners, were not unique to any nationality but reflected problems that were perceived widely in the Soviet Union, although some were given a national coloration in their Tajik context. In addition, Tajiks living in Tajikistan have shown an interest in those developments in other Soviet republics which they see as pertinent to their own concerns. Thus, political change in contemporary Tajikistan is not solely about nationalism, although national assertiveness is an important component of the political processes which have been at work there.

There is a tendency in some quarters to treat the Asian republics of what was the Soviet Union as so exotic as to be incomparable to the rest of the country. Therefore, before taking a closer look at nationalism in Tajikis-tan, it is worth noting that Tajiks who address nationality issues are atten-tive to developments in other republics and at the center. The first Con-gress of People's Deputies demonstrated to such Tajiks how effective representatives from the Baltic and Caucasian republics as well as Moscow and Leningrad were as advocates of their own national or regional interests and how Tajikistan's representatives suffered by comparison.[1] The efforts of nationalists in other republics, including Russia, Armenia, and Lithu-ania, to enhance the position of their respective national cultures as the reform era provided new opportunities for doing so also served as an example to Tajiks.[2] A prominent component of discussions of Tajikistan's economic problems includes comparisons with other Soviet republics (see below).

Reform-minded political groups in Tajikistan, which all advocate Tajik national interests in some form, have cooperated with and been helped by reformers of other nationalities in other republics. The most obvious example of this is the Democratic Party of Tajikistan (DPT) which, according to its leader, Shodmon Yusufov, derived its platform from those of the Democratic Party of Russia and the Social Democratic Association.[3] When Tajikistan's regime refused to allow the DPT to publish the first issue of its newspaper in the republic, the DPT arranged to have it published in Lithuania with the help of Sajudis.[4] Similarly, a Tajik cultural organization, *Mehr*, that faced harassment from the Tajikistani regime was allowed to organize and publish a newspaper by Moscow's reformist city government.[5] In May 1991, the DPT played host to a meeting in Dushanbe, Tajikistan's capital, of reform-minded groups from Russia, Belorussia, and other Central Asian republics.[6] During Tajikistan's presidential election campaign in the fall of 1991, Davlat Khudonazarov was the joint candidate of the DPT and the two other main non-Communist groups, *Rastokhez* and the Islamic Rebirth Party. He had been one of Andrei Sakharov's supporters in the Congress of People's Deputies and won public support for his candidacy from Boris Yeltsin.[7] The rally which these same groups organized in downtown Dushanbe on August 24, 1991 in reaction to the attempted coup by Communist hard-liners included not only the voicing of Tajik interests but also praise for both Yeltsin and Gorbachev. The demonstrators also held a minute of silence for the "national heroes" in Moscow who died opposing the coup.[8]

None of this means that people engaged in Tajik-oriented politics are incapable of formulating objectives or identifying grievances without outside guidance. It does mean that such political leaders, while emphasizing the particular, are well aware of the broader context in which they operate.

The long-standing Soviet condemnation of national feeling, except in the pallid form dictated by the regime itself, continued into the Gorbachev era. The Gorbachev regime continued the practice of its predecessors in presenting "internationalism," which really meant an emphasis on the interests of the center of power, as occupying a lofty moral plane. In contrast, the regime treated nationalism as linked to, and not better than "chauvinism." In practice, the epithets "nationalism" (or "national narrowness") and "chauvinism" were readily applied to any display of interest in one's national heritage or current concerns that fell outside the narrow confines of the officially authorized version. (Given the strongly negative connotations of "nationalist" in Soviet rhetoric, it should be noted that the term will be used in this essay simply to describe people who see themselves as advocates of the interests of the Tajiks as a people and of the worth of their heritage and is not intended to imply that such individuals are necessarily radicals, subversives, or chauvinists.)

Symbolic of this continued Soviet antipathy toward national feeling is the 1986 attack by Tajikistan's leadership, reflecting the attitudes of the center, on Tajik writers for paying too much attention to their own people and republic and not enough to other peoples and internationalism.[9] That same year, the republic's Communist Party First Secretary, Qahhor Mahkamov, one of the Gorbachev-era replacements for the old-guard leadership in Central Asia,[10] told the party to do more to promote internationalism and portrayed nationalism as something pernicious which foreign propaganda encouraged.[11] This approach lasted as late as 1989, by which time nationalist movements were gaining an increased following in various Soviet republics. Reflections of this persistence include Mahkamov's 1989 complaint that Tajiks were too interested in national matters and insufficiently interested in internationalism and the declaration by the plenum of the Central Committee of the Communist Party of Tajikistan that it would fight "nationalism and chauvinism."[12]

Yet this hard line proved unsustainable. In a climate of waning repression and growing nationalism in a number of republics, Tajiks reacted against the long-standing Soviet practice of manipulative nationality politics, as well as Moscow's centralizing and Russianizing practices, to press their national interests with increasing vigor. Even Tajikistan's Communist leadership found it politically useful to espouse Tajik national interests, as changes in the Soviet political system away from the extreme emphasis on command from the center made it desirable for republic-level officials to seek the support of republic-level constituencies.

There is some irony in this in the sense that the contemporary republic of Tajikistan and the emphasis on a Tajik political-national identity are creations of the Soviet era. Yet these have taken on meaning in their own right during the course of this century. The boundaries of the Tajikistan republic reflect neither a traditional Tajik polity nor the distribution of the Tajik population within Soviet Central Asia (or beyond). The territory which now comprises Tajikistan was often part of larger states or divided among a number of regional or supra-regional powers. Even the Samanid kingdom (875–999), which, according to Soviet Tajik historiography, was a Tajik state and presided over the emergence of the Tajiks as a distinct, consolidated people with a flourishing culture,[13] ruled very little of what is now the Tajikistan republic directly. Although part of what is now northwestern Tajikistan (the Panjakent area) was ruled from the Samanid capital in Bukhara, most of the rest of the modern republic's territory was ruled through local vassals; the mountainous southeast (now called Gorno-Badakhshan) was outside the Samanid realm entirely.

During the 1920s, the Soviet regime subdivided its Central Asian holdings into nationally-defined republics. As part of that process, Moscow's fiat established Tajikistan as an autonomous republic within the new Uzbekistan Soviet Socialist Republic in 1924. The core of this Tajikistan ASSR was formed from the eastern provinces of the old emirate of Bukhara (comprising much of what is now central and southern Tajikistan) and, further north (the Panjakent area), a small part of the old governor-generalship (and, briefly, the autonomous republic) of Turkestan. The following year, the remote Pamir Mountain region, along the border with Afghanistan and China, was reassigned from the Turkestan republic to Tajikistan under the name Gorno- ("Mountainous") Badakhshan.[14] In 1929, Moscow separated Tajikistan from Uzbekistan and made it a Union Republic in its own right. At that time part of the populous, economically important Fergana Valley (the Leninobod area) was transferred from Uzbekistan to become the northern-most part of Tajikistan.

Although the idea of a Tajik nation-state is a twentieth-century invention, the ethnic designation "Tajik" has been used for many centuries to refer to Persian-speakers, in contrast to various Turkic peoples, wherever these groups lived in contact with each other. By the twentieth century, the area of its use had contracted to Central Asia, Afghanistan, the eastern-most provinces of Iran, and China's Xinjiang province. According to the 1989 Soviet census there are some 4.6 million Tajiks living within Soviet borders,[15] approximately 3 million of whom live in Tajikistan; the vast majority of the rest live in Uzbekistan, with small numbers of Tajiks living elsewhere in Central Asia or in other Soviet republics. The exact number of Tajik inhabitants of either Tajikistan or Uzbekistan is subject to question for reasons which have to do with ethnic politics (see below). There are also more than 3 million Persian-speakers in Afghanistan, a majority of whom are called "Tajiks." A small number of Tajiks live in the oases of Xinjiang (perhaps a few tens of thousands).

The designation of Tajiks or other Central Asian peoples by ethno-linguistic names does not mean that a majority of them perceived such categories as the proper basis for defining states when the Soviets first reshaped the region into nationally-defined republics. However, decades of Soviet rule in Tajikistan, entailing formal, institutional recognition of national identity and transgressions against national feeling, have made nationality politics extremely important there. Contemporary Tajik nationalists see their people not as the "formerly backward people" they were called for decades in Soviet rhetoric but as heirs to a synthesis of the western and eastern forms of Iranian civilization (representing the Iranian plateau and Central Asia) that has its roots in antiquity. At the same time, many of these nationalists, especially those belonging to the cultural intelligentsia, decry what they perceive as the low level of knowledge about this rich heritage and even of "correct" Tajik among most of their people. They blame Soviet policies for depriving them of their birthright and want to use the power of the state to remedy the situation.[16]

That Tajikistan's Communist leadership perceived such sentiments to have a widespread following in the republic is reflected by its shift in 1989 to policies which addressed nationalist grievances. This has taken various forms, including the appearance of increasingly explicit articles in the official press reflecting nationalist concerns, the establishment of a Tajikistan cultural foundation to preserve the Tajik heritage, the identification of political figures by nationality in the press, and the restoration of the historic name, Khujand, of Tajikistan's second largest city, Leninobod. The republican regime's most important concession to nationalist feeling was the enactment of the language law of 1989, which, among other things, gave Tajik primacy over Russian as the state language, although it did not eliminate the use of Russian. The law also advocated a return to the Arabic alphabet and called for the use of Tajik, not Russianized or Russian personal and place names.[17]

The Communists did not have a monopoly on expressions of Tajik nationalism. For example there was a ground swell of public support among Tajiks, especially in Dushanbe, for improving the status of the Tajik language months before the legislature passed the language law. Tajik public organizations separate from the Communist Party (called "informals" in Soviet parlance) articulate nationalist concerns. Among the common themes are calls for sovereignty, in an economic as well as a political sense, and full, unhindered cultural development of the Tajiks. Such views can be found among the two main secular "informal" organizations in Tajikistan, the DPT and *Rastokhez*, as well as the cultural organization *Mehr*.[18] However, neither the Communist (later Socialist, then again Communist) Party of Tajikistan nor the "informals" extend the concept of national sovereignty or even independence as far as a complete separation from a reconstituted version of what had been the Soviet Union, provided that the new version ensures autonomy for and equality among the republics. The terms in which sovereignty and independence are often discussed give the impression that they are seen in no small part as ways of improving the republic's bargaining position as relations among the constituents of what had been the Soviet Union are renegotiated.[19] There are surely a number of reasons for this stance, among them the daunting prospect that complete independence poses a small republic with neighbors it does not necessarily trust, an economy that is not self-sufficient, and major economic, environmental, and social problems Only after the Soviet Union dissolved in December 1991 did Tajikistan become an independent state.

The strength of nationalism among ordinary Tajiks, especially the rural majority, is harder to gauge because of the dearth of reliable information. Communist Party officials and non-Tajiks living in Dushanbe tend to portray rural Tajiks as a primitive, anarchic menace lacking a full-fledged ideology but capable of xenophobia and Islamic fanaticism. Representative of this are the rumors which circulated in Dushanbe in connection with the February 1990 riots and the anti-Communist demonstrations of

August to October 1991 that rural Tajiks had come or were coming to Dushanbe to commit mayhem. Even many educated, urban Tajik nationalists view ordinary Tajiks, especially those in the countryside, as ignorant of their national heritage and given to a local rather than a national form of identity.[20]

However there are examples of behavior by ordinary Tajiks that suggest that by now their political awareness in general and their sense of national identity may be stronger than they have been given credit for. Mass antigovernment demonstrations in Dushanbe following the collapse of the attempted coup of August 1991, in which rural as well as urban Tajiks (and others) rallied in the heart of the city, were motivated primarily by the kind of opposition to the Communist elite that was widespread in the Soviet Union but also invoked nationalism. The demonstrators who called for the resignation of Party leader and President Qahhor Mahkamov because of his perceived support for the coup carried signs saying "Resign," but at least one sign quoted from the *Shan-nameh*, the Persian national epic set in pre-Islamic times. The point of the sign was the righteousness of the oppressed in overthrowing their oppressor, a point made by referring to two of the most famous characters in the epic, Zahhak, the monstrously cruel tyrant, and Kaveh, the Persian blacksmith whose own sons had been killed by Zahhak and who rallied support for the uprising against him.[21] Much of what was said at the demonstration on September 9, 1991, as Tajikistan's legislature moved to declare the republic's independence, had to do with the concept of national reawakening. One symbol of this was the call for renaming one of Dushanbe's main streets, Putovskii Street, (named for the Polish-born Cheka officer, Ch.A. Putovskii, who played an active role in the Communist victory in what became Tajikistan) after the greatest of the Samanid rulers, Isma'il.[22] The strength of national grievances at the grass-roots levels has also shown itself in another way, in the unfortunate form of antagonism and violence towards members of other nationalities (see below).

Tajik nationalism also affects the discussion of other issues of which it is not the primary component, most notably economic and environmental concerns. The terms in which Tajikistan's standard of living are discussed frequently note that the republic lags far behind other parts of the Soviet Union, especially Russia and the Baltic states, on various points of comparison, including the availability of basic consumer necessities, infant mortality, and the inhabitants' level of education.[23] Both the Tajikistani regime and the opposition blame much of the republic's economic woes on Moscow's policies, which they depict as essentially colonial, although they rarely use that word. According to this argument, Moscow exploits Tajikistan as a producer of raw materials, especially, but not exclusively, cotton, as well as hydroelectric power, and weights the system so that other republics derive most of the benefit from what Tajikistan produces.[24] The solution, according to those inside and outside the Tajikistani regime, is that the republic must have full control over setting economic policy within its borders.

The high level of unemployment in Tajikistan is the target of nationalist criticism on the grounds that Moscow's policies have not provided training for Tajiks to fill new industrial jobs but have relied instead on importing workers from other republics. This is intertwined with Dushanbe's acute housing problem because the imported workers and Russians in general have received priority in housing assignments.[25]

That is why rumors which falsely alleged that large numbers of Armenians had fled to Tajikistan to escape the violence in Azerbaijan and were being given priority housing assignments in Dushanbe touched off a large demonstration in that city on February 11, 1991. The demonstrators' underlying grievances were not about the Armenians but about general dissatisfaction with the standard of living and the unresponsive political leadership, but those rumors struck a raw nerve. When republican Ministry of Internal Affairs forces fired on demonstrators who gathered the following day to continue pressing their demands, rioting swept the city.[26]

Even opposition to the construction (begun in 1976) of what was planned to be Central Asia's largest hydro-electric dam in Tajikistan's Roghun area has been given a nationalist dimension. The opponents' arguments include assertions that the reservoir created by this dam will provide irrigation water for other republics while not only flooding good land Tajikistan itself could have used but also driving Tajiks from their village homes in the lands to be flooded, thus destroying the Tajik cultural traditions that village life had preserved. The analogy between the dam project and the Chernobyl disaster as examples of the environmental damage resulting from flawed technology is another illustration of the way nationalists perceive their particular concerns with an eye to developments elsewhere in the Soviet Union.[27]

Tajik national concerns are not tidily defined by the borders of Tajikistan. Millions of Tajiks and other Persian-speakers live outside that republic while roughly 40 percent of the people living within its borders are not Tajiks but members of many other nationalities, only a few of which are represented in large numbers.

Even some of the inhabitants who are classified as Tajiks for census purposes in fact belong to other ethnic groups which speak eastern Iranian languages (as opposed to western Iranian Tajik). These peoples fall into two main groups, the Yaghnobs and the Pamiris. The Yaghnobs are descended from the Soghdians, who were a powerful, prosperous, highly cultured people of ancient Central Asia. Several of the region's major cities, including Khujand and Panjakent in Tajikistan and Bukhara and Samarkand in Uzbekistan, were originally Soghdian. The modern Yaghnobs are few in number and have suffered considerably from forced relocation from the mountains to the lowlands in the Soviet era. The Pamiris are composed of seven different peoples, all few in number, whose homelands are in the remote Gorno-Badakhshan Autonomous Oblast'. They have traditionally adhered to the Isma'ili sect of Shi'a Islam, which distinguishes them both from the Sunni majority in Central Asia and the Imami ("Twelver") Shi'i majority in Iran. Although policy towards the Yaghnobs and Pamiris, as determined in Moscow as well as Dushanbe, has been rather assimilationist, with education and publications generally being available in Tajik or Russian but not the eastern Iranian languages, at the end of 1991 they had not formed movements which compete with Tajik nationalism.[28]

Tajik nationalism has made at least token gestures towards these eastern Iranian peoples. Nationalist rhetoric points with pride to the role of the ancient eastern Iranians in the making of the Tajik people.[29] Apart from the matter of historical accuracy, this assertion is significant because it supports the nationalists' argument that the Tajiks do not inhabit the periphery of the Persian world, a long-held view among many Persians in Iran, but the center of a world which draws both on eastern as well as western Iranian traditions.[30] Since 1989, some publications in Pamiri languages have been made available and some educational opportunities as well as radio and television broadcasting in these languages have been promised.[31]

Far more significant in terms of sheer numbers is the Uzbek minority. According to the 1979 census, they constituted roughly 23 percent of Tajikistan's population.[32] Unofficial estimates in the wake of the 1989 census still put them at between 20 and 25 percent of the inhabitants of the republic.[33]

Tajikistan's regime asserts that Uzbek inhabitants are well treated in the republic and point to the use there of the Uzbek language to some extent in schools and the mass media. However, there are no token Uzbeks in the republic's highest political offices. The very size of the Uzbek minority, and the fact that they belong to a nationality which numbers some 6 million in Central Asia as a whole, means that it has the potential to pose a serious problem for Tajikistan's rulers if it should ever organize a nationalist opposition. However, that has not yet come to pass, despite the occasional friction between Tajikistan and Uzbekistan in recent years, including over the treatment of the Tajik minority in the latter republic. There was a non-violent dispute between Tajiks and Uzbeks on a collective farm (*kolkhoz*) in southern Tajikistan but it was sparked by a pressing economic problem – how farm land should be allocated – rather than ethnic antagonism for its own sake. This incident did not escalate into a broader conflict between the two nationalities.[34]

Russians constitute the next most numerous minority in Tajikistan, and in terms of positions of influence occupied by its members, a more powerful one than the Uzbeks. According to the 1979 census, Russians comprised just over 10 percent of Tajikistan's population.³⁵ Their relations with the Tajiks have become increasingly uneasy since 1989. Tajiks have been increasingly open about their resentment of Russians over various matters including the preferential treatment in employment and housing mentioned above and the inability of most Russian inhabitants to speak Tajik.³⁶ Russians' worries increased because of the 1989 law making Tajik the primary state language. This did more than raise the prospect Russians being required to learn a language few had shown any interest in learning. It also raised fears of Russian children being denied a good education in their own language which would stress the Russian cultural heritage and train them well for desirable careers. The Russians' concerns have intensified in the wake of the Dushanbe riots of February 1990. Although it is not certain that Russians were singled out for attack, some certainly were hurt during the riots and have been assaulted or threatened in subsequent individual incidents. Rumors have magnified the dangers still further. As a result, many Russians now perceive themselves at least as living in a hostile environment created by Tajik nationalists and probably at physical risk.³⁷

There has been a wave of emigration from Tajikistan since 1989. However, the number, motives, and national identity of the emigrants are subjects of controversy. Accounts which emphasize that large numbers of Russians and members of other non-indigenous nationalities emigrated imply that they were driven out because of abuses inflicted on them by the Tajiks. Some Tajik accounts not only put the total number of emigrants much lower but also cite other motives for emigration, including increased opportunities for Germans and Jews to leave the Soviet Union altogether, and the desire to escape Tajikistan's low standard of living, a concern which is said to have motivated many Tajiks as well as others to leave the republic. Not surprisingly, Armenians, who comprised only a small fraction of the republic's population, were alarmed by the anti-Armenian sentiments expressed on the eve of the Dushanbe riots of February 1990 and subsequently emigrated from Tajikistan in increased numbers. Even the number of emigrants, *in toto* or by nationality, is disputed, from several thousand of all nationalities to 100,000 Russian-speakers alone by late 1990, according to the Russian leader of a group which aids emigration from Tajikistan.³⁸

Communist hard-liners in Tajikistan, including ethnic Tajiks, have played on the Russians' fears to strengthen their own hand in the power struggle with more reform-minded members of their own party as well as non-Communists. Their alarmist message is that they, the hard-liners, are the only people standing in the way of a take over by Islamic extremists.³⁹ This tactic seems to have served the hard-liners well, especially Rahmon Nabiev, the 61-year-old former republic-level party boss (1982–1985), who lost his job in Gorbachev's purge of Brezhnevite party leaders in Central Asia and had been trying to make a come back. Nabiev got his chance in the fall of 1991, at the head of the hard-liners' backlash against proponents of change who had briefly prevailed in the aftermath of the August coup attempt. Many Russians in Dushanbe are said to have supported this restoration of the old guard.[40]

The fact that the Central Asian republics are not ethnically homogeneous is one of several factors which now complicates relations between Tajikistan and its neighbors. The Stalinist approach to inter-republican relations, which survived until the Gorbachev era, was to minimize them and focus all republics' dealings on Moscow. The changing climate of reform-era politics made possible increased direct contacts and cooperation among republics. However, the weakening of the old controls also allowed more inter-republican antagonism to surface.

In some ways, Central Asians have found advantages to cooperation on governmental and non-governmental levels. Representatives of the Central Asian republics, Tajikistan included, began working on a cooperation agreement in 1989 and signed the final draft in June 1990. The pact addressed primarily economic and environmental issues. These included the high level of unemployment, the way the centrally-planned economy had assigned these republics the role of raw-materials producer, and the environmental disaster in the Aral Sea area. On this last point, the republics vowed to cooperate in seeking help from outside sources, both the Soviet central government and the United Nations, and revived the argument that diverting Siberian rivers southward could solve the problem.[41] Tajikistan and Uzbekistan also concluded a bilateral agreement at the end of 1989 for cooperation between their respective Academies of Sciences. Tajikistan already had such agreements with ten other countries, many with the former Soviet bloc but also with the United States, France, and India.[42] All of these apparently predated the agreement with neighboring Uzbekistan, a small reflection of the extent to which the old, centralized Soviet system oriented republics toward Moscow and away from each other.

On a less lofty level, the Communist leaders of Tajikistan (Mahkamov) and Uzbekistan (Islam Karimov) neither of whom could be described as democratic reformers, were alleged to be on good terms personally.[43]

Cooperation exists at lower levels of power as well. For example, in 1989, a delegation from Turkmenistan, where cotton is a major crop as it is in Tajikistan, visited a large cotton-growing *kolkhoz* in southern Tajikistan to discuss issues of deep concern in much of Central Asia: water pollution and methods of cotton cultivation.[44] In September 1991, representatives of city and district (*raion*) governments in northern Tajikistan and neighboring parts of Uzbekistan and Kyrgyzstan concluded a cooperation agreement in the spheres of economics and education.[45]

Inter-republican cooperation does not hinge solely on common bonds among Central Asians. As the old Soviet centralized command economy broke down, the Central Asian republics each negotiated agreements with Soviet republics outside the region. In the case of Tajikistan, this included plans for exchanges with Russia, Belorussia, Georgia, and Armenia in economic and cultural spheres.

Non-Communist Party groups have also expressed a desire for cooperation across republican borders. The reasons for this are not limited to the varying degrees of cultural kinship among the Central Asian peoples and the economic and environmental problems that transcend republican borders. Reformist organizations face a common problem in much of Central Asia: hostility towards them by those republican regimes which are controlled by Communists who in some cases want to limit economic reforms and in all cases want to prevent political democratization. A spokesman for the Democratic Party of Tajikistan told representatives of Helsinki Watch in 1990 that a "regional association" of reform-minded parties existed in Central Asia.[46] Representatives of pro-reform groups in the Central Asian republics have met a few times to address issues of mutual concern.[47]

Some indication of the significance of such contacts, at least for one group of Tajikistani reformers, the Democratic Party of Tajikistan, can be seen by specific actions taken at the May 1991 meeting and immediately afterward. Those attending sent telegrams to the governments of Uzbekistan and Turkmenistan urging them to end their repressive measures against non-Communist organizations.[48] At the end of the meeting, members of the DPT and its Kyrgyzstan counterpart went to Isfara, in northern Tajikistan, to discuss a territorial dispute in that area which had been festering for two years between the two republics.[49]

While such factors appear to be bellwethers of increased cooperation among Central Asians, other considerations reflect the obstacles to regional cohesion. Some of the problems which are widespread in the region, such as the low standard of living, the degraded environment, and the pressure of a rapidly rising population on scarce water, farm land, and housing, pit the republics – and the dominant nationalities within them – against each other. Republican governments have hurt each other's inhabitants by measures designed to keep goods in high demand within their own borders. Thus, oil-producing Turkmenistan and Kazakhstan halted fuel shipments to Tajikistan at harvest time, with the results that trucks could not bring crops to market.[50] Tajikistan banned the export from the republic of food, certain consumer goods and other high-demand items and tried to enforce that with checkpoints on roads leading to neighboring republics as well as railway stations, post offices, and Dushanbe airport.[51]

Access to water is a particularly contentious issue in this region plagued not only by natural aridity but also by the policies of central economic planners which misused and polluted much of the water that is most readily available. Both Tajikistan and Kyrgyzstan, in the mountains of which many of Central Asia's rivers originate, mistrust the designs of the down-river republics, Uzbekistan and Turkmenistan, on their water.[52] A dispute over claims to irrigation water and farm land led to violence between Tajik and Kirghiz villagers on the border between the two republics. According to official Tajik sources, about a thousand people fought over this on June 13 and 14, 1989; one person died and more than a score were wounded. Although the water dispute was eventually resolved, recriminations between the leaders of Tajikistan and Kyrgyzstan over the territorial dispute continued into 1991.[53]

There is another kind of ethnic dimension to the tensions between Tajikistan and the neighboring republics. Alone among the major indigenous nationalities of Soviet Central Asia, the Tajiks are culturally Iranian rather than Turkic. Even though there is a long tradition of close contact and mutual cultural influences between the Tajiks and the Turkic peoples of the region, especially the Uzbeks, the tensions between them now are significant. Part of the problem is related to the concern that Uzbekistan will use the fact that it is far more populous and powerful than Tajikistan to take advantage of the latter in the kinds of economic disputes already mentioned. However, another important factor in the discord is the Tajik nationalists' belief that Uzbeks have, throughout the Soviet period, denied that the Tajiks are a distinct nationality, characterizing them instead as Uzbeks who have stopped speaking their original tongue. Similarly, Tajiks accuse Uzbeks of either claiming as part of the Uzbek heritage or simply neglecting the achievements of any Iranian peoples who lived at any time in the area which is now Uzbekistan.[54]

The main expression of this dispute in contemporary terms is over the status of the Tajik inhabitants of Uzbekistan. Tajiks and Uzbeks do not even agree about the number of Tajikis involved. An official Uzbekistani source put the Tajik population of the republic at about 700,000 in 1988, out of a total population of about 20 million.[55] Tajikistani estimates are higher, although they vary among themselves. The largest figure, offered among others by an Uzbekistan-born Tajik ethnographer who has made his career in Tajikistan, is 3 to 3.5 million.[56] The discrepancy in population figures is part of the larger argument made both by Tajik mainstream Communist and reformist sources: that the cities of Bukhara and Samarkand and their environs were inhabited predominantly by Tajiks in the 1920s, when they were made part of the new republic of Uzbekistan, and remain predominantly Tajik today. According to this argument, the Uzbeks have deliberately undercounted Tajiks and have used various methods to assimilate them, from denying them access to sufficient education or publications in Tajik to forcing them to list their nationality as Uzbek.[57]

In the past few years, Uzbekistani officials have tried to conciliate the Tajik minority, particularly by expanding access to education and the mass media in Tajik. They also announced that Tajiks who had been forced to identify themselves as Uzbeks on official documents would be allowed to change their formal nationality listing to Tajik.[58] (Changing one's official national registration in Soviet documents used to be virtually impossible.)

Such moves have not defused tensions. Indicative of the mistrust at work in both directions was the suspicion among educated, urban Uzbeks that a particularly unpopular, hard-line secretary of the Communist Party of Uzbekistan, who was finally ousted in 1987, was really a Tajik.[59] Tajik intellectuals took umbrage at particularly extreme statements by a few Uzbeks, who claimed that certain great medieval Persian authors were really Turks or, in one case, who faulted Tamerlane for allowing non-Turkic peoples to survive in Central Asia.[60] There have allegedly been at least two occasions when Tajiks in Tajikistan called for Bukhara and Samarkand to be transferred to Tajikistan.[61] Given that the Uzbeks outnumber the Tajiks several times over, any attempt to turn this irridentist rhetoric into action would be reckless indeed.

In a region in which Sunni Islam is an important part of the cultural as well as spiritual traditions of the great majority of indigenous inhabitants, one may wonder whether this supra-national common bond can serve as a unifying force despite all the factors which divide them. The answer may be that some Central Asians want this to be so but that many others think differently. Certainly this has not been the case until now. A shared religion did not prevent conflicts between political, tribal, or other social units in the pre-Soviet era or between those nationalities under Soviet rule. One reason is that Islam means different things to different Central Asians. For some it is at least as important in a cultural and social sense as in a strictly religious one. For some, Islam means the traditional practices of their particular family, village, or urban quarter and not of people outside those groups. Others seek a break with traditional practice in the pursuit of a more thoroughly Islamic society; however they do not all agree on what that alternative ought to be. Still others have begun to take advantage of the waning of Soviet anti-Islamic policies since 1989 to learn more about the teachings of their faith, a process which began so recently that its outcome cannot yet be predicted.[62]

Another reason Islam has not been as powerful a unifying force in practice as it is in theory is that it has become strongly linked to national identity among Central Asians in the past half century.[63] If anything, this linkage strengthens the legitimacy of the comparatively new concept of national identity in this region. One reflection of this national coloration of Islam is that, as the power of the Soviet system eroded, the authority of the Muslim Spiritual Adminstration of Central Asia and Kazakhstan, a Stalinist creation, weakened considerably while religious figures in individual republics gained in authority. That is certainly the case in Tajikistan, where the chief *qadi*, Haji Akbar Turajonzoda, is widely respected because of his personal qualities, not because he is part of a bureaucracy which is nominally headed by the Mufti of Tashkent. Although he used his position in Tajikistan's legislature to seek official recognition of the role Islam plays in Tajik society (such as recognizing Muslim holidays as legal holidays),[64] he chose not to run for president in the fall 1991 campaign, despite widespread enthusiasm for his candidacy. He has publicly disavowed the notion of establishing an Islamic republic in Tajikistan.[65]

Once again, the fact that the Tajiks are an Iranian people worried about domination by the Turkic majority plays a role. A number of Tajik intellectuals have expressed the concern that any supra-national Islamic movement in the Soviet Union would be dominated by the Turkic peoples.[66] Even one of the founders of the Tajikistan branch of the all-Union Islamic Revival Party (subsequently a separate party), Davlat Usmonov, voiced no interest in the creation of a supra-national Islamic state. Apart from the fact that he considered such a state impracticable, he also saw it as undesirable. To him, it is significant that Muslims belong to different nationalities; he thinks their national differences matter.[67]

Culture also links Tajiks to the much larger number of Persian-speakers living outside the former Soviet Union, in Iran and Afghanistan. Soviet policy toward this kinship was oddly ambivalent. On the one hand, the official line designated the Tajiks a distinctive Soviet nationality, separate from peoples living outside the Soviet Union. On the other hand, Moscow's foreign policy found uses from the 1920s to the 1980s for the fact that Tajiks share in the Persian cultural heritage. The Tajiks' interest in the Persian cultural world ought not to be interpreted simply as a desire to emulate Islamic political activists in the Islamic Republic of Iran or among Afghanistan's *mujahidin*. This interest predates the emergence of Islamic political activism by decades. In its current manifestation, it entails a variety of particulars, culture and economics being prominent among them, religion far less so.

Since World War II, Tajik intellectuals found ways, often indirect ones, to evade Moscow's strictures designed to separate them from Persian history, language and culture.[68] As glasnost and perestroika gained strength in Central Asia since the late 1980s, intellectuals and political figures have become much more open in asserting the links between Tajiks and Persians. For example, Tajikistan's 1989 language law also equated Tajik and Persian.[69] Tajik "informal" organizations also see the Persian connection as important, especially in a linguistic and cultural sense.[70] Tajiks in Uzbekistan expressed similar sentiments in a 1989 rally in Samarkand.[71] Both the 1989 Tajik language law and the program of the *Rastokhez* popular front organization advocate a return to the use of the Arabic alphabet, which had been dropped in 1929 as part of Moscow's attempt to erect barriers between the various Muslim peoples of the Soviet Union and kindred peoples abroad. The justification for the change is that it will allow Tajiks direct access both to works which are part of their heritage and contemporary writing in Persian, since so little of this has been translated into the modified cyrillic alphabet in which Tajik is written in the Soviet Union. (Knowledge of the Arabic alphabet would not be sufficient to enable a Tajik to read with comprehension the Koran or any other work in the Arabic language since the two languages belong to separate linguistic families.) The transition has proceeded very slowly thus far, at least in part because of the sheer logistical difficulty involved.[72]

Tajiks' curiosity about Iranians extends beyond those living in Iran or representing the Tehran regime to those living in Western countries, whether as refugees from the Islamic Republic or students.

Much of the Tajiks' attention now directed towards the wider Persian world reflects practical concerns over developing Tajikistan's economy. For example, Tajikistan's regime announced a conference for Tajiks from around the world to meet in Dushanbe in March 1992. The organizers were especially interested in attracting people who had technical expertise, familiarity with the workings of a market economy, and the prospect of investing in businesses in Tajikistan.[73] In 1990 and 1991, delegations traveled in both directions between Iran and Tajikistan. Economic relations, such as prospects for joint ventures, trade, and the application of Iranian textile manufacturing technology to Tajikistan-produced cotton, as well as cultural relations, figured prominently in the discussions on those occasions.[74] Some Tajik intellectuals are interested in learning from revolutionary Iran for what it can show about how a country can make itself economically self-sufficient after having been, in Iranian revolutionaries' terms, dependent on foreign powers.[75] That is an issue of immediate practical relevance for Tajiks who want to reform Tajikistan's economy and end what they see as in essence a colonial relation to the broader Soviet economy.

Interest in things Iranian from the Soviet side of the border is not contingent upon kinship of the Tajiks and Persians. Several predominantly Turkic republics of the former Soviet Union, in addition to Tajikistan, have made *No ruz* a legal holiday, even though this new year's day celebrated on the vernal equinox is of pre-Islamic Persian origin. Over the centuries it was incorporated into the customs of various Turkic peoples, who nevertheless retained their distinctive identities. Since the late 1980s, officials on both sides of the Soviet-Iranian border have shown an interest in increased trade, joint ventures, the exploitation of natural resources in northern Iran, the opening of new transportation routes, and, from Iran's point of view, the pursuit of increased influence in the predominantly Muslim republics of the Soviet Union. All this led to exchanges of delegations and talks between the Iranian government and both the Soviet central government and individual republics, in addition to Tajikistan.[76]

Soviet Tajiks' attitudes toward Afghanistan are in many ways similar to their attitudes toward Iran but are complicated by the war the Soviet army fought in support of the Communist regime in Kabul. In consequence of the increasing decentralization of Soviet power in the Gorbachev era and the concomitant rise in the importance of the republican governments, the Kabul regime opened a consulate in Dushanbe. During the war years, the proximity of and the cultural similarities between Tajikistan and Afghanistan made the former useful to Moscow as it strove to solidify Communist rule in the latter. Moscow used Soviet Tajiks (and other Central Asian peoples) to work in Afghanistan's government, educational, and scholarly systems. It had publications from Tajikistan sent to Afghanistan. It used Tajikistan as an example to show organized delegations from Afghanistan and as a place to educate young Afghanistanis. Cultural exchanges between these two republics continued throughout the war years. Tajiks from Tajikistan saw tours of duty in the Soviet military in Afghanistan from the invasion in 1979 to the Soviet withdrawal in 1988.[77]

This last point is an extremely sensitive one for some Soviet Tajiks. In the period following the August 1991 coup attempt, when various people in Tajikistan expressed their opinions more openly in public than before, a Tajik poet and advocate of reform, Bozor Sobir, ignited a controversy by stating in the republican legislature than no Tajik ought to take pride in being named a "Hero of the Soviet Union" for having fought in Afghanistan. Sobir's objection was that the title came at the price of fighting ones' brothers. Not surprisingly, there were indignant responses from people who spouted cliches of Soviet "internationalist" rhetoric.[78] However, one Tajik who served in the Soviet army in Afghanistan from 1985 to 1987 was able to have published in the official press a letter in which he endorsed Sobir's view and added that Tajiks who fought in Afghanistan were fighting people of the "same race, same blood, and same language."[79] Political conditions have not yet changed enough in Tajikistan to permit a full and free public discussion of this issue or a reliable sampling of public opinion on the subject.

Tajik nationalists also see Afghanistan as important to them culturally, for much the same reason as they do Iran: as a source of examples of good usage of literary Persian to counterbalance the harmful effects of Soviet language policy and of literature in the Persian language.[80]

Since the Soviet military withdrawal, Tajikistan has had direct and indirect dealings with Afghanistan's government on cooperation in various spheres. Tajikistani officials have signed economic agreements with representatives of the Kabul regime and a private company acting with that regime's permission for such things as trade between the two countries, development projects, and joint ventures.[81] There are also plans for exchanges of students and publications and for increased scholarly contacts. Representatives of one of Afghanistan's northern border provinces offered to allow Tajikistanis to study in *madrasahs* there.[82] Small numbers of Soviet Muslim religious figures have been going abroad to study, with Moscow's approval, for years. Opportunities for foreign study are particularly important now because the recent, substantial increase in religious freedom in Central Asia has brought with it an increased demand for Islamic instruction, which cannot be satisfied in full by the *madrasahs* in the region.

The extent and nature of religious influence which passes from Afghanistan to Tajikistan are controversial subjects and also ones on which there is more propaganda than reliable information. An attempt to resolve the controversy lies beyond the scope of this essay. Various Soviet sources, including V.V. Petkel', head of the KGB in Tajikistan from 1985 until 1991, saw Islam in wholly negative terms and linked it to anti-Soviet subversion from abroad, especially via Afghanistan.[83]

Such assertions owe so much to the ideological biases and self-interest of those who make them that it is difficult to discern whether there is any basis for them in fact. Claims by some Afghanistani *mujahidin* to have supporters in Soviet Central Asia cannot be confirmed independently. Although the perseverant battle by Afghanistani *mujahidin* against the Soviet invaders and the Communist regime in Kabul may well have won admiration from at least some people in Tajikistan or elsewhere in Central Asia, that does not by itself prove that Tajiks feel a particularly loyalty to or draw their ideas from any *mujahidin* group. The assumption that *mujahidin* influence plays a crucial role implies that Tajiks are merely passive objects to be manipulated by others.

Further, the *mujahidin*, while agreeing that Islam is a part of their way of life, disagree among themselves on what kind of Islamic country Afghanistan ought to be. There is a big difference between a state which is Islamic, in the sense that Islam is practiced freely in accordance with local traditions, and an "Islamic state" which seeks a radical transformation of society to purge it of injustices, deviations from proper Islamic practice, and non-Islamic influences (all as defined differently by different groups of radicals). Afghanistan's *mujahidin* organizations are divided along these and other lines; several of the organizations are also associated predominantly with a particular ethnic group. Thus, one of the groups that is more radical in its approach to Islam, the Hizb-i Islami, is largely Pushtun and is at odds with the Jami'at-i Islami, which is more moderate on the nature of the role of Islam in Afghanistani society and is predominantly Tajik. Afghanistan's Tajik population lives primarily in the northeast, across the border from Soviet Tajikistan, while the Pushtuns live predominantly in southern and southeastern Afghanistan (and across the border in Pakistan.)[84]

The anti-Communist demonstrations in Tajikistan between late August and early October 1991 may reflect something about the limits there of

Islamic radicalism of any type, including as inspired by Afghanistani *muja-hidin*. Former KGB commander Petkel' had alleged that at the time of the February 1990 riots in Dushanbe, Afghanistani *mujahidin* had marshalled near the border, ready to invade Tajikistan in support of Islamic extremists there. Yet, in the aftermath of the failure of the August 1991 coup, when the Soviet regime was the weakest it had been since the Nazi invasion, there was no uprising by Islamic radicals in Tajikistan and no armed intervention by Afghanistani *mujahidin*. Although the anti-Communist demonstrations were large, they remained orderly. No one was attacked physically. There was no declaration of an Islamic republic and no decision to make a complete break with the Soviet Union.

As important as national consciousness is now to many Soviet Tajiks, they do not look at the rest of the world solely in terms of ethnicity. Tajiks in the republican regime and in opposition to it do not limit their curiosity about foreign lands to those where Persian-speakers are numerous. They also favor developing economic relations with a host of other countries, many of which do not share a Persian cultural link, from Europe and the United States to Turkey and China.[85]

This reflects two fundamentally important characteristics of nationalism as it now exists among the Tajiks of Tajikistan: it is subject to diverse interpretations and is not necessarily exclusivist. The nationalist camp contains Communists and anti-communists, the secular and the religious. It is virtually impossible now for any one to find political support among Tajiks without addressing issues in nationalist terms. The very fact that this is so means that people use nationalist rhetoric for a variety of motives and interpret it in multiple ways. For example, the Communist Party veteran, determined to survive in changing conditions by adapting, the urban intellectual who links pride in his Tajik identity with a desire for political democratization and economic reform, and the unemployed youth who vents his frustration by expressing hostility toward "Europeans" all talk about similar issues but draw sharply different conclusions. For now, the mainstream of the nationalist movement is more interested in working out solutions than in fostering conflict. They look for effective remedies for their problems in the West and elsewhere in the former Soviet Union as well as in lands to the south inhabited by kindred peoples. Their future orientation will be affected significantly by how helpful a response they receive from these varied sources.

Notes

1 S. Davlatov, "Vaqti amal ast," *Tojikistoni soveti*, July 16, 1989, p. 3; R. Ataev and D. Kabiliov, "Kto idet nevernoi dorogoi?", *Komsomolets Tadzhikstana*, September 6, 1989, p. 1; A. Vahhobov, "Khomushi ba ki lozim?", *Tojikistoni soveti*, June 13, 1989, p. 2; T. Barki, "Vstrechaias' s deputatom," *Komsomolets Tadzhikistana*, December 20, 1989, p. 6.

2 S. Ayub, "Nomo niz ta"rikhand," *Adabiyot va san"at*, October 13, 1988, p. 11; B. Karimov, "Dar poyai vaizfahoi nav," *ibid.*, November 9, 1989, p. 12; A. Mukhtorov, "Ta"rikhdoni khudshinosist," *Gazetai muallimon*, March 4, 1989, p. 3; "Mas"uliayati buzurg meboyad," *Tojikistoni soveti*, July 25, 1989, p. 2.

3 M. Khudoiev, "Gotovnost' k dialogu, no na printsipial'noi osnove," *Kommunist Tadzhikistana*, July 3, 1990, p. 1.

4 Foreign Broadcast Information Service [FBIS], *Daily Report. Soviet Union*, October 5, 1990, p. 105.

5 "Izhoroti ishtirokkunandagoni konferentsiyai ta"sisi sozmoni umumimillii tojikon 'Mehr'," *Sogdiana*, 1990, no. 3, p. 1; "Pora obnovleniia," *ibid.*, no. 1, p. 1; "Obshchestvo v 1989 godu," *ibid.*, p. 4.

6 F. Karimov, "Muloqoti namoyandagoni quvvahoi demokrati," *Tojikistoni soveti*, May 15, 1991, p. 2.

7 R. Evans and R. Novak, "Moscow: Periphery of Power," *Washington Post*, September 25, 1991, p. A25.

8 TadzhikTA, "Shikasti suiqasdchiyon – piruzii demokratiya," *Tojikistoni shuravi*, August 27, 1991, p. 2.

9 S. Tabarov, "Sarvati bebehoi ma"navi," *Tojikistoni soveti*, December 12, 1986, p. 3; "Kalomi navisanda – vositai muhimi tarbiyai internatsionali," *Adabiyot va sn"at*, June 11, 1987, p. 3.

10 He fell from his offices as party leader and republican president in September 1991, in the backlash against the attempted coup of August 19–21, 1991.

11 TadzhikTA, "Vospityvat' ubezhdennykh bortsov za delo partii," *Kommunist Tadzhikistana*, September 3, 1986, p. 2.

12 "Politicheskii kharakter partiinogo rukovodstva: opyt i problemy," *Komsomolets Tadzhikistana*, April, 14, 1989, p. 2; "O prakticheskikh merakh po realizatsii v respublike reshenii sentiabr'skogo (1989 g.) Plenuma TsK KPSS," *Kommunist Tadzhikistana*, 1990, no. 2, February, p. 19.

13 From the perspective of Persian-speaking Iranians, the Samanids presided over the revival of Persian culture after the Arab conquest.

14 The historic name "Badakhshan" is also used now for a province in northeastern Afghanistan.

15 A. Sheehy, "Ethnic Muslims Account for Half of Soviet Population Increase," *Report on the USSR*, vol. 2, no. 3, January 19, 1990, p. 16.

16 M. Atkin, "Tajiks and the Persian World," in *Soviet Central Asia in Historical Perspective*, ed. B.F. Manz (Boulder, CO: Westview Press, forthcoming).

17 "Qonuni zaboni Respublikai Sovetii Sotsialistii Tojikiston," *Tojikistoni soveti*, July 30, 1989, p. 1.

18 "Az rui aqli solim," *Adabiyot va san"at*, August 16, 1990, p. 1; "Ustav i programma organizatsii 'Rastokhez' (Vozrozhdenie) Tadzhikskoi SSR," *Rastokhez*, 1990, no. 5, pp. 2, 3; "Izhoroti," p. 1.

19 "Izhorot," *Tojikistoni shuravi*, September 10, 1991, p. 1; "Az rui aqli solim," *Adabiyot va san"at*, August 16, 1990, p. 1; "Navtarin Khabarhoi Ruz," *Tojikistoni shuravi*, September 4, 1991, p. 1.

20 B. Berdieva, "Hama rosti juyu mardonagi," *Omuzgor*, July 25, 1989, p. 7; Atkin, "Tajiks."

21 Photograph of the demonstrators, *Tojikistoni shuravi*, August 30, 1991, p. 2.

22 E. Muhammad, "Maromi mo: khudshinosi, bedorii millat," *Tojikistoni shuravi*, September 10, 1991, p. 2.

23 Representative of the voluminous literature on this subject are: Sh. Sultonov, "Maromnomai partiya," *Tojikistoni soveti*, September 5, 1989, p. 2; H. Umarov, "Iqtisodi tijorati: ovoza, vohima va haqiqat," *ibid.*, June 3, 1990, p. 3; Sh. Shoismatulloev, "Progress – ne"mati azim," *ibid.*, March 1, 1990, p. 2; A. Vahhobov, "Khomushi ba ki lozim?"; Berdieva, "Hana rosti juyu mard-onagi"; A. Istad, 'Iqtisod – sarchashmai mas"alahoi milli," *Adabiyot va san"at*, September 7, 1989, p. 3; R.K. Alimov, Sh. Shoismatulloev, and M. Saidov, "Migratsionnye protsessy i natsional'nyi vopros," *Kommunist Tadzhikistana*, 1990, no. 5, May, p. 12.

24 A few examples of this oft-repeated argument are: "Durnamoi rushdi mo," *Adabiyot va san"at*, July 13, 1989, p. 2; H. Muhammadiev, "Barodari man boshi, barobari man bosh!", *ibid.*, September 7, 1989, p. 3; N. Yodgori, "Narkhi pakhta va sathi zindagi," *Tojikistoni soveti*, January 6, 1990, p. 2; R. Bobojonov, H. Botirov, and M. Mavlaviev, "Mo hama farzandi yek oilaem!", *Tojikistoni soveti*, July 30, 1989, p. 3; S. Mirzoev, "Tadzhikistan! Kakov tvoi zavtrashnii den'?", *Sogdiana*, 1990, no. 3, October, p. 1; "Natsional'nyi vopros," p. 84.

25 "Natsional'nyi vopros," p. 9; A. Sattorov, "Dardhoi miyonshikan," *Omuzgor*, October 3, 1989, p. 4; "Soobshchenie komissii prezidiuma Verkhovnogo Soveta Tadzhikskoi SSR po proverke sobytii 12–14 Fevralia 1991 g. v Dushanbe," *Sogdiana*, 1990, no. 3, October, p. 3; R.K. Alimov, Sh. Shoisma-tulloev, and M. Saidov, "Migratsionnye protsessy i natsional'nyi vopros," *Kommunist Tadzhikistana*, 1990, no. 5, May, p. 11; Q. Kholiqov, "Oilai bara-daroni mo: tajriba, problema, peshomadho," *Adabiyot va san"at*, April 13, 1989, p. 3; Helsinki Watch, *Conflict in the Soviet Union. Tajikistan* (New York and Washington, DC: Human Rights Watch, 1991), p. 13; Bobojonov, Botirov and Mavlaviev, "Mo hama";

26 "Soobschchenie komissii," pp. 2–4; Helsinki Watch, *Conflict*, pp. 22–23, 25, 40, 41.

27 H. Atokhonov, "Azamati navbati dar Vakhsh," *Tojikistoni soveti*, October 19, 1989, p. 2; M. Mirrahim, "Tazodhoi madaniyati dehot," *Sadoi Sharq*, 1989, no. 1, p. 119.

28 L.F. Monogarova, "Evoliutsiia natsional'nogo samosoznaniia pripamirskikh narodnostei," *Etnicheskie protessy u natsional'nykh grupp Srednei Azii i Kazakhstana* (Moscow: Nauka, 1980), pp. 128–130, 132–134.

29 Representative of this view are: "Tojikon,", *Entsiklopediyai Sovetii Tojik*, vol. 7 (Dushanbe: Sarredaktsiyai ilmii Entsiklopediyai Sovetii Tojik, 1987), pp. 428–429; S. Aini, "Ma"noi kalimai tojik," *Sadoi Sharq*, 1986, no. 8, p. 85; B.Gh. Ghafurov, *Tojikon* (Dushanbe: Irfon, 1983), vol. I, pp. 494–496.

30 Atkin, "Tajiks."

31 "Mas"uliyati buzurg," p. 2.

32 Tsentral'noe Statisticheskoe Upravlenie SSSR, *Chislennost' i sostav naseleniia SSSR* (Moscow: Finansy i statistika, 1984), pp. 132–133.

33 I. Zokirov and Kh. Bobojonob, "Isfara: konferentsiyai matbuot dar huzuri Q.M. Mahkamov," *Tojikistoni soveti*, July 21, 1989, p. 1; "Mas"uliyati buzurg," p. 2.

```

34 TadzhikTA, "Dar Prezidiumi Sovetii Olii RSS Tojikiston," *Tojikistoni soveti*, June 23, 1989, p. 2.
35 Tsentral'noe Statisticheskoe Upravlenie SSSR, *Chislennost'*, pp. 132–133.
36 Muhammadiev, "Barodari man boshi,"
37 A.Istad, "Ba ki ta"na mezanem?", p. 7; Helsinki Watch, *Conflict*; Alimov, Shoismatulloev, and Saidov, "Migratsionnye protsessy," p. 13.
38 Helsinki Watch, *Conflict*, pp. 8, 13, 53, 62; FBIS, *Daily Report. Soviet Union*, January 4, 1991, p. 58; Alimov, Shoismatulloev, and Saidov, "Migratsionnye protsessy," pp. 11–13, 17; Dzh. Kabilov, "Domoi, po 'natsional'nym kvartiram'?", *Komsomolets Tadzhikistana*, December 20, 1989, p. 6.
39 I. Rotar', "My khotim islamskoi demokratii," *Nezavisimaia gazeta*, September 11, 1991, p. 3.
40 M. Fineman, "Fearful Christians and Jews Leaving Troubled Soviet Tajikistan," *Los Angeles Times*, October 13, 1991, p. A10.
41 "Regional'noe ekonomicheeskoe sotrudnichestvo: opyt, problemy, perspectivy," *Agitator Tadzhikistana*, 1989, no. 18 (September), p. 3; FBIS, *Daily Report. Soviet Union*, July 17, 1990, pp. 86–88.
42 TadzhikTA, "Dar safi pesh," *Tojikistoni soveti*, December 9, 1989, p. 3.
43 P. Pons, "Communists versus Islam," *Manchester Guardian Weekly*, October 6, 1991, p. 15 (from *Le Monde*, September 25, 1991.)
44 "Az rui maslihati dustoni hammusobiqa amal mekunem," *Tojikistoni soveti*, August 16, 1989, p. 3.
45 "Hamkori duston," *Tojikistoni shuravi*, September 10, 1991, p. 2.
46 Helsinki Watch, *Conflict*, p. 58.
47 P. Goble, "Central Asians Form Political Bloc," *Report on the USSR*, July 13, 1990, pp. 19–20; F. Karimov, "Muloqoti."
48 FBIS, *Daily Report. Soviet Union*, July 9, 1991, p. 74.
49 Karimov, "Muloqoti," p. 2.
50 FBIS, *Daily Report. Soviet Union*, August 22, 1990, p. 91.
51 *Ibid.*, June 4, 1990, p. 116; *ibid.*, June 11, 1990, p. 119.
52 H. Atokhonov, "Azamati navbati dar Vakhsh," p. 2; "Regional'noe ekonomicheskoe sotrudnichestvo"; I. Khisamov, "Voda kak prichina pozhara," *Literaturnaia gazeta*, January 16, 1991, p. 8; G. Gleason, "The Struggle for Control over Water in Central Asia: Republican Sovereignty and Collective Action," *Daily Report. Soviet Union*, vol. 3, no. 25, June 21, 1991, pp. 16, 17.
53 "Konflikt na granitse Kirgizii i Tadzhikistana," *Turkestan*, 1990, no. 1, January–February, p. 5; M. Popov, "Janjol metavonist sar nazanad," *Tojikistoni soveti*, June 28, 1989, p. 3; TadzhikTA, "Dar sharoiti vaqti komendanti," *Tojikistoni soveti*, July 19, 1989, p. 1; Zokirov and Bobojonov, "Isfara"; FBIS, *Soviet Union. Daily Report*, May 28, 1991, p. 76.
54 M. Atkin, "Religious, National, and Other Identities in Central Asia," *Muslims in Central Asia*, ed. Jo-Ann Gross (Durham, NC: Duke University Press, 1992), pp. 50–52.
55 Joint Publications Research Service, *USSR. Political Affairs*, November 18, 1988, p. 97.
56 "Natsional'nyi vopros," p. 33; for a similar estimate, see also Muhammadiev, 'Barodari man boshi."
57 R. Masov, "Far'yodi qurboniyon: nido as safhai ta"rikh," *Omuzgor*, July 18,
```

1989, p. 6; B. Firuz, "Didu bobide muborak!", *Adabiyot va san"at*, April 20, 1989, p. 4; A. Istad, "Qonuni madaniyat zarur," *Adabiyot va san"at*, August 10, 1989, p. 10; D. Ruziev, "Ki durugh meguyad? Vazir yo vakili anjuman?", *Tojikistoni soveti*, October 20, 1989, p. 3; Q. Davlatov, "Seb ne, olma," *Omuzgor*, November 7, 1989, p. 3; A. Mardon, "Barodari boyad barobari boshad," *Omuzgor*, December 5, 1989, p. 9; N.B. Khotamov, "Iz sovetskoi pressy," *Sogdiana*, 1990, no. 1, February, p. 3; "Na ruinakh ambitsii," *ibid.*, p. 3; "Pora obnovleniia."

58 FBIS, *Daily Report. Soviet Union*, September 24, 1990, p. 104; *ibid.*, September 28, 1990, p. 104.

59 W. Fierman, "Policy toward Islam in Uzbekistan in the Gorbachev Era," *The National Question in the Soviet Union*, ed. J. Jaworsky (Waterloo, Ontario: University of Waterloo Press, forthcoming.)

60 M. Umarzoda, "Ma"nii 'Tojik'," *Tojikistoni soveti*, September 25, 1988, pp. 3, 4; R. Sobirov, "Na"lgare, ki zargari kunad . . ." *ibid.*, October 21, 1988, p. 3; S. Halimsho, "Darakhti jovidonkhirad," *Adabiyot va san"at*, August 24, 1989, p. 5; I am grateful to Professor William Fierman for confirming that such an argument is indeed found in the Uzbek-language original of Ahmadali Mahmudov's novel, *Immortal Cliffs*.

61 Barki, "Vstrechaias'"; Helsinki Watch, *Conflict*, p. 12.

62 Atkin, "Islamic Assertiveness and the Waning of the Old Soviet Order," *Nationalities Papers*, vol. 20, no. 1, Spring 1992, p. 62.

63 A. Bennigsen and C. Lemercier-Quelquejay, *L'Islam en Union Soviétique* (Paris: Payot, 1968), pp. 188, 216.

64 A. Lukin and A. Ganelin, "Podpol'nyi obkom deistvuet," *Komsomol'skaia pravda*, March 23, 1991, p. 2.

65 V. Vyzhutovich, "Krasnoe zhamia kommunizma ili zelenoe znamia islama?", *Izvestiia*, October 5, 1991, p. 2.

66 Helsinki Watch, *Conflict*, p. 13; statements made in this author's presence.

67 "Partiia, kotoroi ofitsial'no u nas net," *Komsomolets Tadzhikistana*, November 21, 1990, p. 2.

68 Atkin, "Tajiks."

69 "Qonuni zaboni."

70 "Ustav," p. 3; "Az rui aqli solim"; "Izhoroti," p. 1; "Pora obnovleniia"; "Obshchestvo," p. 1.

71 "Na ruinakh ambitsii."

72 Atkin, "Tajiks."

73 FBIS, *Daily Report. Soviet Union*, August 6, 1991, p. 73.

74 *Ibid.*, April 25, 1991, p. 75; 'Bozargononi Iron dar Tojikiston," *Tojikistoni shuravi*, August 27, 1991, p. 3; Atkin, "Tajiks."

75 Atkin, "Tajiks."

76 FBIS, *Daily Report. Soviet Union*, February 15, 1991, p. 91; *ibid.*, July 22, 1991, p. 88; *ibid.*, May 29, 1991, p. 16; *ibid.*, June 17, 1991, p. 18; *ibid.*, June 13, 1991, p. 12; *ibid.*, November 21, 1990, pp. 18–19; UzTAG, "Gosti Uzbekistana," *Pravda Vostoka*, March 29, 1991, p. 1.

77 Atkin, "Religious, National, and Other Identities," p. 58; TadzhikTA, "Dar safi pesh."

78 "Madar ashk merekhtu duo mekard . . .", *Jumhuriyat*, September 20, 1991,

p. 1; H. Kiromov, A. Ruziev, and S. Iskandarov, "Nadidam mehrubon dilhoi az insof kholiro," *Tojikistoni shuravi*, September 14, 1991, p. 4.

79 M. Shukurzoda, "Haghighat zahr ham boshad, niyush!", *Tojikistoni shuravi*, September 14, 1991, p. 4.

80 Atkin, "Tajiks."

81 Kh. Qodir, "Mekhohem masdari khidmat ba mardumi du kishvar boshem," *Tojikistoni shuravi*, August 27, 1991, p. 4; FBIS, *Daily Report. Soviet Union*, November 1, 1990, p. 106.

82 FBIS, *Daily Report. Soviet Union*, May 7, 1991, p. 76.

83 A typical Petkel' tirade is available in translation in FBIS, *Daily Report. Soviet Union*, April 12, 1991, pp. 74–75; see also Atkin, "Islamic Assertiveness," pp. 56–57.

84 O. Roy, "The Mujahidin and the Future of Afghanistan," in *The Iranian Revolution: Its Global Impact*, ed. J.L. Esposito (Miami: Florida International University Press, 1990), p. 184; M.N. Shahrani, "Introduction: Marxist 'Revolution' and Islamic Resistance in Afghanistan," in *Revolutions and Rebellions in Afghanistan*, Research Series no. 57, ed., M.N. Shahrani and R.L. Canfield, eds. (Berkeley, Institute of International Studies, University of California, 1984), pp. 45–49.

85 N. Asadullo, "Dudi khonaro ravzan dedonad," *Adabiyot va san"at*, June 21, 1990, p. 3; S. Mirzoev, "Tadzhikistan!"; "Oshkhonai chekhi dar Farkhor," *Tojikistoni shuravi*, August 29, 1991, p. 3.

16 Turkmenistan: searching for a national identity

DAVID NISSMAN

When the Soviet Union was intact, Turkmenistan was the fourth largest union republic in terms of territory and one of the smallest in terms of population. Prior to the Russian Revolution, the dominant political forces in the region were the khanates of Khiva and Khokand, to whom the Turkmens were subordinate; the dominant force in Turkmen life was the tribe, the clan, the family and Islam. This has not changed. It is clear that Sovietization for seventy years exerted only a superficial influence on Turkmen life, and then primarily in terms of economics; Turkmenistan's economy came to be based on cotton and, to a lesser extent, energy resources and its vast sulfur reserves.

The August 1991 coup in the USSR changed nothing in Turkmenistan: the Turkmenistan Communist Party was dismantled in name only; S.A. Niyazov, formerly first Secretary of the Central Committee of the Turkmenistan Communisty Party, retained his position as the duly elected president (in an election in which he was the only candidate), and dissent movements, including non-communist democratic reform movements, continue to be either suppressed by authorities or, in general, passed over in silence by the Turkmen media.

Tribalism is still strongly felt in Turkmenistan. A "Round Table" discussion among prominent social activists touched on this in 1988 in the context of nationalism: one participant maintained that nationalism per se was not a problem in Turkmenistan but that "among Turkmens themselves incorrect tribal-clan relations and tribal prejudices . . . are not only disturbing, but also do considerable harm." He noted that at the opening of the academic year at the Turkmen State University students were allocated rooms without regard to their rayon or oblast "but only a short time later only people from the same villages occupy the same rooms."[1]

Turkmen political unity can be said only to have become a reality in the twentieth century. The two factors which transcend tribal and the putative Soviet national concept imposed on the Turkmens in the Stalin period are language and religion, Islam. To be added to this, perhaps, is a third, somewhat more elusive factor – "Turkmenism" – which has only recently been raised for public discussion and not defined. Basically, it is an attempt to define what makes an individual exclusively a Turkmen, as opposed to a

Turk, a Muslim, a communist or a democrat.[2] Since nations have risen and fallen throughout history without defining, or even contemplating, what made them unique, it can be assumed that this question is peripheral to the main issue, which is Turkmenistan's potential future as a nation.

Turkmenistan was the last Central Asian territory conquered by the advance of the Tsarist armies, which smashed the defending forces assembled by the Teke Turkmen tribal confederacy in the late nineteenth century, at the battle of Gokdepe in 1881. The Anglo-Russian Treaty of 1895 established the present borders between Turkmenistan, Iran and Afghanistan. A consequence of this treaty was that a significant part of the Turkmen population which lived, and lives, in Iran and Afghanistan was isolated from Turkmen territory. There are now approximately 2.5 million Turkmens in Turkmenistan, and it has been estimated that there are between 1 and 2 million Turkmens directly across the border in Iran, and another million in Afghanistan. Only since the onset of glasnost in Turkmenistan (somewhat later than in other parts of the Soviet Union) have contacts between the Turkmens of Iran, Afghanistan and the USSR been revived. Of equal or, in the short term, perhaps even greater importance, is that renewed contact with the exile Turkmen community – those who had fled to the West or Middle East from Bolshevism – provides the formerly isolated Turkmens of the Soviet Union with a greater diversity of economic and political views than ever before in the twentieth century.

Turkmenia was proclaimed a republic of the Soviet Union in October 1924, when Central Asia was divided administratively by the Bolshevik government in Moscow. This process was officially termed national-state demarcation (*razmezhevanie*). Before the creation of the Turkmen Soviet Socialist Republic, Soviet policy aimed at repressing nationalist and bourgeois forces, purportedly exemplified by the *bais*, who were wealthy landowners, stockraisers, and merchants, and the *manaps*, clan leaders in control of armed military groups. The Islamic clergy, too, was repressed for insisting on the existence of a single Turkic nation. A coordinated anti-Islam drive launched by the center in 1928 was especially intense. Between 1928 and 1932 opposition to Stalin's collectivization policies also surfaced and even ministers in the Soviet Turkmen government were implicated in a supposed plot to establish an independent state under British protection. One final anti-Soviet uprising, in the Kara Kum in 1931, was brutally suppressed by security forces.

A national opposition movement, called the Turkmen *Azatlygi*, appeared in the 1930s in response to Stalinist excesses and, as elsewhere in the USSR, local party and government leaders were charged with fomenting such sedition and were executed. Chief among those named in the alleged anti-Soviet conspiracy was Premier Gaygisiz Atabay, the subject of a later novel by Turkmenistan's leading writer Berdi Kerbbabayev. An extensive purge of the Turkmen party organization followed but, simultaneously, the replacement of *korenizatsiya* (or Turkmenization) of leadership functions with Sovietization led to the discrediting of the Communist movement for decades. The Turkmen Communist Party had originally been hastily put together in 1925, just before Turkmenistan was officially admitted into the USSR as a union republic, and its credibility was never great.

In the Stalin era, cultural relations among Central Asian republics were limited by Russian suspicions about emergent Pan-Turkism and Pan-Islamism. As in other republics, the Arabic alphabet was replaced in 1929 with a Latin one adapted to Turkmen phonemes. By 1940, however, Latin was, in its turn, replaced by a modified form of Cyrillic. The Stalinist policy of industrialization applied in the republic brought some of the benefits of modernization: emergence of a modest working class and national intelligentsia, increased socio-economic mobility, new employment patterns, some urbanization. Expansion of irrigated agriculture and accelerated development of the cotton industry (already thriving under Nicolas II) also marked Turkmenistan as a region different from Islamic peoples across the Soviet border. Construction beginning in 1954 of the Kara-Kum canal (the largest irrigation project in the USSR) subsequently changed the lifestyle of much of the republic's rural population and caused severe damage to the Aral Sea.

Accusations of nationalism and Pan-Turkism – as different as they are from each other – were regularly leveled at prominent Turkmen politicians after World War II. In the *Zhdanovshchizna* the Turkmen historian Gayip Nepesov was forced to rewrite a too-sympathetic depiction of local opposition to Bolshevik rule after 1917. Under Khrushchev, Turkmen Communist Party head Suhan Babayev was removed from office following his advocacy of *korenizatsiya*. In the Brezhnev period republic party head Muhammetnazar Gapurov exhorted the party to guard against nationalism; among his victims was dissident poet Annasoltan Kekilova, who was hospitalized for "nervous tension" after criticizing the party.

But resistance to the highly-centralized Soviet state seemed inexorable in the political climate following Khrushchev's destalinization speech of 1956. In the early 1960s Turkmen participation in the Central Asian Economic Region revived interest in cooperation with the other republics in non-economic areas as well. By the 1970s some Turkmen officials, while being careful not to attack Soviet leaders, were seeking more powers from the all-union government in budgetary and planning matters. The division of labor among republics mapped out by the Kremlin was meeting with less local cooperation as Turkmen officials sought to give priority to industrial development that served the republic's needs first. In particular, the Soviet policy of treating cotton, gas and oil as raw materials to be exported from Turkmenistan and processed elsewhere in the USSR was increasingly criticized by Turkmen Communist leaders themselves. The fact that industrial development in Turkmenistan lagged behind all other republics exacerbated the sense of deprivation.

Like other Central Asian republics, Turkmens demonstrated extraordinarily high retention of the native language into the 1980s (over 98 percent). About one-third of the republic's population belonged to other nationalities, however. Half of these were Russians, and smaller minorities included the Baluchis, Kurds, and Iranians. Let us now examine the policies of Turkmen leaders in the Gorbachev period that led to independence following Soviet collapse in December 1991.

Turkmen nationhood and sources of dissent

Turkmenistan declared itself a sovereign nation on August 22, 1990 and attained independence slightly more than a year later; at the same time, the Niyazov government stressed its willingness to remain within the Soviet Union. No voices of direct dissent were raised in the media but, in fact, an organized movement searching for political alternatives had already begun to take shape. Unlike most of the other Central Asian republics, the Turkmen democratic and anti-communist movements have received no coverage in the Turkmen mass media, save the occasional denunciation directed at either the movements themselves or their more active members. In January 1990, the director of the Ideology Department of the Central Committee of the Turkmen Communist Party assailed a group of "nonformals" within the Turkmen Academy of Sciences by claiming that they were misusing glasnost and pluralism in their attacks on the Communist Party.[3] A month later, Turkmenistan's First Deputy Procurator announced that "measures" were to be taken against "juridically unregistered movements." Specifically, he mentioned a movement called *Agzybirlik* ("Solidarity") as a target of these "measures."[4] The attitude of the party elite towards political pluralism was expressed clearly by a party official in the Academy of Sciences: he opposed any party which is "unable to make a contribution to perfecting socialism."[5] Despite the frequent criticism directed at such organizations, political and social dissent continued to spread. An official Turkmen Writers Union spokesman noted that "tendencies to deny the political primacy of the CPSU and its organizational and political leadership are not developing without a significant influence on Turkmen literature and writers."[6] The failure of the August 1991 coup clearly caught the Turkmen ruling hierarchy unprepared, although in the coup's immediate aftermath no important Turkmen official lost his position.

Along with democratic movements such as *Agzybirlik*, nationalism and extremism also have found fertile soil in Turkmenistan. In May 1989 citywide riots took place in Ashkhabad and Nebitdag. While these were initially attributed to hooliganism on the part of youths, later interpretations of these events cast a different light on the occurrences. A "round table" discussion at the Turkmenistan Council of Trade Unions stressed efforts by "scandalmongers and extremists" to stir up feelings of nationalism among Turkmen youth.[7] A few months later, a commentator on social issues complained that "windbags" are aiding and abetting nationalism and "exploiting the quarrelsome nature of petty chauvinist groups."[8] On the other hand, the TuSSR Procuracy has admited that the May riots were attributable to a number of "unresolved," but unspecified social problems;[9] shortly thereafter, a "letter to the editor" asserted that the emergence of nationalism was not only built on "unresolved social problems, but also the distance between the party leadership and the people."[10] If that is indeed the case, this distance has not closed in post-coup Turkmenistan.

Events in other parts of the Soviet Union had an impact in Turkmenistan. The press carried the report of a meeting between a people's judge and students in Gokdepe allegedly in response to students' expressions of support for "extremist forces in Uzbekistan" and other parts of the country.[11] In an effort to counter this type of influence, the press started printing "letters to the editor" decrying the Baltic independence movements.[12] This campaign, however, was unable to counter the effect of news of independence movements and alternative political approaches in other republics: a year later, a discussion between historians, political scientists and journalists debating the advantages of remaining in the Soviet Union said that it was "regrettable" that there were some people in the republic under the influence of media coming from dissident republics.[13]

Islam in Turkmenistan

There is also an Islamic dissent movement in Turkmenistan. Statements like "if you are not a Muslim, you are not a Tajik; in Uzbekistan they say . . . not an Uzbek; in Turkmenia they say . . . not a Turkmen, etc"[14] have appeared frequently in past Soviet ethnographic and anti-religious media, and often observers of Central Asian Islam, Soviet and Western, have attempted to link Islam with various forms of Turkic nationalism on that basis. Until the late 1980s, it would have been safe to say that in Turkmenistan, Islam, especially the unofficial kind which has predominated and now is merging with the officially recognized state structure headed by the Kazi-Imam Ibadullayev, was closely linked with the tribal-clan structure. For the last few years, Turkmen Islam has also been subject to external influences: for example, there have been reports that Hekmatyar's Islamic Party of Afghanistan has been successful in bringing its ideology across the border into Turkmen[15] and that an attempt was made by two alleged Tajik "apple sellers" in a kolkhoz market in Ashkhabad to recruit soldiers among the Turkmens to conduct a *jihad* (holy war).[16] In the light of the statements in Dagestan of Abdureshid Saidov (published in Turkmenistan's Ministry of Education newspaper), head of the Islam Democratic Party, that Islam was incompatible with Marxism-Leninism,[17] one can readily understand that Turkmenistan's government, which is staffed almost completely by members of the former Marxist-Leninist regime, is treading very carefully when it comes to Turkmenistan's Muslims, especially in view of the "illegal religious pamphlets" now circulating in the country.[18]

Islam manifests itself in almost every facet of life: brideprice, the *gaytarma*, the pilgrimages to the Muslim shrines (often the burial place of an alleged Muslim saint who also happened to be a tribal patriarch sometime in the near or distant past), burials, marriages, births and major religious holidays (Ramadan, etc).

It would not be inaccurate to say that anti-Muslim propaganda conducted in Central Asia has been relatively ineffective. At the present time Islam is especially powerful among women and the youth. In 1988 an article in the Turkmen CP daily pointed out that mollas, ishans and faith healers are still active, "especially in the vicinity of 'holy' places" and added that "primarily, unemployed women and certain other groups of the population have fallen under their influence." Above all, "it has been demonstrated by sociological studies conducted in rural regions that more than 46 percent of nonbelievers follow religious traditions when they get married and during the course of religious holidays." The same survey established that 61.2 percent of female believers are housewives. Another survey conducted at three Turkmen schools found that 80 percent of the students "wear beads against the evil eye, multicoloured strings, amulets, talismans and other religious ornaments because it is in style."[19] In other words, Islam is not only a "harmful remnant of the past," it is also in style.

Communist officials have not been exempt from Muslim practices either. A report on the need to combat Islam and its influences in Turkmenistan states that

> facts have surfaced to the effect that at the time of death of wellknown high-ranking Communist officials pseudomollas demonstrate an unstinting "activism": they take over the burial and supervise it. By so doing, they create feelings of wonder and all kinds of false impressions among the people in the vicinity. Large mausoleums and monuments built of scarce materials are erected over their graves . . . On one hand, these attract the attention of religious believers and exert a harmful influence on the youth; on the other, they give rise to unhealthy attitudes among the population.[20]

Now that Islam has become more socially acceptable, it will be interesting to observe its impact on post-coup Turkmen graveyard architecture and mausoleum design.

In the last decades two new factors have entered the religious game in Turkmenistan. The first was the major propaganda effort being made by

Iran to reach fellow believers in Turkmenistan, the second was the marking of the millenium of Russia's acceptance of Christianity which, as noted by Imam-Kazi Nasrullo Ibadullayev, leader of Turkmenistan's Muslims, marked a turning point in church-state relations in the Soviet Union.[21]

With regard to the successes of Iranian propaganda, a report by the head of the Turkmenistan House of Scientific Atheism says it all:

> foreign Muslim groups are taking part in broadening bourgeois-clerical propaganda in our republic's border rayons. Broadcasters in the Turkmen departments of Iran's radio stations "Gurgen" and "Bender Turkmen" are discussing this constantly. Now television stations, working in tandem with these radio stations ... have begun to direct Turkmen language programs to the population of Krasnovodsk Oblast. Iran's Islamic centers have also begun to send letters to the oblast's inhabitants certifying that they have been awarded the title "hajji" externally.[22]

On December 16, 1988 two unprecedented events took place. First, Imam-Kazi Ibadullayev (he also leads the congregation at the Shalyka mosque in Tashauz) met with party workers who were taking an advanced course at the House of Political Education in Ashkhabad: the report noted that "as a result of perestroika this is the first time that such an open conversation between party workers and the clergy has taken place. Despite the contradictions between the idealistic and materialist worldviews, religious believers and confirmed atheists found some common ground."[23] The second unprecedented event was that a report on this event was published in party media. It must be noted that not all letters to the editor about the appearance of statements by representatives of the clergy in the party press felt it to be a positive step. A response was published at the end of March 1989 by a scientific worker in the Philosophy and Law department of the TSSR Academy of Sciences in which he defended the move, claiming that good relations with the clergy were necessary because, in many cases, the "progressive-thinking clergy" were heirs to a vast experience in dealing with the population's concern.[24]

According to Ibadullayev, these "progressive-thinking" clergy can also include members of the non-official clergy, referred to generally as "pseudomollas." He pointed out that "official religious representatives are still unable to serve all religious believers, especially those in distant places. In one of my articles I talked about the positive experience collected in Uzbekistan in attracting mollas able to perform religious services to this work. I think this experience could be used in places where there are no mosques."[25] In a subsequent statement made at a meeting in Kalinin Rayon, he claimed that the bad mollas, or "pseudomollas," are those "who do not refrain from cheating people in their own self-interest, who make no distinction between virtue and vice, who do not understand genuine religious views and cannot tell the difference between good deeds and sin."[26]

Turkmen as a state language of the TSSR

Statements in the "letters to the editor" column of the Turkmen daily and weekly newspapers generally make the claim that the key to a strong national identity is a strong national language, and that the national language is only strong when it acquires the status of the "state language." To this end, after a debate lasting over a period of several months, at the end of May 1990 Turkmenistan passed a language law which in effect placed Turkmen on a par with Russian. The debate on the language question was and is extremely intense and covers a number of issues aside from its acquisition of official status as well as a host of other basic, language-oriented issues: language purification and its opposite, russification, and the returkmenification of place and personal names.

Immediately after the creation of a Soviet government in Turkmenistan, Turkmen was declared as a state language, and various measures were taken to assure that cadres coming into the republic had the opportunity to learn it. Pygam Azymov, a leading Turkmen linguist and academician, pointed out in a recent article that "enthusiasm for and interest in studying Turkmen began to weaken" in the late 1930s and 1940s. As a consequence "Turkmen knowledge among Turkmen urban intelligentsia between the ages of 30 and 40 and their chidlren is extremely low" at the present time. Side effects of this decline in the use of the language are that the language is rarely used as a mode of communication in ministries and leading organizations and, as claimed by Azymov, is "misused" by the media. He places the blame for the present situation on "we linguists, the Turkmen intelligentsia, party and Soviet workers."[27] (He incidentally cites as a positive development the success of measures aimed at bringing Kazakh in wider official use in Kazakhstan and makes special reference to a promise made on television by G.V. Kolbin, then first secretary of the KazCP, that he was going to study Kazakh "over the next six months.") Azymov's article, which appeared in the republic party daily, attracted many letters supporting his position. Two weeks later, the same newspaper carried letters from a writer who, expressing his support for Azymov, complained that "most meetings and gatherings are not held in Turkmen, and not even Turkmen feasts in this city [Ashkhabad] are held in Turkmen"; on the same page, the chairman of the Young Scholars council at the Magtymguly Institute of Language and Literature maintained that "local youth in the city view the study of Turkmen with indifference" and proposed that Turkmen language requirements be imposed on all institutions of higher learning because "if entrance and graduation examinations in Turkmen were to be introduced nobody would look on the study of Turkmen with indifference."[28] Five days later it was urged in another letter that the requirement that dissertations be submitted in Russian be eliminated.[29] On March 7 the newspaper devoted a whole page to thirty-four letters containing various recommendations directed at making Turkmen a state language and widening its sphere of public usage.[30] Enhancing these proposals are comparisons with other union republics: a letter to the editor from a reader noted that while on jobs in Kishinev (Moldavia) and Lvov (Ukraine) he saw that Ukrainian and Moldavian were used on street signs, in retail stores and offices, and stated that "at a time when we are breathing the clean air of glasnost" Turkmen should receive the same status.[31]

It would not be unusual to draw the conclusion from the complaints enumerated above that a form of linguistic russification was taking place in Turkmenistan. Nothing could be further from the truth. According to the director of the department of Scientific Atheism at the Turkmen State University Russian knowledge in the republic has lost ground over the last thirty years. He notes that the 1979 All-Union census revealed that only 25.4 percent of the local population could speak Russian freely, and these were mostly in the cities; in short, "the basic component of our [younger] population does not know Russian." He concludes that "the fact that the younger generation in Turkmenistan today knows less Russian than the middle generation gives pause for thought. This situation creates difficulties in exchanging cadres between republics and in enlisting the aid of specialists and workers in mastering new regions."[32] One immediate consequence of this lack of Russian knowledge has manifested itself in Turkmen representation in the officer corps of the Soviet Armed Forces. The chief of the political department of the TSSR Military Commissariat supplied some recent data on this:

> In 1986 133 youth from local nationalities entered a higher military school, 164 in 1987 and 175 this year [1988]. At the same time 124 of these youth abandoned their studies in the higher military schools. Thus, only 0.5 percent of youth from our republic become officers. According to these data we hold one of the last places in the country.

He added that "poor Russian" is one of the primary reasons for this.[33] Numerous articles point out that Turkmen recruits into the army had similar Russian language problems.

A movement rapidly gaining strength and intimately connected with the Russification issue is language purification, which is taking place in two sectors, geographical names and the vocabulary of Turkmen itself. Detailed debates on this question are apparently taking place at meetings and other forums closed to the media but enough information is emerging to reveal that purification advocates, meaning those who wish to expel Russian words from the media, have been winning their campaign. Begench Kerimi, an opponent of and commentator on the purification question, advocated a greater reliance on Russian loanwords in Turkmen largely due to Russia's highly developed technical vocabulary and used as one of his examples the Russian word *poyezd* (train) which had been used in Turkmen until recently; over the last year Turkmen *otly* (lit. 'firebel-cher'), an archaic word for train, had been revived in the media. Kerimi's argument is that *poyezd* has been used for years and everyone understands it so why change it.[34] Since the publication of his article the debate on Turkmen as a state language began to develop in two directions: geo-graphical names, many of which bore the names of luminaries of the Stalin period, began to be changed back to their original names and the Russian transcription of the rendering of Turkmen names was changed to conform to a 1988 directive from the TSSR Supreme Soviet; and the stripping of the Turkmen vocabulary of Russian technical terms (including *poyezd*).

Soltansha Atanyyazov, Turkmenistan's leading toponymist, argued against the trend of changing place names under the rubric "a village's name is a village's history" as far back as 1988; he suggested that it would be more appropriate to name schools or streets after "state and party officials."[35] Subsequently, as director of the terminology department of the Magtymguly Institute of Language and Literature, he pointed out numer-ous violations of the TSSR Supreme Soviet decree on the Russian tran-scription of Turkmen place names.[36] That this is not a debate conducted among the Turkmen nationalist elite was proven by the appearance of seven letters complaining about the "russification" of Turkmen place names a few months later.[37] It is worthy of note that this "Russification" process occurs solely in the Russian language media, not in the Turkmen.

If the place name issue began to take on unusual significance within the national processes occurring in the TSSR, language purification took on even more. As an example, the 1988 publication of the *Short Dictionary of Turkmen Economic Terms* was strongly attacked by two Turkmen econo-mists who claimed that the primary deficiency of the work was that the words were all Russian and not Turkmen at all; therefore, the work was virtually useless.[38] Kerimi, who a year earlier had advocated using Russian technical and other vocabulary, began to back down: in an article appearing in March 1989 he noted that "those fighting to purify the Turkmen language have increased considerably recently" and asked that this process not be carried to the extreme.[39]

Finally, attacks on the use of loanwords do not include Arabic and Persian elements, which may add up to 25 percent of the local Turkmen lexicon. A recent work on Arabic and Persian elements, in fact, was praised for its content and criticized for its limited edition (1,000 copies).[40] In addi-tion to Arabic and Persian words in current use, there is also a huge reser-voir of them in Turkmen classical poetry; it has been suggested that a specialized dictionary devoted to them be published to facilitate the reading of these poets.[41] The language purification movement is directed only against the Russian elements.

The issues cited above can be tracked through the media easily. By examining the implementation of many of these proposals, the victory or defeat of "nationalist" blocs within the republic can be charted. These include: the success in imposing Turkmen language requirements at institutions of higher learning, in expanding the urban national language kindergarden networks, increasing national language academic publishing, establishing language purification (or "translation") commissions, the increase in introducing national language courses for non-local bureaucrats working in predominantly national areas. All of these are required in order to comply with the language law, but the extent to which they can be implemented in a short time is open to question. For these moves to be effective, full cooperation between all institutions within the republic is a basic requirement. A number of recent articles in the press point out that there are many shortcomings in the execution of the massive language program.

Turkmen diaspora relations

Following official, and hence public, recognition that it had become politically feasible to establish contact with Turkmens abroad, the Central Committee of the Turkmen Communist Party passed the decree "On The Establishment Of A Turkmenistan Society For Relations With Co-nationals Abroad" in July 1990.[42] A few months later, the Vatan ("Fatherland") Society was established with the stated goal of focusing on the "close to three million Turkmens" of Iran and Afghanistan.[43] A three-day First International Conference of World Turkmens was convened in Ashkhabad in May 1991, which was attended by Turkmens from Afghanistan, Turkey, Syria, Great Britain, Germany and Iran.[44] At the conference, a mixture of Turkmenistan and foreign Turkmens created the World Humanitarian Association of World Turkmens to which the Vatan Society claims to subordinate itself.[45]

Turkmenistan's relations with Turkmens abroad have not, until recently, been a matter of discussion outside of very narrow circles. Until the Afghanistan war and the upsurge of Turkmen language religious propaganda beamed at the TSSR from the two Iranian senders Gurgen and Bender-i Turkmen, the issue was rarely mentioned in the mass or scientific media, at all. As late as 1958 a Turkmen historian noted that "not one ethnographic study of Turkmen ethnography exists in the Turkmen language if one doesn't count articles published in journals of the 1930s."[46] The Turkmens abroad were, it appears, incidental victims of Stalinism. The significance of this omission in Turkmen research into their own ethnogenesis became apparent when articles began to appear in the Turkmen literary newspaper in the mid 1960s, announcing at first the presence of Turkmens in Turkey and Xinkiang, and then the presence of large numbers in Iraq who were even publishing works in their own language in the multilingual Iraqi literary journal *Yengi Yraq*.[47] Since the Iraqi

Turkmen may be Azeris instead of ethnolinguistic Turkmens, reference to them was subsequently reduced to almost nothing for the next twenty years, as were all efforts to establish contact. In 1966 a work on the Turkmens abroad was to have been published by the Institute of History of the TSSR Academy of Sciences because "the production of scientific work dealing with the Turkmens living in foreign countries has great scientific, theoretical and political importance."[48] The work never appeared, and the Turkmens abroad were forgotten until the Soviet march into Afghanistan.

Prior to the formation of the Vatan Society, there was a section for working with countrymen abroad under the Turkmenistan Society for Friendship and Cultural Relations, but very little is known about it (it was probably more KGB than Turkmen).[49] For several years there has been a section in the Institute of Language and Literature of the Turkmenistan Academy of Sciencies responsible for working with the Turkmen of Afghanistan in laying the groundwork for an Afghan Turkmen literary language and providing other forms of advice.

One can only speculate that the reason why Turkmenistan lagged behind other union republics in establishing relations with their own countrymen abroad is that most foreign Turkmens live either in Iran or Afghanistan (500,000–1,000,000 in Iran, 1–2 million in Afghanistan). They are related by blood with the Soviet Turkmens, but the primary reason for the lack of contact is that many of the Afghan and Iranian Turkmens are descendants of former Basmachis. These relationships did not surface in the public media until recently, and did so on the basis of a decision by Moscow which established direct trade and other relations between oblasts of the TSSR with the Afghan provinces of Badkhyz, Farab and Herat. The latter two contain substantial numbers of Turkmens.

Turkmen media began a campaign, stimulated primarily by Moscow, for the establishment of closer relations with Afghan Turkmens. The first objective was to begin a dialogue with Afghan Turkmens. On February 11, 1989 G.A. Borovik, chairman of the Soviet Committee for the Defence of Peace and vice president of the World Peace Council, met with activists from the TSSR republic Committee for Defence of Peace in Ashkhabad to discuss the role of Turkmenistan, which shares a common border of "more than a thousand kilometers" with Afghanistan, in helping to regulate the Afghan situation following the withdrawal of Soviet troops. He urged that "republic writers, artists, war and labor veterans must join widely in peaceful, creative action . . ., maintain relations with organizations in Afghanistan, Iran and Pakistan and with certain people, including Turkmens living in these countries, and be especially active." He added that "local activists in Tajikistan have talked with Afghan *mujahidin*; it is possible that such meetings can be very useful"; in this context Borovik also pointed out that "we must broadly exploit the participation of religious workers" in this movement.[50]

The movement's purpose was to develop cultural, especially language ties, with Afghan compatriots. For several years a Turkmen newspaper in the Arabic script has been published in Kabul (GORESH) for distribution to Turkmens throughout Afghanistan. In a 1988 visit to Chardzhou its editor, Mukhammet Emin Khemra, discussed the language problems involved in putting out the newspaper (which has a circulation of 5,000 and is distributed in eleven provinces), especially after the Soviet withdrawal. He said: "At the present time the language problem has turned into one of the most pressing questions before press and state workers. The Afghan Turkmens consist of representatives from various tribes, each of them speaking its own dialect. In short, Afghan Turkmens are still far from developing a common Turkmen literary language. Thus . . . Turkmen linguistic scholars must provide help in this urgent problem."[51] Present at these discussions were a number of Turkmen linguists involved in the Afghan Turkmen language problem. One of the reasons behind the formation of the Vatam Society is to provide the necessary help for Afghan Turkmens to develop in concert with the Turkmenistan Republic. Similar developments are occurring in relations with the Turkmens of Iran.

The Vatan Society has the potential to play an important role in Turkmenistan's future, not only as a channel for new ideas, but also as a source of industrial develpment and new markets for Turkmenistan's raw and finished materials. To the extent that it can offset divisive forces such as Muslim radicalism or a resurgent totalitarianism, it will serve as one of the forces, along with language, religion and perhaps "Turkmenism", for defining the Turkmens as a people and a nation distinct from the other Turks of Central Asia.

Notes

1 *Soviet Turkmenistany*, November 19, 1988.
2 The discussion was launched in a two-part essay by the Turkmen commentator on sociopolitical affairs, Tirkesh Jumageldiyev, which appeared in the then Turkmen language daily *Soviet Turkmenistany*, September 22–23, 1990.
3 B. Soyunov, *Soviet Turkmenistany*, January 28, 1990.
4 Shamukhammet Khojamberdiyev, *Soviet Turkmenistany*, February 17, 1990.
5 Babysh Mammetyazov, deputy secretary of the party bureau at the Magtymguly Institute of Language and Literature, *Mugallymlar Gazeti*, March 25, 1990.
6 A. Atabayev, acting chairman of the TSSR Writers Union, *Soviet Turkmenistany*, February 27, 1991.
7 *Soviet Turkmenistany*, July 22, 1989.
8 Yilgay Durdyyev, *Mugallymlar Gazeti*, September 2, 1989.
9 *Soviet Turkmenistany*, July 18, 1989.
10 *Soviet Turkmenistany*, July 26, 1989.
11 S. Atamukhammedov, *Mugallymlar Gazeti*, December 3, 1989.

12 See *Mugallymlar Gazeti*, January 5, 1990; *Soviet Turkmenistany*, March 27, 1990.
13 *Soviet Turkmenistany*, April 10, 1991.
14 M. Zhabarova, "Vperedi mnogo del'," *Nauka i Religiya*, August, 1967, p. 38.
15 Interview with P.M. Arkhipov, chairman TuSSR KGB, *Soviet Turkmenistany*, February 25, 1990.
16 S. Khanov and A. Yusubov, *Soviet Turkmenistany*, April 7, 1989.
17 *Mugallymlar Gazeti*, March 11, 1991.
18 Report from the Ideology Commission of the Turkmenistan Communist Party, *Soviet Turkmenistany*, June 7, 1991.
19 B. Saryyev, *Soviet Turkmenistany*, August 10, 1988.
20 N. Kulyyev, *Soviet Turkmenistany*, January 8, 1989.
21 Imam-Kazi Nasrullo Ibadullayev, *Soviet Turkmenistany*, January 8, 1989.
22 N. Kulyyev, *Soviet Turkmenistany*, January 8, 1989.
23 V. Gordeyev, *Soviet Turkmenistany*, December 16, 1988.
24 M. Annanurov, *Soviet Turkmenistany*, March 31, 1989.
25 *Soviet Turkmenistany*, January 8, 1989.
26 Unsigned, *Soviet Turkmenistany*, January 22, 1989.
27 Pygam Azymov, *Soviet Turkmenistany*, February 9, 1989.
28 *Soviet Turkmenistany*, February 23, 1989.
29 Anegul Ashyrova, *Soviet Turkmenistany*, February 28, 1989.
30 *Soviet Turkmenistany*, March 7, 1989.
31 *Soviet Turkmenistany*, February 28, 1989.
32 A. Atayev, *Soviet Turkmenistany*, November 11, 1988.
33 Lt. Col. I.Ya. Tkachenko, *Soviet Turkmenistany*, December 2, 1988.
34 Begench Kerimi, *Soviet Turkmenistany*, May 5, 1988.
35 *Soviet Turkmenistany*, February 18, 1988.
36 *Soviet Turkmenistany*, August 7, 1988.
37 *Soviet Turkmenistany*, January 13, 1989.
38 A. Choshanov and A. Nazarov, *Soviet Turkmenistany*, November 15, 1988.
39 Begench Kerimi, *Soviet Turkmenistany*, March 10, 1989.
40 B. Aydogdyyev, *Mugallymlar Gazeti*, October 14, 1988.
41 R. Arjykov, *Mugallymlar Gazeti*, February 15, 1989.
42 *Soviet Turkmenistany*, July 1, 1990.
43 *Soviet Turkmenistany*, October 13, 1990.
44 *Mugallymlar Gazeti*, May 22, 1991.
45 Interview with M. Aydogdyyev, member of the directorate of the World Humanitarian Association of World Turkmens and advisor to the President of Turkmenistan on Nationality Affairs, *Soviet Turkmenistany*, May 22, 1991.
46 Sh. Annakylchev, *Turkmenskaya Iskra*, August 16, 1958.
47 Ata Jykyev, *Adebiyat Ve Sungat*, November 3, 1965; and Ashyr Meredov, *Adebiyat Ve Sungat*, January 8, 1966.
48 B. Myradov, *Mugallymlar Gazeti*, March 24, 1967.
49 *Soviet Turkmenistany*, April 16, 1988.
50 *Soviet Turkmenistany*, February 15, 1989.
51 *Mugallymlar Gazeti*, February 19, 1989.

17 Kyrgyzstan: the politics of demographic and economic frustration

GENE HUSKEY

Introduction

In May 1991, the first competitively-elected parliament in Kyrgyz history adopted a new land law, an unremarkable document save Article Two, which described the land and natural resources of Kyrgyzstan as the wealth (*dostoianie*) of the ethnic Kyrgyz. The declaration by itself had no legal force, and detailed provisions of the law made clear that all ethnic groups in the republic, from Russians to Uzbeks to Dungans, enjoyed equal rights in the use, possession, and exploitation of land. Yet the political and psychological fallout from Article Two was immediate. The non-titular nationalities of the republic vigorously protested this special claim of the ethnic Kyrgyz. To prevent a worsening of the already tense ethnic relations in the republic, the new president of Kyrgyzstan, the reform-minded scholar, Askar Akaev, vetoed Article Two as contrary to the constitution.[1] Ethnically neutral language was later substituted for the offending article.

In Kyrgyzstan and the other former Soviet republics, episodes such as this pose the most fundamental questions about the use of state power to establish, or reassert, the identity and preeminence of the titular nationality. If an ethnic group gives its name to a territory, is it entitled to craft policy on language, land, citizenship, and political representation that assures it a leading role among the ethnic groups of the republic? This question assumes special urgency in republics such as Kazakhstan, Latvia, and Kyrgyzstan, where the titular nationality represents a minority or bare majority of the territory's population. Whereas in the Russian Federation or Georgia the assertiveness of the titular group in the transition from Communist rule smacks of superiority complex nationalism,[2] in Kazakhstan, Latvia, and Kyrgyzstan, one may view it as an effort to sustain a fledgling, or threatened, nation. To understand the relationship between the contemporary Kyrgyz state and nation, let us begin with a brief review of the political, cultural, and demographic heritage of the Kyrgyz.

The prehistory of Kyrgyz nationalism

The modern Kyrgyz formed as a people in the mountain ranges and foothills of inner Asia. Their ancestors were the Turkic tribes of the Altai and Irtysh, the Mongols, and the ancient peoples of the Tian-Shan, the mountain range that has been home to the Kyrgyz for at least five centuries.[3] By the end of the eighteenth century – late in comparison to the peoples of Europe and the Caucasus – the Kyrgyz had developed an ethnic consciousness, which was linked to a common territory around the Tian-Shan, to a nomadic, or semi-nomadic economy, and to a legend, Manas, that told of the group's glorious past.[4] One must not confuse, however, the rise of an ethnic consciousness with the rise of nationalism, if by nationalism one means the desire "of a community to assert its unity and independence vis-à-vis other communities and groups."[5] The loyalties of the Kyrgyz, like those of other Central Asians, most notably the Kazakhs, lay first with family, clan, and tribe. It was only their subordination to Russian rule, beginning in the mid-nineteenth century, that planted the seeds of nationalism among the Kyrgyz. As Donald Carlisle argues, "the history of Soviet Central Asia should be read as an attempt to create modern nations . . . where previously there were only ethnic groups."[6]

Lacking a national ideal as well as modern arms and organization, the Kyrgyz offered little resistance to the expansion of the Russian Empire into Kyrgyz lands in the 1860s and 1870s. In effect, the encroachment of the Russians presented the Kyrgyz with a Hobson's choice: remain loyal to the rulers of the Kokand kingdom, the Central Asian khanate that had been governing the Kyrgyz and neighboring groups with increasing brutality, or submit to the domination of the technologically and culturally advanced Russians.[7] While Soviet historiography clearly overstated the welcome extended to tsarist rule in Kyrgyzstan (with such titles as *The Voluntary Entry of Kyrgyzstan into Russia and its Progressive Consequences*[8]), post-Soviet historiogrpahy must be careful not to exaggerate the scale of opposition to Russian suzerainty over the region.

Relations between the Kyrgyz and Russians deteriorated rapidly, however, after the turn of the century, in part due to the encroachment of Russian settlers into traditional Kyrgyz grazing lands. In northern Kyrgyzstan, then a part of the Semirech'e district of the Russian Empire, the indigenous population declined by almost 9 percent from 1902 to 1913 while that of Russian settlers increased by 10 percent.[9] Predominantly Russian cities sprung up where Kokand forts had once stood. Among these was Pishpek (later Frunze, most recently Bishkek), the future capital, which had 14,000 residents by 1916, 8,000 of them Russian.[10]

Mounting resentment against Russian expansionism exploded in the summer and fall of 1916, following the tsar's infamous decree of June 25. To fill labor divisions for the war in Europe, the decree ordered the mobilization of all Central Asian men aged nineteen to forty-three. The Central Asians responded to this "requisition of aliens" (*rekvizitsiia inorodtsev*) for a distant war by attacking the symbols and representatives of Russian authority. Fierce, if lopsided, battles occurred throughout Kyrgyzstan between the local Kyrgyz and the tsar's punitive brigades. None was more alarming for the authorities than the siege of Tokmak in northern Kyrgyzstan, where 5,000 crudely-armed Kyrgyz repeatedly attacked a small garrison of Russian troops. The siege, beaten back with the loss of 300 Kyrgyz and two Russians, was followed by massacres of the civilian Kyrgyz population, carried out by armed Russian settlers as well as by Tsarist reinforcements.[11] The result was what one contemporary Kyrgyz writer called "the unknown genocide." Out of an estimated population of 780,000 in 1916, 100–120,000 Kyrgyz are believed to have been killed in the uprisings.[12] An equal number sought refuge in China through the treacherous, icy passes of the Tian-Shan.[13] Many refugees perished en route; others died in the first winter, having lost their herds. The survivors would return to their former grazing lands in Soviet Kyrgyzstan by the mid-1920s and formed a rallying point for national unity.[14]

The uprisings of 1916 were followed only a year later by the Bolshevik Revolution, whose legacy for the Kyrgyz nation will remain a subject of dispute well beyond the collapse of the Soviet Union.[15] At least through the prism of Western historiography, with its emphases on nation building and state formation, the creation of the Soviet state was in some respects a godsend for the Kyrgyz. Once the resistance to the Bolsheviks had been defeated in the region, the Kyrgyz acquired for the first time their own political community. Formed originally on October 14, 1924 as the Kara-Kirgiz autonomous region within the Turkestan republic of the USSR, Kyrgyzstan underwent several name changes and administration redesignations before emerging in 1936 as the Kirgiz Soviet Socialist Republic. Formal constitutional provisions notwithstanding, the Kirgiz republic was not an autonomous political community. Yet the very linkage of the Kyrgyz to a proto-state and the development of at least the symbols of Kyrgyz cultural and political identity created important pre-conditions for the rise of a Kyrgyz national consciousness.

In the formative years of Soviet Kyrgyzstan, the central authorities in Moscow seemed intent on creating the foundations for indigenous rule in the region, within the parameters of Soviet power.[16] A law of 1924 mandated the translation of all government documents in the region into Kyrgyz and other major Central Asian languages. Furthermore, ten of the thirteen members of the Communist Party's first Orgburo in the Kara-Kirgiz region were ethnic Kyrgyz, as were thirteen of the seventeen members of the highest state body in the region, the oblast revolutionary committee (*oblrevkom*).[17] But the demographic features of the region insured that the ethnic Kyrgyz would at first play only a limited role in the formation of a modern state bureaucracy. In the early 1920s, there was not a single ethnic Kyrgyz with a higher education; at best 20,000 (less than 5 percent) were literate, and many of these were from so-called hostile classes.[18] Thus, the administration of the territory fell largely to the Slavs. In May 1925, ethnic Kyrgyz accounted for only 319, or 10.8 percent, of the 2,950 regional and local administrative personnel in the region.[19]

A gradual indigenization of political life in Kyrgyzstan continued, however, until the mid-1930s. To prepare the rising generation of Kyrgyz for leadership positions in Soviet Kyrgyzstan, the new regime offered short courses and, in a few cases, more extensive training in educational institutions of European Russia. These freshly-trained "Soviet" Kyrgyz cadres were then enlisted in large numbers during the *vydvizhenstvo* campaign of the late 1920s to manage the local economy and society. An edict of December 1932 envisioned a full indigenization of the republican apparatus by June 1934. But in 1933, the first wave of Stalinist repression intervened to halt the indigenization drive, and by 1938, the first generation of the Soviet Kyrgyz elite had been swept away in the purges.[20] Many of the purged had combined a commitment to Bolshevism with a desire to nourish their Kyrgyz and Turkic heritage.

While maintaining the symbols of Kyrgyz national autonomy, Stalinism launched policies that deepened Slavic domination of the region. Perhaps the most important of these was a cadres policy that placed Kyrgyz who were obsequious toward Russian culture and central political authority in leading party and governments posts. It also placed in oversight positions in Kyrgyzstan Slavic personnel, usually seconded from posts in Russia, to serve as the republic's second party secretary, its KGB head, and its procurator. Few republics could match Kyrgyzstan for the malleability and sycophancy of its leaders. Especially notable in this regard were the illiterate miner, Turabai Kulatov, a prime minister and Supreme Soviet chairman of the republic under late Stalinism, and T. Usubaliev, the Communist Party first secretary from 1961 to 1986. Usubaliev's praise of the Russians seemed to reach a crescendo in the waning years of Brezhnev.

> We once again express our gratitude to the great Russian people, whose inexhaustible revolutionary energy and labor heroism, patriotic selflessness and profound internationalism, disinterestedness, ardent love and devotion to the socialist motherland and to Lenin's glorious party have always been and will be a source of inspiration and a splendid example and model for the Kirgiz people.[21]

On the eve of the Gorbachev era – and his own removal from office – Usubaliev noted that:

> Sixty years is just a brief moment in the history of Kirgizstan . . . but it was indeed during this period that its age-old dream of happiness became a reality.[22]

The rhetoric of subservience masked, of course, the inexorable conflicts between center and republic over investment and resource allocation. In a planned economy, Usubaliev and other Kyrgyz leaders believed that political fealty and reliable deliveries of output to the center strengthened their claims to new projects and scarce supplies. To remind the center of its obligation to its faithful vassal, Usubaliev deluged Moscow ministries with claims for resources.[23] Obseqiousness had its limits, which were quickly crossed when economic development of the region was at stake.

In general, the terms of exchange between center and periphery were highly unfavorable for the Kyrgyz, as indicated by linguistic, economic, and demographic developments in the republic. Russification of the Kyrgyz language began in earnest immediately after Stalin's first wave of terror against the Kyrgyz elite. A party directive of June 1934 ordered the further enrichment of the Kyrgyz language "by the maximum use of sovietisms and international, multinational terminology through the Russian language . . ."[24] This policy was facilitated by the adoption in 1940 of the Cyrillic alphabet for written Kyrgyz (its script had been Arabic until 1926, Latin thereafter). Increasingly in the postwar era, Russian began to displace Kyrgyz as the language of politics and commerce in the republic. A new generation of Kyrgyz urban residents was brought up on Russian and was often unable to converse with rural Kyrgyz. Many older Kyrgyz in the cities reserved their native language for private discourse. In short, Kyrgyz was rapidly marginalized in its homeland. Not a single new Kyrgyz-language school was opened in the capital of Frunze (Bishkek) after the 1930s.[25] By the 1980s, only three of Frunze's sixty-nine schools used Kyrgyz as the primary language of instruction.[26] At the end of Soviet rule in Kyrgyzstan, only 4 percent of the 5.6 million books in Frunze's Lenin Library were in Kyrgyz, and of books requested by readers, only 2 percent were in Kyrgyz.[27]

The Russification of the Kyrgyz language had its parallels in economic development in the republic. In the postwar era, Soviet power brought modern industry and transportation to a traditional society that lacked the most rudimentary physical infrastructure. Yet economic modernization of the region largely bypassed the ethnic Kyrgyz. The most advanced enterprises were built in the cities, staffed largely by Slavs, and managed by all-union ministries in Moscow. At the end of the 1980s, enterprises of all-union subordination accounted for 38 percent of the republic's economy and offered employees access to the best housing and social services.[28] Relatively few employees of such enterprises were ethnic Kyrgyz. The Kyrgyz made up only 6.3 percent of employees in the electric energy sector and 11 percent of personnel in machine construction and metal-working.[29] In all, only 13 percent of the republic's engineers and technicians were Kyrgyz.[30] Of particular concern to many Kyrgyz was the reluctance of the central ministries to train an indigenous working class, preferring instead to import Slavic workers *en masse*.[31]

The influx of Slavic workers into Kyrgyzstan in mid-century created one of the conditions for the rise of Kyrgyz nationalism at the end of the century.[32] The demographic challenge to the Kyrgyz had several dimensions. First, it rendered the titular nationality, the Kyrgyz, a minority within its own republic. If the Kyrgyz accounted for two-thirds of the territory's

Table 17.1. *National composition of Kyrgyzstan, 1926–1989*

	1926	1937	1939	1959	1970	1980	1989
Total population	1,001,700	1,370,503	1,458,200	2,066,100	2,933,200	3,588,500	4,257,755
Kyrgyz	668,700	731,026	754,300	836,800	1,248,800	1,687,400	2,229,663
	66.8%	53.3%	51.7%	40.5%	42.6%	47.0%	52.4%
Russians	116,800	269,531	302,900	623,600	855,900	911,700	916,558
	11.7%	19.7%	20.8%	30.2%	29.2%	25.4%	21.5%
Uzbeks	106,300	139,154	151,600	218,900	333,000	426,200	550,096
	10.6%	10.2%	10.4%	10.6%	11.4%	11.9%	12.9%
Ukrainians	64,200	121,481	137,300	137,000	120,000	109,300	108,027
	6.4%	8.9%	9.4%	6.6%	4.1%	3.0%	2.5%
Germans	4,300	NA	11,800	39,900	89,800	101,100	101,309
	0.4%		0.8%	1.9%	3.1%	2.8%	2.4%
Tatars	4,900	17,483	20,000	56,300	69,400	72,000	70,068
	0.5%	1.3%	1.4%	2.7%	2.4%	2.0%	1.6%
Kazakhs	1,700	25,541	23,900	20,100	22,000	27,400	37,318
	0.2%	1.9%	1.6%	1.0%	0.8%	0.8%	0.9%
Dungans	6,000	5,346	5,900	11,100	19,800	26,700	36,928
	0.6%	0.4%	0.4%	0.5%	0.7%	0.7%	0.9%
Uighurs	8,200	14,224	9,400	13,800	24,900	29,800	36,779
	0.8%	1.0%	0.6%	0.7%	0.8%	0.8%	0.9%
Tajiks	7,000	NA	10,700	15,200	21,900	23,200	33,518
	0.7%		0.7%	0.7%	0.7%	0.6%	0.8%
Others	13,600	46,717	30,400	93,400	91,600	108,000	137,491
	1.4%	3.4%	2.1%	4.5%	3.1%	3.0%	3.2%

Source: Narodnoe Khoziaistvo Kirgizskoi SSR (Frunze, 1982), p. 16. *Vestnik Statistiki*, no. 4, 1991, pp. 76–78.

population in 1926, their share of the population had dropped to 40.5 percent by the end of the 1950s (see table 17.1). At this time the Kyrgyz outnumbered the Russians by a margin of only four to three. Although the in-migration of Slavs continued after the end of the 1950s, by 1989 the higher birth rate among the Kyrgyz and other indigenous Central Asian peoples in the republic allowed the Kyrgyz to claim a bare majority of the republic's population (52.4 percent).

The uneven distribution of ethnic groups across the republic exacerbated the effects of Slavic in-migration. Certain areas were largely unaffected by the influx, notably the Naryn oblast, a mountainous region where the Kyrgyz still make up 97 percent of the population.[33] By contrast, Frunze developed, in effect, as a Russian city. In 1959, less than 10 percent of Frunze's population was ethnic Kyrgyz, and even as late as 1989 the Kyrgyz represented less than 23 percent of the capital's population.[34] With Russians and Ukrainians comprising 45 percent of the urban population outside of Frunze, and the Uzbeks accounting for a majority of the population in Osh, the Kyrgyz cannot even claim a plurality of the urban population of the republic. While it is an exaggeration to assert, as one Kyrgyz did recently, that the Slavs have created in the cities of Kyrgyzstan an "impenetrable national boundary,"[35] they have certainly dominated urban life in the republic. For the majority of the Kyrgyz, who live in the countryside, the cities have been, if not quite impenetrable, at least alien and inhospitable.

The emergence of Kyrgyz nationalism

Because the first stirrings of Kyrgyz nationalism appeared in the second half of the 1980s, it is tempting to view them as outgrowths of Gorbachev's policies of glasnost and democratization. That assertion would be a mistake. The policies of the center did, on occasion, arouse national indignation, as in the appointment of the Russian Gennadii Kolbin in December 1986 to head the Communist Party in neighboring Kazakhstan, whence discontent spread briefly to Kyrgyzstan. The policies associated with Gorbachev also facilitated the expression of national interests and the organization of groups to press national claims, both within and outside the state apparatus. But the origins of the national explosion in Kyrgyzstan at the end of the 1980s lie in a volatile mixture of economic and demographic frustration.

Even before Gorbachev assumed power in 1985, rural areas in Kyrgyzstan were in crisis. Coupled with a stagnant economy, the high birth rate of preceding decades had produced a generation of rural youth without jobs in the village or the skills and desire to find work in the cities. Whereas the rural population of the USSR from 1959 to 1989 declined by 18 percent, it doubled in the same period in Kyrgyzstan.[36] By the end of the 1980s, at least 110,000 persons were unemployed in the republic, with the highest concentration among village youth.[37] Many more rural folk were underemployed. In the Osh oblast, the largest and most agriculturally-oriented region in Kyrgyzstan, 45 percent of the employed earned 125 roubles a month or less at a time when the average monthly salary was 180 roubles.[38] The collapse of the Soviet economy in the early 1990s only deepened the crisis in the countryside. According to President Akaev, by 1991, 140,000 persons were unemployed – three-quarters of them under thirty years of age – and 500,000 had a monthly income of less than 75 roubles.[39]

In a pattern long familiar in the developing world, the excess population of the Kyrgyz countryside reluctantly sought work and shelter in the cities.[40] But the cities had neither space nor service for them. Most of the new Kyrgyz settlers in the cities lived not in carefully-rationed apartments but in overcrowded dormitories or the "corners" of private homes. Some set up hovels in open land on the outskirts of the cities only to have them torn down by the authorities. Conscious of the relatively well-housed Russians in the cities, one Kyrgyz complained that he felt "a guest in his own home."[41]

In the summer of 1989, frustrated Kyrgyz settlers in Frunze formed Ashar, the first major independent association in the republic. Ashar soon counted among its members 5,000 of the 20,000 families waiting for suitable housing in the city.[42] Exploiting rumors of the resettling in Frunze of Armenian refugees from the crisis in the Caucasus, Ashar seized land on the outskirts of the city for the construction of a shanty town (*samostroi*), an action that threw the party and government leadership in Kyrgyzstan into a panic. Since succeeding Usubaliev in 1986, the first secretary of the Communist Party of Kyrgyzstan, Absamat Masaliev, had prided himself on the maintenance of traditional politics and a quiescent society in the republic. As recently as the spring of 1989, Masaliev had suppressed attempts to form a Kyrgyz national front akin to those already in place in other Soviet republics. But proscribing Ashar threatened to alienate a desperate and growing segment of Kyrgyz society and set it against the ruling Kyrgyz and Russian elites. After reportedly lengthy discussions with the authorities in Moscow, Masaliev acquiesced in the recognition of Ashar, though he was soon frustrated by the inability of the local authorities to limit its activities to housing matters.[43]

The recognition of Ashar in the summer of 1989 represented the takeoff point for social movements in Kyrgyzstan. By the beginning of 1990 there were thirteen independent associations in the republic; a year later the number exceeded thirty-six. Many of these groups were explicitly nationalist in orientation. In terms of membership, they were generally segregated along ethnic lines, although a few Russians joined predominantly Kyrgyz groups.[44] A defining moment in the development of the Kyrgyz national movement came in late May 1990, when twenty-four informal groups favoring democratic reform and Kyrgyz national revival formed the Democratic Movement "Kyrgyzstan." Over 300 delegates from throughout the republic met in Frunze to advance a program that called for, *inter alia*, a sovereign republic, a civil society and market economy, and a reassessment of Kyrgyz history, especially the uprisings of 1916.[45] Within three months, membership of the movement was estimated at 100,000, with half of that number drawn from Frunze.[46]

In the summer of 1990, competing claims advanced by new ethnically-based associations in the Osh region led to inter-ethnic violence that fundamentally transformed the political landscape in Kyrgyzstan. In contrast to Frunze, land claims by the ethnic Kyrgyz were handled with less success in Osh, where unemployment and land hunger were more acute and local politicians were more willing to support openly Kyrgyz nationalism. The ethnic Kyrgyz in Osh resented the relative wealth and prominence of the local Uzbeks, who controlled, according to one estimate, 80 percent of the city's trade. The Uzbeks, for their part, claimed that their economic and demographic presence in the region was not translated into political power.[47] Only one of the twenty-five party first secretaries of local districts and cities was an Uzbek and only 4.7 percent of leading department posts in soviets in the region were held by Uzbeks (85 percent were occupied by Kyrgyz).[48] This perception of political disenfranchisement fed Uzbek irredentism, which had deep historical roots in the region.

In May 1990, Ashar's counterpart in Osh, Osh Aimagy, demanded land on which to settle ethnic Kyrgyz families who were unable to find housing. The regional party first secretary, U. Sydykov, agreed to allot Osh Aimagy thirty-two hectares of a predominantly Uzbek collective farm on the outskirts of Osh. The reaction of local Uzbeks was swift and dramatic. They seized the occasion to advance a range of political claims, including home rule for an Uzbek region in southern Kyrgyzstan and the recognition of Uzbek as the official language of the territory. There were even calls for the incorporation of parts of Kyrgyzstan into Uzbekistan.[49]

The refusal of the Kyrgyz political leadership to satisfy the Uzbek demands or to reverse its land grant ignited widespread violence between the Kyrgyz and Uzbek communities in the Osh region, the latter supported by compatriots from Uzbekistan who crossed the republican border in the early stages of the fighting. Facing what one observer called "10 Sumgaits,"[50] the republic called in the Soviet Army and MVD to restore order. During a week of rioting in early June, thousands of homes and buildings were destroyed and 230 persons were killed, 161 in the Uzgen district alone. The Osh events exposed and deepened divisions in the republic's political leadership and hastened the downfall of First Secretary Masaliev, who had been one of the most vocal opponents of perestroika in the USSR.

Disputes over land and water resources were the most violent inter-ethnic encounters in the first years of national strife in Kyrgyzstan,[51] but no question excited more debate than the revival of the Kyrgyz language. Following the lead of other republics, Kyrgyzstan began to draft a new law on language in the summer of 1989.[52] The debate surrounding the language law, adopted by the republic's Supreme Soviet in September 1989, brought into the open long-suppressed ethnic tensions. Whereas the Kyrgyz welcomed the elevation of their language to a preeminent position in the republic, Slavic residents viewed with alarm the recognition of Kyrgyz as the state language, despite the simultaneous recognition of Russian as the language of inter-ethnic communication.[53] One of the most controversial elements of the law was Article Eight, which required management and professional personnel – a stratum that the Slavs dominated – to have the ability to speak Kyrgyz to their workers or clients. Unlike most provisions of the law, which were to be phased in by 1999, Article Eight was to take effect immediately.[54] Responding to the draft law, Russian managers of all-union enterprises in the republic organized letter-writing campaigns that criticized the law as divisive. One collective letter, signed on September 16, 1989, bore 1,623 signatures.[55]

The language debate destroyed the official discourse on ethnic relations in Kyrgyzstan, a discourse that had for decades denied tensions or conflicts of interests among ethnic groups in the republic. For the first time, recriminations against Russians became commonplace in the press. In an intemperate article in *Literaturnyi Kirgizstan* at the beginning of 1990, a Kyrgyz writer complained that the Russians despoiled the rural landscape with their trash-strew picnic sites and the urban landscape with their queues. It was the Russians' hoarding genes (*geny zapasaniia*), she insisted, that kept them in lines.[56] The Russian response to such criticism ranged from chauvinist to internationalist. A Russian from the Alamedinsk district wrote that he did not feel guilty before the Kyrgyz people because his ancestors brought with them to Turkestan agriculture, infrastructure, and civilization.[57] Most of the Russians quoted in the press, however, took the moral high road by restating the official discourse's call for internationalism and by advocating in vague terms a policy of bilingualism.[58]

Even if the language law increased the use and visibility of Kyrgyz only modestly in the first years after its adoption – due both to the reluctance of non-Kyrgyz to study the language and the absence of instructional materials and qualified teachers[59] – it spawned symbolic changes that served a rising Kyrgyz nationalism. Shops, squares, and cities gave up their Russian and Soviet labels to assume Kyrgyz names. The republic itself acquired a spelling in Russian that more closely approximated its pronunciation in Kyrgyz.[60] At the end of 1991, a new tote board, in Kyrgyz only, was installed in the Parliament. And the number and edition size of Kyrgyz-language periodicals rose in comparison with those in Russian. Such reforms inspired among the ethnic Kyrgyz a new sense of ownership of the republic.

While the deepening bond between nation and state in Kyrgyzstan represented a renaissance for the Kyrgyz, it alienated many other ethnic groups in the republic, in the first instance the Slavs. The Russians and Ukrainians began to form their own national organizations, such as the Fund for Slavic Literacy and Culture (*Fond slavianskoi pis'mennosti i kul'tury*). This organization, designed to promote Slavic languages and culture in the republic, received assistance directly from the government of the Russian Federation.[61]

Reacting to the indigenization of cultural policy and the violence in Osh, Slavs began to leave Kyrgyzstan in significant numbers in the early 1990s. For the first time in the contemporary history of Kyrgyzstan, the exodus of Slavs from the republic exceeded the in-migration. During the first six months of 1990, Russians left Kyrgyzstan at a rate 2.6 times that of the previous year.[62] From the Osh region, 3,200 Slavs departed the republic in the first months after the riots. The stationmaster in Osh reported in September 1990 that containers were filled until the following summer, and notices of houses for sale could be seen in unprecedented numbers along the streets of Osh.[63] To be sure, the republic's political leadership – and the Slavs themselves – seemed intent at times on exaggerating the scale of Slavic out-migration as a way of moderating the pace of indigenization. The republic must not lose the brains and skills of the Slavs, such was the message underlying alarmist articles on the exodus of the Russians and Ukrainians. But by the beginning of 1992, the exodus was at least serious enough to merit debate in the Supreme Soviet of the Russian Federation, which was apparently concerned about the influx of new residents from Central Asia at a time of economic crisis.[64]

Democratization, marketization, and nationalism in Kyrgyzstan

The discussion above emphasizes the cleavages between the Kyrgyz and other ethnic groups in the last years of Soviet rule, cleavages deepened by the rise of electoral politics, the more liberal rules concerning political expression and association, and the collapse of central authority in Moscow. But as national agendas are formed and acted on, other forces are at work that restrain the development of a pure politics of cultural pluralism. The sources of these restraints lie both in social attitudes and state policy. Kyrgyz attitudes toward the Russians, for example, are by no means unswervingly hostile. To the contrary, the Kyrgyz have generally exhibited respect toward Russians and Russian culture, sometimes to the point of deference. In a letter to ethnic Kyrgyz living in Moscow, a Kyrgyz woman invoked the folk wisdom: "where there are Russians there is truth" (*tam, gde russkie, est' i pravda*).[65] In his own way, a reformist member of the republic's parliament, also an ethnic Kyrgyz, expressed a similar sentiment in regard to Russian language.

I would not have the right to call myself a son of my people without knowing the Kyrgyz language. But without a deep knowledge of Russian, I would not consider myself a complete man [*polnotsennym chelovekom*].[66]

For a century, Russian has been the touchstone for the development of Kyrgyz language, culture, and politics. While that psychological dependency is in part a source of Kyrgyz nationalism, it also binds Russians and Kyrgyz to an extent that is unparalleled in Russian-titular national relations in other non-Slavic republics, with the possible exception of Kazakhstan.

Kyrgyz attitudes toward the Uzbeks, the other major national minority in the republic, are more ambivalent. While sharing a Turkic and Islamic heritage[67] with the Uzbeks, the Kyrgyz have been suspicious of calls for pan-Turkic or pan-Islamic unity, fearing that such movements could lead to the hegemony in Central Asia of the larger and more historically prominent Uzbek nation.[68] The Kyrgyz fear of uzbekization was evident in a 1991 article that pointed to the decline of persons claiming Kyrgyz ethnicity in the Andizhan district of Uzbekistan, from 107,000 in 1906 to only 72,900 in 1989.[69] For the Kyrgyz, uzbekization appears more insidious than russification. The latter affects language and culture, the former ethnic identity itself.

Relations within as well as between ethnic groups have shaped the course of Kyrgyz nationalism. If Kyrgyz national claims have been more modest than those of most titular nationalities of the former USSR, it is in part because of the lack of unity among the Kyrgyz, and especially their elite. Clan and tribal loyalties continue to temper Kyrgyz nationalism.[70] Equally important barriers to Kyrgyz solidarity may be found in regional and urban-rural distinctions. Party and government elites in Kyrgyzstan have long been divided into northern and southern "families," a division that since the purges of the 1930s has facilitated central control of the republic.[71] Long-simmering tensions between the northern and southern Kyrgyz elites boiled to the surface at the end of 1990 following the ouster of the southerner Masaliev as republican leader. Distressed by the erosion of their traditional dominance of key republican posts, some southern Kyrgyz began to agitate for structural changes that would insure greater autonomy for their region. These proposals ranged from dividing the republic into two regions, with equal representation from each in republican bodies, to the formation of a Kyrgyz federation, with northern and southern republics.[72] Pushing the case for political devolution even further, one Kyrgyz writer favored the creation of five autonomous regions in the republic, one for each oblast. Such a confederation would have been coordinated by a rotating collective presidency.[73] The advocates of devolution and power sharing seem to be motivated less by a desire to promote regional social and economic development than to protect local political networks.

Potentially the most serious division among the Kyrgyz runs along urban-rural lines. The urbanized quarter of the ethnic Kyrgyz population has appropriated the language and at least some of the cultural values of the Russians, who dominate the cities of Kyrgyzstan, especially its northern tier. As suggested earlier, Kyrgyz urban youth raised in the postwar era resemble in many respects second generation immigrants. They know smatterings of the language and traditions of their elders but feel more at home in their russified surroundings. In short, they have assimilated. The rise of a Kyrgyz national consciousness stranded many of these urbanized Kyrgyz between two cultures. The predicament has been especially acute for the rising generation of Kyrgyz politicians, typified by an incident in 1991 involving Ulukbek Chinaliev, the first secretary of the Frunze city Communist Party committee. Not knowing Kyrgyz, Chinaliev could only address his Kyrgyz audience in Russian, while immediately after his speech, an ethnic German, raised in the countryside, spoke to the audience in Kyrgyz.[74]

Whether the tensions between urbanized and rural (or recently urban) Kyrgyz can be contained is as yet unclear. At the beginning of 1992, the urbanized Kyrgyz elite appeared to be in firm control of the state apparatus and leading nationalist organizations. As one might expect, they showed considerable sensitivity to the economic and cultural claims of non-urbanized Kyrgyz. But a russified – some would prefer the term sovietized – elite must remain vulnerable to a new and more atavistic wave of Kyrgyz nationalism that could be unleashed by populist politicians or movements. That President Akaev is aware of this threat is indicated by his repeated disparaging references to populist leaders in the republic.

To minimize conflict within and between ethnic groups in Kyrgyzstan, Akaev has sought to incorporate the leaders of all ethnic communities into a grand coalition committed to measured political and economic reform. A surprise winner in the republic's first presidential election in October 1990, Akaev has charted a middle course in nationality policy, shunning both the naive internationalism of traditional leaders of Soviet Kyrgyzstan as well as the inflammatory Kyrgyz nationalism pursued by Sydykov in Osh in 1990.[75] Akaev has made numerous symbolic gestures to the Kyrgyz, especially those in rural areas, adopting special measures for the "defense" of the shepherds and restoring traditional folk holidays and customs.[76] He actively solicits the support and understanding of the Slavic community, reminding it of his long tenure in Russia – he worked for seventeen years as a researcher in Leningrad – and of his respect for the Slavic contribution to the Kyrgyz economy.[77] He frequently points to Russia under the leadership of Boris Yeltsin as a model of political and economic reform. And Akaev appointed two Russians to his twelve-man cabinet, the State Council, which conducts its sessions in Russian.[78] He has also cultivated good relations with the leader of Uzbekistan, Islam Karimov, and with Uzbek religious leaders in southern Kyrgyzstan, who have encouraged quietism in Osh.

To prevent electoral politics from exacerbating national divisions in a democratizing Kyrgyzstan, President Akaev supported the formation in the summer of 1991 of a Gaullist-like presidential party, National Unity. Drawing its leaders from the reform-minded members of the old nomenklatura as well as from "democratic structures and the reform wing of national democratic movements," National Unity is a multi-ethnic party devoted to the politics of consensus.[79] It has ties to "For Democratic Reform," the reform organization founded in Moscow by Eduard Shevardnadze and Alexander Yakovlev.[80] In its first months of existence, National Unity served as a faithful supporter of the presidential program in parliament and as the organizational core of Akaev's campaign for re-election in October 1991, this time by popular vote. The presidential campaign was a remarkable display of Akaev's skill in rallying the most diverse segments of Kyrgyzstan behind his candidacy.[81] Under the banner of "Civil Consensus and National Unity – YES; Chauvinism, Nationalism, and Extremism – NO," Akaev stood unopposed for election to a five-year term, gaining over 90 percent of the vote.[82]

The challenge for Akaev is to hold together this diverse coalition in the face of newly-emerging political parties, the indigenization of language policy, and a market reform that is increasing economic hardships and social stratification. The ethnic Kyrgyz will be especially vulnerable in the transition to a market-oriented economy. As a group, they have neither the education and skills of the Slavs nor the commercial traditions of the Uzbeks or the Koreans living in Kyrgyzstan. In 1990, for example, over 55 percent of Russian applicants were admitted to higher education institutions in the republic; the figure for the Kyrgyz was less than 30 percent.[83] Furthermore, the ethnic Kyrgyz account for 75 percent of agricultural labor in Kyrgyzstan and only a quarter of the industrial workforce, where the jobs and conditions are superior.[84] Perhaps more disturbing, Kyrgyz youth have been reluctant to pursue careers in industry and construction.[85] In a more competitive and open economy, then, ethnic Kyrgyz as a group may fall further behind the Uzbeks, the Koreans, and the Russians in terms of economic well-being. This prospect will undoubtedly create strong pressures on a Kyrgyz-dominated state to adopt measures to "defend" the titular nationality. Already, the more nationalist elements in a new political party, Erkin Kyrgyzstan, have proposed the granting of 65 percent of the republic's property to ethnic Kyrgyz during the process of privatization.[86] If the state adopts such affirmative action policies, it risks a new round of disturbances and the flight of Slavs from the republic.[87] Given current conditions, it will be difficult for Akaev, or any subsequent leader in Kyrgyzstan, to maintain the middle course. Economic deprivation and instability are not conducive to the politics of consensus.

Notes

1 "Zemel'nyi kodeks respubliki Kyrgyzstan," *Slovo Kyrgyzstana*, June 11, 1991, p. 3; "Veto Prezidenta otvechaiet chaianiiam vsekh liudei dobroi voli," *Slovo Kyrgyzstana*, June 28, 1991, p. 3. President Akaev was one of the few leaders of Soviet republics to publicly condemn the August 1991 coup in its initial stages.

2 No one better exemplifies the ugly face of Russian nationalism than Vladimir Zhirinovskii, the right-wing politician who ran unsuccessfully for the presidency of Russia in the summer of 1990. In an interview with an American correspondent in January 1992, Zhirinovskii claimed he would pursue the following policy if in power. "I would immediately change the foreign policy radically. In two days, I would do away with such countries as Kazakhstan and Kirghizia, because . . . there is not a single scholar in the USA or elsewhere in the world who would be able to locate such political entities as Kazakhstan and Kirghizia on the map of the world." *MacNeil/Lehrer Newshour*, January 13, 1992.

3 "The question of the origins of the Kyrgyz nation is among the most complex and controversial aspects of the ethnic history of Central Asia." With these words S.M. Abramzon opens his seminal work on the Kyrgyz. *Kirgizy i ikh etnogeneticheskie i istoriko-kul'turnyi sviazi* (Leningrad: Nauka, 1971), p. 10. As this and other works illustrate, the question of the ethnogenesis of the Kyrgyz is by no means closed. See *Istoriia Kirgizskoi SSR*, vol. 1, ed. V.M. Ploskikh *et al.* (Frunze, "Kyrgyzstan," 1984), and Esen Uluu Kylych, "K dinastii karakhanidov – Kirgizov?," *Slovo Kyrgyzstana*, September 7, 1991, p. 10. Among non-specialists the identity of the modern Kyrgyz is confused by the use of the name to describe an older tribe along the Enisei River in southern Siberia and by the Russians' use of the term well into this century to describe the Kazakhs. The Kyrgyz were often referred to as the Kara-Kirgiz to distinguish them from the Kazakhs.

4 Abramzon, *Kirgizy i ikh etnogeneticheskie i istoriko-kul'turnye sviazi*, pp. 22–23.

5 D. Thomson, *Europe since Napoleon* (Harmondsworth: Penguin, 1966), p. 119.

6 Donald S. Carlisle, "Uzbekistan and the Uzbeks," *Problems of Communism*, September-October 1991, p. 24.

7 A. Arzymatov, "V sostav Rossii: Vkhozhdenie? Prisoedinenie? Zavoevanie?," *Slovo Kyrgyzstana*, June 1, 1991, p. 10; Helene Carrere d'Encausse, "Systematic Conquest, 1965 to 1984," in *Central Asia: 120 Years of Russian Rule*, ed. E. Allworth (Durham: Duke University Press, 1989), p. 134. It should be noted that the southern Kyrgyz were more hostile to the encroachment of the Russians than the northern Kyrgyz.

8 This is the subtitle of the second volume of the authoritative Soviet history of the republic. *Istoriia Kirgizskoi SSR*, vol. 2, ed. S.I. Il'iasov *et al.* (Frunze: "Kyrgyzstan," 1986).

9 Osmon Ibraimov, "Neizvestnyi genotsid," *Slovo Kyrgyzstana*, April 20, 1991, p. 10.

10 Ian Murray Matley, "Population and Land," in *Central Asia: 120 Years of Russian Rule*, ed. E. Allworth (Durham: Duke University Press, 1989), p. 105.

11 Osmon Ibraimov, "Neizvestnyi genotsid," *Slovo Kyrgyzstana*, April 20, 1991, p. 10.
12 "Znaia pravdu istorii, ne pred'iavliat' drug drugu schet za svoikh predkov," *Slovo Kyrgyzstana*, April 6, 1991, p. 3; G. Rongard, "Spravedlivost' trebuet pravdu," *Slovo Kyrgyzstana*, July 13, 1991, p. 3.
13 Osmon Ibraimov, "Neizvestnyi genotsid," *Slovo Kyrgyzstana*, April 20, 1991, p. 10.
14 An authoritative Soviet account of the 1916 uprisings in Kyrgyzstan may be found in *Istoriia Kirgizskoi SSR*, vol. 2, ed. S.I. Il'iasov *et al.* (Frunze: "Kyrgyzstan," 1986), pp. 337–345.
15 For a Soviet account of the revolution itself in Kyrgyzstan, see A.G. Zima, *Velikii Oktiabr' v Kirgizii* (Frunze: "Ilim," 1987).
16 *Istoriia Kirgizskoi SSR*, vol. 3, ed. K.K. Karakeev *et al.* (Frunze: "Kyrygzstan," 1986), pp. 319–337.
17 Dzh. Dzhunushaliev, "Politika korenizatsii: opyt i problemy," *Kommunist Kirgizstana*, no. 1, 1990, pp. 69–70.
18 *Ibid.*
19 *Ibid.* On the background of members of "elected" bodies in early Soviet Kyrgyzstan, see Z. Kurmanov, "Tochka zreniia," *Slovo Kyrgyzstana*, July 13, 1991, p. 6.
20 One member of this elite was Torekul Aitmatov, the father of the internationally-known novelist, Chingiz Aitmatov. For a discussion of Torekul Aimatov's life and its influence on his son's work, see Joseph P. Mozur, *Doffing "Mankurt's Cap." Chingiz Aitmatov's "The Day Lasts More than a Hundred Years" and the Turkic National Heritage* (Pittsburgh: The Carl Beck Papers in Russian and East European Studies [no. 605], 1987).
21 "Usubaliyev Gives Report to Kirgiz CP Congress," *Foreign Broadcast Information Service (Soviet Union)*, February 4, 1981, R46, citing *Sovetskaia Kirgiziia*, January 21, 1981, pp. 2–8.
22 "Vorotnikov Speaks at Frunze," *Foreign Broadcast Information Service (Soviet Union)*, October 15, 1984, R9, citing Moscow Domestic Service in Russian, 1600 GMT, October 13, 1984.
23 See "Kirgiz Party Chief Usubaliev Retires," *Radio Liberty Research Bulletin*, November 7, 1985, p. 3.
24 Dzh. Dzhunushaliev, "Istoki 'belykh piaten' istorii," *Kommunist Kirgizstana*, no. 5, 1990, p. 65.
25 Ch. Aitmatov, "Voronii grai nad opolznem. Oshskie razdum'ia, god spustia," *Slovo Kyrgyzstana*, August 2, 1991, p. 2.
26 Even in the approximately 1,000 schools in the republic where Kyrgyz was the language of instruction, the teachers trained in Russian in their substantive fields. ". . . chtoby v kazhdoi dushe byl pokoi," *Sovetskaia Kirgiziia*, September 13, 1989, p. 3.
27 "Na osnove svobodnogo razvitiia i ravnopraviia iazykov," *Sovetskaia Kirgiziia*, September 28, 1989, p. 3. In general, Kyrgyz-language works were poorly represented in every cultural field. Of the fifty works in the repertory of the Kirgiz Theater of Opera and Ballet in 1989, only four were in Kyrgyz; and of the 5,577 films in the inventory of Kirgizkiioprokat, only 9 percent were dubbed into Kyrgyz. *Ibid.*

28 R. Osmonalieva, "Ob'ektiven li voliuntarizm?," *Kommunist Kirgizstana*, no. 10, 1990, p. 81. Only in light industry, where the Kyrgyz comprise 35 percent of the workforce, does the titular nationality make up at least a third of an industrial sector. *Ibid.*

29 *Ibid.*

30 Dzh. Dzhunushaliev, "Politika korenizatsii: opyt i problemy," *Kommunist Kirgizstana*, no. 1, 1990, p. 75.

31 On the correlation between ethnicity and employment in Central Asia, see Nancy Lubin, *Labor and Nationality in Soviet Asia: An Uneasy Compromise* (Princeton: Princeton University Press, 1984).

32 For an excellent overview of demographic trends in Central Asia, see M. Rywkin, *Moscow's Muslim Challenge: Soviet Central Asia*, revised edition (Armonk, NY: M.E. Sharpe, Inc., 1990), chapter 5.

33 A. Zhakypov, "Komuz ne dlia frantsuvoz," *Sovetskaia Kirgizia*, September 10, 1989, p. 2.

34 M. Guboglo, "Demography and Language in the Capitals of the Union Republics," *Journal of Soviet Nationalities*, no. 4, 1990, p. 7.

35 "O prioritetakh," *Murok*, no. 1, November 1990, p. 2. *Murok* is an irregularly issued newsletter published in Moscow by ethnic Kyrgyz who seek more rapid reform of the republic's political and economic system. For insightful articles on the Kyrgyz communities in Moscow and St. Petersburg, numbering about 3,000 in each city, see A. Gorodzeiskii, "Moskovskie kirgizy," *Literaturnyi Kirgizstan*, no. 11, 1990, p. 82, and N. Ablova, " 'Belyi parokhod v ust'e Nevy, ili kirgizy goroda Pitera," *Literaturynyi Kirgizstan*, nos. 7–8, 1990, pp. 112–117.

36 E. Abildaev, "Rabochii klass Kirgizii: osobennosti razvitiia," *Kommunist Kirgizstana*, nos. 8–9, 1990, p. 135.

37 V. Rumiantsev, "Sluzhba zaniatosti i rynochnaia ekonomika," *Kommunist Kirgizstana*, no. 11, 1990, pp. 42–48.

38 "Ozdorovit' i stabilizirovat' obstanovku (s plenuma oshkogo obkoma Kompartii Kirgizii)," *Sovetskaia Kirgiziia*, August 15, 1990, p. 2.

39 "Deistvovat' vzveshenno, obstoiatel'no, soobshcha," *Slovo Kyrgyzstana*, January 15, 1991, p. 2.

40 On the problem of overpopulation of the Central Asian countryside, see Boris Z. Rumer, *Soviet Central Asia: "A Tragic Experiment"* (Boston: Unwin Hyman, 1989), chapter 6.

41 S. Usenov, "Vozvrat k srednevekov'iu?," *Murok*, no. 1, 1990, pp. 2–3.

42 V. Ponomarev, *Samodeiatel'nye obshchestvennyi organizatsii Kazakhstana i Kirgizii, 1987–1991 (opyt spravochnika)* (Moscow: Informatsionnoe agentstvo 'Aziia,' 1991), p. 84.

43 "Na osnove svobodnogo razvitiia i ravnopraviia iazykov," *Sovetskaia Kirgiziia*, September 28, 1989, p. 5; S. Usenov, "Vozvrat k srednevekov'iu?!," *Murok*, no. 1, 1990, pp. 2–3. By the beginning of 1991, a corporatist-style relationship existed between Ashar and the local authorities in Frunze (Bishkek). E. Denisenko, "Ashar deistvyet, i on prav," *Slovo Kyrgyzstana*, May 8, 1991, p. 7.

44 Russian reformers began to leave these groups, however, after the Osh events and after the rise of Yeltsin in the Russian Federation, which attracted many of

them to Russia. A. Kniazev, "Russkii vopros," *Literaturnyi Kyrgyzstan*, no. 1, 1991, pp. 109–115. An exception was G. Kaliuzhnaia, a Russian elected chairman of the Sokuluk branch of the DDK. "Lider DDK v raione – russkaia," *Slovo Kyrgyzstana*, September 6, 1991, p. 1.

45 "Programma Demokraticheskogo dvizheniia 'Kyrgyzstan'" [document in possession of the author]. The rules of the organization may be found in *Frunze shamy*, 28 August 1990.
46 V. Ponomarev, *Samodeiatel'nye obshchestvennye organizatsii Kazakhstana i Kirgizii, 1987–1991*, pp. 96–97. For biographies of the co-chairmen of the Democatic Movement "Kyrgyzstan," Topchubek Turganaliev and Zhypar Zheksheev, see "Portrety bez ramok," *Literaturnyi Kirgizstan*, no. 12, 1990, pp. 89–94. Turganaliev was among a number of members of the DDK who went on a hunger strike outside the parliament building in Frunze to demand reform of what until that time had been an unreconstructed political system. The defeat of Masaliev and the election of Akaev coincided with this hunger strike.
47 For the result of opinion polls among local residents on the origins of the Osh disturbances, see A. Elebaeva, "Mezhnatsional'nye otnosheniia: mif i real'-nost'," *Slovo Kyrgyzstana*, August 3, 1991, p. 4.
48 "Ozdorovit' i stabilizirovat' obstanovku (s plenuma oshkogo obkoma Kompartii Kirgizii)," *Sovetskaia Kirgiziia*, August 15, 1990, p. 2.
49 Since the 1920s, when Turkestan was divided, the boundaries between Kyrgyzstan and Uzbekistan have been disputed. See T. Ozhukeeva, ". . . i rezali derzhevu, kak tort (istoki territorial'nykh konfliktov v SSSR)," *Slovo Kyrgyzstana*, November 2, 1991, p. 10.
50 Dzhamin Akimaliev, "Igra bez pravil," *Literaturnyi Kirgizstan*, no. 11, 1990, p. 88.
51 Disturbances on a smaller scale broke out on the Kyrgyz-Tajik border concerning water rights. This dispute, whose roots go back to the drawing of territorial boundaries in the 1920s, soured relations between Kyrgyz and Tajik leaders in the late 1980s and early 1990s. For a brief review of the dispute, see A. Kniazev, "Zalozhniki zakholustiia," *Literaturnyi Kirgizstan*, no. 5, 1990, pp. 98–104. At stake is 24,000 hectares of Kyrgyz territory claimed by Tajikistan. "Zachem vvodit' liudei v zabluzhdenie?," *Slovo Kyrgyzstana*, May 24, 1991, p. 1.
52 See A.S. Pigolkin and M.S. Studenkina, "Republic Language Laws in the USSR: A Comparative Analysis," *Journal of Soviet Nationalities* (forthcoming). Reform of language policy had begun in Kyrgyzstan in October 1988 with the adoption of a party directive "O national'no-russkom dvuiazychii, uluchshenii prepodavaniia i izucheniia kirgizskogo, russkogo i drugikh iazykov narodov SSSR v respublike." "O proekte Zakona o gosudarstvennom iazyke Kirgizskoi SSR (Doklad sekretaria TsK Kompartii Kirgizii, predsedatelia Komissii zakonodatel'nykh predpolozhenii Verkhovnogo Soveta Kirgizskoi SSR deputata M.Sh. Sherimkulova)," *Sovetskaia Kirgiziia*, September 28, 1989, pp. 2–3.
53 See, for example, the comments of the ethnic Russian procurator of Kyrgyzstan, G.I. Ivantsov. "Na osnove svobodnogo razvitiia i ravnopraviia iazykov," *Sovetskaia Kirgiziia*, September 28, 1989, p. 4.
54 "O gosudarstvennom iazyke Kirgizskoi SSR," *Sovetskaia Kirgiziia*, September 29, 1989, pp. 1–2.

55 "Obsuzhdaetsia proekt Zakona o iazyke," *Sovetskaia Kirgiziia*, September 12, 1991, p. 1.

56 U. Midinova and E. Turaliev, "O 'piknikakh,' dlinnykh ocherediakh . . . i drugikh malopriiatnykh veshchakh," *Literaturnyi Kirgizstan*, no. 1, 1990, pp. 123–126.

57 V. Ermakov, "Ostat'sia, chtoby vozrodit'sia," *Literaturnyi Kyrgyzstana*, no. 5, 1991, pp. 104–105. See also E. Chernova, "Trudoresursnyi faktor i mezhnatsional'nye otnosheniia," *Kommunist Kirgizstana*, no. 6, 1990, p. 61.

58 The reaction of the Central Asian minorities to the law was less immediate and less alarmist. The law did provoke resentment, however, among the Uzbeks in southern Kyrgyzstan. Uzbeks objected that they already knew a second language, Russian, and Kyrgyz would be a third. In their compact ethnic community in the Fergana valley, many argued, Uzbek and not Kyrgyz should be the official language.

59 "Nuzhen dialog, a ne protivosostoianie," *Sovetskaia Kirgiziia*, December 16, 1989, p. 3.

60 "Respublika ishchet imia," *Slovo Kyrgyzstana*, December 13, 1990, p. 1. Changing the spelling of the republic in Russian from Kirgizstan to Kyrgyzstan caused considerable resentment among the Russians, who claimed their language was being interfered with by forcing it to deny Russian rules of pronunciation. "I dukh, i bukva," *Sovetskaia Kirgiziia*, December 9, 1990, p. 3.

61 V. Alekseev, "'Slavianskie vesti,'" *Sovetskaia Kirgiziia*, December 19, 1990, p. 1.

62 "Russkie uezzhaiut iz Kirgizii," *Izvestiia*, September 17, 1990, p. 2; N. Zenkov, "Budut li garantii?," *Sovetskaia Kirgiziia*, September 22, 1990, p. 1.

63 *Ibid.*; "Vyryvat' s korniami – eto bol'no," *Sovetskaia Kirgiziia*, September 22, 1990, p. 1.

64 Report on Soviet evening news, *ITA*, 1900 GMT, January 23, 1992. The demonstrations held in various Kyrgyz cities to mark the 75th anniversary of the 1916 uprisings stirred up ethnic hatred, according to some Slavs. "Na rozni narodov schast'ia ne postroit'," *Slovo Kyrgyzstana*, August 7, 1991, p. 3.

65 A. Gorodzeiskii, "Moskovskie kirgizy," *Literaturnyi Kirgizstan*, no. 11, 1990, p. 82.

66 Dzhamin Akimaliev, "Igra bez pravil," *Literaturnyi Kirgizstan*, no. 11, 1990, p. 92.

67 The roots of Islam are less deep in Kyrgyzstan than among the more sedentary peoples of Central Asia. As Abramzon points out, although Islam came to Kyrgyzstan in the sixteenth and seventeenth centuries, it had hardly taken hold even by the nineteenth century. Abramzon, *Kirgizy i ikh etnogeneticheskie i istoriko-kul'turnye sviazi*, pp. 255–275. For a sophisticated analysis of the role of Islam in the rise of a Kyrgyz ethnic consciousness, see Guy Imart, "The Islamic Impact on Traditional Kirghiz Ethnicity," *Nationality Papers*, nos. 1–2, 1986, pp. 65–88. It is still unclear to what extent Islam will serve as a catalyst in the formation of contemporary Kyrgyz nationalism.

68 Recent meetings of independent democratic associations and parties in Central Asia have called for retaining the territorial status quo. The leaders of these organizations specifically rejected the idea of a pan-turkic state, Turan. E. Denisenko, "Slozhenie sil na ostrove demokratii," *Slovo Kyrgyzstana*, May 31,

1991, p. 2. The permanent headquarters of this federation of Central Asian democratic organizations is to be in Frunze (Bishkek), remarkable testimony to the pace of reform in Kyrgyzstan, which as late as the fall of 1989 was seen by many to be the most backward republic politically in Central Asia.

69 K. Bobulov, "Pravda i lozh'," *Slovo Kyrgyzstana*, March 1, 1991, p. 3.

70 For a discussion of Kyrgyz tribes and clans, see Abramzon, *Kirgizy i ikh etnogeneticheskie i istoriko-kul'turnye sviazi*, pp. 24–34, 189, and *passim*.

71 Azamat Altay, "Kirgiziya During the Great Purge," *Central Asian Review*, no. 2, 1964, p. 102. I am grateful to Joseph Mozur for bringing this source to my attention.

72 "Diestvovat' vzveshenno, obstoiatel'no, soobshcha," *Slovo Kyrgyzstana*, January 15, 1991, p. 2.

73 A. Biialinov, "Kirgizskaia Federativnaia Respublika: byt' ili ne byt'?," *Sovetskaia Kirgiziia*, November 24, 1990, p. 2.

74 K. Mambetaliev, "Uvazhitel'noe gostepriimstvo – ili bratskoe sokhoziaistvovanie?," *Literaturnyi Kirgizstan*, no. 8, 1990, p. 87.

75 Akaev's victory was remarkable because of the generally conservative composition of the supreme soviet that elected him. On the limits of competitiveness in the supreme soviet elections of February 1990, see E. Huskey, "Politics and Elections in Kirgizia, 1989–1990," in *Elections in the Soviet National Republics*, ed. D. Slider (forthcoming).

76 See, for example, the presidential *ukaz* on "the guardians of the centuries-old Kyrgyz shepherding culture" in "Tak, kak zhivut chabany, zhit' nel'zia!," *Slovo Kyrgyzstana*, March 6, 1991, p. 3. On the reviving of the traditional holiday of Nooruz, see "Segodnia – Nooruz!," *Slovo Kyrgyzstana*, March 21, 1991, p. 1.

77 See, for example, "Brat'ia na vse vremena," *Slovo Kyrgyzstana*, July 23, 1991, pp. 1–2, and "Glavnoe – grazhdanskii mir, natsional'noe soglasie," *Slovo Kyrgyzstana*, July 24, 1991, pp. 1–2, both speeches by Akaev on the occasion of Yeltsin's visit to Kyrgyzstan.

78 "Pod parusom nadezhdi vpered, prezidentskii sovet!," *Sovetskaia Kirgiziia*, November 17, 1990, p. 1.

79 In the wake of the August 1991 coup, National Unity launched a campaign to recruit departing members of the Communist Party into its ranks. The leading Russian-language newspaper of the republic printed on its first page a membership form for National Unity, an indication of the extent to which the press had been incorporated into the presidential camp. "Dvizhenie otkryto dlia vsekh," *Slovo Kyrgyzstana*, August 28, 1991, p. 1. On the politics of National Unity, see "K chemu zovet 'Narodnoe edinstvo'?," *Slovo Kyrgyzstana*, October 23, 1991, p. 2. For an attack on National Unity as a party of the apparatus, see O. Olzhobaeva, "Pis'mo Prezidentu: ot bespartiinykh s liubov'iu," *Slovo Soviet Kyrgyzstana*, July 27, 1991, p. 7.

80 "'Narodnoe edinstvo' o sebe i svoikh tseliakh," *Slovo Kyrgyzstana*, August 6, 1991, p. 2.

81 An assessment of Akaev's consensus-oriented politics – eschewing "communist and religious fanaticism" – may be found in N. Andreev, "Askar Akaev: svobodnyi Kyrgyzstan dolzhen byt' sil'nym," *Izvestiia*, October 10, 1991, p. 2. A brief biography of the Kyrgyz president may be found in "Portrety bez ramok

(Prezident Kirgizstana Askar Akaev)," *Literaturnyi Kyrgyzstan*, no. 1, 1991, pp. 116–118.

Like Yeltsin in the Russian Federation, Akaev sought to dominate local government by bringing its leaders under the direct control of the president. The limitation of democracy was necessary in local soviets, Akaev argued, because "they are not prepared to receive full power from the party apparatus," having worked for years in a secondary role behind the party. "Nuzhny delovitost' i initsiativa," *Slovo Kyrgyzstana*, February 12, 1991, pp. 1–2.

82   "Kredit doveriia ne ischerpan," *Slovo Kyrgyzstana*, August 29, 1991, p. 2.

83   R. Achylova, "Natsiia – sub'ekt, a ne rudiment istorii," *Kommunist Kirgizstana*, no. 6, 1990, p. 37.

84   E. Abildaev, "Rabochii klass Kirgizii: osobennosti razvitiia," *Kommunist Kirgizstana*, nos. 8–9, 1990, p. 134. On the educational "lag" of indigenous Central Asian nationalities, see Martha Brill Olcott, "Central Asia: The Reformists Challenge a Traditional Society," in *The Nationalities Factor in Soviet Politics and Society*, ed. L. Hajda and M. Beissinger (Boulder, CO: Westview Press), pp. 266–267.

85   Even in the urban vocational training schools, only 15 percent of ethnic Kyrgyz opt for industrial courses, with most preferring trade-related subjects. *Ibid.*, pp. 135–138.

86   B. Malikova, "Takie raznye demokraty," *Slovo Kyrgyzstana*, December 3, 1991, p. 2. Some Kyrgyz oppose the privatization of property altogether because it violates the Kyrgyz nomadic tradition and may place too much of the republic's wealth in the hands of "foreigners." See R. Achylova, "Natsiia – sub'ekt, a ne rudiment istorii," *Kommunist Kirgizstana*, no. 6, 1990, p. 36. On the ambivalent attitude of the Kyrgyz toward market reform, see the results of survey research in D. Slider, V. Magun, and V. Gimpel'son, "Public Opinion on Privatization: Republic Differences," *Soviet Economy*, no. 3, 1991, pp. 236–275.

87   Limited affirmative action programs have already begun, though they appear to target rural youth as a whole and not just the Kyrgyz. A presidential *ukaz* of late July 1991 ordered the creation of special schools for the training of gifted rural youth, especially those from the homes of shepherds and tobacco workers (the latter category would presumably embrace some Uzbeks and other non-Kyrgyz). Fifty percent of the places in the preparatory faculties of higher educational institutions are to be set aside for the children of agricultural workers. "O nekotorykh neotlozhnykh voprosakh usileniia sotsiali'noi i pravovoi zashchishchennosti molodezhi v respublike Ky'rgyzstana," *Slovo Kyrgyzstana*, July 30, 1991, p. 1.

Part VII
Nations without States

18 The Middle Volga: ethnic archipelago in a Russian sea

RON WIXMAN

The Middle Volga region, comprising a number of Turkic, Finnic, Hunnic, and Russian-speaking peoples, represents one of the most ethnically diverse areas of the Soviet Union. Situated at the juncture of European Russia, the heartland of the Russian people, and the Siberian Plain, it is the only major non-Russian area within the former USSR which was an enclave surrounded by Russian territory. Its conflictual history of ethnic assimilation centering on the struggle for supremacy between Moslem Tatar and Eastern-Orthodox Russian cultures left the various Finnic and Hunnic peoples trapped between the "Tatar wolf" and the "Russian Bear."

The Middle Volga is distinctive in a number of important ways in terms of ethnic tensions arising between the peoples of the Soviet Union and the Soviet state. It was the first significant non-Russian area incorporated into the Muscovite State. Prior to the fifteenth-century conquest of the Volga Tatars by Tsar Ivan IV, Muscovy was almost exclusively composed of ethnic Russians, with only a few Finnic settlements scattered on the eastern frontier.[1] The region also holds special significance as the site where the Moslem-Turkic Tatars were defeated, which signalled the beginning of the Russian *reconquista*.[2] Indeed, St. Basil's Cathedral – an image which is synonymous with the city of Moscow – was constructed in commemoration of the defeat of Islamic forces by Christian Muscovites. In recognition of this victory, as well as of the liberation of all formerly-Christian lands which at the time were held by Islamic peoples (notably Constantinople and Jerusalem), a new Christian symbol appeared atop Russia's churches – *the cross over the crescent*.[3]

It was also in the Middle Volga that the Russians, under the precedent set by Saint Steven of Perm,[4] enacted the policy of creating literary liturgical languages and tolerating, to some extent, the minorities for whom they were created. This was done less out of a sense of Christian benevolence than as a stop-gap measure to impede the "Islamization" of the local populations by the culturally-dominant Tatars. In order to prevent such assimilation, the Russian (and later the Soviet) government supported ethnic groups by providing them with institutions of their own. This support included the preservation of their spoken languages; the establishment of

Map 18.1 Administrative divisions of the Middle Volga

literary native languages; the recognition of non-Russian, ethnic liturgical languages by the Eastern Orthodox Church; and, at times, even the creation of ethnic territories.[5]

By the late fifteenth century, it had already become apparent to the Russians that ethnic, linguistic, and cultural "Tatarization" was associated with the spread of Islam. As the animist Finnic and Hunnic peoples (and even a significant portion of Slavs) adopted the Moslem religion, they also assumed a Tatar identity. The Tatars, like the Turks of the Caucasus, Turkey, and Central Asia, maintained an open ethnic system under which one could become a legitimate member of the dominant ethnic group by accepting and adopting their cultural norms and language.[6] The same was true of the Russians, in that the acceptance of the primacy of Russian Orthodox religion and the Russian language led to the ethnic assimilation of non-Russians.[7] Thus, the ethnic leitmotif of the sixteenth century through to the twentieth was characterized by the Tsarist and Soviet regimes in competition with the Tatars for cultural, territorial, and ideological (both political and religious) control of the non-Russian peoples of the Middle Volga.[8]

The geographic location of the Middle Volga region is not insignificant. It is situated along the Volga River – the main fluvial transportation artery of the country – which connects central Russia with the rich agricultural steppes to the south; the Urals; northern Kazakhstan; Central Asia; and Siberia. Along its banks millions of Russians have settled, erected towns and trading areas, and, more recently, developed the region into one of the country's primary industrial and transportation hubs. In fact, no other region of the USSR, except Siberia, experienced such a vast migration and settlement of Russians as the Middle Volga. Generally speaking, the indigenous peoples became small minorities in a sea of Russians (see table 18.4), which led in turn to the ascendancy of Russian language and culture in the region. It is no wonder, then, that the Volga is often referred to as *mat' volga* – Mother Volga – in the Russian language.

During the Soviet period, the process of economic development and ethnic "Russianization" of the Middle Volga intensified. In an effort to improve the hinterlands of the country, the government developed industrial centers in Siberia, the Urals, and Kazakhstan, which led to a greater degree of development in the Middle Volga, itself rich in coal, oil, natural gas, and agricultural resources. The discovery of plentiful oil and gas fields (especially those of Bashkiria and Tatarstan) and rich coal deposits in the Komi area restimulated Russian economic development and attracted an increased number of Russian workers. Both the establishment of Gorkiy (Nizhny Novgorod) as the leading automative center of the USSR and the rise of the Kama area as the leading Soviet producer of trucks and other transportation vehicles in the mid twentieth century have contributed to the development and integration of this once-remote and isolated area into mainstream Russia.

One can still find the remnants of widespread non-Russian ethnic groups in the Middle Volga, all of whom have undergone profound changes during the past five centuries. For each of the groups survival as distinct cultures and ethnicities has been problematic. For example, this has been particularly true for the descendants of the Finnic-speaking peoples, who were the earliest inhabitants of the region. The vast majority

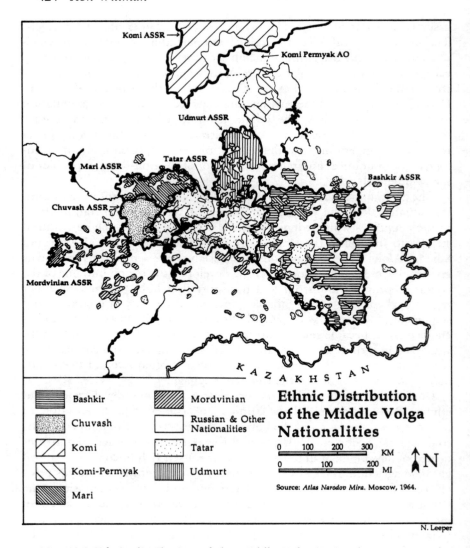

Map 18.2 Ethnic distribution of the Middle Volga nationalities. From *Atlas Narodov Mira* (Moscow, 1964).

of Finnic speakers today have been completely assimilated by the Russians. If current policies and practices toward ethnic minorities do not change, few of these surviving groups will remain as viable, distinct peoples in the future.

The Hunnic Chuvash and the Turkic Tatars and Bashkirs are in different ethno-cultural positions. Having had very different cultural origins and identities and not having been closely tied to Russia and Russian culture, these groups have fared somewhat better than their Finnic countrymen. The Tatars in particular have been able to preserve the image of the greatness of their past, including their ties to the great Mongol Empire of Genghis Khan, cultural and ethnic connections to other Moslem and Turkic peoples in the USSR and the Middle East, and long literary and cultural traditions. As a result, the primary issue facing the peoples of the Middle Volga today is continued cultural and ethnic survival in a region in which the dominant language and culture were linked to Soviet ideology, economic, and cultural development.

In order to appreciate fully the current status of the peoples of the Middle Volga, it is important to consider several factors: who the people are; what Soviet policies were applied to them; and how they have pursued their cultural and ethnic agendas. Demographic trends are important to this analysis, especially since these peoples do not enjoy the same territorial integrity as the titular nationalities of the constituent republics. The following sections treat each of these issues in more depth.

Ethnic groups of the Middle Volga[9]

The earliest known inhabitants of the Middle Volga region were Finnic speakers who practiced animism as their religion, and prior to the eighth century, they alone inhabited the entire area between the Ural mountains and the Baltic Sea. Between the eighth century and the thirteenth, the region witnessed an influx of Hunnic speakers from the steppes of the North Caucasus (the Bolgars) to their south, and of Slavs (Proto-Russians) from the west and south-west. The defeat of the Hunnic Bolgars by the Khazars led to the Bolgars' northward migration and settlement on the Volga in what became the Chuvash and Tatar Autonomous Soviet Socialist Republics (ASSRs). There, among the Finnic peoples, they founded the Volga Bolgar state and made Kazan its capital. Their conversion to Islam led them to assimilate many of the Finnic peoples, and this, coupled with an influx of Turkic nomads, added further to the area's ethnic complexities. The Chuvash people are the descendents of these mixed Funnic, Hunnic and Turkic peoples. The Hunnic language formed the basis of the Chuvash language. This process continued until the thirteenth century, when the entire region was conquered by Tatar Mongols. This unique mixture of Bolgar, Turkic, Finnic, and Mongol peoples produced the ancestors of the people known today as the Tatars.

Upon their arrival to the Middle Volga, the Tatar Mongols (themselves of mixed Kypchak Turkic, Mongol, and other Siberian origins) settled the lands of the Volga Bolgars, adopted Islam from them, and began to usurp their cultural and political primacy. The Tatars spoke a Kypchak Turkic language which was mutually intelligible with all other Kypchak Turkic languages and dialects (e.g. Kazakh, Kyrgyz, Nogai, Bashkir, etc.). Having established themselves at Kazan, they were able to maintain a great military and trading empire. Kazan came to function as a political and commercial center, connecting Russia, Scandinavia, Siberia, China, the Caucasus, Central Asia, and Persia. The Tatar state, which also ruled much of European Russia, flourished throughout the thirteenth, fourteenth and fifteenth centuries, and continued to exert itself as a center for commerce and learning until the nineteenth century, and through the assimilation of Turkic, Mongol, Siberian, Finnic, Hunnic, and Slavic peoples, it came to comprise one of the most ethnically-mixed populations in the world.

While the Tatars engaged in the process of assimilation, the heads of both the Tsarist government and the Russian Orthodox Church plotted to counter the growing Tatar influence. They established literary and liturgical languages for the Turkic and Hunnic-speaking peoples of the region in the dual hope of converting them to Eastern Orthodoxy and reversing their "Tatarization," and their efforts on behalf of the non-Tatar peoples lasted until the reign of Catherine the Great. It is interesting to note that neither the Church nor the tsar pursued a policy of "Russification"; both recognized that such action would probably have produced a negative reaction among those peoples who disliked both Tatars and Russians. Thus, a policy which supported native languages and religions ensued, and it even succeeded in establishing a group of Christianized Tatars (Kryashen) who later developed a Tatar literary language employing the Cyrillic alphabet.[10]

East of the Tatars reside the Bashkirs, a formerly nomadic people of debatable ethnic origin. Most likely, they represent a group of Turkic or Uralic peoples whose ancestors either were linguistically "Tatarized" or shifted to the use of a Kypchak dialect resembling Tatar. Interestingly enough, the Bashkirs fell under strong Tatar influence during the reign of Catherine the Great, who employed Tatars in the settlement and education of nomadic Bashkirs and Kazakhs. As a result, the Bashkirs are only nominally Islamic in culture, much less so than the Tatars. During the 1917 Revolution, the Bashkirs could have been classified easily as a social subgroup (e.g. semi-nomadic peoples) of Tatars rather than as a distinct nation. To varying degrees, however, the Bashkirs resented the cultural and economic dominance of the Tatars who lived among them, including Tatar administrators and teachers employed by the Tsarist regime; conservative Tatar religious leaders who opposed many Bashkir animist religious practices; and Tatar merchants who pursued exploitative business practices. The extent to which the Bashkirs should have been treated as a distinct nationality rather than as a subdivision of the larger Tatar whole thus remains debatable. As late as 1989, approximately one-fourth of all Bashkirs considered Tatar to be their native language in spite of considerable efforts to preserve the Bashkir language and culture. Clearly, the decision by the government to support the distinctiveness of the Bashkir language and culture was political in nature.[11]

Like the Tatars, the Bashkirs also included a group of people that had been Christianized by the Russians. These Christian Bashkirs were called Nagaibak (Noghaibaq) and were officially recognized as a distinct national entity until the 1930s. Similar to the Krayshen-Tatars, they were provided a distinct literary language of their own which employed the Cyrillic alphabet rather than the Arabic. Although small in number (only 11,219 in 1926), their existence further demonstrates the great complexity of ethnicity and ethnic identity in the Middle Volga region.

The current Finnic-speaking peoples of the Middle Volga are a remnant of what was once a greater and more widespread population. The largest of these, the Mordvinians (Mordva), at one time formed a continuous band from the Moscow area in the west to what is now the Tatar ASSR in the east.[12] The western Mordvinians were converted to Eastern Orthodoxy and became Russians, while the eastern Mordvinians were converted to Islam and were assimilated by the Tatars; some of them even became Chuvash. Thus, the Mordvinians have the distinction of having been instrumental in the formation of the Chuvash, Tatar, and Russian peoples.

Today, the remaining Mordvinians comprise two diverse groups – the Erzya (about two thirds of the total population) and the Moshka (about one third of the total population). The languages of these groups are mutually unintelligible, and each maintains its own literary form; thus, in order to communicate with one another, the Erzya and Moshka must either employ Tatar or Russian. Since the Mordvinians are highly dispersed, scattered widely among the Russians, Tatars, and other ethnic groups, they experienced one of the highest rates of assimilation of any peoples in the USSR, in spite of having had a sizable and distinct civilization of their own. Accordingly, their population has continued to decline throughout each successive census period.[13] As a result of their shrinking size and general fluent command of Russian, the Mordvinians lost a great deal of support from the Soviet government for maintaining their ethnic and cultural institutions (e.g. native-language schools and publications).

The Mari people find themselves in a situation not unlike that of the Mordvinians. Linguistically, the Mari are divided into two groups whose languages are mutually-unintelligible and possess two distinct literary forms. The majority of the Mari belong to the highland Kuryks, the minority to the lowland Olyks. The literary languages of both peoples were formed by the Eastern Orthodox Church in the early mid nineteenth century in an attempt (which failed) to convert the population to Christianity (as early as the 1870s, a group known as the Kugu Sorta, or Great Candle, developed, whose purpose was to prevent the conversion of the Mari to Christianity). In fact, the primary distinguishing characteristic of the Mari is their unwillingness to convert to either Christianity or Islam in spite of intense missionary efforts by both the Russians and the Tatars. The majority of Maris today maintain their animist/shamanist beliefs, and their national movement continues to strive toward the preservation of their ancient religion. The movement is quite strong, and its strength, in part, may explain how the Mari have been able to enjoy one of the highest levels of native-language retention and one of the lowest levels of Russian assimilation of any of the USSR's Finnic peoples.

The other three Finnic-speaking peoples of the Middle Volga region – the Komi, Komi-Permyak, and Udmurt – are closely related to one another. All of these peoples share a common religion (Eastern Orthodox), speak mutually-intelligible languages, and share many cultural traits. The Komi and Komi-Permyak peoples are especially closely related and often even refer to themselves as being one people who speak one language.[14]

Although they are officially Eastern Orthodox, the Udmurts have varied somewhat in their religious beliefs depending upon the relative exogenous influence of other ethnic groups surrounding them; i.e. those living closest to the Russians became Eastern Orthodox, and those living among the Tatars and Bashkirs frequently embraced Islam. Furthermore, regardless of these influences, many Udmurts continue to practice the old Finnic animist traditions, which makes them, in this respect, much more like the Mari and less like the Komi and Komi-Permyak.[15]

The Middle Volga, then, presents a rather varied ethnic appearance. It comprises not only a large number of diverse and distinct ethnic groups but also a complicated set of transitional and/or partially-assimilated peoples, all of whom are trying to preserve their respective cultural identities in the face of Russian political, social, economic, cultural, and linguistic domination.

Ethnic and national inspirations

One of the results of the Middle Volga's ethnic history is that no single dominant ethnic movement emerged. Given the cultural, linguistic, and territorial overlap they experienced, as well as being situated deep within the heartland of the USSR, the peoples of the region had little opportunity to pursue independence. Indeed, few, if any, of these peoples had developed either the sense of national consciousness or the great leaders necessary in order to provide and sustain the impetus for a nationalist fervor.

No ethnic independence movements arose among the Komi, Komi-Permyaks, Udmurts, or Mordvinians. Essentially, they accepted the dictates of the Russian, and later Soviet, government and benefitted from the latter's fear of Tatarism. The same could also be said of the Chuvash and Bashkirs.[16]

At the time of the October Revolution, many Tatar intellectuals and conservative religious leaders were thoroughly in support of either Pan-Islamic or Pan-Turkic movements (the former more religious in nature, the latter more secular, nationalist and modernist). In virtually all cases, the

Tatar leadership demanded strong ties with other Turkic and Islamic regions of the USSR, and from this grew a movement to create a great Tatar state in the Middle Volga region that would comprise the lands of the Tatars, Bashkirs, Chuvash, Mari, and Udmurt peoples. Their goal was to achieve autonomous republic status within the framework of the Soviet system; the republic was dominated by the Tatars. The name of this state was to have been Idel Ural (Idel is the Tatar name for the Volga, and Ural was for the Ural mountains and river). Since the failed coup of 1991, many Tatars have either demanded an independent Tatar Republic, or have resurrected the idea of a greater Tatarstan on the basis of the old Idel-Ural state idea in which the Tatars would be a dominant group in a multi-cultural Middle Volga state.

Although Bashkirs expressed strong dislike for the culturally-dominant Tatars, they were more concerned with the threats posed by Russian agricultural settlements in Bashkir territory and the consequent loss of pasture land which ensued in the 19th century. Nevertheless, a handful of Bashkir nationalists, including Zeki Valedi Togan (Zeki Validov), continued to press for the creation of a separate Bashkiria. They opposed both the "Tatarization" of the Bashkirs and the incorporation of Bashkir lands by the Tatars, but they did not demand the creation of a separate Bashkir literary language. The Bashkirs themselves used the Tatar literary language and made no request to alter this. The Soviets were able to exploit the Bashkir nationalists in simultaneously supporting the establishment of a separate (but weak) Bashkir state and undermining the Tatar movement to create the Idel Ural state. This Soviet policy of division (*razmezhevania*) was designed to split the Moslem peoples of the USSR into groups that were large enough to maintain distinct ethnic identities yet small enough to be controlled absolutely by the Soviet center. As Benningsen and Lemercier-Quelquejay state, "the policy involved breaking up the large mass of Muslim and Turkic-speaking populace into fragments and then putting the pieces together into the required number of units, each of them having an exact territorial demarcation."[17]

The Middle Volga was the first region of the USSR in which this policy of central planning was administered. It is not by accident, then, that the first ethnically-based territory established in the Russian Soviet Federated Socialist Republic (RSFSR) was the Bashkir ASSR, proclaimed on March 23, 1919, a full year before the creation of the Tatar ASSR. The maintenance of separate Bashkir and Tatar territorial and administrative divisions was clearly aimed at undermining the Pan-Turkic movement and preventing the creation of the Idel Ural State which, at the time, was supported by a majority of the peoples indigenous to the Middle Volga. The Soviets even created a distinct Bashkir literary language and allowed the Bashkirs access to education in their native Bashkir tongue until the tenth grade as a means to prevent a Bashkir-Tatar merger. It need be considered that over a third of all Bashkirs considered Tatar their native language already, by the time of the Russian revolution.

The primary reason for the creation of many of the Middle Volga autonomies was not merely to recognize the rights of local ethnic groups to territorial and cultural integrity (although this explains support afforded the Tatars). As has been mentioned, the fact that the Bashkirs received the first ASSR clearly indicates the calculated political nature of the decision to single out that specific group for support at that time; i.e. at a time when it would have the best chance to thwart the creation of the Idel Ural state. In fact, the policies to grant limited autonomy and cultural identity to all of the ethnic groups of the region appeared to be designed for one ultimate purpose – to diminish Tatar influence.

The majority of the peoples of the Middle Volga actually benefitted as a result of Soviet anti-Tatarism and anti-Pan-Turkism. In spite of their self-serving motives, the Soviets' actions resulted in a positive externality for the ethnic groups – namely, official support for the native languages and cultures of the Chuvash, Komi, Komi-Permyaks, Mordvinians, Mari, Udmurts, and Bashkirs – without which many of these peoples would have become "Tatarized" or "Russianized."

The Soviets also hindered the progress of "Tatarization" through the careful manipulation of official (versus actual) history. Historiographic examination of official histories of the Tatars and their ethnic relations point out that the peoples of the Middle Volga were ruthlessly subjugated and brutalized by the Tatar Mongol hordes; exploited shamelessly by Tatar merchants; and forced to practice Islam against their will by Tatar mullahs. They were liberated from this heartless oppression only by the grace and benevolence of the Soviet government.[18]

Historiography, in general, has been an important component of ethnic relations in the USSR. The Tatars, specifically, resent the depiction of both their ancestors and themselves in official history books. They object to the negative descriptions of not only their activities in the Middle Volga, Kazakhstan, and Central Asia, but also their conquest of Kiev and Russia itself. While the Tatars freely admit to their Mongol ancestors' having conquered other peoples, they prefer to characterize their rule as a period of benevolent empire and not ruthless oppression. They view themselves as builders of civilization, improving the lives of the less-advanced peoples much as the Europeans, Japanese, and Chinese tried to do with their empires. There is some evidence to support this point of view, as during the 300 years of Tatar rule over what is now central Russia and Ukraine, Slavs were permitted to maintain their language, religious practices (in fact, about 200 Russian monasteries were constructed during this time), and local leaders – a sharp contrast to the rule of the Europeans and the Russians.

At a meeting at the Institute of Ethnography in Moscow in the summer of 1985, a number of papers were presented by American and Soviet ethnographers on ethnicity and nationalism. In one of the papers presented, I discussed the role of education (with an emphasis on historiography) on the rise of nationalism and heightened ethnic self awareness among various peoples. The examples of the defeat of Native Americans, of the Serbs at Kosovo Polje by the Turks, and of the Tatars by Ivan the Terrible were presented. Although the Soviet scholars present at the meeting were quick to recognize the importance of how history treating the conquests of the Native Americans, Serbs, and Russians produced the rise of nationalism among these same groups, they failed to recognize the same for the rise of Tatar nationalism in the USSR. They simply did not see a correlation between the depiction of Ivan IV as conqueror of Tataria in the history books (described as the liberation from the Tatar yoke) and the rise of Tatarism, much in the way the defeat of Sitting Bull and other great Native American leaders and nations portrayed in American history books led to a feeling of nationalism among the Native American peoples.

The official Russian histories depict Ivan IV as a virtual demon. On every issue he is portrayed negatively, except that he is praised for accomplishing the unification of Russia and the defeat of the Tatars. Although Russians may celebrate Ivan's role in defeating the Tatars of old, today's Tatars are not afforded the opportunity to share in what they consider to be the glorious past of their ancestors; e.g. the defeat of the Kievans, and the establishment of a Tatar empire. Although the official Soviet histories denigrated the Tsars, the Orthodox Church, capitalism, the old Russian aristocracy, and feudalism, they almost always extolled the incorporation of non-Russian lands into the Russian state because it brought Russian language and culture to the "culturally less fortunate" inhabitants. According to official Soviet texts (the only texts sanctioned for publication in the USSR during its existence), the defeat of the Kazan, Astrakhan and Crimean Tatars was progressive because it brought Russian culture to them. The process of incorporation is always referred to as either liberation from oppression or a benevolent offer of an improved quality of life, neither of which was an offer that could be refused. At worst, incorporation could be seen as the lesser of two evils, as "enlightened" Russian culture (such as it was) had to be preferable to Tatar "enslavement." Furthermore, Tatars are now taught that their ancestors' defeat by Ivan IV was even good for the Tatar people. Yet, the same Soviet ethnographers who were expert on the rise of nationalism in the US and Serbia could not accept that a strong Tatar movement of ethnic nationalism arose from officially-sanctioned anti-Tatar feelings and stereotypes in the USSR. With the possible exception of the Jews, it is difficult to find a people of the Soviet Union as vilified in the official histories of a nation or country as the Tatars.[19]

Most of the people of the Middle Volga feel threatened by the increas-

ingly large number of Russians in their midst, a problem compounded by
the Soviet policy of language assimilation in the schools. These peoples are
relatively small in number, live in scattered settlements, and are witnessing
the evaporation of their respective languages and cultures. The sole exception to this trend seems to be the case of the Bashkirs, whose native language (through the tenth grade) has been officially sanctioned and
employed in the schools for reasons mentioned above. Yet, even though
they continue to benefit from institutionalized Soviet anti-Tatarism (e.g.
they receive job preference over Tatar candidates in the Bashkir ASSR), the
increased immigration of Russians to the urban areas of Bashkiria as a
result of the boom in the petrochemical industry did little to endear the
Russians to the Bashkirs.

Although the Bashkirs realize that the very existence of a distinct
Bashkir people, language, and ASSR is a product of Soviet anti-Tatarism,
few (if any) view this state of affairs as permanent. Today, the Bashkirs fear
the Russians more than the Tatars, as the Soviet government made clear it
would withdraw support for local ethnic entities when they no longer
served a useful purpose for it.[20] In the summers of 1985, 1989, and 1990, I
interviewed a number of Bashkirs in Bokhara, Tashkent, Moscow, and St
Petersburg (Leningrad). These Bashkirs openly discussed their concerns
about what they stated as the *tenuous* situation regarding continued
Russian or Soviet support of Bashkir ethnic institutions (native language
use in printing, the media, and education) in their ethnic autonomy. In the
Bashkir ASSR, Bashkirs comprise only about one fifth of the total population, and they are outnumbered by both Russians and Tatars in their
own autonomy. They cited the examples of the other Middle Volga
peoples (Komi, Chuvash, and Mari) who, from the late 1950s through the
early 1970s, lost almost all of their ethnic privileges. Many Bashkirs firmly
believed that the same would happen to them when the Soviets no longer
felt threatened by the Tatars. As such, the Bashkirs have good reason to
maintain close ties (or at least the appearance of such) with the Tatars.
This gave them two advantages: (1) it ensured that the Bashkirs would
continue to receive high levels of support from the Soviet government, and
(2) in the event that Soviet support was withdrawn, an alliance with the
Tatars offered the Bashkirs a countervailing force.

The Tatars, too, are keenly aware of this precarious situation. One of
the primary problems is that only a very small percentage of the entire
Tatar population resides in the Tatar ASSR (1,765,000 people or 26.5
percent of all Tatars in the USSR). Even if one adds to this the approximately 1,121,000 Tatars who lived at that time in the Bashkir ASSR (where
they comprised 28.4 percent of the ASSR's population), as well as the
Tatars of the Chuvash (36,000), Mari (44,000), Mordvinian (47,000), and
Udmurt (110,000) ASSRs, one is still only talking about 47.0 percent of all
Tatars in the USSR. If, however, one adds these figures to those of the

Table 18.1. *Population growth of the peoples of the Middle Volga 1959–1989 (in 1,000s)*

Nationality	1959	1970	1979	1989
Tatars	4,765[a]	5,931[a]	6,185	6,646
Chuvash	1,470	1,694	1,751	1,839
Bashkirs	989	1,240	1,371	1,449
Mordvinians	1,285	1,263	1,192	1,154
Udmurts	625	704	714	776
Mari	504	599	622	670
Komi	287	322	327	345
Komi-Permyaks	144	153	151	152

[a] In the 1959 and 1970 censuses, no distinction was made between Volga and Crimean Tatars. The Tatar population in this table for 1959 and 1970 includes the Crimean Tatars as well.

Tatar population of the Middle Volga and its surrounding environs, the total would equal 4,326,000, or about 65.1 percent of all Soviet Tatars.[21] It is not difficult to understand, then, why the Tatars maintain a broader conception of what constitutes their "traditional" territory, and why they have and will continue to strive toward the creation of the Idel Ural state.[22]

Since the settlement pattern among the peoples of the Middle Volga has been scattered (see table 18.4), it has been difficult for them to maintain coherent ethnic communities, and the presence of Russians in the region in increasing numbers has only compounded the difficulty of preserving local languages and culture. In the following section, these demographic patterns are examined in more detail.

Demographic trends

In order to appreciate fully the sense of security (or insecurity) experienced by these various peoples in terms of their ethnic survivability, one must examine their populations and rates of population growth. In cases where one finds large and rapidly growing populations (e.g. the Uzbeks increased by 177.4 percent between 1959–1989), one can assume a high degree of security in their ethnic survivability. Conversely, where one finds a group with a relatively small population and a low rate of natural increase (e.g. the Estonians increased only 0.7 percent between 1959–1989), one would expect a relatively higher feeling of insecurity.

Table 18.2 reflects the population change among the peoples of the Middle Volga region from 1959–1989. The figures for Russians, Latvians, and Estonians (Balts with low rates of natural increase), and Uzbeks

Table 18.2. *Percent rates of population change among selected Soviet nationalities 1959–1989*

Nationality	1959–1989	1979–1989
Tatars	39.5	7.4
Chuvash	25.1	5.0
Bashkirs	46.5	5.7
Mordvinians	− 10.2	− 3.2
Udmurts	19.5	4.6
Mari	32.9	7.7
Komi	20.2	5.5
Komi-Permyaks	5.6	0.7
Russians	27.1	5.6
Estonians	3.8	0.7
Latvians	4.2	1.4
Uzbeks	177.4	34.0

(Central Asians with high rates of natural increase) are compared and contrasted.

Tables 18.1 and 18.2 illustrate one major demographic obstacle for many of the peoples of this region. Only the Tatars, Chuvash, Bashkirs, and Mordvinians had populations equal to or greater than one million persons in 1989. The Udmurts and Mari had between three-fourths and two-thirds million persons, and the Komi and Komi-Permyaks only totalled about one-half million persons. Table 18.2 indicates the rates at which these populations have grown between the 1959–1989 census periods. The Bashkirs and Tatars experienced high rates of growth (46.5% and 39.5% respectively); the Mari (32.9%), Chuvash (25.1%), and Komi (20.2%) experienced moderate growth; and the Komi-Permyaks (5.6%) and Mordvinians (− 10.2%) saw markedly low rates of expansion, indicating a significant rate of Russian assimilation.

Table 18.2 also indicates that between 1979–1989, all of the peoples of the Middle Volga experienced a rapid decline in population growth. To some extent, the lower figures reflect not only a shrinking birth rate but also a recently-intensified degree of Russian assimilation (especially among the Komi-Permyaks and Mordvinians). Similarly, the lower rate of growth among the Bashkir people may represent a significant level of Tatar assimilation. For all of the peoples examined, the annual rate of natural population growth for the period 1979–1989 is below 1 percent, and only the Mari and Tatars experienced rates which are analytically significant.

It is also important to examine patterns of population distribution. With few exceptions, a member of an ethnic group is not entitled to native lan-

Table 18.3. *Population (in 1000s) and percent of total population of each nationality residing within its own autonomy 1959 and 1989*

Nationality	Population (in 1000s)		Percent	
	1959	1989	1959	1989
Tatars	1,345	1,765	27.1	26.5
Chuvash	770	907	52.4	49.2
Bashkirs	738	864	74.6	59.6
Mordvinians	358	313	27.9	27.1
Udmurts	476	497	76.2	66.5
Mari	279	324	55.4	48.3
Komi	245	292	85.4	84.6
Komi-Permyaks	126	95	87.5	62.5

guage education, media, or other materials which promote the preservation of native language and culture when s/he resides outsides of his or her own ethnic autonomy (the only exception in this region is the Tatar people, who have ethnic institutions in both the Tatar and Bashkir ASSRs). Table 18.3 indicates the percentage of each ethnic group residing within the borders of its respective ethnic autonomy in 1959 and 1989. The figures provided for the 1959 and 1989 censuses indicate a decline in all cases of peoples residing within their own autonomies. The most significant changes are those of the Komi-Permyaks (87.5% to only 62.5%), the Bashkirs (74.6% to 59.6%), and the Udmurts (76.2% to 66.5%). Only among the Tatars, the Mordvinians, and the Komi was this change not significant. One can also see that only the Komi (84.6%) have a significant majority of its population residing within its own autonomy, and only the Komi-Permyaks, Bashkirs, and Udmurts have approximately 60% or more of their people residing within their homelands. Among the Chuvash and Mari, the percentage was slightly less than 50%, and among the Mordvinians a mere 27.1%. The situation of the Tatars is slightly more complicated since they have ethnic rights in both the Bashkir and Tatar ASSRs.

Given such a dispersed population, and coupling this with the fact that outside their own autonomies the members of these Middle Volga ethnic groups are not entitled to ethnic institutions of their own, their situations are not good. To this we must add that by the early 1960s the use of Komi, Komi-Permyak, Mari, Mordvinian, Udmurt, and Chuvash was eliminated as a medium of instruction in the schools even within their own autonomies. In all, there is a tremendous pressure on these peoples to shift to the use of Russian as their primary language of daily life. In the above cases, these native languages are offered only as electives in the school systems.

Table 18.4. *Population (in 1,000s) and percent of total population of select nationalities in Middle Volga administrative units, 1959 and 1989*

	Population (in 1000s)		Percent	
Nationality	1959	1989	1959	1989
Tatar ASSR	2,850	3,642		
Tatars	1,345	1,765	47.2	48.5
Russians	1,252	1,575	43.9	43.2
Chuvash	144	134	5.0	3.7
Mordvinians	33	29	1.2	0.8
Udmurts	23	25	0.8	0.7
Chuvash ASSR	1,098	1,334		
Chuvash	770	907	70.2	68.0
Russians	264	357	24.0	26.8
Tatars	31	36	2.9	2.7
Mordvinians	24	19	2.2	1.4
Bashkir	3,340	3,943		
Bashkirs	738	864	22.1	21.9
Russians	1,417	1,548	42.4	39.3
Tatars	769	1,121	23.0	28.4
Chuvash	110	119	3.3	3.0
Mari	94	106	2.8	2.7
Mordvinians	44	n/a	1.3	n/a
Udmurts	25	n/a	0.8	n/a
Mordvinian ASSR	1,000	964		
Mordvinians	358	313	35.8	32.5
Russians	591	386	59.1	40.0
Tatars	39	47	3.9	4.9
Udmurt ASSR	1,337	1,606		
Udmurts	476	497	35.6	30.9
Russians	759	945	56.8	58.8
Tatars	72	110	5.4	6.8
Mari	6	10	0.4	0.6
Mari ASSR	648	749		
Mari	279	324	43.1	43.3
Russians	310	356	47.8	47.5
Tatars	39	44	6.0	5.9
Chuvash	9	n/a	1.4	n/a
Udmurts	2	n/a	0.4	n/a
Komi ASSR	806	1,251		
Komi	245	292	30.4	23.3
Russians	390	722	48.4	57.7
Tatars	8	26	1.1	2.1
Chuvash	3	11	0.4	0.9

Perm Oblast	2,993	3,091		
Russians	2,420	2,592	80.9	83.9
Tatars	166	150	5.5	4.9
Komi-Permyaks	136	123	4.5	4.0
Bashkirs	40	52	1.3	1.7
Udmurts	22	33	0.7	1.1
Chuvash	15	n/a	0.5	n/a
Of which:				
Komi-Permyak AO	217	159		
Komi-Permyaks	126	95	58.1	59.7
Russians	71	57	32.7	35.8
Tatars	6	n/a	2.8	n/a
Gorkiy Oblast	3,591	3,720		
Russians	3,382	3,522	94.2	94.7
Tatars	67	59	1.9	1.6
Mordvinians	64	37	1.8	1.0
Kirov Oblast	1,916	1,694		
Russians	1,761	1,532	91.9	90.4
Mari	53	44	2.8	2.6
Tatars	41	46	2.1	2.7
Udmurts	22	23	1.1	1.4
Ulyanov Oblast	1,117	1,396		
Russians	869	1,017	77.8	72.9
Tatars	97	159	8.7	11.4
Mordvinians	73	61	6.5	4.4
Chuvash	60	117	5.4	8.4
Penza Oblast	1,510	1,505		
Russians	1,312	1,296	86.9	86.1
Mordvinians	109	86	7.2	5.7
Tatars	62	81	4.1	5.4
Chuvash	6	n/a	0.4	n/a
Kuibyshev Oblast	2,258	3,263		
Russians	1,848	2,720	81.8	83.4
Mordvinians	115	116	5.1	3.6
Chuvash	102	117	4.5	3.6
Tatars	74	114	3.3	3.5
Orenburg Oblast	1,829	2,171		
Russians	1,297	1,568	70.9	72.2
Tatars	121	159	6.6	7.3
Mordvinians	95	69	5.2	3.2
Bashkirs	30	53	1.6	2.4
Chuvash	21	21	1.1	1.0
Chelyabinsk Oblast	2,977	3,618		
Russians	2,372	2.930	79.7	81.0
Tatars	190	225	6.4	6.2

Table 18.4. (cont.)

	Population (in 1000s)		Percent	
Bashkirs	88	161	3.0	4.4
Mordvinians	31	n/a	1.0	n/a
Chuvash	11	n/a	0.4	n/a
Sverdlovsk Oblast	4,044	4,707		
Russians	3,560	4,177	88.0	88.7
Tatars	158	184	3.9	3.9
Mari	20	31	0.5	0.7
Mordvinians	18	n/a	0.4	n/a
Bashkirs	15	42	0.4	0.9
Chuvash	15	n/a	0.4	n/a

Only among the Tatars and Bashkirs is native language education available to the tenth grade within their own autonomies. The situation of the Mordvinians and the Mari is particularly bad as a high proportion of their populations reside outside of their native territories (about three fourths of the Mordvinians and half of the Mari); and in both cases their native language is divided into two non-mutually intelligible dialects. To make matters yet worse, in most cases even within these so-called ethnic homeland autonomies the titular group is not even in the majority. The Mordvinians, for example, comprise only 32.5% of their autonomy. Similar statistics are present in the Komi ASSR, where thousands of Russians have flocked to the rich forests and the Pechora coal fields. All of these peoples thus live in isolated territories in which power is vested in the surrounding Russian majority (and often in Moscow itself) and not with the titular nationality groups.

Table 18.4 indicates the distribution of peoples in the Middle Volga and adjacent territories (oblasts) in 1959 and 1989. One can see both the extent of population dispersion among the various ethnicities and the degree to which they form tiny enclaves surrounded by great numbers of Russians. This pattern suggests that the promotion and retention of native language and culture is problematic. Also, although the table states that the Russians actually form a minority in the Komi-Permyak AO, the situation is somewhat misleading. The Komi-Permyak AO, relatively small in both size and population, is a division of Perm Oblast, which as a whole contains 2.6 million Russians and only 123,371 Komi-Permyaks. In fact, in 1989, Perm Oblast contained more Tatars (150,460) than Komi-Permyaks.

Distribution of nationalities in the Middle Volga and adjacent regions, 1959 and 1989

In 1959 the titular groups of the Middle Volga autonomies, with the exceptions of only the Tatars, Chuvash, and Komi-Permyaks, were out-numbered within their own autonomies by ethnic Russians. The same pattern appears in the 1989 period. The only significant change that took place between these two periods was that of the Bashkir ASSR, where the combined population of the Tatars and Bashkirs rose to slightly over 50 percent of the population of that region. Even there, however, the Russians out-numbered either the Bashkirs or Tatars as separate groups. Only in the Chuvash ASSR and the Komi-Permyak AO is the titular group in a sig-nificant majority position (68.8% for the Chuvash and 59.7% for the Komi-Permyaks). In 1989 the titular groups in all other cases comprised less than 50% of the total populations within their own autonomies. In some, like the Bashkirs in Bashkiria (21.9%), the Mordvinians in Mord-vinia (32.5%), the Udmurts in Udmurtia (30.9%), and the Komi in their autonomy (23.3%), the titular groups comprised less than one third of the total population of their own autonomies.

Table 18.4 also indicates the great Russian presence that exists throughout the Middle Volga and adjacent areas. In all of the oblasts (i.e., non-autonomous national territories), the Russians comprised a minimum of 72% of the local populations. More important is their total populations in these oblasts – 21,297,000. If one adds the total population of ethnic Russians within the autonomies themselves (5,946,000) to those in the sur-rounding oblasts, their population of 27,243,000 in 1989 gives them total dominance over the "island" populations of these relatively small Middle Volga peoples. Even the Tatar population, the only people of the Middle Volga with a sizeable population, in this region totalled only 4,326,000 and pales in comparison with that of the Russians.

Russian domination of the Middle Volga does not merely consist of numerical superiority. Most important decisions concerning major economic issues, policies regarding education and media, and virtually all other important matters are made in Moscow and not locally. This includes issues of what language is to be used in the schools, and what form that takes. According to a number of Tatar, Bashkir, and Chuvash informants throughout the region, Russians control virtually all industry and commerce. Russian is the official language, and Russian culture is promoted both officially and unofficially. Little, if any, educational or media materials are available in native languages. Even the Tatars and Bashkirs, who do have access to native language education, often send their children to Russian schools because the quality of native language schools is markedly inferior, and because attending Russian schools will

Table 18.5. *Total populations (1,000s) of select nationalities in the Middle Volga and surrounding areas, 1989*

	1989	
	In autonomies	In entire region
Russians	5,946	27,243
Tatars	3,149	4,326
Chuvash	1,171	1,426
Bashkirs	864	1,172
Mordvinians	361	730
Udmurts	522	578
Mari	430	505
Komi	292	292
Komi-Permyaks	95	123

Based on population statistics available in the 1989 census.

allow their children greater opportunity to succeed in the Russian-dominated society. It is important to note that even in the native language schools some subjects, such as science, are only taught in Russian, and they might be more appropriately referred to as bilingual schools.[23]

The rates of linguistic Russianization – the process by which individuals shift to speaking Russian as their primary language – and ethnic Russification – the process by which non-Russians acculturate to the point that they take on the Russian ethnic identity – are relatively high among those Eastern Orthodox peoples in close cultural contact with the Russians and for whom Russian language and culture represented "high" culture in society. This is true for the Mordvinians, Udmurts, Komi, and Komi-Permyaks, as all of the other Finnic peoples share common cultural traits with the Russians. A weaker Russian influence was in evidence among the Mari, as they are not Eastern Orthodox and lack the same cultural ties to Russian culture as the other Finnic peoples. However, by 1989 the rate of Russianization even among the Mari had become significant.

The Chuvash are one of the most interesting peoples in this regard, as they form a transition between Eastern Orthodox Russians and Finnic peoples on the one hand and Turkic Moslem Tatars on the other. Historically, the Chuvash formed the base on which the modern Tatar nation was formed (Volga Bolgars), and from them, the Tatars adopted Islam. The western Bolgars, as was previously discussed, rejected Islam and adopted Eastern Orthodoxy under the auspices of the Russians, who supported them in order to prevent their "Tatarization." The Chuvash, then, derive a strong identity from their Bolgar past which makes them somewhat dissimilar to the Russian peoples, and although they feel no strong ties to the Tatars, there was something of a historical bond between these peoples. In spite of this, by using native language retention as a measure, they now display a significantly lower level of linguistic assimilation (Russianization). They, however, continue to form a distinct majority in their own ASSR (68.0% in 1989), and the Chuvash ASSR has the lowest relative Russian population of any ASSR in the region (only 26.8%).

A clear trend is discernable among virtually all of the peoples of the region in terms of native language retention. Between 1959 and 1989 there was a significant decline among members of each group listing the language of their own nationality as their first language. There was also a corresponding increase in the percentage of peoples declaring Russian to be their native tongue. In all cases except that of the Bashkirs, the levels of native language retention fell significantly between 1959 and 1989. The level of decline ranged from 11% among the Mordvinians to 18.9% among the Komi.[24]

The statistics on the Bashkirs are indicative of the success of Soviet nationality policy in preventing "Tatarization." As was discussed above, the Russians actively pursued policies designed to prevent the spread of Tatar influence. As a result, they not only created the Bashkir ASSR, they also created a Bashkir literary language in 1923. In granting the Bashkirs a distinct territory, history, and language, the Soviets seemed to have realized the fruits of victory against the Tatars. The Bashkirs thus have been very proprietary where their language is concerned, and the percentage of Bashkirs listing their native tongue as primary rose from 61.9% in 1959 to 72.3 in 1989.

It is interesting to note, however, that the rate of linguistic assimilation among Bashkirs is higher within their ethnic autonomy than without. This would seem to indicate that although Bashkir language and culture are strong and important influences, they are still heavily affected by the presence of large numbers of Tatars in Bashkiria; in fact, almost exactly as many Tatars as Bashkirs lived in Bashkiria in 1989. That there are no Bashkirs living in the Tatar ASSR is further evidence of the potency of the Tatar assimilation practices.

In general, however, language retention rates within the various ethnic autonomies tend to be higher than those outside these regions. In 1989 the Tatar ASSR boasted one of the highest rates of native language retention for any people within their own ethnic autonomy in the entire USSR (96.6% of all Tatars declared Tatar their native language). Nonetheless, the proportion of the populations among the Middle Volga nationalities maintaining their own native languages, even in their own autonomies, has eroded greatly since even 1979 (see tables 18.6 and 18.7). Only among the Tatars is native language retention over 90.0%, and among the others in 1989 it ranged from between 74.4% among the Komi to 88.5% among the

Table 18.6. *Native language retention among the Middle Volga nationalities (i.e. percentage considering the language of their own people to be their native tongue) 1959 and 1989*

Nationality	1959	1970	1979	1989
Tatars	92.1	89.2	85.9	83.2
Chuvash	90.8	86.9	81.7	76.4
Bashkirs	61.9	66.2	67.0	72.3
Mordvinians	78.1	77.8	72.6	67.1
Udmurts	89.1	82.6	76.4	69.6
Mari	95.1	91.2	86.7	80.8
Komi	89.3	82.7	76.2	70.4
Komi-Permyaks	87.6	85.8	77.1	70.1

Mordvinians. But even among these two peoples, in the 10 years between the 1979 and 1989 censuses the proportion of peoples speaking their own languages as native tongues declined from 93.8% to 74.4% and from 97.3% to 88.5% respectively.

The last column in tables 18.6 and 18.7 indicates the levels of native language retention for the Middle Volga nationalities in the USSR on the whole in 1989. Here we see significant levels of native language loss (in all cases except among the Bashkirs to Russian). These figures coupled with the relatively high rates of peoples living outside their own autonomies (see table 18.3) indicate a fairly high rate of "denationalization" among all of the non-Turkic Moslems of this region.

On the eve of the attempted coup in 1991, only among the Tatars could one say there is a strong national movement that presents any challenge to Russian authority and control. It is only among the Tatars that we hear a call for "independence" from Russia. But the Tatar leaders themselves are divided. *Izvestiya*, on October 16, 1991, reported a meeting of two distinct Tatar national parties in Kazan: (1) the Tatar Society Center (*Tatarskiy Obshchestvenyy Tsentr*) – a group of fairly moderate Tatar leaders, and (2) the Party for National Birth – a group of Tatar nationalists far more radical than their rivals. Five thousand representatives (from both parties) met at the Parliament Building in Independence Square (*Ploshchad' Svobody*) and demanded that the issue of full Tatar independence (i.e. independence for Tatarstan) be addressed in the parliament itself. The next day, it was reported in *Izvestiya* that the Tatar nationalists, carrying green banners, had forced their way into the Parliament itself.

To what extent the Tatar populace supports such movements is unknown. It can be assumed that most Tatars, especially given the extremely high rate of cultural and native language retention, as well as the

Table 18.7. *Percentage native language retention among the Middle Volga nationalities within their respective autonomy (1979, 1989) and within the USSR (1989)*

Nationality	In own autonomy		In USSR
	1979	1989	1989
Tatars	98.9	96.6	83.2
Chuvash	97.6	85.0	76.4
Bashkirs	57.7[a]	74.7[b]	72.3
Mordvinians	97.3	88.5	67.1
Udmurts	93.2	75.7	69.6
Mari	97.8	88.4	80.8
Komi	93.8	74.4	70.4
Komi-Permyaks	92.2	82.9	70.1

[a] Within their own autonomy, 1.0 percent considered Russian and 41.4 percent considered Tatar to be their native language.
[b] Within their own autonomy, 4.6 percent considered Russian and 20.7 percent considered another language of the USSR (most Tatar) to be their native language.

pronounced Tatar ethnic awareness, support greater cultural autonomy not only for Tatars in the Tatar ASSR, but also throughout the Middle Volga. But the degree to which they would seek independence can only be determined after a plebiscite.

Regardless of this desire by Tatars for autonomy or independence, one cannot overlook the presence of 1,575,000 Russians in the Tatar ASSR (43.2 percent of the total population of that region) and the positions of the non-Tatar/non-Russians there as well. Tatars comprise only 48.5 percent of the total population of that region. In addition, unlike the Union Republics located on the border of Russia, or even Chechen-Ingushetiya and Dagestan which are within Russia but located on the border with Moslem Azerbaijan, Tatarstan is surrounded by Russians and Russia.

Little is available on the "national" positions of the Finnic peoples of the Middle Volga, or of the Chuvash or Bashkirs. Even if they were to desire independence, such an accomplishment is virtually impossible given the facts that: (1) in general, they form minorities in their own autonomies; (2) the populations are quite small; (3) so many of the members of each people reside outside of their own autonomies; and (4) all form island settlements in a vast sea of Russians (27,243,000 in the Middle Volga and surrounding areas). It is more likely that their demands will manifest themselves in the realm of native language, religious, and cultural institutions.

The Mari religious movement is a good example of what might be seen in the future among the other Middle Volga peoples. *Izvestiya*, on October 31, 1991, carried an article entitled "Pagans defended their belief (*Yazych-nichki otstoyali svoyu veru*)" regarding a demonstration by Mari people in Oshmari-Chimar, the religious center for the animist Mari, where thousands came and registered themselves as 'believers.''

But it is doubtful that peoples of the Middle Volga, an island region within the heart of Mother Russia, will be able to achieve levels of real independence in the foreseeable future. Even now that the Soviet regime has collapsed, they are still at the mercy of the ethnic Russians who form a vast majority of the region's population. This ethnic imbalance will continue to characterize the Middle Volga region well into the future.

Notes

1 This, however, was neither true of Kiev nor Novgorod, the latter especially possessing a large Finnic population.
2 This *reconquista* is as important in Russian history as that of Spain under Ferdinand and Isabella in Spanish history. The seizure of Kazan symbolized more than the defeat of the Tatars and the liberation of the Russian lands; it marks the beginning of an expansion into Islamic lands that culminated with the seizure of the Crimea, Transcaucasia, the North Caucasus, and the Khanates of Central Asia. This push against Islam also manifested itself in Russian support for liberation movements by various Christian peoples within the Ottoman Empire and a series of wars against Ottoman Turkey in the nineteenth century.
3 This is a feature which any visitor to the major Russian churches in the Soviet Union cannot fail to miss. Indeed, even inside the Kremlin it is the dominant cross figure.
4 Saint Steven of Perm both singlehandedly converted the Komi peoples to Eastern Orthodoxy and established a Komi liturgy (and thereby a Komi literary language) in the fourteenth century.
5 The success of this policy in preventing the "Tatarization" of the peoples of the Middle Volga led to its being repeated later in the Baltics, where the Germans, Swedes, and Poles threatened Russia as a result of their influence on the Finns, Latvians, Lithuanians and Estonians. The policy was also applied in the Caucasus region in order both to weaken the Persian influence upon the Georgians and Azerbaijanis and to prevent the unification of the North Caucasian Moslem peoples into a single, anti-Russian (later Soviet) group. See Ronald Wixman, *Language Aspects of Ethnic Patterns and Processes in the North Caucasus* (Chicago: University of Chicago Department of Geography Research Series, no. 191, 1980).
6 This system is distinctly different from the French and English systems, which promoted the adoption of their respective languages, religions, and cultures, but which precluded the actual ethnic assimilation of non-Europeans into their nations. Thus, no North African, Asian, or Arab could be considered an Englishman or a Frenchman.
7 This was the mechanism by which a great number of Finnic and Baltic peoples

were added to the native Russian and Belorussian peoples between the tenth and nineteenth centuries.

8 One of the most interesting manifestations of this conflict was the establishment of Nizhny Novgorod (Gorkiy) as a trading city to rival the great Tatar trading city of Kazan. It was hoped that the new city would weaken Tatar influence in the Middle Volga, and it proved to be a valuable source of competitive information about the Tatars to the Russian/Soviet governments.

9 For further information on the ethnogenesis, languages and cultures of these peoples see: *Ocherki obshchei etnografii evropeiskaya chast' SSSR*, ed. S.P. Tolstov, N.N. Cheboksarov, and K.V. Chistov (Moscow: Institut etnografii im. N.N. Miklukho-Maklaya, Akademiya nauk SSSR, 1968; *Narody evropeiskoy chasti SSSR*, 2 vols. ed. V.A. Aleksandrov (Moscow: Institut etnografii im. N.N. Miklukho-Maklaya, Akademiya nauk SSSR, 1964); and S.A. Tokarev, *Etnografiya narodov SSSR* (Moscow: Izd. moskovskovo universiteta, 1958).

10 Prior to the 1920s, Tatar was written among the Moslem Tatars in the Arabic and among Russian Orthodox Tatars in the Russian script. Also, in addition to the Krayshens, it is worthy to note the existence of another ethnic subgroup – the Mishars. The Mishars are Tatar Meshchera Mordvinians who practiced Islam and spoke Tatar. Prior to and during the 1920s, they were treated as a distinct nationality and were even listed separately in the 1926 Soviet census. Since the 1930s, both the Krayshen and Mishar peoples have been officially designated simply as Tatars.

11 For a more thorough discussion on this question see Alexandre Bennigsen, "Islamic or Local Consciousness Among Soviet Nationalities?" in *Soviet Nationality Problems*, ed. E. Allworth (New York: Columbia University Press, 1971, pp. 168–182; Alexandre Benningsen, "Le probleme linguistique et l'evolution des nationalites musulmanes en URSS, in *Cahiers du monde russe et sovietique*, vol. 1, no. 3, 1960, pp. 418–465; Alexandre Benningsen and Chantal Lemercier-Quelquejay, *Islam in the Soviet Union*, trans. Geoffrey E. Wheeler (London: Pall Mall Press, 1967); Ronald Wixman, "Applied Soviet Nationality Policy: A Suggested Rationale," in *Turco-Tatar Past, Soviet Present*, ed. Chantal Lemercier-Quelquejay, G. Veinstein, and S.E. Wimbush (Paris: Editions Peeters-Louvin-Paris, EHESS, collection Turcica, 1986), vol. VI, pp. 449–468; and Serge A. Zenkovsky, *Pan Turkism and Islam in Russia* (Cambridge: Harvard University Press, 1960).

12 The city of Moscow was itself established upon the site of the Mordvinian village of Moskaava. Its inhabitants, the Meshchera, were a western Mordvinian group who were completely assimilated (as were most Mordvinians) by the Russians, and for whom the Meshcheran Upland is named.

13 Between 1926 and 1989, the Mordvinian population declined from about 1.34 million to 1.15 million persons. In 1989, only 27.1 percent of all Mordvinians lived in the Mordvinian ASSR.

14 Experts are divided over the issue of whether the Komi and Komi-Peryaks are close-but-distinct ethnic groups or simply divisions of a single Komi nation.

15 Among the Udmurts, one also finds a group of former Volga Bolgars, the Besermen, whose ancestors became "Udmurtized," and whose dialect today contains many Chuvash and Tatar linguistic forms. In 1926, only 10,035 individuals

listed themselves as Besermen, although many more may have listed themselves as Udmurts.

16 The Chuvash, without making any specific demands, let it be known that they favored the establishment of a Middle Volgan state in line with Tatar proposals in order to exploit the government's fears. In 1918, leaders of the Chuvash and Mari peoples formally requested that the Soviet government create this Middle Volgan state, as they claimed the Russians to be of greater danger to Chuvash and Mari ethnic interests than the Tatars. The Bashkirs also benefitted from this situation as the Soviets adamantly wished to prevent a Bashkir-Tatar merger. See Serge A. Zenkovsky, op. cit. pp. 165–208; Pipes, *The Formation of the Soviet Union*, pp. 155–172; and E.H. Carr, "Some Notes on Soviet Bashkiria," in *Soviet Studies*, vol. 8, no. 3, 1957, pp. 217–225.

17 Alexandre Benningsen, Chantal Lemercier-Quelquejay, op. cit., p. 126.

18 See *Ocherki po istorii Bashkirskoi ASSR* (Ufa, Akademia nauk SSSR, Bashkirskii filial institut istorii, yazyka i literatury, 1959).

19 Many years ago, a demonstration protesting the rector of the school's remarks was led by Tatar students at the university in Kazan. The Tatars apparently objected to his continued use of the Russian saying, "*ne zhdanny gost' khuzhe Tatarina* (an uninvited guest is worse than a Tatar)." This remark had followed a proclamation which stated that anti-ethnic slurs would no longer be tolerated, especially anti-Russian statements. There had been an attempt to purge the academic community of the commonly-used ethnic stereotypical proverbs and sayings common to peoples of the Middle Volga. The rector of the school did not, however, think that the Russian language and proverbs should receive the same treatment. After the demonstration by the Tatar students, he proclaimed that the Russian proverb should not be expurgated; rather, it should be changed to "*ne zhdanny gost' luche Tatarina* (an uninvited guest is *better* than a Tatar)." A riot among the Tatar students ensued.

20 In the last 30 years, this was true of Soviet policy toward the peoples of the North Caucasus, the Middle Volga, and Siberia. Until the mid-1960s, education was provided in native languages in these regions through the fourth grade (through the tenth grade in Bashkiria and Tatarstan), but in the latter part of the decade, the Soviet government eliminated completely the use of those languages for educational purposes.

21 This area would include all of the ASSRs in the region, as well as the Gorkiy, Kirov, Kuibyshev, Orenburg, Penza, Perm, Saratov, Sverdlovsk, Ulyanov, and Chelabyinsk Oblasts, in which about 1,071,000 Tatars resided in 1989 (see table 18.4).

22 The Tatars have not been static in their desire for change. In 1990, they demanded greater ethnic rights and even full republic status for the Tatar ASSR. They have also insisted that Tatar become the official language of the republic and that all inhabitants be forced to learn Tatar. For a more thorough examination of the ethnic demands of the Volga Tatars, see Ayse-Azade Rorlich, *The Volga Tatars: A Profile in National Resilience* (Stanford: Hoover Inst. Press, 1986).

23 The presence of Russians correlates isomorphically with the percentages of non-Russians who employ Russian as their second language. It is important to recognize, however, that the influence of the Russians over others is not equal

with respect to all peoples. For example, Russian influence on kindred Belorussians and Ukrainians is far greater than it is on the Turkic-speaking, Moslem Uzbeks and Kazakhs. See Ronald Wixman, "Territorial Russification and Linguistic Russianization in Some Soviet Republics," in *Soviet Geography: Review and Translation*, vol. 22, no. 10, 1981, pp. 667–675. Accordingly, one should expect to see that Russians have a much stronger influence on those peoples of the Middle Volga whose cultures are closer to their own (i.e. Eastern Orthodox and not Moslems). This hypothesis is substantiated by the information in tables 6 and 7, which indicate the levels of native language retention for the peoples of the Middle Volga in 1959, 1970, 1979, and 1989.

24 The 11.0 percent change among the Mordvinians masks the relatively rapid rate of their ethnic assimilation by the Russians. One can reasonably conclude that the decline in the Mordvinian population took place primarily among those Mordvinians who had listed Russian as their primary tongue in earlier census periods and through marriage. The same is true for the Komi-Permyaks.

19 North Caucasus: fragmentation or federation?

JANE ORMROD

History, nation and identity

Embracing nineteen native national groups which were recognized on the Soviet census of 1989,[1] as well as a significant ethnic Russian diaspora,[2] the North Caucasus region is one of the most ethnically and linguistically diverse regions in the world. Three main ethno-linguistic groups – Altaic, Indo-European and Ibero-Caucasian – are represented in the region. The diversity of linguistic subgroups renders many of the national languages, even some within the same ethno-linguistic group, mutually incomprehensible.[3] The geography of the North Caucasus facilitated the preservation of this diversity: the mountainous terrain isolated the population groups, creating conditions conducive to the persistence of a multiplicity of languages and dialects.

At least until the mid twentieth century, the diversity of the North Caucasus was also expressed in tribal or clan identity. For example, decisions to fight against the Russians in the Caucasian Wars of the nineteenth century were made not by Caucasian national groups, but rather, by tribal federations.[4] While the tribal federations had begun to dissolve by the early twentieth century, the clan structure remained strong, and social identity based on a local, clan consciousness was prominent in the early decades of Soviet power.[5]

Despite the fragmentation of the North Caucasian population into various linguistic, ethnic, tribal and clan groups, the inhabitants are unified by broad, cultural similarities. Contact between North Caucasian groups extends back for centuries, and various cultural and economic practices were broadly adopted throughout the North Caucasus.[6] Hence, the North Caucasian ethnic groups exhibit similar wedding rituals, family customs, building designs, styles of dress, forms of epic narrative in folklore, notions of justice, and even the retention of pagan practices in Christian or Muslim rituals.[7]

The broad, North Caucasian *gorskii* (mountaineer) identity was realized in a variety of alliances. The North Caucasian force, led by the Imam Shamil, opposed Russia in the nineteenth-century Caucasian Wars and embraced most of the North Caucasian Muslim groups. The Christian

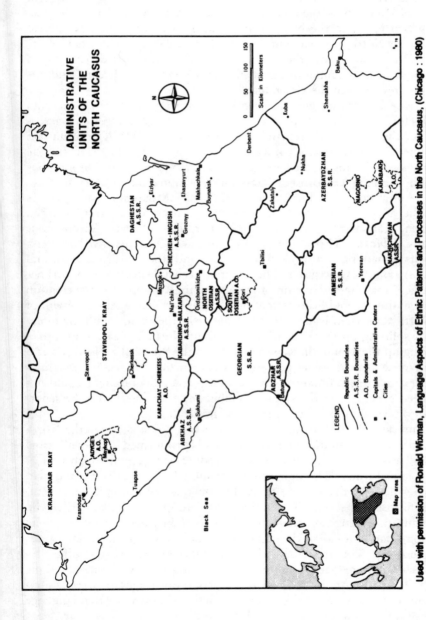

ADMINISTRATIVE
UNITS OF THE
NORTH CAUCASUS

N

Scale in Kilometers
0   50   100   150

KRASNODAR KRAY

STAVROPOL' KRAY

DAGHESTAN
A.S.S.R.

CHECHEN - INGUSH
A.S.S.R.

KABARDINO-BALKAR
A.S.S.R.

KARACHAY - CHERKESS
A.O.

ABKHAZ
A.S.S.R.

NORTH
OSSETIAN
A.S.S.R.

SOUTH
OSSETIAN A.O.

GEORGIAN
S.S.R.

ADZHAR A.S.S.R.

ADYGEI
A.O.

ARMENIAN
S.S.R.

AZERBAYDZHAN
S.S.R.

NAGORNO
KARABAKH
A.O.

NAKHICHEVAN
A.S.S.R.

Black Sea

Krasnodar
Tuapse
Stavropol'
Cherkessk
Maykop
Sukhumi
Nal'chik
Mozdok
Ordzhonikidze
Tskhinvali
Gori
Tbilisi
Kizlyar
Khasavyurt
Grozny
Makhachkala
Buynaksk
Derbent
Zakataly
Nukha
Kuba
Shemakha
Baku
Yerevan

LEGEND
_____ Republic Boundaries
///// A.S.S.R. Boundaries
- - - A.O. Boundaries
■ Capitals & Administrative Centers
• Cities

■ Map area

Used with permission of Ronald Wixman, Language Aspects of Ethnic Patterns and Processes in the North Caucasus, (Chicago : 1980)

Map 19.1 Administrative units of the North Caucasus. From Ronald Wixman, *Language Aspects of Ethnic Patterns and Processes in the North Caucasus* (Chicago, 1980).

Ossetians, perhaps wary of Shamil's aim to establish a North Caucasian emirate governed by strict adherence to *shariat* (Koranic law), did not join his forces.[8] Regardless, the Ossetians were caught up in the Russian repression which followed the North Caucasian defeat. Ossetians later joined the wave of North Caucasian immigration to Turkey in the last half of the nineteenth century.[9] And the civil war struggle – in which diverse North Caucasian peoples united under sheik Uzun Khadzhi to defeat Denikin's forces – drew in even the Ossetians.[10]

The *gorskii* identity was sufficiently strong that the North Caucasian peoples formed a relatively independent political alliance, extending across the Caucasus, that would remain intact from 1918 to 1921. The Mountain Republic (*Gorskaia respublika*) was created in early 1918. In 1921, after the Bolsheviks had consolidated power, it was made into an Autonomous Republic, and the territories of Dagestan were united into a separate, Dagestan Autonomous Republic. In 1922, the Mountain Autonomous Republic was reduced further, with the creation of separate Adygei, Chechen, Karachai-Cherkessian and Kabardino-Balkarian Autonomous Regions (*Oblasti*). The Mountain Republic was fully dissolved in 1924, when its remaining territories were divided into the North Ossetian and Ingush Autonomous Regions. The emigré Chechen historian A. Avtorkhanov argues that the destruction of the Mountain Republic and the creation of new national republican formations was undertaken against the will of the North Caucasian leaders at the initiative of the center, with the intention of splitting up the historically rebellious North Caucasian groups.[11] Breaking up the Mountain Republic reduced the threat of a North Caucasian alliance against Soviet power. Less convincingly, some Soviet ethnographers have argued that the diverse North Caucasian nations could not be settled peaceably into a single republic, and therefore had to be separated into several autonomous republics and regions.[12]

In any case, the new national formations had no analogue in the North Caucasian past. Until this time, alliances had been formed on a local, tribal or clan basis or, at other times, were a product of a general North Caucasian *gorskii* loyalty. The new groupings united various dialect and clan groups which had distinct identities. The Balkars, for example, were actually comprised of several Turkic linguistic groups: the Balkan, Chegem, Khulamtsan, Bezeng and the actual Balkars.[13] In Dagestan, where there was no titular nationality (the name "Dagestan," like "Yugoslavia," refers to a territory, not an actual ethnic or national group), the officially-recognized national groups sometimes contained more than one ethnic group. Thus, the Andi-Dido and Archi peoples of Dagestan were assimilated into the Avar national group: they shared the Avar written language and cultural institutions, and were listed in the 1959 census as Avar.[14]

Soviet efforts to foster these new "national" identities were considerable. The creation of written languages for many of the groups was a first step in this direction, and was underway in the 1920s.[15] Knowledge of Arabic was widespread among Muslim clergy, but most of the North Caucasian native population was illiterate.[16] By the end of the 1920s, newspapers were being published in many of the national languages. However, throughout the 1920s and early 1930s, the written languages and national language schools met with little enthusiasm from the local population. The local regimes had difficulty finding people who were willing to work (or to train for work) as teachers or newspaper correspondents. Publishing activity was minimal.[17] Furthermore, enrollment of children in schools was low.[18]

Indifference on the part of native groups – both peasants and intelligentsia – to participate in the development of their "national" cultures suggests that these cultures were not, at least in the 1920s and early 1930s, an important part of their identity. The Soviet scholars N.G. Volkova and L.I. Lavrov have characterized North Caucasian national consciousness in this period as a local, clan-consciousness, together with a "parallel consciousness" of a "huge ethnic society" of North Caucasian *gorskii*. The North Caucasian peoples exhibited little consciousness of themselves as members of their officially recognized, national groups.[19]

During the years of Soviet power, official national identity gradually emerged as the basis of current ethnic and political discourse in the North Caucasus. This transformation in ethnic consciousness has been fostered by a number of developments which served, on the one hand to distinguish the particular national groups from the sea of culturally and historically similar groups of *gorskii* and, on the other hand, to supplant clan loyalties with a vision of a larger national community.

Although not embraced with immediate enthusiasm by their national groups, literary languages were an important prerequisite for the development of a modern national community. Fellow nationals, most of whom – unlike members of a village or clan community – will probably never actually meet, are, through the printed word and the dissemination of the idea of the nation, joined in an abstract community.[20] By the mid-1930s, North Caucasian national groups were showing signs of cultural development. A national intelligentsia had become active. Using the national languages, scholars and writers recorded native folklore and wrote literature.[21] Significantly, the Chechen rebellion of the late 1930s was led by members of the intelligentsia: the writer Khasan Israilov, and the jurist Mair-Bek Sharipov.[22] However, events of the late 1930s, particularly the cyrillization of the national languages and the Stalinist purges of the national intelligentsia, hindered the development of North Caucasian national cultures.[23] The curtailment of national language education under Khrushchev in the late 1950s posed another obstacle to cultural development.

During the Gorbachev era, the future of national languages and national language education became an important issue throughout the

North Caucasus. In the late 1980s and 1990, a group of Karachai linguists compiled a new Karachai-Russian dictionary and wrote school textbooks; they are currently working with other representatives of the local intelligentsia to implement a national language education programme in Karachai schools.[24] Similar reforms are underway in Chechen schools: the grade one class of 1990 was the first class of students in a new curriculum.[25] A Chechen thesaurus and a new Ossetian dictionary are being prepared.[26] National cultural development is a concern of virtually every national political movement in the North Caucasus, and the demand for national sovereignty or enhanced republican status is, in part, a demand for cultural sovereignty.

A crucial event in the development of national identity in the North Caucasus was the deportation, in 1944, of the entire populations of the Karachai, Balkar, Ingush and Chechen national groups. The official explanation for this policy was that these groups had conspired with the occupying German forces during the Second World War. However, a more likely motive was the Soviet government's desire to weaken the force of rebellion and eliminate possible Turkish sympathizers in the region.[27] The groups were resettled in Central Asia, Kazakhstan and Siberia, and their former territories were merged into the lands of the surrounding republics and regions.[28] This tragic event served to further enforce notions of national identity: on the basis of official nationality, some peoples were deported and others were not. If it was possible to speak of the North Caucasian nationalities as groups without distinct national histories in the earlier decades of the twentieth century, this was no longer true after 1944.

In 1956, the Khrushchev government granted the deported peoples the right to return to their homelands.[29] The names of their former regions were restored, and the exiled peoples returned, in massive numbers, almost immediately. However, the actual process of resettlement did not always proceed smoothly. In many cases, returning people arrived in their former territories only to find that their villages had, during the years of their exile, been resettled by others. Former territorial divisions and boundaries were not always restored.[30] As a consequence, clashes between peoples ensued and, to this day, disputes about borders between national territories have not been resolved. North Caucasians were drawn into conflict on the basis of national identities which had begun as ethno-linguistic designations with little resonance in popular consciousness. The circumstances of the resettlement brought historically new, hostile and competitive relations between titular national groups in the North Caucasus and non-titular groups in Dagestan.

In the wake of perestroika and the collapse of the Communist regime, the discourse of national and ethnic identity among the peoples of the former Soviet Union is based almost entirely on concepts of the national state, whether fully sovereign or part of a republican structure. In the North

Caucasus, national identity – rather than tribal or broadly North Caucasian – is the framework for discussion among North Caucasians, and between North Caucasians and other groups. Notions of national states based on official nationality circulate in print and on television, and are received by broad audiences.

Historically, the relations of the North Caucasian *gorskii* to Russia have been hostile, and the historical memory of the North Caucasian peoples is closely tied to struggles against the Russians.[31] As the Soviet Union crumbled and the new Commonwealth began to emerge, these relations began, at least as manifest in political relations between the republics, to change. Cooperation with Moscow has been perceived by some North Caucasian national politicians as a means to enhance their national independence with respect to other North Caucasian groups. However, the roots of current Russian-North Caucasian relations lie not only in recent demands for increased national status, but also in territorial disputes and demographic conditions which preceded the Gorbachev era.

The situation of titular nationalities in the North Caucasus has been complicated by the sharing of territory by more than one titular nationality. This is the case for Chechens and Ingush (in Checheno-Ingushetia), Kabardinians and Balkars (in Kabardino-Balkaria) and Karachai and Cherkess (in Karachaevo-Cherkessia). All of these groups are currently in the process of negotiating their separation. After the creation of Checheno-Ingushetia in 1934, only the Adygei and the Ossetians retained unshared, titular nationality status. Dagestan is distinguished by a lack of titular national groups, and instead incorporates ten non-titular national groups, which are officially recognized as Peoples of Dagestan: the Avars, Aguls, Dargins, Kumyks, Laks, Lezgins, Nogai, Rutul', Tabasaran and Tsakhurs.[32]

The following section will focus more closely on events in each of these regions. Because of the current, uncertain status of many of the proposed republican and sovereign formations, the territories will be identified by the names and status that they had prior to the August 1991 coup attempt. In addition, three large, non-titular national groups – the Nogai, the Cossacks and the Russians – will be considered separately as non-titular diaspora groups. The populations of these groups are spread throughout various areas of the North Caucasus and do not live compactly within a single republican territory.

The Autonomous Regional and Republic Territories

Adygeia

From the time of its creation in 1922 until 1991, the Adygei territory had Autonomous Region (AO), rather than Autonomous Republican status,

Table 19.1. *Concentration of ethnic groups in North Caucasus and Dagestan, 1989*

Territory	National group	% of territorial population
Dagestan	Avar	27.5
	Agul	0.8
	Dargin	15.6
	Kumyk	12.9
	Lak	5.1
	Lezgin	11.3
	Nogai	1.6
	Rutul'	0.8
	Tsakhur	0.3
	Russian	9.2
Adygei	Adygei	22.1
	Russian	68.0
Checheno-Ingushetia	Chechen	57.8
	Ingush	12.9
	Russian	23.1
Kabardino-Balkaria	Kabardin	48.2
	Balkar	9.4
	Russian	32.0
Karachaevo-Cherkessia	Karachai	31.2
	Cherkess	9.7
	Russian	42.4
North Ossetia	Ossetian	53.0
	Russian	29.9

Source: 1989 census data, *Argumenty i fakty*, no. 13, March 1991, p. 1.

within the Krasnodar District (*Krasnodarskii krai*). According to the 1989 census, the region had the highest percentage of ethnic Russians – 68 percent – of all of the North Caucasian national territories, and the titular nationality, Adygei, constituted only 22.1 percent of the population.[33] Nevertheless, the change in status from the Adygei Autonomous Region to the Adygei SSR appeared to evoke no hostility from ethnic Russians.

The Kuban Cossacks have, for over 200 years, lived in close proximity to the Adygei. Indeed, the Kuban Cossacks, in national dress and cultural practices, resemble more closely the Adygei than the Don Cossacks. Historically, the two groups have had peaceful relations.[34] At their All-Kuban

Table 19.2. *The populations of North Caucasian ethnic groups, 1989*

Ethnic group	Population
Abazin	34,000
Avar	601,000
Agul	19,000
Adygei	125,000
Balkar	85,000
Chechen	957,000
Dargin	365,000
Ingush	237,000
Kabardin	391,000
Karachai	156,000
Kumyk	282,000
Lak	118,000
Lezgin	466,000
Mountain Jews	19,000
Nogai	75,000
Ossetian	598,000
Rutul'	20,000
Tabasaran	98,000
Tsakhur	20,000

Source: Naselenie SSSR: po dannym vsesoiuznoi perepisi naseleniia 1989 (Moscow, 1990), pp. 37–40.

Founding Meeting of the Cossack Union in October 1990, the Cossack delegates addressed an announcement to their "Adygei brothers," expressing their desire for "mutual support," "respect and council" between the two, and hopes that "no provocation" between them would arise. The Kuban Cossacks, who have endeavored to establish their own Cossack region in the Krasnodar District, have appeared to be supportive of the autonomous status of Adygei.[35]

Perhaps in response to their demographic minority in the Republic, the Adygei Republic created in August 1991 a special commission "for the return of expatriot Adygei to their ethnic homeland" in hopes of creating a "national-cultural rebirth" and "economic flourishing" in the republic.[36] The Adygei share with the Kabardinians and Cherkessians a mutually understandable Caucasian language, and all three groups refer to themselves as "adyghe."[37] However, there is no evidence to suggest that any sort of union of these national territories is forthcoming: the Adygei were, more likely, appealing to the expatriot communities in Turkey and expressing their own desires to create a national community and to foster national culture.

Checheno-Ingushetia

The Chechen and Ingush groups are linguistically related, and were both deported in 1944. The two national groups are, in both the Russian and Western press, occasionally treated as one and the same.[38] The Chechens and Ingush, however, have mutually unintelligible languages, distinct political and cultural agendas, and have differed in their demands for sovereignty and in their relations to Russia. Prior to 1934, each was the sole titular nationality in its own Autonomous Region. The merged, Chechen-Ingush territory was granted autonomous republic status in 1936, dissolved with the deportation of the titular nationalities in 1944, and then re-established, but with new borders, in 1957.

The Chechens are characterized by their aggressive nationalism and strong sense of national identity. As early as the 1960s and 1970s, the Chechen national intelligentsia was active. Its more vocal and nationalist elements called for respect for Chechen ethnic and religious practices, an enhancement of Chechen language education accompanied by a curtailing of Russian language education, and even discouraged the performance of folk songs in non-traditional, orchestral arrangements. Islam has remained a strong force among Chechens.[39]

The Chechen All-national Congress, led by General Dzhakhar Dudaev, has called for a sovereign Chechen republic since November 1990.[40] Dudaev and the Congress came into prominence after the August 1991 coup attempt, when he and his supporters overthrew the existing republican (Soviet) government. He was able to mobilize rapid support for his nationalist platform. A large demonstration blockaded the square of the Council of Ministers and while the demonstrations continued for several months, Dudaev's forces formed a National Guard and occupied many of the important government buildings. Dudaev appealed to the Muslim consciousness of the Chechen people. At meetings, the daily prayers (*namaz*) were announced over loudspeakers.[41] Russian families, fearing the creation of an Islamic Checheno-Ingushetian state, began to leave the Checheno-Ingushetia, and many moved to the neighboring territory of Stavropol'. In the course of 1991, over 19,000 people, mainly ethnic Russians, left Checheno-Ingushetia.[42]

Despite the opposition of the Checheno-Ingushetian Supreme Soviet and the Russian Republic, Dudaev declared an election for 9 November 1991. Dudaev won the election,[43] swore his oath of office on the Koran, and the day was declared a national holiday.[44] Dudaev's victory and the declaration of Checheno-Ingushetian sovereignty was contested by Boris Yeltsin. However, Yeltsin's decisions to issue a warrant for Dudaev's arrest and to send Russian troops to Groznyi proved to be a mistake. Dudaev's National Guard blocked the Russian troops at the airport. The Russian Parliament, which had not been consulted, reversed Yeltsin's decision, recalled the troops, and the Russian challenges to Checheno-Ingush sovereignty faded.[45] The incident fuelled Dudaev's anti-Russian, nationalist rhetoric, and provided a rallying point for Chechen nationalists.

In December, a referendum provided evidence of the desire of the Ingush people to separate from Chechnia and remain within the Russian republican structure. This divergence of Chechens and Ingush was a product of the demographic situation of Ingush within Chechnia, and the distinct political aspirations of the two nations. In 1989, Chechens represented 57.8 percent of the republic's population, while the Ingush amounted only to 12.9 percent.[46] Furthermore, Dudaev's movement has been directed primarily at the fulfillment of Chechen national aspirations and Chechen concerns, with little attention to the concerns of the Ingush. Dudaev's government is called the All-National Chechen Congress.

One prominent concern of the Ingush which has entered Dudaev's national agenda is to restore an autonomous Ingush territory separate from Chechnia. The Ingush deputy Kh.A. Fargiev, in a speech on May 29, 1989 at the Congress of USSR Peoples' Deputies, argued that Ingush autonomy was essential to the cultural and economic development of the Ingush people. According to Fargiev, a total of 60,000 Ingush signatures had been collected on petitions circulated in 1988 and 1989.[47]

The Chechens and Ingush have had distinct relationships with the surrounding national groups. Territorial conflicts between Ingush tribes and Terek Cossacks have been ongoing since the 1860s.[48] The Ingush are also involved in territorial disputes with the North Ossetians. Following the deportation of the Ingush in 1944, some of the former Ingush territory was granted to the North Ossetian ASSR, and was not restored to the Ingush following their return from exile in 1957. Even in the 1970s, the Ingush wrote petitions to the government asking for the return of this territory, and complained of Ossetian discrimination against Ingush living in the region. Armed clashes between Ossetians and Ingush have occurred periodically since the Ingush returned from deportation.[49]

In September 1990, the Supreme Soviet of the North Ossetian ASSR suspended the right of Ingush to live in North Ossetia.[50] In March of 1991, clashes broke out as armed Ingush attempted to seize Ossetian homes in the disputed Prigoridnyi region.[51] The situation flared up again in November 1991. In the Ingush city of Nazrani, thousands of Ingush demanded the restoration of their territories, and were willing, if necessary, to use armed force.[52] In the village of Maiskoe, a group of Ingush seized an Ossetian bus and took the passengers as hostages. In response, the Ossetians imposed a curfew and formed a National Guard.[53]

The Ingush are demanding not only their own autonomous territory, but also the territories (the Prigorodnyi region of North Ossetia, and part of the territory of the North Ossetian capital, Vladikavkaz) that had belonged to them prior to their deportation. In a referendum held on 30

November 1991, 92.5 percent of the Ingush voters supported "a sovereign Ingushetia within the Russian Federation and the restoration of the original Ingush territories."[54] The referendum was declared illegal by the Chechen and the Ossetian parliaments. The Chechen government, which had earlier declared the complete independence of Checheno-Ingushetia, argued that the referendum constituted an "illegal act" and "contradicted the territorial integrity of Chechnia, in so far as the [Ingush] region constitutes a part of Chechen territory."[55] The North Ossetian reaction was similar, condemning the referendum as "gross interference in the internal affairs of the North Ossetian republic."[56] The Ingush, then, have been in conflict with two neighboring titular nationalities: a long-standing conflict with the Ossetians on issues of territory, and a more recent conflict with the Chechens on the issue of sovereignty.

The Ingush have been unable to count on Chechen support in their struggle against the Ossetians: Dzhakhar Dudaev has shown no willingness to participate in this conflict, and reportedly told the Ossetians that his government would not involve itself in the affair.[57] The Ingush have, since Boris Yeltsin addressed a group of Ingush in Vladikavkaz in March 1991 and spoke of plans for the full rehabilitation of the deported peoples, inclined to turn to the Russians for support against the Ossetians. The Ingush have argued that a true rehabilitation must involve the restoration of the former Ingush land.[58] Yeltsin has not discouraged Ingush hopes for a territorial rehabilitation; nor has he been willing to enter into a direct conflict with the Ossetians on this issue. The Ossetians, for their part, insist that the rehabilitation should not involve the loss of territories currently within the Ossetian border.[59]

Initially, Dudaev reacted angrily to the Ingush-Russian relations, accusing the Russians of deliberately provoking an Ingush-Chechen confrontation and attempting to interfere with Chechen territory.[60] At the same time, he did not directly interfere in Ingush affairs. By blaming the Russians for the current conflicts between Ingushetia and Chechnia, Dudaev is attempting to avoid a direct confrontation with the Ingush. In general, Dudaev has avoided hostilities with the neighboring North Caucasian states. For example, he did not become involved in the clashes between Avars, Laks and ethnic Chechens living in Dagestan, nor has his government joined the Ingush in their struggle to regain territorial struggles with North Ossetia.[61]

Having successfully seized power in Chechnia, Dudaev's government began to concern itself with the restoration of social and economic order in the republic.[62] By late December 1991, Dudaev indicated a desire for peace and stability. The Chechen parliament approved the creation of separate Chechen and Ingush territories, and created a commission to determine the boundaries between the two republics.[63] He has supported the notion of a general North Caucasian assembly to foster cooperation between the North Caucasian republics.[64] Furthermore, Chechen-Russian relations show signs of improvement: according to a Tass report, Dudaev has indicated a willingness to participate in talks with Russia.[65]

Nevertheless, relations between the titular nationalities of Checheno-Ingushetia are tense: the tensions involve not only territorial disputes among the groups, but also questions of political authority. The surprising Ingush appeal to Russia (given the traditional animosity of these two peoples) indicates that the competition between North Caucasian titular nationalities has defined a new role for Russia in the region. Russia has emerged as a power that can be annexed by national republics in the efforts of the latter to further their own claims over those of other North Caucasian republics. However, as symbolized by the failure of Russian intervention in Dudaev's rise to power, Russian control in the region is limited. These emerging relations also indicate that a consciousness of nation based on titular nationality is beginning to take precedence over the historical memory of the broad North Caucasian solidarity against Russia.

Kabardino-Balkaria

The creation, in 1922, of a republic which combined Kabardians and Balkars as the two titular nationalities was puzzling. Their languages are not mutually understandable. The Kabardians have closer linguistic and historical ties to the neighboring Cherkess, while the Balkars are closer to the Karachai.[66]

The Balkars are a demographic minority in the Republic. In 1989, they comprised only 9.4 percent of the population, while the Kabardinians accounted for 48.2 percent.[67] The total population of these groups was 85,000 and 391,000 respectively.[68] The Balkars were deported in 1944 and their territories turned over to the Kabardinian ASSR. While they were permitted in 1956 to return to the reconstituted Kabardino-Balkar ASSR, they were not permitted to rebuild their homes in their former regions. Rather, the Balkar population was assigned to new locations and dispersed throughout Kabardino-Balkaria.[69]

While conflicts between Kabardians and Balkars have never approached the violence of the Ingush-Ossetian conflict, there were, in the late 1950s, reports of tension between Balkars and Kabardinians in some of the collective farms in which the Balkars had been resettled.[70] Balkar dissatisfaction with the 1956 repatriation was not confined to territorial grievances. The Balkar press has reported that, following the repatriation, Balkars were the objects of discrimination within the Republic and the USSR generally. Balkar students had more difficulty gaining admission to universities and receiving permission to defend dissertations than groups which had not been deported.[71]

The Balkar movement for national independence met with cooperation from the Kabardino-Balkar government. In November 1990, the Supreme Soviet of the ASSR established a commission to study the "restoration of the historically Balkar regions." A year later, the First Congress of the Balkarian People announced that the Balkar Republic would be formed within the Russian Republican structure by February 1, 1992.[72] Timur Ul'bashev, a member of both the National Congress of the Balkar People and the Kabardino-Balkar Supreme Soviet, indicated that the Balkarian movement represented no threat to the territorial integrity of Kabardia, as no significant Kabardian population groups live on the land in question. Ul'bashev added that Balkar autonomy was necessary, for "the national state structure of the Kabardino-Balkarian Republic did not permit [the Balkarian People] to realize in full measure their rights as full subjects of the Republic." Balkarian nationalism and national identity is expressed in terms of the national state. The many references to the deportations and repatriations indicate that the historical memory of these experiences is an important part of Balkar national identity.

The destruction of Balkar cemeteries and monuments during the time of exile has been a point of great resentment on the part of the Balkarian people.[73] The press has accused both Kabardinians and Ossetians of responsibility in this regard.[74] In their relations to the neighboring North Caucasian peoples, Balkarians exhibit solidarity with other deported peoples. In particular, the Balkarian press has condemned Ossetia for retaining lands that formerly belonged to the Ingush. This anti-Ossetian perception found expression in claims that Stalin and Beria (who organized the deportations) were actually Ossetians and that the objective of their nationalities policies in the North Caucasus was to secure advantages for Ossetia. Apparently, similar sentiments have been echoed in the Chechen and Ingush presses.[75] Aside from the common experience of deportation, the Balkars have nothing more in common with Chechens and Ingush than with other peoples of the North Caucasus. However, by virtue of a perceived solidarity based on a common history, the three groups share resentment toward Ossetia, and the Balkars support the Ingush claims against Ossetia. It is significant that the Balkars have no competing, territorial claims with the Chechen and the Ingush which would challenge the Balkarian solidarity with these groups.

Karachaevo-Cherkessia

In 1989, the two titular nationalities of the republic, Karachai and Cherkess, accounted for 31.2 percent and 9.7 percent of the population respectively. Russians comprise an ethnic plurality, with 42.4 percent of the republic's population.[76] In addition, two national minority groups – the Abazin and Nogai – have populations of approximately 30,000 and 20,000.[77]

Inter-ethnic relations in the republic have been relatively peaceful. Perhaps as a consequence of this, representatives of the non-Russian nationalities have devoted much attention to the development of national culture. In the 1988–1989 school year, many national-language schools were opened: 817 Karachai schools; ninety-one Cherkessian schools; 115 Abazin schools and thirty-nine Nogai schools. As non-titular national groups, the cultural development of Abazinians and Nogai has, in the years of Soviet power, suffered great neglect. Most of the Abazinian and Nogai activity has been centered in the republican capital of Cherkessk. In the countryside, however, popular interest in these national cultures has been slow to develop.[78]

As in Kabardino-Balkaria, the most prominent movement for national sovereignty in Karachaevo-Cherkessia is that of a formerly deported group – the Karachai. Like the Balkar, Karachai have perceived themselves as victims of prejudicial treatment, particularly with respect to entrance to universities and even employment. Furthermore, the Karachai have been unable to assume socially or politically sensitive positions within the Karachaevo-Cherkessian republic. Since the repatriation of the Karachai, no Karachai has occupied the post of *gorkom* secretary, chief of police, procurator, judge, dean of the university, or even a rank-and-file KGB member in the city of Karachaevsk. The directors of many Karachai schools have been Russians.[79] As early as August 1989, a Karachai delegation to the Central Committee requested autonomy in the form of an independent ASSR. In late November 1991, the request was posed with greater insistence. A general meeting of the Karachai announced to the Russian Supreme Soviet their desire to secure their separate autonomy and secure "complete rehabilitation." According to a Radio Moscow report, the Karachai group decided that, if their demands were not met, an Extraordinary Council of People's Deputies of Karachai would simply create republican structures on its own authority, as Dudaev's government had done in Chechnia.[80] The Karachaevo-Cherkessian Supreme Soviet has supported the Karachai demands and potentially conflicting teritorial claims appear to have been resolved peacefully.[81]

North Ossetia

The ethnocultural situation of the Ossetian people in the North Caucasus is complicated by religious factors. Unlike the majority of the North Caucasian peoples, who are Muslim, the majority of Ossetians are Orthodox Christian. While this religious difference may have deterred the Ossetians from joining Shamil's struggle against the Russians in the nineteenth century, they nevertheless allied with other North Caucasian groups during the civil war and were included in the broad, North Caucasian Mountain Republic of 1918 to 1922. The cultural similarities and shared history of the Ossetians and the other North Caucasian peoples has made a common identity among these groups possible despite religious differences.[82]

The Ossetian national community includes three dialect groups. The Tual have lived mainly in South Ossetia, which was, until it declared its independence in late 1991, a region within Georgia. The Digor and Iron dialect groups occupy the northern parts of the Ossetian territories, where the Iron constitute the vast majority. The Digor account for only about one-eighth of North Ossetians,[83] and they were eliminated as an officially recognized group in the late 1930s.[84] Among the Digor, some 30 to 40 percent are Muslim. Although only 15 to 20 percent of Iron are Muslim, they are a numerically larger group than the Digor Muslims.[85] Christian and Muslim Ossetians have in common many traditional cultural practices: the wedding ceremonies, avoidance customs within the family, and wake rituals are identical and are "national rather than religious" in character.[86] While Christian and Muslim Ossetians retain distinct religious identities, and Iron and Digor retain a consciousness of linguistic distinction, there is – according to Ossetian informants from all of these categories – little friction between the groups, and intermarriage is socially permissible.[87]

The Christian Ossetians, then, are not strangers to Islam: indeed, various Muslim names have been adopted by Christian Ossetians.[88] The religious differences of the Christian Ossetians and the Muslim peoples of the North Caucasus have not recently appeared to play a divisive role in political relations, and have not entered the discourse between these groups, nor has the Ossetian government expressed concern about the rising Islamic consciousness in the North Caucasus. The Ossetians do not appear to see Islam as a threat to their national identity.

In December 1990, the Supreme Soviet of the North Ossetian Autonomous Republic issued a declaration changing its status to that of a Soviet Socialist Republic within the RSFSR. Its state languages are Ossetian and Russian. As elsewhere in the North Caucasus, educational reforms to enhance national language education have been underway.[89]

Ossetian discussion of national identity has been framed by the struggle of South Ossetia with Georgia. Until dissolved by Georgia in 1989, South Ossetia had existed as an Autonomous Region (oblast) within Georgia. The two sides have been engaged in armed conflict since South Ossetia's autonomous status was annulled. North Ossetia has rallied to the defence of the South Ossetians. North Ossetians have been sending food, medical and military aid to the South, and North Ossetian volunteers have joined the South Ossetian guard. North Ossetia has housed masses of South Ossetian refugees. By September 1991, the number of South Ossetians registered as refugees in the North Ossetian capital of Vladikavkaz had exceeded 80,000.[90] As a consequence of this struggle, concepts of the Ossetian nation and Ossetian national identity are a focus of attention.

The Ossetian intelligentsia views North and South Ossetia as a single nation, which was divided after the Bolshevik Revolution in a genocidal

"Bolshevik experiment" intended to weaken the Ossetian nation and assimilate its people into the Georgian and Russian nations. The competing Georgian and Ossetian claims have revitalized the study of the history of the region, and both groups use history to justify their territorial claims. Georgians have argued that the South Ossetian territory was historically Georgian, with Ossetians settling there only 200 years ago. Ossetians, for their part, identify themselves as descendents of the Alans, which, they claim, had occupied South Ossetian territory for centuries.[91]

In August 1991, Georgian president Zviad Gamsakhurdia demanded that North Ossetia rename itself "Ossetia" and thus renounce the notion of an Ossetian nation which embraces North and South Ossetia. The North Ossetian Supreme Soviet decisively rejected this demand, describing it as a gross interference in North Ossetian affairs.[92] The question of the unification of North and South Ossetia has been tabled at sessions of the North Ossetian Supreme Soviet, but a decision has yet to be made.[93] It is possible that North Ossetia does not wish to open itself to accusations of direct interference in the affairs of Georgia. However, in late November 1991, South Ossetia had declared itself to be an independent republic and changed the name of its capital from the Georgian "Tskhinvali" to the Ossetian "Tskhinval."[94] South Ossetian independence may enhance the possibilities for the creation of a united Ossetia.

While the relations between the Ossetians and the Russians have historically been more peaceful than those of Russia with the other titular nationalities of the North Caucasus, recent events have caused some tension between the two. In March 1991, Boris Yeltsin signed, together with Zviad Gamsakhurdia, an agreement to eliminate all "illegal armed formations" (which would include the South Ossetian guard) in "the territory of the former South Ossetian autonomous region." Given the wording of the agreement, Yeltsin implicitly acknowledged the elimination of the South Ossetian region.[95] Further, the Russian Republican decree "On the Rehabilitation of the Repressed Peoples" indicated that the restoration of former territories would be included in the rehabilitation process.[96] This added strength to the Ingush claims on territories which had been turned over to North Ossetia after the deportation of the Ingush in 1944. In one survey, 97 percent of Ossetians polled felt that the borders of North Ossetia should not be altered.[97] While North Ossetian discontent with Russia may not lead to open conflict, the North Ossetian government declined to participate in the March 1991 RSFSR Referendum, thus indicating its opposition to the creation of an RSFSR presidency.[98]

Dagestan

Throughout the Soviet period, none of the ten national groups of Dagestan recognized in the 1989 census has been a titular nationality within a territory. The majority of the national groups of Dagestan appear willing to remain in the Dagestan structure. In April 1991, thirty-nine out of fifty-four regional soviets (*raisovety*) in Dagestan supported a resolution for sovereignty and the creation of a Dagestan republic. For the most part, the fifteen regional soviets opposing the creation of a sovereign Dagestan represented national groups which had expressed aspirations to form their own national states.

In Dagestan, the expression of ethnicity through the discourse of the national state has not assumed the dominance that it has had elsewhere in the Soviet Union. With few exceptions, the peoples of Dagestan are drawn together through years of common history and through Islam. Dagestan is, in some respects, the center of Islam in the North Caucasus: Makhachkala, the capital of Dagestan, is the seat of the Muslim Spiritual Board of Dagestan and the North Caucasus. Islamic, inter-ethnic political movements, such as the Islamic Democratic Party and the Muslim Society, have emerged.[99] A number of large demonstrations in Dagestan in 1991 were religious and not national in character. 4,000 people attended a January 1991 rally in protest against American and Soviet aggression in the Persian Gulf war.[100] In June 1991, members of diverse national groups united to protest the rising cost of airplane tickets for the pilgrimage to Mecca.[101] Only three of the peoples of Dagestan – the Kumyk, the Lezgins and the Nogai – have begun to take steps toward separation from the republic. The Kumyk and Lezgin populations live in relatively defined territories: the Nogai, however, are spread throughout various regions of the North Caucasus and will be considered in the discussion of diaspora groups.

The Kumyk and the Lezgins, respectively comprising 12.9 percent and 11.3 percent of the Dagestan population, are the third and fourth largest national groups.[102] Their demographic situation may be a factor in their aspirations to separate. They are not large enough to have a strong voice in republican affairs. However, the Kumyk and Lezgin populations (282,000 and 466,000) are sufficient for national states of a relatively (in the North Caucasian context) large population. This latter consideration does not apply to some of the smaller Dagestan groups, such as the Tsakhury and Agul, with populations of only 20,000 and 19,000 respectively.[103]

The Lezgin movement *Sadval* ("Unity") held its founding congress in the Derbent district of Dagestan in July 1990. The Lezgin territory is clearly divided, with almost half of ethnic Lezgins living in the neighboring republic of Azerbaijan. At the congress, delegates called for unification, on the grounds that the Lezgin people "had been denied the opportunity to develop [their] culture and economy on a common basis."[104] The 1990 congress had not resolved the form that a unified Lezgin entity would assume. In December 1991, however, the All-national Congress of Lezgins issued a declaration calling for the creation of a "national-state formation Lezgistan," which would unite the Lezgin populations of Azerbaijan and Dagestan.[105]

The Kumyk movement *Tenglik* ("Equality") announced their intention to create a national state in 1990. In November of that year, the Congress of People's Deputies of the Dagestan Autonomous Republic agreed to create a Kumyk republic within the Dagestan republican structure, provided that Kumyk deputies agreed to support the creation of a Dagestan republic. The Kumyk representatives, however, were not satisfied and called for greater sovereignty than the proposed formation would permit.[106] The proponents of Kumyk independence have argued that the years of Soviet power and Russification have stunted the development of Kumyk language and culture, and that cultural sovereignty is the only way to rectify this situation.[107]

Aside from the Lezgin, Kumyk and Nogai movements, there is little agitation in Dagestan for the creation of new national state formations. Furthermore, a significant group supports the notion of a multi-national, Dagestan federation. The proponents of the Dagestan federation argue that this sort of structure offers the best protection for the cultural rights of the many national groups.[108] Nevertheless, some tension between the national groups of Dagestan is apparent. Abdurashid Saidov, the leader of the Islamic Democratic Party, said that his efforts to create a multi-national party have been challenged by the reactions of non-Avar peoples to the Avar majority in his party. The non-Avars, Saidov observed, are inclined to be suspicious of the Party and fear that it may actually be "some kind of Avar formation."[109] In Northern Dagestan, ethnic Chechens (called Akkintsy), who were deported in 1944, have entered into violent clashes with Avars and Laks in efforts to recover their former territories. The Akkintsy, however, are demanding neither sovereignty nor unification with Chechnia. They appear content to remain within Dagestan, provided that their territories are restored.[110]

For the most part, national identity among the peoples of Dagestan has not led to movements for independence. The Lezgin and Nogai movements represent, in part, efforts to unite national populations that extend beyond the borders of Dagestan. Neither movement has cited cultural repression within the Dagestan republican formation as a reason for separation. R. Ramazanov, a member of the Congress of Lezgins, expressed approval for Dagestan: while Lezgins in Dagestan were granted "full constitutional rights," this was not the case in Azerbaijan.[111] The small percentage of ethnic Russians in Dagestan may contribute to the satisfaction of some of the national groups of Dagestan.[112] This may have allowed representatives of non-Russian groups to hold positions of authority which, in other regions of the North Caucasus, were occupied by Russians. Significantly, only the Kumyk have based their claim for sovereignty on a need for greater cultural autonomy.

For the most part, the relations of the groups of Dagestan are remarkably less competitive than those of the titular nationalities in the other

North Caucasian republics. This may change if nationalism, as expressed in the concept of the national state, gains greater currency among the larger national groups, such as the Avars or Dargins. However, a number of factors help to unify the population of Dagestan. The organized, multi-ethnic Islamic political movements foster a consciousness of identity among the peoples. The peoples of Dagestan are bound by the same cultural similarities that characterize the peoples of the North Caucasus. However, the histories of the Dagestan peoples have been less divergent than those of other North Caucasian groups. For example, excepting the relatively small group of ethnic Chechens, the Akkintsy, living in Northern Dagestan, the Dagestan peoples were not deported. Perhaps paradoxically, the non-titular nationalities of Dagestan appear to have had greater opportunities for cultural development and self-expression than the titular nationalities of some of the other North Caucasian republics, and the relations of the former are relatively less adversarial.

The non-titular diaspora groups: Nogai, Cossacks, Russians

Among the non-titular national groups of the North Caucasus, diasporas constitute an important subgroup. The diaspora national groups are distinguished by the dispersal of their population throughout the North Caucasus, and they lack a geographically focused, single homeland. The Nogai – the remnants of a great nomadic steppe people – are spread throughout various North Caucasian republics, occupying a territory that was once the huge Nogai steppe, and live mainly in Dagestan, Checheno-Ingushetia and Kabardino-Balkaria.[113]

The Nogai in Kabardino-Balkaria and Checheno-Ingushetia have had little opportunity for cultural development, for they have lacked the cultural institutions – such as theatres, schools and clubs – that would facilitate this. Futhermore, positions of social or political leadership have, in the years of Soviet power, generally been assigned to ethnic Russians or, less frequently, to representatives of the titular national groups of these regions.[114] As a non-titular national group in territories with titular nationalities, the Nogai have been dominated and their cultural development has been stunted.

In Dagestan, where all the national groups are non-titular and the ethnic Russian population is small, the Nogai have had greater cultural and political independence. Furthermore, in Dagestan, the Nogai lived more compactly and experienced less interaction with other ethnic groups. Only in the Nogai region of Dagestan, where Nogai represent up to 75 percent of the student population in schools, has Nogai language education been available at all educatonal levels.[115]

Because the Nogai community in Dagestan has been able to preserve its national culture more successfully than the Nogai in other regions of the

North Caucasus, it is not surprising that the impetus for the Nogai national movement has come largely from the Dagestan group. The Nogai movement *Birlik* ("Unity"), was opposed to Dagestan sovereignty in May 1991, on the grounds that the borders of Dagestan would become less open to negotiation.[116] *Birlik* called for a Nogai national state from the Dagestan territory. However, *Birlik* resolved that the Nogai state should separate from Dagestan and be established as a sovereign republic within the Russian Republican structure.[117] Presumably, this would facilitate the migration of expatriot Nogai from the other regions of the North Caucasus to the new Nogai republic.

Soviet ethnographers K.P. Kalinovskaia and G.E. Markov report that all of their informants – who ranged from teenagers to the elderly, and who included representatives from all the Nogai communities in the North Caucasus – support the creation of an autonomous Nogai state.[118] Nevertheless, the question of the creation of a Nogai sovereign state has not yet been resolved. The demographic situation of the Nogai has made their claim difficult. As a diaspora group, the Nogai cannot isolate and define any one region as a historic, national homeland in the manner that the Ossetians, for example, have endeavored to do.

The demographic situation of the Cossack groups in the North Caucasus is even more challenging. There are Cossack populations in all of the North Caucasian republics. Furthermore, the Cossacks have never been recognized by the Soviet government as a national or ethnic group, and generally have listed themselves as either Russian or Ukrainian on Soviet censuses. The Cossacks suffered severe repression during the years of Soviet power: in 1919–1920, entire Cossack settlements were eliminated and their populations deported to Siberia, in fulfillment of an official policy of "decossackization" (*raskazachivanie*); during collectivization, alleged Cossack kulaks were resettled in Central Asia and Kazakhstan.[119]

Cossacks began arriving in the North Caucasus regions as early as the last half of the sixteenth century.[120] In 1860, the Black Sea Cossack band divided itself into the Kuban and Terek bands. In 1916, when Cossacks were last enumerated, the populations of these bands were 1,367,000 and 255,000 respectively.[121] Prior to the Revolution, the Cossacks offered military support to Russia, and they fought against Shamil in the Caucasian Wars. This historical alliance has complicated their relations with other North Caucasian groups. However, they do share a history of repression at the hands of Soviet power.

The Kuban Cossacks, who inhabit the territories of Stavropol' and Krasnodar, do not live in the mountainous heart of the Caucasus, and their contact with non-Russian North Caucasian nationalities is mainly confined to those of the Adygei and Karachaevo-Cherkessian territories. Despite a history of pre-revolutionary enmity between the groups, their more recent relations have been friendly. The Kuban Cossacks have declared their friendly intentions toward Adygeia and their support for its sovereignty.[122] The Supreme Soviet of Karachaevo-Cherkessian, on December 3, 1991, appealed to the RSFSR to initiate the complete, and presumably territorial, rehabilitation of the Cossacks.[123] The Kuban Cossack relations with the RSFSR, however, have been less cordial. In December 1991, the Kuban Cossacks announced that, unless the RSFSR government agreed to support their territorial claims in the Krasnodar region, they would form a national guard and seize the territories by force.[124]

The Terek Cossacks, with populations in North Ossetia, Dagestan and Checheno-Ingushetia, have experienced greater friction with the North Caucasian national groups. On one hand, almost five centuries of contact between mountaineers and Cossacks have led to the development of common cultural traits: for example, the male national costumes are very similar.[125] The North Caucasian peoples have at times exhibited a cultural solidarity with "our" Terek Cossacks, saying that "we are all one people."[126]

On the other hand, the aggressiveness with which the Terek Cossacks have pursued their territorial claims has drawn them into armed conflict with the Ingush.[127] The Don Cossacks have supported the Terek Cossacks, threatening that "our force will be retaliatory: for every shot fired in Checheno-Ingushetia, a shot will ring out from the Don."[128] In Chechnia and in Dagestan, Terek Cossack populations have threatened to transfer their settlements to the Russian Republic in the event that these republics declare their full sovereignty and separation from the RSFSR.[129] The Terek Cossacks have declared their support for "a single united Russia" and "the widening of Russian boundaries." In response to the departure of 2,773 ethnic Russians from the Sunzhenskii region of Ingushetia, the Terek Cossacks announced their intention to establish a new settlement (stanitsa) of Cossacks in the territory.[130] Vocal pro-Russian sentiments and aggressive actions serve to draw the Cossacks further into conflict with the neighboring North Caucasian groups.

However, Cossack irritation with Russia is growing as a result of Russia's hesitation to grant their territorial claims. In a letter to Dzhakhar Dudaev, one group of Terek Cossacks wrote that, "in the case of armed conflict [between Checheno-Ingushetia and the Terek Cossacks], neither the President nor the Supreme Soviet [of the RSFSR] will come to our defence. This means that we will have to defend ourselves."[131] It is unlikely, however, that the Cossacks will in the near future be able to forge firm alliances with North Caucasian nationalities, given the suspicion of Islam and Russian nationalism among the Cossacks.

As a diaspora group, the Cossacks are faced with the same challenge that confronts the Nogai: no single territory appears as a natural homeland. Unlike the Nogai, who have proposed the delineation of one Nogai territory as the site of the Nogai national state, the Cossacks have been inclined to demand autonomy in the form of relatively small, dispersed territories. They are perhaps the most aggressive group in the North Caucasus and are likely to alienate both Russia and the North Caucasian nationalities. However, they can probably count on the support of a considerable network of equally aggressive Cossack bands, which extend from Ukraine to Kazakhstan.

Ethnic Russians are the largest diaspora group of the North Caucasus. In all territories but Dagestan, Russians account for more than 25 percent of the total population. In Karachaevo-Cherkessia and Adygeia, they out-number any of the titular nationalities. Despite their numbers, the Russians (excepting, of course, the Cossacks) do not appear to have established any form of political organization apart from the traditional Soviet state struc-tures. In Checheno-Ingushetia, confronted by emerging Islamic political movements and the anti-Russian rhetoric of Dudaev's government, Russians felt sufficiently threatened to leave the republic in large numbers in the last half of 1991. The Terek Cossacks offered some support to the Russians, and the Groznyi section (*otdel'*) of the Terek Cossack band endeavored to make the Russian plight known to the press.[132]

While the Checheno-Ingushetian government has, thus far, been alone in its vocal hostility toward Russians, anti-Russian sentiment is a tradi-tional component of the North Caucasian *mentalité*. Hostility and resentment toward Russians has historically acted as a rallying point, bringing the North Caucasian ethnic groups together in a variety of alli-ances. If North Caucasian nationalist sentiment or expressions of Muslim identity rise, then conflicts between ethnic Russians and the North Cauca-sian nationalities could also escalate. Russian behavior in Checheno-Ingushetia suggests that, if inter-ethnic tension increases, the Russians will elect to leave the North Caucasus rather than to organize themselves poli-tically. Unlike the other diaspora groups – the Nogai and the Cossacks – Russians exhibit no consciousness of a North Caucasian homeland but continue to identify themselves with the territories of Russia.

Conclusion: fraternity or Balkanization?

On October 22, 1991, in the heat of Dzhakhar Dudaev's confrontation with the Russian government, a pronouncement by the emigré Chechen historian A. Avtorkhanov – who is revered throughout the North Cauca-sus – was broadcast on Chechen television in both Russian and Chechen languages. Avtorkhanov appealed to the Chechen people to support North Caucasian solidarity:

> The Ingush are our brothers; the Ossetians are our brothers; the Terek cossacks and peoples of Dagestan are our brothers. We must unite in a federation, or else we will never be able to administer our affairs free from the Russians.[133]

Given the cultural similarities of the North Caucasian peoples and the economic and political advantages that could be secured in such a union, the notion of a North Caucasian federation does not appear entirely unfeasible. Indeed, the Dagestan Republic exemplifies such a federation: it unites several North Caucasian nationalities on an equal, non-titular basis, and appears to satisfy the majority of its peoples.

Efforts to realize a North Caucasian federation have been undertaken. The Assembly of the Mountain Peoples of the Caucasus was created in August 1989 and drew in representatives of sixteen North Caucasian national groups. The aim of the Assembly is to create a North Caucasian Federal Republic which would incorporate the North Caucasian national republics, Dagestan and Abkhazia. The republic would be fully sovereign and would exist outside the Russian Republican structure. While the Assembly sees the economic necessity of maintaining close ties with Russia, it has resolved to do so "on an equal basis," as a sovereign republic.[134]

In January 1991, representatives of the Karachai and Balkar expressed their unwillingness to enter the Federation. At that time, these peoples shared titular republican status with the Cherkess and Kabardin groups respectively and were unwilling to enter a federation before their independence was secured.[135] In February 1991, the leader of the Popular Democratic Union of North Ossetia expressed his reservations about the proposed Federation, on the grounds that the challenges posed by the breadth and depth of unresolved difficulties in the North Caucasus would prove too great for North Caucasian unity. However, the Progressive Democratic Party of North Ossetia seemed willing to consider the federation.[136] Later, in December 1991, Dzhakhar Dudaev announced his intention "to consider the question of the creation of a Caucasian commonwealth."[137]

Despite the efforts of the Assembly, none of the governments of the North Caucasian republics aside from Chechnia has indicated an active interest in joining a North Caucasian federation. Is such a federation, then, a sort of "fraternal illusion," with roots not in Soviet propaganda about "the brotherhood of peoples," but rather, in a historical memory of alliances which are no longer possible given the evolution of national consciousness in the North Caucasus? In October 1991, the Chechen folklorist and ethnographer I.Iu. Aliroev felt that a North Caucasian federation was possible, "but not in the near future."[138] Disputes are ongoing among various North Caucasian groups, and some show no sign of speedy resolution. Furthermore, the concept of the national state has captured the imaginations of politicians and intelligentsia alike. Even diaspora groups, whose demographic configurations are unsuitable to a national state formation, expressed their cultural programs in terms of political sovereignty.

For much of the first half of the twentieth century, the ethnic consciousness of the North Caucasian peoples was expressed in either narrow clan loyalties, or a broad, North Caucasian Mountaineer identity. The Soviet period, however, has witnessed a gradual emergence of national identity in the North Caucasus. The histories of various peoples began to diverge, through such events as the deportations of 1944, and such circumstances as the splitting of national groups between two Union Republics. Furthermore, the intellectual histories of the various nations have grown more nationally specific as authors and scholars write in the national languages and distinct national narratives emerge. The cultural self-representation of the North Caucasian peoples has also evolved: a general North Caucasian consciousness is still present, but the national groups also perceive themselves as peoples with distinct cultures. Among some groups, national sovereignty is perceived as the only means to protecting these cultures.

Political agendas of the North Caucasian nationalities are also divergent and, consequently, relations with Russia have changed. In the nineteenth century and the first half of the twentieth, animosity toward Russia was a common factor among North Caucasians, and one which drew them together into alliances. More recently however, with the overt competition of titular nationalities and the efforts of some non-titular groups to enhance their political power, the potential gains of collusion with Moscow can overcome the traditional hostility.

For the most part, the priority of the North Caucasian national groups has not been to define themselves with respect to Moscow, but rather, to define themselves both culturally and politically with respect to each other. Expressions of nationalism have been complicated by the persistence of a common, North Caucasian identity. Relations of competition and alliance among and between the titular and non-titular national groups are fluid, shifting with changing circumstances. North Caucasian national governments may, in the coming months, begin to follow Dzhakhar Dudaev's lead and support North Caucasian federation or commonwealth. On the other hand, unresolved sovereignty claims, territorial disputes and fears of cultural weakness and vulnerability are factors which contribute to divisive, nationalist sentiment in the North Caucasus.

Notes

I would like to thank the McArthur Foundation for the financial assistance that made my research and fieldwork in the Soviet Union in 1991 possible. I also acknowledge the useful contributions of James R. Harris in the preparation of this chapter.

1 *Naselenie SSSR: po dannym vsevoiuznoi perepisi naseleniia 1989* (Moscow, 1990), pp. 37–40. These native groups are: Abazin; Avar; Agul; Adygei; Balkar; Dargin; Mountain Jews (*Evrei gorskie*); Ingush; Kabardin; Karachai; Kumyk; Lak; Lezgin; Nogai; Ossetian; Rutul'; Tabasaran; Tsakhuri; and Chechen.

2 *Argumenty i Fakty*, no. 13, March 1991, p. 1. Data from 1989 census shows the percentage of ethnic Russians to range 9.2 percent in the Dagestan ASSR to 68 percent in the Adygei AO.

3 Ronald Wixman, *Language Aspects of Ethnic Patterns and Processes in the North Caucasus* (Chicago: University of Chicago, Dept. of Geography, Research Paper No. 191, 1980), pp. 86–98.

4 *Ibid.*, pp. 89–90.

5 N.G. Volkova, L.I. Lavrov, "Sovremennye etnicheskie protsessy," E.P. Prokhorov, ed., *Kul'tura i byt narodov Severnogo Kavkaza* (Moscow: Nauka, 1968), p. 330; Wixman, *Language Aspects*, p. 113.

6 V.S. Uarziati, *Kul'tura Osetin: sviazy s narodami kavkaza* (Ordzhonikidze: Ir, 1990), pp. 6–7.

7 Ethnographical and historical study of the broad, North Caucasian culture has been considerable. See especially Uarziaty, *Kul'tura Osetin*; Volkova and Lavrov, "Sovremennye etnicheskie protsessy," p. 330; A. Avkesent'ev, *Islam na Severnom Kavkaze*, p. 168; Ia.S. Smirnova and A.I. Pershits, "Izbeganie," in *Sovetskaia etnografiia*, no. 6, 1978, pp. 61–70; Ia. Smirnova, *Semia i semeinyi byt narodov Severnogo Kavkaza* (Moscow: Smirnova, 1983); Wixman, *Language Aspects*, pp. 102–103; A. Bennigsen and S.E. Wimbush, *Muslims of the Soviet Empire* (Bloomington, Indiana: Indiana University Press, 1986), p. 149.

8 P. Henze, "Fire and Sword in the North Caucasus," *Central Asian Survey*, vol. 2, no. 1 (July 1983), pp. 17, 32–33.

9 Dzeps Kimmer, "Severnyi Kavkaz: god 2000," *Sovetskii Dagestan*, no. 1, 1991, pp. 41–44.

10 A. Uralov (A. Avtorkhanov), *Narodoubiistvo v SSSR* (Munich, 1952), p. 10.

11 Uralov (Avtorkhanov), *Narodoubiistvo*, pp. 10, 21–22; see also Kh.M. Berbekov, *K voprosu ob obrazovanii natsional'noi gosudarstvennosti Kabardino-Balkaria* (Nal'chik), 1960, pp. 15, 20; Wixman, *Language Processes*, p. 137; Robert Conquest, *The Nation Killers: the Soviet Deportations of Nationalities* (London: Macmillan, 1960), p. 23.

12 Volkova and Lavrov, "Sovremennye etnicheskie protsessy," p. 330; "Scholars Identify Pressing Ethnic Issues," *Izvestiia*, 22 March 1988, p. 3, in *Current Digest of the Soviet Press* (*CDSP*), 13 April 1988, pp. 1–4 (interview with ethnographer L.M. Drobizheva and demographer Iurii Poliakov).

13 V. Kozlov, *The Peoples of the Soviet Union*, trans. P.M. Tiffen (Bloomington, Indiana: Indiana University Press, 1988), p. 156.

14 Wixman, *Language Aspects*, pp. 172–174.

15 In the 1920s, the languages were written in Latin script; in 1938, the Latin languages of the North Caucasus were changed to Cyrillic.

16 A.G. Trofimova, "Razvitie literatury i isskustva," in *Kul'tura i byt narodov Severnogo Kavkaza*, p. 303.

17 *Ibid.*, p. 310.

18 V.I. Fil'kin, *Partiinaia organizatsiia Checheno-Ingushetiia v gody bor'by za uprochenie i razvitie sotsialisticheskogo obshchestva* (Groznyi: Checheno' Ingushstoe Kuhkhnoe Izdatelstvo, 1963), p. 98.

19 Volkova and Lavrov, "Sovremennye etnicheskie protsessy," p. 330.

20 Benedict Anderson, *Imagined Communities* (London: Verso, 1983), p. 15.

21 Trofimova, "Razvitie literatury i isskustva," pp. 311–312.

22 V. Kharlamov, "Kogo razdeliaet Terek," *Pravda*, November 4, 1991, p. 2.

23 A. Avtorkhanov, "Forty Years of Sovietization of Checheno-Ingushetia," *Caucasian Review*, no. 10, 1960, p. 8.

24 Interview, Cherkessk, October 9, 1991.
25 Interview, Groznyi, October 23, 1991.
26 Interviews, Vladikavkaz, October 16, 1991; Groznyi, October 21–23, 1991.
27 Wixman, *Language Patterns*, p. 148.
28 A. Nekrich, *The Punished Peoples*, New York, Norton, 1978; Discussion of the deportations in the Soviet literature began to appear only in the late 1980s. See especially N.F. Bugai, "K voprosu o deportatsii narodov SSSR v 30–40kh godakh," *Istoriia SSSR*, no. 6, 1989, pp. 135–144; N.F. Bugai, "Pravda o deportatsii chechenskogo i ingushskogo narodov," *Voprosy istorii*, no. 1, 1990, pp. 32–44; V.N. Zemskov, "Massovoe osvobozhdenie spetsposelentsev i ssyl'nykh (1954–1960 gg.)," *Sotsiologicheskie issledovaniia*, no. 1, 1991, pp. 5–26.
29 V.N. Zemskov, "Massovoe osvobozhdenie spetsposelentsev," p. 26.
30 A. Nekrich, *The Punished Peoples*, p. 149.
31 L.I. Klimovich, "Bor'ba ortodoksov i modernistov v Islame," *Voprosy nauchnoi ateizma*, no. 2, 1966, p. 85.
32 *Argumenty i Fakty*, no. 13, March 1991, p. 1 (Information from 1989 census). The Rutul', Aguls and Tsakhurs have no written language; the Agul use Lezgin as a written language, while the Rutul' and Tsakhur use Azeri. See A. Bennigsen and S.E. Wimbush, *Muslims of the Soviet Empire*, p. 169.
33 *Argumenty i fakty*, no. 13, March 1991, p. 1.
34 S. Shipunova, "Kazaki Kubani," *Sovetskaia Rossiia*, April 13, 1991, p. 3.
35 *Ibid.*, p. 3.
36 Valerii Khabilevskii, "Adygeia," *Nezavisimaia gazeta*, August 13, 1991, p. 3.
37 Dzeps Kimmer, "Severnyi Kavkaz: god 2000"; R. Wixman, *Language Aspects*, p. 128.
38 For example, TASS, cited in *Radio Liberty: Report on the USSR*, May 10, 1991, p. 28, reported clashes between Ossetians and "Chechen-Ingush." These conflicts arose from border disputes between Ingush and Ossetians, and did not directly involve Chechens.
39 Kh.Kh. Bokov, *Internatsionalizm na dele* (Moscow, 1984), pp. 152–169.
40 Timur Muzaev, "Checheno-Ingushetiia," *Nezavisimaia gazeta*, April 26, 1991, p. 3.
41 Field observations, Groznyi, October 1991; Chechen National Television, Groznyi, October 1991.
42 *Izvestiia*, November 27, 1991, p. 1.
43 There were accusations that only his supporters were permitted to run.
44 *Pravda*, November 11, 1991, p. 1.
45 *Nezavisimaia gazeta*, November 20, 1991, p. 3.
46 *Argumenty i fakty* no. 13, March 1991, p. 1.
47 *Izvestiia*, May 30, 1989, reported in CDSP, vol. 41, no. 24, 1989, p. 17.
48 Iu. Karpov, "K probleme ingushskoi avtonomii," *Sovetskaia etnografiia*, no. 5, 1991, p. 29.
49 A. Nekrich, *The Punished Peoples*, pp. 158–159.
50 B. Kotikov, "Zakon o pomilovanii?," *Nezavisimaia gazeta*, April 25, 1991, p. 3.
51 "Kavkaz," *Nezavisimaia gazeta*, March 28, 1991, p. 3.
52 *Izvesttiia*, November 21, 1991, p. 1.

53 A. Grachev, "Severnaia Osetia: dolzhno khvatit' mudrosti," *Pravda*, November 29, 1991, p. 1.
54 Ali Kazakhanov, "92.5 protsenta golosov – za suverennuiu Ingushetiiu," *Izvestiia*, December 4, 1991, p. 2. 73.7 percent of the Ingush population registered for the referendum.
55 "Ne podelili raion," *Pravda*, November 30, 1991, p. 3.
56 "Referendum o suverenitete Ingushetii priznan nezakonnykm Severnoi Osetiei," *Izvestiia*, December 6, 1991, p. 2.
57 "Otkrytie vtorogo fronta," *Argumenty i fakty*, no. 46, November 1991, p. 1.
58 B. Kotikov, "Zakon o pomilovanii?," *Nezavisimaia gazeta*, April 25, 1991, p. 3.
59 Liana Minasian, "Shest' rublei za patron," *Nezavisimaia gazeta*, May 12, 1991, p. 3.
60 Anatolii Grachev, "K chemy gordoe odinochestvo?," *Pravda*, December 13, 1991, p. 2.
61 Liana Minasian, "Shest' rublei za patron," *Nezavisimaia gazeta*, May 12, 1991, p. 3.
62 A. Grachev, "Groznyi uspokaivaetsia," *Pravda*, December 2, 1991, p. 2.
63 *Izvestiia*, December 26, 1991, p. 1.
64 *Pravda*, December 14, 1991, p. 1.
65 *Pravda*, December 27, 1991, p. 2.
66 R. Wixman, *Language Aspects*, pp. 137–139.
67 *Argumenty i fakty*, no. 13, March 1991, p. 1. Russians accounted for 32 percent of the Kabardino-Balkarian population.
68 *Naseleniia SSSR: po dannym vsesoiuznoi perepisi naseleniia 1989*, pp. 37–38.
69 Iuliia Moshkovich, "V polchasa, mama, c Kavakza sela ischezaiut," *Nezavisimaia gazeta*, March 14, 1991, p. 3.
70 Fadeev, A.V., ed., *Ocherki istorii Balkarskogo naroda* p. 98.
71 Valerii Dzidzoev, discussion of Balkarian nationalism and attitudes toward other North Caucasian peoples as represented in the Balkarian press. Presentation delivered at the *Pervaia mezhdunarodnaia konferentsiia po osetinovedeniiu*, October 1991, Vladikavkaz.
72 Iu. Moschkovich, "V polchasa," p. 3.
73 Similarly, this was an important issue among Karachai informants, and the Karachai expressed strong resentment of the Svanetians (an ethnic group of Georgia), who they accused of the destruction. (Interviews conducted in the city of Cherkessk and the village (*aul*) of Nizhnyi Uchkulan, October 1991.)
74 V. Dzidzoev, Presentation at *Pervaia konferentsiia po osetinovedeniiu*.
75 *Ibid.*
76 *Argumenty i Fakty*, no. 13, March 1991, p. 1.
77 S.A. Arutiunov, Ia.S. Smirnova, G.A. Sergeeva, "Etnokul'turnaia situatsiia v Karachaevo-Cherkesskoi Aftonomnoi Oblasti," *Sovetskaia etnografiia*, no. 2, 1990, p. 28.
78 *Ibid.*, p. 23.
79 *Ibid.*, p. 27; also, interviews with Karachai intelligentsia in Cherkessk, October 1991.
80 Radio Moscow, November 27, 1991, *Radio Liberty: Report on the USSR*, no. 49, December 6, 1991, p. 34.

81 TASS, *Radio Liberty: Report on the USSR*, December 13, 1991, p. 33.

82 See V.S. Uarziati, *Kul'tura Osetin: sviazy s narodami kavkaza*, Introduction.

83 Ruslan Bzarov, *Pervaia mezhdunarodnaia konferentsiia po osetinovendeniiu*, October 1991.

84 N.G. Volkova, L.I. Lavrov, "Sovremennye etnicheskie protsessy," p. 333.

85 I am indebted to the Ossetian historian Ruslan Bzarov for his information. The figures are approximate, as no official statistics have been compiled for these categories.

86 Kh.V. Dzutsev, Ia.S. Smirnova, *Semeinye obriady osetin* (Vladikavkaz, 1990), pp. 35, 56–72.

87 Supported by all scholars with whom I spoke at the *Pervaia mezhdunarodnaia konferentsiia po osetinovedeniiu*.

88 E.Kh. Apazheva, presentation on Kabardinian-Ossetian connections, *Pervaia mezhdunarodnaia konferentsiia po osetinovedeniiu*, October 1991.

89 Interviews, Vladikavkaz, October 1991.

90 TASS, "Iz Vladikavkaza," *Sovetskaia Rossiia*, September 17, 1991, p. 1.

91 Declaration composed at Plenary Session of the *Pervaia mezhdunarodnaia konferentsiia po osetinovendeniiu*.

92 A. Semenianka, "Iuzhnaia Osetiia: problemy vse eshche ne resheny," *Pravda*, August 19, 1991, p. 6; See also TASS, August 10, 1991, *Report on the USSR*, August 23, 1991, p. 24.

93 *Izvestiia*, October 23, 1991, p. 1.

94 *Pravda*, November 30, 1991, p. 1; *Pravda*, December 3, 1991, p. 1; *Pravda*, December 21, 1991, p. 1.

95 "Krestovyi pereval Gamsakhurdia i El'tsina," *Nezavisimaia gazeta*, March 26, 1991, p. 3; Liana Minasian, "Shest' rublei za patron," *Nezavisimaia gazeta*, May 12, 1991, p. 3.

96 "Zakon Rossiiskoi Sovetskoi Federativnoi Sotsialisticheskoi Respubliki o reabilitatsii repressirovannykh narodov," text published in *Sovetskaia Rossiia*, May 7, 1991, p. 3.

97 Liana Minasian, "Shest' rublei za patron," *Nezavisimaia gazeta*, May 12, 1991, p. 3.

98 Ann Sheehy, "The All-Union and RSFSR Referendums of March 17," *Report on the USSR*, March 29, 1991, p. 20.

99 A. Glebova, "Musul'mane sobiraiutsia v khadkh," p. 12; "My khotim rasshatat' monolit," *Nezavisimaia gazeta*, February 26, 1991, p. 2.

100 *Report on the USSR*, February 8, 1991, p. 39.

101 Alla Glebova, "Musul'mane sobiraiutsia v khadzh," *Novoe vremia*, no. 30, June 1991, pp. 12–14.

102 *Argumenty i fakty*, no. 13, March 1991, p. 1.

103 *Naselenie SSSR*, pp. 37–40.

104 *Izvestiia*, July 23, 1990, p. 2, reported in *CDSP*, vol. 42, no. 29, 1990, p. 27.

105 *Pravda*, December 9, 1991, p. 1.

106 Murad Zargishiev, "Chetvertyi put'," *Nezavisimaia gazeta*, January 24, 1991.

107 Den'ga Khalidov, "K soglasiiu cherez reformy," *Sovetskii Dagestan*, no. 2, 1991, p. 20.

108 "My khotim rasshatat' monolit," p. 3; Murad Zargishiev, "Chetvertyi put'," p. 3.

109 "My khotim rasshatat' monolit," p. 3.
110 "Vstrecha s delegatsiei," *Sovetskaia Rossiia*, April 9, 1991, p. 2; Vladimir Kosiakov, "S armaturoi na sovetskuiu vlast'," *Nezavisimaia gazeta*, April 15, 1991, p. 3.
111 *Izvestiia*, 23 July 1990, p. 2, reported in *CDSP*, vol. 42, no. 29, 1990, p. 27.
112 According to the 1989 census, ethnic Russians represent only 9.2 percent of the population of Dagestan. *Argumenty i fakty*, no. 13, March 1991, p. 1.
113 K.P. Kalinovskaia and G.E. Markov, "Nogatsy – problemy natsional'nykh otnoshenii i kul'tury," *Sovetskaia etnografiia*, no. 2, 1990, p. 15.
114 *Ibid.*, p. 17.
115 *Ibid.*, p. 18.
116 Murad Zagrishiev, "Respublika Dagestan," *Nezavisimaia gazeta*, May 18, 1991, p. 3.
117 Murad Zagrishiev, "Chetvertyi put'," p. 3.
118 K.P. Kalinovskaia, G.E. Markov, "Nogaitsy," p. 20.
119 Svetlana Shipunova, "Kazaki Kubani," *Sovetskaia Rossiia*, April 13, 1991, p. 3.
120 S.A. Kozlov, "Popolnenie vol'nykh kazach'ikh soobshchestv na Severnom Kavkaze v XVI–XVII vv.," *Sovetskaia etnografiia*, no. 5, 1991, pp. 47–55.
121 "Kazachestvo," *Bol'shaia sovetskaia entsiklopediia* (Moscow, 1973), pp. 175–177.
122 S. Shipunova, "Kazaki Kubani," p. 3.
123 TASS, reported in *Report on the USSR*, December 13, 1991, p. 33.
124 *Izvestiia*, December 4, 1991, p. 1.
125 S.A. Kozlov, "Poplnenie vol'nykh kazach'ikh," p. 54.
126 *Ibid.*, p. 48; "1000 'stvolov' – ne problema," *Argumenty i fakty*, no. 47, November 1991, p. 3.
127 M. Lisina, Zh. Marukian, "Kazaki pishut pis'mo generalu Dudaevu," *Nezavisimaia gazeta*, September 15, 1991, p. 3.
128 Mariia Lisina, "My poidem drugim putem," *Nezavisimaia gazeta*, July 24, 1991, p. 3.
129 Murad Zagrishiev, "Respublika Dagestan," *Nezavisimaia gazeta*, April 18, 1991, p. 3.
130 M. Lisina, Zh. Marukian, "Kazaki," p. 3.
131 *Ibid.*
132 *Izvestiia*, November 27, 1991, p. 1.
133 Groznyi, Chechen Republican Television Station, October 22, 1991.
134 "Proshchai, oruzhie?," *Nezavisimaia gazeta*, January 31, 1991, p. 3.
135 *Ibid.*
136 "Korotko: Severnaia Ossetia," *Nezavisimaia gazeta*, February 12, 1991, p. 3.
137 *Pravda*, December 14, 1991, p. 1.
138 Interview, Groznyi, October 23, 1991.

20 Siberia: Native peoples and newcomers in collision

GAIL FONDAHL

Siberia, the land beyond the Urals (and north of Kazakhstan), comprises 75 percent of Russia. Rich in fossil fuels, minerals, timber, hydropower potential, and furs, it is relatively sparsely populated. But while it is people-poor, with only 22 percent of Russia's population,[1] it is peoples-rich. Over thirty peoples, numbering from a few hundred to several hundreds of thousands, claim part of Siberia as their homeland (see table 20.1), and essentially all of the Commonwealth's other nationalities can be found here in small or large numbers. Over half a millennia of Russian colonization has left its mark on the demographic makeup of this vast area: the Native peoples currently constitute a mere 4 percent of the total population of Siberia.

It is this combination of great wealth of resources and small numbers of Native peoples which fuels the national conflicts that are increasingly evident in Siberia. The indigenous peoples have nominal autonomy but no real control over the development of their homelands. Resources flow west from their lands to the center, with little remuneration. They see the environmental degradation that accompanies the exploitation of these resources undercutting the basis of their traditional economic activities – reindeer, sheep, and cattle pastoralism, hunting and trapping, and fishing. They question the benefits of services provided by the state, such as universal education, which develops aspirations for a "more civilized" way of life while providing few opportunities for upward mobility in either "traditional" or newer professions. With heightened expectations, and greater contacts with the outside world, indigenous Siberians are weighing the gains from membership in a powerful empire against the losses in terms of their cultural vitality. Here, as elsewhere in the former USSR, the myth of fraternal relations has unravelled, to be replaced by accusations of internal colonialism. As these peoples attempt to regain control over their lands and its resources, they increasingly propound a separation of Native and non-Native geographies.

The preceding chapters of this book for the most part have focused on nationalities which form the majority of the population in their own titular areas. In Siberia *prishlie* – "newcomers" (mainly Russians, but including Ukrainians, Tatars, Jews, and individuals from essentially every other

477

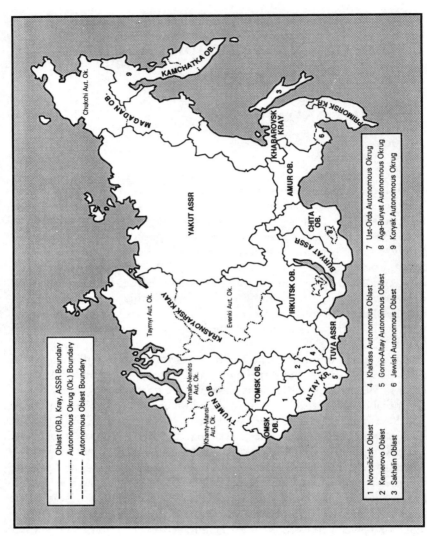

Map 20.1 Administrative-political divisions in Siberia

nation of the former USSR) – dominate numerically. Indeed, Russians have outnumbered Native peoples for over two centuries.[2] The percentage of indigenous representation varies by area, but in almost all political-administrative divisions above the *rayon* level Natives constitute less than one-quarter of the population (table 20.2). Only in Tuva are there more Natives (Tuvans) than *prishlie*. Where rapid industrial development and concomitant large-scale immigration of laborers has occurred, such as that experienced in the West Siberian oil fields, the Native population's representation has dropped most precipitously: the Khants and Mansi now make up only 1.4 percent of their titular territory's population, a mere one-tenth of their relative representation in 1959.

Thus, for most cases in Siberia, were we to examine the majority policy toward minorities we would be examining the policy of the *prishlie* or more narrowly, the Siberian Russian policy toward the Buryats, Khanty, or Chukchi, rather than Buryat, Khanty or Chukchi policy toward the *prishlie* or Russians. But the *prishlie* have no readily identifiable, coherent policy toward minorities. Likewise, virtually no distinctive minority (Native) *policy* toward the majority can be identified in the various autonomous administrative units until very recently. Rather than focus on policy, I will examine practice: how can the relations between Natives and non-Natives themselves be characterized?

Of course simple characterization of these relations poses an impossible task. Relations between Native and newcomer groups and individuals at various times and in various regions have evidenced hostility, friendship, awe, disdain, trust, distrust, exploitation and charitable aid. Instances can be pointed to where individuals of each group viewed members of the other as saviors or destroyers.

Further exacerbating the problem is the fact that throughout the whole history of Russia and the USSR we have very few sources which give us the uninterpreted, unedited, uncensored Native view of Native–non-Native relations. Accounts of "historical" relations between the Native and immigrant population of Siberia are reconstructed largely, if not exclusively, from the writings of non-Native observers. Indeed only in the last several decades, with the creation of literary languages by the Soviets, have most of the Siberian Natives been able to write, and thus record their observations and feelings. And only much more recently have they been allowed to openly express in the press any opinions critical of relations between the Russians and themselves.

Finally, there is a dearth of information on Native–Native relations within the Soviet-period literature, with that available mainly limited to statistics on intermarriage. Due to all of these constraints, this chapter will concentrate on Native–non-Native relations, and deviate from the general framework of this book in its considerations of center–periphery relations and "majority"-foreign relations, focusing not on the numercial majority (Russians) but on the autochthonous Siberians.

For the purposes of this chapter the Siberian peoples lend themselves to classification in five groups: the "peoples of the North," the Southern Siberian Turkic peoples, the Buryats, the Yakuts and the Tuvans. I will consider the peoples of the North in greatest detail, then draw parallels and contrasts with developments in inter-ethnic relations which characterize the other peoples of Siberia.

The peoples of the North

Twenty-five small-numbered nations (under 35,000 persons each) inhabit the taiga and tundra zones of Siberia[3] (see table 20.1). Linguistically represented are the Ugrian (Khanty, Mansi) and Samoedian (Nentsy, Entsy, Nganasany, Sel'kupy) branches of the Uralic family of languages; the Turkic (Dolgan, Tofalar) and Tungus/Manchu (Evenk, Even, Nanay, Negidal, Orochi, Oroki, Udegey, Ul'chi) branches of the Altaian family of languages, the Kett language group (Kets), the Eskimo-Aleut language group (Eskimo, Aleut), and the Paleoasiatic grouping of little internal coherence (Chukchi, Chuvan, Koryak, Itel'men, Yukagir, Nivkhi). Economically, these peoples depended on reindeer pastoralism, hunting and trapping, sea mammal hunting, or fishing, or most commonly a combination of these activities. Land use thus was based on harvesting locally available renewable resources. Because of the environmental conditions of Siberia, the peoples of the North required large territories to support small populations.

As early as 1918 the Soviet state categorized these linguistically, racially, and economically differentiated peoples as a group to be handled with one set of policies.[4] Peoples from the Arctic littoral to the Amur Basin, those living on the eastern flanks of the Urals and those of the western rim of the Pacific, were all designated "small peoples of the North" (*malie narody Severa*).[5] The uniformity of the state's policy towards these peoples has evoked similarities in development of their national consciousness. Of course differences also are evident, in part stemming from their varied geographies, histories and economies. For purposes of manageability, but also because the "peoples of the North" themselves are now employing this grouping in order to develop a political program demanding increased rights and recognition of their distinct cultures, I will discuss these peoples together.

Historical background: inter-ethnic relations in the pre-Soviet period

In 1581, with Yermak's crossing of the Urals to attack Kuchum's Siberian khanate, the Russian state officially began its conquest of Siberia. However, for almost 500 years prior to this historical watershed, Nentsy, Khants and Mansi had conducted trade across the northern Urals,

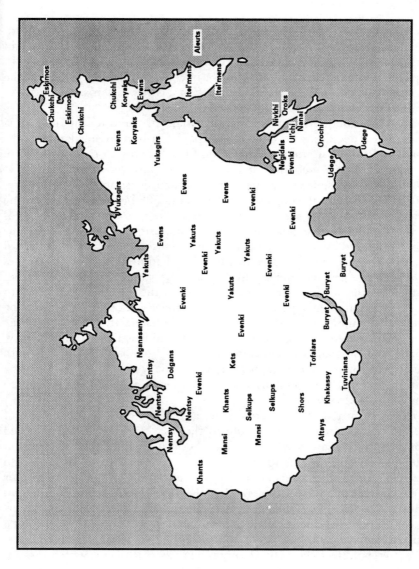

Map 20.2 Ethnic distribution in Siberia

exchanging fur, walrus ivory, and other products of the northwestern Siberian forests and Arctic littoral for western goods from Novgorod and then Muscovy. In fact, while a desire for more furs stimulated the Russian expansion into Siberia, one impetus for opening a *southerly* route was the increasing hostility of the Nentsy to Russian incursions across the northern Urals at the end of the fifteenth century.[6]

The more southerly route brought Russians first into Khant and Mansi lands. These peoples, who were already paying tribute to the khan of Sibir, responded to initial attempts at levying further taxes on them with fierce resistance.[7] Using superior military technology (firearms), but also promises of release from payments to the khan, Russian forces soon prevailed. Throughout the taiga and tundra zones of Siberia this would be the model for conquest: a show of strength was often enough to achieve compliance of the Native population to the imposition of *yasak* – the fur tribute required by the Tsar, especially when accompanied by offers of aid against other perceived oppressors. Russians had firearms; Native peoples didn't. Native groups soon saw Russians as possible (and powerful) allies in their battles against each other and joined these well-armed forces to crush long-standing opponents. Russians quickly learned to exploit the inter-tribal animosities to their own advantage. Lantzeff, in a review of the seventeenth-century literature, found Khants and Russians fighting Nentsy, Khants and Russians allied against Mansi, Yukagirs battling Chukchi with the help of Russians, and Evenks joining Russians in subjugating Buryats. Within nations, the Russians exploited inter-clan hostilities as well to conquer recalcitrant groups.[8]

Russians moved rapidly across Siberia. By 1650 most of the peoples of the North were paying fur tribute to the Tsar's coffers. *Ostrogs* raised alongside Native towns, at the confluences of rivers and at portage termini, acted as collection points for the fur tribute as well as foci for trade and retreats during times of rebellion. For Native compliance with the demands of yasak and other burdens imposed by the Tsarist state was neither unanimous nor continuous. When dealt with unfairly, an all-too-frequent occurrence, Native peoples rebelled. An attempt to raise the yasak in 1606 caused Nentsy in the region of Mangazeya, and Khanty along the Ket River to revolt. In 1609–1610 Khanty tried to evict Russians who had occupied their homelands.[9] Further to the east the Evenks and Evens revolted in 1662. The Chukchi most effectively resisted Russian domination, and continued to function as a semi-independent nation well into the nineteenth century.

Native responses to the conquest and imposition of tribute were not limited to armed revolts. When provincial officials increased yasak rates or demanded other services, the hunters often petitioned Moscow to rule against local corruption. A second line of recourse was simple refusal to pay yasak. To avoid the inevitable confrontation which this resulted in, some Native groups migrated deeper into the taiga, temporarily escaping their economic tormentors. More drastic measures involved assassinations of Russians, and in at least one case mass suicides in protest.[10]

Moscow's greatest interest in Siberia, and more specifically, in its autochthonous peoples, was in ensuring an uninterrupted flow of furs from the hinterland to the center.[11] To achieve this, the Tsarist government repeatedly issued decrees denouncing exploitative practices. In the initial stages of conquest, yasak paid to the Tsar was to be no higher than that levied by former powers (khans); later on the yasak collectors were strictly prohibited from addending levies for their own profits. Unregulated trade was prohibited in order to protect the Native population. However, stories abound of highly usurious practices, the most common being unfair trading deals, especially those involving Russians attempting to get Natives drunk before negotiating. Deceit was not a Russian monopoly, however. We may read of Native trappers rubbing sable pelts with coal in order to garner the higher prices paid for the more valuable, darker species.[12]

The preceding depiction of Native–Russian contact in the Siberian North draws a picture of conflict and animosity. As the immigrant population of Siberia grew Native northerners and Russians increasingly lived in relatively close proximity and dealt with each other in realms other than trade. While laws expressly prohibited many Native–Russian contacts, including unregulated trade, land leasing by Russians from Natives, and the cohabitation of Natives and common Russians in the same village,[13] these laws were difficult to enforce. Native and Russian villages were often separate but adjacent. Intermarriage became increasingly common, and Russians employed Natives to fish, herd deer, cut hay, gather firewood and berries, and carry out innumerable other tasks. Natives adopted some items of Russian dress, domestic implements and tools, and other elements of material culture, and an increasing number learned to speak Russian. At the same time, Russians adopted much indigenous technology for surviving in the severe Siberian environment: clothing, transport and hunting equipment, foodstuffs and preparation techniques, etc. Some Russians learned to speak the local language; most often the terminology of work incorporated many words from the Native language.

Unlike many other parts of the world, the state enacted no large-scale policy of genocide; in fact, as mentioned, tsars repeatedly issued protective measures in order to ensure that Native peoples would be able to continue to provide the state with furs. However, these decrees were often not realized *in situ*, and the indigenous northerners met oppressors both in government agents and individual traders and colonizers. Officials at the local level overlooked crimes against Natives by private traders and other immigrants, and themselves frequently ignored state decrees on humane treatment. They mistreated hostages (whom they were officially allowed to keep to ensure continued yasak payments by fellow tribesmen), even starving them at times, and condoned the use of alcohol in trading. Military campaigns against Native settlements involved rape, murder, kidnapping and pillaging. The conquest and colonization of northern Siberia severely impacted the Native population. Introduced diseases to which Native peoples had no immunity caused phenomenal death rates. Moreover, the demand for fur tribute in areas where there had been none before meant a restructuring of the indigenous economy away from purely subsistence concerns and a decrease in food production. When and where this contributed to declining nutritional status, the depredations of disease were even more greatly felt. Finally, cultural anomie in the face of foreign incursion and subjugation undoubtedly further undermined peoples' resistance to the new diseases. Populations of a number of the peoples (Khants, Mansi, Evenks, Nanay) by the Revolution had declined by as much as 30 to 40 percent.[14]

The Soviet period: inter-ethnic relations

Before the Revolution, we might surmise that many Natives had little reason to distinguish between state official and individual trader or colonist in terms of the treatment they could expect to receive. Any initial impressions of the Tsarist government as ally or protector would have faded quickly. This view of government changed temporarily after the Revolution. During the early years of Soviet power, the peoples of the North did invest hopes in the new government as a better ruler and even as a protector of Native interests. Many Native people still accept the 1920s and early 1930s as a period of great cultural development which the new Soviet state supported. To the 1920s and 1930s date the creation of literary languages, the establishment of educational institutions, universal suffrage, and many other institutions which are viewed as positive. In 1924 the state created a special "Committee for the North" to protect the interests and oversee the development of these peoples. This group, dedicated and relatively effective in its early years, helped institute the state's policy of *korenizatsiya* in Siberia, encouraging Native political participation in the new governmental structures (*soviets*). It most likely played a large role in defining the identity of many of these peoples as nations, both in the eyes of the state and among the peoples themselves.[15] The culminating step was the establishment of national *okrugs* for a number of the peoples of the North in 1930 (map 20.2).[16]

If paternalistic, the state policy was at least nurturing. The Committee for the North espoused what is now referred to as "internationalization" (*internatsionalizatsiya*), a process combining the best specific, national (*natsional'no-osobennoe*) traits of these "primitive" cultures with the universal (*internatsional'no-obshchee*) traits of the more advanced (Russian) culture.[17] Internationalization would in theory avoid both extremes of complete assimilation and complete isolation.

Native people initially looked to the Committee and to the new Bolshevik government to resolve some of their conflicts with the growing Russian population. Paramount in the list of protestations in the early twentieth century were the issues of Russian encroachment on Native lands and of hunting competition and habitat destruction. For instance, delegates to a 1926 meeting in the Turukhansk region complained that "Russians, invading the taiga, ravage the graves of our ancestors, rob Native caches, steal foxes from Tungus [Evenk] traps. Hunting dogs of the Russians chase the easily frightened Tungus reindeer through the taiga . . . And there have been cases where Russians have killed domestic reindeer."[18] At this meeting, and at regional meetings fo the Evenks of southeastern Siberia as well, Native persons appealed to the state to exclude Russians (and also Buryats) from hunting, and to protect the forest from burning by non-Natives.[19] Soviet officials responded by assigning clans specific hunting areas (allegedly the most valuable), and prohibiting access to these by Russians. However, enforcement of the prohibition was nigh impossible. Russians continued to penetrate into indigenous hunting areas, complaining that it was unfair that the Natives had special areas set aside, but could also hunt on "free lands" (i.e. the ones open to the Russians) and that they began hunting prior to the official commencement of hunting season.[20] When Native persons pleaded with Soviet officials to totally halt colonization by Russians, governmental officials flatly condemned this attitude.[21] The only answer left appeared to be self-imposed isolation, a retreat beyond the borders of Russian settlement. In some instances Native groups assumed a "scorched earth" policy, burning winter hunting grounds to stop the advance of Russian hunters and stabilize the boundaries of their shrinking territory.[22]

The creation of eight national okrugs for seven of the peoples of the North must have seemed a promising step in terms of gaining a degree of geographic autonomy. However, the majority of peoples of the North received no such titular administrative unit.[23] Moreover, for those who did, the gains were limited. As immigrants continued to pour into Siberia, the population of the national okrugs became increasingly non-Native. Native peoples usually received figurehead posts in the okrug government and party apparatus, but exercised minimal power over decisions on the development of resources and allocation of lands to the various state ministries and their enterprises.

By the 1930s any hopes of autochthonous northerners must have faded, with state pursuance of policies of collectivization and sedentarization in the North. It also became clear that the state not only did not intend to limit Russian colonization, but indeed encouraged it. Local control over local affairs increasingly eroded, and two autonomous okrugs were actually disbanded.[24] Moreover, cooptation replaced integration as the state's policy toward a number of the peoples of the North. Several nations were

486   *Gail Fondahl*

Table 20.1. *Population of Native peoples of Siberia, 1926–1989*

	1926	1959	1970	1979	1989
Buryats (000s)	238.0	253.0	314.7	352.6	421
Yakuts (000s)	240.5	236.7	296.2	328.0	382
Altays (000s)	47.7	45.3	55.8	60.0	71
Khakasy (000s)	52.8	56.6	66.7	70.8	80
Tuvans (000s)	60.0	100.1	139.4	166.1	207
Shors	17.0	15.3	16.5	16.0	na
Peoples of the North					
Nentsy	16,217	23,007	28,705	29,894	34,675
Evenks	38,805	24,710	25,149	27,294	30,247
Khanty	17,334	19,410	21,138	20,934	22,531
Evens	2,044	9,124	12,029	12,523	17,193
Chukchi	12,221	11,727	13,597	14,000	15,182
Nanay	5,860	8,026	10.005	10,516	12,021
Koryaks	7,439	6,287	7,487	7,879	9,237
Mansi	6,095	6,449	7,710	7,563	8,461
Dolgans	656	na	4,877	5,053	6,931
Nivkhi	4,076	3,717	4,420	4,397	4,673
Sel'kups	1,630	3,768	4,282	3,565	3,611
Ul'chi	723	2,055	2,448	2,552	3,234
Itel'mens	859	1,109	1,301	1,370	2,480
Udegey	1,357	1,444	1,469	1,551	2,011
Eskimos	1,293	1,118	1,308	1,510	1,718
Chuvans	705	na	na	na	1,511
Nganascans	867	748	953	867	1,279
Yukagirs	443	442	615	835	1,142
Kets	1,428	1,019	1,182	1,122	1,113
Orochi	647	782	1,089	1,198	915
Tofalars	413	586	620	763	731
Aleuts	353	421	441	546	702
Negidals	683	na	537	504	622
Entsy	482	na	na	na	209
Oroks	162	na	na	na	190

Sources: Barbara Anderson and Brian Silver, "Some Factors in the Linguistic and Ethnic Russification of Soviet Nationalities: Is Everyone Becoming Russian?" in L. Hajda and M. Bessinger, eds., *The Nationalities Factor in Soviet Politics and Society* (Boulder: Westview Press, 1990), pp. 95–130, table 2.
V.I. Boyko, "Chislennost', rasselenie i yazykovaya situatsiya u narodnostey Severa na sovremennom etape," in *Problemy Sovremennogo Sotsial'nogo Razvitiya Narodnostey Severa* (Novosibirsk: Nauka, 1987), pp. 37, 38.
I.S. Guvrich, ed., *Etnicheskoe razvitie narodnostey Severa v sovetskiy period* (Moscow: Nauk, 1987), p. 67.
Osnonvye . . . 1990. *Osnovnye Pokazateli Razvitiya Ekonomiki i Kul'tury Malochislennykh Narodov Severa (1980–1989 gody)* (Moscow: Goskomstat RSFSR, 1990), pp. 5, 16.

deemed by central authorities too small to deserve their own literary language: the development of these was halted, and indigenous language
presses closed or not developed. Some peoples (e.g. the Chuvans, Entsy,
and Oroks) actually lost official recognition as distinct nationalities, as
witnessed by their disappearance from the censuses (table 20.1). On the
other hand, the peoples of the North continued to receive a number of
benefits from the state, such as affirmative action policies for admittance to
universities and free travel to medical care facilities. These benefits have
served to encourage Native peoples (including children of mixed mar-
raiges) to identify themselves as such, at least officially, and may have even
played some role in keeping the identity of the non-recognized peoples
alive.[25]

Recent accounts by Native northerners have identified the 1960s and
1970s as especially damaging periods for their cultural vitality.[26] During
these decades the pace of industrial development of Siberia greatly
increased, and with it the degradation of their homelands. Other state-
initiated practices also are condemned. The conversion from collective to
state farms throughout the North meant the consolidation of small single-
nation villages into larger multinational ones; in the 1960s the number of
farms decreased by 60 percent.[27] With increasing rarity did indigenous
persons hold leadership positions in the farms. Removed from their birth-
place, torn from the resource base upon which they depended, large
numbers were alienated from employment in traditional activities. The
state also became increasingly effective in enforcing its compulsory education policy, which meant that more and more Native children ended up
in boarding schools, often far removed from their parents. Northerners
condemn this sytem as nurturing a culture of dependency on the dominant
nation; indeed by the late 1950s, Natives passively accepted harmful state
policies.[28]

Interference proceeded hand in hand with neglect: while forcing sedentarization and compulsory education, the state failed to provide the needed
infrastructure in terms of housing, medical care facilities, transport, etc.
Living conditions in the rural areas of Northern Siberia, where most of the
Native population lives (74.1 percent), are among the worst in the USSR.[29]
Native people have routinely suffered un- and underemployment, with
trivial compensation for low-skilled work.[30] Inter-ethnic conflict is exacerbated where job discrimination favors *prishlie*, especially in "traditional" activities: for instance, in the northern Chita Oblast, qualified
Evenks greatly resented the loss of well-paid positions as state hunters to
Russians.[31] The disorientation that accompanies current conditions in the
North increasingly finds its expression in high rates of alcohol usage, violence, homicide and suicide.[33] Life expectancy for Native northerners runs
16–18 years lower than the average for the RSFSR, largely due to alcohol-
related accidents and violent deaths.[34]

Besides the malaise caused directly by state policies, Native northerners now also openly condemn that caused by the *prishlie* themselves. In areas where non-Native immigration has been greatest and resource exploitation activities most dramatic, tensions are most severe. These tensions are expressed in violence and other criminal activities of the *prishlie* against the Natives. For instance, Aypin, a Khant, tells of immigrant workers in the oil rich areas of Western Siberia stealing sleds and winter clothing, poaching domesticated reindeer, and desecrating Native burial grounds.[35] One Khant recently (1990) announced to a foreign visitor that he would shoot any oilman that entered his hunting territory.[36] To date accounts concentrate on non-Native attacks on Natives and fail to mention any widespread retaliation, as has occurred between the Yakuts and Russians and the Tuvans and Russians (see below).

To escape the social and psychological malaise endemic in the economic and cultural surroundings crafted for them by the state, and exacerbated by individual immigrants, some Native groups again have considered retreat, and the separation of things Native and non-Native. For example, a number of Evenks living in the northern Irkutsk oblast, who had been settled in a *sovkhoz* (state farm) central village, returned to the taiga with their deer to work as state hunters. One measurable indicator implied a better life in the bush: alcohol consumption dropped to 12–20 percent of that of the Evenk village population.[37] Other non-quantifiable indices also suggested that this separation had improved, rather than detracted from, the herders' living standard.[38] The desire to regain such separation has been expressed by others: Nivkh and Orok reindeer herders living on Sakhalin Island petitioned to be allowed to return to their abandoned Native villages and hunting grounds, from which they had been resettled into a larger sovkhoz central village,[39] and the political platform of the Khanty-Mansi cultural revival movement, *Spacenie Yugri*, includes provisions for resettling the indigenous population into Native villages of no more than 150 persons, surrounded by zones of protected land.[40] The Chukchi have instituted an even bolder program which encourages the resettlement of *prishlie* rather than Native persons: the program attempts to induce Russians to re-emigrate to other parts of the USSR. More generally, the idea of establishing national parks, reservations or some other form of protected territory for the exclusive use and occupancy by indigenous persons has gained wide acceptance among Northern groups.[41]

This desired separation addresses the demographic problem facing the Native northerners. Ironically, with "democratization," their political power base has deteriorated due to large numbers of immigrants and the current integration of Native and non-Native spheres of activity. With free elections, Native peoples can no longer hope to achieve a majority of votes in the soviets, and thus their power base further erodes. Both the absolute and relative number of elected representatives of the Native northerners decreased in the 1989 and 1990 elections, most markedly at the lower (regional and settlement) levels of government.[42] In less than 43 percent of all settlements registered as "national" do Native northerners comprise more than 50 percent of the population. Moreover, many of these settlements are considered "futureless" (*neperspektivnye*) by the government, and are slated for closing.[43] In proposing a geographic separation of nationalities, Native groups hope to achieve control over at least their immediate surroundings.

To address the above threats and promote "liberation," at least in the sense of greater cultural and geographic autonomy, the peoples of the North have formed associations at both the regional and all-Union level. The latter evidences the consolidation of the supra-national identity fomented by the state: representatives of the northerners have used this government-assigned category to organize an "Association of the Small-numbered peoples of the North." Here, referring back to Bremmer's Table 1.1, we see not competition among "non-titular" groups but rather cooperation for a common goal. With only advisory powers, the Association, formed in 1989, nevertheless has successfuly attained high visibility in policy circles. It puts forward a platform of juridical guarantees of traditional land use and control of all resources, surface and subsurface, for the Native population of the North.[44] It also asks for veto power over any large-scale construction on Native homelands. Where legislation to ensure such rights is lacking, the Association seeks protection of Native rights to land, resources and cultural survival under international codes, especially statutes of the United Nations. At present it is lobbying for Russian ratification of the recently adopted Convention 169 of the International Labor Organization, which upholds Native peoples' rights to control their "economic, social and cultural development," and requires the state government to "guarantee effective protection of their rights of ownership and possession" of their land and resources.[45] However, individual Native northerners increasingly question the Association's ability to efficaciously promote such a platform.[46]

Regional associations (*Yamal-potomkam, Spacenie Yugri, Arun*,[47] etc.), though promoted by the all-Union Association, for the most part have been more grass-roots, bottom-up, organizations. These have received little attention in the press; their effectiveness in successfully negotiating for greater rights for their constituents is yet unknown.

Decrees of greater autonomy put forward by the soviets of some of the autonomous okrugs might be seen as a further move towards demanding, indeed asserting, indigenous rights in the North. The Chukchi okrug soviet, for instance, has declared itself an ASSR and has announced its intention to secede from the Magadan oblast'.[48] Likewise, the Koryak okrug council has declared its intention to break away from the Kamchatka oblast. We must question however the assumption of indigenous power carefully. For instance, the deputies declaring a new Chukchi

Autonomous Republic sought to "define more clearly the status of the native peoples of the Chukotsky Peninsula, to ensure their social protection, and to use the area's natural resources more efficiently."[49] However, they did not explicitly tie the issue of resource use to Native control or even input. In reaction to the Koryak okrug's seccession, Kamchatkan officials emphasized that the indigenous people's opinion was not necessarily reflected.[50] To assume that the upgrading of the status of autonomous territories (okrugs, oblasts, and ASSRs) is in all cases a move in favor of greater sovereignty for Native peoples is to incautiously ignore the demographic reality of the territories and their leadership. What Bremmer refers to as "matrioshka nationalism" is nowhere more evident than in the Yamalo-Nenets Autonomous Okrug. Inhabitants of this region claim rights to the gas and oil over which the Tyumen oblast, RSFSR, and USSR each also assert ownership. Yet it is the *prishlie*, not the Nentsy and other Native peoples of the okrug, who rallied to upgrade the autonomy of, and therefore their control over, the okrug and its hard-currency generating resources.

Relations to the international circumpolar community

The Association of the Peoples of the North is now looking towards inclusion of its member nations in the World Council of Indigenous Peoples and other international fora for Fourth World rights. Sami (Lapps), Greenlanders, and Inuit (Eskimo) observers from abroad were invited to the first congress of the Association, and members are familiarizing themselves with the benefits and drawbacks of land claims settlements and other political agreements negotiated by foreign nations of the Arctic and Subarctic with their respective states.[51]

As individual nations, the northern peoples have few connections with outside states, or nations within these states. The notable exception is the Siberian Eskimos.[52] Cut off from communications with their kinspeople across the international border only in 1948, these people are now reestablishing ties with the American Yupik (Eskimos), with a great potential for politicized common agendas. With much publicity, relatives were allowed once again to visit each other in 1988. Since its formation in 1977 the Inuit Circumpolar Conference (ICC)[53] has invited the Soviet Eskimos to participate at its tri-yearly meetings: they were finally able to do so in 1989. Interestingly, the head of the delegation, which had observer status at the meeting, was not Eskimo but Chukchi.[54] One Native governmental representative from Chukotka suggested that the Association of Peoples of the North should seek membership in the ICC, an idea rejected by the ICC's president, who sees no place for non-Eskimo peoples in this specifically Eskimo group.[55] Rather, the ICC hoped that *Eskimo* delegates from Russia would join by the next meeting (1992) as full members.

The Southern Siberian Turkic peoples: Altays, Khakassy, Shors

As in Northern Siberia, the indigenous peoples of southwest Siberia identify the most significant threat to their continued cultural viability as stemming from incursions of an industrialization program over which they have had no control, and the concomitant loss of land and degradation of the environment which has threatened "traditional" activities. Southwestern Siberia, an area of high mountains alternating with undulating plains, is home to nomadic pastoralists of Turkic linguistic stock, who traditionally herded sheep, cattle, and horses. Over the course of the last century and a half, immigrants have streamed into the area, both as agricultural colonists and in association with the development of mining centers and metalworks. Most recently, *prishlie* have come to mine ores which utilize in their processing the coal of the nearby Kuznetsk Basin (Kuzbas). As with the "Peoples of the North," the numerical inferiority, ever increasing, of the South Siberian Turkic peoples holds little promise for any type of real political autonomy based on the present titular administrative units.

The identities of these peoples as Shors, Altays, and Khakassy were forged, fairly successfully, during the Soviet period. Here, as elsewhere in the USSR, the creation of one literary language for each of these peoples contributed to the internal unification of a number of related groups as self-conscious nations. Prior to the October Revolution none of these three (groups of) peoples identified themselves with a single, encompassing name. The Altay and Khakassy were divided into a number of tribes and territorial groups, and the Shors identified themselves primarily by clan, one of the more numerous of these being the eponymous clan. This did not however, preclude pan-nationalist aspirations even before the Revolution. The national histories of these peoples are similar enough to consider together; in fact, nationalist aspirations have coalesced in both the earlier part of this century and more recently.

The Altays actually consist of two groups with distinct languages, a northern group comprising the Tubulars, Chelkans and Kumandas, and a southern group comprising the Telengits, Telesy, Teleuts, and Altay.[56] These various groups fell under Western Mongol (Oirot) rule from the fifteenth century to the eighteenth century. The defeat of Dzhungaria by China signified a change in rulership. Then, in the mid nineteenth century, the Russian Empire wrested this area from China, and the Altays became subjects of the Tsar. Venerating their Mongol connections, nationalists of the early twentieth century would borrow "Oiro," the term initially also used by the state to identify the peoples now known collectively as the Altay.

With the establishment of Russian power, Russian peasant immigrants, attracted by the rich pasture lands, soon began to flow into the area. Land reform in 1899 stipulated a redistribution of land based on needs for sub-sistence family farming (18 *desyatins*, or approximately forty-nine acres per family).[57] This of course greatly eroded the land base of the semi-nomadic indigenous herders, whose needs were for extensive tracts of pasture and who did not recognize private ownership in any event.

The Khakass nation included the Kacha, Sagay, Bel'tir, Kyzyl and Koybal "tribes."[58] Their union with the Russian empire dated to the early 1600s, when the various tribes pledged allegiance to the tsar in return for protec-tion from multiple tribute payments (to Mongols and Kyrghyz as well as Russians).

Nationalist movements developed among the Altay and Khakass intelli-gentsia in the late nineteenth century and early twentieth. Among the Altay, the movement was tied to a messianic religious movement, Burk-hanism, which acknowledged the visitation of Oirot Khan to an Altay shepherd.[59] This Khan preached a doctrine that was both anti-Christian and anti-Russian. The movement among the Khakassy apparently did not have the same religious character, though the choice of the name, Kha-kassy, for the fledgling nation evoked a history of great depth, referring to the Khyagasy of Chinese chronicles.[60] In the early twentieth century, with the Tsarist regime weakened by the 1905 revolution, Khakass nationalists attempted to free themselves from Tsarist control by a transfer of land and administration to clan organizations.[61] However, Tsarist officials refused to recognize the indigenous reforms.

During the tumultuous months following the October Revolution, Altay and Khakass nationalists joined to consider the creation of an independent Turkic peoples' republic, which would have included these two groups as well as perhaps the Tuvans or the Kazakhs.[62] While the new Bolshevik government forbade the formation of such an independent unit, the People's Commissariat for Nationalities initially accepted the concept of an Oirot-Khakass autonomous territorial unit within Russia. However, in the early 1920s the state established two separate administrative units, the Oirot Autonomous oblast and the Khakass *Uezd*. The latter was given national okrug status in 1925, then elevated to an autonomous oblast in 1930.

The Soviet state also established a Shor National Okrug, Gornaya Shoriya, in 1929. In all three areas the autochthonous populations may have been a majority at the time of creation of the national administrative units.[63] Rapid influx of Russian and other immigrants during the early years of the Soviet industrialization drive quickly changed this situation. By the end of World War II the Khakass people constituted less than 20 percent of the population of its designated homeland; prior to the war (1938), Shors had decreased to 13 percent of Gornaya Shoriya's inhabit-ants.[64] This national okrug was disbanded in 1939 and the land became part of the Kemerovo oblast. Here we have a situation analogous to that of the Even-Okhotsk National Okrug: Gornaya Shoriya's existence may have been seen as an impediment to the development of the rich coal deposits of the Kuzbas as well as the associated iron deposits of the okrug itself, and the titular population considered small enough to disenfranchise without consequence to the state.[65]

The consequences to the Shors, though, were significant. In simple demographic terms the growth of the Shor population was almost three percentage points below that of the RSFSR average between 1959 and 1970 (7.98 percent vs. 10.7 percent),[66] and between 1970 and 1979 the Shor population actually declined by almost 3 percent. Besides the abolishment of their autonomous territory, the Shors faced the closing of predominantly Shor farms and of Shor villages.[67] Forced emigration from rural areas increased the number of Shors working in the mines of the region. Social malaise of the indigenous population was expressed as it was further north: suicide rates and fatal accidents grew, especially in the wake of increased alcohol and drug abuse.[68]

The Altay suffered a less dramatic, but none the less telling fate. Too obviously an echo of lingering aspirations, the designation "Oirot" was changed to "Altay," and "Gorno Altay" substituted for "Oirot" in the autonomous oblast's name in 1948. Altay nationalists had apparently continued to nurture the idea of a sovereign Oirotia, and remained in contact with "Oirots" in Xinkiang.[69] By renaming this nation, the state sought to sever psychological as well as tangible connections to related peoples beyond the boundaries of the USSR.

Today we see both divisive and unifying movements among these South Siberian peoples. On one hand, the consolidation of the various tribes or territorial groups into cohesive nations has not been complete: the Teleuts, for instance, request recognition from the Russian state as a nation distinct from the Altays.[70] On the other hand, we see cooperation in the creation and development of the Siberian Cultural Center (SCC) as a union of nationalist activists from these three peoples.[71] To date the SCC has lobbied for increased national autonomy of the South Siberian peoples, an improvement in the situation of native languges, and protection from degradation caused by industrialization. Within the SCC, founded in 1989 by Khakass intellectuals, there appears to be "an increasing consensus about the necessity of restoring the historical unity of these three nationalities, separated from each other by centuries of Russian colonial administration."[72]

SCC membership spans the political spectrum from radical separatists to more conservative "sovereignists." Some dream of an independent South Siberia Turkic republic, reminiscent of the vision of Oirotia earlier in this century. Pragmatists point to basic demographic problems inherent in establishing such a republic – the indigenous peoples are now minorities throughout their homelands. A somewhat less radical component of this movement proposes establishing Native administration over an archipelago of rural areas which do still have a Native majority. There is talk of attempting to close these areas to further non-Native immigration.[73]

The SCC, and its regional counterpart, "Toon," centered in the Khakass Autonomous Oblast, have made appeals to Native Americans for closer ties, suggesting joint conferences, youth and tourist exchanges, and joint publication programs. To this end a North American support group has been established in Canada.[74] The SCC also suggests establishing ties with indigenous peoples of Oceania, and with these and other "First Peoples," organizing meetings and demonstrations.[75]

Meanwhile, the government of Gorno-Altay has worked independently for greater sovereignty. In 1990 it adopted the higher status of ASSR within the RSFSR, which would remove it from one "matrioshka" of administrative nesting, the Altay *kray*. In its sovereignty decree, it claimed exclusive rights to its natural resources.[76] *Vis-à-vis* the case of the Yamal Nenets okrug discussed above, we cannot be sure to what extent this can be considered a "national movement" by the Altays.

The Buryats

The Buryats, living to the west and east of southern Lake Baikal, and north of the border with Mongolia, are one of the former USSR's two Mongol and Buddhist peoples (the Kalmyks being the other). Traditionally pastoral nomads, raising sheep, horses and some cattle, they adopted agriculture in increasing numbers during the last century. Buryats living to the west of Lake Baikal were most heavily influenced by Russians, and many even converted to Eastern Orthodoxy. The Buryats differ little ethnically from the Mongols across the international border: in fact Caroline Humphrey describes them as "those northern Mongol tribes who decided they wished to remain in the Tsarist Russian Empire" in the eighteenth century.[77] This choice stemmed from lower taxes and greater freedom of movement under the tsar than under the Khalka Mongol leadership.

While Russians began to penetrate Buryat homelands as early as the seventeenth century, contact between the two peoples remained limited. Russians settled in villages, Buryats continued to nomadize. This difference in lifeways, which limited interaction between the two peoples, would become the basis for conflicts between them, for the Buryat economy depended on the extensive use of land for grazing livestock.

Inter-ethnic conflicts over land had begun by the late eighteenth century as increasing numbers of (mainly Russian) immigrants moved into the Buryat homelands and gradually dispossessed the Buryat of their ancestral territory. Disputes reached a critical level in the early twentieth century when the Tsarist government proposed a land reform similar to that proposed for the Altay region, which granted equal territory to each household regardless of ethnic identity or economic activity. The area to be allocated, as in the case of the Altay, was calculated to meet the needs of the peasant farmers (fifteen *desyatins*, or roughly forty-one acres, per male), not the transhumant pastoralists, and would be owned individually, not collectively.[78] Under this reform indigenous communities would lose up to half of their lands and their nomadic lifeway would be threatened. Tsarist reforms also did away with an administrative system which guaranteed distinct Buryat governance of predominantly Buryat areas.[79]

In response to these reforms, to continued Russian immigration, and especially to the land tenure issues, a vital Buryat nationalist movement developed around the turn of the century.[80] Members of the Buryat intelligentsia in vain petitioned St. Petersburg to regain local self-government. They condemned the Tsarist government in countless meetings for its land policies and unwillingness to limit Russian colonization. Within the intelligentsia grew increasingly schismatic factions. One supported a separate Mongolian state, essentially a re-creation of the Mongol Empire.[81] Another worked for greater political and cultural autonomy within the Russian state. The latter held greatest power at the time of the Revolution, with most Buryat leaders subscribing to socialism, but not Bolshevism.[82]

As a first step towards territorial autonomy under the new regime, the Buryats in 1918 were given *aimaks* – their own administrative areas, equivalent to *rayons*, scattered among the Russian villages. Two years later, with the formation of the Far Eastern Republic, the Buryat nation was temporarily split politically. In 1921 the constitution of the Far Eastern Republic created an "Autonomous Buryat-Mongol Oblast"; the following year the Soviet government established a Buryat-Mongol Autonomous Republic. These two were merged to form one single Buryat-Mongol ASSR in 1923. From the very beginning, Buryats were outnumbered in the ASSR; in 1926 Russians already constituted 53 percent of the population of the republic, Buryats only 44 percent.[83]

It was not the demographics, however, but rather retribution for supposed nationalist and even pan-Mongolist "deviations" that in 1937 caused the reduction of Buryat titular territory. Most of the members of the Buryat intelligentsia, who had played a critical role in shaping the early policy of the Buryat-Mongol ASSR, were denounced as Japanese spies and purged. The ASSR was carved up into three titular units (see map 20.2), with 12 percent of its former territory given to the Chita and Irkutsk oblasts.[84] This lost land constituted some of the richer agricultural and pastoral areas of the republic. During 1937 the state also instituted a number of new privileges for settlers in the Eastern reaches of the country, which increased the flow of Russians into Buryatia.[85] By 1959 Buryats only accounted for 20 percent of the ASSR's population,[86] though since then the indigenous population has grown faster than the Russian population.[87] The two groups tend to remain separate, living in different villages or different sections of the villages and towns. Inter-ethnic relations can be strained: Humphrey writes that it is "apparently unsafe for Russians to venture at night into Buryat quarters, and vice versa,"[88] and more recent visitors among the Buryats note a marked disdain for, if not hostility towards, Russians.

A recent resurgence in nationalist activity in Buryatia is evidenced in demands for the return of the *aimaks* and re-consolidation of the Buryat homeland to its pre-1937 borders. Nationalists also have lobbied for a return to the original name, from which "Mongol" was dropped in 1958.[89] Buryats apparently support the 1990 declaration of sovereignty put forward by the republic's Supreme Soviet, which upgraded the republic to SSR status and claimed control over all natural resources. Perhaps more indicative of national aspirations is the growing Buryat participation in environmental groups which support the preservation of the homelands and the creation of a variety of Buryat groups to promote cultural revival.[90]

Buryat links with Mongolia

The relationship between Buryats and Khalka Mongols has often been one of uneasy alliance, relying on cultural ties to overcome political hostilities. At the turn of the century, pan-Mongolists on both sides of the border sought the creation of a separate Mongol state. Meanwhile, both the Tsarist and the Soviet government attempted to make use of the Buryats' close linguistic and cultural affinity to Mongolians to draw Outer Mongolia into an ever closer dependency relationship. As the Mongolian People's Republic had little of its own educated elite, Buryats were sent by the Soviets to staff major positions.[91] Members of the Buryat intelligentsia straddled the divide, sometimes to advance their own nationalist political agendas, trying to "extract favorable treatment for Buryats at home in return for political work carried on in Outer Mongolia."[92] While some Buryats probably felt their role as brokers and intermediaries between the Russian and Mongol cultures to be a positive one, promoting progress while buffering against cultural anomie, Mongols allegedly resented the dominance of a westernized, modernized leadership and considered the Buryats traitors to true Mongolian culture.[93]

In 1990 a Buryat-Mongol People's Party held its first congress in Ulan-Ude; this new party echoes the visions of the pan-Mongolists at the beginning of this century. It advances a platform for the cultural rebirth of the Buryat-Mongol people and the formation of a single Mongol state, and in the short term demands a cessation of Russian immigration into the republic.[94]

The Yakuts

Yakutia is one of Russia's most richly endowed regions in terms of natural resources. From this republic comes essentially all of Russia's diamonds and much of its gold, as well as coal, timber and other resources. The titular nation, the Yakuts, comprise about 33 percent of the population; various peoples of the North another 2 percent.[95] Turkic in origin, the Yakuts migrated from the southwest to their current home with horses and cattle, and retained transhumant pastoralism, substituting reindeer in the northernmost regions of Yakutia, where the other animals failed to thrive. They both fought and intermarried with the local population (Chukchi, Evenks, Evens and Yukagirs).

Russian penetration of this area began in the early 1600s. The Yakuts initially welcomed the newcomers, but due to repressive governmental actions soon began to clash with them. A major revolt against Russian occupation occurred in 1642, and the town of Yakutsk was burned in 1681.[96] Eventually, though, the Yakut began to work for the government as tribute collectors and in other official positions. Increased contact between the two peoples led to assimilation, but this did not always mean Russification: Russian colonists were often "Yakutisized," adopting the native language and economic activities.[97]

By the early twentieth century, a Yakut intelligentsia preached a strongly nationalist doctrine. The Yakut Union, founded in 1906, demanded the return of all lands which had been expropriated by the state, by monasteries, and by other Russian groups.[98] Subsequent Tsarist repression of the Union's leaders only further fueled interest in revolutionary ideas. During the prolonged civil war in Yakutia, Yakuts participated on both sides, hoping that the new order which each side promised would bring greater self-determination.

In 1921, in the midst of the civil war, the Yakuts founded a cultural organization, *Sakha Omuk*,[99] to promote their interests. Members of this organization spanned the political spectrum, the most "radical" preaching pan-Turkism. The organization survived until the late 1920s, when the state initiated an anti-nationalist campaign. Many members of the Native intelligentsia were purged over the course of the next decade. This and the collectivization drive met with much resistance in Yakutia.

The Yakut ASSR was established in 1922. In 1924, with the discovery of gold in its southerly region (the Aldan), Russians began to immigrate in large numbers. While in 1926 the Yakuts still comprised the vast majority (82 percent) of their titular republic's population, by 1959 their share had dropped to less than half (table 20.2).[100] Once again, it is this demographic situation, and the feeling that Russian industry is ruining the Yakut environment for Russian profit, which has fueled the resurgence of overt nationalism in the last decade. Yakuts feel that they have benefited little

Table 20.2. *Percent of population belonging to titular nation, 1926–1989*

	1926	1959	1970	1979	1989
Gorno-Altay Aut. Obl. (Altays)	42.5	24.2	27.8	29.2	
Buryat ASSR	33.5	20.2	22.0	23.0	24
Aga Buryat Aut. Okrug	88.0	47.6	50.4	52.0	
Ust-Orda Aut. Okrug	60.0	33.7	33.0	34.4	
Tuva ASSR	75.0	57.0	58.6	60.5	64
Khakass Aut. Ob.	49.2	11.8	12.2	11.5	
Yakut ASSR	81.6	46.6	43.0	36.8	35
Taymyr (Dolgan-Nenets) Aug. Okrug	na	na	17.3	14.8	13.7
Yamalo-Nenets Aut. Okrug	na	22.4	21.9	11.0	4.2
Khanty-Mansi Aut. Okrug	na	13.8	7.0	3.1	1.4
Chukchi Aut. Okrug	na	21.4	10.9	8.1	7.3
Koryak Aut. Okrug	na	18.5	19.1	16.2	16.5
Evenki Aut. Okrug	na	33.7	25.3	20.3	14.0

Sources: Marjorie Mandelstram Balzer, "Yakut," *Encyclopedia of World Cultures, USSR Volume* (New Haven: Yale University Press, forthcoming).
V.I. Boyko, ed., "Chislennost', rasselenie i yazykovaya situatsiya u narodnostey Severa na sovremennom etape," in *Problemy Sovremennogo Sotsial'nogo Razvitiya Narodnostey Severa* (Novosibirsk: Nauka, 1987), pp. 41.
Boris Chichlo, "Histoire de la formation des territoires autonomous chez les peuples Turco-Mongols de Siberie," *Cahiers du Monde Russe et Sovietique*, vol. xxvii, nos. 3–4, p. 391.
Daria Fane, "RSFSR's Nationalities Problems: The Autonomous Republics," typescript.
Table 2, prepared for US/USSR Area X Workshop on Rational Development in the Arctic, Dartmouth College, Hanover, NH, May 22–25, 1991, by Lyudmilla Ilina, from *Economic and Social Development of Autonomous Republics, Autonomous Oblasts and Autonomous Okrugs* (Moscow: Goskomstat, 1990).

from the mineral wealth of their republic. Indices of living conditions fall well below the Soviet average. Major mining areas have been deemed ecological disaster zones, unfit for the pursuance of traditional activities. Conversely, Russians resent the affirmative action programs which benefit the Yakuts (and other indïgenous nations) in both higher education and job placement.

Records of severe inter-ethnic clashes in Yakutia date to 1979. A Ukrainian human rights activist, who was exiled to Yakutia, recounted incidents of ethnic hostility between Yakuts and Russians, such as beatings and attacks, as well as rancorous graffiti.[101] Racial incidents, including mass brawling and large demonstrations, continued to occur throughout the 1980s in the capital city of Yakutsk. The demonstrations mainly involved young Yakuts protesting police inaction over the inter-ethnic clashes.[102]

The year 1990 saw the revitalization of *Sakha Omuk* as an organization for preserving and reviving Yakut culture. In the autumn of the same year, the Yakut Supreme Soviet upgraded the status of the ASSR and renamed it the Yakut-Sakha SSR. Since Yakuts dominate the political positions of the republic, this pronouncement can be read more certainly as a nationalist move as well as a regionalist move than similar pronouncements of increased status from the other Siberian administrative units. The draft constitution of the SSR declares exclusive ownership of the land, minerals, and other resources of Yakutia, and the Supreme Soviet has transferred all enterprises to Yakut ownership.[103] Yakutia plans henceforth to charge the Russian Federation for mining in the republic, and has already begun to negotiate directly with foreign enterprises for resource development.[104]

Inter-ethnic relations: Yakuts and the Peoples of the North

The little information available on titular–non-titular relations in Yakutia suggests that Yakuts indeed have "dominated" the peoples of the North (see table 1.1, in this volume). When in 1930 a number of the peoples of the North received national okrugs, fifteen national rayons were set up within the Yakut ASSR for the Evenks, Evens, Yukagir and Chukchi.[105] Five national rayons for the Evenks alone covered one-third of the Yakut ASSR's territory. However, in 1933 Yakuts held the highest administrative position in ten of the fifteen rayons.[106] The peoples of the North have been increasingly Yakutisized: the number of Evenks who speak Evenk, for instance, continues to decrease, but it is Yakut which is often adopted, not Russian.[107]

"For minorities in the Yakut republic, assimilation is complicated and perhaps less advanced because the surrounding dominant population is not Russian but Yakut."[108] Nevertheless, the peoples of the North are demanding greater political and cultural rights from the Yakut government, including legal protection of their political and cultural rights. That it is willing to meet at least some of the demands is best attested to by the creation in 1989 of a new titular unit for the Even people, the Even-Bytantaisk rayon, within the Yakut ASSR.[109] Top leadership positions in this rayon have gone to Evens. It is also of interest to note that of four contenders in the 1991 Yakut presidential election, one was an Evenk, while none was Russian (the rest being Yakut).[110]

The Tuvans

The Tuvans are primarily pastoralists, herding sheep and cattle and horses in isolated highland pastures of this alpine republic. Linguistically turkified Mongols, with some Turkic, Samoyed and Ket ancestry, most subscribe to the Buddhist faith.

Tuva presents a special case in the study of national relations in Siberia and indeed in the USSR. Firstly, nominally independent from 1921 until 1944, Tuvans remember a recent past of greater sovereignty. Secondly, of all the autonomous units (above rayon level) in Siberia, only in Tuva does the titular nationality predominate. Indeed, Tuvans form a substantial majority (64 percent) of the republic's population. Thirdly, inter-ethnic conflicts, specifically those between Tuvans and Russians, have in the last few years taken a particularly violent flavor, stimulating a massive exodus of Russians from the republic.

These unique characteristics do not negate the fact that the same tensions which fuel inter-ethnic discord in other areas of Siberia are also at work here. Tuvans have watched their traditional way of life erode under policies of collectivization of the pastoral economy, attempted annihilation of the Buddhist faith, and denial of Mongolian elements of their culture. The area, like the rest of Siberia, has experienced large-scale non-Native immigration. Receipts from the extraction of mineral resources, a major source of the area's wealth, have not profited the indigenous population, which experiences high unemployment and one of the lowest standards of living in Russia.

While most of Siberia has been under Russian rule since the seventeenth century, Tuva was never militarily conquered by the Russians. Wedged between Russia, China and Mongolia, and separated from them by lofty mountains of the Sayan, Altay and Tannu-Ola ranges, it enjoyed periods of relative independence from external subjugation. In its worst years its population fell victim to taxation by both the Russian and Chinese empires.

Russian settlement of Tuva accelerated in the early nineteenth century, as peasants, traders and miners were drawn to the area. Manchu China considered Tuva a natural extension of Mongolia, over which it exerted control, and tried to control Russian penetration into the area. The Treaty of Peking (1860) allowed Russians to trade in Uryankhai, as Tuva was then known, as well as throughout Mongolia, but forbade permanent Russian settlements. However, China was unable to enforce such restrictions. Meanwhile, the loss of land to Russian settlers increased tensions between the indigenous and immigrant population. Moreover, Russian merchants employed exploitive practices similar to those used elsewhere in Siberia. Tuvans implored the local government officials to limit this exploitation, and then began to protest more vehemently, at times resorting to violence. In turn, Russians called for Tsarist military protection against "native attacks and revolts."[111] Eventually (1885) the Tsar decreed that a Russian frontier okrug with a Russian administration be set up to deal with issues of Russian trade in Tuva.

Gold mines attracted Russians as early as the 1830s and by the 1870s drew large numbers of immigrants. Permanent settlements could now be established if limited to 200 Russians. Tuvans provided the mines with foodstuffs and were occasionally hired as miners.

While increasingly tied economically to Russia, Tuvans still looked south to their cultural roots. Many aspired to a united Tuva and Mongolia. With the onset of the Chinese Revolution, Tuva provided forces to fight for Western Mongolia's independence. The question of its own fate arose. Tuvan leaders turned to Moscow to ask that Tuva be included in Russia, and in 1914 the Tsarist government proclaimed a protectorate over Tuva. This appears to have encouraged Russian settlement, for the Russian population grew from 2,100 to 8,200 between 1910 and 1916.[112]

During the years immediately prior to and after the October Revolution the political status of Tuva was unclear.[113] Shortly after the February Revolution Russians in Tuva held a congress to support the Provisional government. Meanwhile, at least some members of the Tuvan elite looked elsewhere for leadership, entering into relations with both Mongolia and China. Others sought independence:

> the Uryankhai people declare that from now on they are free from the Russian government, that they will govern themselves in full independence and consider themselves a free people, dependent on no one.[114]

Shortly after the Revolution, Soviet power was declared, and the new Soviet government proposed that Tuva join the Russian Federated Republic as a national territory. Relations with Russians, however, deteriorated during the course of the civil war when both Red and White forces confiscated Tuvan livestock for food and transport. Tuvans retaliated by destroying Russian settlements.[115] Meanwhile both Chinese and Mongols used the breakdown of order to increase their presence in Tuva and to put forward claims to the region.[116]

In 1921 the Uryankhai *kray* soviet allowed the Tuvan people to democratically decide their future: they voted for the establishment of an independent government. Thus a nominally independent Tannu-Tuva (Tuva People's Republic) was established, under Soviet supervision, and viewed by both the USSR and China as a buffer state. Russians living in Tuva were given the status of privileged foreigners rather than granted full citizenship. The first political leader of the Tuvan People's Republic, Prime Minister Donduk, was a confirmed pan-Mongolist and Buddhist. His government declared Lamaism the state religion, required religious training for young Tuvans, and argued for reunification with Mongolia.[117] Buryat and Kalmyk church leaders supported this revivalist movement and played an active role in its propagation.[118] Fearful of a pan-Mongolism allying the Tuvans with the Khalka Mongols, Buryats and Kalmyks, the Soviet government decided to act. It encouraged the substitution of Tuvan geographic names for Mongol ones, and emphasized the Turkic ancestry of the Tuvans by introducing a literary language based not on a Mongol, but on a "neo-Turkic latinized alphabet."[119] In 1929 a Soviet-orchestrated purge replaced Donduk with Solchak Toka, a Moscow-trained, dependable communist.[120] The USSR also successfully encouraged the granting of full citizenship to the Russian inhabitants.

In 1944 the Little Khural, a body of thirty persons parallel to the USSR's Central Committee, petitioned the latter body for Tuva's admission into the USSR. Tuva was incorporated as an autonomous oblast in the RSFSR. It was elevated to ASSR status in 1961. Kolarz, analyzing the reasons for the Soviet take-over, suggested that the economic resources the region offered and the strategic position it held *vis-à-vis* some of the Soviet Union's other resources ("a fortress guarding the approaches to the Kuzbas") were not the only reasons prompting absorption.[121] He noted that the Tuvan communists, following the Soviet policy of stressing the Turkic elements of Tuvan culture, emphasized their ethnic links to the Altay and Khakassy when lobbying for a merger with the USSR.[122] Kolarz surmised that the Altay and Khakassy might similarly stress these links in arguing an opposite movement:

> From the point of view of Oirot nationalists in particular, there was no reason why these peoples should belong to the Russian Empire instead of uniting with the Tuvinians in an independent State. As long as there was an independent Tuva, there was always the possibility that Oirots and Khakassians might gravitate towards that country.[123]

The absorption of Tuva into the USSR stimulated a large influx of Russians: by 1959 they constituted 40.1 percent of Tuva's population. Since then, with strong population growth among the indigenous population,[124] the Russian share has decreased. In the last few years, the relative Tuvan majority has even grown faster, as Russians leave the ASSR. The exodus has been provoked by increasingly numerous and violent attacks by Tuvans. While malicious actions toward Russians by Tuvans have been dated to the 1970s by an article in *Literaturnaya Rossiya* (August 3, 1990), conditions have worsened recently: the Soviet press attributed eighty-eight deaths in the first months of 1990 to inter-ethnic hostility.[125] During the first half of 1990, about 3,000 Russians left Tuva.[126]

A Tuvan Popular Front formed in 1989, with members spanning much of the political spectrum. Within the Front, there are those who question the validity of Tuva's absorption into the USSR. While it is unclear whether some members hold a vision of a pan-Mongol state, as does the Buryat-Mongol Peoples' Party, relations with Mongolia may rest on a shaky foundation. Chairman of the Supreme Soviet of Tuva and a leader of the Front, Kaadyr-ool Bicheldey, has challenged Tuva's frontiers, and put forth territorial claims to areas of the Mongolian People's Republic (as well as of the Krasnoyarsk *kray*).[127] A separate, independent Tuva is more likely the goal of the more radical elements.

According to various Soviet newspapers,[128] many young Tuvans support priority access to jobs and housing for Tuvans; an oath of loyalty to the ASSR from all non-Tuvans, the emigration of Russian-speaking people who have arrived since 1944; proportional representation of Tuvans in the management of all economic agencies; and an election to the capital city's soviet from the whole of Tuva, to ensure a Tuvan majority.[129] A survey in one mining town, carried out in 1989, found 23 percent of the Tuvan respondents in favor of only Tuvans living in the republic.

Conclusion

Walker Connor has suggested that "ethnonationalism appears to feed on adversity and denial," but "also appears to feed on concessions."[130] Confronted with the overwhelming physical and cultural degradation which the last several decades of Soviet power have wrought in their homelands, but recently freed from a fear-imposed silence to protest, Native groups now seek the power to reverse these processes of decline. In what is in effect a bioregionalist analysis, they identify the foundations for the environmental and cultural destruction in the alienation of these lands from their guardianship. Without intimate ties to the land, *prishlie* have violated it, threatening long-term sustainability. With severed ties, Natives have suffered a disorientation strong enough to threaten cultural survival. National movements seek to restore Native control over land and resources, and in doing so, to regain command of their cultural, social and economic environments as well as their physical one.

Espousing a separation of native spheres from those non-Native, indigenous Siberians do not necessarily refute the process of internationalization but seek to realize its first stage, that of the full "flowering" of national identity. This they feel is requisite to true multiculturalism, as distinct from assimilation or acculturation. Currently, to partially withdraw from the external state is to draw on internal cultural strengths – and hopefully to develop these. Nationalists also look outward, past state boundaries, to forge alliances, cultural and political, with sororal nations in their quest for self-determination.

The quest for true self-determination is surely a futile one, given the demographic makeup of Siberia. Rather, Native groups for the most part will remain part of Russian-dominated territorial units, whether these continue to answer to the Russian government, or to another political entity. They will thus remain subordinated to the very system, rooted in a colonial history, which has gradually disempowered them. What negotiated arrangements for partial recovery of control can be reached remain to be seen.

Notes

I would like to thank Ken Bilski for comments on a draft of this chapter, and Amanda Tate and Hilary Rose for making the maps. Much of the information on the "Peoples of the North" was gathered during the tenure of a Title VIII post-doctoral fellowship at Hoover Institution, 1989–1990.

1 The corresponding figures for Siberia's share in the former USSR are 60% of the territory, 8 percent of the population.
 2 See Alan Wood, "From Conquest to Revolution: the Historical Dimension," in Alan Wood, ed., *Siberia: Problems and Prospects for Regional Development* (London: Croom Helm, 1987), p. 42, for population figures.
 3 The North or regions "equated with the North" due to climate and demo-graphic-economic characteristics. For the definition of the Soviet "North," see S.V. Slavin, *The Soviet North. Present Development and Prospects* (Moscow: Progress Publishers, 1972). A twenty-sixth people, the Sami (Lapps), live on the Kola Peninsula, in the European North of the RSFSR.
 4 During the Tsarist period they had also been lumped together for policy pur-poses, but with other peoples as well.
 5 Later simply "Peoples of the North" (*narody Severa*), as distinguished from the more numerous "Peoples of Siberia" (*narody Sibiri*), including the Altays, Buryats, Khakassy, Tuvans, and Yakuts. Most recently the former have adopted the term "Small-numbered peoples of the North" (*malochislennie narody Severa*).
 6 Henry R. Huttenbach, "Moscovy's Penetration of Siberia: the Colonization Process 1555–1689," in Michael Rywkin, ed., *Russian Colonial Expansion to 1917* (London: Mansell, 1988), p. 76.
 7 *Ibid.*, p. 78.
 8 George V. Lantzeff, *Siberia in the Seventeenth Century. A Study of the Colonial Administration*, University of California Publications in History, vol. 30 (Berkeley: University of California Press, 1943), pp. 90–91.
 9 Huttenbach, "Muscovy's Penetration," p. 86; Lantzeff, *Siberia*, pp. 107–110.
10 Huttenbach, "Moscovy's Penetration," p. 86.
11 Though Russians hunted furs, most of Siberia's "soft gold" was taken by indig-enous peoples and turned over to the state as tribute or traded for Russian commodities.
12 Vladilen A. Tugolukov, *Idushie Poperek Khrebtov* (Krasnoyarsk: Krasnoyarskoe knizhnoe izdatel'stvo, 1980), p. 101.
13 Marjorie M. Balzer, *Strategies of Ethnic Survival: Interaction of Russians and Khanty (Ostiak) in Twentieth Century Siberia* (Ann Arbor, Mich.: University Microfilms, 1980), pp. 334–335.
14 Zoya Sokolova, *Na prostorakh Sibiri* (Moscow: Izdatel'stvo "Russkiy yazyk," 1981), p. 17.
15 The issue of national consciousness among the peoples of the North is not well studied. Available Soviet sources which hold that these peoples had no national consciousness, but identified only with the clan, are suspect due to their adher-ence to a strict Morganian social evolutionary bias (e.g. M.G. Levin and L.P. Potapov, eds., *The Peoples of Siberia* [Chicago: University of Chicago Press, 1964]). However, if a national consciousness did exist prior to the Revolution among some or all of these peoples, it was none the less much strengthened by the creation of a literary language (a single one, in more than one case, for groups speaking a large number of dialects), a national elite, and the desig-nation of official homelands for a number of the peoples.

16 Renamed *autonomous* okrugs in 1977.
17 See Yu. V. Popkov, 1990, *Protsess internatsionalizatsii u narodnostey Severa* (Novosibirsk: Nauka, 1990), esp. chapters 2, 3; V.I. Boyko, *Sotsial'no-economischeskoe razvitie narodnostey Severa* (Novosibirsk: Nauka), chapter 4.
18 N. Amyl'skiy, "Kogda zatsvetayut zharkie tsvety (O rabote tuzemnykh sovetov i sudov v Turukhanskom rayone)," *Severnaya Aziya*, 1928, no. 3, p. 55.
19 Tsentralnyy Gosudarstvennyy Arkhiv Oktyabrskoy Revolutsii (TsGAOR). Fond 3977: Komitet Severa pri VTsIKe. Op. 1. Delo 300. "Protokoly tuzem-nykh sobraniy Dal'ne-Vostochnogo kraya, Irkutskoy gubernii, Arkhangel'skoy gubernii i Buryato-Mongol'skoy ASSR." II.77, 104.
20 K.A. Zabelin, K.A., "Ocherki po ekonomike Severo-Baykal'skogo rayona," *Zhizn' Buryatii*, 1930, no. 4, pp. 35–37.
21 TsGAOR, f. 3977, op. 1, d. 300, I. 100.
22 Amyl'skiy, "Kogda zatsvetayut . . .," p. 55; Zabelin, "Ocherki po . . .," p. 42.
23 For some national *rayony* were identified, but these low-level political-adminis-trative units soon lost any designation as specifically "national" territories.
24 The Vitimo-Olekma (Evenk) and the Okhotsk-Even National Okrugs were abolished late in the 1930s. The disappearance of the latter has been explained by the fact that its center, Nogaevo, became a transit point for Gulag-bound prisoners, and Dalstroy (the Main Construction Administration of the Far North), preferred to have complete control over the area. This explanation is not fully satisfactory; for further discussion, see Gail Fondahl, *Native Economy and Northern Development: Reindeer Husbandry in Transbaykalia* (Ann Arbor, Mich.: University Microfilms, 1989), p. 109, note 44.

The remaining national okrugs were renamed autonomous okrugs in 1977. At present Evenk activists in the region of the former Vitim-Olekma National Okrug seek to re-establish the administrative unit (David Anderson, "Social Movements of the Zabaikal'skie Evenks. State, Civil Society and Economy in a Siberian Province," unpublished Masters thesis, University of Wisconsin, Madison, 1990, p. 85).
25 Affirmative action policy also "invites accusations of reverse discrimination by increasingly nationalistic Russians" (Marjorie M. Balzer, "Ethnicity without power: the Siberian Khanty in Soviet Society," *Slavic Review*, 1983, vol. 42, no. 4, p. 648).
26 E.g., Alitet Nemtushkin, "Bol' moya, Evenkiya," *Sovetskaya Kul'tura*, July 28, 1988; Yuriy Rytkheu, "Lozungi i Amulety," *Komsomol'skaya Pravda*, May 19, 1988; Vladimir Sangi, "Otchuzhdenie," *Sovetskaya Rossiya*, September 11, 1988.
27 I.S. Gurvich, ed., *Etnicheskoe razvitie narodnostey Severa v sovetskiy period* (Moscow: Nauka, 1987), p. 94.
28 N.V. Isakova and V.V. Markhinin, "Vsaimodeystvie natsional'nykh kul'tur: problemy i poiski resheniy," typescript of paper presented at the II Soviet-Canadian colloquium "Russia–Quebec," July-August 1990, pp. 10–11.
29 *Osnovnye Pokazateli Razvitiya Ekonomiki i Kul'tury Malochislennykh Narodov Severa (1980–1989 gody).* (Moscow: Goskomstat RSFSR, 1990), p. 9; A.I. Pika and B.B. Prokhorov, "Bol'shie problemy malykh narodov," *Kommu-nist*, 1988, no. 16, p. 77.
30 Unemployment in 1987 ran betwen 15–18 percent, and was on the increase

among eleven of the twenty-six peoples of the North. V.I. Boyko, ed., *Kont-septsiya sotsial'nogo i ekonomicheskogo razvitiya narodnostey Severa na period do 2010 g.* (Novosibirsk, 1990), p. 45. See also Yeremey Aypin, "Ne neft'yu edinoy," *Moskovskie Novosti*, January 8, 1989, pp. 8–9.

31 Anderson, "Social Movements," pp. 65–66.

32 *Ibid.*, p. 65ff, esp. 66n.

33 Pika and Prokhorov, "Bol'shie problemy . . .," p. 80.

34 *Ibid.*

35 Aypin, "Ne neft'yu edinoy."

36 Asen Balikci, "The Process of Internationalization and the Political Renaissance Movement Among the Khazim River Khanti (Western Siberia)," typescript, p. 9.

37 M.A. Kolesnikov, "Orientatsii evenkov Severa Irkutskoy oblasti na traditsionnye i netraditsionnye vidy zanyatii," in *Narodnosti Severa: Problemy i Perspektivy ekonomicheskogo i sotsial'nogo razvitiya.* (Novosibirsk, 1983)., p. 19.

38 *Ibid.*

39 Vladimin Sangi, *Antologii folklora narodnaste i Sibitii Severa i Dalnego Vostoka* (Krasnoiarsk: Kn. izd-vo, 1989).

40 Balikci, "Process of Internationalization," p. 10. Similarly, the Evenks of the Severnyy *sovkhoz* in the northern Chita Oblast have established a thirty-kilometer radius "independent zone" around their farm (Anderson, "Social Movements," pp. 86, 107).

41 E.g., E.A. Oborotova, "Narody severa v sovremennom mire. Vzglyady i pozitsii," *Sovetskaya etnografiya*, 1988, no. 5, pp. 146–151; O. Voronin and L. Shinkarev, "Dayte slovo Kukagiru," *Izvestiya*, April 7, 1989.

　The idea of reservations has been hotly debated in the press. See, for instance, Yuriy Rytkheu, "Beloe Bezmolvie?," *Ogonek*, April 1989, no. 17, pp. 20–21, for the opposing viewpoint. Kathleen Mihalisko gives an overview of the discussion ("North American-style Native reservations in the Soviet North?" *Report on the USSR*, 1989, no. 29, pp. 31–34). At present, the Khants and Mansi are looking at the Sosva River Basin as an area in which to try out this form of territorial protection (Andrey Golovnev, pers. comm., April 10, 1991).

42 V.I. Boyko, "The Peoples of the North of the USSR on the Way to Self-Government," typescript of paper presented at the II Soviet-Canadian colloquium "Russia–Quebec," July-August 1990, p. 11.

43 *Ibid.*, p. 15.

44 *Materialy S"ezda Malochislennykh Narodov Severa* (Moscow: Sovromenik, 1990). This document has been translated, with preface, in *Indigenous Peoples of the Soviet North*, IWGIA Document 67, Copenhagen, July 1990.

45 "International Labour Organisation: Convention Concerning Indigenous and Tribal Peoples in Independent Countries," *International Legal Matters*, 1989, no. 28, pp. 1386, 1387; M.I. Mongo, "The Legislative Foundations of the National Policy in the Period of Perestroika and the Destiny of Small-Numbered Peoples of the North," report prepared for the II Soviet-Canadian colloquium "Russia–Quebec," July-August 1990, p. 14.

46 Indeed, many question the true representativeness of its members, who are for the most part members of the Native intelligentsia who have spent the larger part of their lives in Moscow or Leningrad.

47 "Yamal-for our progeny" (a mainly Nentsy association on the Yamal Peninsula); "Salvation of Yugria" (the Khant and Mansi area); "Revival" (the association of Native peoples of the Evenk Autonomous Okrug).

48 *Report on the USSR*, November 15, 1991, p. 36.

49 *Report on the USSR*, October 12, 1990, p. 28.

50 FBIS-SOV-91-215, 6 November 1991.

51 For instance, *Golos Sterkha* [The Bulletin of the Finno-Ugrian Peoples of the USSR], featured an article about the Nordic Sami Council in Fennoscandia, as an example of how effective cross-border alliances can be. (*Golos Sterkha*, first edition, 1990.)

52 The Sami of the Kola Peninsula, one of the people of the North (but not of Siberia) have contacts across the border with Sami of Fennoscandia, and have participated in several pan-Sami conferences in the last couple of years.

53 A non-governmental organization of Inuit and Yupik (Eskimos) from Alaska, Canada and Greenland, with NGO status at the UN.

54 The Chukchi, long in a position of dominance *vis-à-vis* the Eskimos of the Chukotka Peninsula, now feel somewhat jealous over the attention being paid to this small nation by Alaska in particular, and America more generally. Here we see an example of the competition between non-titular groups which Bremmer suggests in table 1.1 of the introduction to this volume.

55 Lars Toft Rasmussen, "Completing the Circle: The Inuit Circumpolar Conference and the Soviet Eskimos," *Questions Sibériennes Bulletin N° 1, Peuples autochtones*, 1990, pp. 83–86.

56 Ronald Wixman, *The Peoples of the USSR. An Ethnographic Handbook* (Armonk, NY: M.E. Sharpe, 1984), p. 9.

57 L.P. Potapov, "The Altays," in M.G. Levin and L.P. Potapov, eds., *The Peoples of Siberia* (Chicago: University of Chicago Press, 1964), p. 320.

58 Wixman, *Peoples of USSR*, p. 101.

59 Walter Kolarz *The Peoples of the Soviet Far East* (New York: Frederick A. Praeger, 1954), p. 172.

60 L.P. Potapov, L.P., "The Khakasy," in M.G. Levin and L.P. Potapov, eds., *The Peoples of Siberia* (Chicago: University of Chicago Press, 1964), pp. 345, 351.

61 *Ibid.*, p. 370.

62 Kolarz, *Peoples of Soviet Far East*, pp. 173, 175.

63 Though barely – see table 20.2 for 1926 figures.

64 Kolarz, *Peoples of Soviet Far East* pp. 169, 177.

65 See note 23 above.

66 Most other Turkic peoples of the RSFSR were growing at rates between 15 and 25 percent during this period.

67 A. Tchoudoïakov, "La tragédie des Chors," *Questions Sibériennes Bulletin N° 1, Peuples autochtones*, 1990, p. 31.

68 *Ibid.*, p. 32.

69 Kolarz, *Peoples of Soviet Far East*, p. 175.

70 Wixman, *Peoples of USSR* p. 189.

71 Juha Janhunen, "Ethnic activism among the South Siberian Turks," *Questions Sibériennes Bulletin N° 1, Peuples autochtones*, 1990, pp. 57–60. The SCC is based in St. Petersburg.

72 *Ibid.*, p. 59.

73 *Ibid.*
74 "NativeNet: An Invitation from Siberia!" electronic mail message from Gary S. Trujillo, dated December 14, 1989.
75 *Ibid.*
76 The Soviet of the Gorno-Altay ASSR also declared the establishment of an "ecological economic zone." Foreign investment will be solicited in this zone to develop such relatively low-impact commercial activities as medicinal herb collection and tourism (FBIS-SOV-90-212).
77 Caroline Humphrey, *Karl Marx Collective. Economy, Society and Religion in a Siberian Collective Farm* (Cambridge: Cambridge University Press, 1983), p. 28.
78 K.V. Vyatkina, "The Buryats," in M.G. Levin and L.P. Potapov, eds., *The Peoples of Siberia* (Chicago: University of Chicago Press, 1964), p. 209.
79 Humphrey, *Karl Marx Collective*, p. 27; Robert A. Rupen, "The Buriat Intelligentsia," *Far Eastern Quarterly*, 1956, vol. X, no. 3, pp. 385, 386.
80 Rupen, "Buriat Intelligentsia," p. 385.
81 *Ibid.*, p. 384. The Japanese sponsored a pan-Mongol congress in Chita in 1919, attended by Buryats, which promoted a Greater Mongol State and called for the expulsion of Russian colonists living east of Lake Baikal (Kolarz, *People of Soviet Far East*, p. 119).
82 Humphrey, *Karl Marx Collective* p. 31.
83 Kolarz, *Peoples of Soviet Far East*, p. 123.
84 See Boris Chichlo, "Histoire de la formation des territoires autonomes chez les peuples Turco-Mongols de Sibérie," *Cahiers du Monde Russe et Soviétique*, 1987, vol. XXVII, nos. 3–4, especially p. 369, for "before" and "after" maps.
85 Kolarz, *Peoples of Soviet Far East* p. 123.
86 Twenty-five percent of all three titular areas, taken together.
87 Buryats now constitute 24 percent of the ASSR's population.
88 Humphrey, *Karl Marx Collective*, p. 33.
89 The Buryat SSR Council of Ministers adopted a resolution to this effect in September 1991, which evoked demonstrations from opposed parties. FBIS-SOV-91-77, September 12, 1991, p. 81; FBIS-SOV-91-194, October 7, 1991, p. 61.
90 Daria Fane, "RSFSR's Nationalities Problems: The Autonomous Republics," typescript.
91 Kolarz, *Peoples of Soviet Far East*, p. 116. The Soviet government also early on encouraged contact between the Buryats, Khalka Mongols, and the other Mongol people of the USSR, the Kalmyks. For instance, in 1931 Moscow hosted a conference for these three nations, the topic of which was language reforms, including the adoption of a Latin alphabet for all three groups (p. 115n).
92 Rupen, "Buriat Intelligentsia," p. 388.
93 *Ibid.*, p. 392, esp. p. 394, n. 24.
94 Fane, "RSFSR's Nationalities Problems."
95 Goskomstat RSFSR, *Natsional'nyy Sostave Naseleniya RSFSR po dannym vsesoyuznoy perepisi naselenie 1989 g.* (Moscow: Respublikanskiy informatsionno-izdatel'skiy tsentr, 1990), p. 152.
96 Terence Armstrong, *Russian Settlement in the North* (Cambridge: Cambridge University Press, 1965), p. 113.

97 *Ibid.*
98 Kolarz, *Peoples of Soviet Far East*, p. 103.
99 Sakha is the self-designation of the Yakut.
100 The Yakut population actually dropped between 1926 and 1959 (table 20.1). This is attributed primarily to severe losses during the collectivization drive (Wixman, *Peoples of USSR* p. 220).
101 Ann Sheehy, "Racial Disturbances in Yakutsk," *Radio Liberty Research Report* 251/86, July 1, 1986.
102 Marjorie M. Balzer, "Yakut," *Encyclopedia of World Cultures, USSR Volume* (New Haven: Yale University Press, forthcoming). Less dramatic but telling events also evidence the inter-ethnic tensions. Izvestiya published an article in 1987 about a number of Yakut teachers who had been allegedly fired for incompetency, but claimed that their dismissal was due to their nationality. Complaints against one centered around her grading Russian students more harshly than Yakut students; her response was that Russian teachers did the same to Yakuts. Yakut teachers were also accused of "preaching nationalism". *Izvestiya*, July 22, 1987; excerpted in *Current Digest of the Soviet Press*, vol. XXXIX, no. 29, p. 20.
103 FBIS-SOV-90-231, November 30, 1990, p. 87; *Report on the USSR*, August 23, 1991, p. 36.
104 Fane, "RSFSR's Nationalities Problems."
105 Kolarz, *Peoples of Soviet Far East* p. 102.
106 *Ibid.*
107 Almost half of the Evenk population of the USSR lives in the Yakut ASSR (only 14 percent live in the Evenk Autonomous Okrug). In 1979, 85 percent of the Evenks living in the Yakut ASSR spoke Yakut as their first language. (V.I. Boyko, "Chislennost', rasselenie i yazykovaya situatsiya u narodnostey Severa na sovremennom etape," in *Problemy Soveremennogo Sotsial'nogo Razvitiya Narodnostey Severa* [Novosibirsk: Nauka, 1987], pp. 40, 47.)
108 Piers Vitebsky, "Reindeer herders of Northern Yakutia: A Report from the Field," *Polar Record*, 1989, vol. 25, no. 54, p. 217.
109 *Sovetskaya Rossiya*, August 19, 1989. National rayons were abolished in the 1930s; this is the first instance of this level of national territorial recognition being granted since then.
110 FBIS-SOV-91-224, November 20, 1991, p. 63.
111 Robert A. Rupen, "The Absorption of Tuva," in Thomas T. Hammond, ed., *The Anatomy of Communist Takeovers* (New Haven: Yale University Press, 1975), p. 149.
112 Rupen, "Absorption of Tuva," p. 150.
113 Chichlo, "Histoire," pp. 380–381.
114 Statement made by "representative of the Russian and Tuvan peoples," June 18, 1918, during the concomitant meetings of the Fifth Congress of Russian Population of Uryankhai and the Congress of Uryankhai Khoshuns (Native leaders). Quoted in Yu. L. Aranchyn, *Istoricheskiy put' tuvinskogo naroda k sotsializmu* (Novosibirsk: Nauka, 1982), p. 74.
115 Chichlo, "Histoire," p. 381.
116 *Ibid.*
117 Kolarz, *Peoples of Soviet Far East* p. 156.

118 Aranchyn, p. 107.
119 Aranchyn, *Istoricheskiy* . . ., p. 167. The alphabet was changed to Cyrillic in 1941.
120 Rupen, "Absorption of Tuva," p. 151.
121 Kolarz, *Peoples of Soviet Far East*, pp. 167–168.
122 See also L.P. Potapov, "The Tuvans," in M.G. Levin and L.P. Potapov, eds., *The Peoples of Siberia* (Chicago: University of Chicago Press, 1964), p. 388.
123 Kolarz, *Peoples of Soviet Far East*, p. 168.
124 The rate of growth among the younger Tuvan population between 1959 and 1970 appeared low, though during this period, Tuvan population grew from 57 to 59 percent of the Republic's population. Anderson and Silver suggest that one explanation for the apparent low rate of growth is the permeable border with Mongolia which allowed emigration during this period. This might have been one way which Tuvans dealt with threats to their cultural integrity in the past. See Barbara Anderson and Brian D. Silver, "Some Factors in the Linguistic and Ethnic Russification of Soviet Nationalities: Is Everyone Becoming Russian?" in L. Hajda and M. Beissinger, eds., *The Nationalities Factor in Soviet Politics and Society* (Boulder; Westview Press, 1990), p. 118.
125 *Report on the USSR*, August 10, 1990, p. 27, from *Izvestiya*, July 3, 1990.
126 Ann Sheehy, "Russians the Target of Interethnic Violence in Tuva," *Report on the USSR*, September 14, 1990, p. 16.
127 *Ibid.*, p. 15; FBIS-SOV-91-212, November 1, 1991, p. 59.
128 Tuvans have condemned the accounts of events in their republic in Russian newspapers as highly biased, portraying the Tuvans very unfavorably (Sheehy, "Interethnic Violence," pp. 16–17).
129 *Ibid.*, p. 17.
130 Walker Connor, "The Politics of Ethnonationalism," *Journal of International Affairs*, 1973, vol. 27, no. 1, p. 21.

Part VIII

Conclusion

21 Conclusion: making sense of matrioshka nationalism

RAY TARAS

The rise of nationalist assertion among the many peoples that formed part of the USSR is a complex phenomenon not easily susceptible to generalization. Whether we look at the roots of such assertion, the processes that carried such assertion forward, or the political outcomes that have resulted and are by no means final, the tasks of understanding unique cultures and making sense of their political aspirations are daunting. It is little consolation to scholars that the number, scope, and variation of explanatory theories concerned with modern nationalism is equally imposing. Terminologies, taxonomies, and etiologies abound; mnay of these have universalist pretensions.

An array of definitions of nationalism exists. In tackling the subject, Louis Snyder's *Encyclopedia of Nationalism* acknowledges: "The term nationalism admits of no simple definition. It is a complex phenomenon, often vague and mysterious in character."[1] One classification of nationalism described in the *Encyclopedia* included a 1921 typology that identified, *inter alia*, "precaution nationalism" and "marginal nationalism" to go along with more obvious kinds like hegemonic or irredentist nationalisms.

If nationalism is a complex phenomenon that often induces an equal degree of scholastic obfuscation, it has engendered complex schema intended to capture its many manifestations. Few could be more complex than one designed by John Armstrong seeking to depict the emergence of national identity. Stressing boundary properties of peoples rather than the "essence" of identity, the result was a typology that included such categories as terrestrial reflection polities, nomad and sedentary nostalgias, mythomoteurs, and other factors serving to differentiate Islamic and Christian cultures from antiquity to the nineteenth century.[2] In Armstrong's defense, the complexity of empirical findings may have required such a conceptually-loaded framework.

What seems most desirable in a paradigm constructed to study the elusive topic of nationalism is parsimony and clarity. In these respects, it would be difficult to improve on the approach taken by Jewish theologian Martin Buber. The historical context in which he was writing had much in common with the post-Soviet era – incipient statehood for Israel. His

513

observations appear, therefore, to be especially salient to the study of nations emerging from the Soviet yolk.

In an essay written in 1949, just after the creation of the State of Israel, Buber rhetorically asked: "We have full independence, a state, and all that appertains to it, but where is the nation in the state? And where is that nation's spirit?"[3] While hardly a popular view to take after the birth of Israel, Buber expressed concern about "group egoism" and the nationalist program it engendered; while accepting its mobilizing efforts, he was alarmed about how egoism could produce extremism, for in hothouse conditions nationalism would know no bounds. For Buber, "formal nationalism" disclaimed that the nation was based on anything other than a national task and as a result "formal nationalism sanctions a group egoism which disclaims responsibility." Buber's critique of official Zionism went further and was, predictably, cast in terms of moral postulates: "A foundation on which the nation is regarded as an end in itself has no room for supernational ethnical demands."[4] Put in theological terms, "To be limited to one's self is to be condemned to die; to live for what is limitless is to be freed from death."[5]

Only encounters with other nations with programs of their own would, in Buber's view, lead to full recognition that other groups have rights. Extrapolating this principle from Talmudic teaching led to a prosaic yet profound conclusion whose relevance is as great today in the post-Soviet landscape: "There is no scale of values for the function of peoples. One cannot be ranked above another."[6]

Buber's approach to the national question was grounded in subtle distinctions: peoplehood involved a unity of fate; nationality, a collective awareness of this unity; and nationalism, an overconscious sentiment. Or as Michael Walzer summarized Buber, "Peoplehood is an impulse, nationality an idea, nationalism a program. The program is conceived in difficulty; it aims to mobilize the nation so as to overcome some deficiency in its common life."[7] Buber was not satisfied with such restrictive teleology and his quest was for the realization of *universalist* values – justice and truth. Walzer sorted out Buber's priorities: "federation and confederation represent something less in his mind; and statehood is entirely open-ended, power and possibility, nothing more."[8] Yet it is power and possibility that characterize the Soviet successor states in their first years of independence. How they make good on the possibilities presented to them is a question for a succeeding generation of scholars to evaluate.

Our study has described the processes that produced nationalist assertion throughout the areas that formerly constituted the Soviet empire, that is, the pathways taken by different peoples to power and possibility. In the case of European peoples more than in the case of Soviet Muslims, the effort was to regain national identities rather than create or define them. In addition to national identity, however, the case studies have examined the less ephemeral issues of political organizing, institution- and state-building. These tasks were in many ways inseparable from the emergence of nationalist agendas. Theoretical investigations of the interconnected nature of these processes, though uncommon, have also been more lucid. Thus Anthony Giddens described how the expansion of state sovereignty helped foster the identity of subjects as *citizens* of a political community. Nationalism was associated with the "administrative unification of the state" and, in turn, "the expansion of state sovereignty means that those subject to it are in some sense – initially vague, but growing more and more definite and precise – aware of their membership in a political community and of the rights and obligations such membership confers."[9] Giddens' important point is that sovereignty and, presumably even more so, state-hood – when attained by peoples who for a long time possessed the status of mere political subsystems – are not the outcomes, but part of the process of national renaissance. It is a point in large part substantiated by our case studies.

Given the resurgence of nationalist movements at the end of the twentieth century – no longer of the spurious kind described by an earlier generation of Leninists as "national liberation movements" but *bona fide* ones – it is crucial that social scientists be armed with powerful theory. Yet, as we have suggested, students may be deterred from operationalizing theories because of the myriad of approaches available, all with varying degrees of applicability to empirical research. Some theories and paradigms appear too grand and others too micro, some too universalist and still others too culturally relativist. Middle-range theories appear to offer most promise, and in this chapter we review some of these. What is clear from the sad experience of exponents of Marx's social science is that we do well to avoid superimposing on complex historical phenomena and processes one schema, one analytical framework, one person's etiology. No single theory can account for the historical path travelled in the early 1990s in the former Soviet Union by Balts and Turkic peoples, Uniates and Buddhists, industrialized sectors and communities of reindeer herders. *Fin de siècle* social science needs to be wary of any form of determinism – historical, economistic, nationalist, even liberal-democratic.

The remainder of this chapter is divided into four parts. First, I briefly assess the value of *comparative social research* of the kind presented in this volume: qualitative case studies offering interpretative, holistic analysis. Political events of the scale that occurred at the beginning of the 1990s are rare in world history: the Roman empire declined but once, the Ottoman empire died after one protracted illness, the Soviet empire also rose and fell once. The opportunity for social scientists to study the process termed state formation presents itself very infrequently, therefore, and it seems important to engage in critical introspection concerning the merits and limitations of our comparative exercise.

Following this brief epistemological exposé, I next consider specific theoretical issues that have particular relevance for making sense of national awakening in what was the USSR. I propose no new explanatory theories; rather, I test the adequacy of selected analytical frameworks in existence. The objective is to suggest ways of seeing the recent political history of fifteen Soviet republics at three points in time: when they were still governed by Moscow; when they began to appropriate power; and when they exercised power in their own right. At each time the focus is on the part played by nationalist assertion.

The second section of this chapter, accordingly, addresses the question of *ethnic political mobilization*. Focusing on the early years of perestroika and glasnost, this analysis seeks to capture the processes of nation-building or -rebuilding. What are the principal theories that offer alternative understandings of this phenomenon? Which framework appears to provide greatest explanatory power for the rise of nationalism in the last years of the USSR? What methodology can most parsimoniously present and order the empirical findings on ethnic political mobilization reported in the individual chapters?

The third section returns to the paradigm advanced in the introductory chapter. It examines the degree to which titular nationalities, non-titulars, and the Soviet center interacted with each other as hypothesized during the process of state formation. This section, then, seeks to describe *strategies* followed and not followed by national groups once it had become clear that the Leninist party-state had begun to unravel. Evidence on these strategies, provided in individual chapters, is aggregated and ordered in terms of different combinations of interaction among titulars, non-titulars, and the center. This syncretic analysis may reveal patterns in an otherwise confusing – the realist school would call anarchic – system of state interaction.

The final section concerns new forms of interaction among the independent states that formerly made up the USSR. It considers the impact that national and ethnic conflicts – tied to a global wave of "subgroupism" – may have on the *international politics* that are emerging and, conversely, the ways that actors in the international system can mediate such conflicts. A distinctive phenomenon of the post-Soviet political landscape is the presence of new minority groups in newly independent states, often having co-nationals in other states. The potential for new axes of ethnic conflict, as well as for conciliating cleavages through third-party mediation, is assessed.

Methodological considerations

We learn from case studies of fifteen ex-Soviet republics and three sub-republic peoples that theories of nationalism alone cannot fully explain the events that occurred in the final months of the USSR's existence. For social scientists examining modern forms of nationalism, matters become complicated when – against the odds and to the surprise of many – nations actually attain statehood. Is there adequate and sufficient social science theory to shed light on this rather exotic process?

Chapters in this book provide a contrast between Soviet republics that began institution-building early on, and those that did not give it high priority. Clearly there is some way to go in mapping out the conditions under which state-building proceeds at a different pace yet the final political outcome – statehood – is identical. None the less our case studies have demonstrated the need to go beyond an exclusive focus on the phase favored by social science – national consciousness-raising and nation-building. The suddenness of the Soviet collapse shifted attention away from this – as it turned out – antecedent phase of state-building and drew it instead to the state-building process itself, with its numerous attendant problems.

At the same time, given the cultural uniqueness and peculiarities of insurgent modern national and ethnic groups – it is, after all, the claim to distinctiveness, to being a "nation-in-itself," that is at the heart of individual groups' ambitions – it is important to produce thick descriptions of previously "hidden" nations and emergent peoples. Cultural sensitivity, proficiency in what seem exotic languages, and extensive fieldwork become crucial components in the writing of ethnographies. Again, in looking at what were Soviet peoples from the bottom up, the individual chapters depicted differing, national roads to statehood or to greater self-determination.

To resolve the double research imperatives of capturing the pattern of state-building cross-nationally while remaining sensitive to national and ethnic idiosyncrasies, the research in this volume had to be case-oriented as opposed to variable-oriented, and historical as opposed to causal. This implies that we have complied with Charles Ragin's strictures about the case method:

> case-oriented methods are holistic – they treat cases as whole entities and not as collections of parts . . . Second, causation is understood conjuncturally. Outcomes are analyzed in terms of intersections of conditions, and it is usually assumed that any of several combinations of conditions might produce a certain outcome.[10]

Accordingly, nationalist assertion – a political outcome common to all Soviet republic – was the product of conjunctural factors (collapse of central authority, appealing mass movements, new leaders, old leaders in new guise) whose combination varied from one republic to the next.

Objections may be raised about the extent to which our volume involves truly comparative inquiry. Przeworski and Teune posited that comparative research had to proceed simultaneously at two levels, within-system and system. The case studies here were concerned with within-system variables – factors that engendered nationalist assertion among peoples – as well as with systemic ones – the parallel processes of the center's collapse and republic state-building. But to satisfy Przeworski and Teune's defintion of comparative inquiry, a system level variable would have to be used to explain variation across systems (that is, republics) in within-system relationships.[11] Our inquiry would have to study how collapse of central authority (a system level variable) explained differences among republics in within-system relationships – the strength of the relationship between nationalist assertion and commitment to achieving statehood by individual republics.

A more accurate description of our approach is contained in Theda Skocpol's summary of alternative strategies for carrying out empirically-grounded research informed by theory:

> one can readily identify three major strategies for bringing history and theoretical ideas to bear on one another. Some historical sociologists apply a single theoretical model to one or more of many possible instances covered by the model. Other historical sociologists want to discover causal regularities that account for specifically defined historical processes or outcomes, and explore *alternative* hypotheses to achieve that end. Still other historical sociologists, who tend to be skeptical of the value of general models or hypotheses, use concepts to develop what might best be called meaningful historical interpretations. Each of these strategies may be applied to a single historical case or to two or more cases through comparative historical investigations.[12]

Our contributors are not historical sociologists. Moreover, the phenomena studied in this book remain too fresh and incomplete to fall under the purview of this subdiscipline of the social sciences. But it should be clear that our epistemological preferences are grounded in the third strategy Skocpol identified – interpretative analysis. Given the complexity and opaqueness of Soviet peoples, a search for *causal regularities* can prove elusive. Rarely do social phenomena have a single cause, and the most we could hope for is to capture convergent causal conditions, that is, a multiplicity of causes combining in some way to produce a specific outcome. Ragin comes to our aid here. Developing John Stuart Mill's idea of "chemical causation" which required the right ingredients for change, he asserted: "It is the intersection of a set of conditions in time and in space that produces many of the large-scale qualitative changes, as well as many of the small-scale events, that interest social scientists."[13]

Given the paradoxical, perhaps even poignant, part played by Gorbachev in the destruction of the USSR, a *functional explanation* that underscores unintentionality may attract some scholars. Applying Jon Elster's account, a functional explanation would read: Institution X is explained by its function Y for group Z if and only if:

1   Y (collapse of Soviet power) is an effect of X (perestroika);
2   Y is beneficial for Z (titular nationalities);
3   Y is unintended by the actor (Gorbachev) producing X;
4   Y, or at least the causal relation between X and Y, is unrecognized by the actors in Z;
5   Y maintains X by a causal feedback loop passing through Z.[14]

While we discover that the first three conditions for functional explanation are readily met, it is stretching credulity to posit that Kravchuk, Landsbergis, and Yeltsin had not recognized the linkage between perestroika and Soviet collapse and, further, did nothing to take advantage of the unintended consequences that followed (condition 4). The fifth condition, too, was not satisfied: Elster argued how successful instances of the paradigm required a lenient interpretation of condition 5 – it was automatically fulfilled whenever the first four criteria were. But consequence laws were not enough, in his view, to assure the validity of functional explanation. Fine-tuning the functional explanation may yet provide social scientists with a viable paradigm for understanding complex and seemingly accidental events.

The interpretative approach used in this book offers a number of advantages. Skocpol observed how, first, "There is no need to move from a highly abstract model to historical specifications that may appear arbitrary or artificially ripped out of context; nor do flows of description need to be repeatedly broken to examine alternative causal hypotheses."[15] If we learn that Tatars, Chuvash, and Mari – all of whom live close to each other – engage in quite different interactions with each other as well as with central authorities, possess different national goals and apply contrasting methods to reach them, no abstract model can be contrived to account for their political behavior. Skocpol identified a second advantage of the interpretive method: "works in this genre necessarily tap into vivid contemporary sensibilities, intellectual trends, and assumptions about how the world works."[16] Put perhaps more positively than Skocpol intended, researchers are informed by state-of-the-art theoretical insights when making sense of their findings. Such an approach stimulates dialogue between ideas and evidence in a way that multivariate analysis does not. Finally, for Skocpol,

> comparative studies in this genre stress the portrayal of given times and places in much of their rich complexity, and they pay attention to the orientations of the actors as well as to the institutional and cultural contexts in which they operate. Consequently, interpretative works can seem extraordinarily vivid and full, like a good Flaubert novel.[17]

Although less lyrical than the French novelist's works, our study has aimed at providing a colorful cultural canvass of former Soviet nations and their politics.

Skocpol acknowledged, then, that "From certain philosophical points of view, the kinds of understanding of social history that interpretative works seek to convey represent the most desirable, and perhaps the only really feasible, kind of knowledge available through historical sociology."[18] Let us move beyond interpretative analysis and, in the next section, consider operationalizing a compelling and relevant methodology–qualitative comparative analysis as advanced by Ragin.

Ethnic political mobilization and the Soviet denouement

A central problem for comparative research is the limited number of cases that are comparable. This follows from the concern of social science for interpreting *significant historical outcomes* – social revolutions, regime changes, collapse of empires. As a result, as Ragin indicated, "when a comparativist interprets significant historical outcomes, he or she selects extreme values on a more general dependent variable." If it is to be manageable, comparative research *has* to adopt a limited perspective: "the problem of having too few societies on which to test theory is compounded by the fact that the interests and goals of comparative social science (and scientists) often dictate the design of studies with a small number of cases."[19] These problems did not affect our research given the felicitous, perhaps fortuitous occurrence of fifteen cases of statehood.

Ragin put forward a methodology for conducting qualitative comparative research based on Boolean analysis. Causal variables in various combinations are identified, thereby revealing key causal conjunctures. In a follow-up exercise, case-oriented elaboration develops causal conjunctures. In this way, causal explanation and historical interpretation are combined.

Ragin tested the explanatory power of three major theories of ethnic political mobilization. The first is the *developmental perspective*. It views ethnicity as a primordial category that manifests itself when regional economic inequality has adverse effects on a subnation. As Ragin summarized this view, "the underlying basis for mobilization according to developmental logic is the failure to integrate the subnation, not its relative poverty per se."[20] Examples from our study are the Muslim republics as well as autonomous areas inhabited by Tatars. These groups appeared not to have been fully drawn into national economic life, leading to alienation and subsequent revindications.

A second theory of ethnic mobilization is the *reactive ethnicity perspective*. In contrast to the developmental approach, it points to the infiltration of a subnational area by members of the dominant cultural group – not its isolation – as engendering a "cultural division of labor" and the ethnic backlash to it. Ragin again: "The dominant strata come to be seen as alien by the lower strata, and the culture of the lower strata becomes stereotyped as inferior by members of the dominant strata."[21] A clear illustration of reactive ethnicity is the Baltic peoples' sense of having been infiltrated by large-scale Russian in-migration.[22]

The third approach to ethnic mobilization is found in the *ethnic competition perspective*. For a non-dominant nation to be competitive, it needs to be large enough to challenge the core. Further, abundant natural resources and wealth enhance the prospect of political mobilization, thereby requiring resource mobilization. Under conditions of competition, "Ethnic political mobilization is sparked when ethnic groups (dominant and subordinate) are forced to compete with each other for the same rewards and resources."[23] Of former constituent republics of the USSR, only Ukraine was in a position to challenge Russian dominance.

Ragin synthesized the causal variables accounting for ethnic political mobilization underlying the three perspectives: (1) size of national groups (from the competition perspective); (2) linguistic proficiency (from the developmental perspective); (3) relative wealth (from the reactive ethnicity perspective); and (4) economic growth or decline (from all three perspectives). Adapting Ragin's coding to the Soviet context, large nations were those titular nationalities representing at least 10 percent of the overall population of the USSR; coding size presented no problem since no nation came close to this figure other than Russia and Ukraine; they were coded as large (1) and remaining nations were coded as small (0) on the size variable (S).

Soviet statistical data over the years concurred that titular nationalities of union republics in overwhelming numbers declared their nationality language to be their native tongue; all, therefore, would have been coded 1 on the linguistic base variable, making the variable insignificant.[24] In the specific context of the USSR, *ethnic homogeneity* of a republic was likely to be a factor producing variations in political mobilization since it tells us something about the degree of unity and cohesiveness of a population. Republics where titulars accounted for at least 75 percent of the population were coded 1 on the ethnic homogeneity variable (H); those with minorities of 25 percent or more were coded 0.

With regard to relative wealth (W), Ragin's measurement was regional variations in production per capita; relative wealth was coded 1 when such production was equal to or greater than the average. Our index was national income per capita during 1981–1985, before economic rot really set in. Those republics with national income levels at or above the Soviet average were coded 1, those below it were coded 0.[25]

Finally, Ragin assessed the growth variable (G) in terms of net in-migration, which he took to signify advancing economic status. Given the relative immobility of the population of Central Asia, which would skew results if this index was applied to the Soviet case, combined with the ready availability of more direct indices of advance or decline, we do not follow Ragin here. One possible measure could be the average annual rate of growth of consumption per capita between 1960 and 1986 – an especially

Table 21.1. *Data on first-order titular Soviet nationalities*

	S	H	W	G	E
Russia	1	1	1	1	1
Ukraine	1	0	1	0	1
Belarus	0	1	1	1	1
Moldova	0	0	1	1	1
Lithuania	0	1	1	1	1
Latvia	0	0	1	1	1
Estonia	0	0	1	0	1
Georgia	0	0	1	1	1
Armenia	0	1	1	0	1
Azerbaijan	0	1	0	0	1
Kazakhstan	0	0	0	0	0
Uzbekistan	0	0	0	0	0
Tajikistan	0	0	0	0	0
Turkmenistan	0	0	0	0	0
Kyrgyzstan	0	0	0	0	0

S = Size of nation
H = Ethnic homogeneity
W = Relative wealth
G = Growth or decline
E = Ethnic mobilization for sovereignty

revealing factor in a centrally planned economy stressing growth of heavy industry.[26] But in keeping with the interpretation of the growth variable offered by Ragin, a region or republic's economic advance or decline would be more accurately measured by levels of gross fixed investment per capita over time. As Gertrude Schroeder put it, "If the central government had been determined to equalize levels of development among nationality groups, this policy presumably would have been most apparent in the allocation of investment."[27] More than migration patterns, growth or decline in the Soviet context seemed more a function of fixed investment. Those republics whose level of investment in 1981–1985 was equal to or higher than 1961–1965 levels were coded 1; those whose share of investment fell over this time were coded 0.

Table 21.1 replicates Ragin's Boolean analysis of minority peoples of Western Europe for the Soviet case. It includes the outcome variable ethnic mobilization (E). While our cases provide abundant evidence of ethnic mobilization, encompassing titular and non-titular nationalities, across the Soviet Union as the center began to disintegrate, our interest here is in ethnic mobilization in support of *national sovereignty*. Where in our cases we have found evidence of a high degree of such mobilization (evidenced in early formation of national fronts, recurrent mass pro-independence demonstrations, extra-constitutional measures to enhance a republic's jurisdiction), we have coded such outcomes as positive (1); lower degrees of mobilization, as evidenced only in our Central Asian cases (and summarized in the following section), are coded negatively (0).

Our account of theories of ethnic mobilization tell us that the developmental perspective emphasizes ethnic homogeneity but also growth or decline: the image is of a culturally distinct but economically isolated nation. It would be represented in Boolean terms as Hg (uppercase letters indicate presence, lowercase indicate absence, and multiplication indicates logical AND). Reactive ethnicity focuses on the predatory behavior of the dominant nation involving erosion of ethnic and economic bases (hw). Ethnic competition would stress the size and wealth of the subordinate nation (SW).

In Boolean analysis the absence of a cause has the same logical status as its presence. From table 21.1 we note that ethnic mobilization for sovereignty did not occur in Central Asia: the combination of causal conditions for lack of mobilization was small population, lack of ethnic homogeneity, limited wealth, and economic decline ($shwg$). Conversely, of our ten instances of mobilization, two combinations of causal conditions explain half of the cases. The first is when relative wealth and economic advance are combined with small size and ethnic heterogeneity (Georgia, Latvia, and Moldova), expressed in primitive (unreduced) Boolean terms as $shWG$. The second is when relative wealth, economic advance, and homogeneity are combined with small size (Belarus and Lithuania), that is, produced $sHWG$.

Boolean minimalization is based on the rule that when two Boolean expressions differ in only one causal condition, then that causal condition can be regarded as irrelevant since the outcome remains the same. Thus, whether or not a nation was characterized by homogeneity still could lead to mobilization, expressed as $sHWG$ combining with $shWG$ to produce sWG. Further minimization[28] produces the final reduced Boolean equation:

$$E = HWG + sWG + hWg + sHg$$

where $+$ signifies logical OR. That is, our studies revealed mobilization took place under causal conjunctures where nations were relatively wealthy and economically growing but were either small (Belarus, Georgia, Latvia, Lithuania, Moldova) or at least were ethnically homogeneous (Russia); *or* they were not advancing but were wealthy and ethnically heterogenous (Estonia, Ukraine) or were small and homogeneous (Armenia, Azerbaijan). No single cause appeared necessary or sufficient to produce mobilization since each appeared only in a subset of a combination of conditions. Relative wealth comes closest to being a necessary condition, appearing in nine of the ten instances of ethnic mobilization.

Azerbaijan was the exception, but it was the "richest" of the republics coded as poor and also represented the only one of the six Soviet Muslim republics that was ethnically homogeneous. Factoring the Boolean expression above would highlight the importance of wealth:

$$E = W(HG + sG + hg) + sHg$$

The equation reveals two contradictory contexts (HG and hg) which require W to be present for E to occur.[29] It therefore draws our attention to the third causal combination, sG in the presence of W and indeed, as we have noted above, a relatively wealthy but small republic that is economically advancing is the most common profile of a politically mobilizing nation in our study (five of ten cases).

Two of the three theories explaining ethnic mobilization receive support from our Boolean analysis. The developmental perspective stressed the probability of mobilization under conditions of ethnic homogeneity but economic decline (Hg). This equation is a prime implicant of sHg identified in Armenia and Azerbaijan. Except for Ukraine, we could not really have expected the ethnic competition perspective (SW) to be substantiated in the Soviet case, given the near-hegemonic position of Russians in the old Soviet Union. And indeed Ukraine with its size and wealth fitted the competition perspective (though heterogeneity and decline were also important factors here). Most surprising is that the reactive ethnicity perspective (hw), which in the Soviet case would highlight Russian infiltration into other republics and their own limited wealth, was not borne out by the analysis. To the contrary, a weak ethnic and economic base was more closely linked with failure to mobilize.

Findings based on our Boolean analysis of Soviet peoples' mobilization patterns contrast with Ragin's findings on the subnations of Western Europe, which mobilized under conditions posited by the ethnic reaction and competition, but rarely the developmental, perspective. Yet given the earlier stage of development nations of the USSR had reached in comparison with those of Western Europe, we can readily understand why developmental explanations were more salient to the Soviet case.

The approach we adopted can, of course, be modified and refined. It is possible, for example, to use other *measures* to describe the variables we employed. Indeed, other *variables* might be sought and defined so as to assess their presence or absence in conjunctural causal explanations of ethnic mobilization. Finally, Boolean analysis seems particularly appropriate to assess mobilization *and* non-mobilization among non-titular peoples. Applying De Morgan's law, which would inversely recode the conditions associated with multiple conjunctural causation of mobilization to identify conditions of non-mobilization, we might test the developmental perspective's salience to smaller, less wealthy nations like Tatars, Ossetians, or Chechens. In our reduced equation for ethnic mobilization, small size produced mobilization when combined either with homogeneity and no growth (*sHg* – the developmental perspective) or with wealth and growth (*sWG*). Holding size constant since we are studying only small nations, recoding of $E = (Hg + WG)$ would produce

$$e = (h + G)(w + g) = hw + hg + Gw.$$

Were the smaller nations of the former USSR which did not mobilize characterized by no homogeneity and no wealth, or no homogeneity and no growth, or no wealth but growth? Generating such hypotheses seems important at a time when a new panorama of national minorities appears in the fifteen independent states that used to make up the Soviet empire.

In conclusion, let us refer to Ragin's account of the merits of Boolean analysis. It is a holistic approach and views cases in terms of combinations of values as well as comparing cases with different combinations. It is also primarily an inductive method, simplifying complexity: "It starts with a bias toward complexity – every logically possible combination of values is examined – and simplifies this complexity through experiment-like contrasts – procedures which approximate the logic of the ideal social scientific comparison."[30] While also variable-oriented, it is easily compatible with qualitative interpretative analysis. Indeed, "the *results* of Boolean-based analysis provide important signposts for more detailed historical examination of specific cases, using a traditional case-oriented approach," as has characterized this book.[31] Finally, in the specific area of interest to nationalism studies, "Boolean analysis does more than simply confirm complexity. It shows the key combinations of causal conditions linked to ethnic political mobilization."[32]

Patterns of interaction in the Soviet ethnic mosaic

Has our study also located key patterns of *interethnic relations* that are part of the process of political mobilization? In the introductory chapter, in table 1.1, four actor-types in the Soviet context were identified: center (Soviet power), first-order titular nationality (of union republics), second-order titular nationality (of autonomous republics), and non-titular nationality (unempowered peoples). There are fifteen conceivable permutations of interactions among the four actor-types (center–center interaction is empirically vacuous). Six general types of interaction characterize such interactions: integration, assimilation, liberation, competition, domination, and collusion. Let me order the data emerging from our case studies in terms of such interactions.

Only central authority – the old USSR – sought *integration*. It aimed at creating *sovietskii narod* which would normatively integrate first- and second-order titular peoples, and it failed in this effort. While attention has focused on the failure of integration with regard to first-order titulars

(Lithuanians, Georgians, Uzbeks), three of our chapters reveal a similar failure of integration among second-order titulars: Tatars, Chuvash, Bashkirs and Mari in the Middle Volga; Chechens, Balkars and Karachai (all deported peoples) in the north Caucasus; and Yakuts, Buryats and Tuvans in Siberia.

When the center sought *assimilation* of non-titulars, however, such as Crimean Tatars, Lithuanian Poles, Volga Germans, or Russian or Moldovan Jews, evidence of some linguistic success was apparent. Crimean Tatars proved exceptional in having a high rate of maternal language retention but, simultaneously, they demonstrated a high rate of knowledge of Russian as a second language. We can suggest, therefore, that central Soviet authority succeeded – and then only partially – when it bullied the weak. One unusual finding in research into second-order titulars was how Soviet authorities sought assimilation of certain groups, but not necessarily into Russian culture. Thus Gail Fondahl described the efforts at "Yakutizing" many peoples of the north, which met with resentment and then resistance.

The inter-ethnic relationship depicted as *liberation* was to characterize interaction initiated by first-order titulars towards the center, second-order titulars towards their first-order cohorts, and non-titulars towards all titulars. Chapters in this volume have documented the origins, methods, and strategies of national liberation from Soviet control by the former union republics. Even the Russian federation, often viewed as isomorphic with Soviet power, engaged in an independence struggle under Yeltsin. But as John Dunlop noted, other types of nationalists with more authoritarian platforms competed with democrats for the same objective. Processes of nation-building (following in-migration beginning in 1976 and accelerating in the late 1980s) and state-building (setting up the same republic institutions in Russia that other republics had had for many years) provided the basis for attaining separate statehood.

In Ukraine, Bohdan Krawchenko observed that an acute sense of economic exploitation propelled the liberation struggle. As in the Baltic republics, nationalist and democratic movements coalesced and expanded the agenda of liberation into national as well as political freedom. Ukraine's institution-building was particularly impressive and was linked to the confidence that a republic with its resources could attain.

In Belarus, apart from collapsing central authority national liberation was given momentum by the republic's economic development producing industrialization and urbanization. Moreover, as Michael Urban and Jan Zaprudnik observed, concern with the status of the native language, then revelations in 1988 about large-scale executions under Stalin which created a Belarus martyrology, strengthened the resolve for an independent, separate, Belarus state. Moldova's national struggle has not, perhaps, been as fully appreciated as that of other peoples. But Daria

Fane noted how it was Moldova that, first among Soviet republics, pro-claimed its own language as the official one of the republic. Indeed, she added that the Moldovan popular front was so nationalist that it made little effort to court the republic's own minorities for use against the Kremlin.

The Baltic republics led the struggle of Soviet peoples for independence, and Lithuania led the Baltics. In much the same way as Poland – first with the Solidarity movement in 1980, then with roundtable talks with anti-Communists in 1988, and finally with free elections in 1989 – pioneered post-Communism in Eastern Europe, so Lithuania pioneered post-Sovietism.[33] Richard Krickus identified the principal factors underlying Lithuania's desire for liberation from the Soviet center: its historic identity and attendant emotional attachments (thereby making explanations centering on economic exploitation or repressive Soviet policies second-order causes); its earlier statehood (and an important state it once had been); and widespread perceptions of russification. In neighboring Latvia, the fact that the republic's ruling Communist Party did not even have a Latvian majority made the sense of being ruled from without more acute. Nils Muiznieks pointed out, in addition, that violence used by Soviet troops to produce submission of Latvian nationalists itself affected the pathway of Latvian nationalism. In Estonia, a more cautious approach to indepen-dence was taken but, Cynthia Kaplan contended, the country's interwar republic remained a social memory. In an assertion confirmed by findings from other republics, she concluded that perestroika did not give rise to nationalism, it only provided a venue for it.

The thrust for liberation from the center characterized the Transcauca-sus as well. Shireen Hunter described the rich history of Azerbaijan, the efforts made to rediscover the past, often requiring mythification of history and identity, and the competing influences of Iran and Turkey. She also pointed to Gorbachev's own incompetence in nationalities' problems and offered the ironic but incisive conclusion that even the Soviet Union was stunned to find out one day that the Soviet Union was nothing but a colonial empire. Nora Dudwick traced Armenia's identity to a distant past as well, but she underscored the importance of a martyrology in Armenian national identity in the Soviet period and noted the influence exerted by a large diaspora in sustaining this identity. Up to 1936 it was not necessary to cease being Armenian, so long as one was Soviet Armenian. But the goal of liberation from the center became central in the Stalin era, and took on renewed urgency when the Nagorno-Karabagh conflict (discussed below) broke out. Georgians shared two characteristics with Armenians: a rich history but insecurity about the integrity of their historical territory. With minorities concentrated in peripheral regions, Georgia's relations with, in particular, Abkhazians and Ossetians could easily be upset. Such was the case under the Mensheviks, Shevardnadze, and Gamsakhurdia. Stephen

Jones described how the "Georgianization" program pursued by Gamsak-hurdia championed majority over minority rights. As in Moldova, other nationalities were not coopted into the new system. When radical Georgian nationalism was coupled with the "old wiring" inherited from the Soviet period – statism, censorship, personalization of politics – conflictual ethnic relations rebounded on other structures and the transition to democracy failed.

Case studies of the Central Asian republics suggest the involuntary nature of statehood that arrived in the region, as well as the curious possibility that statehood had been attained before nationhood. Political mobilization for sovereignty was limited at best, and we need to summarize reasons for this unusual phenomenon. Kazakhs were a minority in their own land and, seeking to make the best of a bad situation, projected with pride their multinational profile. Not surprisingly, as Martha Olcott observed, President Nazabarev was able both to support Gorbachev on the need for a new union *and* remain very popular at home – an improbable scenario in other parts of the old USSR. The influx in earlier Soviet periods of Tatars, Germans, Koreans, kulaks, and exiles of many nations was now viewed by Kazakh intellectuals, however, as a ploy by Russians to make them a minority. Pro-secessionist sentiments in Russian-dominated northern Kazakhstan fueled such suspicions, but the Alma-Ata demonstrations of December 1986 were the catalyst for a rise in nationalist sentiment.

Internal ethnic disunity also was found in Uzbekistan. Gregory Gleason advanced the view that greater contestation occurred among groups within the republic than between Uzbekistan and Moscow. Groups interacted more as coalitions than as nations, a product of a different cultural understanding of national identity. Gleason provided a detailed list of secessionist claims made by various groups in the region and cautioned about the potential for conflict, especially with Russians, Kyrgyz, and Tajiks.

Adding to this account, Muriel Atkin asserted how in Tajikistan referents for a political agenda were the other Soviet republics. Less interference but also less support from the center coupled with waning repression left the Tajik elite with little choice but to obtain endorsement of the local constituency. Under such conditions, nationalist sentiment was likely to grow but, as Atkin made clear, Tajik identity was paradoxically a Soviet creation, and a Tajik nation-state a twentieth-century invention. And though the ethnic group's roots could be traced to antiquity, most of the population was not aware of this. Islam meant different things to different peoples and, in the past, shared religion did not prevent conflicts. But, as Atkin reassured, Tajiks did not look at the rest of the world solely or even primarily in terms of ethnicity and religion. Independence left Tajikstan with neighbors it did not trust, an economy that was not self-sufficient, and social and environmental problems not resolvable by a small country on its own.

In Turkmenistan, too, the republic's population was unclear about nationhood, and the political elite was equivocal about statehood. David Nissman stressed the importance of language in creating a national identity, in particular, the pursuit of a language purification policy. But the campaign was directed almost exclusively at expunging Russian words from the vocabulary. The embryonic "nationalist" orientation was also exemplified by increased contacts with co-nationals in Afghanistan and Iran. While making some strides towards national liberation, politically Turkmenistan was far from liberated and dissent remained limited.

Nationalist sentiment was shaped in Kyrgyzstan, according to Eugene Huskey, by the demographic and economic frustrations of the titular nationality rather than by Gorbachev's liberalization policies. The related phenomena of large-scale Slav in-migration, urban centers with non-Kyrgyz majorities, the declining status of the Kyrgyz language, and an increasing sense of economic inefficacy among titulars challenged not just local language and culture but national identity itself. But nationalist assertions remained, by and large, circumscribed. Tellingly, popularly-elected President Akaev had served a long apprenticeship in Russia, worked closely with Yeltsin, appointed Russians to the State Council, and conducted its sessions in Russian.

To summarize, then, first-order titulars engaged in struggles for liberation from the center, though it was inaccurate to cast the interaction of Central Asian republics with the center in terms of emancipation. What of second-order titulars' approach to their higher-ranking cohorts (and now nation-states)? Disturbances in Yakutia and the northern Caucasus can be interpreted as efforts at liberation from external rule. Tatars number close to seven million and, while relatively quiescent during the *Sturm und Drang* period of Soviet collapse, now seek greater self-determination. The status of these groups as national minorities in new states may provide benefits since they are closer to centers of authoritative decision-making and offer a more visible presence in more compact countries than in the far-flung former Soviet empire. To be sure, the center of the Russian Federation remains as distant from Tatars as before. We still do not know whether peoples whose identities are very distinct (Chuvash, Mari), who are sizeable (Bashkirs, Mordovians), who can count on outside support for their cause (Chechens, Ossetians), or who are sitting on significant natural resources (Yakuts) are likely in the future to seek full liberation from new overlords.

Non-titular nationalities may seek liberation from first- and second-order titulars, which is the quintessential feature of matrioshka nationalism within Russia. Still, whenever it was feasible, emigration rather than liberation was often the personal choice. Thus Jews left Russia and

Moldova in large numbers, and Russians living in other republics sought to escape from new tutelage by returning to their roots. The struggle of Poles in Lithuania and the Gagauz in Moldova for greater rights may serve as prototypes of future interactions of minorities with titulars.

Ethnic *competition* can occur between first-order titulars, second-order titulars, and non-titulars. The conflict between Armenia and Azerbaijan provides a classic illustration of this process but more subtle manifestations were also identified, such as Kyrgyz fears about encroaching "Uzbekistani-zation." In general, however, our studies of the Baltics and Central Asia revealed much *cooperation* among first-order titulars. Further examples included Belarus cooperation with Lithuania, and common interests pressed in Ukraine and Russia by democratic forces.

There is evidence of competition among second-order titulars: Tatars and Chuvash, Chuvash and Mari, Chechens and Ingush, Ingush and Osse-tians, Yakuts and other peoples of Siberia. Indeed, as Ron Wixman stressed, Soviet policy sought to diminish Tatar influence in the Middle Volga region through support of the Chuvash. And Jane Ormrod found Soviet dissolution of the North Caucasus Mountain Republic in 1924, then the wartime policy of deportation of entire regional peoples, as efforts to split up rebellious groups. As she observed, over time the peoples of the North Caucasus were drawn into conflicts on the basis of national identi-ties which had begun as ethno-linguistic designations and which still had little resonance in popular consciousness. Competition between neigh-boring groups was, therefore, in many cases throughout the USSR, scripted by central authorities where cooperation might have been the rule. At one level lower, among non-titulars, a considerable degree of cooperation among non-titulars was found where we might least expect it – in Dagestan with its ten distinct national groups. But also in the North Caucasus Ormrod detected competition between scattered Cossack groups on the one hand and, predictably, all comers – other non-titulars, second-order titulars, and Russians – on the other.

Domination may be at the heart of relations pursued by first-order titu-lars with second-order counterparts or with non-titulars living in their region, and by second-order titulars with their non-titulars. In the Soviet period the hierarchy of nations was embodied in constitutional provisions according different status to each. Revindications today by Tatars, Buryats, Chechens, Poles, and Jews indicate they felt oppressed not only by the center but by their own union republics. Not surprisingly, this at times may lead to *collusion*: ethnic interaction between second-order titulars and the center against first-order titulars, and between non-titulars and the center against titulars, were especially likely. Evidence we have found of such collusion include Ossetians aligning with the center against Geor-gians, Ukraines and Gagauz seeking central support against Moldovans, and Poles aligning themselves with the center against Lithuanians.

The hypothesized relations between nationalities with different standing within the old Soviet hierarchy of nations were largely substantiated by empirical research. Notable exceptions were the half-hearted struggle of Central Asia for liberation from the center and the pattern of cooperation rather than competition between titular nations, at least under conditions where central power was under assault.

There are three general findings that run across the case studies and merit separate treatment. One is the significance of environmental causes in crystallizing national awareness. The 1985 Chernobyl disaster was a catalyst for organizing environmental movements in Ukraine and Belarus, but ecological concerns were heightened in distant Central Asia, too, as the scale of the Aral Sea disaster became known. In addition, the Brezhnev administration's scheme to divert Siberian rivers to southern regions triggered off concern in many parts of the USSR. In Kazakhstan the Nevada-Semipalatinsk Anti-Nuclear Movement, and in Tajikstan organized opposition to the Roghun hydro project that would have flooded villages were important catalysts. In Armenia, protests organized originally against a chemical plant located near Yerevan were converted into solidarity marches with Nagorno-Karabakh Armenians. And in the case of Latvia, in the early years of glasnost the environmental movement was able to address topics that were relatively safe politically while exhorting rational employment of resources and greater efficiency. Often, then, ecological movements provided Soviet citizens with their first arena for undertaking political action. The actions of environmentalists empowered new social groups and served as springboards for engaging in even more politicized behavior subsequently.

By contrast, a second finding concerns the *limited* role played by religion, in particular Islam, in fomenting ethnic strife under Gorbachev. Our contributors were uniformly cautious about interpreting conflicts in terms of religious struggles. Where Islam and Christianity intersected, patterns of ethnic interaction were generally harmonious. Our account described how most Central Asians adopted respectful, even deferential, attitudes to Russians. Explaining the most tragic manifestation of nationalisms in collision – the Nagorno-Karabakh conflict – Hunter held that religion and ethnicity were less important than the legacy of Soviet mismanagement and colonialism. Dudwick concurred that had Nagorno-Karabakh recorded economic growth, conflict would have been unlikely. After all, before the troubles Armenians had prospered in Baku and their presence was welcomed by Azerbaijani leaders. Here was the closest approximation of "Soviet citizens" sharing common interests that overshadowed differences in ethnic backgrounds. By contrast, when Uzbeks prospered in Osh, in Kyrgyzstan, their presence *was* resented by fellow Muslims and, in 1990, rivalry was on the verge of being transformed into violence of the magnitude of "ten Sumgaits." Although more susceptible to centrally-organized divisions, even second-order titulars were not alienated from each other by the Christian-Muslim cleavage. Ormrod noted how differences between the mainly Muslim populations of the North Caucasus and the Christian Ossetians did not lead to conflicts along those lines. In sum, while religion served frequently as a galvanizing force for *asserting* national identity (Armenia, Lithuania, Ukraine), it did not appear to be a divisive force *instigating* communal-based violence.

The third issue underscored in many of our case studies was the concern for native languages. In the last years of their existence as Soviet republics, many legislatures passed bills giving priority to the use of native languages. While most of these republic laws (for example, Kazakhstan, Kyrgyzstan, and Tajikistan) were sensitive to the position of Russian speakers and provided reassuring provisions for continued use of Russian, they caused enough concern nevertheless to precipitate discernable Russian out-migration. In the high drama that marked the Soviet empire's collapse, it was easy to overlook the long-term significance of the new language laws. Interestingly, language laws can provide cultural security for beleaguered national communities when they convert the mother tongue into the official language of work, education, communication, and business. By providing security, language laws can help defuse, at least for a time, nationalist movements whose appeals for defense of national identity lose their urgency.[34]

Post-Soviet ethnic conflict and international politics

What were, a short time earlier, internal affairs of the USSR suddenly became transformed into foreign policy questions for Soviet successor states. It is important to consider briefly international relations theory that focuses on ethnic conflicts. As this volume has documented, the last years of the USSR witnessed a process of nationalist awakening that engendered ethnic-based conflicts. What does international relations tell us about the metamorphosis of ethnic-grounded conflicts into international problems?

Ethnic conflict is the dominant form of contemporary political violence and occurs in most parts of the world.[35] Stephen Ryan described how such conflict was commonplace in the first world, manifested as ethnic revival; in the second world, triggered by erosion of central authority; and in the third world, saddled with the legacy of decolonialization (artificial borders, dominant cultural groups as neo-colonizers).[36] He then outlined how regional powers became involved in ethnic disturbances. In our study we considered the probability that Turkey, Iran, and even Afghanistan would be lured into the politics of Soviet Central Asia. Azerbaijan, too, was making pivotal choices in seeking Iranian or Turkish influence in its development. In all these areas, the existing ethnic balance of power was fragile and even subject to attack.

Ryan's argument is that states may intervene in an ethnic conflict for affective and instrumental reasons. Affective links range from ethnic solidarity with another state's minority to irredentist claims on that other state. Instrumental concerns focus on a state's pursuit of its own national interests; this includes the interrelated subjects of national security, balance of power, and geopolitics. For Ryan, "Rarely . . . will affective concerns prompt action without fears relating to security and loss of geopolitical advantage."[37] Further, third party management by a regional actor often has the effect of escalating rather than deescalating conflict, rendering it more complex and intractable.

Spillover of ethnic conflict into the international arena can occur under any of four sets of conditions. First, ethnic conflict and resulting instability may tempt outside powers to intervene in order to maximize their self-interest. Understandably, any Russian efforts at mediating conflicts in Central Asia or the Caucasus might be perceived by regional actors as manifestation of Russian neo-imperial self-interest. Secondly, when an ethnic group is spread over more than one state but is a majority in none, it can cause ethnic strife arising in one state to spill over to another. National assertion by Tatars, Ossetians, and Meshketians in any number of former republics could produce a chain reaction. Thirdly and probably most commonplace, conflict can arise in situations where a dominant group in one state is separated from co-nationals making up a minority in another state. Political assertion by Russians resident in the other republics of the old USSR but also Ukrainians in Belarus and Moldova could be magnified in scale if endorsed by the governments of independent Russia or Ukraine. Fourthly, disaffected ethnic groups can resort to terrorism in their efforts to attain their objectives.

In the post-Soviet context, additional factors affecting violence-proneness need to be investigated. The most likely victims of ethnic conflicts are the many minority groups found on the territory of the former USSR. Some colluded with the center in the distant or recent past, thereby inviting ostracization in the new political order. In addition, a sense of relative deprivation may be greater when certain formerly subject peoples regain independence but others do not. Best known is the threat posed by the massive inventory of the former Red Army which, when combined with the desperate need for hard currency, can facilitate arms transfers to disaffected ethnic groups.

There can be a positive side to ethnic conflict. It can result in a process through which minority rights are asserted and their grievances addressed. As this study has shown, cross-national coalition building in striving for independence was a common feature, and matrioshka nationalism allowed some minority groups to ally or bandwagon with titular nationalities against the Kremlin, creating a positive sum game for both. However as Jacob Bercovitch reported, the crucial factor that determines "whether a conflict relationship is expressed through acts of violence and hostility, or whether it produces a more fruitful form of interaction [is] the way it is managed." Conflict management efforts need to devise "a range of mechanisms to limit the destructive effects of a conflict and increase its potential benefits."[38] This role is increasingly falling upon the Conference on Security and Cooperation in Europe (CSCE).

Ultimately the assessment of the new ethnic order carved out of the Soviet shell depends on one's vantage point. "Inside-out" accounts of nationalism, compiled by the ideologues of a national community, are usually kind to the phenomenon; "outside-in" analyses, carried out by external observers, are generally harsher. Some political theorists are skeptical of all forms of nationalism and a political philosopher like Michael Walzer is quick to point to the inadequacy of both socialist as well as nationalist ideologies. Suggesting that national liberation and socialist revolutions can each establish regimes as bad as those they replace, he observed:

> The movements they create, heroic in their origins, turn out later on to be lethargic, bureaucratic, corruptible. The victories they win are incomplete and compromised; and often they don't win. If the masses can be mobilized, they can also be demobilized and dominated. And, what is most striking, they can be demobilized and dominated by militant elites acting in their own name – though also in the name of detachment, science, and a false universalism.[39]

A pessimistic interpretation of the post-Soviet order would highlight how nationalism – in contrast to socialism – will not be blamed for a country's economic failures, cultural shortcomings, and social pathologies, thereby avoiding the accountability that Buber considered a central criterion. Yet nationalist programs in the new states are not immune from the virus that killed Marxism. It will not be surprising, then, if the incidences of injustice, poverty, and conflict in the region remain largely unchanged.

A more positive conclusion might be reached if we follow James Rosenau's reasoning about the road to postinternational politics. Characterizing turbulence in international politics in terms of a clash between centralizing and decentralizing tendencies, he recognized a global shift to subgroupism – a concept broader than but related to nationalism. Fragmentation of whole systems into subsystems was occurring more commonly, and "whether such changes stem from systemic planning or subsystem stirrings, they amount to movement in the direction of what has here been called "subgroupism," a direction contrary to that of 'nation-statism.'"[40] Rosenau gave examples of this distinction: "some subgroups, such as the Armenians, Kurds, and Tamils, are 'nationalities' that coexist with other groups within nation-states. It is in order not to confound the demands of nationality groups for autonomy and recognition with the orientations focused on states as whole systems that the term 'nationalism' has been eschewed here in favour of 'subgroupism.'" Thus "the Armenian pressure for autonomy in the Soviet Union is viewed as a form of subgroupism, even though Armenian 'nationalism' is the impetus behind the pressure."[41]

Rosenau wrote before the Soviet breakup and presciently detected the forces that produced proliferation of subgroups. The global tendency towards decentralization accelerated as "illusion of states as omnicompetent collectivities has been revealed by technological developments that render people ever more interdependent."[42] James Mayall captured the paradoxical and contradictory nature of this same process: "Ostensibly, the world has been made safe for nationalism," yet "the ideal of 'true' popular national sovereignty has never been wholly domesticated." If it had been, Mayall pursued, then a world consisting of about 8,000 identifiably separate cultures would not have been compressed into under 200 independent states.[43]

Mayall was sanguine about the possibilities of the international system being able to develop beyond the nation-state. By contrast Rosenau perceived the beginnings of postinternational politics in increased cooperation between and among sovereignty-bound and sovereignty-free actors. Global norms would crystallize as societies used performance criteria to evaluate governments. Virulent patriotism was on the decline and "Unabashed assertions of sovereign rights will diminish in frequency and intensity as adequate proof and appropriate performance become increasingly salient as criteria of national conduct."[44]

Whether the future world order was to consist of a restored state-system, a pluralist world order, or the emergence of a global society was not clear to Rosenau. It thus remains for future research to discover whether, in the Soviet case, triumphant subgroupism may lead more effectively than Marxism did to an order grounded in consensual norms. Francis Fukuyama's postion was decidedly on the side of stressing the compatibility of nationalism with liberalism. Nationalist struggles were "the birth pangs of a new and generally (though not universally) more democratic order" in the states that used to make up the Soviet external and internal empires. He contended that "Nationalism in these cases is a necessary concomitant to spreading democratization as national and ethnic groups long denied a voice expressed themselves in favor of sovereignty and independent existence." At the same time, he was convinced that nationalism would have a transitional character and fade in political importance over time.[45]

Fukuyama may have equated nationalism's transitional nature with the ebb and flow of national assertion. It is conceivable, then, that nationalism (or subgroupism) was just a wave that broke in the early 1990s, to be succeeded by more placid political development. But it seems risky to suggest nationalism will never revisit the region.

In a vast empire brutalized by Tsarist autocracy and Stalinism, observers have been unclear about how much subgroupism exists and how deep nationalism is rooted among the various peoples that were subject to Moscow's rule. Our collective endeavor has been to explore the richness of this ethnic mosaic and to track the directions that many peoples set out for at a remarkable moment of history.

Notes

1 Louis L. Snyder, *Encyclopedia of Nationalism* (New York: Paragon House, 1991), p. 145.

2 John A. Armstrong, *Nations Before Nationalism* (Durham: University of North Carolina Press, 1982), pp. 288–289. On external and internal boundaries, see Anya Peterson Royce, *Ethnic Identity: Strategies of Diversity* (Bloomington, IN: Indiana University Press, 1982), pp. 17–33.

3 Martin Buber, "Should the Ichud Accept the Decree of History?" in Paul R. Mendes-Flohr, ed., *A Land of Two Peoples: Martin Buber on Jews and Arabs* (Oxford: Oxford University Press, 1983), p. 250.

4 Martin Buber, "Nationalism," in Buber, *Israel and the World: Essays in a Time of Crisis* (New York: Schocken, 1978), p. 225.

5 Martin Buber, "The Gods of the Nations and God," in Buber, *Israel and the World*, p. 198.

6 Buber, "Nationalism," in Buber, *Israel and the World*, p. 221.

7 Michael Walzer, *The Company of Critics: Social Criticism and Political Commitment in the Twentieth Century* (New York: Basic Books, 1988), p. 66.

8 Walzer, *The Company of Critics*, p. 78.

9 Anthony Giddens, *The Nation-State and Violence* (London: Macmillan, 1985), p. 210. The transformation of citizens from passive into active political actors was already anticipated in the pioneering work of Almond and Verba who, in cross-national investigations, distinguished between subject and participant cultures. See Gabriel A. Almond and Sidney Verba, *The Civic Culture* (Princeton: Princeton University Press, 1963).

10 Charles Ragin, *The Comparative Method* (Berkeley: University of California Press, 1987), pp. ix–x.

11 Adam Przeworski and Henry Teune, *The Logic of Comparative Social Inquiry* (New York: Wiley, 1970), pp. 50–51.

12 Theda Skocpol, "Emerging Agendas and Recurrent Strategies in Historical Sociology," in Skocpol, ed., *Vision and Method in Historical Sociology* (Cambridge: Cambridge University Press, 1987), p. 362.

13 Ragin, *The Comparative Method*, p. 25.

14 Jon Elster, *Explaining Technical Change* (Cambridge: Cambridge University Press, 1988), p. 57. Other works by Elster (cited in his bibliography to this volume) also critically examine functional explanation.

15 Skocpol, *Vision and Method*, p. 371.

16 *Ibid.*

17 *Ibid.*
18 *Ibid.*
19 Ragin, *The Comparative Method*, p. 11.
20 Ragin, *The Comparative Method*, p. 134. Three expositions of the developmental perspective are Clifford Geertz, *Old Societies and New States: The Quest for Modernity in Asia and Africa* (New York: Free Press, 1963); Talcott Parsons, "Some Theoretical Considerations on the Nature and Trends of Change of Ethnicity," in Nathan Glazer and Daniel Moynihan, eds., *Ethnicity: Theory and Experience* (Cambridge: Harvard University Press, 1975), pp. 56–71; Stein Rokkan, *Citizens, Elections, Parties* (New York: McKay, 1970).
21 Ragin, *The Comparative Method*, p. 135. Elucidation of the reactive ethnicity perspective can be found in Ernest Gellner, *Thought and Change* (Chicago: University of Chicago Press, 1969); and Michael Hechter, *Internal Colonialism: The Celtic Fringe in British National Development* (London: Routledge and Kegan Paul, 1975).
22 The strength of reactive ethnicity is associated in large measure with the strength of central oppression. But was anti-Sovietism strongest in those republics where Stalinism was most brutal? For a start in making this connection, see Jim Nichol, *Stalin's Crimes Against the Non-Russian Nations: The 1987–1990 Revelations and Debate*, Carl Beck Papers in Russian and East European Studies, no. 906 (Pittsburgh: University of Pittsburgh, 1991). For national grievances articulated in speeches at the May-June 1989 Congress of People's Deputies session that could be compared in terms of reactive ethnicity, see Oleg Glebov and John Crowfoot, eds., *The Soviet Empire: Its Nations Speak Out* (London: Harwood Academic Publishers, 1989).
23 Ragin, *The Comparative Method*, p. 136. Examples of the ethnic competition approach include Michael Hannan, "The Dynamics of Ethnic Boundaries in Modern States," in Hannan and John Meyer, eds., *National Development and the World System* (Chicago: University of Chicago Press, 1979), pp. 253–277; Francois Nielsen, "Toward a Theory of Ethnic Solidarity in Modern Societies," *American Sociological Review*, 50, 1985, 133–149. The resource mobilization view is described in Charles Tilly's magisterial *From Mobilization to Revolution* (Reading, MA: Addison-Wesley, 1978).
24 See 1959 through 1989 data on nationality language use in table 4 of Graham Smith, ed., *The Nationalities Question in the Soviet Union* (New York: Longman, 1990), pp. 366–367. Only Belarus, as reported in this table as well as in Urban and Zaprudnik's chapter, had some cause for linguistic security.
25 The source for these data is table 2 on average annual growth of national income and industrial production by republic reported by Gertrude E. Schroeder, "Nationalities and the Soviet Economy," in Lubomyr Hajda and Mark Beissinger, eds., *The Nationalities Factor in Soviet Politics and Society* (Boulder, CO: Westview Press, 1990), p. 47. If personal income distribution was used, the coding would not vary; see table 8 of Smith, *The Nationalities Question*, p. 371. Note that Ukraine's national income (as well as personal income) was just marginally below the Soviet average. If we also take into account that the really significant interval is between Ukraine and the republic ranked below it (Azerbaijan), Ukraine should be coded 1 on relative wealth.

26 A source on per capita consumption is table 4 of Schroeder, "Nationalities and the Soviet Economy," p. 51. If instead of rate of change, *relative* levels of per capital consumption were employed, differences would be seen to have widened in the twenty-five year period, in particular between the Baltics at one end of the spectrum and Central Asia on the other. But republic *rankings* remained very stable over this time.

27 Schroeder, "Nationalities and the Soviet Economy," pp. 52–53. My source for republic levels of gross fixed investment per capita, 1961–1965 to 1981–1985 compared, is table 5 of Schroeder, p. 53.

28 *SHWG* is combined with *sHWG* to produce *HWG*; *ShWg* is combined with *shWg* to produce *hWg*; and *sHwg* is combined with *sHWg* to produce *sHg*.

29 Ragin suggested that when faced with such contradictions, we should search for an additional variable to include in the causal combination. One possible factor might be industrial or agrarian society. Thus wealth combined with homogeneity, growth, and an agricultural economy could produce mobilization (Belarus, Lithuania) as when it was combined with no homogeneity, no growth, but sizeable industrial enclaves (Estonia, Ukraine). For more on resolving contradictions in Boolean analysis, see Ragin, *The Comparative Method*, pp. 113–118.

30 Ragin, *The Comparative Method*, p. 101.

31 *Ibid.*, p. 170.

32 *Ibid.*, p. 149.

33 For a study of how Polish Communists sought unsuccessfully to harness nationalism in support of their project but how it instead led to their self-destruction, see Raymond Taras, *Polish Communists and the Polish Road to Socialism* (Stanford, CA: Stanford University Press, 1993).

34 For a study of the extensive language legislation of the 1960s and 1970s that secured the position of French in North America's only francophone bastion, see Donat Taddeo and Raymond Taras, *Le débat linguistique au Québec* (Montréal: Presses de l'Université de Montréal, 1986).

35 For an overview, see Rodolfo Stavenhagen, "Les conflits ethniques et leur impact sur la société internationale," in *Revue Internationale des Sciences Sociales*, no. 127 (Février 1991), pp. 123–138.

36 Stephen Ryan, *Ethnic Conflict and International Relations* (Aldershot: Dartmouth Publishing, 1990), pp. x–xi.

37 Ryan, *Ethnic Conflict and International Relations*, p. 36.

38 Jacob Bercovitch, "Third Parties in Conflict Management: The Structure and Conditions of Effective Mediation in International Relations," *International Journal*, 40, no. 4 (Autumn 1985), 736–737.

39 Walzer, *The Company of Critics*, p. 227.

40 James N. Rosenau, *Turbulence in World Politics* (Princeton, NJ: Princeton University Press, 1990), p. 403.

41 *Ibid.*, pp. 135–136n.

42 *Ibid.*, p. 418.

43 James Mayall, *Nationalism and International Society* (Cambridge: Cambridge University Press, 1991), pp. 50, 64.

44 Rosenau, *Turbulence in World Politics*, pp. 435–436.

45 Francis Fukuyama, *The End of History and the Last Man* (New York: Free Press, 1992), pp. 215, 272.

Appendix A
Chronology of ethnic unrest in the USSR, 1986–1991

This chronology was compiled from various sources including: *Report on the USSR, FBIS Daily Report, The New York Times, Nationalities Papers,* and *The Economist.*

June 1986	Ethnic tensions between Russians and Yakuts in city of Yakutsk.
December 1986	Dinmukhamed Kunaev replaced as party leader of Kazakhstan by Gennadii Kolbin, an ethnic Russian. Riots in Alma-Ata.
August 1987	Demonstrators turn out in all three Baltic capitals to mark the 48th anniversary of the Nazi-Soviet pact which resulted in their incorporation into the USSR.
January 1988	A petition is signed by 75,000 Armenians demanding the annexation of Nagorno-Karabakh by the Armenian Republic.
February 1988	One million Armenians participate in protests and strikes in the Armenian capital of Erevan. Clashes in Sumgait, Azerbaijan, result in the deaths of at least thirty-one people.
	Police and civilian auxiliary officers prevent demonstrations to mark Lithuania's twenty years of independence.
April 1988	Estonia forms a Popular Front. Latvia and Lithuania soon follow suit.
July 1988	100,000 Lithuanians attend a rally in Vilnius to hear a report from Lithuanian participants in the party conference.
November 1988	The Estonian Supreme Soviet declares its right to veto all-union laws passed in Moscow by a vote of 258-1 (with several abstentions). Gorbachev assails this decision.
January 1989	A rally in Lithuania calls for the removal of all Soviet troops from the Baltic. Estonia and Lithuania make Estonian and Lithuanian their official state languages. Latvia and Moldavia prepare for similar action.

March 1989	20,000 demonstrate in Riga against the Latvian Party Central Committee's condemnation of "anti-Soviet and separatist" currents in the republic.
April 1989	Nineteen demonstrators are killed and 200 are wounded in clashes with Soviet troops at a pro-independence rally in Tbilisi. Attempts are made to distance Gorbachev from the massacre, leading to the replacement of Georgia's party secretary and premier.
	Soviet troops pour into Tashkent, the capital of Uzbekistan, following a nationalist meeting.
	Soviet tanks roll into the Estonian cities of Tallinn and Tartu and the Latvian capital of Riga.
	2,000 members of the Democratic Union rally in Moscow to protest the killings in Tbilisi; forty-seven are arrested.
May 1989	The Estonian Supreme Soviet votes for an economic autonomy program. The Lithuanian Supreme Soviet votes for constitutional amendments, granting Lithuania the right to veto Soviet laws.
June 1989	70,000–80,000 demonstrators participate in a rally by the Popular Front of Moldavia to protest the 1940 annexation of Moldavia by the USSR.
	Rioting breaks out in the Fergana region of Uzbekistan between Uzbeks and Meskhetian Turks. Seventy-nine are killed and 800 injured.
July 1989	Ethnic riots break out in Tajikistan, Uzbekistan, and Kazakhstan, as well as in Abkhazia, Georgia. In Abkhazia, eighteen are killed and 239 injured.
	Gorbachev warns the Union in a television broadcast that ethnic conflict poses a great threat to continued state stability.
	20,000 Georgians march for independence in Tbilisi.
August 1989	Approximately one million demonstrators in the Baltics participate in a human chain of protest against the 50th anniversary of the Nazi-Soviet pact. Lithuania declares that the 1940 annexation to the USSR is invalid.
	Estonia passes a voter-registration law.
	Representatives of several pro-independence groups gather at Riga Conference to make radical demands.
	Moldavians rally to make Moldavian the official language of the republic.
	Thousands of Russian factory and shipyard workers in Tallinn walk off their jobs in protest against perceived discrimination. Language and residency requirements are cited.

September 1989   Founding conference of the Ukrainian Popular Front for Perestroika (*Rukh*) in Kiev.

Ukraine announces that Ukrainian will become the republic's official language.

Azerbaijan passes an extensive sovereignty law.

October 1989   The Latvian Popular Front declares a goal of "complete independence" at their 2nd Congress.

November 1989   Lithuania moves to have a popular referendum on the question of secession.

December 1989   The Lithuanian Communist Party secedes from the USSR Communist Party. The Lithuanian legislature votes 243-1 to abolish the clause in its constitution which grants the Communist Party a monopoly on power.

The Armenian Supreme Soviet votes to unite with Nagorno-Karabagh region.

Nationalist and Popular Front movements achieve victory in Latvian and Estonian elections.

January 1990   Fierce fighting breaks out between Armenians and Azerbaijanis. Sixty-six are killed and 220 injured. 10,000 Armenians and many Russians are evacuated from Azerbaijan. Soviet troops attack Baku, using artillery, tank, and naval gunfire to break a blockade of Baku's port and raid the offices of the Azerbaijani Popular Front.

Ukrainian Popular Front mobilizes 400,000 to form a human chain from Lviv to Kiev.

February 1990   Thousands participate in riots in the Tajik capital of Dushanbe. Thirty-seven are killed and eighty wounded. The clashes are provoked by false rumors that thousands of Armenians were to be given preference for apartments in the capital.

Lithuania requests talks with Moscow to discuss ending all constitutional ties to the Soviet Union.

Ethnic violence occurs in Samarkand, Uzbekistan after 10,000 people demonstrate to demand an end to persecution of Uzbek Popular Front members.

March 1990   The Lithuanian Supreme Soviet declares Lithuania to be an independent state by a vote of 124-0 (with six abstentions). A non-communist, Vytautas Landsbergis, is elected president. Gorbachev claims acts are "illegal and invalid." Soviet tanks and personnel carriers rumble through the streets of Vilnius. Lithuania appeals for international recognition.

Tens of thousands of Ukrainians defy a ban by the Kiev

authorities and answer a call by *Rukh* for mass meetings in support of Lithuanian independence.

Estonia declares its independence.

April 1990   Moscow imposes severe economic sanctions on Lithuania, implementing embargoes of oil and gas supplies.

Estonia supports Lithuanian independence in a resolution.

200,000 rally in Tbilisi to press for independence and to protest the April 1989 massacre.

May 1990   Latvia declares its independence.

The Baltics decide to coordinate independence movement policies.

Commission on Tatars adopts a program to return Tatars to their historical homeland in the Crimea between 1991 and 1996.

More ethnic violence occurs in Armenia while tens of thousands demonstrate demanding formal political ties with Nagorno-Karabakh.

June 1990   The RSFSR Congress of People's Deputies votes overwhelmingly for sovereignty.

Uzbekistan declares sovereignty.

139 people are killed in inter-ethnic violence over a land dispute between Uzbeks and Kyrghyz in Kyrghyzan's Osh *oblast*.

July 1990   Ukraine declares sovereignty and rejects the "deployment, production, and use of nuclear weapons on its territory."

Ethnic violence continues in Osh, Kyreyzstan.

Belarus declares sovereignty.

August 1990   Karelia becomes the first ASSR to declare its sovereignty. Komi and Tataria soon follow.

3,000 people flee Tuva because of conflict between ethnic Russians and locals.

September 1990   "Dniester-Soviet" and Gagauz leaders proclaim secession from Moldavia and recognize each other.

A state of emergency is declared in Mordvinia banning all rallies, meetings, and city and *rayon* soviet sessions in response to mounting public movement against the republican leadership.

Turkmenistan Parliament declares sovereignty.

75,000 to 100,000 rally in Kiev for greater independence from Moscow.

October 1990   Ukrainian students declare a hunger strike in Kiev, demanding rejection of the new union treaty, full sover-

	eignty and independence, an end to Communist party domination, and radical social and economic reforms. Ukrainian prime minister Masol tenders his resignation. Yakutia, Chukchi, Chuvash, Mari, Khanty-Mansi, Yamal-Nenets, and Udmurtia move to declare sovereignty.
November 1990	Following the proclamation of an independent Dniester republic, the Moldovan militia clashes with an "internationalist detachment" of Russian workers. Six are killed, thirty injured.
December 1990	Lithuania and Estonia boycott the Federation Council Meeting. North Ossetia declares itself a union republic.
January 1991	Attempting to take control of local radio and television stations in Vilnius, Soviet troops kill fourteen Lithuanians. Gorbachev claims he did not order the violence. 200,000 rally in Moscow to protest Lithuanian crackdown and call for Gorbachev to resign. Ten are killed in ethnic conflict in Nagorno-Karabakh. Six Georgian policemen are killed. in a South Ossetia shootout. Moldova revokes a Soviet conscription law declaring Moldova's youth are not obliged to serve in Soviet armed forces. Moldovan Popular Front decides to boycott the all-Union referendum to be held in March. Georgia boycotts the March referendum. The Georgian Supreme Soviet moves to create a National Guard.
February 1991	Lithuanians vote 9:1 in favor of a "democratic and independent state of Lithuania." Ukraine discusses the possibility of an independent army. North Ossetia requests presidential rule. Ukraine Supreme Soviet supports Crimean independence. A national referendum is slated on the question. Lviv, Ivano-Frankovsk, and Ternopol oblasts decide to hold separate ballots. Turkmenistan makes plans to create foreign consulates. Gagauz opens its own university. 500,000 rally in Nagorno-Karabakh for a transfer of Nagorno-Karabakh to Armenian control. Two are killed there in continuing ethnic violence. Shooting occurs among national militias in Tskhinvali, South Ossetia.

March 1991	Latvians and Estonians turn out for a referendum on independence. Both have large majorities in favor.
	Armenia decides to hold a referendum on secession.
	Georgians hold a referendum on independence, 98 percent vote for secession.
	Moldova creates a presidential style government.
	Chechen-Ingushetia ASSR issues a statement that they will not participate in the referendum.
	Ethnic Germans in the USSR hold a conference to request the re-creation of a German ASSR on the Volga.
	South Ossetian extremists burn four Georgians to death.
	Latvia approves a law to protect minorities in the republic.
	Ukraine approves private land ownership.
	Armenians attack the village Kheyrimli, Azerbaijan; casualties result.
April 1991	The Georgian government demands that Gorbachev withdraw troops from South Ossetia and in a unanimous vote declares full secession from the Union.
	Soviet troops and Azerbaijani militia begin a crackdown on Armenian insurgents in Western Azerbaijan. Thirty-five Armenians are killed by Soviet troops and Azerbaijani police during an attack on the village of Getasen in Azerbaijan.
	Armenia, Estonia, Latvia, Lithuania, Georgia, and Moldova propose cooperation in independence efforts.
	The Kyrghyz Supreme Soviet refuses to sign the Union Treaty.
	Communist Party property in Armenia is nationalized.
	100,000 workers strike in Belarus asserting political demands.
	The Peoples' Front of Latvia drafts a plan for a transition period in the move toward Latvian independence.
	Eight are killed and sixteen wounded in ethnic clashes between Chechen-Ingush and Cossaks in Cossak settlement 80 km. from Grozny in the Checheno-Ingushetia ASSR.
May 1991	Armed Georgians kill seven in South Ossetia, secession conflicts are cited.
	200,000 rally for Lithuanian independence in Vilnius.
	The New Ukrainian Constitution draft is published. An independence referendum is planned for Ukraine.
	Checheno-Ingushetia declares a National "Justice Day" for the rehabilitation of repressed peoples.

The Congress of People's Deputies of Dagestan declares the autonomous republic to be the Sovereign Dagestan SSR.

1,500 Armenians are forcibly deported from Nagorno-Karabakh by Azerbaijanis; 1,200 more are forced to leave their homes and live in tents.

Anti-election protests in Tatarstan. Protestors do not want the RSFSR presidential elections to take place as scheduled for June 12.

Independence-seeking republics set up a coordinating body. Six republics are involved: Moldavia, Lithuania, Latvia, Estonia, Georgia, and Armenia.

June 1991 Soviet troops set up checkpoints in Vilnius. Lithuanians hold a vigil around the parliament building in Vilnius to help prevent an army attack.

Moldova founds a National Bank, separate from the Union.

The Congress of the Chechen People reaffirms the decision to rename Checheno-Ingushetia the Chechen Republic of Nakhnichichi, to exist within historical boundaries.

President of Georgia, Zviad Gamsakhurdia, states that Georgia wants membership in the European Community.

The RSFSR Supreme Soviet approves a draft law "On the Languages of the Peoples of the RSFSR."

Crimean Tatars vote for sovereignty.

A Ukrainian Workers' Union is formed. During a protest in Kiev demonstrators demand that Ukraine reject the proposed Union Treaty.

A German National Raion is created in Altai Krai.

July 1991 An opinion poll in Lithuania shows that 85 percent of the population supports independence, with only 4 percent opposed. A similar poll conducted in Armenia indicates that 80 percent of Armenians support secession from the USSR.

Troops order the inhabitants of three Armenian villages in the Geranboi region to leave their homes.

Several Russian democratic groups within the RSFSR oppose Azerbaijan's signing of the Union Treaty because of human rights violations in the republic. They demand guarantees of minority Russian rights within Azerbaijan as a pre-condition to Azerbaijan's participation in the new union.

Crimean ASSR drafts a constitution which is adopted by the Crimean Supreme Soviet.

Uzbeks set up an International Association, *El*, to develop cultural and economic cooperation between Soviet Uzbeks and Uzbek diasporas.

1,000 Meskhetians, Muslim ethnic Georgians who were deported by Stalin, demonstrate outside the Kremlin.

August 1991   The National Independence Front is formed in Lithuania.

The International Israeli Organization opens a branch in Kiev to promote Jewish culture, tradition, and customs in Ukraine.

A proposal to create a Siberian Soviet Federal Republic is published in *Narodnaya Tribuna*.

The self-styled "Dniester SSR" moves to separate all enterprises and institutions from Moldova.

"Gang of Eight" Soviet hardliners stage a coup, detaining President Gorbachev in the Crimea. Coup fails to gain popular and military support.

Baltic governments in exile are planned in case the elected governments are unable to function after the coup. Lithuania demands removal of Soviet forces from the republic. Latvia asserts that the coup leaders have no authority in the Latvian Republic. Estonia condemns the coup and declares independence.

Moldova issues a statement condemning the coup and calls for independence.

Anti-coup protests are organized in Ukraine, and the Ukrainian parliament declares independence.

Turkmen President Niyazov declares coup authority in Turkmenistan.

Uzbek President Karimov declares coup initiatives invalid.

Yelstin issues a decree recognizing Estonia's and Latvia's independence.

September 1991   Belarus declares independence and decides to form its own defense system.

Uzbekistan moves to break away from the Union. Later both Uzbekistan and Kyrgyztan declare independence.

Demonstrators in Azerbaijan call for independence. The Azerbaijani Supreme Soviet votes to restore the independent status the republic had in 1918–1920. Nagarno-Karabakh declares independence from Azerbaijan. Azerbaijan Popular Front demonstrations in Baku call for dissolution of the republic's Supreme Soviet.

Lithuania demands that the Soviet army withdraw completely from its territory. Estonia nationalizes all Soviet property. Baltic states are recognized internationally, and the Council of Europe grants all three guest status.

Moldova proclaims independence and receives diplomatic recognition from Romania and Georgia.

Ukraine seeks diplomatic ties with the United States, Canada, Israel, and all states with which it shares a border. Demonstrations occur in Western Ukraine in support of Ukrainian independence. Ukrainian nationalists also protest against the proposed economic union. Ukraine calls for its own army.

Tajikistan declares economic sovereignty and later declares independence.

Armenia nationalizes all Communist Party property and votes for secession. 95 percent of the electorate participates in referendum on secession.

The self-proclaimed Gagauz Republic declares independence.

The Georgian parliament breaks ties with the USSR.

Turkmenistan decides to hold a referendum on independence.

October 1991   The Baltic council, comprised of the leaders of Lithuania, Latvia, and Estonia, issue a joint statement demanding the withdrawal of Soviet troops from their respective territories to begin immediately. The Baltic states join UNESCO. Later they are admitted as associate members of the North Atlantic Assembly. Lithuania declares it does not intend to take on USSR debts.

The Ukrainian Parliament passes a law on citizenship requirements. Ukraine insists on having its own armed forces.

Northern Ingush Republic is proclaimed.

An overwhelming majority in Azerbaijan votes against signing an interrepublican economic treaty.

The Supreme Soviet of Tatarstan adopts a resolution on state independence. A national referendum is called on the status of the republic.

In Turkmenistan 94 percent vote for independence in a referendum.

The Belarus Supreme Soviet prepares a draft proposal for a republican national guard.

Uzbek Popular Front proclaims itself an official political party. Uzbeks try to retrieve the throne of the Khans in the Hermitage in St. Petersburg, claiming it belongs to the Uzbek people.

The Kazakh government derives a plan to issue its own currency in the republic.

The Georgian Supreme Soviet rejects Georgian participation in the new treaty on economic union.

November 1991 The Moldovan First Deputy Prime Minister and Economics Minister asserts that Moldova intends to cancel her initial adherence to a proposed Treaty on the Economic Community of Sovereign States. The Moldovan Popular Front calls for reunification with Romania. Moldova takes over Soviet army property and establishments in Moldovan soil and moves to form a professional army.

Parliamentary elections occur in Checheno-Ingushetia. Parliament decides to nationalize all enterprises, departments, and associations of Checheno-Ingushetia.

An Independent Association of Ukrainian Officers is formed. Ukraine moves to place military units in its territory under the republic's control. A Ukrainian independence poll indicate, a majority of people support the August declaration of independence.

Uzbekistan nationalizes all gold mines within the republic.

Magadan Oblast opposes move by Chukchi Autonomous Okrug to secede.

Lithuania and Latvia introduce national currencies. Latvia claims property occupied by the Soviet army. Estonia adopts a citizenship law which is in essence a re-adoption of the 1938 citizenship law and tightens border controls by restricting crossings. Lithuania establishes diplomatic links with NATO.

Belarus makes initiatives for a separate currency and establishes a defense ministry.

Balkar Republic is proclaimed by Balkar people in Nalchuk, the capital of Kalbarden-Balkar Republic in the North Caucasus. A Confederation of Mountain Peoples of Caucasus is proclaimed.

Azerbaijan tries to abolish the Autonomous state of Nagorno-Karabakh.

December 1991 Ukraine votes 9:1 for independence.

Kravchuk becomes the first president of independent Ukraine receiving 61 percent of the popular vote. Kravchuk declares he will not sign a Union Treaty, economic or otherwise. Crimea supports an independent Ukraine with 51 percent in favor. Poland, Hungary, and Canada recognize independent Ukraine.

Leaders of the three Slav republics, Russia, Belarus, and Ukraine, declare a new Commonwealth of Independent States. Minsk is chosen capital of this new Commonwealth. The agreement of the three republics states that the Soviet Union no longer exists. Gorbachev resists dissolution of the Union.

Announcements are made that on December 31, 1991 the Soviet flag will be lowered from atop the Kremlin. Gorbachev says he is prepared to resign.

Five Asian republics, Kyrghyzstan, Kazakhstan, Turkmenia, Uzbekistan, and Tajikistan, join the plan for a Commonwealth.

Russia, Belarus, and Ukraine ask the United States for recognition. Yeltsin declares Russia wants to join NATO.

Eleven states, all of the former republics except the Baltics and Georgia, formally establish the Commonwealth of Independent States.

Russia assumes the Soviet seat on the United Nations Security Council

Ethnic violence erupts in Georgia as Georgian nationalists demand resignation of President Gamsakhurdia.

Gorbachev resigns marking the formal dissolution of the Soviet Union.

Note:

This Appendix was compiled by
SIOBHÁN FISHER.

Appendix B
Soviet census data, union republic and ASSR, 1989

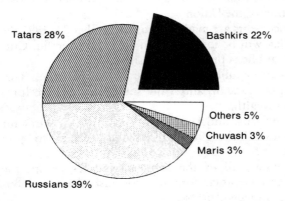

1. Bashkir ASSR 1989 population 3,043,133

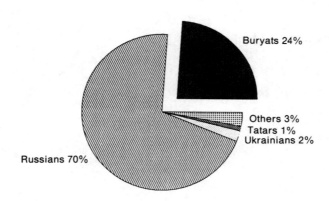

2. Buryat ASSR 1989 population 1,038,252

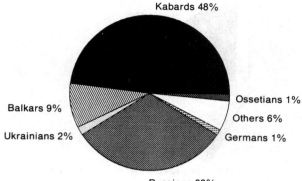

Kabards 48%

Ossetians 1%

Others 6%

Germans 1%

Balkars 9%

Ukrainians 2%

Russians 32%

3. **Kabardino-Balkaria ASSR 1989 population 753,531**

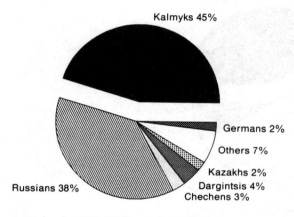

Kalmyks 45%

Germans 2%

Others 7%

Kazakhs 2%

Dargintsis 4%

Chechens 3%

Russians 38%

4. **Kalmyk ASSR 1989 population 322,579**

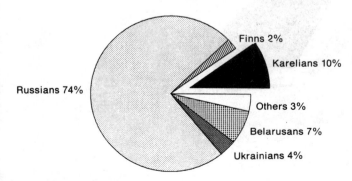

Finns 2%

Karelians 10%

Others 3%

Belarusans 7%

Ukrainians 4%

Russians 74%

5. **Karelia ASSR 1989 population 790,150**

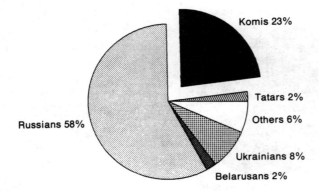

6. Komi ASSR 1989 population 1,250,847

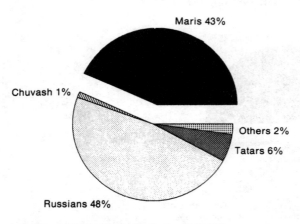

7. Mari ASSR 1989 population 749,332

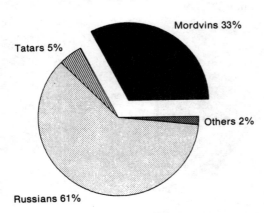

8. Mordvinian ASSR 1989 population 963,504

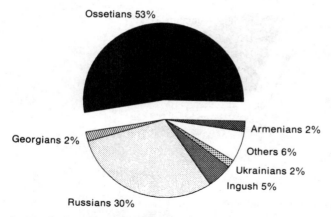

9. North Ossetia ASSR 1989 population 632,428

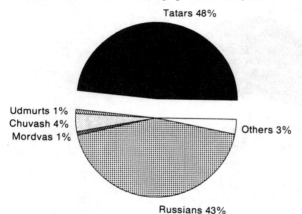

10. Tatar ASSR 1989 population 3,641,742

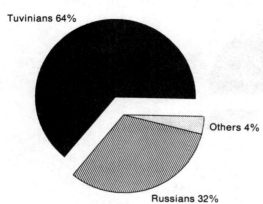

11. Tuva ASSR 1989 population 308,557

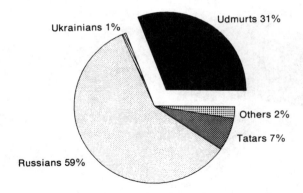

12. Udmurt ASSR 1989 population 1,605,663

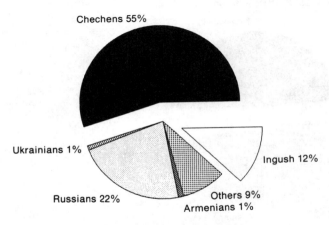

13. Chechen Ingush ASSR 1989 population 1,338,023

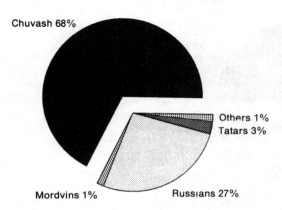

14. Chuvash ASSR 1989 population 1,338,023

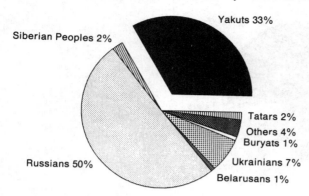

15. Yakut ASSR 1989 population 1,094,065

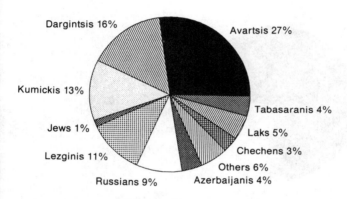

16. Dagestan ASSR 1989 population 1,802,188

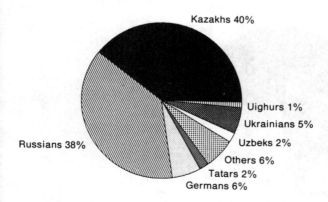

17. Kazakhstan 1989 population 16,463,115

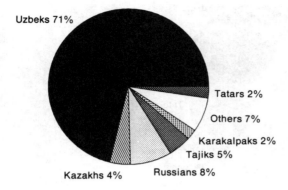

18. Uzbekistan 1989 population 19,808,077

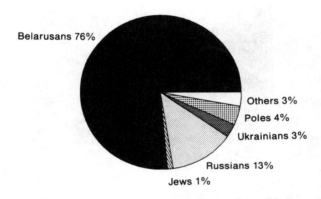

19. Belarus 1989 population 10,149,248

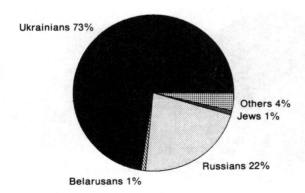

20. Ukraine 1989 population 51,449,479

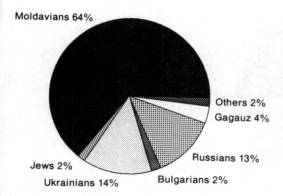

21. Moldavia 1989 population 4,322,363

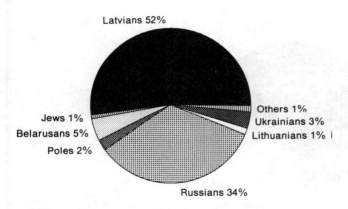

22. Latvia 1989 population 2,666,567

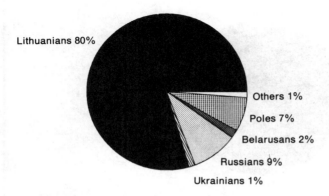

23. Lithuania 1989 population 3,673,362

24. **Estonia 1989 population 1,565,662**

25. **Turkmenistan 1989 population 3,512,190**

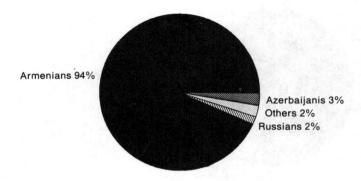

26. **Armenia 1989 population 3,304,353**

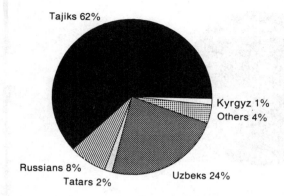

27. Tajikistan 1989 population 5,089,593

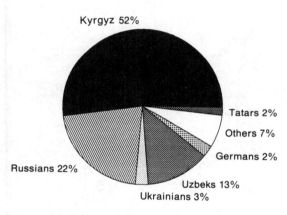

28. Kyrgyzistan 1989 population 4,257,755

29. Georgia 1989 population 5,395,841

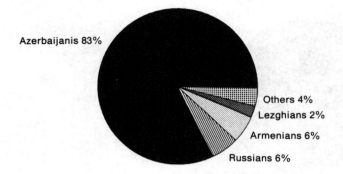

Azerbaijanis 83%

Others 4%
Lezghians 2%
Armenians 6%
Russians 6%

30. **Azerbaijan 1989 population 7,019,739**

Note:

This Appendix was compiled by
DARIA FANE.

Further reading

The creation of fifteen independent states in place of the Soviet Union has changed the research agenda for Western scholars. Where studies of the center made most sense in the past and research on "peripheral" nations was treated as indeed peripheral to the field of Soviet studies, examination of the new countries is the future of ex-Sovietologists as well as of the new wave of scholars who will specialize exclusively in the Soviet successor states.

A list of further reading on the states and nations studied in this volume is bound to be skewed by the past Moscow-oriented research bias. There are more books available on the center that no longer exists, than on the periphery that now is a series of centers. The list below is selective, encompassing book-length studies published over the past two decades that focus primarily on the political aspects of nationality questions. Corresponding in large measure to the organization of this volume, the bibliography is divided into parts treating the center, Russia, the Baltic region, the new Eastern Europe, the Caucasus, Central Asia, and non-independent nations. Some of the books included under the center are comparative studies of two or more republics that are usually informed by "top-down" or "outside-in" perspectives (Karklins' volume is an exception). Several guides to nations of the USSR and to Marxist theories of nationalism are also included in this section.

Very soon scholars will redress the balance that, until now, weighed in favor of the perspective from Moscow. We can expect many new monographs on the politics of individual sovereign states. Russia's politics will receive special attention but political science research on the other countries will also expand. At the same time, cross-national comparative research (shorn of the Moscow perspective) will also prove an interesting field of inquiry for post-Soviet scholars.

The Center

Amalrik, Andrei. *Will the Soviet Union Survive Until 1984?* New York: Harper and Row, 1970.

Azrael, Jeremy R. (ed.). *Soviet Nationality Policies and Practices.* New York: Praeger, 1978.

Bahry, Donna. *Outside Moscow: Power, Politics, and Budgetary Policy in the Soviet Republics.* New York: Columbia University Press, 1987.

Bialer, Seweryn (ed.). *Politics, Society, and Nationality inside Gorbachev's Russia.* Boulder, CO: Westview Press, 1989.

Bremmer, Ian and Norman Naimark (eds.). *Soviet Nationalities Problems.* Stanford, CA: Center for Russian and East European Studies, 1990.

Carrere d'Encausse, Helene. *Decline of Empire: The Soviet Socialist Republics in Revolt*. New York: Newsweek Books, 1979.

Conner, Walter. *The National Question in Marxist-Leninist Theory and Strategy*. Princeton, NJ: Princeton University Press, 1984.

Conquest, Robert (ed.). *The Last Empire: Nationality and the Soviet Future*. Stanford, CA: Hoover Institution Press, 1986.

Denber, Rachel (ed.). *The Soviet Nationality Reader*. Boulder, CO: Westview Press, 1992.

Diuk, Nadia and Adrian Karatnycky. *The Hidden Nations: The People Challenge the Soviet Union*. New York: William Morrow, 1990.

Gleason, Gregory. *Federalism and Nationalism: The Struggle for Republican Rights in the USSR*. Boulder, CO: Westview Press, 1990.

Glebov, Oleg and John Crowfoot (eds.). *The Soviet Empire: Its Nations Speak Out*. London: Harwood Academic Publishers, 1989.

Hajda, Lubomyr and Mark Beissinger (eds.). *The Nationalities Factor in Soviet Politics and Society*. Boulder, CO: Westview Press, 1990.

Huttenbach, Henry R. (ed.). *Soviet Nationality Policies: Ruling Ethnic Groups in the USSR*. London: Mansell Publishing Company, 1990.

Karklins, Rasma. *Ethnic Relations in the USSR: The Perspective from Below*. Boston: Allen and Unwin, 1986.

Katz, Zev, Rosemarie Rogers, and Frederic Harned (eds.). *Handbook of Major Soviet Nationalities*. New York: Free Press, 1975.

Kozlov, Victor. *The Peoples of the Soviet Union*. Bloomington, IN: Indiana University Press, 1988.

Mandel, William M. *Soviet but not Russian: The 'Other' Peoples of the Soviet Union*. Palo Alto, CA: Ramparts Press, 1985.

Motyl, Alexander. *Will the Non-Russians Rebel? State, Ethnicity and Stability in the USSR*. Ithaca, NY: Cornell University Press, 1987.

—— *Sovietology, Rationality, Nationality: Coming to Grips with Nationalism in the USSR*. New York: Columbia University Press, 1990.

Motyl, Alexander J. (ed.). *Thinking Theoretically about Soviet Nationalities*. New York: Columbia University Press, 1992.

Nahaylo, Bohdan and Victor Swoboda. *Soviet Disunion: A History of the Nationalities Problem in the USSR*. New York: Free Press, 1990.

Olcott, Martha Brill (ed.). *The Soviet Multinational State: Readings and Documents*. Armonk, NY: M.E. Sharpe, 1990.

Simon, Gerhard. *Nationalism and Policy Toward the Nationalities in the Soviet Union*. Boulder, CO: Westview Press, 1991.

Smith, Graham (ed.). *The Nationalities Question in the Soviet Union*. New York: Longman, 1990.

Szporluk, Roman. *Communism and Nationalism: Karl Marx Versus Friedrich List*. New York: Oxford University Press, 1991.

Tillett, Lowell. *The Great Friendship: Soviet Historians on the Non-Russian Nationalities*. Chapel Hill, NC: University of North Carolina Press, 1969.

Wixman, Ronald. *The Peoples of the USSR: An Ethnographic Handbook*. Armonk, NY: M.E. Sharpe, 1988.

Zaslavsky, Victor. *The Neo-Stalinist State: Class, Ethnicity, and Consensus in Soviet Society*. Armonk, NY: M.E. Sharpe, 1982.

Zwick, Peter. *National Communism.* Boulder, CO: Westview Press, 1983.

Russia

Allworth, Edward (ed.). *Ethnic Russia in the USSR: The Dilemma of Dominance.* New York: Pergamon Press, 1980.

Carter, Stephen K. *Russian Nationalism: Yesterday, Today and Tomorrow.* London: Pinter, 1990.

Dunlop, John. *The Faces of Contemporary Russian Nationalism.* Princeton, NJ: Princeton University Press, 1983.

Krasnov, Vladislav. *Russia Beyond Communism: A Chronicle of National Rebirth.* Boulder, CO: Westview Press, 1991.

Smith, Hedrick. *The New Russians.* New York: Random House, 1991.

Yanov, Alexander. *The Russian New Right: Right-Wing Ideologies in the Contemporary USSR.* Berkeley, CA: Institute of International Studies, 1978.

—— *The Russian Challenge and the Year 2000.* Oxford: Basil Blackwell, 1987.

Baltic States

Allworth, Edward (ed.). *Nationality Group Survival in Multi-Ethnic States: Shifting Support Patterns in the Soviet Baltic Region.* New York: Praeger, 1977.

Misiunas, Romuald and Rein Taagepera. *The Baltic States: Years of Dependence, 1940–1980.* Berkeley, CA: University of California Press, 1983.

Parming, Tonu and Elmar Jarvesoo. *A Case Study of a Soviet Republic: The Estonian SSR.* Boulder, CO: Westview Press, 1978.

Raun, Toivo. *Estonia and the Estonians.* Stanford, CA: Hoover Institution Press, 1987.

Trapans, Jan Arveds (ed.). *Toward Independence: The Baltic Popular Movements.* Boulder, CO: Westview Press, 1991.

Vardys, V. Stanley. *The Catholic Church. Dissent and Nationality in Soviet Lithuania.* Boulder, CO: Westview Press, 1978.

Vardys, V. Stanley and Romuald J. Misiunas. *The Baltic States in Peace and War.* University Park, PA: Penn State University Press, 1978.

von Rauch, Georg. *The Baltic States: Years of Independence, 1917–1940.* Berkeley, CA: University of California Press, 1974.

The "New" Eastern Europe

Bruchis, Michael. *Nations – Nationalities – People: A Study of the Nationalities Policy of the Communist Party in Soviet Moldavia.* Boulder, CO: East European Monographs, 1984.

Dzyuba, Ivan. *Internationalism or Russification? A Study in the Soviet Nationalities Problem.* New York: Monad, 1974.

Krawchenko, Bohdan. *Social Change and National Consciousness in Twentieth-Century Ukraine.* London: Macmillan, 1985.

Krawchenko, Bohdan (ed.). *Ukraine after Shelest.* Edmonton, Alberta: University of Alberta, Canadian Institute of Ukrainian Studies, 1983.

Lewytzkyj, Borys. *Politics and Society in Soviet Ukraine, 1953–1980.* Edmonton, Alberta: University of Alberta, Canadian Institute of Ukrainian Studies, 1984.

Manoliu-Manea, Maria (ed.). *The Tragic Plight of a Border Area: Bessarabia and Bucovina*. Arcata, CA: Humboldt State University Press, 1983.

Urban, Michael. *An Algebra of Soviet Power: Elite Circulation in the Belorussian Republic 1966–1986*. Cambridge: Cambridge University Press, 1989.

Vakar, Nicholas P. *Belorussia: The Making of a Nation*. Cambridge, MA: Harvard University Press, 1956.

Transcaucasia

Allen, W. *A History of the Georgian People*. New York: Barnes and Noble, 1971.

Lang, David M. *The Armenians: a People in Exile*. London: Unwin Hyman, 1988.

Libaridian, Gerard J. (ed.). *Armenia at the Crossroads: Democracy and Nationhood in the Post-Soviet Era*. Watertown, MA: Blue Crane Books, 1991.

Matossian, Mary K. *The Impact of Soviet Policies in Armenia*. Leiden, Holland: E.J. Brill, 1962.

Suny, Ronald G. *The Making of the Modern Georgian Nation*. Bloomington, IN: Indiana University Press, 1988.

Suny, Ronald G. (ed.). *Transcaucasia: Nationalism and Social Change*. Ann Arbor, MI: University of Michigan Press, 1983.

Swietochowski, Tadeusz. *Russian Azerbaijan 1905–1920: The Shaping of National Identity in a Muslim Community*. Cambridge: Cambridge University Press, 1985.

Walker, Christopher J. *Armenia: The Survival of a Nation*. New York: St. Martin's Press, 1990.

Central Asia

Akiner, Shirin. *Islamic Peoples of the Soviet Union*. London: Kegan Paul International, 1983.

Akiner, Shirin (ed.). *Cultural Change and Continuity in Central Asia*. London: Kegan Paul, 1991.

Allworth, Edward. *The Modern Uzbeks: From the Fourteenth Century to the Present*. Stanford, CA: Hoover Institution Press, 1990.

Allworth, Edward (ed.). *The Nationality Question in Soviet Central Asia*. New York: Praeger, 1973.

Bennigsen, Alexandre and Marie Broxup. *The Islamic Threat to the Soviet State*. New York: St. Martin's, 1983.

Bennigsen, Alexandre and S. Enders Wimbush. *Muslim National Communism in the Soviet Union*. Chicago: University of Chicago Press, 1979.

—— *Muslims of the Soviet Empire*. London: Hurst, 1986.

Critchlow, James. *Nationalism in Uzbekistan: A Soviet Republic's Road to Sovereignty*. Boulder, CO: Westview Press, 1992.

Fierman, William (ed.). *Soviet Central Asia: The Failed Transformation*. Boulder, CO: Westview Press, 1991.

Lubin, Nancy. *Labor and Nationality in Soviet Central Asia*. Princeton, NJ: Princeton University Press, 1984.

Manz, Beatrice (ed.). *Soviet Central Asia in Historical Perspective*. Boulder, CO: Westview Press, 1992.

Olcott, Martha Brill. *The Kazakhs*. Stanford, CA: Hoover Institution Press, 1987.

Rakowska-Harmstone, Teresa. *Russia and Nationalism in Central Asia: The Case of Tadzhikistan.* Baltimore, MD: Johns Hopkins University Press, 1970.

Rywkin, Michael. *Moscow's Muslim Challenge: Soviet Central Asia.* Armonk, NY: M.E. Sharpe, 1990.

Rumer, Boris Z. *Soviet Central Asia: "A Tragic Experiment".* Boston: Unwin Hyman, 1989.

Nations without States

Allworth, Edward (ed.). *Tatars of the Crimea: Their Struggle for Survival.* Durham, NC: Duke University Press, 1988.

Conquest, Robert. *The Nation Killers: The Soviet Deportation of Nationalities.* London: Macmillan, 1970.

Fisher, Alan W. *The Crimean Tatars.* Stanford, CA: Hoover Institution Press, 1978.

Gitelman, Zvi. *A Century of Ambivalence: The Jews of Russia and the Soviet Union. 1881 to the Present.* New York: Schocken Books, 1988.

Humphrey, Caroline. *Karl Marx Collective: Economy, Society and Religion in a Siberian Collective Farm.* Cambridge: Cambridge University Press, 1983.

Nekrich, Aleksandr M. *The Punished Peoples: The Deportation and Fate of Soviet Minorities at the End of the Second World War.* New York: Norton, 1978.

Pinkus, Benjamin. *The Jews of the Soviet Union: A History of a National Minority.* Cambridge: Cambridge University Press, 1988.

Ro'i, Yaacov. *The Struggle for Soviet Jewish Emigration, 1948–1967.* Cambridge: Cambridge University Press, 1990.

Rorlich, Azade-Ayse. *The Volga Tatars: The Profile of a People in National Resilience.* Stanford, CA: Hoover Institution Press, 1986.

Index